I0816183

Gun Digest® PRESENTS

RELOADER'S HANDBOOK OF WILDCAT CARTRIDGE DESIGN

2ND EDITION

BY FRED ZEGLIN

Foreword by Philip P. Massaro

Published by

Gun Digest® Books, an imprint of Caribou Media Group, LLC
Gun Digest Media
5583 W. Waterford Ln., Suite D
Appleton, WI 54913
gundigest.com

To order books or other products call 920.471.4522
or visit us online at gundigeststore.com

CAUTION: Technical data presented here, particularly technical data on handloading and on firearms adjustment and alteration, inevitably reflects individual experience with particular equipment and components under specific circumstances the reader cannot duplicate exactly. Such data presentations therefore should be used for guidance only and with caution. Caribou Media accepts no responsibility for results obtained using these data.

ISBN-13: 978-1-959265-07-8

Edited by Corey Graff
Cover Design by Gene Coo
Interior Design by Jon Stein

Printed in the United States of America

10 9 8 7 6 5 4 3 2 1

ACKNOWLEDGMENTS

The author would like to thank the following people and institutions for their invaluable assistance with this handbook.

Dean Arnold, Murray State College
Mike Brady, North Fork Technologies
Don Cantwell, Wood Products
Pete Cardona, Quality Cartridge
John Cargill, Kaltron/Pettibone
Robert Dunlap, Pacific International Service Co.
Max Dunlevy, Wildcatter
William Eichelberger, Eichelberger Cartridges
Phil Filing, Glenrock Blue
Pete Folk, Pacific Tool & Gauge
Ken Green, SAAMI
Andy Hill, Hawk Bullets
Mike Horstman, Snoozin' Moose Guide Service
Ken Howell, Author
Bill Kemmerer, Wildcatter
Dave Kiff, Pacific Tool & Gauge
Todd Kindler, *Small Caliber News*
Jeff Lawrence, Lawrence Rifle Barrels
Jim Leahy, James Calhoon Bullets
Dave Manson, Manson Precision Reamers
Greg Mushial, GMDR, Inc.
Bruce Nichols, Mountain Sun Photo
Michael Petrov, Author
Ron Reed, RAR
Ed Reynolds, AEM Software
Jim Ristow, Recreational Software, Inc.
Dave Scovill, Wolfe Publishing
Graydon Snapp, Hunter Extraordinaire
Ed & Deb Stevenson, Sheep River Outfitters
Wayne van Zwoll, Author
Steve Wright, Testing
Dewain Zeglin, 4D Reamer Rentals, Ltd.

TABLE OF CONTENTS

INTRODUCTION

Have you ever wondered at what point a shooter crosses the line and becomes a gun nut? Most wives would argue that the crossing occurs somewhere between acquiring the second and third firearm—then you're an official one.

Another obvious definition of a gun nut is; when the mild-mannered gun enthusiast is overcome with an uncontrollable urge to design a cartridge all their own. If you're reading this, you have, in all likelihood, already crossed that line. You've become a certified "Gun Nut." Welcome to the club!

It was 2005 when I finished the first edition of this title. The primary changes to this second edition are new cartridges wildcatted since then (Chapter 19), an update to current component suppliers and the newest tools (Appendix I), a review of the Armscor M22 rifle in .22 TCM and associated wildcat experiments and modifications (Chapter 25); expanded information about comparing parent cases by water weight capacity (Appendix II); The latest specialty reloading tools (Appendix III); and, homebrew options for .22 ammunition during shortages (Chapter 24). In the intervening years, we had a huge scare and shortage of .22 rimfire ammo, caused mainly by speculators buying up every round they could find, like an investment. This chapter presents ideas to repurpose your .22 LR.

The *Reloader's Guide to Wildcat Cartridge Design* aims to help the would-be cartridge designer along the path to success. No other book has provided the reader with the necessary information to properly design a new wildcat cartridge. In these pages, you'll find processes, dimensions and information that took years to assemble. Even if you're not planning to design your own wildcat, the information in this volume will be invaluable in your reloading and shooting experience.

I made every effort to collect accurate information for this book. I often used the original—or at least the earliest-published—data to ensure accuracy. I preferred to spend more time locating original details over repeating long-standing errors found in other works. Even so, there are likely still errors in this book; after all, human hands assembled it.

Reloading is a hobby that offers the gun nut a way to spend numerous additional hours with their favorite rifle, handgun or shotgun. Wildcatting extends that hobby even further. When you begin loading for a new wildcat with no published load data available, it takes long hours of careful testing and provides hours of enjoyment as you prove out your cartridge. Hopefully, this book will help you discover exciting new territory in the hobbies of shooting and reloading.

Here's to many more happy days in the field and at the bench!

—Fred Zeglin, Kalispell, Montana
October, 2023

FOREWORD

In many aspects of my life, from music to firearms to cartridges to movies, I've heard the repeated phrase, "*It's all been done*." My dear father—affectionately known as Ol' Grumpy Pants—adopted the .308 Winchester as his cartridge of choice before I was born; his experiences in late 1968 at Fort Leonard Wood in Missouri made an indelible mark on him and that stuck for over three decades. Whenever I'd peruse a reloading manual and bring up a different hunting round in conversation, he'd repeat the mantra: "A good .308 Winchester with a 165-grain bullet is all you need."

He wasn't entirely incorrect, as many African safaris have proved (I have killed an exorbitant amount of game with GP's chosen load). However, if we all subscribed to his thinking, I'd wager we would all be wielding a .30-06 Springfield, as we'd never have moved past that development. The various rifle and ammunition manufacturers have brought us many interesting and effective rifle and pistol cartridges over the years; some have a certain panache associated with them, which may inspire the user based upon the exploits of those who have come before. Others check the boxes in the performance department and are relied upon as a tool. Nonetheless, many of those cartridges we've all come to accept as 'standard offerings' began life as wildcat cartridges, the result of someone's desire for something different.

"Wildcat." In the cartridge world, the word has come to mean a cartridge for which ammunition is unavailable and, more specifically, one for which the ammunition must be made. So many of our favorite cartridges began life on the drawing boards of hunters and shooters like you and me—someone interested in creating a unique development that offers something previously unavailable. For example, the .22-250 Remington, .243 Winchester, .280 Remington, .25-06 Remington, and .17 Hornet all began life as wildcats, and some retained that status for a half-century. Some wildcats have been commercialized and retain the name of the developer, such as the .257 Roberts, .458 Lott, 7-30 Waters and .280 Ackley Improved, or are named after a well-known figure, such as the .35 Whelen, which James Howe reportedly developed and dedicated to Col. Townsend Whelen. All pay homage to the experimenters and developers who—unsatisfied with the cartridges available in their eras—sought to improve their hunting and shooting experience.

All of this fascinating history is contained and well-documented within the covers of this book, laid out in an easy-to-read fashion by Fred Zeglin. To tackle a project of this magnitude, you need to be well-versed in the history of cartridge development and equally experienced in what makes a cartridge and firearm tick. And while I know many shooters who are excellent handloaders and gunsmiths, they cannot clearly and concisely convey the ideas with which they are so familiar. Fred Zeglin is one of those rare examples of a man who can both 'teach' and 'do.' His association with the Hawk series of cartridges is known across the industry, and custom rifle builders often lean upon him as he sits at the helm of 4D Reamer Rentals.

Fred has taught the NRA gunsmithing courses at universities in several states and hosted video courses on reloading ammunition. He is an excellent writer, having been published in numerous hunting/shooting periodicals (including contributing to the *Gun Digest* annual). He has authored some great books; I especially enjoyed his *P.O. Ackley, America's Gunsmith*. The bottom line is that Fred Zeglin knows of which he speaks or, in this instance, writes. As the saying goes, you need to do something 10,000 times to become an expert. In nearly every aspect of cartridge and rifle design, Fred has done it many more times than that.

Obviously, if you're reading these words, you're interested in wildcatting cartridges, and I encourage you to pursue your interest. Within this book, you'll find cartridge schematics, a healthy discussion of tools and techniques, and insights into creating wildcat cartridges and their correlative chambers—all presented in simple language. While I truly hope this book inspires you to take the plunge and create your own wildcats, even if you don't, I'm certain you'll come away with an appreciation of the process. I'll guarantee that you'll have a much better understanding of the history of many of our favorite rifle cartridges, with insight into what the shooting world desired and that we may take for granted now. After all, it wasn't all that long ago that the .35 Whelen transformed a long-loved wildcat into one of Remington's most beloved designs.

Fred Zeglin has done an excellent job paying homage to the wildcatters of the past, men like Ned Roberts, Rocky Gibbs, Grosvenor Wotkyns, Townsend Whelen, Ken Waters, P.O. Ackley and Charles Newton—as well as bringing wildcatting into the 21st century. He debunks myths and employs mathematics to save time, keep you safe, and, most of all, get you on the road to creating something entirely new.

And what of the claim that "*It's all been done*"? That is nonsense, for if that were the case, the major manufacturers wouldn't continue to release new cartridges almost yearly. Cartridge design trends are changing as the 21st century progresses, making room for longer, sleeker, more efficient projectiles and giving wildcatters many more options.

Grab those dies, head to the bench, and be proud of whatever you've chosen to create as your own unique cartridge. Who knows? With Zeglin's guidance, your dream wildcat might take off as the next hot design.

–Philip P. Massaro, Editor-in-chief
Gun Digest
December, 2023

CHAPTER 1

What is a Wildcat?

In gunsmithing terms, a wildcat is any cartridge that is not now a factory-offered caliber. Cartridges frequently make the jump from wildcats to factory offerings. In rare cases, cartridges that were once factory offerings become obsolete. Some shooters may consider them wildcats when the factory drops them, later developing a following. In other words, no factory source for the brass or ammo exists.

In *Wildcat Cartridges*, Al Miller offered another definition of wildcatting.[1]

"Exactly when the terms 'wildcat cartridge' and 'wildcatting' were first applied and who applied them is anybody's guess," Miller said, "but the practice is as old as the metallic cartridge itself. Basically, the history of cartridge development is the history of wildcatting. From the very beginning, ballisticians, military ordnance experts, gunmakers, and others interested in improving small arms ammunition based their experiments on their predecessors' success. Each military or commercial cartridge introduced served as a point of departure, spurring improvements, not only in case shape and bullet construction but in primers and propellants as well."

In the simplest explanation, wildcats are an opportunity for gun nuts to express themselves ballistically. Every gun nut has a pet caliber or project that they wonder (often aloud), "Why doesn't the factory do this? It's so obvious!" In many cases, these pet projects would appeal only to a limited number of shooters and, therefore, are not likely to attract the attention of the big factories. On the other hand, there can easily be enough interest to keep an individual custom shop busy.

1 Miller, Al, *Wildcat Cartridges*, 1992

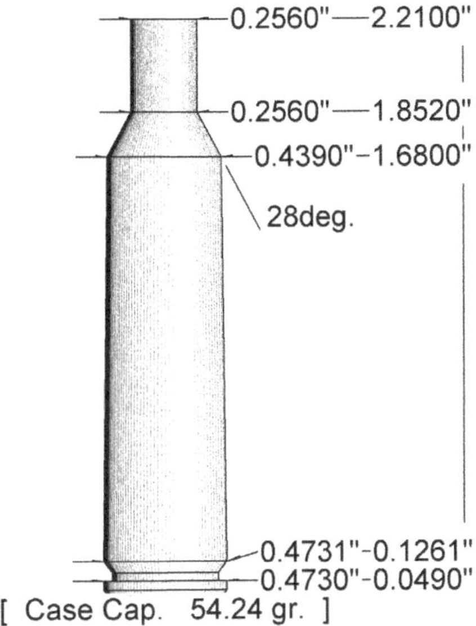

The .228 Ackley Magnum is an excellent example of a wildcat that will never be a factory offering; the case dimensions are on the right.

Wildcat All the Way

Cartridges in this category have never been factory offerings and probably never will. For them, brass must be cold-formed in dies before fireforming.

The .228 Ackley Magnum is well-suited to heavy-for-caliber bullets to help burn slow-burning powders. These powders did not exist when the cartridge was designed. Frankly, quality bullets in the 70- to 90-grain range were rarely available. Today, there are options.

There are many reasons why a wildcat will not attract the factories like a new production cartridge. First and foremost is marketability. The factories want a broad-appeal cartridge, and wildcats are often specialized rounds that attract a relatively small segment of the shooting public. The second is for mechanical reasons. Cases with sharp shoulders and minimum body taper do not fit well with the factories' chambering and ammunition production methods. (This is changing as factories offer the .280 Ackley Improved with a 40-degree shoulder.)

Modern production ammunition tends to run close to the minimum specifications allowed by the Sporting Arms and Ammunition Manufacturers' Institute (SAAMI). Factory chambers tend to run toward the maximum limits of SAAMI specifications. This system works exceptionally well with cases having shoulder angles of 30 degrees or less and a fair amount of body taper; it's a forgiving combination. The use of minimum dimension brass has become so pervasive in the industry that shooters frequently have concerns about how the case web swells when fired in their gun; they overlook the factory dimensions of new brass.

You can get a minimum-dimension chamber reamer custom-made. The problem with that approach is that someday, you will get brass closer to the maximum tolerance, and then it will fail to chamber. Everything in life is a trade-off.

From Wildcat to Factory Cartridge

An example of a wildcat becoming a factory cartridge is the .243 Rockchucker;

Note that the swollen body and thin brass in the body move to fill the chamber when fired. The solid head and part of the web are too thick to expand. This is a visual example of minimum-dimension brass fired in a maximum-dimension chamber.

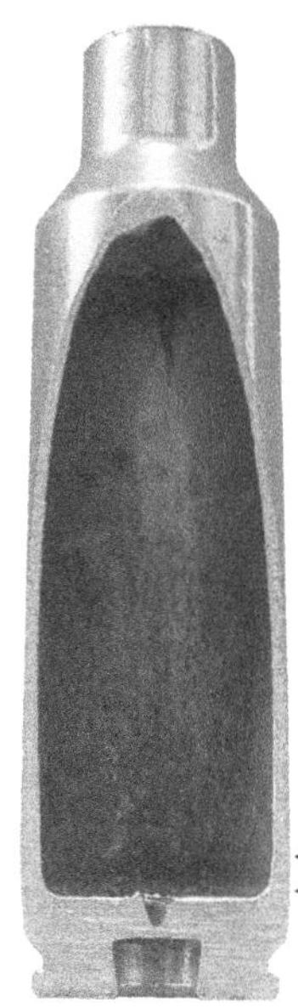

The web area is between the two arrows below. The expansion will be spread over this area in the form of a taper. The uppermost arrow is fully expanded to the dimesions of the chamber. The solid head remains the same diameter as it was prior to firing.

it was the most popular .243/6mm wildcat available before Remington introduced the .244 Remington in 1955. The original Rockchucker was based on the 7x57 case necked to .243, with a 32-degree shoulder. Remington chose a 26-degree shoulder for the .244. In the same year, 1955, Winchester introduced the .243 Winchester with its 20-degree shoulder as a factory answer to the popularity of the .243/6mm wildcats, which, along with Remington's offering, spelled death for the .243 Rockchucker. However, there are still people shooting that wildcat today.

Some wildcat cartridges break the *no-factory production rule* through no fault of their own. The .35 Whelen was a wildcat for about 75 years before Remington standardized it in 1987. Unfortunately, commercial acceptance can damage a cartridge's reputation. In the case of the .35 Whelen, today's factory ammunition produces relatively low velocity by reloading standards. Some reloaders say, "You could use a sundial instead of a chronograph on such loads."

Of course, that's an exaggeration, but Remington publishes its factory load for the .35 Whelen with a 250-gr. bullet at 2,400 fps. A quick check of published loading data revealed numerous listings for the same weight bullet over 2,500 fps. That is not to say you should jump straight to that level in your gun. Use appropriate testing methods; see Chapter 17 for a detailed explanation.

These factory loadings, which some would call anemic, are designed for two valid reasons: First, to accommodate the most recent factory gun manufactured in .35 Whelen, which was a pump-action (a relatively weak design compared to modern bolt guns). Secondly, many of the guns built in this caliber over the past 75 years are of questionable strength.

Headspace may vary somewhat on wildcat rifles built over the years. By offering low-pressure ammo, the manufacturer minimizes liability. A well-built modern commercial bolt-action rifle will handle substantially higher pressure and give much better ballistics.

Still, reloaders should use common sense. If the .30-06 is loaded to 60,000 PSI according to an Oehler Model 43 or a Pressure Trace system, then any variant of the '06 case is limited to the same "factory pressure." Since these systems are limited by design and provide an indirect method of determining pressure for any given load, they should be used as a comparative tool. Where factory ammo is available, you can use it as a standard; if you never exceed factory pressure, you should be within safe limits.

Another example of a wildcat finding its way into factory production is the .300 Remington Ultra Mag., which arrived in 1999 and was soon followed by its brethren. Popular wildcats preceded the Ultra Mag in the market. North American Shooting Systems and Dakota Arms offered their own cartridges based on the .404 Jeffery case—the .300 Canadian Magnum and the .300 Dakota, respectively. Some would argue that the Dakota offerings are not wildcats; however, since they were only available in semi-custom or custom-built firearms, it is safe to call them wildcats.

Heavy Express was a wildcat based on the .348 Winchester case with the rim modified to a rimless design, and comparing it to the .300 WSM, it's not hard to see the similarity. Going back even further, grab P.O. Ackley's Volume 1 off the shelf and on page 428, there is a .30 Howell— a shortened, rimmed case that delivered 3,100 fps with a 180-grain bullet. Ackley also tells us of a line of cartridges with the rims turned down to create a rimless case called the 7mm, 8mm and .375 Express. There is nothing new under the sun.

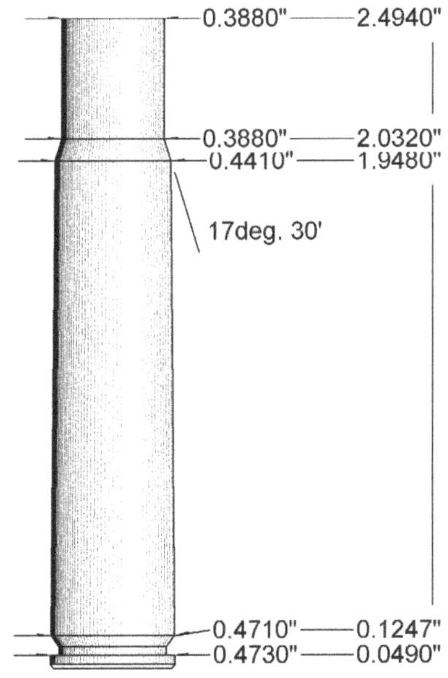

The .35 Whelen.

From Factory to a Wildcat (Obsolete)

Charles Newton had a great idea for a line of cartridges in the first decade of the 20th century. Newton was decades ahead of his time; he designed the first high-velocity commercial cartridges for the U.S. market. The most famous of which are the .256 Newton and .30 Newton. He convinced more than one ammunition manufacturer to produce ammunition for his cartridges. The reasons for his failure as a firearms maker are varied.

Apparently, he was a genius as an engineer and ballistician but lacked good business acumen. As a result, the rifles produced under his name were diverse in quality, from beautiful, well-built ones to cheap junk that would put any business under. Newton produced very lightweight rifles for his cartridges, which have respectable recoil (especially the .30 and .35 Newton), which only added to the marketing problems. Eventually, the reputation for heavy recoil and questionable quality rifles killed Newton's companies, and ammunition makers dropped the ammo from their lines as the demand slipped.

Newton's cartridges are good designs even by today's standards, but they are relegated to wildcat status by the lack of available factory brass.

Modern Wildcats

Today's wildcatters seem willing to spend far more than in the past on their pet cartridges. One example is the .470 Mbogo, based on the .416 Rigby case.

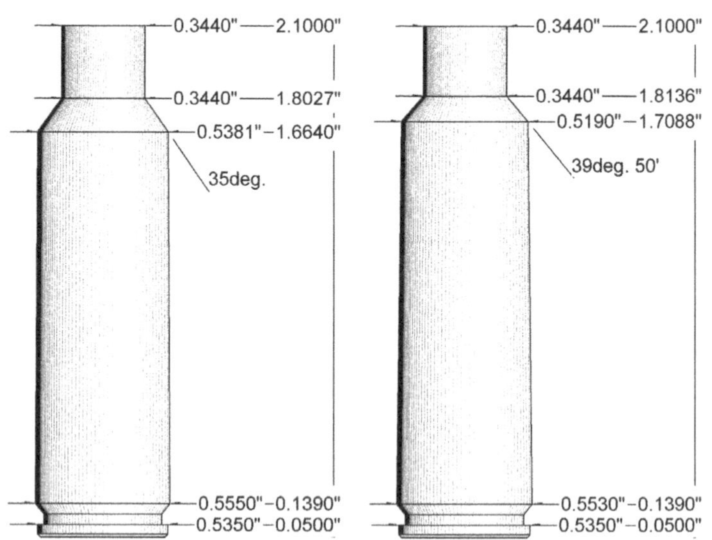

The .300 Winchester Short Magnum (left), .300 Heavy Express (right).

The designer, Dave Estergaard, had a website (470mbogo.com, you can look it up on the "Internet Archive" waybackmachine) devoted to the round with a surprising amount of information about its development and loading, not to mention the story of its first major field test in Africa. An unusual effort by Estergaard went into making correctly headstamped brass for the wildcat. He also had a bunter made (the stamping tool used to put the headstamp on the brass). Not many wildcatters go to this extreme for their babies.

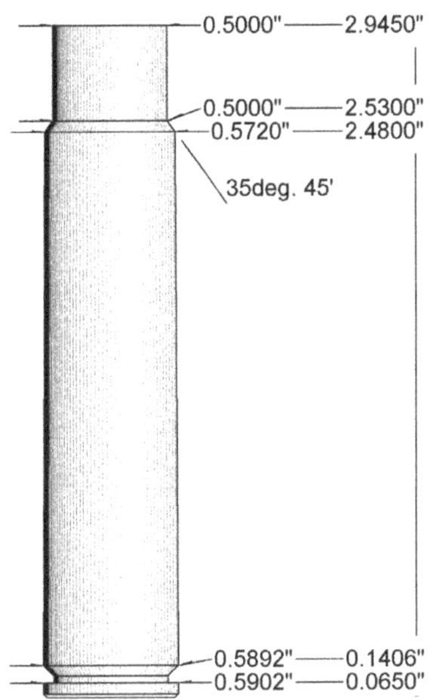

The .470 Mbogo.

Examples of cartridges born out of one man's interest in a challenge and his abilities as a designer are the .19 Calhoon and the .19-223 Calhoon. James Leahy of James Calhoon Bullets from Havre, Montana, was looking over the results of the 1970s NATO ammunition trials. He noted that the British had entered a 4.85mm cartridge in the competition, which had faired very well. Unfortunately for this .19-caliber offering, those were the same trials where the Germans offered the SS109 loading for the 5.56mm NATO. When all was said and done, the 4.85mm had performed well. Still, the difference between it and the SS109 did not convince NATO to change to a new cartridge. It would have necessitated either rebarreling all the 5.56mm guns in the arsenal or replacing them with new firearms in 4.85mm.

Leahy saw some interesting data in the test results. The .19 caliber offered superior sectional density with ballistic coefficients similar to the .22 caliber. Add to that the velocities, which approach the .220 Swift with far less powder and, therefore, longer barrel life and less recoil. Two cartridges emerged from Calhoon's efforts; the .19 Calhoon is a .22 Hornet necked to .19 with the shoulder blown out to 30 degrees and the body taper at minimum. This little darling will send a 27-grain bullet downrange at 3,600 fps. The .19-223 Calhoon will send a 32-grain bullet out at 4,100 fps and a 44-grain at 3,600 fps. While Calhoon did not invent the .19-caliber bore, he saw a missed opportunity and developed some respectable cartridges and, equally important, quality varmint bullets to fill the niche.

Hawk Cartridges is a line of 11 wildcats. Originated in 1988 by Robert Fulton of Hawk Bullet fame, he started with a .375-06 Improved and was unsatisfied with the results. Fulton attempted several variations on the chambering until he finally had a case with minimum body taper, and the shoulder moved forward. When he was done, the .375 Hawk (so named for his company) had about 9% more case capacity than the parent .30-06 cartridge he had started from. Dave Scovill, the long-time editor for *Rifle* and *Handloader* magazines, found his name intertwined with the .375 Hawk when he did an article on the cartridge.

Trends in the industry at the time were toward large-capacity magnum cartridges. As a result, some shooters began to see that big muzzle blast, heavy recoil and belted cases left something to be desired. In effect, the factories created a market for cartridges with moderate case capacity and decent ballistics as they moved toward large-capacity cases. In 1995, a client of mine, Graydon Snapp, introduced me to the .375 Hawk/Scovill and Bob Fulton. Just a few months later, the whole line of cartridges was developed around Bob's original work, with his blessings. The calibers range from .240 to .411 and offer something for nearly every shooter or hunter. Success for the Hawk line came from filling a niche in the market: low recoil, magnum velocities, no belt, work in a standard-length action and inexpensive standard brass can be used to form them.

That gives you three examples of successful wildcats; note they represent three different ways of looking at them. You can use the cartridges for anything from small varmints to the "Big Five." The availability of brass, bullets, barrels, actions and accessories has significantly expanded; today, there are more to choose from than ever. Consequently, new wildcats are inevitable. You're only limited by your imagination.

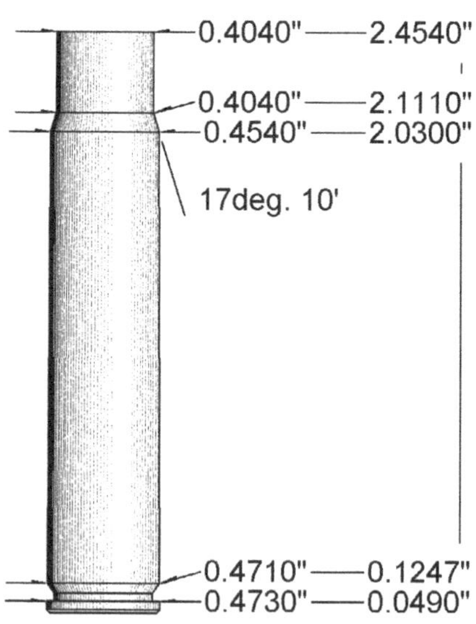

The .375 Hawk Scovill.

"Why Bother?"

This is the second most common question concerning wildcat cartridges, "Why bother?"

There are as many excuses as there are wildcats. Like most excuses, some are good, some are not so good and some outright stink.

The best excuses involve a new combination of a specific firearm and a caliber that the factory will not produce any time soon or, more likely, never produce. Look back at our earlier examples to see the excuses for those wildcats. The .243 Rockchucker came about in the years following World War II. In those days, the factories did not build rifles or ammunition for .243/6mm cartridges in the United States.

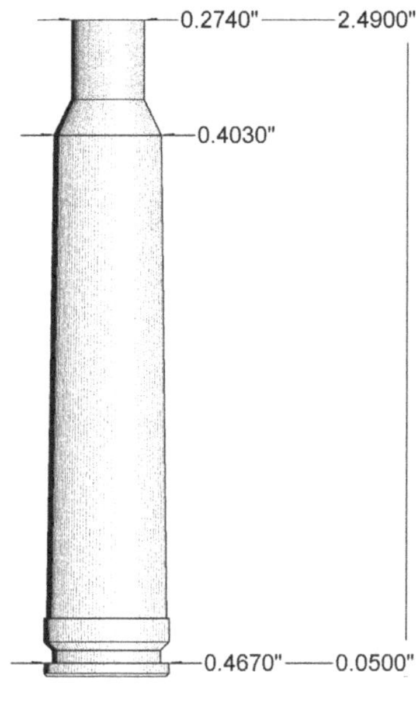

The .240 Apex.

During the 1920s, the British worked with several 6mm cartridges. In the early 1920s, Holland & Holland introduced the .240 Magnum Rimless, also known as Holland's 240 Apex. At the same time, Holland introduced a rimmed version of the cartridge, which is the .240 Magnum Flanged. These cartridges boasted a 100-gr. bullet at 2,900 fps in the factory loadings. In 1923, Kynoch, in conjunction with Manton & Co., introduced the .242 Rimless Nitro Express, marketed initially as the .242 Manton. Factory data indicates that this cartridge would push a 100-gr. pill at 2,800 fps.

The earliest of all 6mm cartridges came from the Germans. In 1895, the 6x57 Mauser was the earliest known commercial endeavor into the 6mm bore. As the name indicates, the 6x57 is based on the 7x57, first introduced in 1893.

The U.S. largely ignored small calibers, with few exceptions, until the end of World War II. The 6mm Lee Navy, originated in 1895, was one notable entry from this side of the ocean. The last factory ammo for it was probably made around 1939. The most successful of the pre-war small-caliber cartridges is the .220 Swift, still in production today.

Following World War II, gun folks found themselves in a unique position. With the post-war economy, people had more time for leisure, so hobbies grew, including hunting, shooting and reloading.

During the war years, shooters needed to learn to make do with what was available. As a result, many gunsmiths learned to make tools, reloading equipment and even bullets. One such person was Fred T. Huntington. Fred became an expert at making dies and eventually started RCBS. On a visit to Huntington's in Oroville, California, in 1983, Huntington showed our group some bullet-making dies that he had made in the 1940s. A customer had donated them back to him for display in his store, and Huntington talked about the tools he had designed and the reasons they were necessary at the time.

In those post-war days, military surplus powder became available, and not long after, commercial powders followed. For the first time, reloaders had a choice of powders, allowing for more experimentation. Before the war, the gunpowders available could not deliver the burning characteristics that cartridges smaller than .308 needed to perform at their best. Armed with these new powders, Huntington and many other wildcatters developed several new wildcats. Among the most successful was the .243 Rockchucker.

When Fred Huntington developed the .243 Rockchucker, few competing cartridges were in the market. The correct time and place had come together for the Rockchucker to succeed. Gunpowder was now available to deliver good ballistics, and the .257 Roberts was popular, so the interest in smaller bores was there, ready to be exploited. The Rockchucker filled a niche for the shooting public. However, it would be several years before Remington and Winchester recognized the opportunity the 6mm bore offered for marketing.

Now, let's bring this full circle. Why bother?

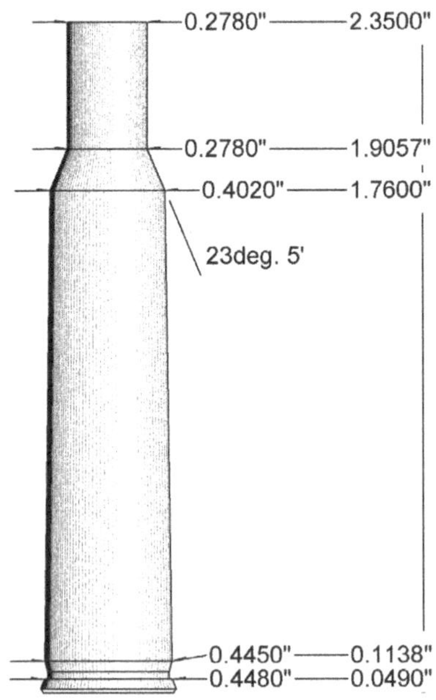

The 6mm Lee Navy.

First, to fill a perceived need. Second, to take advantage of technological changes in firearms, brass or other components. Third, you see a combination of a gun and a caliber that would work well together for a specific purpose. Finally, just because it's fun.

Who Can Design a Wildcat?

Anyone who has the desire can design a wildcat cartridge. It's a way of having something no one else has. It's a challenge to work out the details, and it's interesting to design a cartridge that will do something that no other will do in that same way. Wildcatting can be the biggest challenge shooting sports offers if you're so inclined.

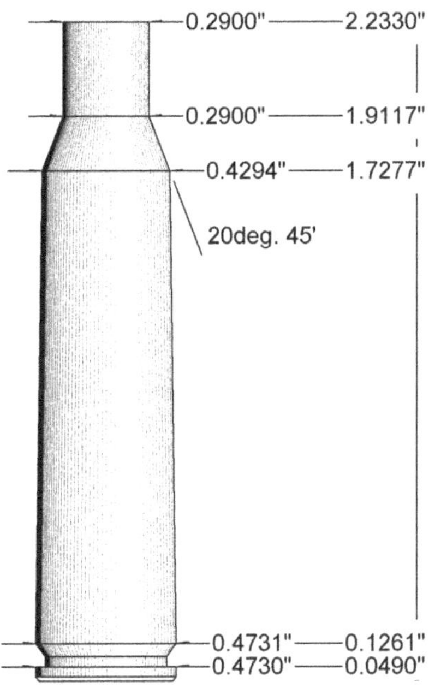

The .257 Roberts.

What Do You Need?

Nothing, well, almost nothing. You need a goal. Which niche do you want your cartridge to fill? Then you need some basic knowledge. What type of firearm will work with your wildcat? Seek advice from a competent gunsmith, though remember that not all gunsmiths are experienced wildcatters.

A chamber reamer will have to be made to meet your needs. Then, you build a test gun. It's OK to make it a nice gun because even if the wildcat turns out to be less than you expected, you can rebarrel it to something else, and no one will ever know but you.

Next, work up loads, which can take time. With a true wildcat, there is no reloading manual to follow (some manuals contain data for the more popular wildcats). Testing a new wildcat and getting more than you bargained for is exciting.

Chronograph your loads. If you don't know the actual velocity, it is difficult to compare your loads to any other cartridge and to know if you have a better mousetrap.

Now, some easy-to-use software products can help you design the cartridge of your dreams. RCBS.Load contains a "Cartridge Designer" that is simple to use, and future releases will contain a load estimator. Quick Design, from Neco, is another valuable product to the wildcatter for cartridge design. Their advantage is that they provide information instantly that you would spend a fair amount of time calculating. For instance, case capacity (Quick Design will import data directly into Quick Load, the internal ballistics software from Neco). For more on software, see Chapter 8.

Welcome to the wonderful world of wildcatting!

CHAPTER 2

Nomenclature (What's That *Thingamabob?*)

Widgets, whogeewhats and *thingamajigs* are commonplace words used in conversation. But no two of these figurative terms are ever the same when pointed out. That's because words mean things. The words above are used when we can't think of the correct name or simply as a placeholder in the conversation so we can concentrate on the concept rather than a specific product or item.

So, what does this all have to do with wildcatting? Again, words mean things; we have names for cartridge components, which allow for concise and specific communication in an article, discussion or written report. Below is a collection of terms that reloaders and wildcatters will often use, along with diagrams to display and name the various parts, cases and bullets.

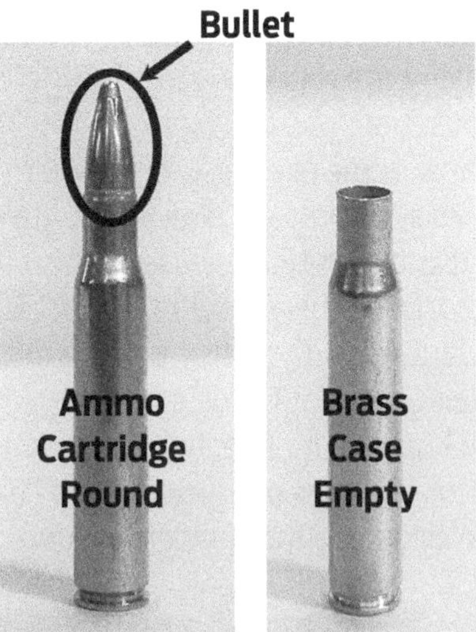

accuracy: In firearms, using single projectiles at a given distance, the measure of the dispersion of the group of projectiles fired. The optimum would be one hole no larger in diameter than a single projectile. See *mean radius.*

accurate life: An estimated or empirically determined number of

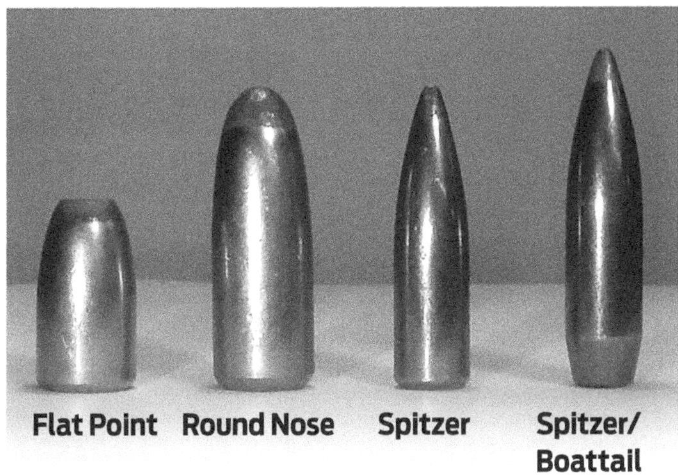

rounds that can be fired in a particular gun of a particular caliber before it fails to meet a particular accuracy specification. Wide variations may occur due to caliber, ammunition characteristics, firing schedules, maintenance and firearm design.

action: The portion of the firearm that performs the action of handling and firing the ammunition.

air gauge: A pneumatic device for measuring diameters, such as a barrel bore.

average pressure: The arithmetic mean of pressure measurements for several rounds in a single test.

back thrust: The force exerted on the breechblock by the head of the cartridge case during propellant burn. Also known as *bolt thrust.*

ballistic coefficient: An index of how a particular projectile decelerates in free flight expressed mathematically as: $c = w/id^2$ where: c = ballistic coefficient, w = mass, in pounds, i = coefficient of form (aka form factor), d = bullet diameter, in inches. It represents the bullet's ability to overcome the air resistance in flight.

ballistic table: A descriptive and performance data sheet on ammunition. Information usually includes bullet weight and type, muzzle velocity and energy, downrange velocity and energy, and trajectory data at various ranges.

ballistics: The science of projectiles in motion. Usually divided into three parts: 1.) interior ballistics, which studies the projectile's movement inside the barrel of a firearm; 2.) exterior ballistics, which studies the projectile's movement between the muzzle and the target; and 3.) terminal ballistics, which studies the projectile's movement in the target.

barrel time: The elapsed time from the contact of a firing pin with a cartridge primer to the emergence of the projectile(s) from the firearm's muzzle.

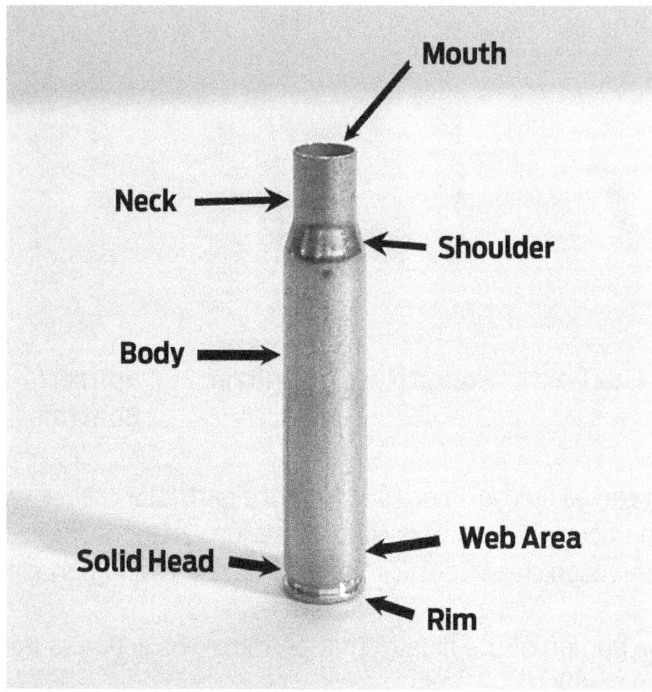

Nomenclature.

bearing surface: That portion of a bullet's outer surface that comes into direct contact with the interior surface of the barrel bore when moving through the barrel.

bell: To flair a case's mouth to receive a bullet easily.

big-bore: A non-technical term generally referring to any firearm using a centerfire rifle cartridge with a bullet .30 inch or larger diameter.

bolt-action: An action in which the bolt is in line with the bore at all times, manually reciprocated using a handle attached to the bolt to load, unload and cock. There are two principal types of bolt-actions: the turn-bolt and the straight-pull type.

bolt face: Forward face of the bolt, which rests against the back of the cartridge when the firearm is loaded. Also called the *breechface*.

bolt throw: The distance the bolt travels from the "fully open" to the "fully closed" position.

bullet: A projectile formed from lead, copper or bronze. It may be homogonous or an amalgamation of various metals.

bullet swaging: To form a bullet in a die.

caliber:

1. Approximate diameter of the bullet or gun bore.
2. A specific cartridge design, i.e. .30-06 is one caliber, .25-06 is another.

cannelure: One or more grooves cut or rolled into the circumference of the bullet where the crimped case mouth can grip the bullet.

cartridge: A completely loaded, ready-to-fire piece of ammunition.

case: A metal cylindrical container that holds the primer, powder and bullet. Also called brass.

caseforming: To form cases for one cartridge case from a different case.

case head: The solid portion of the case at the breech end. Also called the base of the case.

chamber: The breech end of the gun's bore, which receives and supports the cartridge for firing.

chamber insert: A device placed in the chamber to safely fire a smaller cartridge, i.e., .308 Winchester in a .30-06.

chamber reamer: Same as a finish reamer.

chamfer: To ream or bevel the case mouth, primarily inside.

chronograph: An instrument used to measure the velocity of a bullet.

CIP: In 1914, the Liège Proof Master (1908–1946) M. Joseph Fraikin, was involved from the very beginning in creating the **Permanent International Commission (CIP)** for the proof of small arms.

The CIP established standard rules and regulations for the proof of weapons and ammunition to ensure the mutual recognition of proof marks by its member states. As of 2023, 14 European countries are CIP member states.

components: The parts that make up a cartridge.

crimp: To bend inward the mouth of the case to grip the bullet. Used only with bullets having a cannelure or crimping grove.

datum line: The point along the shoulder where the length of the camber or case is measured for headspace. It varies from one cartridge to another. Specifications can be located from SAAMI or your reamer maker.

deburr: To remove the small metal burrs from inside and outside the case mouth.

decapping: Removal of spent primers from fired cases.

decapping pin: Slim needle-like rod in the resizing die, which pushes the spent primer out of the case.

decapping rod: Normally found in the resizing die, the decapping rod carries the expander ball and the decapping pin.

Diplock's Syndrome: In an article by Samuel Clark Jr., originally published in

Twenty-two Caliber Varmint Rifles by Charles Landis in 1945, Clark tells a story about shooting accurate rifles and the good-natured jabbing that will inevitably erupt among shooting buddies. Here is an excerpt:

> *The writer (Clark) had often remarked how frequently it is that we read of rifles capable of shooting into a minute of angle or how often we hear of ¾" or even ½" groups shot from rest or a machine rest at 100 yards, or 2" or less than 2" groups at 200 yards. It has also been frequently noted that although shooting, as just described, causes no great stir among the shooting fraternity, nevertheless, such shooting even in the hands of well-known experimenters, equipped with the most accurate rifles obtainable, has not been the rule on the range described above—in fact far from it—actually, quite the contrary, and if all groups fired by each individual shooter were averaged, the result would indicate the progress along the lines of accuracy was a very dubious matter indeed.*
>
> *Among visitors to the range who had not neglected to observe this point, was Clark's good friend and genial shooting companion, John Diplock. In fact, Diplock had so often been disappointed when rifles which were described as tack drivers failed to shoot in the vicinity of the tack, let alone shooting group after group measuring 1" or under, that he had lost a great deal of faith in the expressed opinions of his fellow man.*
>
> *Another illusion, which Diplock had learned to discount about 99%, was that of the dependence that could be placed in the 5-shot groups as a test of accuracy. The whole matter had been discussed from all possible angles and the opinion was firmly held that a group of 10 shots fired from any rifle from bench or machine rest at 100 yards, which measured 1" from center to center of bullet holes farthest apart, was still a mighty fine group, and despite claims to the contrary, that the rifle and rifleman, who could sit down and do such shooting when the chips were down, with spectators present, and continue to do it for 10 shot group after 10 shot group, just had not come along yet.*
>
> *Diplock, sensing an opportunity to turn the weekend into a payday, pounded his fist on the loading bench and stated that he had listened to all this 1" talk he wanted to, and he had seen all the selected groups he wanted to see, but what he did want to see was a shooter who was man enough to demonstrate before witnesses and with money on the board, what he could do about this 1" business ... Peeling a big bill off his*

roll, Diplock laid it on the loading bench and announced that he had "had his say."

False shoulder.

Why repeat all this here? For years, gunsmiths have had the reputation of being grumpy, opinionated old duffers. I contend that the above story is a good explanation for the attitudes displayed by many long-time gunsmiths. Professional gunsmiths are forced to endure fantastic tales of accuracy and hunting prowess, most of which no 5-year-old would believe. After some exposure to such comments, stories, statements, anecdotes, yarns, legends, and outright lies, even the kindest heart will become hardened to these tales. This hardened condition the author has dubbed Diplock's Syndrome.

By the way, Diplock lost his bet ... nobody's perfect.

Designation- metrics: Most foreign and some American commercial cartridges are identified by their nominal bullet diameter and cartridge case length, which are given in millimeters-e.g., 5.7x28, 7x57, 9.3x62.

discharge: To cause a firearm to fire.

double-based powders: A propellant composed of colloided nitrocellulose and nitroglycerin as its base as opposed to a single-base powder, which has colloided nitrocellulose only as its base material. The percentage of nitroglycerin added ranges from a low of 3% to a high of 39%.

draw mark: In ammunition, a longitudinal scratch on a cartridge case caused by foreign material on either the draw punch or die during fabrication.

dropped primer: A primer that is separated from the cartridge or shotshell after firing without obvious distortion of the primer pocket and head.

dummy cartridge:

1. An inert cartridge that cannot be fired. In America, an inert cartridge for gun functioning is usually black oxidized and may or may not have holes in the case's sidewall.

2. An inert cartridge for display may be natural-colored and should have a hole in the primer cup, with holes in the sidewall of the case optional.

Belted.

3. An inert cartridge used as an example for the seating depth of the bullet.

duplex load: A cartridge case containing a single projectile with two types of powder. Elmer Keith and Charlie O'Neil extensively tested this process before WWII.

encapsulated bullet: A bullet with a metallic core entirely covered with another metal or polymer.

expander: The part of the die that expands the case mouth to receive the bullet. It is also called *expander-ball* or *expander plug.*

explosion: The sudden release of energy of sufficient magnitude to create a pressure wave. The energy to produce an explosion may come from various sources, including nuclear, pressure or chemical reactions.

1. Examples of pressure-related explosions include a rapid change in state (liquid to gas, for example) or the over-pressurization of a container (i.e., the failure of a gas cylinder).

2. A chemical explosion occurs when a quantity of matter is instantaneously converted to a gaseous product, generating high temperature and pressure.

exterior ballistics: The branch of Applied Mechanics related to the motion of a projectile from the muzzle of a firearm to the target.

extractor: Device for withdrawing the cartridge or fired case from the chamber.

extractor groove: A groove turned in the sidewall of a cartridge case just forward of the rim for extraction.

false shoulder: When forming a wildcat from parent brass of a larger neck diameter, a new shoulder is formed in a sizing die at the correct point to properly headspace the new case in the wildcat chamber for fireforming. See photo.

finish reamer: A chamber reamer used to ream the chamber to the final dimensions. Often referred to as a *chamber reamer.*

fire control: The mechanism that utilizes trigger action to release the energy to initiate the primer. It may include but is not limited to the trigger, hammer, sear, disconnector or safety.

fireforming: The process of fully forming cases by firing them in a larger chamber. Headspace must be observed.

firing pin indent:

1. The impression made by the firing pin in the primer cup of the centerfire primer or the rim of rimfire cartridges.
2. A measure of the kinetic energy delivered by the firing pin.

firing pin protrusion: The distance the firing pin protrudes from the breechface when it is in its most forward position.

flake powder: A type of smokeless propellant in the form of thin discs or cut squares.

flash hole: The hole in the center of the primer pocket that allows the fire from the primer to ignite the powder in the case.

flat trajectory: A relative term for minimal arching in the flight of a projectile. Generally, the faster the projectile's speed, the flatter its trajectory.

flattened primer:

1. A condition where the typical rounded corners of a fired primer cup are squared due to internal pressures.
2. A primer cup configuration in which the crown is flattened to alter sensitivity.
3. A primer that has backed out due to excessive headspace and has been reseated when the case stretches under pressure.

flyer: A shot considerably outside the regular group on a target.

form dies: Dies that form brass into a new shape. Such dies are common to wildcatting.

forming: The process of shaping brass in form dies.

freebore: A portion of the chamber, usually cylindrical, forward of the case mouth, which rifling has been cut away to allow the bullet to move freely before engaging the rifling when fired. See *throat*.

full-length sizer: A die used to resize the entire length of the case to minimum specifications.

gas cutting: An erosive effect in a firearm caused by the high-velocity, high-temperature propellant gases.

glass bedding: Applying a mixture of fiberglass and resin between the action, barrel and stock.

Rebated.

grain:

1. A unit of weight (avoirdupois), 7,000 grains per pound. The grain unit is commonly used in American and English ammunition practice to measure the weight of components.

2. A term sometimes applied to a single particle of propellant powder. Used this way, *it does not* relate to charge weight. It is more appropriately called a *kernel* or *granule*.

gram: A metric unit of mass equal to one-thousandth (.001) of a kilogram.

groove diameter: The major diameter in a barrel that is the diameter of a circle circumscribed by the bottom of the grooves in a rifled barrel. Equal to the nominal diameter of the bullet for that caliber barrel.

group: A series of consecutive shots fired at the same aiming point without changing the sight adjustments of the firearm.

group size: The determination of the statistics of a particular group. Examples of measurements include extreme spread, mean radius, and vertical and horizontal extreme spread, to name a few. Most sporting shooters are interested in extreme spread.

hammer forged: The process of forming the interior and/or exterior shape of the barrel of a firearm by pneumatic or hydraulic hammers. Also called *hammered barrel, hammered-forged rifling.*

handloading: The process of loading ammunition by hand. Also known as *reloading.*

hangfire: Slang term for any detectable delay in cartridge ignition.

head: The end of the cartridge case in which the primer or priming is inserted and the surface upon which the headstamp identification is imprinted. The part of the case that contacts the breechface.

headspace:

1. Ammunition: Measured distance from the bolt face to a predetermined point on the case. Rimmed cases headspace on the rim. Rimless, semi-rimless and rebated cases headspace on the shoulder of the case at a point called the datum line. Belted cases headspace on the belt.

2. Chamber: the space between the bolt face and the rear face of the Go gauge within its most forward position in the chamber. (Bolt-actions work best with .000-inch headspace. Some guns, like revolvers, need a small amount of headspace to function correctly.)

headspace gauge: Solid steel tool made to measure headspace for specific cartridges by inserting the gauge in the chamber and checking the fit. Designs vary by cartridge type.

ignition: The action of setting the powder charge on fire.

ignition time: The elapsed time from the moment of firing pin contact on the primer to the point on the X (time) axis equal to the point where the pressure-time curve indicates propellant burning has initiated.

instrumental velocity: The velocity of a projectile or shot charge that is recorded by suitable instrumentation located a predetermined distance from the muzzle of a test barrel or firearm.

interior ballistics: The science of ballistics in thermochemical and physical events from primer ignition through projectile exit from the muzzle.

jacket: The outer skin of the bullet, with different core material.

Rimmed.

keyhole, keyholing: An oblong or oval hole in a target produced by an unstable bullet striking the target at an angle to the bullet's longitudinal axis.

land, lands: Raised portion of the bore (the uncut, smaller-diameter portion), creating rifling.

lap: The process of polishing a metal surface, such as the interior of a barrel, with a fine abrasive substance. Also known as *lapping*.

leade: The distance between the mouth of the cartridge (firearm) and the point at which the rifling engages the bullet. Also called 'throat.'

legacy cartridge: Factory cartridges of old school design, i.e., do not fit the current concept of cartridge design with minimum body taper, sharp shoulders and short/fat bodies.

lipped mouth: If a bullet is incorrectly inserted into the mouth of a case, it may deform the case mouth rearward and downward, causing this defect.

load:

1. The combination of components used to assemble a cartridge or shotshell. It could be considered a *recipe*.
2. The act of putting ammunition into a firearm.

load density: The relationship in a cartridge of the volume of the propellant to the available case volume. Usually expressed as a percentage.

lock-time: The time interval between the sear release and the firing pin striking the primer.

loose primer: A primer that does not fit properly in the primer pocket of a cartridge case. Cause: The case has been overloaded and expanded the head during firing, or the primer pocket has been damaged.

lot of powder: A homogeneous powder blend with defined chemical and physical properties and performance characteristics.

LRP: Large Rifle Primer pocket. Sometimes seen with brass denoting the primer pocket size.

magnum: A non-technical term commonly used to imply higher performance than standard cartridges or shells of a given caliber or gauge. Rifles, handguns or shotguns designed to fire magnum cartridges or shells may also be described as magnum.

maximum charge: The greatest charge weight, in grains, of a particular propellant that may be used with other specified ammunition components without exceeding the safe, maximum allowable pressure limit for the specific cartridge or shell being loaded.

meplat: A term for the blunt tip of a bullet, precisely the tip's diameter.

mid-range:

1. A term that defines a specific point in the trajectory of a projectile that is half the distance between the firearm and the target.

2. A reduced-velocity centerfire cartridge used principally in target shooting.

mid-range trajectory: The distance, measured in inches, that a projectile travels above the line of sight at a specific point in the trajectory that is half the distance between the firearm and the target.

misfire: Failure of the cartridge to ignite after the firing pin has struck the primer.

mouth: The open end of a cartridge case from which the projectile is expelled in firing.

muzzle energy: A projectile's energy when it leaves the muzzle of a gun.

muzzle velocity: The velocity of a projectile as it exits the muzzle of a firearm.

neck: The portion of the case that retains the bullet. In bottleneck cases, that portion of the case forward of the shoulder.

neck clearance: The dimensional difference between the diameter of the neck of a loaded cartridge case and the chamber. The average is .004 inch.

neck-sizer die: A die used to size only the neck of the case.

neck thickness: The average thickness of the wall of a cartridge case surrounding the bullet.

neck down: Using caseforming dies to reduce the outside and inside diameter of a cartridge case neck for smaller-diameter bullets.

neck up: Using an expander ball in reloading dies to open the neck for a larger-diameter bullet.

ogive: The curve of the bullet ahead of the bearing surface.

obturation:

1. The momentary expansion of a cartridge case against the chamber walls, minimizing the rearward flow of gases between the case and the chamber wall when the cartridge is fired.

2. When enough pressure is applied to the base of a projectile, it will obturate to match the bore of the barrel.

origin of trajectory: When a bullet exits from the barrel of a firearm, the location of the center of the bore at that specific point in time is called the origin of the trajectory.

overall length: The greatest dimension of a loaded cartridge, i.e., from the face of the head to the tip of the bullet for centerfire. Also known as *OAL*.

overbore capacity: The point where the powder charge of a particular propellant's burning rate exceeds the capacity of a barrel of a specific caliber and length to convert the propellant gas pressure to velocity.

Parkerizing: A non-reflecting, rust-resistant finish used on metal surfaces of some firearms. Also called *phosphate coating*.
partition bullet: A bullet designed for controlled expansion, having a jacket divided into two cavities enclosing the bullet's forward and rear cores. It is designed so the first cavity expands and the rear cavity holds together for penetration.
peak pressure: That maximum instantaneous pressure measured in the firearm's chamber produced by the expanding propellant combustion gases.
pierced primer: A fired primer that the firing pin has perforated.
piezoelectric pressure transducer: A device that generates an electrical charge proportional to the pressure applied to its crystal element. Used to measure chamber pressure.
powder: The propellant used in cartridges to generate energy to push the bullet through the bore.
powder burn rate: The speed with which a propellant burns inside a cartridge case. It is affected by physical and chemical characteristics and conditions under which the powder is burned.
powder charge: The specified amount of powder loaded in the cartridge.
pressure: In a gun or cartridge, the force imparted to various components developed by the expanding gases generated by the deflagration of the propellant when fired.
pressure curve: A graph of the relationship of chamber pressure to time or travel in a firearm when a cartridge or shell is fired.
pressure gauge: A piston and crusher system or a piezoelectric transducer system used to measure internal barrel pressure in a firearm or test device.
primer: A small cap containing a detonating mixture used to ignite the powder charge in the case. Boxer and Berdan are the most common types.
primer pocket: The cavity in the base of the case where the primer is seated.
priming: The process of installing new primers in cases. Also known as *primer seating*.
projectile: An object propelled from a firearm by the force of rapidly burning gases or other means.
ram: The part of the reloading press that holds the shell holder and moves up and down to accomplish the tasks of sizing and seating.
rate of twist: The distance required for the rifling to complete one revolution. In the U.S., measured in inches.
rebarrel: The replacing of a barrel with another barrel.
rebated head: A centerfire cartridge case whose rim diameter is smaller than

the diameter of the body of the case at the head.

receiver: The firearm part that houses the firing and breech mechanism and to which the barrel and stock are assembled. It is called the *frame* in revolvers, pistols and break-open guns.

recoil: The rearward movement of a firearm resulting from firing a cartridge. Sometimes informally called "kick."

recoil lug: A block or plate on the bottom of a receiver and/or barrel to transfer the recoil to the stock.

reduced charge: A less than nominal powder charge.

reference ammunition: Ammunition used to qualify and calibrate velocity and pressure measuring systems.

reloading: Reassembling a fired cartridge case with a new primer, propellant, bullet, or wads and shot. Also called *handloading* when performed manually.

reloading data: A description of recommended relationships of reloading components.

reloading dies: Tools that hold and/or reform cartridge cases during a reloading operation.

reloading press: A tool used to perform the main tasks of the reloading process.

resize: Pushing cases into sizing dies will resize the case to the minimum specification necessary to be loaded and fired again.

resize reamer: A special reamer made to specifications for resizing die dimensions.

rimless case: A centerfire cartridge whose case head is of the same diameter as the body and has a groove turned forward of the head to provide the extraction surface.

rimmed case: A cartridge having a rimmed or flanged head that is larger in diameter than the body of the case. It may be either rimfire or centerfire.

roughing reamer: An undersized chamber reamer used to rough out the chamber; it saves time in production situations.

round: A military term for a loaded cartridge.

rupture: A generally circumferential separation in the sidewall of a cartridge case. It may be complete or partial. Also known as *case head separation*. It is always related to excessive headspace.

SAAMI: The acronym for the Sporting Arms and Ammunition Manufacturers' Institute.

seater die: Used to seat the bullet in a primed and charged case.

seating depth: The depth to which a bullet is seated in the case mouth.

sectional density: The ratio of bullet weight to its diameter.
semi-rimmed case: A centerfire cartridge having a case head only slightly larger in diameter than the case body and an extractor groove just forward of the head.
shell holder: An interchangeable part used in a reloading press to hold the rim of the case during the reloading process.
shoulder:

1. Act of placing a shotgun or rifle to a shooter's shoulder to properly align the sights and fire at a target.
2. The sloping portion of a metallic cartridge case that connects the neck and body of a bottleneck-type cartridge.
3. The square or angular step between two diameters on a barrel, pin, stud, or other part commonly used in sporting firearms.

single-based powder: Smokeless propellant powder with colloided nitrocellulose as its main ingredient and no other major energy-producing component. The nitrogen content of the nitrocellulose is usually between 13.1% and 13.2%. In the United States, single-base powders contain no nitroglycerine, whereas in some European countries, powders containing less than 10% nitroglycerine are considered single-base. See *double-base powder* for comparison. Also known as *nitrocellulose powder.*
sizer die: A die used to return brass to minimum specification.
slugging (bore): A process of determining the interior dimensions of a barrel or cylinder by measuring a deformable material that has been pressed through the bore.
small bore: A general term applied in the United States to .17- through .22-caliber cartridges.
smokeless powder: A propellant containing mainly nitrocellulose (single-base) or both nitrocellulose and nitroglycerine (double-base).
spent primer: A fired primer.
spherical propellant: A smokeless propellant manufactured by a process in which nitrocellulose is first lacquered with solvents and then processed into a sphere. The finished product may be a sphere, flattened sphere or cylinder.
spin: The rate of spin of a projectile fired from a rifled barrel.
split neck: A longitudinal rupture in the neck of a metallic cartridge case. Also known as a *cracked neck*.
squib load: A cartridge or shell that produces projectile velocity and sound substantially lower than usual. It may result in the projectile or wads remaining in the bore.
SRP: Small Rifle Primer pocket. Sometimes seen with brass denoting the

primer pocket size.

strain gauge: An electronic device to measure stress and strain in mechanical devices. Also known as a *piezoelectric pressure transducer.*

sub-caliber: Generally refers to calibers smaller than .17 caliber.

terminal energy: The remaining energy of a projectile at the point of impact.

terminal velocity: The remaining velocity of a projectile at the point of impact.

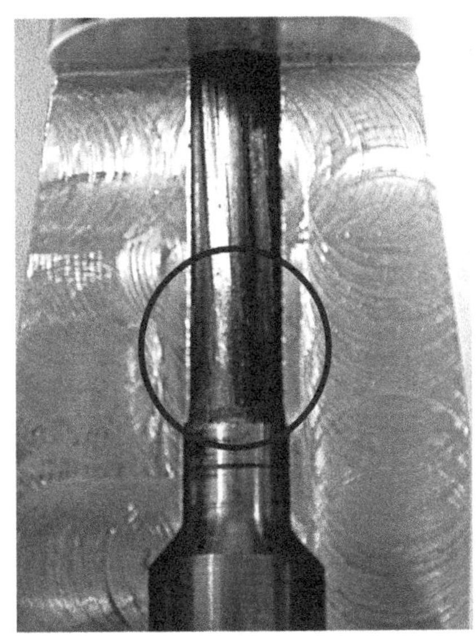

Throat.

throat: The tapered portion of the barrel's bore, immediately ahead of the chamber, which is sized to provide clearance for the bullet of the loaded cartridge. It is also referred to as *leade* and is associated with *freebore*. See photo.

time of flight: A projectile's total elapsed time to travel a specific distance from the muzzle (generally to the target).

trajectory: The curved path of a projectile from the muzzle to the target.

triple-based powder: A propellant composed of colloided nitrocellulose, nitroglycerine and nitroguanidine. Generally used in large-caliber military ammunition.

twist: The distance required for one complete turn of rifling, usually expressed as a ratio, e.g., 1:10 inches.

velocity: The speed of a projectile at a given point along its trajectory.

web: The portion of the case toward the muzzle, just ahead of the solid head, which tapers out quickly to the thickness of the main wall of the case.

wildcat cartridge: Cartridges designed by individual inventors that have never been commercially manufactured. See Chapter 1 for a complete discussion.

witness mark: A line on each of two mating parts indicating proper alignment. Also known as an *index mark*.

yaw: The angle between the longitudinal axis of a projectile and a line tangent to the trajectory through the center of gravity.

An excellent reference book for defining firearms terms is *The Firearms Dictionary*, by R.A. Steindler, Stackpole Books, 1970.

CHAPTER 3

Improved Cartridges

A nearly universal description of an "improved" case is one in which you create a larger (than original) chamber that will safely allow the firing of factory cartridges to fireform them to the larger dimensions. The new chamber will have a sharper shoulder angle and decreased body taper, combining to provide greater case capacity.

P.O. Ackley was probably not the first person to improve a cartridge, but he was the guy who made the process both uniform and popular. As a result, Ackley's name is synonymous in the gun industry with this form of cartridge.

It is widely accepted that sharp-shouldered cases are less prone to stretching; in other words, the brass does not flow forward as much as with commercial cartridges. Reloaders perceive this as an advantage because they must trim brass less frequently. The most significant advantage of improved cartridges is that no forming dies are required to make the brass. Firing an appropriate factory cartridge in the improved chamber will result in a fully formed case.

It is common to read claims that an improved cartridge is more accurate than its factory counterpart. This is highly unlikely; it is more likely that careful work by a qualified gunsmith will remove imperfections in the fitting of the barrel to the action, improving accuracy. There is a quote in an old P.O. Ackley pamphlet that says, "I have never seen an inaccurate cartridge when chambered in an accurate barrel."

Upon reloading the fireformed cases, the increased case capacity boosts velocity and flattens the projectile's trajectory. It's easy to see why the term improved became attached to this process. Logically, most reloaders are looking for enhanced performance, and because improved cases are so simple to work with, they're the first step shooters take toward wildcatting.

Some would argue that necking a case up or down in diameter from the original factory caliber is a form of an improved cartridge. It is a form of wildcat because the caliber is changed, but it's not an improved case because it doesn't alter the case capacity.

The earliest example of a "necked" cartridge that remains popular today is the .257 Roberts—originated by Major N.H. Roberts before World War I. It is essentially a 7x57 case necked down to .257 caliber. In 1938, the factory loadings for the .257 Roberts were an 87-gr. bullet at 3,200 fps, a 100-gr. at 2,900 fps and a 117-gr. at 2,650 fps[1]. The standard factory loadings at that time for the 7x57 included a 175-gr. bullet at about 2,300 fps, so you can see why some would consider the .257 Roberts, with its higher velocities, to have better ballistics over the 7x57, but that does not make it an improved cartridge.

Regarding cartridges with increased case capacity, the .22 K-Hornet is probably one of the best-known examples. It continues to be popular well over half a century after its introduction. Lysle Kilbourn of Whitesboro, New York, developed his design for an improved .22 Hornet case in about 1940. With the help of a Canadian gunsmith, G.B. Crandall, Kilbourn designed a cartridge to fire factory .22 Hornet ammunition in

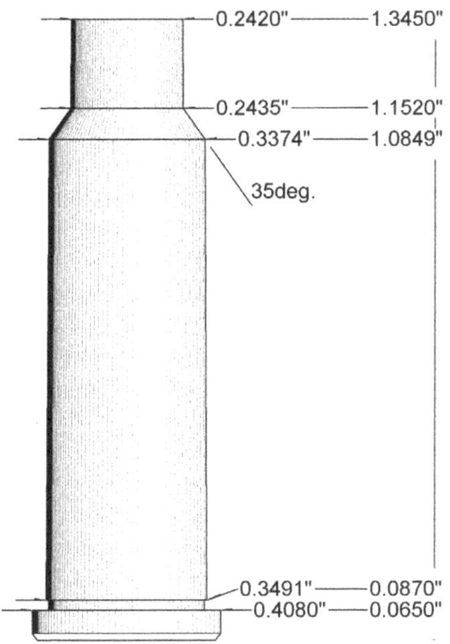

The .218 Mashburn Bee.

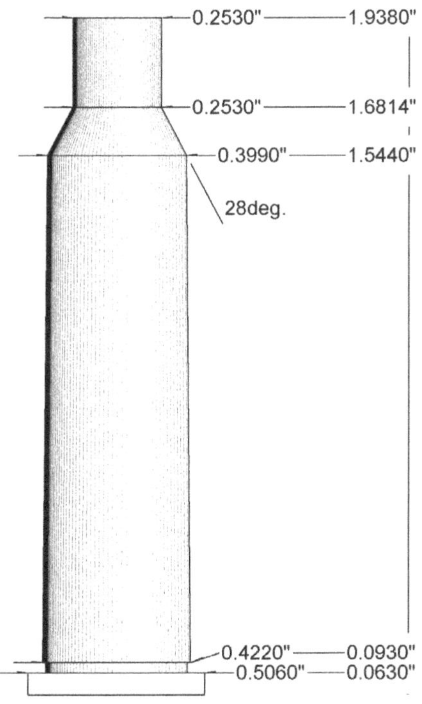

The .219 Zipper AI.

1 Sharpe, Philip B., *The Rifle in America*, 1938

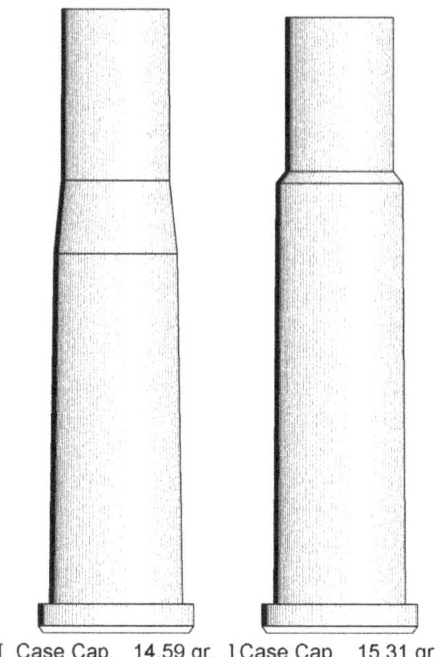

The .22 Hornet (left), .22 K-Hornet (right).

the new chamber, which sported a minimum taper body and sharp shoulder.

Two advantages came with the K-Hornet "Improved" case; first, case capacity was increased, adding about 10% more room for powder. Second, except for the comments about inherent accuracy on the previous pages, accuracy was improved over the original cartridge. The reason for this exception is straightforward; the original Hornet design was from the days of blackpowder cartridges with its long, tapered case, undefined shoulder and minimal case capacity. The K-Hornet had increased capacity, making it less finicky about load selection. Less body taper and a well-defined shoulder made the K-Hornet less susceptible to imperfections in the brass or dirt in the chamber pushing the case off center.

Research indicates that Kilborn was one of the first to develop this simple method of forming improved cases for a wildcat. One researcher suggests that Art Mashburn was the first in 1937 with his .300 Mashburn based on the .300 H&H case.[2] Mashburn also created the .218 Mashburn Bee in about 1940, so he is clearly in the running as the first to develop fireformed improved cases. These improved cartridges were important because they could safely fire factory loads in the wildcat chamber.

It's impossible to overstate Lylse Kilborn's and Art Mashburn's contributions to wildcatting in creating these improved cases.[3] These guys and at least a half dozen others were all working on the concept at the same time. Most of them knew each other, or at least of each others' work, so it's not likely we will ever know who was first.

Efficiency is not a word that writers often choose when describing cartridge designs. The reason is simple enough: readers are looking for superlatives in the descriptions of cartridges. They want a cartridge that can be described as flat shooting, having extreme velocity, screaming, powerful, amazing, accurate,

2 Lucas, Rob, "P.O. Ackley's Wildcats", *Gun Digest*, 1996

3 Waters, Ken, "22 K-Hornet", *Wildcat Cartridges*, 1992

smoking, or any of a dozen other adjectives that indicate fantastic external ballistics. However, efficiency is an exciting thing in the proper context.

For example, in the case of the .22 K-Hornet, the increased case capacity is converted into significantly increased velocity over the parent case. At the same time, it doesn't have so much fuel capacity as to be wasteful. The clearest example of this efficiency is a 45-gr. bullet in the factory Hornet loaded with 9.5 gr. of 2400 powder, which delivers 2,400 fps. The same bullet and powder in a K-Hornet with 10.5 gr. of powder will deliver 2,700 fps.[4] That's a 300 fps increase in velocity in exchange for one grain more powder, or to put it another way, a 12.5 percent increase in velocity in exchange for a 10.6 percent increase in powder charge.

Generally, when you look at statistics for increased case capacity, it is fair to say that a 10 percent increase in capacity will deliver a 3 to 5 percent increase in velocity. So, the K-Hornet far outstrips the average. That's what we mean by efficiency—a cartridge that utilizes the fuel available to it efficiently. As we look at larger bore diameters, other efficiency benefits, such as lower recoil, become noticeable. Therefore, efficiency in a cartridge is desirable, just like accuracy and knockdown power. More importantly, one does not preclude the other.

Inefficient cartridges will have higher felt recoil for two reasons. First, higher capacity means higher charge weights, and if you look at the math involved in calculating felt recoil, the powder charge is a substantial factor. Second, more fuel means more gas at the muzzle. Hot expanding gases escaping the barrel after the bullet exits turn into rocket thrust, driving the rifle back against your shoulder. That is why muzzle brakes work: They redirect the thrust to reduce felt recoil.

To calculate approximate recoil in foot-pounds:

$$E = 1/2\left(\frac{Wr}{32}\right)\left(\frac{Wb \times Vb + 4700 \times Wp}{7000 \times Wr}\right)^2$$

E is energy in foot-pounds, Wr is the weight of the rifle, Wb is the weight of the bullet in grains, Wp is the weight of the powder charge in grains, and Vb is the bullet's muzzle velocity. The constant of 4700 results in *approximate* recoil, as it does not precisely suit all calibers.[5] Recoil in foot-pounds will be very close +/– a few foot-pounds of the actual energy delivered. Felt recoil is subjective and will vary significantly from one shooter to another and is greatly affected by the design of the individual stock. However, the above formula does not account for the effect of rocket thrust.

---

4 Harvey, Nick, *Practical Reloading Manual*, 1993

5 *Lyman Reloading Handbook, 43rd Edition*, 1964

As you can see, the powder charge is a major factor in felt recoil. So, if we can reduce the powder charge and get the same result velocity-wise, we will also get less recoil.

It's interesting to note that improved cartridges are close enough in capacity to the parent cartridge that the increased recoil is negligible compared to the increased velocity. Efficiency comes into play here: a slight increase in capacity for a well-balanced commercial cartridge equates to increased velocity. However, if the original commercial case is already inefficient (overbore), then improving the case will deliver little or no increase in ballistics (it will increase recoil and muzzle blast).

Other "Improvements"

Years ago, I was working in a large gunshop in North Idaho as a gunsmith, and we had a client who always wanted to push the envelope ballistically with every rifle he owned. One of the gunsmiths in the shop inadvertently overcut the throat in one of this client's rifles (it's a long, stupid story), an 8mm Remington Magnum. The throat length was .750 inch (standard length would be about .150 inch). The client found that he could push the envelope. The throat was so long that he could load well beyond published data, so much so that it scared him, and, after years of wanting to have such a rifle, he disposed of it. Be careful what you ask for!

(The use of freebore in cartridge design will be covered in more detail in Chapter 13.)

At this point, failing to mention P.O. Ackley could be considered a valid reason to have the author flogged or even shot. I wish to avoid such consequences, so Ackley will have the last word on improved cartridges.

P.O. Ackley took factory offerings, expanded the body to a minimum body taper and changed the shoulder angles. The resulting case design provides increased case capacity. The idea was to give you more velocity from the case yet allow you to fire factory (parent) ammo in the chamber. The ability to fireform the brass easily using factory ammo is attractive to many shooters.

You can buy factory ammo in the parent caliber to shoot the rifle in a pinch; this can be a lifesaver (or at least a tripsaver) when traveling. It is purely my opinion that improved cartridges are not true wildcats. Wildcats must be formed in dies before being fired, and no factory cartridge can safely be fired in the wildcat chamber.

Ackley tested and retested his ideas and the cartridges he developed from those concepts. He wrote numerous articles, brochures, and the two books for which he is well known, *Handbook for Shooters & Reloaders, Volumes I & II.* Interestingly, Ackley did not particularly like the term "improved" concerning his cartridges, yet he did not suggest an alternative moniker for them. Here is what he had to say about it.

"The word 'improved' is an unfortunate selection because any 'improved' cartridge has little relation to its commercial counterpart except for the fact that the 'improved' chamber will accept factory ammunition without any danger to the shooter.

"Cases for an 'improved' cartridge are made by simply firing factory ammunition in the 'improved' chamber which does away with the necessity of using forming dies which are required for a pure Wildcat."[6]

There is much more to say about P.O. Ackley and his accomplishments. See Chapter 4 for a more complete story, or if you're curious about all the details, read *P.O. Ackley, America's Gunsmith* by Fred Zeglin, ISBN# 978-1-4402-4759-0. Available at Amazon.com and GunDigestStore.com.

Design rules for improved case design:

1. The minimum body taper is .0075 inch per inch of body length.
2. It must be able to safely headspace factory ammunition.
3. The shoulder angle has far less to do with case capacity than body taper.
4. A shoulder angle of 40 degrees is optimum for controlling brass flow (a shallower shoulder angle is more conducive to reliable feeding).
5. Fireforming will shorten the overall case length.
6. A balanced case and bore capacity will deliver the best ballistics vs. powder charge.

Improved cartridges do not allow the would-be designer to develop something original. As soon as the factories offer new chamberings, the improved designs are drawn up and made available by most reamer makers even before you can buy the parent brass. Many new cartridges at this writing are so close to improved designs that the gains from improving cases are hardly worth the effort with new factory offerings.

Wildcatting will no doubt take you into more complex designs. However, knowing the basic rules of improved chambers is very useful for the wildcatter in designing cartridges that feed and extract well. Velocity is of no value without reliability, and if you have both of the former but poor accuracy, you are wasting powder and time.

6 Ackley, P.O., *Handbook* and catalog, 1951

The author with his son Dewain in front of the "Chicken Coup," P.O. Ackley's shop in Salt Lake.

CHAPTER 4

Parker Otto Ackley, Undisputed King of Improved Cartridges

To this day, P.O. Ackley is the most famous of all Wildcat cartridge designers. Ackley was a native of Granville, New York. He graduated from Syracuse University, Magna cum Laude, in 1927. Following his marriage to Winnefred Ross in 1928, the couple established a farm and trucking business, and she stopped teaching to raise a family. During his career, Ackley was a barrel maker, gunsmith, firearms importer, college professor, experimenter, author, and, most important to those reading this book, a wildcatter extraordinaire.

During the Great Depression, Ackley moved to Roseburg, Oregon, where, in 1936, he established his gunsmithing and barrel-making business. The business flourished there until 1942 when Ackley went to work for the Small Arms Division of the Ogden Arsenal to support the war effort until 1944. Upon leaving the Arsenal, he moved to Cimarron, New Mexico, for a year, where he re-established his gun business. In 1945, Ackley moved his gun business to

Trinidad, Colorado. From 1946 to 1951, he taught the theory of gun making and metallurgy at Trinidad State Junior College. During this time, Ackley performed his famous experiments in case design and blowing actions apart.

In 1951, Ackley sold his gun business in Trinidad and moved his family to Salt Lake City, Utah. His wife Winn opened a branch of Tandy Leather Co., becoming the first female in a management position for the company, from which she retired in 1968.

P.O. Ackley regularly contributed to *Guns & Ammo* and *Shooting Times* magazines. He worked carefully to develop a reputation for telling the truth. These magazine articles contributed significantly to his fame in the gun industry and helped to build his business. In 1962, Ackley published his magnum opus, *Handbook for Shooters & Reloaders Volume I* (Volume II followed in 1966). These books are still handy and valuable resources for would-be wildcatters. Knowing what has been done and the results can be helpful when considering a new design.

P.O. Ackley died in 1989 at the age of 86.

Ackley's Contributions

Ackley showed unusual professionalism as a gunsmith as his use of a scientific approach to testing cartridges, barrels and actions set him apart from the pack. He carefully recorded and collected test results to find empirical evidence to verify or refute longstanding theories concerning internal ballistics. To this day, his collection of information stands as the most extensive published body of evidence describing the strengths and weaknesses of various actions and case designs. He went beyond theory to prove what would happen under various conditions with real-world tests.

In Volume I, Ackley explored the question of pressure. To prove his points concerning case design and bolt thrust as important issues, when discussing pressure, he describes tests he did with a Savage 99 and a Winchester 94 action. He asserted that he proved three major points by creating a condition of grossly excessive headspace in the 94 action.

1. That minimum body taper cases transfer more pressure to the chamber walls, minimizing the amount of bolt thrust.
2. That an oily chamber or cartridge will increase bolt thrust.
3. That brass cases will contain some pressure; otherwise, the unsupported cases would have ruptured in his test.

Many shooters consider Ackley's tests inconsequential or outdated, but neither could be further from the truth. He proved that many of our accepted axioms are little more than wives' tales.

How could this be? Well, it's simple. Over the years, various sources have written down with "authority" that some information is gospel fact. The truth is, all too often, the information represented as supposed facts is little more than an assumption on the part of the originator, most often a gun writer.

That is not to say you have a license to pack powder in cases without fear of reprisal. The point is that the wise use of design principles, proper headspace of firearms and ammunition, and attention to pressure signs will serve you well when developing a new wildcat. This is perhaps P.O. Ackley's most crucial contribution to wildcatting.

To further illustrate the value of the improved case design, Ackley reports on his tests with a Savage 99 initially chambered in .250-3000. He indicates that a specific load of HiVel #2 and a 100-gr. bullet delivered 2,900 fps, a peak chamber pressure of 52,000, and extracts fine. The method used to collect pressure data is not mentioned. Ackley states that any increase in powder will lock up the action from the increased pressure. Next, he rechambered the Model 99 to his improved .250-3000 and fireformed the brass before testing full-power loads. The result is interesting. The load mentioned above, which previously froze the action, was fired in the improved chamber, and extraction was easy.

Ackley wanted to demonstrate that his improved chamber would handle pressure differently than the factory-style chamber. He added one grain of powder at a time to the load until trouble appeared. He states that with the improved chamber, seldom will the action lock up before something else fails. In his account, Ackley goes into much more detail, the point being that improved cases—which have minimum body taper—are subject to much less bolt thrust.

With two separate tests, Ackley proved that minimum body taper will change how pressure is handled by the action (more on this in Chapter 9).

In Volume II, Ackley published the results of some very interesting tests. Titled "The Strength of Military Rifle Actions," the article runs 22 pages. It details the results of tests in 18 actions, including the Arisaka M38, Mauser 98, Enfield

P-17, Springfield, Krag, Lee-Enfield and various 6.5 Jap actions. First, he laid out the test data for each action and then provided a narrative for the tests. Here again, P.O. Ackley provided actual tests to develop an informed opinion, whereas most of his contemporaries parroted what they had heard from other gun buffs or "experts."

In short, Ackley worked hard to dispel rumors and misinformation. He designed tests as close to the real world as possible to ascertain the truth of any discussion. Over and over, he disproved long-standing statements, like, "Krag actions are weak; they will not handle a .22 wildcat." The funny thing is that many of the fallacies that Ackley disproved are still popularly retold as gospel—proving that it's easier to create a myth than to kill one.

Ackley's books did a better job of recording the wildcatting that was going on during his time than any book did. So, for historical purposes, they are extremely interesting. By seeing the successes and failures of those who went before us, we can see how design features and trends have performed. It may be possible to predict the popular trends by looking back at previous experiments.

If you want to know about wildcats before P.O. Ackley's books, check out *Wildcat Cartridges* by Richard F. Simmons, 1947.

What and When

It makes perfect sense that Ackley would start with a rimmed case. Rimmed cartridges headspace on the case's rim, so when fireforming a wildcat, the rim is trapped between the bolt and the barrel breech. There is no better safety valve for a young wildcatter learning the ropes. Headspacing on the rim leaves the rest of the case free to fireform without the need to headspace on a shoulder or apply special fireforming techniques. Here, Ackley would have learned about brass stretch and how the brass will shorten when fired in an improved chamber.

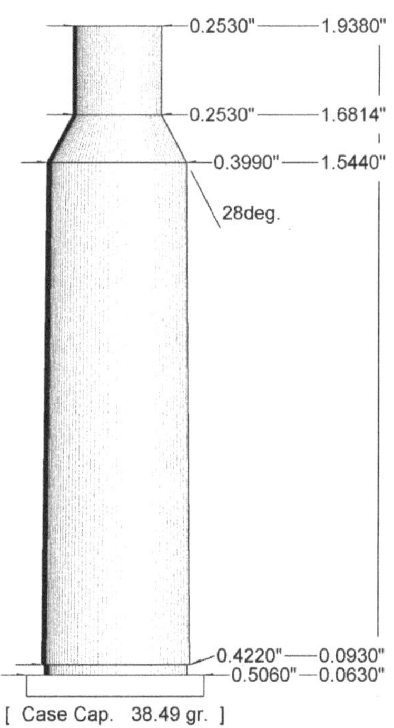

The .219 Zipper Improved.

In the first edition of this book, I stated that "In 1938 Ackley offered his first wildcat, the .219 Zipper Improved. Like most wildcatters, the first attempt for Ackley was not perfect. He made three versions of the .219 Zipper Improved before being satisfied with the design.[1] Ultimately, Ackley suggested using .30-30 brass to form this cartridge because of the factory's changes in the cases after World War II. Finally, he designed the .22/30-30 Ackley improved apparently to simplify the making of brass."

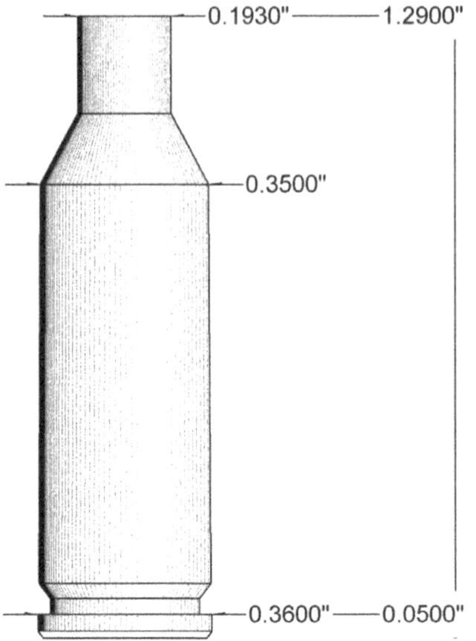

The .17 Ackley Pee Wee.

While researching *P.O. Ackley, America's Gunsmith*, I learned that Ackley produced an improved .22 Savage Hi-Power before the creation of the .219 Zipper Improved. Likely, this work was done in 1937–38 since the Zipper Improved was published in 1938.

In an old P.O. Ackley pamphlet (circa 1951), Ackley shows photos of 16 cartridges he was promoting. During his career, he built and sold far more wildcats than that. Reading his comments and articles, no reference was located that he ever said so. Still, I speculate that he felt the cartridges he was selling at that time covered any foreseeable need of any shooter. Over time, the public asks for variations, and any time the factories come out with a new cartridge, it's a wildcatter's delight. Over the years, Ackley added to his line as demand required.

In the late 1940s and early '50s, Ackley pioneered the .17 caliber. At one time, he was the only source for .17-caliber barrels in the industry. In 1946, according to Landis, "Ackley seems to largely control the field on the manufacture of .17-caliber rifles in the United States."[2]

The .17 Ackley Bee was one of P.O.'s earliest attempts at a .17-caliber wildcat, called initially the Rimmed .17 Ackley Pee Wee. The true .17 Pee Wee is based on the .30 Carbine.

Developed in the early 1950s, the .17 Ackley Hornet is a fine example of Ackley putting his lessons learned to work. He achieved maximum case capacity, retained the necessary neck length for good function and created a very

1 Lucas, Rob, "P.O. Ackley's Wildcats", *Gun Digest*, 1996

2 Landis, Charles S., *Twenty-Two Caliber Varmint Rifles*, 1946

efficient cartridge that remained popular with wildcatters until the .17 Hornady Hornet came on the market in about 2011. It is so similar to the Ackley that one could consider the .17 Ackley Hornet obsolete.

Ackley mentioned the .17/222 as the maximum capacity for the .17-caliber bore. Others, such as Paul Marquart, who partnered with Atkinson to develop the .17 Javalina, confirmed this. Marquart said, "The .17-caliber case should not exceed 17 grains capacity." As proof, Marquart would produce his rifle in .17 Javalina, which he proudly pointed out had not been cleaned since the day it was built and still produced tiny little groups. The primary complaint of .17-caliber shooters is that they must clean every 10 to 15 shots to maintain accuracy. They could avoid all that cleaning if they stuck to Ackley's and Marquart's capacity limit for the .17.

Ackley's Thoughts on Shoulder Angle

"Most of our own .22 cases, such as the .228 Ackleys, the Improved Zippers, the .17 caliber, are all 28-degree shoulder. We can see very little difference in small changes in shoulder angle. We have tried the 45-degree shoulders but did not like the results; we can see no increase in efficiency of the 30-degree or even the 28-degree, but with the too-sharp angles, the headspace is hard to maintain. That is, the first shot or two will expand the cases slightly, which causes the bolt to turn down hard because there is little taper on the shoulder, and the case can not be pushed (wedged) into the chamber as easily as with the more tapered design. This necessitates setting the headspace with a full-length sizing, which I do not like to do. This is also in complete agreement with Ashurst, Gipson, and Lovell; they all agree that 28-degree and 30-degree shoulder slopes are the best for satisfactory results[3]," said Ackley in a letter to Charles Landis in about 1945.

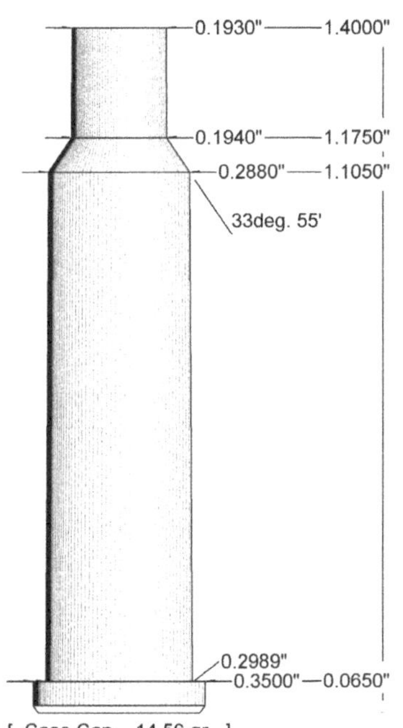

The .17 Ackley Hornet.

If Ackley believed what he said above, there is a discrepancy

3 Ibid.

somewhere; why are most of his improved cases blessed with 40-degree shoulders? Because perception is everything in sales, customers perceived that the sharper shoulder gave them the advantage of greater capacity and less brass flow. The increased capacity is so slight that it makes virtually no difference in ballistics. Sometimes, in business, we have to sell what the customer wants instead of the best possible product. P.O. Ackley understood this better than most gunsmiths. Many gunsmiths were working with shoulder angles close to 30 degrees, and by staking out the ground at 40 degrees, he separated himself from the pack.

I located 101 wildcats tied to Ackley, and there could be more; over 40 of those cartridges are improved cases of one form or another.

Declaring who designed the first fireform-improved case is near to impossible. Ackley himself was never presumptuous enough to take credit for it. The K-Hornet discussed in Chapter 2 of this book was developed in 1939 or '40. Numerous other cartridges were developed in the same period. In the mid-1930s, Harvey Donaldson, Vernor Gipson, Lyle Kilborn, Art Mashburn, and Hervey Lovell were just a few of the guys working on wildcats, fast and furiously. This was a time when wildcatting truly deserved its name. With each development, the designers learned something that would be applied to later designs. The question of who was first to "fireform improve" a cartridge will never be answered. Too many new cartridges were churned out by too many individuals to nail down that detail.

How success is measured is essential. Being the first at something does not make you the best, and Ackley was likely not the first to improve a case. However, by nearly every standard, he was successful. He was prolific in developing cartridges, but more importantly, he knew how to market them. For example, Charles Newton was probably 40 years ahead of his time in terms of the rifles and cartridges he designed. By most accounts, Newton was an engineering genius, but in the marketplace, he failed by nearly every measure because he could not deal with the day-to-day problems of running a business. To be fair, Newton had some bad luck as well.

Not everyone thought of P.O. Ackley as the pioneer of the improved case design. Rob Lucas relates a conversation with Elmer Keith in his article, "Ackley's Wildcats," *Gun Digest*, 1996. He tells how Keith chastised him for considering an Ackley-improved chamber. Keith said, "Charles Newton invented the improved wildcat before 1920; it was the blown-out old .256 Newton. Charlie O'Neil fooled with the Improved '06 before we brought out the .333 OKH after the war. But Charlie Newton beat Charlie O'Neil an' everybody else, including Ackley, by

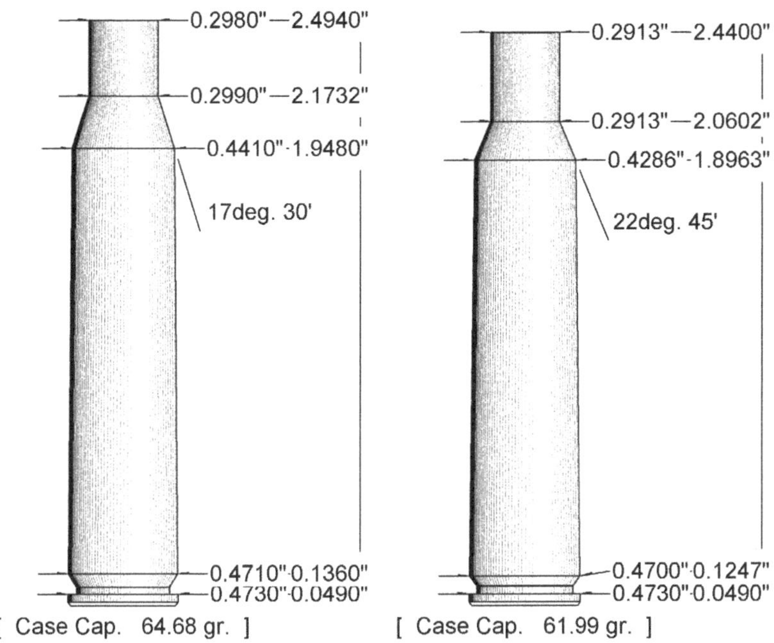

The 6.5-06 (left), .256 Newton (right).

twenty years!"[4]

The problem with these comments is that the .333 OKH came out in 1945—eight years after Ackley began his improved wildcats (and it just so happens the same year that Ackley introduced the .30-06 Ackley Improved). The .333 OKH was not an improved design; it was basically a .30-06 case necked up to .333. The modern equivalent is the .338-06, which no one would call improved.

Second, the dimensions of the .256 Newton are not improved at all. The .256 Newton is a shorter version of the 6.5-06 with a smaller shoulder diameter, and it clearly has less case capacity than the conventional 6.5-06. Maybe the slightly sharper shoulder on the .256 made Keith think it was an improved design. Was Keith referring to some improved versions of these cartridges?

In a cross reference of Newton's designs, you will find no improved cases among his work. So, what was Keith getting at? It probably had more to do with the longstanding disagreements between Keith and Ackley than with who pioneered the improved case design. Each man helped shape the gun industry through his respective labors.

4 Lucas, Rob, "P.O. Ackley's Wildcats", *Gun Digest*, 1996

.17 Ackley Hornet
.17 Ackley Bee
.17 Ackley Pee Wee
.17 Ackley Rimmed Super Pee Wee
.17 Mach III & IV
.17/223 Ackley Improved
.17/222
.17/222 Magnum Ackley
.17/225 Ackley
.17 Flintstone Eyebunger
.22 Ackley Hornet
.22 Ackley Improved Jet
.218 Ackley Bee
.222 Ackley Improved
.222 Rem. Mag. Ackley
.22 Hi-Power Ackley
.219 Zipper Ackley
.22/30-30 Ackley Improved
.22/250 Ackley Improved
.220 Swift Ackley Improved
.224 Ackley Wine Bottle
.228 Belted Express
.228 Krag (Ackley)
.228 Ackley Magnum
.230 Ackley Short
.230 Ackley
.22-06 Ackley Double Shoulder
.22 Eargosplitten Loudenboomer
.224 Belted Express
6mm/30-30 Ackley
.240-250 Savage Ackley
.243 Winchester Ackley
6mm Rem Ackley
6mm Krag Ackley
6mm Magnum Ackley
.25-20 Single Shot Ackley
.25 Short Krag (Ackley)
.25 Belted Express
.25-35 Ackley
.250 Savage Ackley
.25 Krag Improved
.25-06 Improved
.25 Ackley Magnum
6.5x57 Ackley
6.5-06 Ackley
.270/308 Improved
.270/257 Improved
.270 Winchester Improved
.270 Ackley Magnum
.270 Ackley Newton
7x57 Improved
7mm-06 Improved
.280 Ackley Improved
7mm Ackley Newton
7mm Ackley Magnum
.30 Baby Magnum
.30-30 Improved
.30/40 Improved
.30-06 Improved
.30 Short Magnum #1
.30 Short Magnum #2
.30/348 Improved
.300 H&H Improved
(300 Ackley Magnum)
8mm/06 Improved
.333 Short Magnum
.333 Magnum Improved
.348 Improved
.35 Whelen Improved
.35-348 Improved
.35 Ackley Magnum
.35 Ackley Mag. Imp.
.375 Whelen Improved
.375 H&H Improved
.40-348 Improved
.400 Ackley Magnum
.411 Bowman
.450-348 Ackley Improved
.450 Ackley Magnum
.475 Ackley Magnum

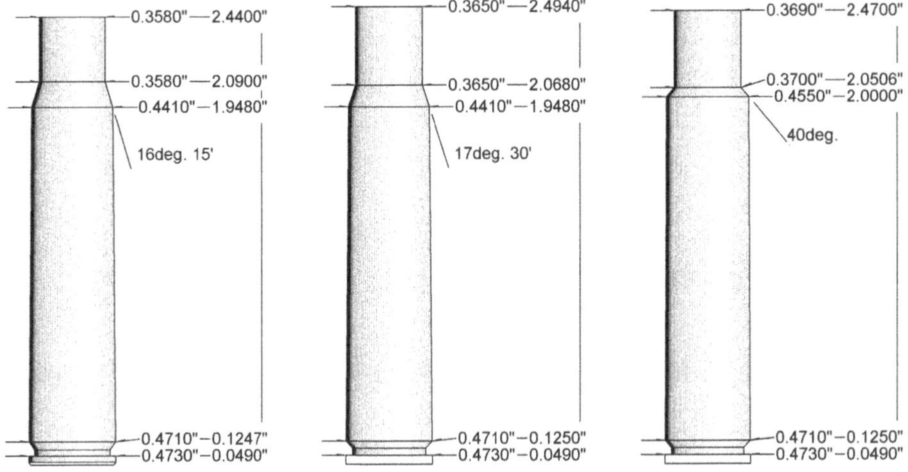

The .333 OKH (left), .338-06 (middle) and .338-06 Ackley Improved (right).

The .333 OKH, .338-06 and .338-06 AI Compared

P.O. Ackley may not have been the first gunsmith to work with improved cases, but he did make a career out of it. Ackley's improved cartridges have become so well known that it is now common for reamer makers or gunsmiths to offer Ackley Improved versions when a new cartridge comes from the factories. Even when called improved, they still use Ackley's basic rules for case improvements. That is quite a compliment to a gunsmith who has long since departed from the range.

On the left is a partial list of the cartridges that Ackley claimed at one time or another in his career. There are others with his name attached, many of which he did not personally build but follow his design rules. He also developed cartridges for others, so they do not all have his name attached.

CHAPTER 5

Case Design and Development

A long and interesting history led to the development of brass cases for cartridges in modern firearms. Some would argue that it is a long and tedious history (obviously, they are not gun nuts). However, we will pick up the story about halfway through, and you will have to do some research if you want to know the rest.

In 1851, Edward Maynard patented his now universal brass cartridge. The original design included a tubular brass case for the body, to which was soldered a large, rimmed flat base. There was a tiny flash hole in the center of the case instead of a primer pocket. The case was used with Maynard tape primers, becoming the first practical brass cartridge breechloader.

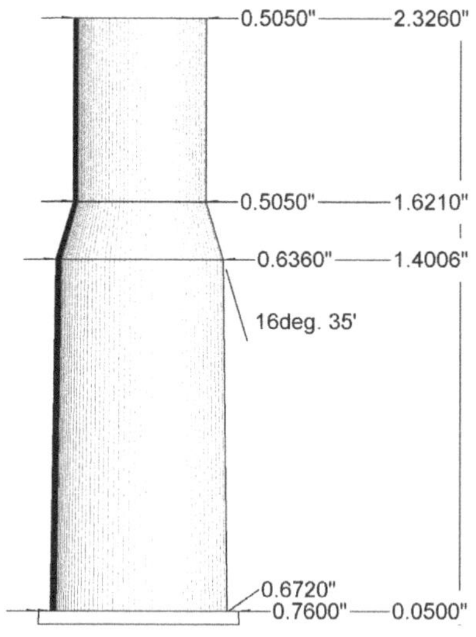

The .577/450 Martini-Henry.

Philip B. Sharpe told a story from his youth about the Maynard cartridge: "They were a pretty poor thing to strike a match on even in wet weather. In building a campfire, one of the boys tried a match. The match lighted—so did the powder charge. There was one vivid explosion and a very surprised youngster who no longer had either the match or the cartridge case in his hand. Fortunately, no injury was caused. We spent several hours looking for traces of that cartridge without success."[1]

(For details on various cartridge case designs and information about the subject for all hobbyists to utilize, see CartridgeCollectors.org.)

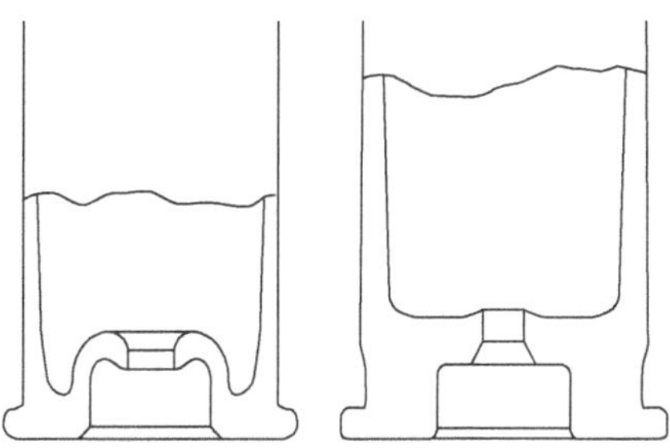

On the left, we have a folded head cartridge case. On the right is a modern solid head cartridge.[1]

1 Col. Whelen, Townsend, *Small Arms Design and Ballistics*, 1945

During the early development period of brass cartridges, the British tried a composite case made of brass foil and paper with a steel head. Later, they tried an all-brass-wrapped case as the cost was much lower than drawn brass. Even into the 1930s, Great Britain produced these wrapped cases for the .577 Snider and the .577/450 Martini-Henry. The reason cited was twofold: cost and the fact that the Crown saw no reason to arm natives in its colonies with more modern arms.

Coiled cases, as they were called, never caught on in America—the earliest attempts at drawing metallic cases used copper rather than brass. Our manufacturers learned early on how to draw solid brass cases. We were years ahead of most countries in this technology.

The first major success for brass cases in the United States was the Burnside. Burnside carbines were widely used during the Civil War through the Battle of the Little Big Horn. This cartridge was straight-walled with a very thin mouth, the bullet was conical with a heavy ring around the base, and the case mouth was crimped around this bulge. The Burnside was unique in its function. In his 1938 book, *The Rifle in America*, Philip Sharpe says "old timers" told how, when fired, the crimped mouth at the bullet's base tore off and stayed with the bullet[2]—not much different than a gas check or a driving band in modern terms. Sharpe was dubious of these claims until a reader of his articles mailed him samples of bullets dredged up in the area of Grand Coulee Dam. Many were identified as Burnside bullets; indeed, they had the brass ring still attached, rifling engraved right over the band. The Burnside used external ignition, either a percussion cap or a Maynard tape primer—a tiny flash hole at the base of the cartridge lined up with the ignition source.

What we would recognize as centerfire cartridges first went into the experimentation phase at Frankford Arsenal in 1864. Starting with a long line

1 Sharpe, Philip B., *The Rifle in America*, 1938

2 *Ibid.*

of folded head cases, numerous experiments led to the balloon head case, then the semi-balloon head, and eventually to the solid head case as we know it today.

The first solid head case was the .45 Hotchkiss. Examples of the Hotchkiss case show signs that lathe turning finished the rim. The Hotchkiss did not have an external primer pocket. Instead, a cup was formed inside the case in the head of the cartridge. An inverted anvil containing the primer compound was inserted into the pocket and crimped. The firing pin then struck the center of the head, causing an indentation and igniting it as with modern primers. These cases were not reloadable.

When did the first solid head case we would associate with modern-day cases go into use? In the late 1860s, the United States Cartridge Co. of Lowell, Massachusetts, submitted a cartridge based on Farington's patent to Frankford Arsenal for testing. In December 1872, Farington received Patent No. 133,929 for a double-cupped primer used in a conventional primer pocket.

Frankford Arsenal (FA) tested 630 cartridges using Farington's new priming system against an equal number of arsenal-fabricated service loads. No failures occurred among the FA rounds; one cartridge failed among the ammunition loaded by the U.S. Cartridge Co. An investigation found no priming compound had been inserted in that one primer. A .50-caliber Gatling gun was used to test another 100 rounds of both ammo types without failure. It was reported that extraction was much easier with the solid head cases.

With the development of the external centerfire priming system, the end of the copper case for any cartridge with centerfire ballistic capabilities arrived. At this point, the development of the centerfire case stagnated. Ammunition manufacturers lacked the knowledge or equipment to produce solid head cases. It took time for manufacturers to learn how to draw brass cases with a solid head.

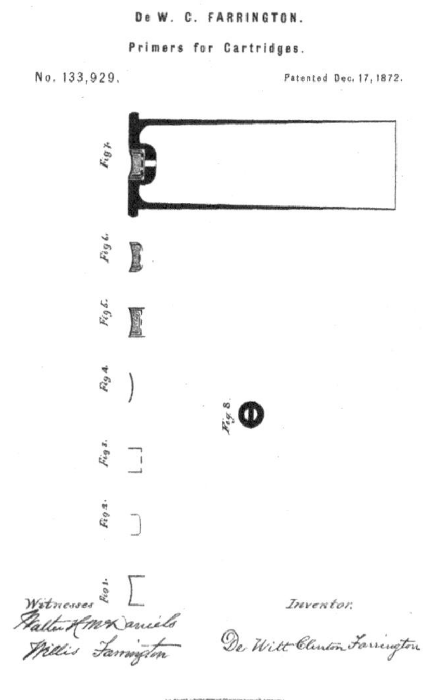

Farington's patent.

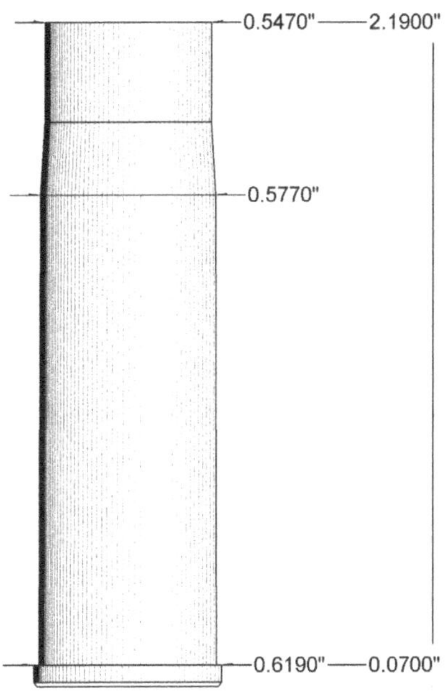

The .50-115 Bullard.

Union Metallic Cartridge Company (UMC) was a pioneer in the development of manufacturing processes for the solid head brass case. Folded head cases were made much like a rimfire: when the rim was bumped onto the case, it created a weak spot at the edge of the rim where ruptures were possible. UMC marked all the early solid head cases it produced with "S.H." on the headstamp to differentiate them from the folded head cases still in production. It took several years to completely replace the old-style cases with the new, stronger design. When the conversion was complete, UMC dropped the "S.H." marking from the headstamp.

The arrival of smokeless powders on the scene was the final death knell for the folded head case. They did not have the strength to handle the pressures the then-new smokeless powders created.

Smokeless powder develops pressure differently than blackpowder—the pressure is built very quickly, placing significant stress on the cartridge case and the rifle's breech. Blackpowder tends to distribute its pressure over the entire length of the barrel. Note that barrels on blackpowder-era guns tended to be approximately the same thickness out to the muzzle. Modern smokeless powder barrels quickly evolved into a heavy breech with a taper to a relatively thin muzzle.

Developing Rimless Cartridges

Cut-and-dried answers are pretty tough to find in the history of cartridge development. Sharpe states in *The Rifle in America* that "Winchester claims they made the first successful rimless cartridge in this country in the 6mm Lee Navy. It is also quite possible that this was the .50-115 Bullard." Then, in Frank C. Barnes' *Cartridges of the World, 8th Edition*, he refers to the Bullard, "It is unique in being both the first semi-rimmed and solid head cartridge produced in the U.S."

Let's assume that Barnes was correct. He also pointed out that the .50-

115 was a semi-rimmed cartridge. Yes, that does make it similar to a rimless case—the mechanics are the same—the difference is a rim slightly larger than the body on a semi-rimless case. Today, we recognize semi-rimless and rimless cases as two separate designs. However, there was little distinction between the two during their early development.

With all that said, the 6mm Lee Navy is likely the first successful rimless case manufactured in the United States. Unfortunately, the Lee Navy was far ahead of its time in design. The powders available in 1895 were not sufficient for this small-caliber cartridge. We know it was a good case because later in its life cycle, Winchester necked it to .224 and increased the rim diameter to work in a standard bolt face, creating the .220 Swift.

Rimmed and rimless cases are basically the same mechanically. Rimless case rims are formed approximately the same diameter as the head, and an extractor groove is cut into the head. This process was not possible on the early solid head cases because there was not enough material in the head of the case. Necessity is the mother of invention, though. Smokeless powders forced thicker head construction and eventually made rimless cases a logical step in development. Rimless cases feed more smoothly in nearly any rifle design than rimmed, and from a military standpoint, that equals speed and reliability. We would inevitably move in the direction of rimless case designs.

The next significant improvement was the elimination of mercuric fulminate primers. Mercury attacks brass, making it brittle and unsuitable for reloading. When Frankford Arsenal introduced its H-48 priming compound for the 1898 .30-40 Krag, the gun industry quickly picked up on it, and it lasted into the 1950s when the first non-corrosive primers went into production.

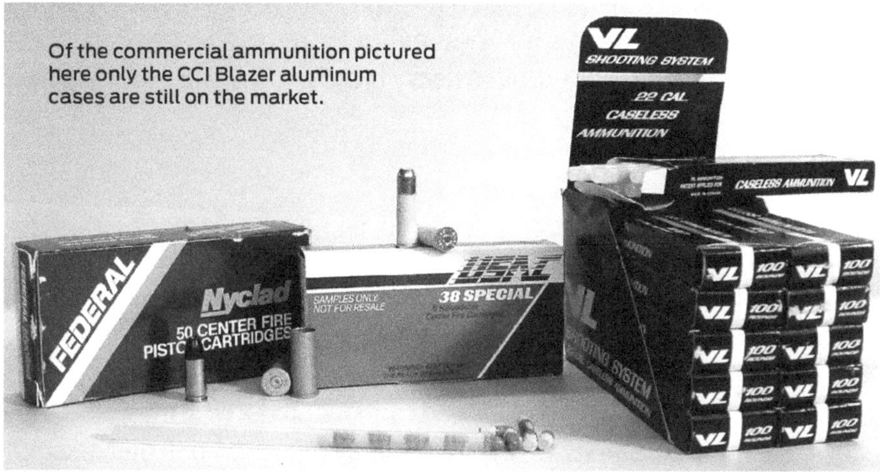

Of the commercial ammunition pictured here only the CCI Blazer aluminum cases are still on the market.

Nov. 30, 1948. R. W. MILLER ET AL **2,455,080**

ORDNANCE CHAMBRAGE AND CARTRIDGE CASE

Filed Dec. 4, 1944

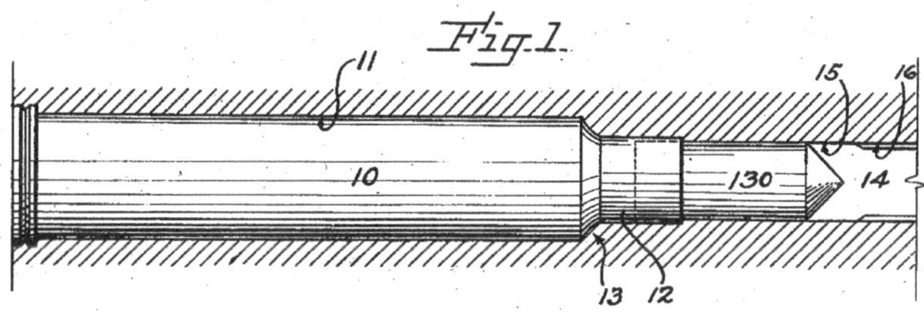

The 7x57 Mauser was put to work in the 1893 Mauser action designated for that year. Winchester introduced the .30-30 in 1895 for the 1894 Winchester lever-action. In 1893, the .30-40 Krag (the .30 U.S.) went into service with the United States Army. Looking at cartridge cases from those days to the present, one might get the idea that the technology of cartridge case design has stagnated. In many ways, it has done just that. Aside from some minor experimentations with steel cases, plastic cases, and even caseless ammo, we are still using brass that an armoror from 1893 would recognize.

One interesting, if not important, change is the development of the venturi-type shoulder. Ralph Waldo Miller taught Roy Weatherby how to reload and develop cartridges. Miller did much of his development work with the .275 H&H case, as he liked the rounded shoulder design that later became synonymous with the Weatherby name. Miller believed the double-radius shoulder allowed gases and powder to slip smoothly out of the cartridge case. Along with E. Baden Powell, he developed a whole line of cartridges while attempting to surpass 5,000 fps. These were the Powell-Miller Venturi Freebore Cartridges (PMVF)[3].

During the last 100 years, the changes in brass cases have been relatively minor. Metallurgy has improved so that the manufacturers now know which material will provide the best combination of traits for a high-pressure case. The case head, body, and neck thicknesses have all trended upwards, primarily to handle the higher pressures of modern loads. This point can easily be proven by chamber casting early blackpowder cartridge guns: the necks are thin compared to modern brass, and 50% less wall thickness is not unusual.

Two examples of these changes would be:

The .219 Zipper Ackley Improved. When Ackley developed his cartridge

3 Stowers, Roger and Jackson, Robert, "Rise and Fall of the 228 Weatherby", *The Weatherby Reference*, 1999

version in the late 1930s, he used .25-35 brass to form it. After World War II, he found that the factory .25-35 brass was too thick in the neck and body to form the .219 Zipper AI properly, so he recommended using .30-30 brass.

A recent example is the .223 WSSM case. A client asked me to wildcat a .25/223 WSSM, which was accomplished by necking the case up to .257 (this cartridge became a factory offering before the first edition of this book was finished). The factory .223 WSSM case neck had a wall thickness of .020 inch (typical thickness in the neck would be an average of .014 inch).

Upon test firing the cases, they could not be resized in a standard reloading press to allow easy chambering. In effect, fireforming had stretched the case slightly longer than the chamber. The case shoulder was so large in diameter and the brass so thick that two standard reloading presses I tried would stretch at least .010 inch. Using an old RCBS A4 press, we ran the brass through the same die. The heavy-duty press made simple work of resizing the beefed-up cases so they headspaced correctly again.

The trend toward short and fat cases like the WSSM has pointed out new problems for those who reload or wildcat them. The added wall thickness, combined with the huge surface area of the shoulder, requires reloading presses with sizing power generally reserved for .50 BMG cases.

Factories face a dilemma; they want to offer the cartridges they believe the shooting public will buy. To make the high-pressure short, fat cases work reliably, the engineers must look for ways to contain the pressure. In a .25-06 chamber, the pressure is distributed over a much larger surface area in the case, so conventional-thickness brass allows some of the pressure to be used up in expanding the case to the chamber walls, creating a gas seal for the breech. Bolt thrust, the amount of pressure against the face of the bolt, is at least in part affected by the amount of surface area inside the chamber. Another significant factor is the diameter of the case head—the bigger the head, the more exposure to the gas pressures in the case.

Engineers thickened the short, fat case of the .223 WSSM and its family to contain the same high pressure as in a .25-06 Remington. The smaller case offers far less surface area for the pressure to work against. Thus, engineers use thicker brass to make up the difference. An unintended consequence is that the case's internal surfaces are slightly reduced.

One problem with this approach is that the brass is so thick that it does not adhere to the chamber walls as it should to seal the chamber against escaping gases. This is proven by the fact that even full-pressure loads will show carbon on the outside of the case neck, a clear sign that the case did not seal when the

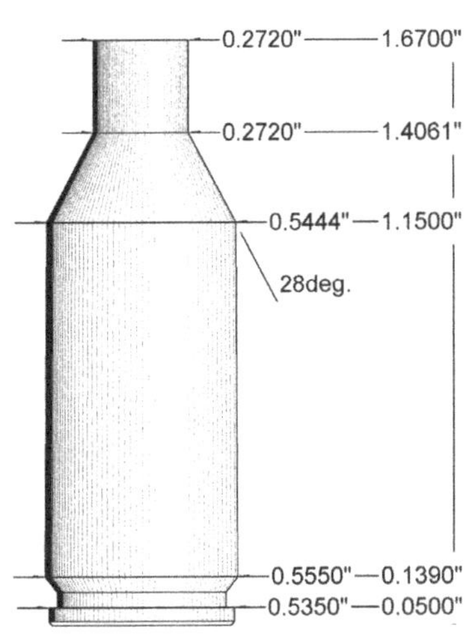

The .223 WSSM.

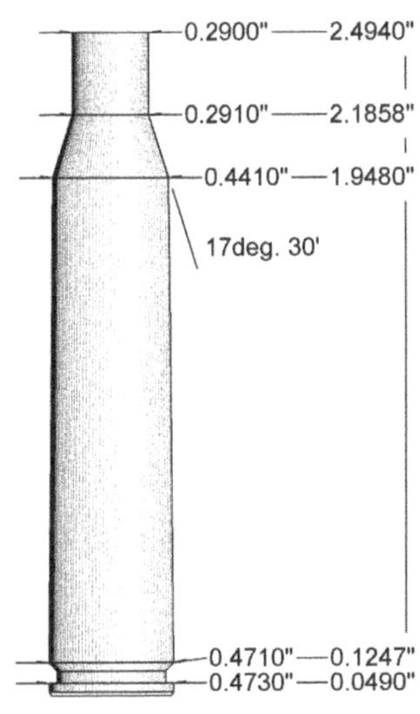

The .25-06.

bullet entered the bore. This is a situation where annealing the case neck and shoulder may help.

Upon hearing about the brass that had grown long, one experienced shooter and reloader commented that he had seen similar problems on other calibers. Even after a case was full-length sized, it would not headspace correctly in the chamber, being too long, making it hard to close the bolt. As a result, I went looking for such brass/gun combinations.

I located a .25-06 and .300 Savage that displayed the problem. The brass for the .300 Savage was so long that the bolt was very difficult to close (we are talking about the length of the case in terms of headspace). Some reloaders might toss these cases because they are unsure of the problem.

There is a solution. Brass annealing has been a mildly controversial subject in the reloading community. Some say it's needed, some ignore it, and competition shooters have tested brass and loaded ammo to find the truth. Annealing makes the brass softer, more malleable. Naturally, this solves our problem with brass that has grown too long at the shoulder, preventing proper chambering.

There are numerous methods for annealing, and many commercial machines provide semi-production setups so that many cases can be uniformly annealed. Until about 2015, nobody had applied much science to the process. It was mostly trial and error until the reloader found a system they liked. What changed?

In 2015, Annealing Made Perfect (AMP) hit the market.[4] Alex and Matt Findlay designed the machine in New Zealand. They worked with the university

4 ampannealing.com

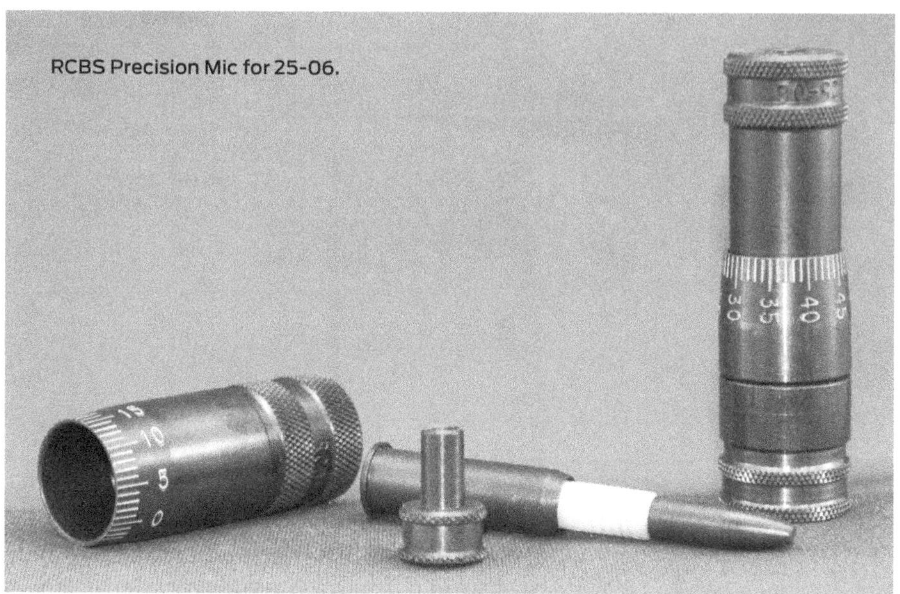

RCBS Precision Mic for 25-06.

in their community to develop a machine that you could calibrate to the exact lot of brass you are working with—delivering uniform and repeatable results. Whether you run out and buy one or not, they learned something important while developing this tool.

It has long been thought that brass can be loaded more than once, and you would need to anneal every three or four loadings to return to proper malleability. AMP proved that brass is notably hardened with just one firing cycle and should be annealed for best uniformity and accuracy. One more wives' tale was disproven.

Can you anneal brass without the AMP machine? Yes, of course! If you are the average shooter/reloader, any methods or equipment traditionally used to anneal will suffice. Results will be less uniform, but unless you are a competition shooter, you may not be able to see the accuracy difference.

For our tests on the .300 Savage and .25-06, we did not anneal the brass because many reloaders would skip that step. First, we lubed the necks and shoulders of the .300 Savage and sized the brass in a full-length sizer. This process did not change the headspace of the brass (shortened the body of the case), and the reloading press sprung noticeably, allowing a gap to appear between the die and the shellholder. Next, the entire case body was lubed and sized again. This time, the case went all the way into the die. The press did not spring nearly as much, and when checked in the gun, the brass would now headspace and the bolt closed easily as it should.

As a result of this first test with the .300 Savage, I worked on the .25-06 to determine if the same dimensional variances caused the problem. After sorting the brass, it turned out that all the cases with the length problem were from one manufacturer. It does not matter which manufacturer, as the problem appears with different brands and calibers. This is one more example of why using brass from one lot is essential when working up loads.

I used an RCBS Precision Mic in .25-06 to check the brass. All the brass that did not chamber properly was .004 inch longer than the standard brass. Again, we skipped annealing. We tried the same process of lubing the neck and shoulder, the shoulder did not budge. The cartridge length quickly returned to the correct length when we lubed the case body. The bottom line is that if reloaders are too stingy with case lube, problems with ammo will result. Annealing is the best solution to this problem as it will allow the shoulder to bump back correctly.

Tools for Measuring Cases

There are numerous commercial tools available for measuring cartridge cases. Forster offers tools like the Datum Dial shown here. You can use it to measure cases from the head to the datum point on the shoulder. That allows you to check cases quickly to ensure they match your chamber or are within standard specifications. I frequently use mine to check that headspace gauges are correct, Go vs. No-Go vs. Field.

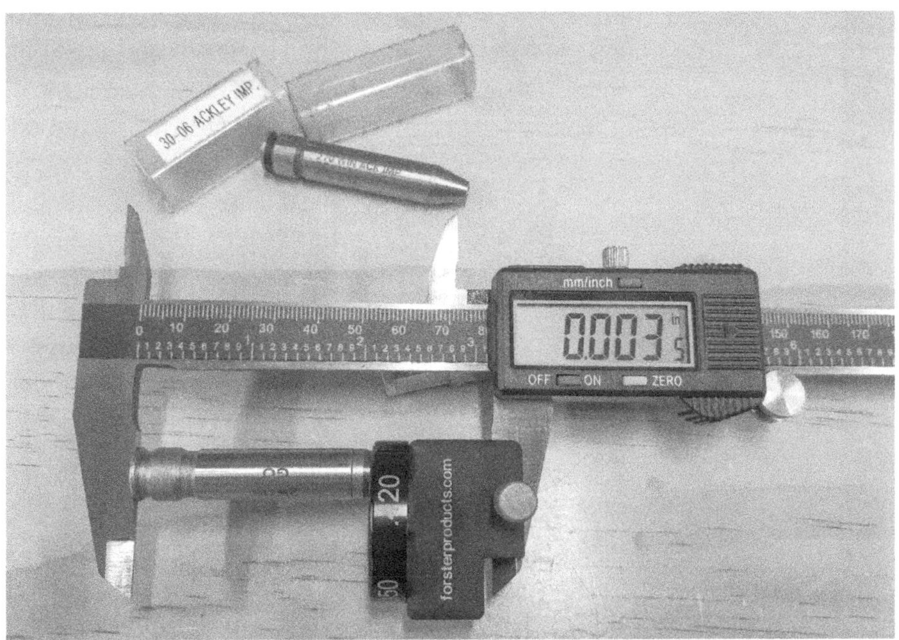

Forster makes caliber-sized dials to check seating depth or measure bullets and ammunition.

The Lyman case length gauge ensures your brass is short enough to chamber correctly in a standard SAAMI chamber, which can be useful for checking your improved cartridges or any wildcat matching the case length dimensions on the gauge.

You do not have to know how to read a dial caliper to use the Lyman gauge. Test fit your cases to the correct point on the gauge. Naturally, if you have a dial caliper and know how to use it, it's the ultimate in case length gauges.

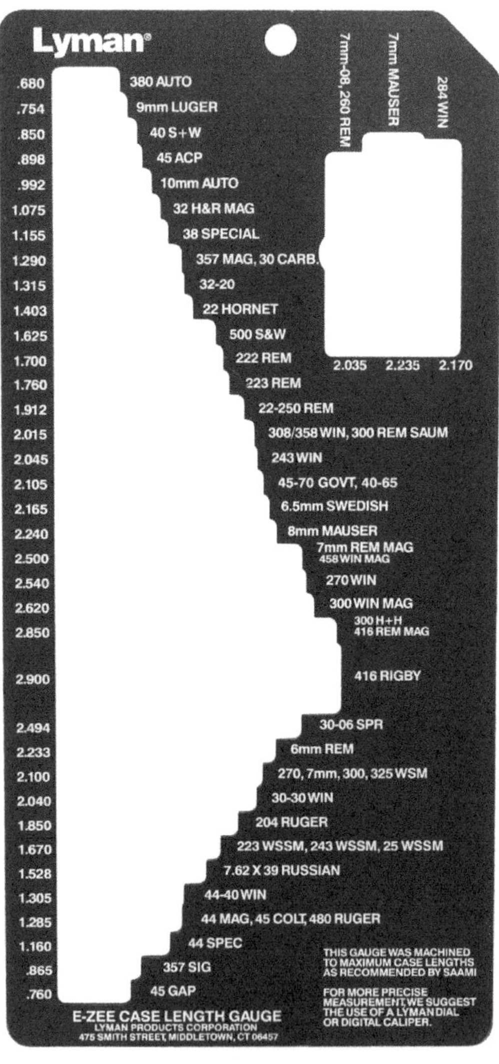

Wilson case gauges allow you to check all critical dimensions at once. First, slide the sized brass entirely into the gauge and headspace. This is simple: the case head must be flush with the base of the gauge. If unsure, you can always put a straight edge on the die base to double-check. It should be self-explanatory that the case slipping into the gauge indicates it will fit in the chamber. Next, look at the opposite end; a step on this end shows the cartridge's maximum and minimum trim length. This gauge type is offered by more than one company; Wilson was the original and is still available.

Many companies offer ammo checkers or ammo blocks. Pictured here is the Lyman version of this product. These are caliber-specific and can check single or multiple rounds to ensure

they will drop into a chamber properly. You could make your own, or many gunsmiths and custom shops will make such tools for you. They are usually made of aluminum and are reamed with your chamber reamer and headspaced with a proper gauge.

The RCBS Precision Mic measures ammunition for headspace and freebore length. Its instructions are well written, and use and application are clear.

I have heard some gunsmiths say that ammunition does *not* have headspace. This is a case where the understanding of headspace is critical. *True headspace is the distance between the breech face with the firearm locked up in the firing position and the back of the gauge or cartridge in the chamber.*

Reloaders can use dies and a reloading press to "bump" the shoulder of the case back. This shortens the distance from the head of the case and the headspace datum line on the shoulder. If you bump it too far, you create headspace in the reloads. Consequently, checking or measuring this dimension when setting up the resize die is crucial. The various tools in this section are designed to measure cartridge cases in several ways. The window for best accuracy is about .001 inch. It is ideal to set headspace in most rifles to zero (.000). The closer to zero, the better.

The difference between a Go gauge (minimum) and a Field gauge (maximum) in most shouldered rimless cases is about .014 inch. Any gun that will close on a Field gauge is considered unsafe and requires service to correct the headspace. Custom gun makers and all accuracy buffs like to set headspace tight, meaning zero, which produces repeatable accuracy and ensures the firearm's longevity. These measuring tools are available to the general shooting public to allow knowledgeable shooters and gunsmiths to ensure ammo matches the chamber with the correct tolerances.

On this subject, factory new ammunition is made to specification with manufacturing tolerances set by SAAMI or CIP. If the gun is made to the minimum chamber length (zero headspace) set with a headspace Go gauge, it should, in theory, accept all factory-loaded ammunition. If factory-made ammunition is made to the maximum tolerance for headspace, it *must* be shorter than the chamber to allow for normal function and cycling of the action. As long as the ammunition is within tolerance, it will function and fire safely. To those gunsmiths who insist ammo does not have headspace, you need to study manufacturing tolerances, as you are too rigid in your thought process. Your statement is only true when everything is perfect, which it seldom is!

All of the measurement information here applies equally to wildcats.

Historical Wildcat Development

Beginning wildcatters gravitate to one of two options. They either neck up or down an existing cartridge for their first attempt or start with rimmed cases. While selecting the most commonly available cases for experimentation was natural, rimmed cases offered a benefit that early wildcatters needed. Because the case headspaces on the rim instead of the shoulder, it provides a simple safety mechanism for inexperienced wildcatters. With the head trapped between the bolt face and the barrel breech, the wildcatter is free to try all kinds of changes to the shape of the case's body and shoulder.

In 1938, Sharpe said about case design, "Super-power in modern rifles will probably call for an entirely different material for cartridge cases. As yet it is not in sight."[5] We are approaching a century later and still using the same material for our Super-magnums as they used in Sharpe's day. So far, there is no change on the horizon.

For the 2005 edition of this book, Dave Manson of Manson Precision Reamers (8200 Embury Road, Grand Blanc, MI 48439) commented on wildcatting and how the popularity of various cartridges has shifted over 25 years. His comments appear below.

---

5 Sharpe, Philip B., *The Rifle in America*, 1938

It's difficult to list specific wildcats in terms of their popularity. With my daily focus on making reamers for specific cartridges—both standard and wildcat—the relative production figures of reamers for a particular wildcat compared to another get lost. A few chamberings, such as the 7mmSTW or 6.5-08(.260 Rem.), of course, stand out because they've been standardized as factory offerings, but the majority are popular for a while and then fade into wildcatting history.

It is for this reason that I can best answer, "What is the current state of wildcatting?" by describing wildcatting trends then—say 20 to 25 years ago—and now. Some of the discussion will mention standard cartridges in different shooting disciplines because oftentimes wildcats are developed as a competitive edge—an example would be the use of the 6.5-08 in service rifle competition that traditionally used .308 or .30-06. What was hot in the early 1980s?

Ackley Improved chamberings would probably be first on the list, with necked-up or necked-down versions of the .284 Win. a not-so-distant second. Many of these were sufficiently popular that reamers for them were offered as standard items.

The Gibbs family of .30-06-based wildcats were moderately popular but were beginning to fade. Reamers for some of these were standards.

Wildcats such as the 8mm-06 or 6.5-06 were beginning to fade. These chamberings originated as a way war trophies could be converted to use the '06 case—more readily available and cheaper than the cartridges for which the arm had been designed to use. The supply of cheap surplus rifles was also drying up and shooters were beginning to care more about originality than shootability. Increasing disposable income and an aging population of WWII vets probably further reduced the conversion of service rifles.

Silhouette shooting was just becoming popular. Wildcats such as the 7mm Merrill, 7mm-08X, the various TCU chamberings (Thompson Center Ugalde), .357 Maximum, .30 & .357 Herrett and others were popular, with some becoming standardized in factory chamberings and/or loadings.

Handgun hunting was a natural outgrowth of silhouette shooting, if one considers only single-shot pistols such as the Contender or Merrill(RPM). Some hardcore shooters used revolvers to hunt, as well. Dick Casull and Wayne Baker were beginning to produce their .454 Casull in the Freedom Arms single action, and a then-unknown gun crank named John Linebaugh was experimenting with reworked Rugers chambered in his .475- and

.500-caliber wildcats.

Benchrest competitors have always bought tooling way out of proportion to their percentage of the total shooter population. Because of this, reamers for the Donaldson Wasp, 6x45, .22 and 6mm BR and .22 and 6mm PPC were standard offerings; the Donaldson was rapidly being eclipsed by the newer designs.

Bullseye and PPC shooting—mostly used standard chamberings. Blackpowder cartridge shooting—only the rare shooter of old rifles. Action Pistol, IPSC, IDPA—all in their infancy or not yet invented. Cowboy Action Shooting—Huh? In its infancy.

Hot in the 1980 era: Ackley Improved PPC & BR, .284-based wildcats, .219 Don Wasp, .308x1½ .30 and .357 Herrett, .38/45 Auto, .357/44 Bain & Davis, .458 Lott Gibbs wildcats, TCUs 6x45, 7mm/300 Wby—long-range shooting; International series of cartridges for silhouette.

From then 'til now, there have been many changes—even if in many cases the change has not always been progress. The shooting sports, like many aspects of our society, enjoyed tremendous growth in popularity from 1980 to the present. With more disposable income and a greater population of shooters as consumers of new ideas and developments, disciplines that would have been marginally popular before experienced rapid growth as new shooters found niches they enjoyed. Advances in manufacturing processes, i.e. CNC machining, made economically feasible firearms designs that previously would have been too expensive to produce.

New shooting disciplines and firearms spawn new cartridge designs. More hunters use handguns now than 25 years ago, and cartridges have been designed to meet these shooters' demands. Blackpowder cartridge shooters, Cowboy Action buffs, Action Pistol and Rimfire Benchrest have all created demands for specialty cartridges and/or chambers. Older shooting disciplines have been divided into special interests. Benchrest, for instance, no longer is shot at 100 or 200 yards. Many shoot "benchrest" rifles at longer distances for both score and group, with .50-cal. (.50 BMG) and varmint shooting both popular subdivisions. Any specialization such as the above will generate specialized cartridges that better meet the needs of the sport.

One must also be aware of the growing trend of hobbyist gunsmithing. Where avid shooters might once have taken their ideas to the local gunsmith for translation into metal and wood, many now have the time and inclination to attend classes, buy the necessary tools and do the work themselves. Gun-oriented periodicals, such as Precision Shooting (which ceased publication in November of 2012), did a good job educating the shooter on the benefits of precision work. This is not an unalloyed blessing; we often hear from gunsmiths about customers' unreasonable requests and have had to do a certain amount of customer education about what constitutes reasonable precision.

Reinforcing the trend of shooters doing their own work is the tremendous amount of aftermarket and drop-in parts available. The non-professional can easily fit a short-chambered barrel to a receiver if he's willing to buy a few tools and heed instructions. When designing a new tool, we always keep in mind that it will likely be used by a hobbyist as well as someone trained to work on guns.

Finally, the growth of businesses that cater—at least in part—to the cartridge experimenter has facilitated wildcatting today. There are many more die makers today than there were in the 1970s and a large part of their business is "specials." If you want to make your own dies—like many had to do back then—there are makers of various styles of die blanks to make the job easier.

Our end of the market (chambering reamers) has expanded as well. Where there were two primary reamer makers in 1980, there are now four. I'd guess that 30%-40% of our business involves wildcat reamers or alterations of standard reamers in an effort to improve firearm performance. Among the firearms toolmakers, there's also a wider range of associated tooling other than chamber reamers. I feel this reflects the growing interest in performance improvement of stock firearms, whether it's accuracy, reliability or power.

With the above in mind, I offer the following list of what's hot in 2005.

Ackley Improved chamberings continue to be very popular. Many current AI cartridges were, of course, never chambered by Mr. Ackley, but bear his name because they follow his design parameters. Wildcats based on the .284 Winchester have faded significantly in popularity, with the exception of the 6.5/284. Factory ammunition is available and this "wildcat" is exceedingly popular for long-range target work, varmint shooting, as well as hunting.

The Gibbs family of wildcats has become a nostalgic wildcatter's memory, as has the Epps line of wildcats.

The 6.5-06 is a SAAMI cartridge in its own right; the 8mm-06 continues to be a "standard" reamer with us, though I doubt either is used very often *to convert old service rifles.*

Silhouette shooting has faded in popularity, although some new cartridges such as the .270 REN were developed for it 10 or 15 years ago.

Handgun hunting has become very popular in the past 25 years. JD Jones, of SSK Industries, is largely responsible for the proliferation of wildcat chamberings that are available for the T/C Contender and Encore. Two of his wildcats—the .300 Whisper (.300 AAC Blackout has taken its place) and .375 JDJ were offered in 2005 as standard chamberings by T/C. Other companies (Bullberry, Dave Van Horn, and Virgin Valley) have also helped by offering the customer a wide range of barrels and wildcat chamberings.

Handgun hunters haven't ignored revolvers. Freedom Arms continues to make their excellent revolvers and a number of custom gun builders have started to rework Rugers along the lines pioneered by John Linebaugh. John has seen his .475 Linebaugh become standardized as a factory cartridge and Ruger offers a shortened version of it—the .480 Ruger—in its Super Redhawk. Gary Reeder offers custom Contenders and revolvers chambered in his more than 20 wildcats.

Benchrest shooting has grown tremendously, with many subdivisions to the classic 100- and 200-yd. distances. Rimfire Benchrest, Long-Range Benchrest, .50-Cal. Benchrest, and even Blackpowder Benchrest, are all now acknowledged divisions of the original discipline. The PPC and BR cartridges are now commercial cartridges and remain very popular, with specialized reamers being produced for variants by specific manufacturers, i.e. 6mm BR Norma. Additionally, many benchrest shooters are wildcatting the basic case design with changes in neck diameter, shoulder angle, neck and case length to find that magical configuration that will beat other competitors. The .219 Donaldson is history and the 6x45 has re-emerged as a moderately popular varminting wildcat.

BlackPowder cartridge shooting has grown into a popular discipline, with many of the old chamberings resurrected and shooters rediscovering accuracy secrets of 100 years ago. Silhouette shooting with blackpowder is popular as is long-range target competition. Most chambering reamers for blackpowder cartridges are made to suit the shooter's specific loading, but we offer two versions of the .45-90 chambering and one each of the .32-40 and .45-70 as standards.

Cowboy Action Shooting has emerged as a specialty shooting sport. In addition to the period costumes, many competitors shoot guns chambered in period calibers. The .38-40 was almost dead 25 years ago and no one had chambered a new gun in .41 or .44 Colt in many years. These calibers are now quite popular and are even available in commercial ammunition.

Action Pistol sports, such as IPSC and IDPA, have grown significantly. During the late 1990s in IPSC, there was a big push to find the optimum cartridge that combined low recoil with sufficient muzzle energy to "make major," was small enough to allow more rounds per magazine and would work well in compensated pistols. Wildcats such as the 9x21, 9x23, .356 TSW, 9x25 Dillon and others were developed in this search. Existing chamberings, such as the .38 Super and 9mm Luger were altered in this effort. Some of these still exist but more have faded from the scene.

Big-bore "African" cartridges have experienced a revival way out of proportion, I feel, to the actual amount they're used hunting dangerous game. We make a lot of reamers for cartridges such as the .577NE, .500NE, .470NE, 475#2 and so on. Additionally, new dangerous game calibers such as the .416R Chapuis, .470 Capstick, .458 Lott and more are being developed all the time.

Traditional wildcatting—that is, the development of rifle cartridges that don't fall into any of the above categories—is still going strong. There have been a number of wildcatters who have designed families of cartridges in several different bore sizes. Fred Zeglin's Z-Hat Custom has the "Hawk" line of wildcats, the Jamison series of cases for short actions based on the .404 Jeffery, and the Dakota series are several that come to mind. The developers of these cartridges, in my opinion, have done a much better job than their predecessors of load development and dimensional standardization.

Factory adoption of wildcats is, in my opinion, the biggest trend today. Where the wildcatter was once someone with an idea for a new type of cartridge, or simply an improved version of a standard, we now have ammunition and firearms manufacturers working together to create new calibers. All of the new factory cartridges have antecedents in work done previously by individuals, but the factories have the resources necessary to refine the concepts into cartridges the average person can live with as well as the marketing capabilities to ensure their success.

Let's look at a few of the more recent developments and their antecedents:

Winchester Short Magnums—virtually identical to Rick Jamison's cartridges except for changes necessary for manufacturing expedience. The Super Shorts are the same idea taken a little further. All of these derive from the benchrest concept of short, fat, efficient cases. The Short and Super Short cases also serve as a basis for many current wildcat experiments.

Remington Ultra Magnums—very similar to the many long-range cartridges wildcatted on the .404 Jeffery case.

.204 Ruger—a sub-caliber cartridge that has lots of ancestors in the .223-based wildcats (.20 Tactical, etc.) developed by Todd Kindler and others.

.17 HMR, .17 HM2 and .17 Aguila—Terry Kopp, Bill Eichelberger and others have experimented with necked-down rimfire cartridges for years. Federal, in the early '90s, worked on an early version of the .17 RFM, but abandoned it due to pressure and tolerance problems.

.450 Marlin—many shooters have up-loaded the .45-70 in modern rifles. Manufacturers had to figure out how to capture that market and avoid the possibility of blowing up old guns.

I could revise this list every time I review it, as I recall this wildcatter or that variation of a factory cartridge, but I have to stop somewhere. My vote for the most successful wildcat in memory? The PPC lineup.

What's Hot in 2005 :

.22 LR match chamberings PPC & BR

6x45 6.5/284

.458 Lott—now a factory offering

.454 Casull

.22/243 Middlestead, .224 TTH

.17 Mach IV, .20 Tactical

.30/378 Wby., .408 Chey-Tac

.338 Lapua-based wildcats

.404 Jeffery-based wildcats

.45-90, .40-82

.32-40, .40-65

.470 NE, .500 NE

.38-4041 and .44 Colt

.357/44 B&D-mostly chambered by Bain & Davis

.38-45—popular for now as Aussie shooters convert their .45 ACPs to bores .38-cal. or smaller.

WSM and WSSM-based wildcats

AR-15 platform wildcats such as the 6.8 Rem SPC, .50 Beowulf, .499 L-W.

The Remington 6.8mm SPC ammunition is already available at the time of this writing, but no guns have been released. Since this is a slightly different case than is currently available, it will certainly spawn a whole batch of new wildcats.

For an in-depth study of the development of cartridge cases, look at a book by Robert Mermelstein, Mermelstien's Guide to Metallic Cartridge Evolution. *Published by Sinclair International, Inc., 2004. Another great resource is the* Ammo Encyclopedia, 7th Edition, *By Charles F. Priore and Lisa Beuning, Blue Book Publications, 2022.*

What's new from the factories since 2005?

.17 Hornady Hornet
.17 Remington Fireball
.22 TCM
.22 Nosler
.224 Valkyrie
6mm ARC
6mm Creedmoor
6mm GT
.25-45 Sharps
6.8 True Velocity Composite
6.8 Western
6.5 PRC
.26 Nosler
6.5 Creedmoor
6.5x47 Lapua
.27 Nosler
.28 Nosler
.280 Ackley Improved
7mm Blaser Magnum
7mm PRC
.30 Super Carry
.300 PRC
.300 HAM'R
.30 Nosler
.30 Remington AR
.30 Thompson Center (TC)
.308 Marlin Express
.300 AAC Blackout
.300 Ruger Compact Magnum (RCM)
.300 Olympic Super Short Magnum
.327 Federal
.33 Nosler
.338 Blaser Magnum
.338 Federal
.338 Ruger Compact Magnum (RCM)
.350 Legend
.360 Buckhammer
.375 Ruger
.375 Blaser Magnum
.400 Legend
.416 Barrett
.429 Desert Eagle
.450 Bushmaster
.460 S&W
.480 Ruger

CHAPTER 6

Has It Been Done Before?

Research is key if you want to design an original wildcat. There are very few holes in the ballistic universe; a factory cartridge or some other existing wildcat may already do what you have in mind. Most new wildcat ideas come when the factory makes a new case available. Here, we are just trying to find something that has not yet been done. Many clients ask about building a wildcat they dreamed up, while all too often, two minutes of checking will unearth the cartridge they want already in existence. Half of those cases are factory offerings with such minor variations as to be indistinguishable from the factory cartridge.

Probably the most common error new wildcatters make is a lack of research. A small investment in time will save you phone calls and the embarrassment of being told you have reinvented the .308 Winchester. Worse yet, after spending all your money on a new wildcat chamber reamer and custom reloading dies, you realize you invented the .308 Winchester, but it won't accept factory ammo. Research saves money and time, too.

Here are three virtually interchangeable cartridges:

In 1962, Les Bowman, working with Fred Huntington, designed a cartridge that would work in a standard-length action, deliver at least 2,200 fps with a 400-grain bullet, and was powerful enough to deal with anything he might meet in Africa. This collaboration resulted in the .411 Bowman—a .338 Winchester case necked up to .411 with no other changes. Bowman said he selected .411 over the .416 bullet because "at the time, the 411 was more available."[1]

1 Miller, Al, *Handloader 178*, 1996

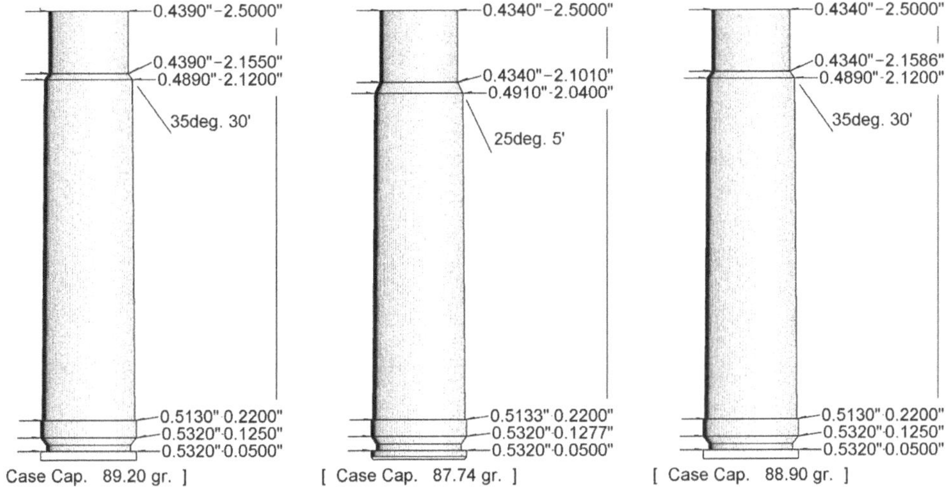

The .416 Taylor (left), .411 Bowman (middle) and .411 KDF (right).

In the 1970s, Robert Chatfield-Taylor used the .458 Winchester case necked down to .416 for his design. The cartridge is moderately popular as wildcats go. There was no .411 Taylor.

Phil Koehne, owner of KDF, said he never looked at the other cartridges in this mix. He worked one out he liked, a hard-hitting wildcat on a standard magnum case. Phil's gun was the newest of the three designs. Ballistically, the .411 Bowman and the .411 KDF are twins based on published load data. The KDF version was born much later. It has the shoulder moved forward about .080 inch, otherwise, they are essentially the same case.

Now for the really interesting question. Was KDF wrong for not just using the .411 Bowman, or was Robert Chatfield-Taylor wrong to put his name on the .416 Taylor? With very little investigation, they would have discovered that they were essentially copying another man's work, although they were probably unaware. The .411 Bowman appeared in Ackley's second book in 1966. You be the judge.

In 1999, when Remington brought out the .300 Ultra Mag., folks were wildcatting it before you could get the parent brass. In the Z-Hat Custom shop, we created a list of cartridges based on the .300 Ultra Mag., called UltraCats. As the factory started offering more calibers, the 7mm Ultra and .375 Ultra, our wildcats became obsolete, and we removed them from the line. But many shooters wanted to be the first to wildcat that case, so it brought us much attention. At the same time, we were just one shop offering variations on this theme. When I stopped gunsmithing, I was still offering the 6.5mm, 8mm, .338, .358, .416 and .458 UltraCat cartridges. The metric numbers are based on the

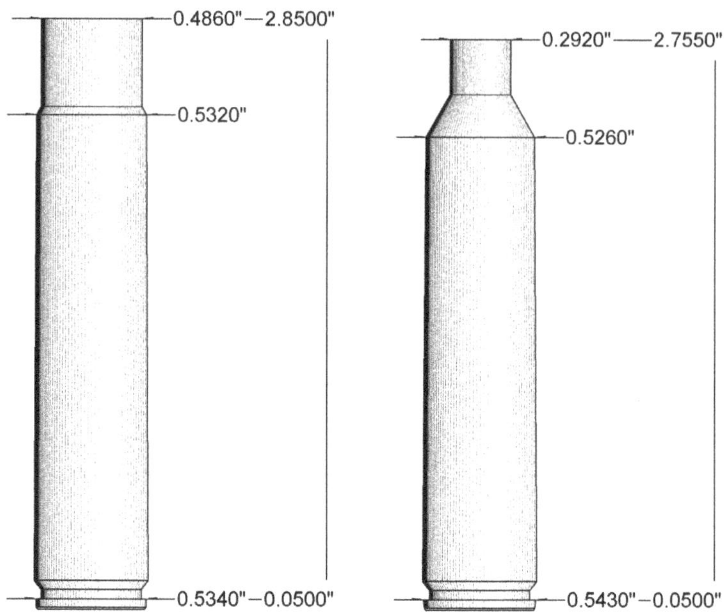

The .458 UltraCat (left), 6.5 UltraCat (right).

.338 Ultra case because of its slightly reduced capacity, which better suits those calibers. The .338 through .458 are based on the .300 Ultra case.

In 2001, Shawn Carlock of Defensive Edge started working with a .338/.300 Ultra. He named it the .338 Edge in part to avoid confusion with the factory .338 Remington Ultra. The .338 Edge is nothing more than the .300 Remington Ultra neck up to .338. Shawn uses a longer-than-standard throat on the factory .338 RUM to accommodate longer, heavier bullets. The cartridge name caught on, and the .338 Edge replaced the .338/.300 RUM and the .338 UltraCat. The Edge uses standard .300 RUM headspace gauges.

Bryce Towsley lays claim to the .358 UMT, which is the .358/.300 RUM. His articles have done much to popularize this wildcat. The .358 UMT and the .338 Edge are examples of a wildcat name catching on with the shooting public. Often, numerous shops are working on the same ideas, and it's just a matter of marketing and a name that people like.

Public response was so strong in the instance of the .300 Ultra and its brethren that Winchester wasted no time offering a new cartridge based on the same case, the .300 WSM. Of course, the Winchester Short Magnum is a much shorter version (we have had short magnums before, such as the 6.5mm

Left to right, the .300 WSM, .350 Remington Mag. and 6.5mm Remington Mag.

Remington Magnum and the .350 Remington Magnum). The WSM has the advantage of a fatter case, increasing case capacity by about 10% over the older generation of short magnums and has no belt.

Before the WSM and the SAUM cartridges, Heavy Express was a small custom manufacturer that proved the shooting public wanted these high-capacity cases based on what amounts to a shortened .404 Jeffery case. The .300 Heavy Express was based on a .348 case with the rim turned down to create a rimless case. As a result of the proven market, big manufacturers introduced similar cartridges (WSM and SAUM), and H.E. is no longer in the market.

Manufacturers rarely introduce products in the middle of the year because they miss the big sporting goods shows, like the SHOT SHOW or the NRA convention, where they get the best press exposure for new items. Winchester wisely knew that it would get the jump on the competition by being first to market with the shortened .404 case. If it had waited, it's hard to say which maker would have won the press wars.

The reality is that even if there is a ballistic twin for your cartridge design somewhere, there is no reason why your idea won't work. The main reason for variations on cartridges is to fit particular uses. JD Jones has made a career

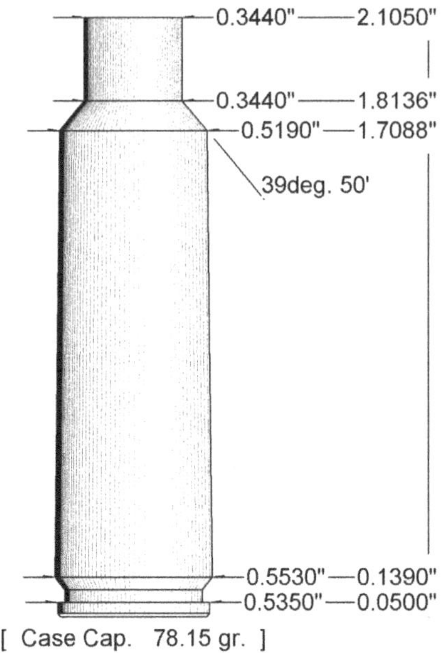

The .300 Heavy Express Mag.

out of rimmed cases with sharp shoulders for single-shot pistols. They would not feed worth a darn in a bolt-action, but who cares? That's not what they're for. Other common reasons for wildcats are to fit a specific magazine length or other factors concerning a specific firearm.

Hawk Cartridges is a line of wildcats based on the '06 case. The .338, .358, .375, and .411 Hawk are all true wildcats—no factory ammo can be fired in the chamber to form them. Originally, the only source of brass was forming it in dies or using a fireforming technique, to be discussed in Chapter 15. Sometime later, correctly headstamped brass and custom-loaded ammo became available for them.

Hawk cartridges filled a niche that developed in the market: non-belted, standard-length, magnum velocity, and relatively low recoil. At the time of development, there was a growing trend toward larger cases, which meant more recoil and louder muzzle reports, hoping for a flatter trajectory. Witness the .300 Remington Ultra, 7mm STW and the like. Because of this trend toward big magnum cartridges, two groups of potential customers naturally developed for Hawk Cartridges.

The first group consisted of shooters who never bought into the bigger-is-better theory and were looking for good performance without suffering recoil. They realized accuracy and realistic hunting distances are better reasons to select a cartridge. Hawk Cartridges are realistic 300-yard rounds that don't require special optics or Kentucky windage. Accuracy is always easier to attain from an efficient cartridge (efficiency will be discussed in detail in Chapter 8). Conversely, an overbore cartridge will present a challenge when finding an accurate load. By design, an overbore cartridge is finicky about what combination of bullets and powders it will perform well with.

The second group has considerable experience. Thousands of rounds downrange will teach you what works and what is merely entertainment or trendy. These knowledgeable gun buffs have tried it all; they have shot the ultra-velocity cartridges and probably just about every factory caliber they could use. So, they know what they like. Here is a partial list of the things they desire in a cartridge:

- Accuracy. Like Townsend Whelen said, "Only accurate rifles are interesting."
- Velocity ranges from the muzzle of 2,400 to 2,700 fps.
- Moderate recoil; roughly equal to a .30-06 with a 180-gr. bullet at 2,700 fps, about 22 ft-lbs of recoil.
- Choose heavy-for-caliber bullets, but not necessarily the heaviest, i.e., 250-grain bullets in a .338 bore will perform well at moderate velocities.
- Efficient design, no wasted powder capacity, minimizes muzzle lift and perceived recoil.

Hawk Cartridges are successful because they work in a standard-length action with cheap brass and no belt, delivering magnum performance and low

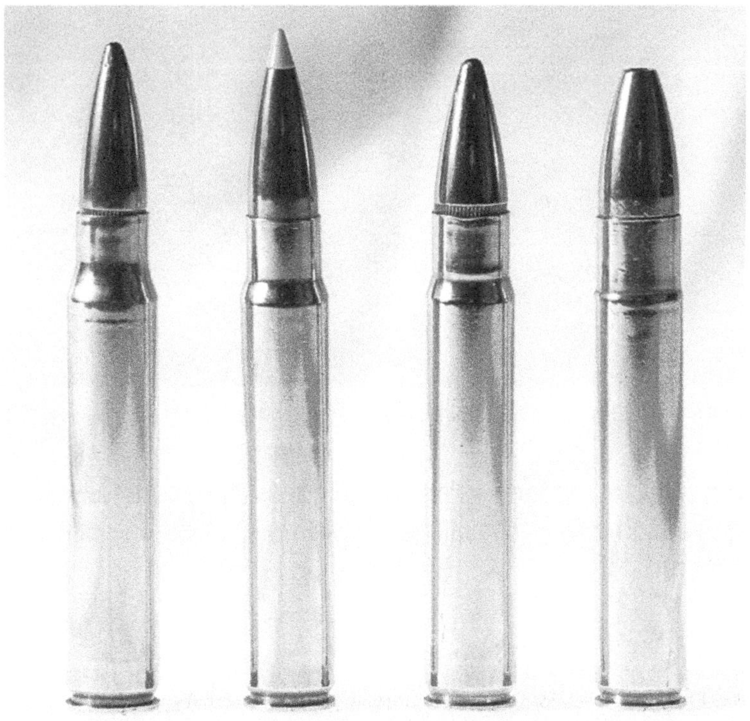

Left to right, the .338 Hawk, .358 Hawk, .375 Hawk/Scovill and .411 Hawk.

Phil Filing with a small part of his research library.

recoil compared to the same caliber magnum cases. In short, they filled a niche all their own, something that will help make a wildcat commercially successful in the long run.

Expand Your Research Library

According to Phil Filing, a retired gunsmith known for starting Glenrock Blue in Wyoming, *"A gunsmith without books is like a room without windows!"* Research requires reference materials. You may already have a small reloaders' library, but you should also add several of the following books.

Cartridges of the World edited by W. Todd Woodard (GunDigestStore.com). While not all-inclusive, this reference will often show if your idea has already been tried. It's broken up into chapters with clear headings to make loading various types of cartridges easier. There is a chapter for wildcats and proprietary cartridges. Each listing includes a short writeup for the cartridge and its history and a small sample of load data. Cartridge dimensions are listed at the end of each chapter. To date, the book is in its 17th edition.

Another good choice would be P.O. Ackley's books, *Handbook for Shooters & Reloaders,* Volumes I and II. The main flaw with Ackley's manuals is that they do not contain dimensions, so comparing cartridges is tough. However, Ackley does a great job of describing most of the cartridges, so at least the parent brass is obvious. The load data is dated, and you should be very careful about using top loads from these books, as powders have changed significantly.

Next would be Ken Howell's *Designing and Forming Custom Cartridges,* which is more of a dimension book with no load data. It features excellent drawings of more than 900 factory and wildcat cartridges and numerous articles of interest. Data allows you to compare case capacitities. Still, the method differs from any other manual: it uses the amount of water that would be displaced if the brass were a solid billet. Case capacity by water weight is not used, and you must recognize this difference if you plan to make comparisons. However, it's one of the more useful books for a wildcatter or reloader and includes suggestions and methods of forming each cartridge.

Ken Waters' *Pet Loads* is another resource to help with your research. It encompasses many years of Waters' research and reloading experience. (A supplement is also available for it.) The author details loading techniques, powder selection, components and more. It includes a wide range of cartridges and is a delightful source of information for reloaders.

John J. Donnelly's *The Handloaders Manual of Cartridge Conversions* combines load data and cartridge dimensions. Over 1,000 pages with information on brass forming methods have been updated and revised with a new, easy-to-reference format. Edited by well-known author, writer and precision shooter Bryce Towsley, it's a superb guide for beginners and experienced handloaders.

Wildcat Cartridges, Volumes I & II is a collection of articles from *Rifle* and *Handloader* magazines and makes for interesting reading while providing useful data and dimensions in most articles. It's historically interesting as the articles span many years of Wolfe's publishing history. The book includes authors such as P.O. Ackley, Les Bowman, Layne Simpson, Steve Timm, Ken

Waters, Sam Fadala, Bob Hagel, Don Zutz and John Wooters—an enjoyable read for any gun lover.

Charles Newton, Father of High Velocity by Bruce M. Jennings, is a source of in-depth information on the man and his designs. Much of this book is made up of the compiled writings of Newton so that you can read about him and his work in his own words. Newton originated many features on his rifles that are now common to factory designs.

Charles S. Landis *wrote Twenty-Two Caliber Varmint Rifles* at the end of World War II. The book is a window into the history of the early days of wildcatting. Landis incorporates cartridge dimensions, so it's a valuable resource for older designs.

Modern Sporting Rifle Cartridges by Wayne van Zwoll includes several articles of interest to reloaders, with a section devoted to descriptions of cartridges (many with dimensions), histories and load data. Popular wildcats are covered.

Some Simplified Interior Ballistics for Handloaders by Wm. C. Davis, Jr. is out of print but contains a clear treatise on internal ballistics that most reloaders can grasp.

Robert A. Rinker's *Understanding Firearm Ballistics, 4th Edition*, *Basic to Advanced—Simplified, Illustrated & Explained* (2002) explains firearm ballistics in understandable terms and is an authoritative and standard reference for advanced studies. It is required reading for wildcatters, from beginner to expert.

Mermelstien's Guide to Metallic Cartridge Evolution by Robert Mermelstein (published by Sinclair International, Inc., 2004) is an interesting book if you like metallic case development's history and details.

Philip P. Massaro's *Big Book of Ballistics,* published by *Gun Digest* (and a 2024 update titled *The Ballistics Handbook*), is worth your time (GunDigestStore.com). Phil has an easy-to-read style, and the book is perfect for shooters who do not want a dry college text. All aspects of ballistics are addressed in a fast-reading and entertaining way. It includes lots of illustrations and photos to help explain complicated information.

Then, to fill out your library, add every loading manual you can afford. You'll find that some offer more information on specific cartridges than others; this is where your interests will help you select the best manuals for your purpose. It's surprising how many reloaders are unaware of the articles in their loading manuals: tons of useful information is at your fingertips. Pull one of your reloading manuals off the shelf and check it out. It can save you an incredible amount of wasted time on the range. It's better to load smart and make every shot count.

Other sources of information include:

SAAMI (Small Arms and Ammunition Manufacturers' Institute)
11 Mile Hill Rd.
Newtown, CT 06470-2359
saami.org

SAAMI offers a list of publications that can be very useful to the wildcatter. They include books that contain all factory-accepted dimensions for commercial and military cartridges. Pressure limits are included for factory offerings.

CIP *(Commission Internationale Permanente)*. The CIP establishes standard rules and regulations for the proof of weapons and their ammunition to ensure the mutual recognition of proof marks by its member states. Fourteen countries are CIP member states.

In compliance with the 1969 Convention, its Rules and Regulations, and CIP Decisions, every small arm, together with all highly stressed parts, must undergo lawful testing in the Proof House of the CIP member state in which the manufacturer is located or, for imported weapons, in the Proof House of the Member State into which they have been imported for the first time. The same applies to commercial ammunition. *cip-bobp.org*

Online chat rooms, forums, or message boards have been left out intentionally as they tend to be soapboxes for a limited number of self-proclaimed "experts." (I call them keyboard commandos.) While forums are fun to participate in, they are not a great source of factual information. If you see something on one of these sites that interests you, check the facts before you dive into building it. After all, bad advice is always worse than no advice at all.

Once you've completed your research, choose the parent cartridge that will allow you to design the wildcat you have in mind. Check the dimensions against the firearm you plan to use to ensure it will function reliably when complete. Decide if the conversion will be worth the cost. With your research complete, you can be sure that your cartridge does not yet exist in a form that will work for your planned use. Now, you're truly ready to start designing and testing.

When you send the drawing to your reamer maker, have them check for existing cartridges. You don't want to be guilty of plagiarizing a 6mm Remington or a .300 WSM, so ask the reamer maker what other cartridges are similar to your design. They will gladly fax, snail mail or email you a drawing for your comparison before you spend all your money on custom tools.

In real estate, the axiom is *Location, Location, Location*. When you stake your claim to territory in the realm of wildcats, the axiom is, *Research, Research, Research!*

CHAPTER 7

Wildcatting History (The Necked Down, Shortened Version)

This chapter examines a representative list of cartridges that have enjoyed varying success. While this list is incomplete, it is sufficient to discuss a wide range of calibers and case designs. Some made it to commercial production, and some are all but dead, but they all enjoyed popularity in their day. We'll examine each one and discuss its history, merits and drawbacks. In short, figure out what made it a good wildcat. Since we're interested in the history, I'll group cartridges by their timeline.

The .25-20 Single Shot is the earliest wildcat I could locate. J. Francis Rabbeth, a gun writer at the turn of the 20th century who went by the pen name of J. Francis, designed it.[1] The wildcat first appeared around 1882, Remington commercialized the round, which may make it the first wildcat to become a factory offering. Maynard, Stevens, and Winchester later chambered it, and it was popular in single-shot rifles (believe it or not) and produced excellent accuracy. The .25-20 WCF came about because the .25-20 Single Shot was too long to fit the 1892 Winchester, the two cartridges are not interchangeable.

In the 1890s, jacketed bullets (then called metal-cased bullets), similar to present-day projectiles, were first used. The first of the smokeless powders came into use about this same time. Yet, it was another 10 years before work was done in earnest with .22- and .25-caliber wildcats.

In 1893, Harvey Donaldson began experimenting with small-caliber cases and smokeless powders.[2] He started with a .22-10-45 Maynard single-shot cartridge and was not alone in using this case for testing. He loaded shotgun smokeless powder but soon realized the case could not handle the pressures the new

1 Barnes, Frank C., *Cartridges of the World, 6th Edition*

2 Landis, Charles S., *Twenty-Two Caliber Varmint Rifles*, 1946

smokeless powder developed. Donaldson then went through a progression of cartridges looking for an accurate and useful case, including the .22-13-45 WCF, .25-21, .25-25, .28-30, .32-40 Ballard and a very accurate .32-35 Stevens. The latter had less case capacity than the .32-40 but produced better accuracy when wildcatted to .22 caliber.

In 1901, the .30-06 appeared in its earliest variant. After extensive experimentation, the U.S. adopted it as the .30-03 or .30 Government. Revised in 1906, it became the .30-06. There is a clear difference between the '03 and the '06. The 1903 version had a long neck, much like the .30-40 Krag, to accommodate the relatively long bullet. The 1906 version used a shorter bullet, so the case was shortened by about 1/10th of an inch. With the advent of the .30-06, the most wildcatted case of all time was born.

The .35-30 (.30-30 WCF necked up to .358) originated around 1900; although not a terribly popular caliber, it has held on and is still used in many lever guns today. It was intended for reboring shot-out .32-40 and .32 Winchester barrels. In the mid-1970s, it saw a slight surge in interest when Paul Marquart built several .35-30 rifles based on the Remington 788 action for silhouette shooting. The cartridge is well suited for lead bullet loads because of its long neck. Single-shot pistol aficionados and lever gun fans keep this cartridge on life support.

The .25 Krag is the next notable wildcat to appear. In *Cartridges of the World*, Frank Barnes credits the .25 Krag as "one of the oldest wildcat cartridges in existence." Notably, it was illustrated in Dr. Mann's book, *The Bullet's Flight From Powder to Target*, where he mentions testing it in 1906. It was popular in the P-14 Enfield action and single shots. (It is not advisable to use the .25 Krag in a Krag action because of the increased pressures.)

Charles Newton was the most notable ballistic experimenter at the beginning of the 20th century. He first developed a cartridge that Savage Arms adopted as the .22 Savage Hi-Power. Later, Newton designed the .250-3000 for Savage. Along the way, he developed a whole line of cartridges for his companies. Most of his design work ended by 1915, although he continued in the gun industry into the mid-1920s.

Newton's cartridges are interesting because they look for all the world like they could have been designed yesterday, but they were developed over a century ago. Newton was so far ahead of his time that the powders that would make his cartridges sing were at least 30 years in the future for him. (For more details on Newton and his arms, see Chapter 20.)

The First World War ran from 1914 to 1918, and during that time, all materials and industrial efforts were redirected to the war effort. So, there were few developments in sporting cartridges during that period.

The .25-06 dates to 1920, when A.O. Niedner began offering it in his custom rifles. There were numerous variations on the wildcat until Remington adopted it in 1969. In 1922, Ned Roberts necked the 7x57 Mauser case down to .257, and it took another 12 years for Remington to standardize the .257 Roberts. In so doing, Remington restored the 20-degree shoulder of the parent cartridge in favor of the 15-degree shoulder that Roberts had used on his wildcat.

No cartridges of consequence appear in the period from the mid-1920s to the mid-1930s. The Great Depression likely had much to do with this lull in activity.

Wildcat Renaissance

In the mid-1930s, the wildcat world had a massive burst of creativity. Below is a list of cartridges that appeared during this renaissance of cartridge development up to about 1940.

R-2 Lovell
.219 Donaldson Wasp
.22 K-Hornet
.218 Mashburn Bee
.22 Varminter (.22-250)
.219 Ackley Improved Zipper
.22-303
.228 Ackley Magnum
.35 Ackley Magnum

The R-2 Lovell and the .219 Donaldson Wasp came about as benchrest cartridges. As later cartridges like the .222 Remington and .222 Remington Magnum came to the market, they replaced these earlier benchrest contenders. This change was due, in part, to the interest in bolt guns over single-shots as technology progressed.

Hervey Lovell developed the .22-3000 around 1933. He used the shoulder angle of the parent .25-20 Single Shot cartridge. Harvey Donaldson and M.S. Risley should get credit for creating demand for the R-2 Lovell, a sharper-shouldered and blown-out version of the case. There were many versions of the R-2, so older chambers are likely to vary in shoulder angle, ranging from 11 to 17 degrees. Many of these variations have different neck lengths as well.

According to Phillip B. Sharpe, Lovell issued an R-2 Lovell design in 1937, illustrated here. Sharpe also states that most original .22-3000 Lovell chambers were converted to the R-2 version.

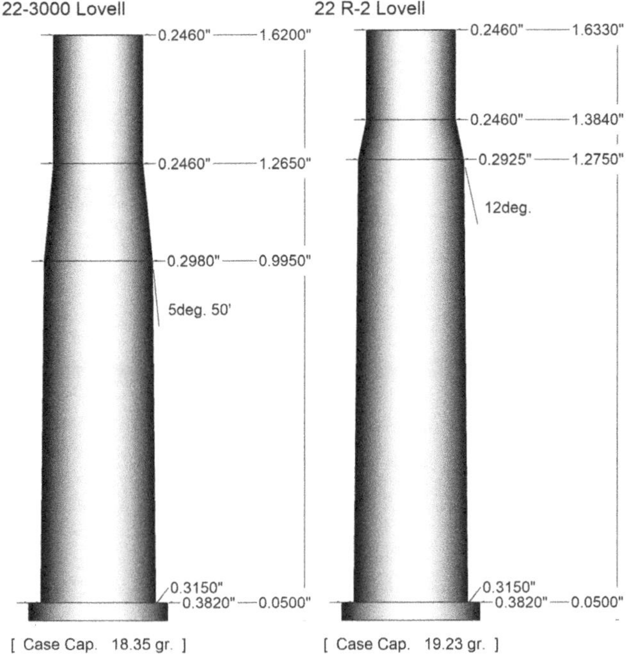

The .22-3000 Levell.

.219 Donaldson Wasp

Here, we have a cartridge that truly played a role in the development of modern wildcats. The .219 Wasp is interesting for several reasons: It was one of the first and the most dominant cartridges designed for benchrest shooting. Popular with the benchrest crowd up through the mid-1950s, it held more accuracy records than any other cartridge up to that time.

The .219 Donaldson Wasp's influence can be seen in several modern benchrest cartridges, such as the Remington BR series and the popular .22 and 6mm PPC. Notably, the Wasp was the first successful cartridge design to incorporate a short and fat shape, a sharp shoulder angle and a propellant capacity balance for the intended powder. This combination allowed for a powder charge that filled the case to nearly 100 percent density, producing the maximum combustion. No doubt it was well ahead of its time.

The .219 Donaldson Wasp's demise was due primarily to a lack of quality brass (when the factories dropped the .219 Zipper). On top of that, the .222 Remington began to set more and more records at the ranges. However, there are still folks shooting this cartridge.

THE .219 DONALDSON (.219 WASP) CARTRIDGE 189

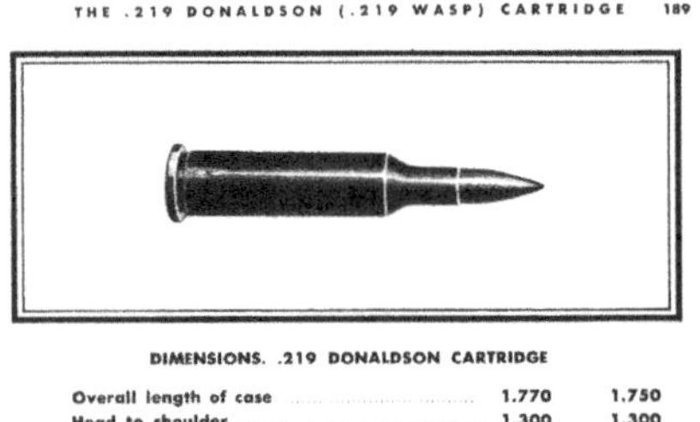

DIMENSIONS. .219 DONALDSON CARTRIDGE

Overall length of case	1.770		1.750
Head to shoulder	1.300		1.300
Head to rear of neck	1.434		1.434
Length of neck			.315
Diameter of rim	.506		.500
Diameter, head of case body	.418		.417
Diameter at shoulder	.407		.406(1)
Diameter, rear of neck	.253		.251(1)
Diameter, front of neck	.252		.250(1)
Angle of shoulder	30°		30°
Groove diameter of barrel	.2235	to	.224
Twist of rifling, I turn in	14.00		
Bullet diameter	.2235	to	.224
Overall length of cartridge			(2)

(1) Varies slightly according to diameter of seated bullet.

(2) Depends upon the depth to which the bullet is seated in the case, which should be such that when the cartridge is seated in the chamber the ogive of the bullet should just touch the lands.

The above dimensions were arrived at by measuring a number of cartridges furnished by various riflemen, from measurements furnished by Samuel Clark, Jr. and from the standard dimensions of the .219 Winchester Zipper Cartridge. They will differ slightly according to the various makes and dimensions of barrels and chambering reamers, and the forming and sizing dies. Particularly there are slight variations in the basic measurements of the .219 Winchester Zipper case because a small tolerance from exact standards is a practical manutacturing necessity.

192 THE ULTIMATE IN RIFLE PRECISION

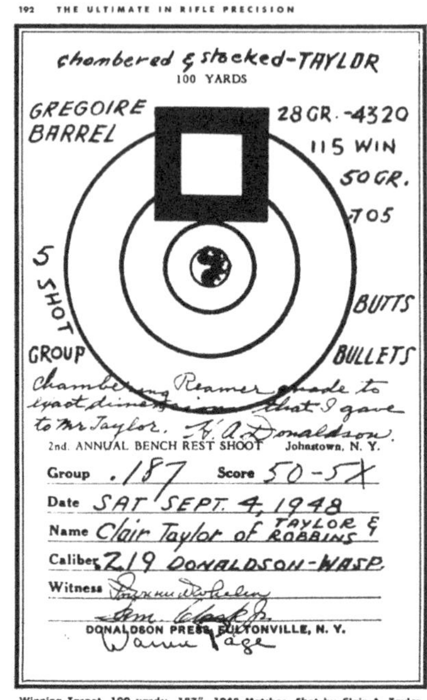

Winning Target, 100 yards: .187". 1948 Matches. Shot by Clair A. Taylor.

The .219 Donaldson Wasp, from the 1951 *Bench Rest Shooter's Annual*.

.22 K-Hornet

One of the first fireformed improved cases, the K-Hornet has stood the test of time, outliving many other cartridges. The .22 Hornet has continued in use for many reasons, chief among them are low recoil and soft report. As we become increasingly urbanized, a relatively quiet cartridge that will efficiently take small game is highly valuable.

In Chapter 3, we discussed Lysle Kilbourn, who, with the help of a Canadian gunsmith G.B. Crandall, designed a cartridge that could fire factory .22 Hornet ammunition in the new chamber, which sported a minimum taper body and sharp shoulder, adding about 10% more room for powder—the .22 K-Hornet. The original Hornet design is from the days of blackpowder cartridges, with its long, tapered case, undefined shoulder and minimal case capacity. Most importantly, Kilbourn retained the important asset of safely firing factory cartridges in the wildcat chamber.

Increased case capacity is the main reason that the K-Hornet is so popular. It provides respectable ballistics and good accuracy, making it popular with varmint shooters. The ballistics for this small cartridge are out of proportion to its size. So long as the factories offer .22 Hornet rifles, the .22 K-Hornet will live on.

.218 Mashburn Bee

The .218 Mashburn was popular with varminters until the .222 Remington arrived. It is a simple fireform-improved case, no special dies are needed to form the .218 Mashburn Bee. There are numerous improved cases based on the .218 Bee. The Mashburn was or is the most popular of these. Likely, much of its popularity came from its radical look, for with a neck length of .170 inch, it was unusual for a time when necks tended to be long.

Ballistically, it was not substantially different from the K-Hornet, but the .218 Bee was chambered in some guns that the Hornet was not. It was available in Winchester Model 65 lever guns. Lever guns are notoriously less accurate than many other designs, which hindered the wildcat. Shooters of the day were looking for the same thing varminters are looking for today: flatter trajectory and longer ranges, which the .218 Mashburn delivered. Benchresters and varminters were likely to chamber the .218 Mashburn Bee in a single shot or bolt-action so they could use spitzer-type bullets.

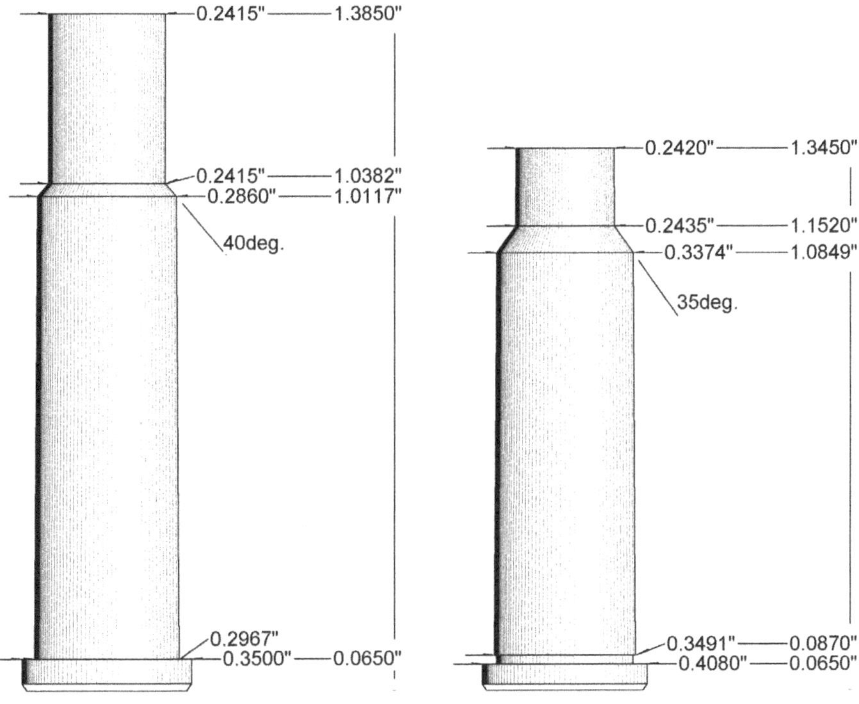

The .22 K-Hornet.

The .218 Mashburn Bee.

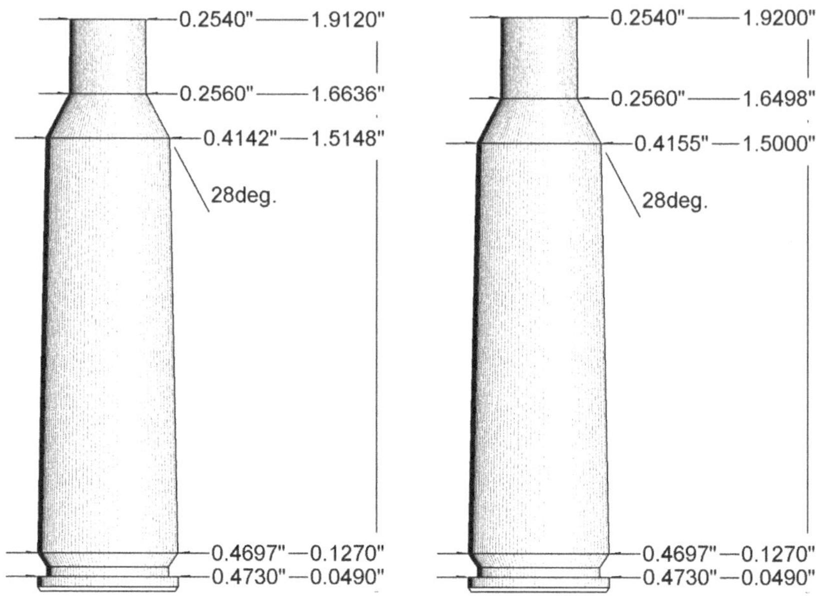

The .22-250 Remington (left), versus the .22 Varminter.

.22-250 Vs. .22 Varminter

From 1925–1928, Captain Grosvenor (Grove) Wotkyns developed a version of the .22-250. However, the most popular version of this wildcat became the .22 Varminter, developed and marketed by J.B. Gebby in about 1937, who is often credited with developing the .22-250. Gebby did a great deal to popularize the cartridge (see Chapter 20). Remington eventually adopted it in 1965 as the .22-250.

.219 Zipper Ackley Improved

Introduced by Winchester in 1937, the .219 Zipper originally came in the Model 64. The Zipper is the .25-35 case necked down to .22 with a slightly shortened neck. Accuracy was limited by the lever-actions it was offered in, just as it was with the .218 Bee. Winchester discontinued the Zipper in 1962, and Remington followed suit shortly after that. P.O. Ackley's .219 Zipper Improved is important because it was his first public trip into the wildcat world. After World War II, Ackley revised it to use .30-30 brass because the factories changed the Zipper cases, making them unsuitable for his improved case design.

The choice of rifles available from factories always limited the Zipper's popularity. Because it was offered in guns with tubular magazines, factory-loaded bullets were always round- or flat-nose, so velocity dropped off quickly. In a strong single-shot or bolt-action, the Zipper is an excellent little cartridge with good accuracy and ballistics.

Ackley wasted no time. In 1938, he brought out his version of the Zipper. Recognizing the shortcomings of limiting the cartridge to lever-actions, Ackley chambered his .219 Zipper AI in single-shot, Krag and Winchester 54 actions. Ackley readily mentioned the existence of other versions of the .219 Improved by his competitors, which he said were equally as good.

Originally, the .219 Zipper Ackley Improved was a simple fireformed wildcat. After World War II, the factories changed the configuration of .219 brass, making it less flexible, so Ackley used .30-30 or .32 Winchester Special cases—a process requiring form dies. While it's a good cartridge, too many similar modern designs do not require complicated forming before use, so it is well on its way to the boneyard. The .22/30-30 Ackley Improved superseded this cartridge.

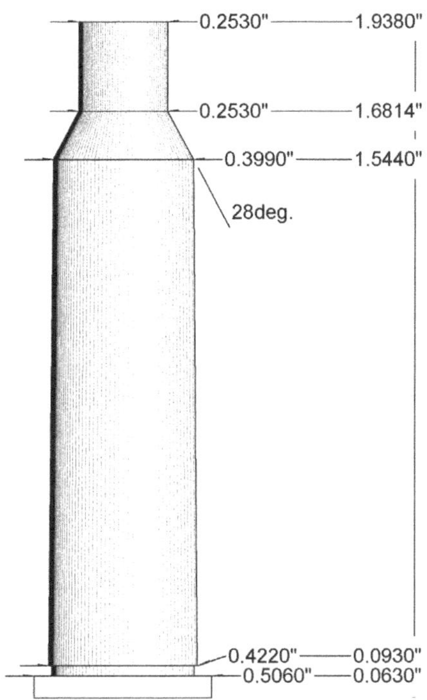

The .219 Zipper Ackley Improved.

.22-303 Varmint-R

Best suited for single-shot rifles, the .22-303 closely approaches the case capacity of the .22-250. Its popularity is mainly in the British

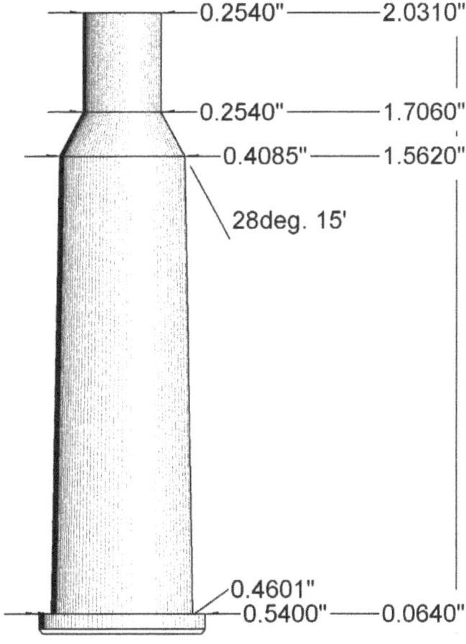

The .22-303 Varmint-R.

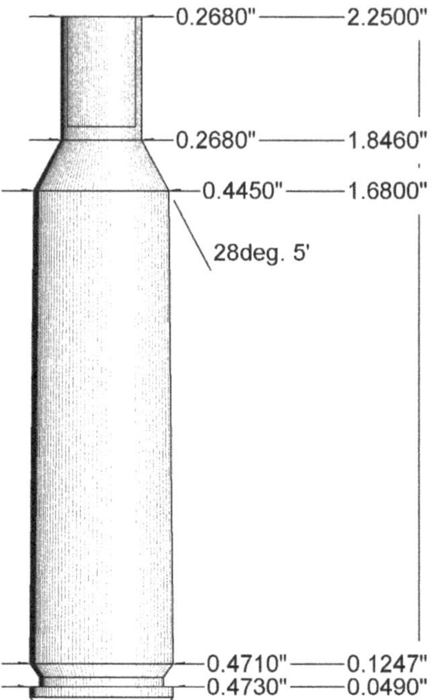

The .228 Ackley Magnum.

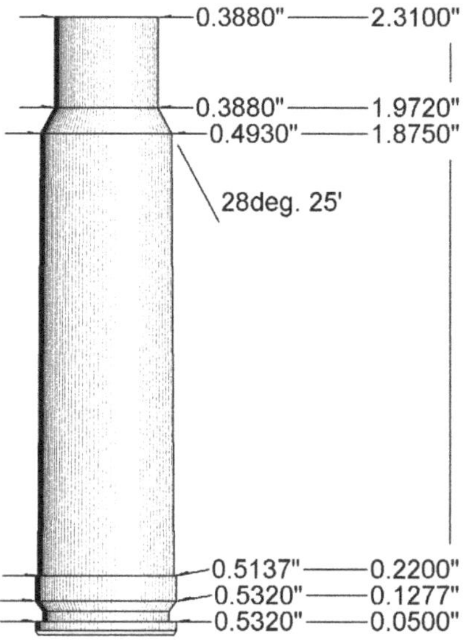

The .35 Ackley Magnum.

colonies, where the .303 was and is in widespread use. It would be an interesting choice in a P-14 Enfield action.

Ackley's .228 Magnum

The .228 Ackley Magnum was designed with both varmint and big game hunting in mind and would be Ackley's first wildcat. In 1936, he built his first gun in this caliber while learning barrel making at Ben Hawkins' shop in Cincinnati when 90-grain bullets were used for deer-class animals and smaller.

According to Ackley, "Its record on big game, including Alaskan and African varieties, has been impressive. This is mainly due to the fact that almost all bullets made for this caliber have been made of heavy tough jacket type of a special controlled expansion design."[3] Later, Ackley prescribed a 70-grain bullet, but they were always the .228 bullet used in the .22 Savage Hi-Power.

Like the .22 Newton that went before it, misuse was the .228 Ackley's biggest detractor. Small calibers require precise shots for a clean kill, and not all hunters have the patience to wait for the right shot.

Currently, many reamer makers offer a tool for this cartridge for both .228- and .224-inch groove diameters, so be sure you know what you are getting. In 2023, several

3 Ackley, P.O., *Handbook for Shooters & Reloaders*, 1962

makers offer heavy, long bullets in .224 inch (70 grains and above) that would work well in this cartridge on deer-size game.

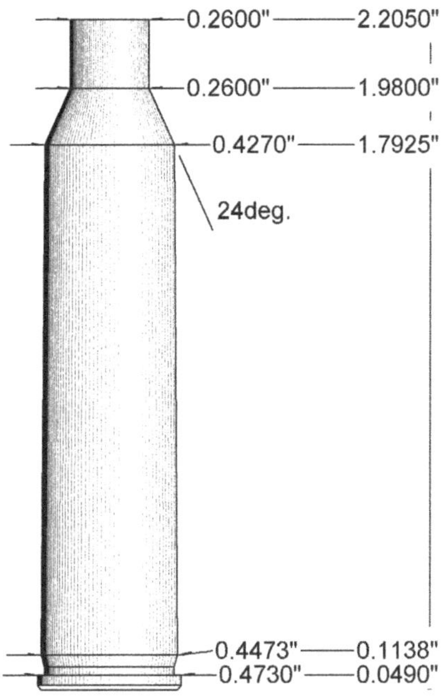

The .220 Weatherby Rocket.

.35 Ackley Magnum

The .35 Ackley Magnum is one of the few medium-bore wildcats of consequence from this time. In about 1946, Ackley redesigned this case; it was originally a necked-up version of his .30 Magnum No. 1. (The later and now standard design was a necked-up version of the .30 Ackley Magnum No. 2, a slightly longer case.) Interestingly, the .358 Norma Magnum nearly duplicates it. According to Ackley, the .35 Short Magnum cases were the best and most efficient of the .35-caliber magnums.[4] He designed the .35 Ackley Magnum with the .35 Newton in mind, and it closely duplicates the ballistics of that early cartridge.

During World War II, new wildcat development was effectively arrested as the country turned all resources toward the war effort. Following the war, wildcatting renewed in earnest.

Other Notable Wildcats

A few more notable wildcats came along from World War II to about 1950.

.220 Weatherby Rocket
.22/30-30 Ackley Improved
.30-06 Ackley Improved
.250-3000 Ackley Improved
.243 Rockchucker
6.5-06, 8mm-06
.333 OKH
.334 OKH
.257 Roberts Ackley Imp.
7mm Mashburn Super Mag.
.300 Mashburn Super Mag.

4 Barnes, Frank C., *Cartridges of the World, 9th Edition*

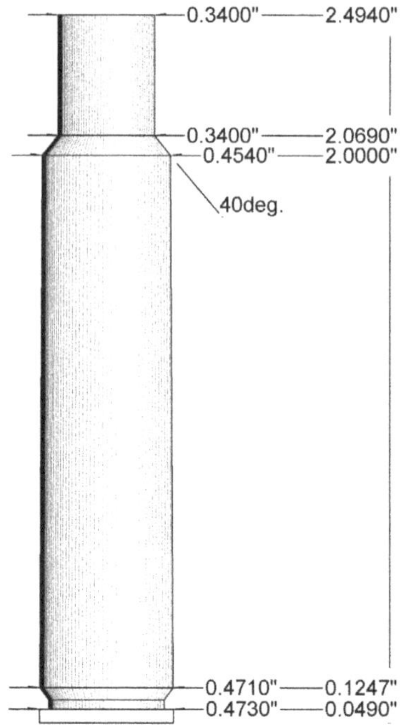

The .30-06 Ackley Improved.

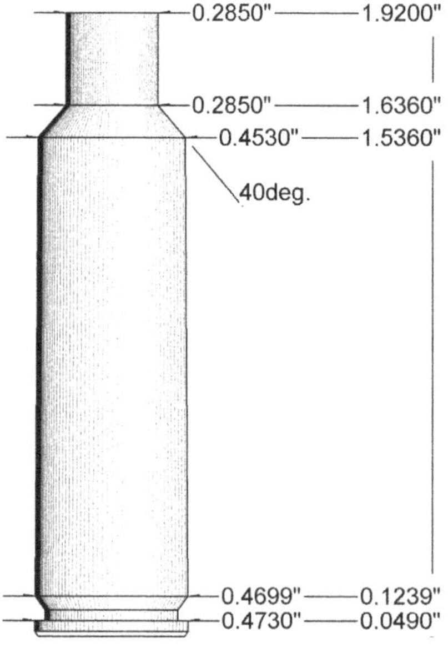

The .250 Savage Ackley Improved.

.220 Weatherby Rocket

Developed in 1943, the .220 Weatherby Rocket was not remarkable as a cartridge but because it was the first of Roy Weatherby's design efforts. No headstamped cases or ammunition are available for this improved .220 Swift case, so it qualifies as a wildcat. It's important mainly because it marked the beginning of the Weatherby legacy.

.22/30-30 Ackley

The .22/30-30 Ackley was developed after the war, largely because the factory brass that Ackley had before the conflict, which he used for his .219 Zipper Improved, no longer worked properly—the post-war production brass was thinner in wall and neck thickness, so Ackley did not feel it worked well with his design. Ackley eventually developed the .22/30-30 AI to resolve this issue. Another notable design change was that Ackley modified the shoulder to 40 degrees to make his customers happy as they had come to identify him with this sharp-shoulder angle.

It was at this time that wildcatters finally started to move away from .22-caliber cartridges: The .22 field was getting crowded, better powders became available, income levels were on the rise, making new rifles more affordable, and big game hunters were interested in cartridges larger than .22.

.30-06 Ackley Improved

The .30-06 Ackley Improved came about sometime in 1945–46. Nearly 80 years later, this cartridge is still very popular with shooters. The folks at JGS Precision Tool Mfg., Coos Bay, OR, list the .30-06 Ackley Improved chamber reamer as one of their best sellers.

Ackley was open about the fact that it was one of many improved designs in the marketplace for the .30-06. Of course, his design is the one that became the go-to. A review of published load data where the pressures are held to standard SAAMI for the .30-06 allows an average increase in velocity of 60 to 75 fps, depending on the bullet design and other variables. So, for those who say the .30-06 AI is a waste of time, it depends on your desire for more velocity and what that is worth.

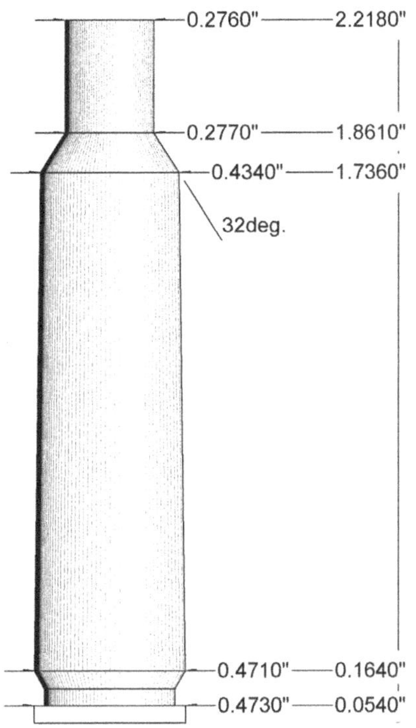

The .243 Rockchucker.

.250 Savage Ackley Improved

In *Cartridges of the World,* Frank Barnes credits P.O.'s improved version of the .250-3000 as "one of Ackley's best wildcats." Whether you call it the .250 Ackley, .250 Ackley Improved or .250-3000 Improved, the results are undeniable. Velocities are increased by the highest percentage of all of Ackley's improved cases, delivering results that exceed the .257 Roberts by a small margin.

.243 Rockchucker

Fred Huntington of RCBS fame created the .243 Rockchucker, perfecting it in the years following World War II. He based it on the 7x57 or .257 Roberts case with a 32-degree shoulder angle. Indeed, the smokeless powder quality and increasing numbers of shooters with money to spend helped make this cartridge a success. It was the primary cartridge leading to the development of the 6mm Remington.

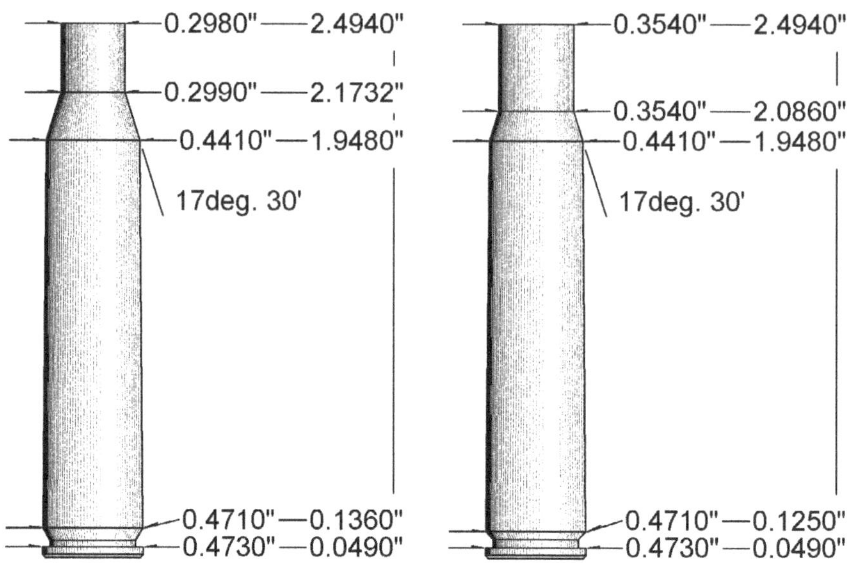

The 6.5-06 (left) and the 8mm-06 (right).

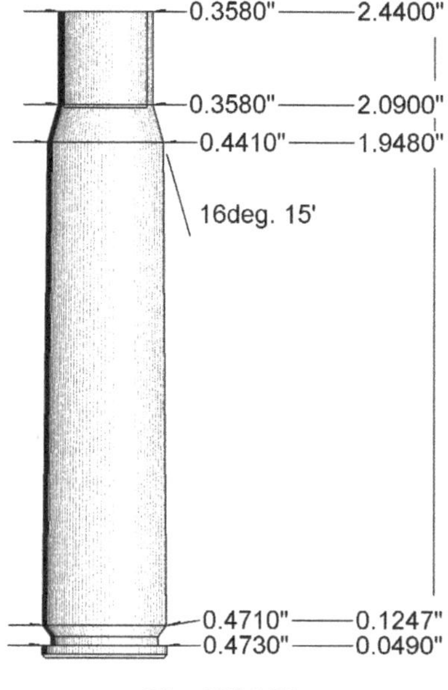

The .333 OKH.

6.5-06 and 8mm-06

Variations on the .30-06 case using 6.5mm and 8mm barrels appeared following World War II. These cartridges were created because of the influx of surplus rifles in these bore diameters. Ammunition was hard to locate in the original calibers, so many rifles were rechambered for the .30-06 case, necked for the appropriate bore diameter. This option made for inexpensive conversions and generally delivered ballistics superior to the original military cartridges, allowing for the use of commonly available brass. Both utilize standard .30-06 headspace gauges.

.333 OKH

The .333 OKH is the direct ancestor of the .338-06, developed by Charles O'Neil, Elmer Kieth and Don Hopkins (OKH) in 1945. This wildcat used the then-available .333-caliber bullets, and the .30-06 case necked up.

In 1958, the .338 Winchester Magnum was introduced, making .338 bullets more available than the .333 and the .333 OKH obsolete. The difference between the .333 OKH and the .338-06 is so tiny that it is possible to interchange load data. Only Hawk Bullets, Inc. and Woodleigh make bullets in .333 caliber today.

Elmer Keith subscribed to the concept that bigger is better, so it's only natural that there would be a magnum version of the OKH cartridges.

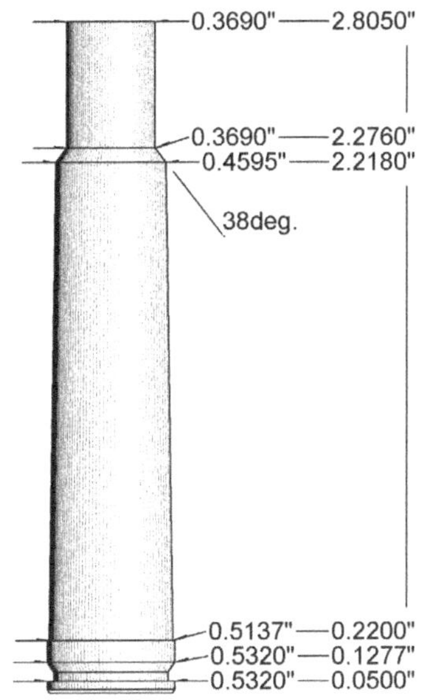

The .334 OKH.

.334 OKH

The .334 OKH was based on the .300 H&H case, somewhat improved in design, and dates from the late 1940s. It was a precursor of the later .338 Winchester.

.257 Roberts Ackley Improved

How about a wildcat, on a wildcat? In 1922, Ned Roberts created the .257 Roberts when he necked the 7x57 case down to accept a .25-caliber bullet. A quarter of a century later, P.O. Ackley improved the .257 Roberts, which Remington had standardized by then. Depending on bullet selection, this improved case will deliver from 100 to 300 fps more velocity than the parent case. The .25-06 only slightly beats the improved case. Because the Roberts case will fit a short action, it has a strong following.

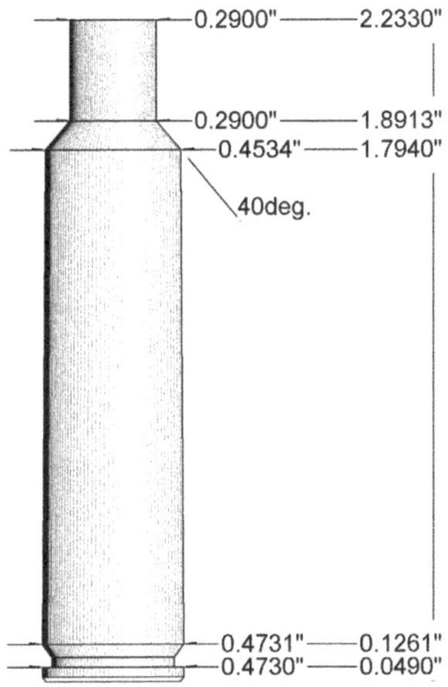

The .257 Roberts Ackley Improved.

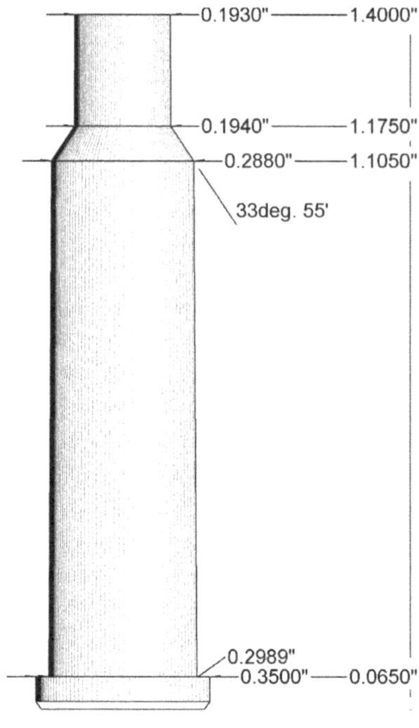

The .17 Ackley Hornet.

7mm Mashburn

A.E. Mashburn of Oklahoma City was a prolific designer. His 7mm Super Magnum, or 7mm Mashburn, was just one of a full line of cartridges. A quick check of Ackley's *Handbook for Shooters and Reloaders* produced a list of 6.5mm Super Mag., .270 Super Mag. and 7mm Super Mag. All are based on the .300 H&H case necked and shortened to 2.630 inches. So, standard-length actions will handle them. Mashburn promoted these calibers nearly 20 years before the factories offered similar ones. There were also "long" (full-length 2.850-inch) as well as "short" (cut-down 2.5-inch) versions, as Mashburn covered all the angles, you might say.

The long version of the 7mm Mashburn is the equivalent of the 7mm STW. Interestingly, there is a .300 Mashburn Super Mag. (long), a ballistic twin of the .300 Weatherby. They were developed at about the same time.

More Wildcat Developments from 1950 to 1960

.17 Ackley Hornet	.17/222
.20-250	.30-30 Ackley Improved
7mm-06, .285 OKH or	.270 Gibbs
7mm-06 Mashburn	.375 Whelen
.450 Alaskan	.450 Watts
.50 Alaskan	

.17 Ackley Hornet

Although it was not Ackley's first wildcat in .17 caliber, it may have been his best. The .17 Ackley Hornet remained popular until 2012, when Hornady adopted a close variation of it as the .17 Hornady Hornet. Ballistically, the Hornady is the same cartridge, even though they are not interchangeable. Part of the Ackley

Hornet's continued interest was the availability of brass and the ease of forming cases.

Its popularity is primarily because it is far less susceptible to fouling than the larger capacity .17s such as the .17/223 and .17 Remington and doesn't require frequent cleaning. A good rule of thumb for case capacity in a .17 is no more than 17 grains of powder. The same holds for .19- and .20-caliber wildcats: one grain per caliber, i.e., 19 grains of powder for a .19 caliber and 20 grains for a .20, will likely produce the best results.

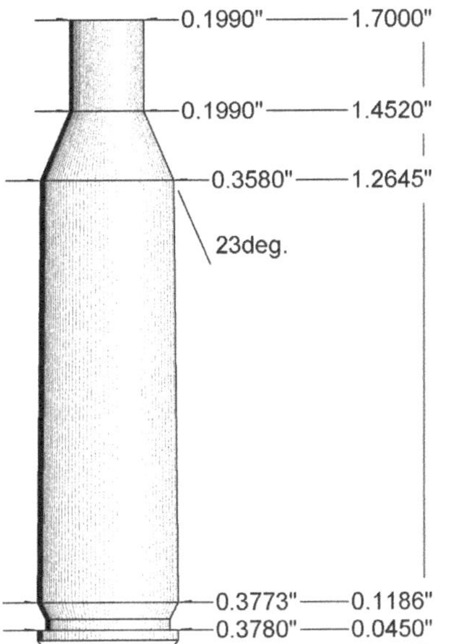

The .17-222.

.17/222

Reportedly, the .17/222 dates from 1957.[5] No specific gunsmith is credited with its development, but it is obviously one of the predecessors of the .17 Remington. Ackley says the .17/222 was about the maximum in case capacity for the .17 caliber and he complained that larger cases lacked flexibility. There is no doubt he was correct.

.20-250

Todd Kindler, who once published the *Small Caliber News*, wrote an article titled "The .20-250—A Long Range Smasher." It included a January 22, 1957 letter from G.R. Douglas (Douglas Barrels) in which Douglas referred to the .20 bore as the "New Two Hundred." Kindler

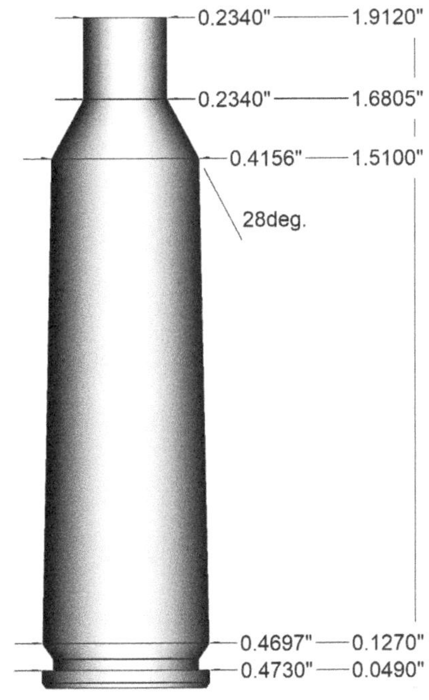

The .20-250.

5 Barnes, Frank C., *Cartridges of the World, 8th Edition*

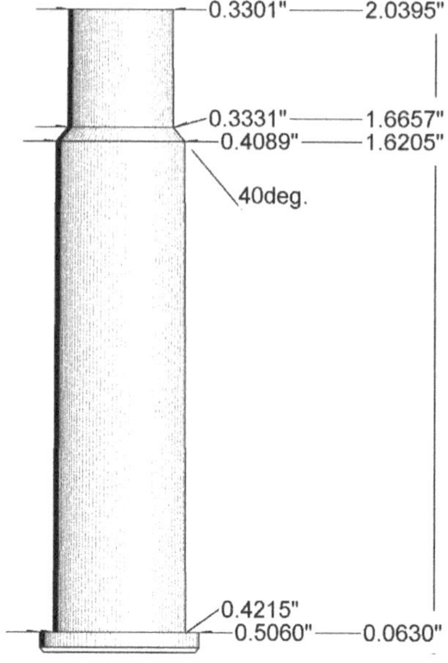

The .30-30 Ackley Improved.

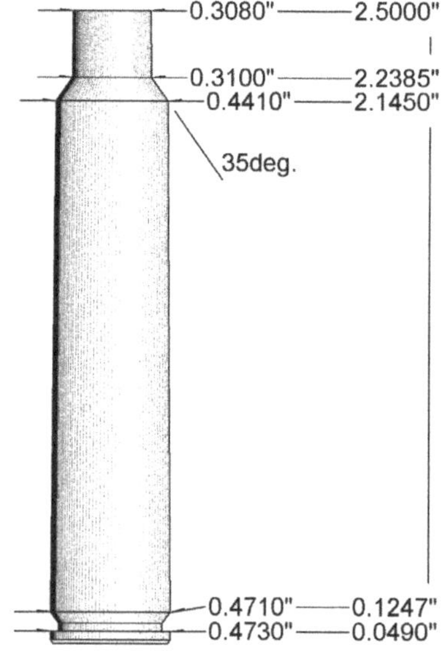

The .270 Gibbs.

was a significant force in developing interest in all sub-calibers, and talked Douglas into bringing the .20 caliber back after a few decades in the attic of the gun world.

The G.R. Douglas letter mentions creating a .20 caliber on the .250 case. This was 10 years before Remington made the .22-250 a factory round. Douglas' first wildcat in this diameter was the .200-222.

Kindler had a reamer made for the .20-250 in 2006, nearly 50 years after Douglas announced his new bore diameter and tooling to the public. Likely, others played with this caliber, but, to be fair, without Todd Kindler, who knows if we would be shooting .20-caliber anything?

.30-30 Ackley Improved

Surprisingly, the .30-30 Ackley Improved originated in the early 1950s. As old as the .30-30 is, you would think Ackley would have worked it over early in his career. Its value comes from the 200 to 300 fps it adds to the original cartridge. Because the .30-30 WCF is one of the most popular factory cartridges ever, it makes sense that this wildcat would have a good following. Lever guns like the 94 Winchester and 336 Marlin can be rechambered to this cartridge with no other work necessary.

When I performed pressure testing on the .30-30 Ackley Improved chambering for my book, *P.O. Ackley, America's Gunsmith*, published by Gun Digest (GunDigestStore.com), I learned that it's possible to get almost 400 fps more

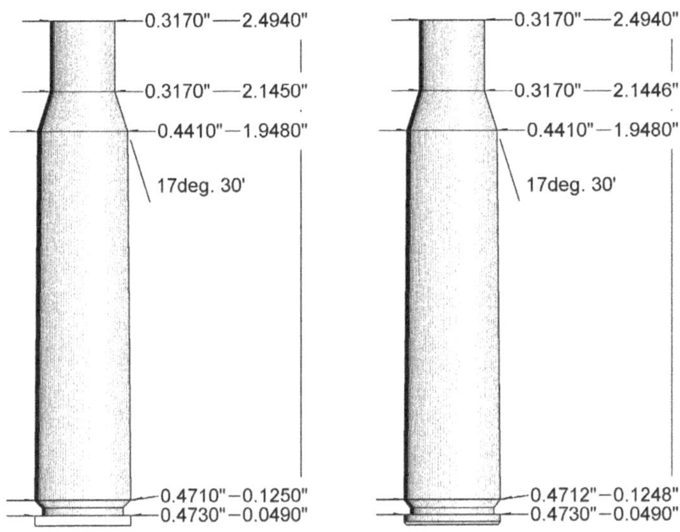

The 7mm-06 (left), .285 OKH (right).

velocity with a 150-grain bullet than the factory advertises for standard .30-30 ammo with the same bullet, while maintaining safe SAAMI pressure limits.

.270 Gibbs

Rocky Gibbs' favorite cartridge. In 1954, Gibbs won a match at the Richmond, CA, Rod and Gun Club—a match that required an accurate and flat-shooting rifle. The rifles were sighted in for 100 yards. First, a group was shot for score at 100 yards, and then a group was shot at 400 yards to measure drop. The drop figure played heavily in determining the winner of the match.

Gibbs' wildcats have always been controversial because their short necks are only .250 inch. Gibbs was famous for squeezing every last bit of velocity out of the '06 case. According to Roger Stowers in his article about the .270 Gibbs, Rocky was a proponent of using brass life as a measure of safe loads. Stowers said, "He (Gibbs) repeatedly cautioned that long case life and snug primer pockets were the secret to safe handloads. Sticky bolt lift and extraction should not be a problem until safe pressures have been left well behind."[6] Sound advice to any reloader.

.285 OKH/7mm-06

The .285 OKH and the 7mm-06 variation seemed a no-brainer. After all, they were the forerunners of the .280 Remington introduced in 1957 (known as the

6 Waters, Ken, "The 207 Gibbs", *Wildcat Cartridges, Volume II*, 1992

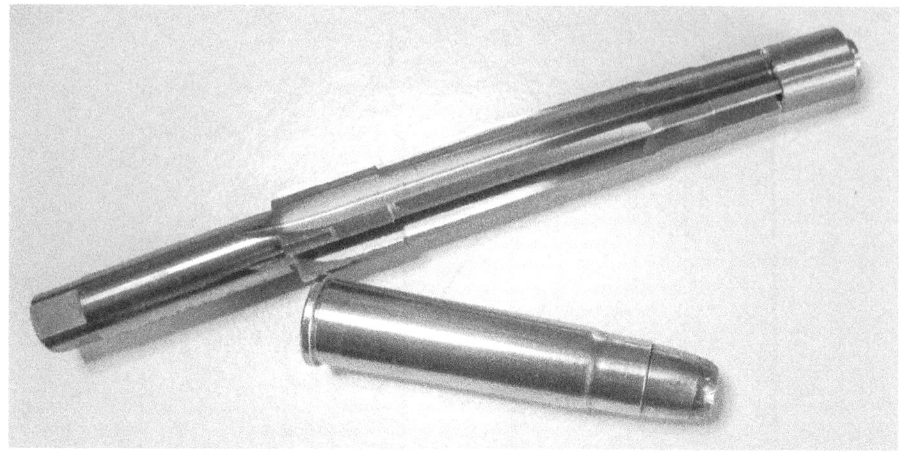

A .450 Alaskan reamer and cartridge.

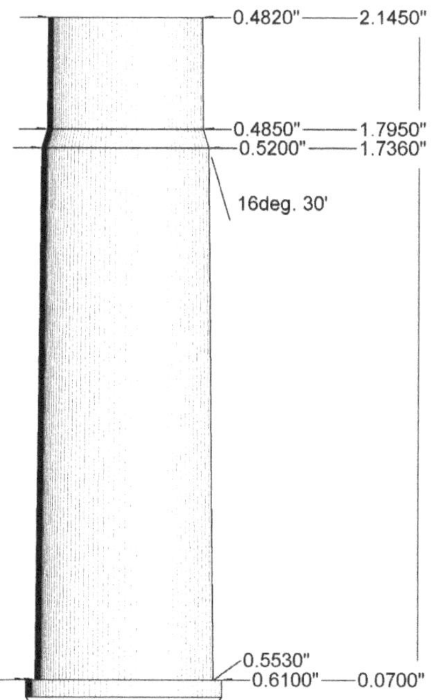

The .450 Alaskan.

7mm Express at one time). There is so little difference between the wildcats and the factory cartridge that there is not much to say about them, just that they were good designs, as evidenced by the success of the factory version. The .280 Remington produces about 95% of the ballistics of the 7mm Remington Magnum with far less powder and recoil. Because the .280 Remington borders on the maximum capacity for the bore, the Ackley version does not produce as large of an increase in velocity as it does with some factory cartridges. Still, the .280 Ackley Improved is extremely popular, especially since Nosler took it to SAAMI.

.450 Alaskan

The 1952 brainchild of Harold Johnson, of Coopers Landing, AK, the .450 Alaskan is the .348 Winchester case necked up with the shoulder blown out. Its success comes primarily because the .450 Alaskan functions well in the Winchester Model 71 action. This combination provides a fast lever-action in a rugged but lightweight package. The ballistics are nearly identical to the .458 Winchester. Reliable and strong, these rifles are prized by Alaskan hunters and guides.

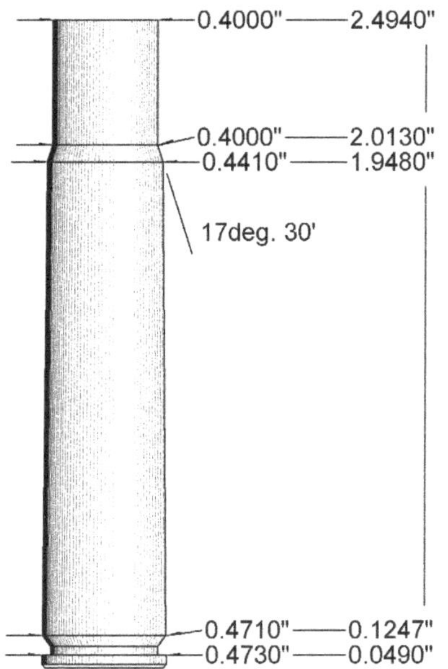

The .375 Whelen.

.375 Whelen

The .375 Whelen is credited by many writers to L.R. "Bob" Wallack as a 1951 development. Wallack necked the .30-06 case up to .375 with no other changes. Over the years, the fact that Townsend Whelen had tested a .38 Whelen was somehow forgotten. However, to Wallack's praise, he chose to name his "new" cartridge after the famous writer and shooter Townsend Whelen as a tribute. In a letter dated August 23, 1919, Whelen wrote to Fred Adolph, saying, "Neidner and I have been trying to develop a .38 caliber high power Springfield for some time, to use the regular Springfield shell." So, Wallack reinvented something that Whelen had tested years before. These facts were brought to light by Michael Petrov during his research into the origins of the .400 Whelen, see Chapter 11.

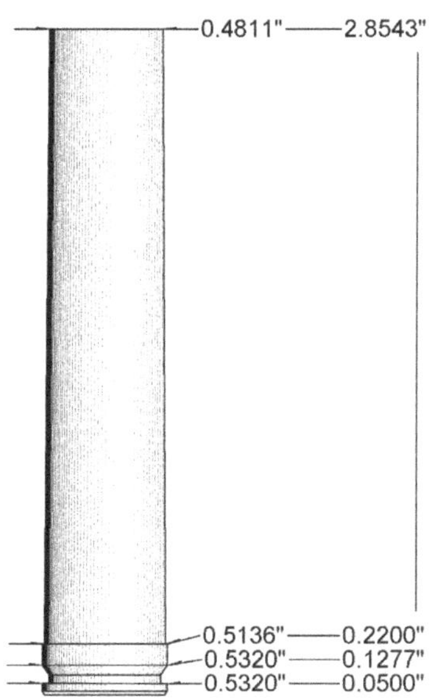

The .450 Watts.

.450 Watts

Originating in the 1950s or earlier by Watts and H.B. Anderson of Yakima, WA, the .450 Watts is a full-length .375 H&H case straightened to accept a .458 bullet.[7] Nearly 3/8-inch longer than the .458 Winchester case and .050-inch longer than the .458 Lott, the Watts easily pushes a 500-grain

7 Ackley, P.O., *Handbook for Shooters & Reloaders*, 1962

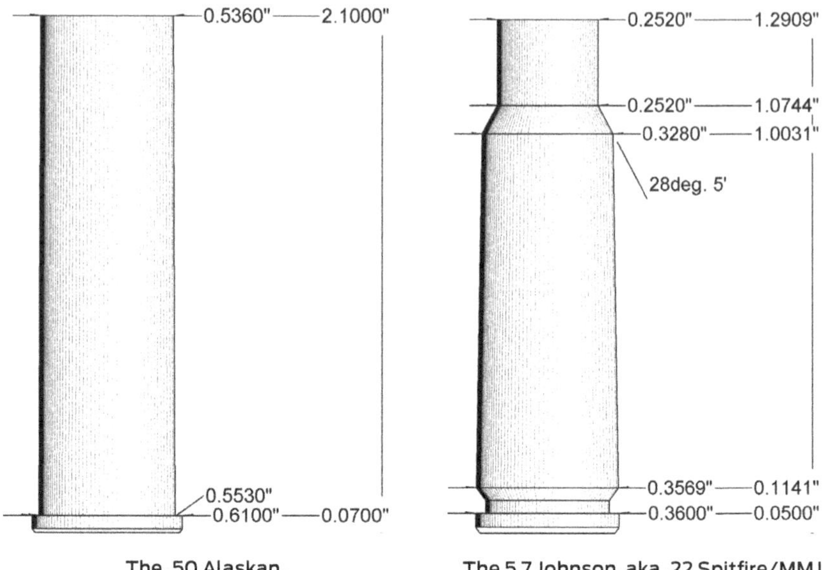

The .50 Alaskan.

The 5.7 Johnson, aka .22 Spitfire/MMJ 5.7mm.

bullet 200 fps faster than the factory .458 Winchester. At the turn of the 21st century, when the .458 Lott became a factory-loaded cartridge, the Watts became obsolete.

.50 Alaskan

Harold Johnson, the .50 Alaskan's originator, called it "The Fifty." Designed shortly after the .450 Alaskan, the .50 Alaskan uses a .510-inch bullet and is a straight-walled case based on the .348 Winchester. Johnson initially used surplus .50 BMG bullets cut in half to get a usable weight, reverse loaded so they became a truncated cone, with the boattail facing out. Today, there is a much better selection of bullets for this cartridge. Big bores, in general, have developed their own following; the .50 Alaskan is a fun cartridge, and like its little brother, the .450, it works in the 71 Winchester with a few modifications. If you prefer a bolt-action, you can convert Siamese Mausers to feed the .50 Alaskan.

Wildcats 1960 to 1970

5.7 Johnson or .22 Spitfire

.22-243 Middlestead

6x47 (6mm-222 Remington Mag.)

6mm-284, .25-284 and .30-284

.308x1.5" Barnes

.458x2" American

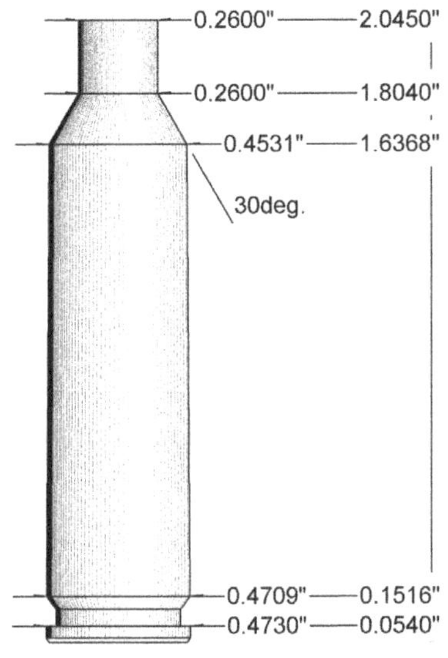

The .22-243 Middlestead.

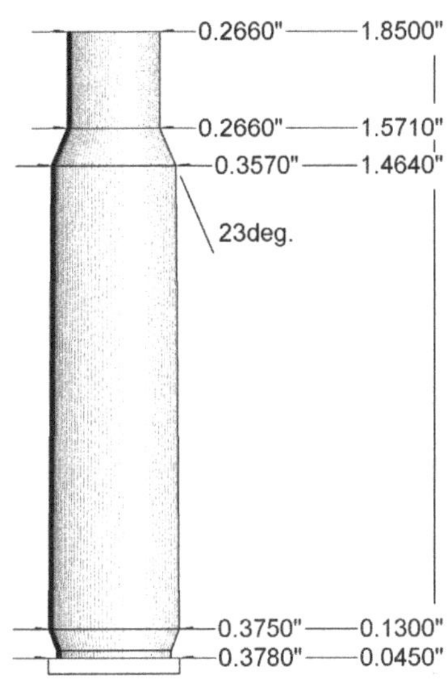

The 6x47mm.

5.7 Johnson/.22 Spitfire/MMJ 5.7mm

Some cartridges have trouble settling on one name. For example, the 5.7 Johnson is also known as the .22 Spitfire and the MMJ 5.7mm. The .30 Carbine, by all accounts, is a fairly worthless cartridge; however, when necked down to .22 to make the Johnson, it suddenly shows some value. Melvin Johnson, Marine Colonel, author and inventor of the Johnson semi-auto rifle and light machine gun used in World War II, designed it to be used in the M-1 Carbine.

The .22 Spitfire never achieved a significant following but seems to hang on year after year as a wildcat. It did see a short time as a factory offering when Plainfield chambered it.

.22-243 Middlestead

Designed by Paul Middlestead in the early 1960s, the .22-243 Middlestead is still a reasonably popular wildcat. The case capacity is about 5% greater than the .220 Swift. Because of its large capacity, it performs exceptionally well with heavier bullets of 60 grains and up. Frank Barnes says, "If any wildcat cartridge deserves to become a commercial round, the .22-243 would certainly fall into that class." Shooters of the .22-243 commonly report groups under ½ MOA.

6x47mm

Intended as a benchrest cartridge, the 6x47mm (6mm-222 Remington Magnum) came to be in the early 1960s. Mike Walker built the first of these for

HUNTINGTON

Fred T. Huntington
President

P.O. BOX 991 · 601 ORO DAM BLVD · OROVILLE, CALIFORNIA 95965 · (916) 534-1210

Aug. 1/90

Fred D. Zeglin
Public Relations
2615 N. 4th St. Suite 603F
Couer d Alene, Idaho 83814

Dear Mr. Zeglin:

I was pleased to get up for the #1 Varmit Assn. Convention and hope to be able to come again.

With regards to the proposed trip and hunt to the Malta, Mt Area-That will all depend on whom I can get to drive for me as I just do not do very well on such long drives. It sounds good if I can work it out!

I might say that.223 Necked up to 6M I bought there just would not groupe its shots after tryung several loads and Bullets. Kimber offered to have me ship it up to them becauae It just was not right. However As it was a poor Wildcat to say the least I just decided to make it into a 223 Caliber rifle with new Barrel. The first goupe shot of 6 Shots turned out to be just a Hair under 1" and five of the shots in 3/4" so I belive that's a better deal than that odd-ball Wildcat Caliber it was! We have our gunsmith here that was capable of a good job. I am now pleased with the way its grouping. The#1 Groupe was with Factory loads and believe some good handloads will keep it within a 1" Groupe.

So far I have not done anything with the .22/250 Riwall Browning Rifle I won there. One of these days I'll get on it and see what it turns out to be.

Keep me posted on the Proposed Varmit hunt and new dates for a convention for 1991.

Cordially,

Fred T. Huntington

(OVER)

Supplier of RCBS Dies, Accessories, and Parts

Bob Hutton and told Hutton he believed "It would probably be more accurate than anything available at the time in 6mm."[8]

Light bullets produce the best accuracy. In the letter reproduced here, Fred Huntington made it clear that he was not impressed with the 6x47mm cartridge—the 6mm rifle he mentions was a 6x47 made by the original Kimber.

6mm-284 Winchester/.25-284/6.5-284 Norma-Lapua/.30-284/.338-284/.35-284

In 1963, when the .284 Winchester came on the scene, it did not take long for wildcatters to work it over. P.O. Ackley made a barrel for Bob Hutton of *Guns & Ammo* magazine. They tested every caliber.

The variations are the 6mm-284, .25-284, 6.5-284 Norma/Lapua, .30-284, .338-284 and .35-284. This case has nearly identical capacity to the .30-06, so it's easy to see the ballistics for each. Offering standard-length ballistics in a medium-action cartridge is the only advantage of this case. It lacks the flexibility of the '06 case because the neck is too short to allow any real improvement in capacity. However, the 6.5-284 verges on being a factory cartridge. Lapua and Norma offer brass (there is so little difference between the two designs that they interchange. They vary a tiny amount from standard .284 Winchester brass, and special chamber reamers are needed for the Lapua/Norma chamber, but they all use the same headspace gauges).

.308x1.5"

Frank C. Barnes developed the 308x1.5" in March 1961, conceived as a varmint through deer cartridge. The idea was to build lightweight short-action rifles for the cartridge, making it a handy hunting caliber. In actual practice, it was adopted by the metallic silhouette crowd and single-shot pistol hunters. While approximately the same size as the 7.62x39, the case capacity is greater, making it more versatile. Producing velocities as much as 300 fps faster than the .30-30 with the same weight bullet, the 308x1.5" would probably be more popular

8 Barnes, Frank C., *Cartridges of the World, 8th Edition*

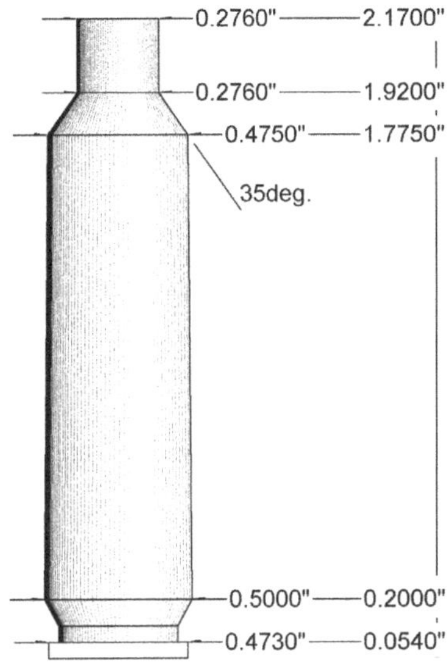

The 6mm-284 Winchester.

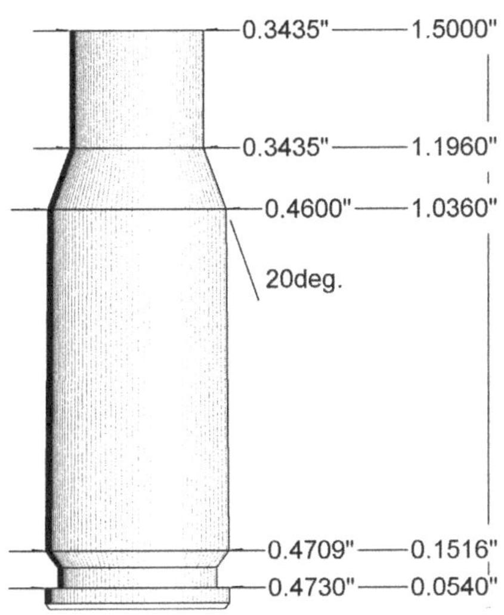

The .308x1.5".

if a good bolt-action was suited to the short cartridge.

The 308x1.5" has inspired many other wildcats, including caliber-necked cartridges in 7mm, 6mm, and .22 up to .375 caliber. It provided the framework from which the BR cases were designed, extremely successful as wildcats go!

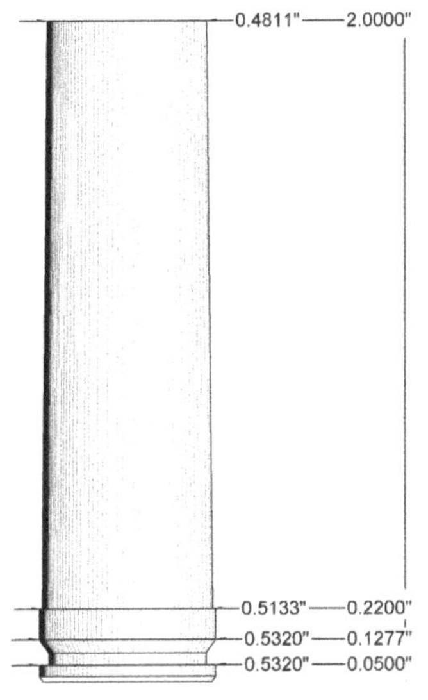

The .458x2".

458x2" American

A year later, in 1962, Frank Barnes developed a cutdown version of the .458 Winchester, known as the "458x2" American." The short overall length makes this cartridge workable in short- or standard-length actions. Barnes felt that the .458 Winchester was overpowered for North American game. The idea of the .458x2" was to create a modern design that would work in a bolt-action rifle and produce ballistics suitable for North American game animals. It is, in effect, a belted .45-70 rather than a shortened .458 Magnum. Ammunition can be made from 458 Magnum cases.[9] While case dimensions and capacity are similar to the .45-70, because the 458x2" is used in modern bolt-actions, it can be loaded to higher pressures.

For a hard-hitting iron-sighted rifle, the 458x2" American was a great candidate until the .450 Marlin came along in 2000.

The .10/222 or .222 Remington necked down to .10 caliber. Yes, that is a standard .224-inch bullet on top of the case.

Wildcats 1970 to 1990

.14-222	.22 Waldog
.22 PPC & 6mm PPC	.22 CHeetah
.22 BR	6mm, .25, 6.5mm, 7mmTCU
7mm STW	.300 Whisper
.30 Herrett, .357 Herrett	.309 JDJ
.416 Taylor	.358 STA
.458 Lott	.577 Tyrannosaur
.585 Nyati	

.14-222

Tiny calibers like the .14-222 became technically possible during this period. I was commissioned to make dies for a .10-222, although barrels for this caliber are as yet unavailable. Some research was done with .14 and .12 calibers in the years following World War II, though a lack of manufacturing or quality barrels was likely the stumbling block that kept interest in small calibers low.

In 1985, Helmut W. Sakschek developed the .14-222. An article in the 1988 20th edition of *Guns Illustrated* covered this cartridge in detail.

.22 Waldog

The .22 Waldog was born in 1980 when gunsmith Dan Dowling named his wildcat for a friend, Waldo G. Woodside, calling it the Waldo-G or Waldog. He fabricated cases from .220 Russian brass shortened in a die to duplicate the .222's case capacity. This short, fat case broke several 100-yard benchrest records. Its similarity to the .22 BR from Remington relegates the Waldog to permanent wildcat status.

.22 PPC & 6mm PPC (Pindell-Palmisano Cartridge)

In 1974, Dr. Louis Palmisano and Ferris Pindell developed the .22 PPC and 6mm

9 *Ibid.*

PPC. They based the wildcats on the .220 Russian case and intended them for benchrest competition. In 1987, Sako introduced ammunition for both calibers and began to offer rifles chambered for them. Later, Norma began making ammunition as well. In 1993, Ruger offered rifles chambered for the PPC cartridges as varmint calibers. They are a fine example of wildcats that filled a niche so well that the factories could not ignore them.

.22-06 Short/.22 K-S-S (Krag Super Short)

It's amazing how sometimes ideas take off. The PPC concept that short, fat cartridges tended to be accurate, was not new. While they developed the PPC calibers without consideration of predecessors, some did exist. Two examples are the .22-06 Short designed by gunsmith Claude Graves of Indianapolis, IN, and the .22 K-S-S or Krag Super short from the well-known L.E. Wilson of Cashmere, WA. Wilson even tried bushing the primer pocket and flash hole for a small rifle primer, like the PPC utilizes. These cartridges are surprisingly similar to the .22 PPC.

The bottom line is that very little has not been done before. However, the PPC cartridges won matches and set records, which is the reason for their extreme success.

.22 BR

The .22 BR was based on Frank Barnes' 308x1.5" and is a rare "factory wildcat"

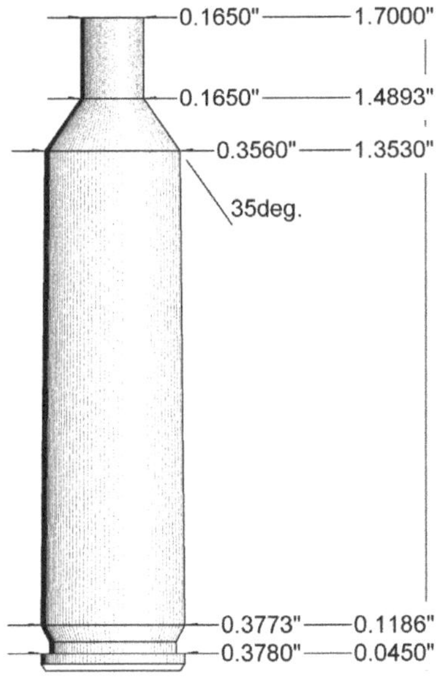

The .14-222 Walker.

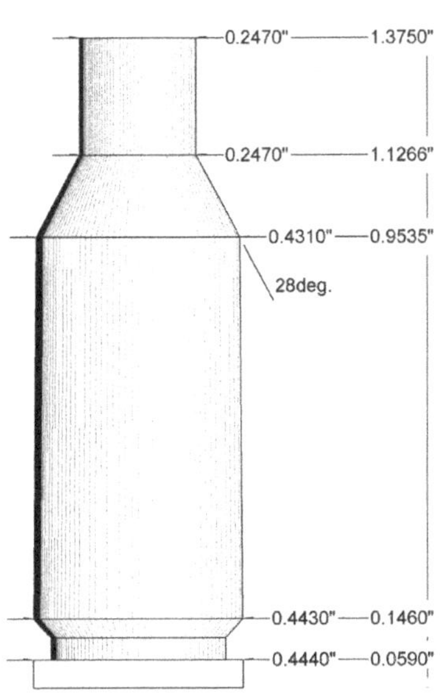

The .22 Waldog.

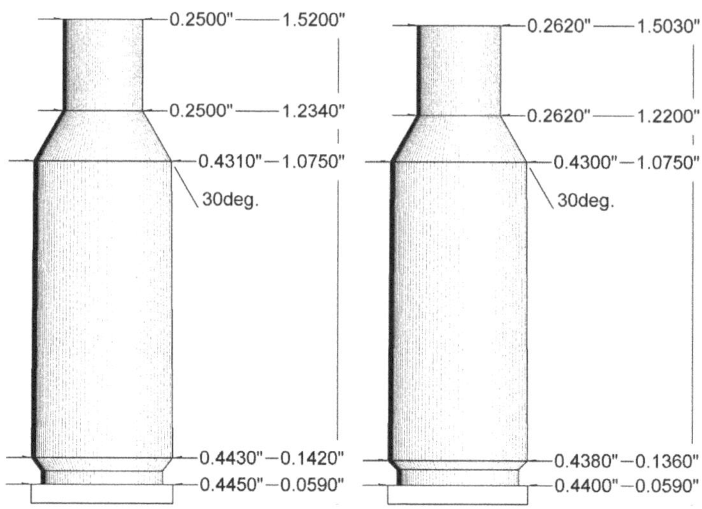

The .22 PPC (left), 6mm PPC (right).

(the factory does not offer loaded ammo for the .22 BR, although brass is available). Because of the easy availability of brass, the BR series of cartridges tend to overshadow similar wildcats. Ordering custom shop guns like the 40X also increased the following for them. Many shooters now select Lapua or Norma brass for BR wildcats (make sure your chamber reamer is correct for that brass as it does vary from the standard BR slightly).

.22 CHeetah

In the late 1970s, Jim Carmichel and Fred Huntington collaborated to design the .22 CHeetah. Their idea was to wring out as much accuracy as possible. What makes this different from the earlier .22 wildcats on the .308 or .243 case? It uses the .308 BR case with a small primer pocket, which is lighter in construction and more uniform than the average brass. A 40-degree shoulder improved brass flow control and maximized case capacity. This cartridge has a shorter neck than the earlier versions, accomplished by moving the shoulder, which also increases capacity.

The .22 CHeetah proved to be accurate but was not sufficiently different from the .22-243 Middlestead to warrant the added costs and efforts. While both wildcats have a following, the Middlestead appears to be gathering new converts more rapidly. The longer neck of the Middlestead should increase accurate barrel life, as the brass takes more of the beating instead of the barrel's throat.

TCU

TCU stands for Thompson-Center/Ugalde. Developed in the 1980s by Wes Uglade of Fallon, NV, the TCU line includes several calibers. Their primary purpose was for use in the Thompson-Contender pistol in metallic silhouette shooting. The 6mm, .25, 6.5mm and 7mm TCU proved effective for hunting up to deer-sized animals using the Contender. They're easy to form since about all that is involved is necking .223 Remington brass to the appropriate caliber. Often overlooked, the TCU cartridges make great choices in ultralight rifles for running trap lines or hunting game up to and including deer or antelope. Smith & Wesson purchased Thompson-Center and eventually shelved the brand, ending production of the Contender and Encore platforms, the primary guns offered in the TCU calibers. Silhouette shooting is not as popular as it once was in the U.S.; consequently, these cartridges have slipped from the shooting public's collective consciousness.

7mm Shooting Times Westerner (STW)

Writer Layne Simpson's baby, 7mm Shooting Times Westerner (STW), is the 8mm Remington Magnum necked down to 7mm. The wildcat is an overbore cartridge, but it's an excellent caliber for those who want velocity at any cost. The 7mm STW is capable of effective long-range shooting, and because of the extreme velocities it can develop, high-quality bonded bullets like those made by North Fork Technologies are essential. Hunters who complain that 7mm cartridges destroy too much meat are often too close to the animal when they

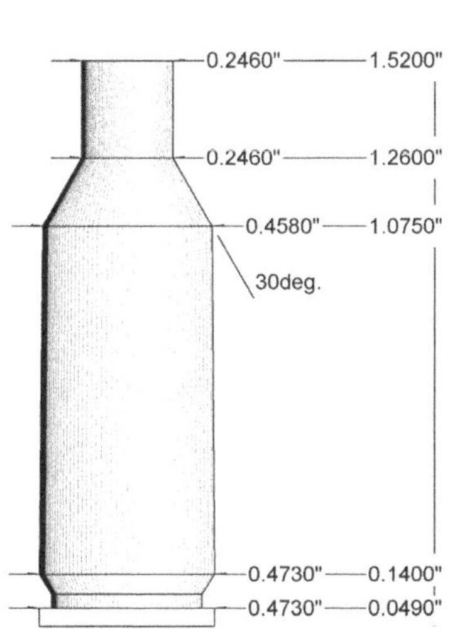

The .22 BR.

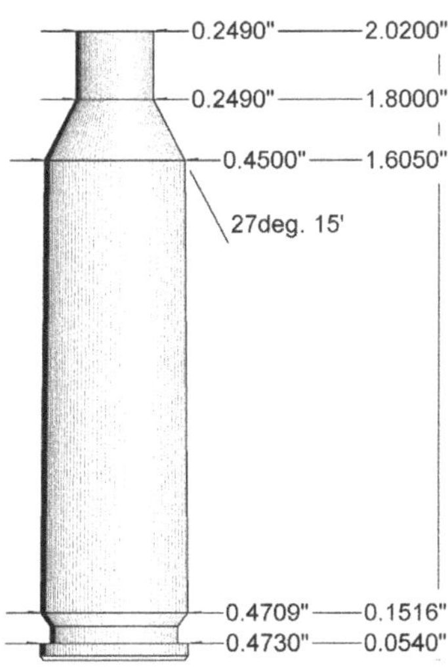

The .22 CHeetah.

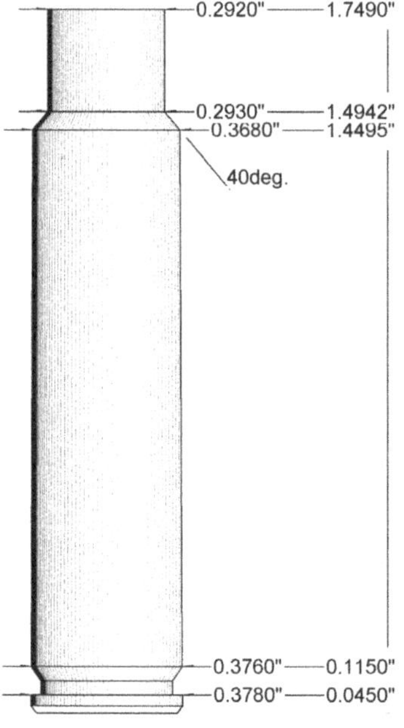

The 6.5 TCU.

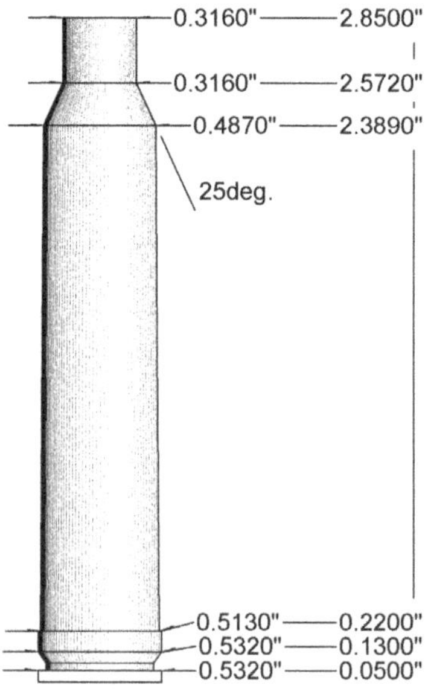

The 7mm STW.

shoot. The best answer, however, is to use premium-quality bullets intended for magnum cartridges.

.300 Whisper

J.D. Jones of SSK Industries developed the .300 Whisper as a special-purpose cartridge. It's based on the .221 Fireball case necked up to .30 caliber. The idea was to use heavy bullets for subsonic loads in a suppressed rifle, delivering excellent accuracy to 200 yards. Such cartridges have obvious uses for military applications, and a less obvious use is for Fish & Wildlife departments in culling operations close to populated areas. Silhouette shooters like this cartridge with bullets from 220 to 240 grains. Performance exceeds that of the .30-30 in silhouette pistols, with far less felt recoil.

Since the first edition of this book in 2005, the .300 Whisper has been superseded by the .300 AAC Blackout or 7.62x35mm (AAC stands for Advanced Armament Corporation). In 2009, AAC introduced this version of the .30/221 wildcat and took it to SAAMI, so it is no longer a wildcat.

.309 JDJ

Another J.D. Jones cartridge that has retained a following is the .309 JDJ. Developed in the late 1970s, it was designed for the single-shot hand cannons for which SSK Industries (J.D. Jones' company) is known. It utilizes the .444 Marlin case necked to handle a .308 bullet. A characteristic sharp shoulder on the .309 JDJ cartridge is common in most JDJ designs. The .309 JDJ is a good handgun hunting caliber for medium-sized, thin-skinned game.

.30 Herrett and .357 Herrett

In 1972, Steve Herrett and Bob Milek collaborated on a wildcat for handgun hunting. The .30 Herrett was intended for use in the Thompson-Contender pistol. Shortening a .30-30 case to 1.6 inches delivers over 2,000 fps from a 10-inch barrel using 125- or 130-grain bullets. Accuracy is excellent, and recoil is very manageable.

The .357 Herrett was a natural next step after the success of the .30 Herrett. It became evident that a heavier bullet was necessary to hunt animals larger than deer. Milek and Herrett combined their talents again to develop the 357 Herrett. Its larger diameter and heavier bullet required a case with more capacity, so the .357 version is .150 inch longer.

Both cartridges were used for metallic silhouette shooting. The .357 proved more popular for silhouette as the heavier bullets are more effective in knocking down the heavy steel ram targets used in silhouette competitions. Thompson chambered barrels for both Herrett cartridges for some time.

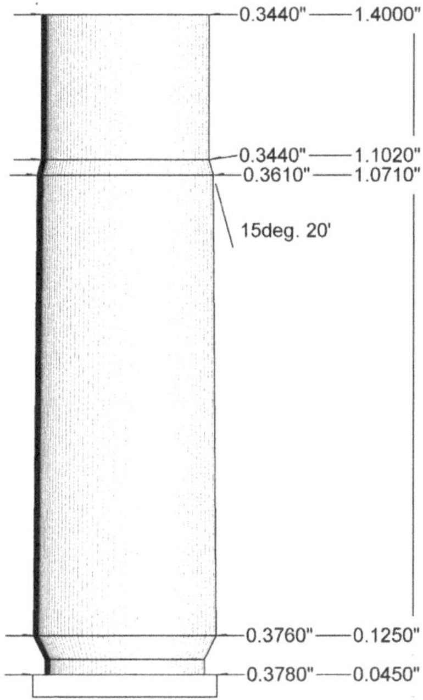

The .300 Whisper.

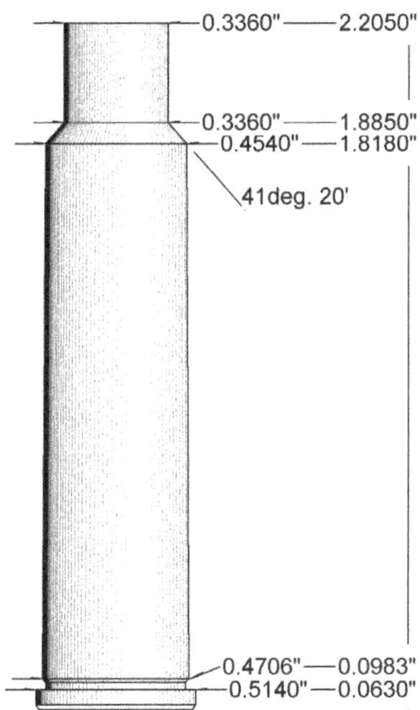

The .309 JDJ.

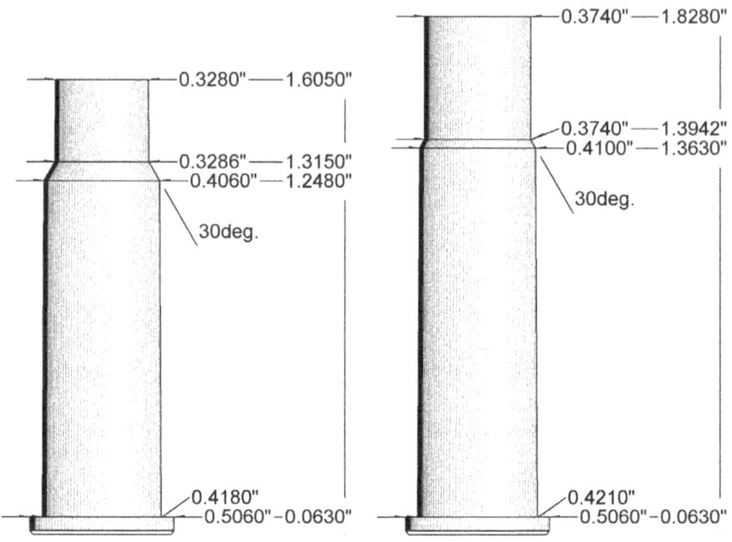

The .30 Herrett (left), .357 Herrett (right).

.358 Shooting Times Alaskan (STA)

Originating in 1990 and the creation of Layne Simpson, writer for *Shooting Times* magazine, the final version of the .358 Shooting Times Alaskan appeared in 1994 with less body taper and a sharp shoulder. The parent case is the 8mm Remington Magnum, left full length it utilizes the long magnum action. For some reason, .35-caliber rifles seem to have trouble getting the respect they are due. To quote a hunter, "When I went to calibers .35 and up, I witnessed an amazing change in the length of blood trails ... in fact, often I have to move dead animals to locate them."

.416 Taylor

Robert Chatfield-Taylor developed his .416 Taylor in 1972. Based on the .458 Winchester necked down to .416, it can also be formed from .338 Winchester Magnum cases. Rumors abounded that one of the factories would commercialize the cartridge, though that never happened. The .416 Taylor was a forerunner of the .416 Remington, which uses a much higher-capacity case. The Taylor has been proven on all sorts of African game, including the most dangerous. At the time of the Taylor's development, .416 Rigby brass and ammo were tough to get, so the .416 Taylor filled a niche in the market. It has the added advantage of working through any standard magnum action.

.458 Lott

In 1971, Jack Lott decided that the .458 Winchester lacked the horsepower he needed for reliable kills on dangerous game. So, he created the .458 Lott from full-length .375 H&H brass. Although it is .300 inch longer than the .458 Winchester, you can fire Winchester ammo in the Lott chamber in a pinch.

The Lott is very popular in safari rifles and has a strong reputation for one-shot kills. Like many big-bore magnums, the recoil is more than most shooters want to handle. Ruger and Hornady have commercialized the Lott. The .450 Watts predates it by about 20 years and has slightly more capacity.

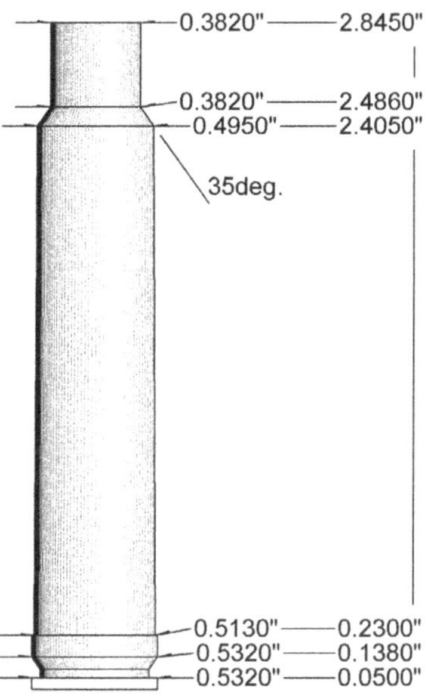

The .358 Shooting Times Alaskan.

.585 Nyati

In the December 1991 *Guns & Ammo*, Ross Seyfried announced his "World's Most Powerful Rifle." Nyati is the name for Cape buffalo in many African languages. Seyfried admitted up front that the recoil from his brainchild was horrendous. After a charging elephant made him feel his .450 Nitro Express was less than adequate, he pined for his .577 Nitro Double. "However the rarity and immense value of a .577-100-750 double rifle dictated that it not be risked to charging elephants, or worse yet, African Governments, any longer," said Seyfried.

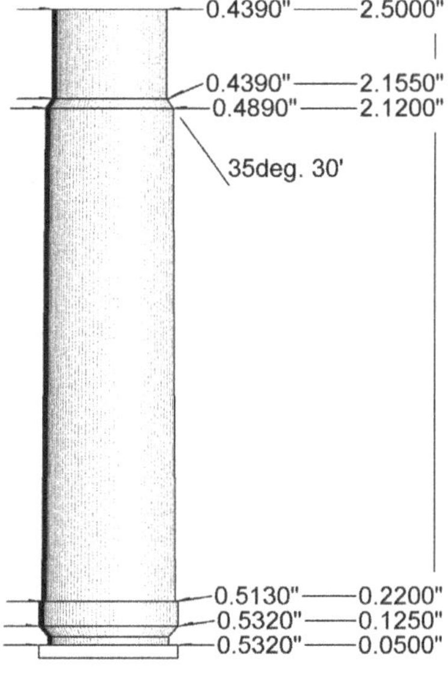

The .416 Taylor.

As a result, he conceived the .585 Nyati as an inexpensive way to bring the power of the .577 Nitro to the hunting field in a less valuable package. The parent

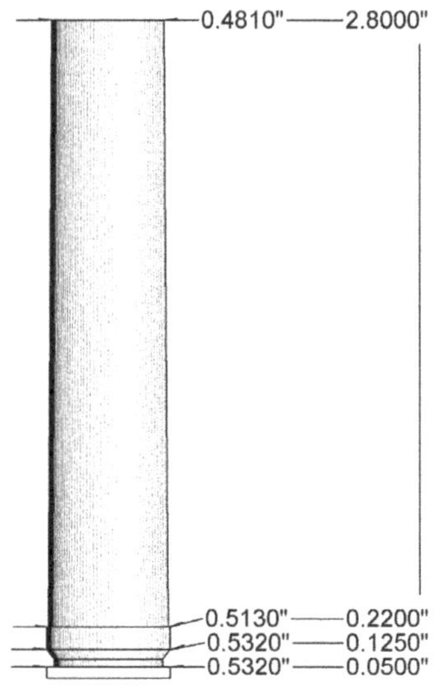

The .458 Lott.

brass is the .577 3-inch Nitro Express. The rim is turned to .505 Gibbs dimensions, creating a rebated rim case, and the body taper is minimal at .045 inch. A 30-degree shoulder is formed, leaving a neck .500 inch long, and the case is cut to 2.800 inches. The .585 Nyati will fit in any .375 H&H-length action with some feeding adjustments. Bertram offers headstamped brass. The Nyati can produce as much as 10,000 ft-lbs of energy at the muzzle. The result is a cartridge that creates a level of recoil most shooters would wish to avoid. At the same time, it's a cartridge that will take on any animal on Earth and probably many other planets with power to spare.

.577 Tyrannosaur

In 1993, two professional hunters contacted Art Alphin of A-Square for a rifle that would equal the .577 Nitro Express in a bolt-action. Ultimately, the design of the .577 Tyrannosaur developed around using the largest cartridge that could be shoehorned into a "Hanibal" (P-14 Enfield action). A-Square designed and produced brass of a unique head size for this purpose, resulting in the Tyrannosaur. A-Square effectively went one up on the most powerful rifle claim, though it appears few people ever noticed.

Ballistically, there is little difference between the Tyrannosaur and the Nyati. With only 7% more case capacity than the .585 Nyati, the only real advantage the Tyrannosaur might have is lower operating pressure for the same velocity load. The availability of brass is much better for the Nyati since A-Square closed its doors. If one dared to bring practicality into the equation, the Nyati is the winner in that department, just in terms of brass.

Reloading tip: When resizing brass for cartridges like the .577 Tyrannosaur and the .585 Nyati, the ideal case lube seems to be a heavy coating of pure testosterone.

In conclusion, this is far from a complete list of all the wildcats of the last 100 years. Historical perspective is the purpose of this information: Placing cartridges in a general timeframe helps us see how wildcatting developed over time. In the early days, .22-caliber cartridges were the primary area of interest. The development of better powders and higher-quality bullets contributed as much, and probably more, to improved accuracy as the improvements in case designs.

Using small, efficient cartridges during the war was expedient because powder and bullets were hard to come by. After the war, when the field for .22 cartridges became crowded, shooters and gunsmiths began looking at wildcatting larger calibers. Interestingly, most new wildcats today seem to be either big bore (.35 caliber and up) or sub-caliber (under .22 caliber).

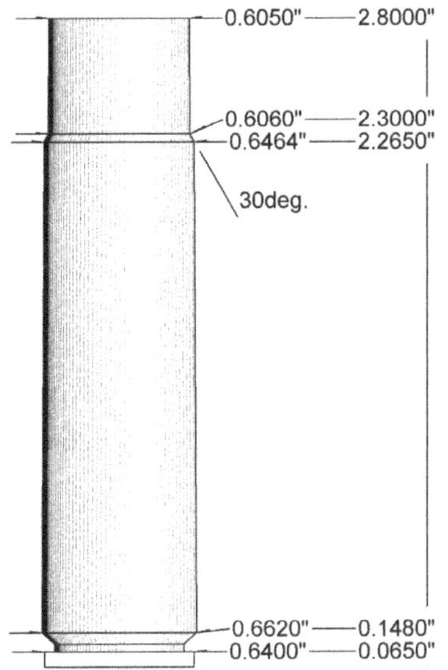

The .585 Nyati.

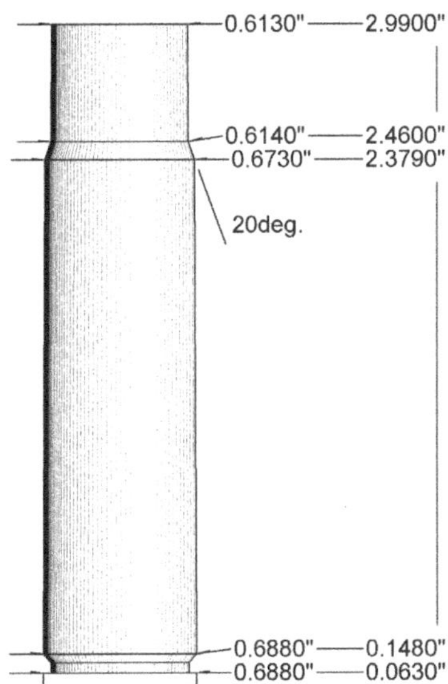

The .577 Tyrannosaur.

At the beginning of the 20th century, the head of the U.S. Patent Office announced, "Everything that was going to be invented had been invented." That turned out to be a myth, but it brings up an important point: new products or improvements to existing ones are inevitable. The same is true for cartridge development. As the shooting public's interests change and the factories offer new cases or revive old designs, wildcatters will continue to try new things.

Someday, brass cases may be obsolete, and who knows what will replace our current form of cartridges. Likely, we will go to caseless ammunition or some kind of energy-based weapons. When that happens, it's safe to say that wildcatting's last chapter will have been written. But until then ...

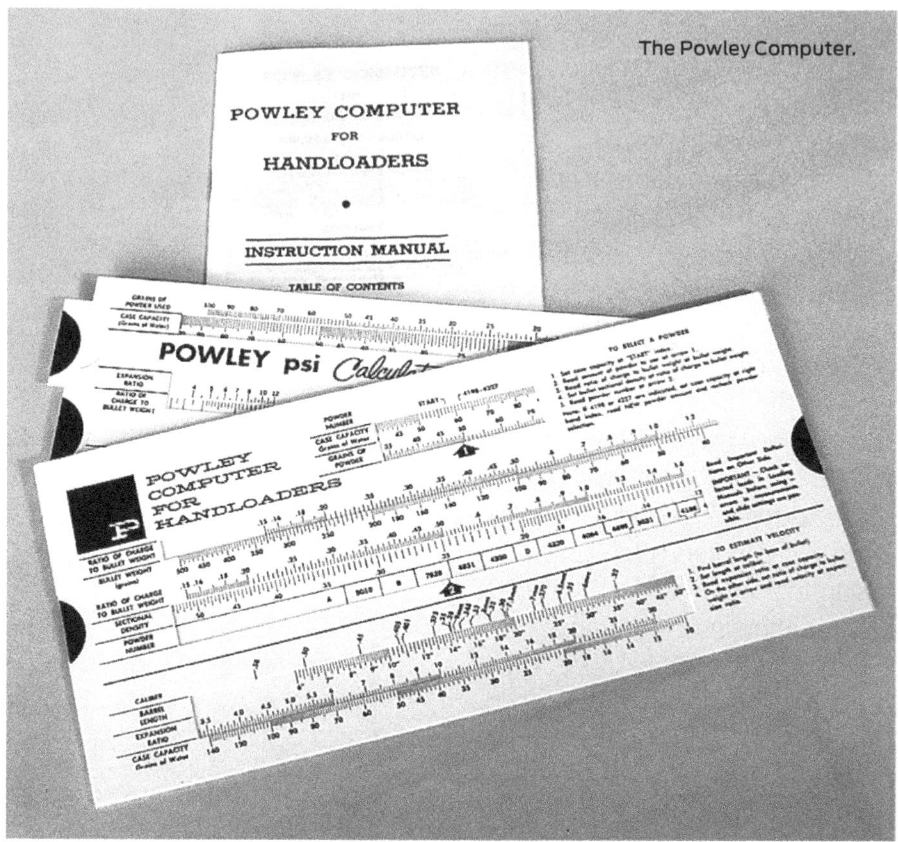

The Powley Computer.

CHAPTER 8

Predicting Results

It's one thing to *predict* the outcome of your new cartridge; it's quite another to *know the real-world results*. Chronographs have become more affordable. Simple models can be had that will produce reliable results for well under $100. At that price, there is no reason not to have one if you reload, and if you're reading this, it's a good bet you're a reloader.

When thinking about a new wildcat, one of the best ways to decide if you want to go to the expense of building one is to run some calculations to determine a design's practicality. There are several ways to do this.

The tried and true method is the "Powley Computer for Handloaders." Developed by Homer Powley in 1961, this simple computer is a slide rule device designed to predict starting loads for IMR powders in any rifle cartridge case. The idea is to provide loads with high load density for uniform pressures, thereby delivering good accuracy. The instructions with the Powley Computer indicate that the load density for all but IMR 4198 and IMR 4227 is 86%.

Powley states, "All loads directly indicated by your computer will result in approximately the same maximum pressure. This preserves one of the computer's central features, giving you maximum velocity with good working pressure. In other words, you will obtain maximum performance from the selected combination."

Although the Powley Computer has not been updated for new propellants, it is still an effective tool for IMR powders. Mine came with an update sheet (dated 1975) that shows comparable powders from various manufacturers, so one can substitute popular propellants. It's still available from:

Hutton Rifle Ranch
P.O. Box 170317
Boise, ID 83717

In 1965, Powley added the Powley psi Calculator. It calculates the chamber pressure based on the loads predicted by the "Powley Computer for Handloaders." It works with IMR powders just like its older brother and is meant to be used with it. Of course, many computer programs will do the same things. The good news is that most of them will now support a much broader range of powders.

Software

Market changes since 2005 have reduced options for in-depth technical information, or has the market shifted to different consumption methods? We have lost publications that offered technical information for the shooting public. Those that remain have reduced the number of pages they produce and lowered the quality of the information provided (some say, dumbed it down). *Small Caliber News* and *Precision Shooting* are two prominent examples.

One programmer told me that the desire to "have an app for that" is killing the market for software that can run valuable calculations. Shooters who want an app on their phones are not interested in taking measurements and analyzing the data. "They are looking for a magic bullet."

I understand where he is coming from. But, there will always be a market for accurate data that aids the user in greater skill-building and success. Another part of this shift is generational: As us old duffers depart the range, the sport moves along with the younger crowd and a different focus. This shift is often technology-driven. Fifty years ago, we did not have the combination of equipment and optics that allowed for PRS, long-range and super long-range competition. But, these are primarily pay-to-play games, requiring expensive equipment. The average shooter will benefit the most from a chronograph, a few good reloading manuals and some software to quickly help analyze their results. So, here are a few to consider.

GMDR.load (previously RCBS.Load) by RCBS—A program that stores data from more than 90 historical and recently published reloading manuals and specialized periodicals over the last 20 years. Several of these resources are included for free with the software. Many more are on the CD; access must be purchased from GMDR, a convenient resource since some manuals have long been out of print and are difficult to locate.

Other features in the program include a database manager for a large handload and factory load performance database; a graphing utility that allows visualization of any data from that database, with filters, slicing and zooming; a kinetic energy calculator, a sophisticated external ballistics calculator; a utility to automate the addition of user load data to the dataset; a cartridge drawing utility; *a cartridge designer utility for the wildcatters*; a ballistic coefficient calculator and many other useful technical charts and tables.

GMDR.Load features a database of technical drawings for more than 412 cartridges, which you can access for reference or as the basis of a wildcat of your own design. The cartridge designer utility allows you to click on any dimension on the screen and vary its value as desired. The program calculates the water weight capacity as you draw your new wildcat. Future versions will also include the ability to calculate load data from this information. This program has become a tool we use daily in the shop.

GMDR.com

Sierra Infinity—an exterior ballistics program for small arms. The Sierra Bullets exterior ballistics program is in its 7th version as of this writing. This program computes all essential elements of any bullet's trajectory in yard, meter or mil increments, with a ballistic coefficient referenced to the "G1" drag function and for any set of firing conditions.

Infinity handles up to five different active bullets at a time. The program stores a complete inventory of bullets and cartridges offered by all major U.S. and foreign manufacturers; each of the five active bullets can be selected from anywhere in the stored inventory list. A vital feature of the program allows you to compare any one of several trajectory parameters for up to five bullets.

You can create custom bullets and save the settings in the custom bullet database. These custom settings function in the program like the manufacturers' bullets. You can save a modification of an existing bullet or create a custom projectile from scratch. The custom bullets database is handled separately from the manufacturer data, allowing future updates without affecting your custom settings.

Infinity Suite is a separate offering that includes the Infinity exterior ballistics program discussed above, additional reloading data programs to calculate cartridge and reloading data and reference material included in the *Sierra 5th Edition* printed manuals.

Sierra Bullets
PO Box 818
Sedalia, MO 65302-0818
660-827-6300
sierrabullets.com

Load From A Disk (Now Defunct)—A program that primarily determines what type and how much powder to use to develop safe starting loads for rifle cartridges. It can also estimate the chamber pressure and muzzle velocity for the given round at various load densities. With a few mouse clicks, you can perform trajectory calculations to determine the downrange energy, velocity, knockdown power and how long the bullet took to get there. Ballistic coefficients for most of the major bullet manufacturers are included in an extensive database. If the BC is missing, you can calculate it given some field data or the shape and size of the bullet. The software will correct the ballistic coefficient for your outside conditions, average a group of velocities, determine your rifle's recoil or figure out the optimum barrel rifling twist.

You can also use Load From A Disk to study the effect of temperature on velocity and pressure, barrel length on bullet velocity, the effect of bullet weight and bullet seating depth on velocity or the performance and ballistics of a new or wildcat cartridge without building a rifle or firing a shot. The suggested starting loads from this program are generally conservative, providing a safe starting point for the wildcatter.

The cartridge case database includes over 650 standard cases with dimensions and case capacity values. You can quickly scroll through the available list and select one for handloading, plus easily create a custom one if your cartridge case is not listed. You can enter dimensions (all or just the ones you know), case capacity and the typical overall cartridge length and the program will draw your case and provide the external dimensions. You can calculate the case capacity if you've taken all the case measurements, including thickness values. Alternately, you can determine its capacity by weighing the case with and without water (the difference is the capacity in grains of water); as always, this is a case full to the top of the neck.

QuickLoad/QuickTarget—Now available in version 3.9, QuickLoad analyzes interior and exterior ballistics. You can enter data for user-created wildcats and compute results. The developer updates the program approximately three to four times yearly as new powders or calibers from manufacturers are obtained.

QuickLoad is fully integrated with QuickDesign, so you can transfer data from the latter to the former to develop load data quickly.

- More than 1,200 cartridges
- More than 250 powders
- More than 2,500 bullets
- Abundance of useful outputs
- Customize cartridge selection for your firearms
- Dimensioned drawings and photos of many cartridges at the click of a button
- Interfaces with the PVM-21 and PVM-08 Chronograph

As the name implies, QuickDesign is a design utility for wildcatters and ballistics buffs. When you modify a design, all the related tables are updated simultaneously to simplify the design process. It's simple to generate a list of starting loads for a design. Support for both programs is fully integrated into the software, with no print manual. These programs take some time to learn (not intuitive for computer nerds) but are powerful.

Drawing options:

- Create your own scale.
- Compare a cartridge to chambers to see if the barrel needs to be reset for a different cartridge of the same caliber.
- On-screen 1:1 scaling for comparison to actual cartridges.
- Draws wire-frame, outline, outline with interior walls, solid model drawings and interference points with the chamber.
- Drawing can be rotated and translated about the X, Y and Z axes.
- Print out data sheets in SAAMI or CIP format standards.

- Import generated data into QuickLoad/QuickTarget for interior/exterior ballistic analysis.

NECO
536C Stone Rd.
Benicia, CA 94510
neconos.com

Oehler Ballistic Explorer—The latest computer techniques and industry-standard drag coefficient tables are combined to replace the old Ingalls tables and Siacci technique. Results are displayed so they are easy to interpret, and it includes a library of 3,300 loads and more than 2,600 bullets with a drawing of each case and bullet.

You can quickly calculate downrange performance and play "what if" to your heart's content. The program handles up to three ballistic situations at once for easy comparisons. You can also print the resulting curves in black and white or color.

You can save your loads—with load data and test results—in a data file for quick replay and comparison to other handloads or catalog loads. The shooting environment is considered: temperature, altitude, barometric pressure, uphill/downhill, wind speed and direction. You can find sight settings for maximum point-blank range and work with yards, inches, or metric.

Oehler lets you download the complete program in Demo Mode to try it before buying. Naturally, it interfaces with all Oehler Chronographs. The retail price is a bargain, in my opinion.

Interior Ballistics: Oehler believes that the interior ballistics of small arms should be measured instead of predicted. They have made lots of measurements and compared measurements to predictions. Predictions for small arms ammo often differ *significantly* from actual measurements. Oehler says, "When all loading manuals agree, we'll start making interior ballistics predictions in our software."

An example of a shrinking market for essential tools is that Oehler no longer offers the system to measure chamber pressure.

Oehler Research
P.O. Box 9135
Austin, TX 78766
oehler-research.com

Gordon's Reloading Tool (GRT)—This free software was designed for the

Windows 7 environment. I've heard that it can be troublesome, which may be due to compatibility issues. (The company has a Discord channel, so you can join to get help from other users.)

You need a chronograph if you choose predictive software for load development like GRT. Otherwise, you are in the dark about your loads' actual pressure and velocity. Remember, pressure and velocity are well correlated, so the chronograph is essential.

A simple way to see if predictive load software is giving safe results is to enter published data from a reliable source, i.e., from a manual. If the software roughly agrees with the manual, then at least with that powder, you are probably getting reliable results. I would do this test with several calibers to be comfortable with the output.

grtools.de

RSI's Shooting Lab—Time will tell if this product continues. As of this writing, the owner and creator, Jim Ristow, is retiring. Ristow tells me he was unsure how many users of his Pressure Trace system use his software, as one is not required to operate the other.

Software is the first component of the Shooting Lab system, which includes full integration with a proprietary method for measuring chamber pressure. Ristow developed RSI to help serious shooting enthusiasts accurately model long-range trajectories, analyze loads and keep proper records.

Shooting Lab is much more than just another "exterior ballistics" program. It bases exterior ballistics on methods developed at the U.S. Army's Ballistic Research Laboratory in Aberdeen, MD. Exterior ballistics is less than 10% of the program! The Shooting Lab is a complete, fully developed software package and valuable tool for any shooting sport. If you reload, it will help analyze components and keep you organized. If you hunt, it will help select calibers, ammo and set gun sights. If you compete, it will help analyze and improve your shooting.

One measure of software quality is its user interface or how easy the program is to use. Shooting Lab is fully developed and packed with features that make it as user-friendly as possible, given the subject matter. You only need to enter information one time, which is accessible throughout the program with a simple mouse click. You can open locations within the program from a navigation palette, menu or keyboard commands. Data is linked between the various segments to reduce entry effort and allow quick retrieval via customizable pop-up menus.

The Shooting Lab takes exterior ballistics several steps further than other programs. Like other products, it compares the trajectories of different calibers and loads under varied shooting conditions. It calculates the optimum sighting range and game for a load or the windage and elevation adjustment needed to hit a target. Most importantly, it reproduces published trajectories and duplicates real-world results for long ranges. Don't trust the BCs provided by bullet companies? (You shouldn't.) The Shooting Lab will calculate perfect sea-level ballistic coefficients for any bullet you fire from your firearms.

Included are drag curves from VLD or very low-drag bullets to rimfire and balls. It matches your bullets to the best drag curve, converts BCs and calculates custom drag curves from bullet dimensions.

In addition to exterior ballistics, the Shooting Lab includes segments for analysis of powder load density with burn rate tables and gyroscopic stability. These help you select bullets, powders and charges to improve your loads. It does not attempt to forecast pressure and velocity using questionable mathematical models. The folks at RSI sell PressureTrace for that purpose; rather than predicting pressure, they measure it (more on this in Chapter 10).

Recreational Software, Inc.
shootingsoftware.com

Reloader USA—Designed from the ground up for the serious or casual rifle or pistol ammo reloader, this Windows-based software allows you to enter and track your inventory of bullets, powder, primers and brass, along with costs and all other necessary data.

There is a built-in spreadsheet that records every component addition and purchase. Select any part of the inventory and have it automatically imported to the "Load Rounds" screen, where, once you complete a reloading session, your inventory is automatically adjusted for what was used. Data is recorded for your archived records.

You can also have your reload session moved to the "Ammo Dump," where it becomes part of your ready-to-fire inventory, along with reload data and costs. From there, you track rounds fired and their performance. You can also add in any factory-purchased ammo.

Reloader USA is designed to track and automatically maintain your rifle and handgun reloading inventory, quickly import data to create reloading sessions, provide detailed reloading records and maintain a powerful and versatile Ammo Dump. This software is not designed to suggest load data recipes or provide ballistic data.

reloaderusa.com

Reloading Studio—An online equivalent of Reloader USA with similar functions and uses, Reloading Studio is different because it is a subscription-based product. You can track your reloading workflow, components and firearms. You can also print everything out for your notebook in the shop.

- Manage and track your entire load development process.
- Automatically track barrel life and component quantities.
- Organize load development into batches and groups.
- Generate labels, summaries and detailed reports.
- Document performance, sighting notes, weather and ballistics.
- Catalog reloading components, cartridges, firearms and more.
- Track brass history, prep process and notes.
- Create recipes, firearms and optics relationships.
- Attach photos and documents to reference targets, firearms and component attributes.

reloadingstudio.com

Ballistic Basics14—Allowing you to analyze and understand various ballistics information, Ballistic Basics14 is like most programs; you can compare a variety of components, up to five loads at a time. All the standard exterior ballistics calculations are supported along with a long list of calculators to help you decide about components, calibers, twist rates, BC, energy and everything else you might want.

Logs allow you to track costs as well as inventory. Numerous logs allow you to track virtually every aspect of the hobby. This is donation software, so you can try it, and if you like it, you can support the author with a donation. At this writing, the programmer continues to update the product actively.

obxballistics.com

BallisticXLR V10.5—A spreadsheet for shooters similar to a TFT (Tabular Firing Table) that creates a set of charts for various conditions. Naturally, this is for you long-range folks. Print out your charts for a field expedient way to handle drop and wind data—an excellent analog backup.

ballisticxlr.com

Final Thoughts

There is an amazing amount of software available for shooters. Those listed in this chapter were selected because of their unique ability to handle and analyze data. Many good exterior ballistics programs are available that we have not mentioned here, and several component companies offer apps to aid the reloader in using their products to the best advantage.

Each program delivers slightly different information, and the interface varies widely from one program to the next. The selection of the appropriate software for your needs depends on several factors; below are just a few important considerations:

1. What information do you want the software to provide?
2. How user-friendly is it?
3. Will it work in conjunction with a pressure-measuring system?
4. Can it produce useful charts and graphs?
5. Can it predict starting loads for any given cartridge?
6. Can it do long-range calculations? (A very popular requirement—most will do this.)
7. Does it have a database of information, i.e., bullets, factory loads, etc?
8. Does it include cartridge dimensions and capacity?
9. Does it have cartridge design functionality?

The best thing about ballistics software is that it allows you to play "What if?" without spending a fortune on guns and equipment. You can test-fly your ideas and have enough information to make an informed decision about that next custom rifle. All that being said, use your brain and be cautious. Any program that predicts loads is only a best guess. There is no way to plug all of your real-world variables into the software, so results in the real world could vary significantly from any predictions. Start low, cross-check data with known sources and be safe.

Warning! *Neither the software developers, the author of this book, nor the publisher accepts any responsibility for the accuracy of the information derived from the software discussed herein. The final responsibility for determining safe load parameters is yours and yours alone.*

CHAPTER 9

Wildcat Design Principles

What makes a practical wildcat design? What produces more capacity, efficiency and barrel life—or, if you prefer, higher velocity and flatter trajectory without the detrimental costs that can push a cartridge beyond the point of diminishing returns? Here, I cover design features like shoulder angles and what attributes various angles bring to design, as well as shoulder diameter and case taper. Plus, how to select parent brass for design purposes while considering neck and throat design and freebore.

Ken Howell once told me, "Simply changing the neck diameter or shoulder angle does not constitute a new cartridge design." He was referring to the fact that many shooters simply neck a factory offering to a new diameter and put their name on it, or worse yet, take another person's well-designed wildcat and, with a tiny change, claim it. Ken's point was well taken; a well-designed cartridge represents research, experience and careful planning. (It's not much different than a well-written book; if I were to take a classic like "Atlas Shrugged" by Ayn Rand and modernize it, would you consider it unethical if I then put my name down as author?) If you're going to bother designing a cartridge and spending the money for custom chamber reamers and reloading dies, don't waste time copying somebody else's work.

In all fairness, it's essential to realize that when you change someone else's design, you should denote it. For instance, if you order a chamber reamer for a 6mm Dasher with a tight neck, you should mark the barrel with the neck dimensions, but it's still a Dasher. Let's say you changed the shoulder dimension; well, then it's a 6mm Dasher 28 Degree, not a 6mm Mine, Mine all Mine!

I teach classes on wildcat design for the NRA Gunsmithing Schools. My teenage son attended one of my classes for the first time and designed his first cartridge. The only centerfire he had much experience with at the time was a .300 Savage, so naturally, he chose it as the starting point for his wildcat. The result was an improved case with a tiny bit more capacity than the parent brass. He dubbed it the .300 NRC (New Raiph Cartridge) after a character in a role-playing game he was interested in at the time. Upon comparing it to the parent case, I teased him that NRC should stand for "No Real Change." That initialization has stuck, and now all such cartridges with minor changes that come across this author's desk are designated NRC.

Desirable Design Attributes

There's no cut-and-dried answer to this question, but here are my rules to avoid mechanically unsound, foolish and repetitive designs.

1. Select parent brass that will suit the rifle action to be used and will likely be available in the foreseeable future. Otherwise, your design's lifespan will be very short.
2. Case capacity should be appropriate to the bore. A .50 BMG necked to .30 caliber is not an appropriate use of case capacity.
3. Increased case capacity comes more from decreasing body taper (expanding the case shoulder) than increasing the shoulder angle.
4. Some taper in the case body is necessary for proper extraction. Ackley found that .0075 inch per inch provided a reliable feeding and extracting case. So, why reinvent the wheel?
5. Neck length should be at least 90% of the caliber. This ratio provides proper neck tension on the bullet for good accuracy. Calibers that use bullets 300 grains and up will probably work better with a neck length equal to the caliber or slightly longer. The increased length provides more contact area with the bullet, making for more uniform neck tension.
6. Neck length should not exceed caliber by more than about 10%. When the neck is too long, it becomes a lever, which can bend the case during feeding and handling.
7. Hunting cartridges need a .004-inch expansion area over the neck in the chamber for the safe release of the bullet. Benchrest or varmint calibers can get away with a tighter neck. Leave .002 inch to allow proper bullet release without erratic variations in pressure.
8. In most factory guns today, some freebore is used to control pressure, allowing the bullet to get a run at the throat before it

> engages the rifling. Factory chambers for blackpowder cartridges like the .45-70 typically have an abrupt throat (some would say no throat) as compared to what we expect to see today. The reason for this abrupt throat is that such cartridges are expected to be used either with lead or jacketed bullets that have minimal contact area ahead of the cannelure or groove diameter surface protruding ahead of the case mouth.

Custom chambers can be cut with little or no freebore, but in most cases, you should have *some*, especially in a hunting rifle. An expanded discussion of freebore will be found later in this chapter.

Selecting Parent Brass

The selection of an appropriate case for the project is the most critical part of the design process for a wildcatter. Brass availability is a crucial factor: If it's difficult to locate, but you're set on using it, buy a lifetime supply when you start. However, it's a better plan to select a case that will likely be available for years.

An appropriate action must be available to house your wildcat. You could design a wildcat and then discover no action will work reliably or make a practical platform for your cartridge. Think about this in advance. Later in this chapter, there is an example of a wildcat design called the .19 Hawk. Only a few currently available bolt-actions are suited for this cartridge, including the CZ 527, Howa Mini action, Mini Mauser and the Remington 40X or equivalent custom for varmint and benchrest shooters.

Many wildcat designs start with a particular purpose, so selecting the action will be a natural extension of that purpose. Choose one that will not require a major overhaul to accept the new cartridge; this will aid in reliability and save on cost and headaches.

Case Capacity

Here is where the bore ratio comes into play. "Overbore capacity" means that the cartridge case holds more powder than the bore can efficiently handle. Homer Powley ties up bore capacity with expansion ratio—the ratio between the total bore volume and the case volume, or the number of times the gas will expand by the time the bullet reaches the muzzle. High expansion ratios mean long barrel life. Low ratios mean short barrel life. Low ratios may result in the highest velocity, but slightly higher velocity is more than offset by significantly reduced barrel life, critical loading and general inflexibility.[1]

There is no set rule or way to determine the proper maximum capacity for a case design. Below is a table of bore diameters, which, through empirical evidence, has proven what is "efficient" and what is "overbore." Of course, not everyone will agree with these numbers, but they make a good guideline.

BORE DIAMETER (IN.)	MAXIMUM EFFICIENT POWDER CHARGE (GR.)
.172	17
.224	35
.243 (6mm)	45
.257	48
.264 (6.5mm)	50
.277	55
.284 (7mm)	60
.308	70
.323 (8mm)	72
.338	75
.358	75
.375	85
.416	90
.458	90

Excessively overbore cartridges suffer from short barrel life. Examples include the .220 Swift, many Lazeroni cartridges, 7mm STW, 7mm Remington Ultra and the .22 CHeetah. In many cases, if the shooter does not try to get every last bit of velocity out of the case, barrel life can be much better. For instance, when loaded to 3,600 fps with a 55-grain bullet, the .220 Swift will produce good accuracy for quite a while. Still, if the reloader insists on getting 4,000+ fps from every shot, accurate barrel life will be very short indeed, likely well under 1,000 rounds. Keep these factors in mind when you think about the capacity of your case design.

It's generally accepted that case capacity expressed in water weight provides a reasonable basis for comparison. Ballistic programs such as Load From a Disk and GRT use this method to develop load data for new case designs. RCBS. Load, now known as GMDR.Load includes a cartridge designer that will give you an estimated water-weight case capacity. Quick Design can provide the estimated case capacity and directly share it to Quick Load. In all cases, you can take real-world water weight and enter that data in the software for more

1 Ackley, P.O., *Handbook for Shooters & Reloaders*, 1962

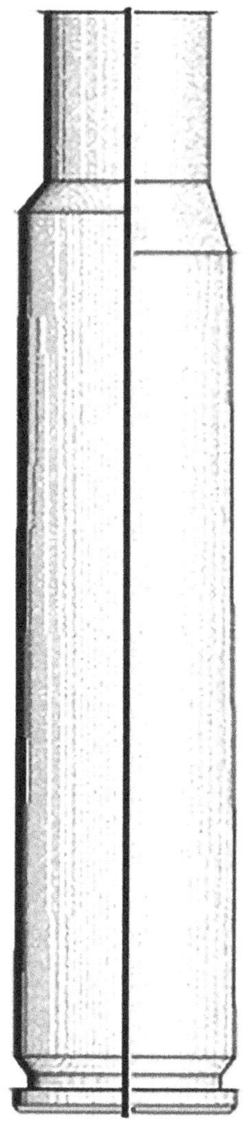

accurate results. Always use starting loads and work up for safety.

Unless all capacity measurements are performed using the same criteria, the data will be flawed and useless for comparisons. The correct method for obtaining the water capacity of any given case is as follows: The Primer pocket must be plugged, either with clay, wax, or a spent primer (so long as you apply the method uniformly). Weigh the dry case and record the weight in grains. Distilled water should fill the case as it provides a uniform medium. Fill the case to *level* with the mouth; an eyedropper helps. Weigh the full case on the same scale and record the results. Subtract the weight of the dry case from the full one, and you have the water-weight capacity for that specific case. To be scientific, measure several cases. Five cases should be sufficient to provide an average. All cases should be from the same lot of brass.

Case Capacity & Shoulder Angle

If you take a .30-06 case and maintain the body taper but increase the shoulder to 40 degrees, you only gain 0.7 of one grain in water capacity. However, if you reduce the body taper to .0075 inches per inch and leave the shoulder angle alone, you would gain 1.8 grains of water capacity—two and a half times more increase in case capacity. You will gain far more capacity by decreasing body taper, but if you decrease body taper to less than .0075, extraction and feeding problems will surface. Of course, low-pressure cartridges are less sensitive to body taper.

One simple way to increase case capacity is to choose a firearm with a long enough magazine box or feed system so that the bullet can be seated only in the neck with no portion of the bullet intruding into the case body, reducing case capacity.

The only real advantage to sharp 35- or 40-degree shoulders is that the sharp angle curtails brass flow. In the firing process, brass tends to flow forward as the case stretches. For this reason, case trimmers were developed to control the neck length and overall case. When you employ a sharp shoulder, the attributes of brass impede flow around those tight turns in the shoulder. The disadvantages to sharp shoulders include rougher feeding, and headspacing is more critical.

Freebore or Leade (Throat Design)

Length, diameter and throat angle can have far-reaching effects. European or CIP chambers have long, tapered throats that stretch over an inch or more. They allow the bullet to gradually engage the rifling, preventing a pressure spike. European thinking revolves more around holding pressure down than accuracy because much of their hunting is done at very short ranges; one could argue that MOA accuracy is not very important to Europeans in hunting rifles.

Factory chambers in the United States use a different approach. The throat transition from groove diameter (projectile diameter) to bore (top of the lands) is much shorter than CIP chambers—1°30' is the standard transition angle. The variation will be found more in the length of the freebored (groove diameter area with rifling reamed out) section of the throat. There must be enough freebore to allow a loaded cartridge to seat in the chamber without the bullet engaging the rifling.

A common (unfired) modern American-style throat.

Many factory chambers will have freebore well beyond the minimum required to clear the bullet. This serves a couple of purposes. Like the CIP chamber, a long freebore will hold pressures down because the bullet can move unimpeded out of the neck and into the rifling. Newton's first law of motion (Sir Isaac, not Charles) states, "An object at rest tends to stay at rest, and an object in motion tends to stay in motion with the same speed and in the same direction unless acted upon by an unbalanced force." The second advantage is that it allows for using a wide range of bullets. There is always someone who wants to use long, heavy bullets or seat shorter ones out long to exploit magazine length and increase case capacity.

Most custom chambers in America today are made with a 1°30^2 throat, with about .060-inch leade plus or minus .100 inch, depending on the caliber. Reamer makers are experienced with this and can suggest the appropriate length for your cartridge. The ideal throat for a hunting rifle would have a diameter equal to the bullet diameter plus .0002 inch, or 2/10,000th of an inch, with no minus. The reality is that chamber reamers have throats with a tolerance of plus .002 inch—2/1,000th of an inch, no minus. For perspective, that's 10 times as much clearance as is necessary. Again, this serves the purpose of avoiding pressure spikes as the bullet starts down the bore. It also aids in aligning the projectile to the bore axis.

In Charles Landis' *Twenty-Two Caliber Varmint Rifles,* the various contributing gunsmiths stated that they were very particular about the throat dimensions of their reamers. Vernor Gipson, Harvey Donaldson, and Fred Ness all subscribed to the concept of a custom tight throat in their .22 varmint-caliber rifles. The idea was to use a bullet that was .001 inch oversized for the bore, i.e., a .224-inch bullet in a .223-inch barrel (.001-inch oversized bullets are sometimes referred to as "super caliber") and a perfectly matched throat diameter and tapered leade into the rifling. (You're probably jumping up and down about that bullet diameter. So long as you understand what is happening, a .001-inch oversized bullet will not cause any danger, and you will need less powder to get up to pressure. This type of throat seals the bore so that no gas can bypass the bullet, thus causing throat erosion; it also supports the bullet, acting as an efficient self-centering bullet guide.)

Landis references the October 1944 issue of *American Rifleman.* The article is reproduced below.

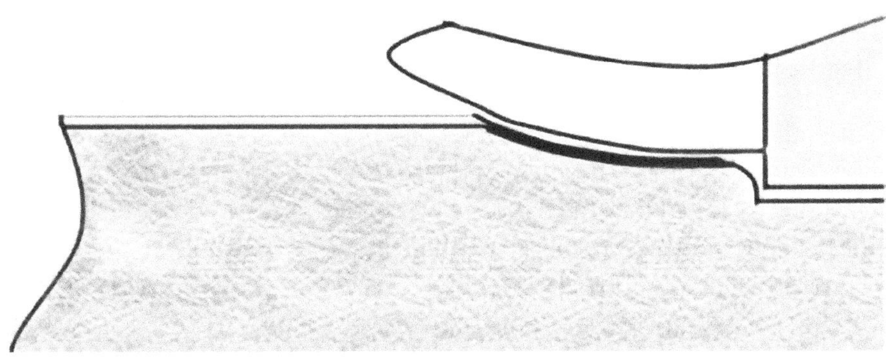

Donaldson Throating Method[2]

Harvey A. Donaldson is an old-timer in the shooting game who was aware of the importance of proper throating in the interests of accuracy and bore life. His design of throat works even better when the groove diameter is .001 inch smaller than the bullet diameter because it emphasizes, what he calls, a "reverse curve."

To ensure getting the throat right and in the correct location, he makes up a checking gauge of a second piece of barrel for a preview. If it has the same groove diameter, the gauge will help get everything right and properly located. The piece of barrel is chambered, and a dummy cartridge of the desired seating depth is used for spotting. In order to see the throat clearly, a section of the barrel, or gauge, is cut away at that point to permit direct observation. By checking with the dummy, the exact depth the throating reamer must enter is readily determined. The throat starts at the mouth of the case and follows the curve of the bullet's ogive. It is such a slight curve that it cannot be clearly shown in a sketch, and it defeats description. Its purpose is to contain and fit the bullet for guidance and still let it slip easily into the bore.

After reaming Harvey laps his throat smooth with a bronze lap, to fit his bullet perfectly. His own rifles shoot well and have long life, and he successfully uses oversize bullets (.001 inch larger than his groove diameter) in the Hornet and R2 Lovell. Harvey gives much if not most, of the credit to his throating.

A.R. Weeks wrote me recently that he could not get his R2 Lovell barrel to shoot until he lapped out the throat, with a dummy cartridge, to fit his bullet, and that is exactly what the Donaldson throat does.

According to the accompanying drawing, Donaldson was seating his bullet so that it perfectly matched the throat—he used no freebore. The description above, along with the illustration, shows that he was seating the bullet to what

2 Ness, F.C., "Dope Bag," *American Rifleman*, October, 1944

I would call a "dead fit." The bullet in a Donaldson throat does not engage the rifling at all when the round is chambered, but neither does it have any jump. This, combined with the super-caliber bullets (.001 inch oversized), produced long barrel life; since the bullet seals the barrel the instant it begins to move (allowing no gas to escape past the bullet), throat erosion would be almost nonexistent. Of course, this type of throat limits you to either one bullet or at least one maker so that the ogive is always the same. You would have to seat the bullet to the same overall length regardless of the weight/length.

Conventional throat length is far less critical than one might think. It must be long enough to clear the longest bullet you plan to shoot, plus .050 inch. Contrary to what you may have read elsewhere, the best hunting accuracy will generally come from a bullet seated between .030 and .070 inch off the lands. When working up a load, start at .050 inch, and when you find the best combination of components, perform the equivalent of a ladder test, varying the seating depth in or out by .005 inch at a time until you find the best seating depth for that load. This process saves time and components, not to mention barrel life; it also provides that all-important safety margin for pressure.

If you're building a benchrest gun, your throat tolerances should be held much tighter than those of a hunting rifle. A special-order chamber reamer will be necessary if you want control over those dimensions. Tight necks and minimum freebore are useful and desirable in a benchrest gun, but they only hinder reliability and safety in a hunting rifle. Many sources cover benchrest processes, so we will not belabor the point here.

Magazine length can be a limiting factor in throat length. When short, it can force you to seat your bullets way off the lands, creating a condition of freebore. On the other hand, if you have a long magazine compared to your cartridge of choice, you will have much more flexibility in setting the throat length to suit your selection of bullets. So, when designing your wildcat, consider the action it will be used in and how that will influence throat design.

Efficiency

An efficient design will deliver practical ballistics, be within standard bore capacity for the caliber and give good case and barrel life. Other efficiency advantages will be flexibility in load development, relatively low recoil, minimal muzzle blast and often better accuracy.

Bore capacity is a measure of efficient powder burning in a restricted space. Six major factors affect the burning of the powder:

1. Type of powder

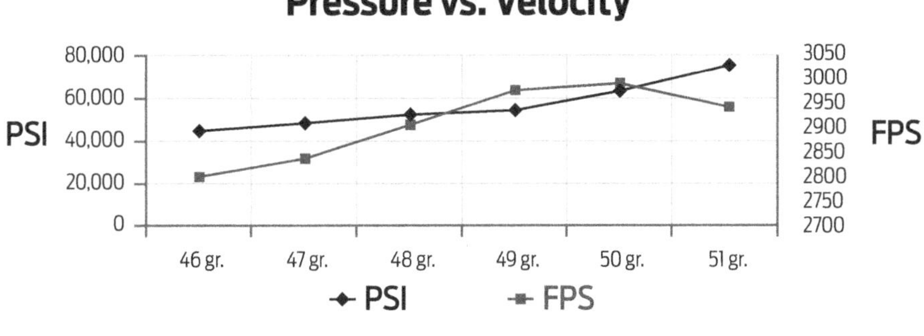

Figure 9-1.

2. Bore and groove dimensions
3. Rate of twist
4. Sectional density of the projectile
5. Maximum permissible pressure
6. Cartridge design (shape)

The law of diminishing returns certainly applies to gun powder. As we increase case capacity for a given bore diameter, there will always be a point at which the increase in velocity per grain of powder added begins to drop off. Chronographs are so inexpensive these days that any reloader can afford one, and it should be as important a tool as the reloading press itself. When you see the velocity fall off (which does not always happen), it's a clear sign that you've reached the maximum pressure for that combination of components. Back off to the best load for accuracy below the point where velocity begins to level off; this process provides a safety margin.

Burning characteristics of powders vary, which is an obvious point, but it affects the ballistics in ways the advanced reloader needs to consider. For instance, each powder has its own efficiency window. One powder will be suitable for straight-walled cases, such as IMR 4198, while another will better suit big cases with small mouths, such as H870. The reason they perform better in specific case designs is that they burn efficiently when used in a situation that provides the correct volume to cause the progressive burning of the powder to occur.

Each powder/cartridge combination has a minimum amount of powder that will reliably and safely produce the pressures needed to move the projectile down the bore. Choosing a powder with the characteristics that best match your case design is essential to getting the most out of your design. If you're testing a powder and the velocity results are in the expected range for your cartridge but are erratic, you likely have the wrong powder for your case.

Let's look at a hypothetical example: We have a .30-caliber wildcat that uses about 50 grains of powder. As we work up the load from 46 grains, moving up one grain at a time, velocity increases by about 35 fps. At 48 grains, we see an increase of 75 fps; at 49 grains, we see an increase of an additional 70 fps, at 50 grains, velocity only jumps by 10 fps; and at 51 grains, velocity *decreases* by 50 fps—we have found the top velocity for that powder and bullet, 50 grains, and in fact, accuracy will likely be better at 49 grains or less. Why? When the velocity doesn't increase at the same rate, we are no longer efficient: more powder at this point will only add to muzzle blast and recoil, and the added ballistics will be minimal at best. See Figure 9-1. We are likely to be near maximum pressure, if not past it when we reach this point. Be sure to watch all other pressure indicators, too.

When increasing a load grain by grain, the pressure curve will take off exponentially at some point. At the same time, the velocity curve will lag far behind. In the graph, where the pressure curve (psi) and the velocity curve (fps) diverge, we have the efficient bore capacity for that particular combination of components. In the graph, the maximum efficient load would be about 49.2 grains of powder because the pressure is safe, and we have reached maximum velocity for this example.

There is a mathematical explanation for the fact that no bullet can exceed a certain velocity at a given pressure. The equation that describes pressure is:

$$P + F \div A$$

Where P is pressure, F is force, and A is area. If we increase A (area), P will fall off instantly, provided F remains constant. No amount of case design will change the area of the bullet; therefore, if you have a pressure limit of 60,000 psi, then you have a velocity limit for the caliber because the bullet's area is unchangeable.

So, the three main ways to increase velocity are:

1. Raise the pressure limit; it's not a good idea!
2. Increase bore volume by using a longer barrel, which raises the expansion ratio (this has obvious limitations).
3. Decrease the expansion ratio via a larger case capacity (this is why improved cases work). See Chapter 22 for the math involved.

The one factor that is not addressed by this equation is the propellant. The maximum velocity in this equation may slowly creep up as powders change. For example, in Charles Newton's time (1905–1920), bore capacity was about 15% less than it is today because the "progressive" nature of powders has improved. In other words, the pressure curve is slower to rise. Friction is a factor that must be overcome in moving the projectile down the bore. Reduction in bearing surface and lubricant coatings or alloys will reduce friction, but inertia is the primary factor that must be overcome. Once the bullet's mass begins to move, it takes less energy to accelerate it; as the bullet moves down the bore, combustion chamber space increases behind the bullet. So, the pressure falls as the bullet accelerates toward the muzzle.

Barrel Life

When barrel life is mentioned, often the mental picture we get is one of a rifle that shoots well, and suddenly, one day, the groups look like they were shot from a shotgun rather than a rifle. Reality is different. Accurate barrel life could be defined as the number of shots that a barrel will maintain accuracy at a specified level. Benchrest shooters are looking for accuracy well under .200 inch, so they would consider a barrel that will not hold that level of accuracy to be "shot out."

Hunting accuracy is a different animal altogether; pardon the pun. Hunters seldom expect accuracy much better than one minute of angle. Quality custom makers today build rifles with ½ MOA accuracy. A hunter will probably consider a barrel shot out when it no longer holds 1 MOA. Some would not complain until the groups open up to 2 or 3 inches. Accuracy is in the target of the beholder, after all.

Several factors go into barrel life: case capacity (see Efficiency above), case design, neck length, throat design (bullet fit), how the cartridge is loaded, cleaning practices and the type of bullet used, to name the most important.

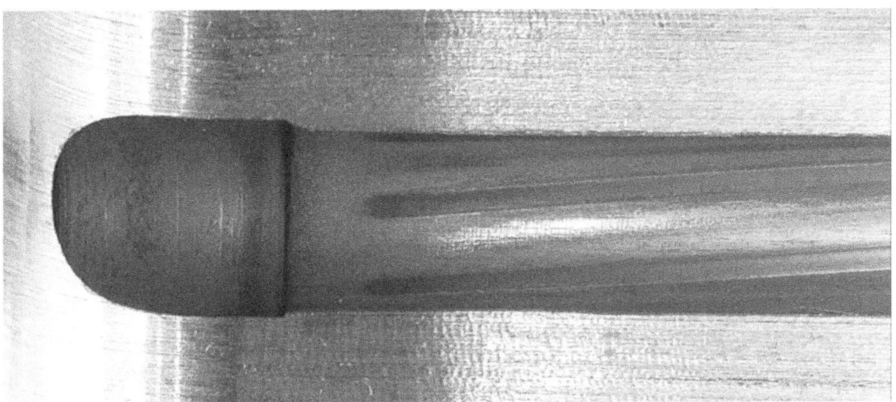

Compare this to the unfired throat pictured a few pages earlier in this chapter. Gases have rounded the case mouth and the transition to the rifling. In person, you can see cracks where the gas has cut away the softer alloys in the steel.

Case design will have some effect on the accurate life of your barrel. An overbore case with a short neck will burn out the throat more quickly than an appropriate bore capacity design. The .240 Gibbs illustrates this point well. It is overbore for a 6mm and, when loaded to full potential, will shoot out a barrel in 1,500 to 2,000 rounds, maybe fewer, depending on your idea of accuracy. That's just a few trips to shoot prairie dogs.

Would a longer neck make a difference? Probably not, although there has been much speculation about the sandblasting effect of powder in the throat as it's forced up the barrel behind the bullet. However, this seems unlikely to be a significant factor. Inspection of barrels with throat erosion indicates that the damage results from gas cutting rather than peening by high-speed powder kernels.

Above 40,000 psi, the flame temperature created by the burning powder is always more than the melting points of all the ingredients of alloy steels (except carbon) and is the reason erosion occurs.

Here is a way to take advantage of this fact: When you break in a new barrel, you can purposefully fill in the microstructure of the steel with carbon in the form of graphite. Neolube No. 1 is a colloidal graphite in an isopropanol carrier and is a dry film lubricant. It conforms to the stringent requirements of Military Specification MIL-L-24131C (Huron Industries, Inc. is the manufacturer). This product fills the microstructure. So, you have a graphite lubricant in the microstructure instead of copper and carbon. This helps to prevent the fowling from sticking to the bore and gives you a longer shot count before needing to clean. According to the maker, it provides non-corrosive, dry adherent lubrication for metal parts with limited clearances in applications where control of impurities is required. Neolube No. 1 resists abrasion and effectively lubricates moving parts, rubbing surfaces, and threaded parts for easier assembly, trouble-free operation and non-destructive disassembly. Sounds a lot like a bullet passing through a bore to me.

High pressure is high temperature and, therefore, hastens erosion. Barrel life depends upon and directly relates to chamber pressure. Although, if the bullet fully seals the bore, it may retard the process as gas is prevented from escaping past the bullet's base (see the discussion on throat design in this chapter).

As mentioned above, the ideal throat for a hunting rifle would have a diameter equal to the bullet diameter with a tolerance of plus .0002 inch. Again, that's 2/10,000th of an inch, with no minus. I say ideally because this throat would produce the longest accurate barrel life. Gas cutting is the principal source of accuracy decline, so by holding the throat tolerance tighter, less gas can escape around the projectile, controlling the jet effect that cuts the bore.

Bullet fit about the throat is an issue that is largely ignored these days. Townsend Whelen had some thoughts on this design feature. "The groove diameter of a barrel has considerable influence on accuracy and barrel life, and this must be understood by the gunsmith who would concern himself with design and specifications for rifle barrels," he said. "Groove diameter must always be considered in connection with the diameters of the bullets that are to be used in the rifles. The diameters of the bullets are usually fixed by the ammunition manufacturer, but different manufacturers may use bullets of slightly different diameters for a given caliber of cartridge, so it is best to find out what the average diameter of all bullets likely to be used is and use that figure in the selection of groove diameter for the barrel. Rifle barrels can often be had with slight variations in groove diameter, thus allowing the gunsmith a certain latitude in fit between bullet and barrel."[3]

In reality, matching barrels and bullets is not very practical. It can certainly be done, and for benchrest shooters, it might be worth pursuing. However, for the average shooter or hunter, it would not be cost-effective. Time is always at a premium, so having to measure all your bullets to be sure they are within specification would be a burden many shooters would not be willing to take on. The truth is that barrel making—as well as bullet making—has improved dramatically since 1932, when Whelen wrote his comments on the subject. Today, both types of manufacturing use improved technology that allows for better control over tolerances, yet variations still exist for many reasons.

Whelen's comments apply here, too. "Of course where barrels and bullets are made in quantities by machinery certain tolerances or allowances from the standard diameters are absolutely necessary, for no company can afford to discard its tools as soon as they show any wear. Thus, a manufacturer, starting with new tools, will cut his barrels to a certain diameter. As the tools wear or have to be sharpened, the diameter changes slightly, and finally the tools are discarded when they are producing barrels to the limit of the tolerance. The same holds true of bullets, the dies for making which are ground to the minimum diameter and are discarded when they are producing bullet of the maximum allowable diameter,"[4] he said.

SAAMI Specs

A well-balanced cartridge like the .30-06 has enough capacity to deliver useful ballistics yet is highly flexible in loading. Every year, there is at least one article

3 Whelen, Townsend, *Clyde Baker's Modern Gunsmithing*, 1933

4 *Ibid.*

written about its flexibility or some variation on that theme. Accurate barrel life with such a cartridge is extraordinarily long.

Bob Fulton is fond of talking about using his original takedown Winchester 1895 in .30-06 to shoot desert jackrabbits. In 1951–54, Fulton was in the Coast Guard based out of the San Diego station and bought the used rifle while stationed there. He had a friend who was in charge of the armory. Part of the armory's responsibility was to destroy the out-of-date ammo not only for the armory but also for the Navy. Most of that ammo had corrosive or semi-corrosive primers.

As a result, Fulton had all the '06 ammo he could shoot, not to mention .22 Long Rifle and .45 ACP. They found a ranch that was overrun with jackrabbits, ground squirrels, and, consequently, coyotes. The rancher was happy to have the help, so about every week, Bob and his shooting buddy took two or three days to camp and shoot. "If you stayed on base on your days off, you were in effect 'on call.' So, if you really wanted time off, you left the base," he said. He figures that in two years, four to five thousand rounds went through his rifle. When he got out of the service, Fulton went off to a four-year college, during which time he continued his habit of shooting on weekends. In discussing all his escapades with that old '95, we concluded that it has had approximately 10,000 rounds through it. Accuracy is still reasonable after 50 years of steady use. It shoots ½ MOD now, a 3-inch group at 100 yards. MOD? Oh, that's "Minute Of Deer," since the kill zone on a deer is about six inches.

For most shooters, 10,000 rounds is a lifetime of shooting, just like it was in Fulton's rifle. Barrel life should probably be measured in years instead of rounds. The average big game hunter shoots no more than 20 rounds a year. The avid hunter may work on loads and practice, shooting about 200 rounds a year. Let's say that you design a barnburner cartridge that will have a 1,600-round accurate barrel life (meaning groups will exceed 1 MOA after 1,600 rounds). If you're an avid hunter, your barrel will last about eight years; by then, you will have a new dream cartridge in mind anyway. If you're an average hunter, your barrel will last 80 years once you work up a load. In either case, barrel life is not a huge issue.

On the other hand, how long does a barrel last in real time, that is, the time bullets travel in the bore?

In 2010, John Farrier published a blog post, "The Life Span of a Gun Barrel is About Six Seconds." From that post, "If a bullet flies at 3,000 fps, it will pass through a 24-inch (2-foot) barrel in 1/1,500th of a second. If you have a useful barrel life of 3,000 rounds, that would translate to just two seconds of actual bullet-in-barrel operating time.

But it's not that simple. Your bullet starts at 0 fps velocity and then accelerates as it passes through the bore, so the projectile's average velocity is not the same as the 3,000 fps muzzle velocity. So, how long does a centerfire bullet (with 3,000 fps MV) typically stay in the bore? The answer is about .002 seconds. Varmint Al, an engineer at the Lawrence Livermore Laboratory, calculated this number. Six seconds! That's how long your barrel actually functions (in terms of bullet-in-barrel shot time) before it's shot out."

Wildcat Design Process

Start the process of design by setting goals.

Example wildcat goal list:

- Build a .19-caliber cartridge that closely duplicates the tried-and-true Donaldson Wasp
- Must be centerfire/reloadable
- Use a standard bore dimension (.198 groove)
- No similar cartridges in .19 caliber
- Easy to form
- About 90% of caliber neck length
- Easy to feed
- Base the design on the 7.62x39 case to take advantage of the CZ and Charles Daly bolt-actions currently available for the parent case

Next, check to see what similar cartridges exist.

Duplicating the general case capacity of the .219 Donaldson Wasp is desirable because this case is well-known for its accuracy. Applying our modern design

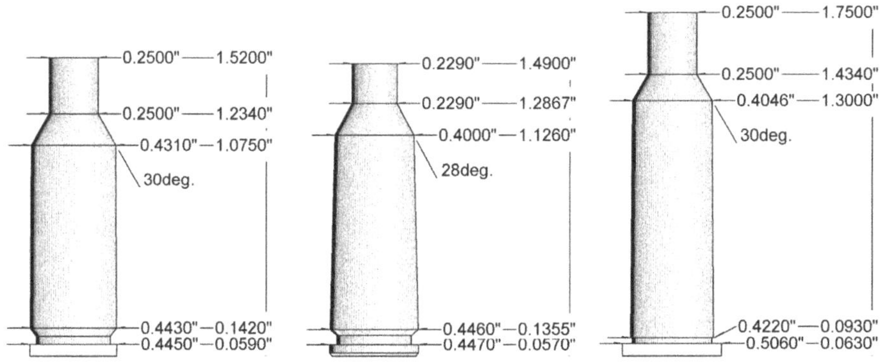

The .22 PPC (left), .19 Hawk (middle) and .219 Donaldson Wasp-L (right).

principles should deliver an updated case that suits today's shooters' needs and the available actions.

In addition, .19 caliber is a relatively new bore diameter, and there are only a few cartridges in existence for it. The folks at Calhoon Bullets of Havre, Montana, have introduced three cartridges in .19 caliber, including the .19 Calhoon (.19 Hornet), .19-223 Calhoon and the .19 Badger based on the .30 Carbine case. At the time of this writing, James Calhoon Bullets was the only source for .19-caliber bullets, but offers a variety of bullet weights ranging from 32 to 44 grains.

In the early stages of development, you can use a computer program to draw the cartridge and estimate the case capacity. Then, using more software to estimate starting loads will help you decide if the cartridge is worth testing. Using RCBS.Load, we developed a case drawing that would deliver just a couple of grains by water weight less capacity than the .219 Donaldson Wasp. Since the bore is .026 inch smaller in diameter than the bore of the .219, a reduction in case capacity would be needed to account for the difference in bore diameter. The closest existing cartridge would be the .22 PPC.

We used Load from a Disk v2.2 and entered case capacity in water weight and other pertinent data, which we previously created using RCBS.Load. These estimated results are interesting enough to encourage actual tests. See Figure 9-1 on page 135.

It's time to give your project a working name if you have not already created a permanent one. In this case, we'll call it the ".19 Hawk."

Typically, after using load estimating software, you will find these programs very good at suggesting a safe starting point. However, they seem to fall short when predicting the top-end pressures. Most likely, this is because of the variables the program cannot address, such as chambering, throat length, actual bore dimensions and numerous others. We have also noted that the software has trouble working with tiny cases like the .17 Eichelberger Dart. The point is you will have to do some careful testing to find the safe limits of any given cartridge. Just because the printout

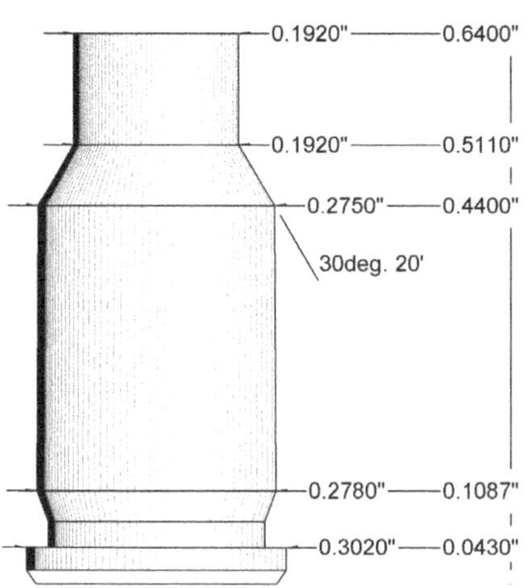

The .17 Eichelberger Dart.

Load From a Disk for Windows, v2.2

Cartridge Load Results

Date: 4/5/05
Cartridge Type: .19 Hawk

Case Capacity = 27.673 gr. water Bullet Weight = 44 gr.
Bullet Diameter (Actual) = 0.198 in.
Barrel Length = 22.7 in. Temperature = 70F
Sectional Density = 0.16 Volume Ratio = 7.3

Powder Class: MEDIUM POWDERS
Powder Type: IMR 4895, H4895, S-4065, AA-2495, N135
Charge/Bullet Weight = .541 Calculated Powder Charge = 23.8 gr.
Load Density = 86% Estimated Peak Pressure = 42,200 psi
Estimated Muzzle Velocity = 3,254 fps

Alternate Powder Class: MEDIUM POWDERS
Alternate Powder Type: IMR 4064, H-380, AA-2520, N140
Charge/Bullet Weight = .568 Calculated Powder Charge = 25 gr.
Load Density = 90.3% Estimated Peak Pressure = 44,300 psi
Estimated Muzzle Velocity = 3,322 fps

WARNING: For starting loads, reduce the calculated powder charge by at least 10%.

Load Information

Powder Type: IMR 4895, H4895, S-4065, AA-2495, N135

Load Density %	Charge Wt. gr	Velocity fps	Pressure psi
75	20.8	2,800	32,200
80	22.1	3,000	36,400
85	23.5	3,200	41,100
90	24.9	3,400	46,200
95	26.3	3,600	51,500
100	27.7	3,800	57,200

Alternate Powder Type: IMR 4064, H-380, AA-2520, N140

Load Density %	Charge Wt. gr	Velocity fps	Pressure psi
75	20.8	2,800	30,700
80	22.1	2,900	34,600
85	23.5	3,100	39,100
90	24.9	3,300	43,900
95	26.3	3,500	49,000
100	27.7	3,700	54,400

* WARNING — HIGH PRESSURE – REFERENCE ONLY!

Figure 9.2.

lists a load does not mean it will be safe in your rifle, so work up carefully.

Before you build a gun, you should ask one more question. With what you know about your new design, is it practical? The answer may or may not matter to the designer. Gunsmiths, as a whole, are relatively practical, though, and will tell you what they think, right or wrong. Remember, we are talking about opinion here, so view the answers in that light.

The .19 Hawk is practical from the standpoint of available actions and efficient ballistics. Some argue it's not practical based on the light bullets it shoots. Others may consider it a barrel burner because it has a relatively large capacity for the bore diameter. To all this, the fan of the .19 Hawk design would say, "Yeah, but wouldn't it be cool to have a .19 that will push 32-grain bullets at 4,000 fps?" That's where practicality often loses out in wildcatting—the "wouldn't it be cool" factor. (For those interested, I ordered the reamers for the new cartridge, so the cool factor of having a Mini Mauser set up for a .19 Hawk won out. It's a good thing that prairie dogs aren't ballistics experts.)

In about 2007, I finished the load testing for the .19 Hawk. The bullets that were available at the time were James Calhoon 36 and 40 grain. The rifle was a CZ 527 with a 24-inch barrel. One could get more velocity in a different action as the bolt lugs on the 527 have a small contact surface. Either way, the results are close to the prediction.

BULLET WEIGHT (GR.)	VELOCITY (FPS)
36	3,719
40	3,564

The Accuracy Question

Townsend Whelen said, "Only accurate rifles are interesting." When we design a wildcat cartridge, a major consideration should be whether or not the design is likely accurate. If you read the history portions of this book, you probably noticed that much of wildcatting has been done in the search for better accuracy. We need to define accuracy for our discussion: An accurate cartridge and load will produce MOA groups at worst. MOA is the arc subtended by an angle of one minute (1/60th of a degree) 1.0471680 inches at 100 yards—so close to 1 inch that, for all practical purposes, most shooters consider it an inch.

There are many wives' tales about accurate design. For instance, belted cases are supposedly less accurate than rimless ones. If there is any truth to this it would have more to do with the manufacture of the brass than the design itself. The process of forming brass from a coin involves the use of multiple dies.

In typical operation, the dies will wear and move slightly out of adjustment in the machine. For this reason, the belt can be out of round, longer or shorter than is desirable but within SAAMI specifications. So, maybe that one has a basis in truth.

Rimmed cases are looked down upon by the accuracy fraternity these days. In reality, the rim or lack of rim has little to do with accuracy. Over time, the bolt-action has taken over from the single-shot, so naturally rimmed cartridges have lost popularity with the benchrest crowd. The only argument one can make against rimmed cases is that the rimmed head is larger and, therefore, has greater contact area with the bolt face, which one could argue offers more opportunity for deflection. The reality is that rimmed cases are harder to work with in a bolt-action, so nobody bothers since a rimless case will provide at least equal results.

Looking back at the last 60 or so years of benchrest shooting, one can see trends in the types of cartridges that win matches. Gradually, the trend has been toward short and fat cases, described by one writer as square designs. Benchresters shoot more rounds in a year than the average hunter in 10 years, so they learn more about inherent accuracy (accuracy of a given design) than most of us ever do. For that reason, we can learn from the benchrest crowd and save a lot of time and powder if we recognize the aspects of that discipline that apply to hunting cartridges and are limited to the benchrest universe.

Benchrest shooters have an unofficial motto: "Short and fat is where it's at!" The truth is that no matter what the popular trends are at the moment, more accuracy comes from the way the firearm is assembled than from case design. Give a well-built gun in any caliber to a top competitor, they will get results.

At the same time, we are not all benchrest shooters, and hunting conditions are not conducive to some of the unique techniques and efforts such specialists must apply to be competitive at a match. Sitting at a shooting bench, the competitor has more time to watch for problems developing with his gun or ammo. In the field, a hunter might drop ammo in the snow or dirt and need to clean and use it. If the chamber and ammo were as precisely fit in a hunting rifle as in a benchrest gun, dirty ammo could be a severe safety problem. That is not to say that dirty ammo is ever a good idea, just that it will happen.

Benchrest guns have a tight-dimensioned chamber, and the brass will be much more closely fit to the chamber—to the extent that, for some matches, the same case is loaded over and over at the bench to shoot the match. Accuracy buffs in the blackpowder cartridge fraternity will even mark cases to be oriented the same way in the chamber for each shot for the best accuracy. This will not happen with a hunting gun in the field.

What's the Point?

Some general features of case design work well in any rifle. Neck length near caliber length, no less than 90% of the caliber if possible, will provide proper and even neck tension to the projectile. Neck tension is a significant factor in accuracy. Crimping bullets can improve accuracy by making neck tension more uniform. When you increase crimped tension on the bullet, you allow the burning of the powder to progress slightly before the bullet is released into the throat of the chamber. A crimped neck usually produces a more consistent result, often leading to good hunting accuracy.

Concentricity is a massive issue with both benchrest and hunting ammunition. There are several ways that ammunition can be made non-concentric. Hard

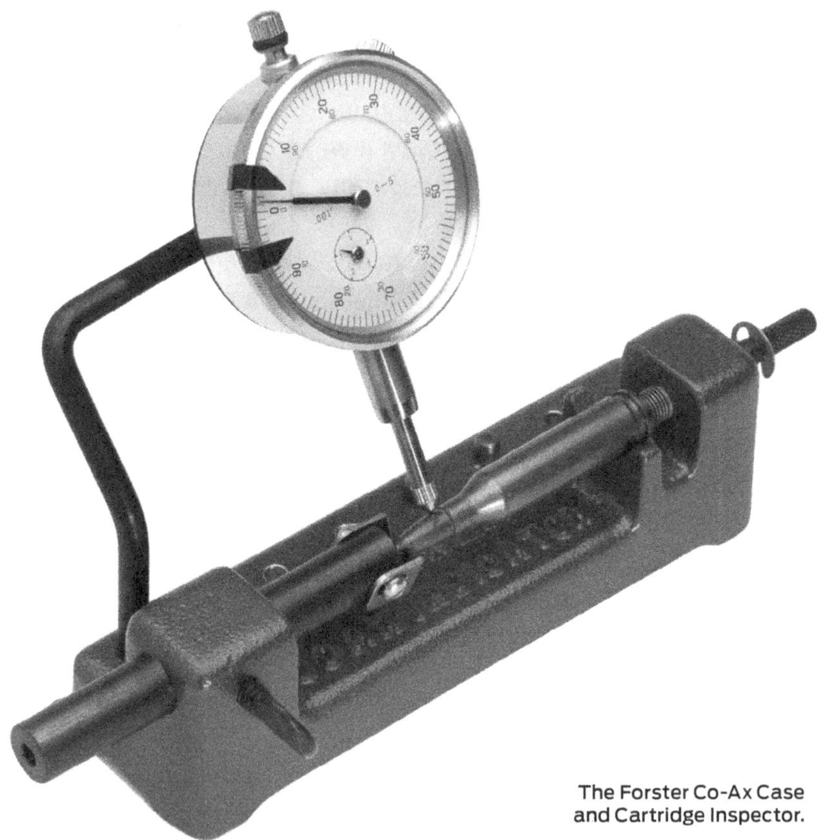

The Forster Co-Ax Case and Cartridge Inspector.

brass will tend to be less malleable and, if out of alignment, will not easily be corrected in the die. RCBS offers its X-dies as one way to attempt to control brass flow. A mandrel supports the neck during sizing, forcing the brass to stay uniform in the neck area. Outside neck turning will make the brass uniform around the circumference of the neck; when such brass is to be used in a standard chamber, all that is necessary is to turn the brass so that, visually, 90% of the brass is trimmed. If you used a tube micrometer to check brass neck turned this way, you would find it extremely uniform (less than a .0002-inch variation).

Using fired brass from another rifle can provide a hidden problem if the bolt face or chamber of the other gun is out of square or misaligned. The most common alignment problem is bent necks. Most often, the bullet seater causes this: in a conventional seater, the bullet lays over to one side as it is raised into the die. Not so in an inline bullet seater. When the bullet is bound between the die and the case, it tends to push the neck out of alignment until the force finally overcomes the tight mouth of the brass and allows the bullet to be seated.

There are several solutions to the problem of crooked ammunition. Annealing the brass before resizing it can make it more malleable. High-quality sizing dies will ensure the best possible brass before bullet seating. Using an inline seating die will avoid bending the neck during seating. As a last resort, some shooters report good results by bolting an aluminum plate to the loading bench and drilling a hole the same diameter as the case neck. Once the ammo is loaded, it is checked for concentricity, and those rounds that are more than .001 inch out of alignment are inserted in the plate and bent in the proper direction to remove the misalignment. It's low-tech, but it works. Then, check the concentricity on a gauge until you get the desired results.

Brass of nearly any design can be made accurate. What most affects accuracy is the degree of sizing the brass undergoes, as well as how the brass fits the chamber. The selection of components will certainly affect accuracy, but these factors come after the fit of the brass to the chamber. Neck sizing is popular with shooters because it leaves the brass fully formed to the chamber from which it was fired. It's important to know that benchrest shooters have abandoned the practice of neck sizing, as they found it did not provide the pinnacle of accuracy.

Most full-length resizing dies are designed to take the brass back to SAAMI minimums or very close to them. The problem with such extreme full-length sizing is that it makes the ammo so small that it can float in the chamber side to side or up and down, just the opposite of what neck sizing provides (although different makes of dies can vary wildly). The happy medium for the best possible hunting accuracy is a set of custom dies closely matched to the chamber (more on this in Chapter 16) so that the brass is only minimally sized. Such custom dies will allow reliable feeding and function while delivering the best possible accuracy.

Hunting Cartridges

What is the most effective velocity range for a hunting cartridge? This question has probably been the most debated issue among shooters and hunters. There are essentially two schools of thought on this issue.

School #1—Ultra velocity (3,000 to 4,000 fps, more is better!). This crowd believes that the sheer shocking power of a high-velocity bullet will deliver killing power even on large game animals. Numerous folks have used such flat-shooting cartridges effectively on a variety of game and would argue the efficacy of their choice. Another reason for using these high-velocity cartridges is the ability to shoot long-range and relatively flat trajectories.

Modern, high-quality bullets make this train of thought more sensible than it was in the past. A bullet that retains its weight and stays on course during the kill is much more effective.

School #2—Moderate velocity (2,400 to 2,700 fps) and relatively heavy bullets for the caliber. Proponents of this philosophy are usually experienced hunters who have taken (or seen taken) a variety of game under a range of conditions. The idea is simple: deliver energy to the target. The reasoning is that heavy bullets in the moderate velocity range will allow the bullet to penetrate and, equally as important, to expend the majority, if not all, of its power inside the animal.

Interestingly, the same high-quality bullets mentioned in School #1 are of equal value to School #2. A quality projectile offers all the same benefits of accuracy, penetration and energy delivery to the target.

Comments on School #1 (Ultra Velocity)—There are several problems with the idea that velocity is the answer to every hunting situation. On animals of any real mass, such as western mule deer, elk, or moose, not always, but all too often, a light bullet at high velocity will explode on the surface or against a bone and never penetrate the body cavity. A shallow surface wound will not kill quickly or humanely. This is where the cost of premium bullets can make high-velocity cartridges more practical and effective.

Wayne van Zwoll writes in his book *Elk Rifles, Cartridges and Hunting Tactics* about a survey he took from elk hunters. The survey included a question about which bullets hunters used. Most entered the name of the bullet maker along with the weight and design information, but one response was "dentmatter." Van Zwoll pondered that response for a while, then realized that the respondent was saying the choice of bullets "don't matter."[5] That's not true. Experience will teach you that not all bullets are created equally.

Using light bullets on big game requires two things many shooters can't or won't bring to the sport. First, a high degree of accuracy that only comes from extensive practice. This is important because you must deliver a light bullet directly to the kill zone. If a heavy bone is encountered or if the bullet strays too far back and misses the heart and lungs, it will do very little damage, and while the animal may still die, it could be in the next time zone by the time it drops. Of course, that's the beauty of ultra-high-velocity cartridges—they were designed for shooting into the next time zone (if you can still see the animal).

Gary Sitton, a well-known gun writer and hunter, did some testing with a .300 Magnum. He was preparing for a mule deer hunt and ordered 180 gr. Hawk bullets from Bob Fulton, who suggested that the 200-gr. bullet would be a better choice for big mule deer, and the trajectory would still be acceptable for typical shooting distances. Being open-minded, Sitton gave the 200-gr. bullet a try. As luck would have it, he had a shot at a big buck from above, and when he pulled the trigger, the deer took a step forward, so the bullet hit in the back just behind the rib cage. Sitton knew it was a lousy shot and figured they would have to do some tracking. To his surprise, they found the buck lying right where he had shot it. Sitton was of the opinion that, with a lighter bullet and a poorly placed shot, he would have been tracking that deer for a while, and Fulton agreed.

Bullet construction is essential. If you insist on shooting light bullets fast, you need the best bullets money can buy, those designed for high-velocity use. Part of the problem is that darn few bullets are constructed to function at extreme velocities. Most open too fast, and others are of such heavy construction that there is a chance they will remain largely intact and penetrate the animal. The cost of custom controlled-expansion bullets is low compared to your investment in time, equipment, license fees, hunting guides, etc.

Cartridges like the .30-378 Weatherby, .338-378, and .300 Ultra Mag. are good examples of the problem of finding bullets that will perform at extreme velocity.

Many of the bullets on the market today are not designed to perform at extreme velocity, and some manufacturers have put velocity ranges right on

5 Van Zwoll, Wayne, *Elk Rifles, Cartridges and Hunting Tactics*, 1992

the box of bullets. North Fork Bullets are designed to work with a broader velocity range than any other available today, and they have done the testing to prove it. Morally, we owe it to the game we seek to see that they do not suffer unnecessarily. Good shot placement and quality bullets will help to meet this obligation.

Finally, these same folks, if offered a choice when hunting dangerous game, will invariably select the big bore with a heavy bullet over their favorite ultra-velocity case. So, even they know that reliable terminal ballistics result from mass times velocity rather than ultra-velocity times mini-mass. The hydrostatic shock will knock down smaller game animals, but it's not as effective on large ones; if it were, all professional hunters would carry .220 Swifts.

If you're a fan of the Ultra-Velocity school, you're probably plum ticked off by now. Well, let me share some real-world experiences that will help you to cool down and hopefully see where these comments originated. Discussions of caliber selection with guides over the years are a significant source. In the years before the large-capacity magnums, the 7mm Remington Magnum was a popular choice among hunters. Guides almost universally expected trouble when a hunter arrived with a 7mm Mag. for two reasons. 1. The hunters could seldom shoot well with these guns, likely due to lack of practice. 2. They reported that with animals shot at ranges of less than 150 yards (where most of the game is taken), the bullets had trouble penetrating. When the ranges were longer, the problem was far less noticeable. The reason? Velocity had dropped back into the proper range for the projectile to function as designed.

Interestingly, there is a way around the 7mm Remington Magnum issue. Since this cartridge operates at the low end of the Ultra-Velocity spectrum if you select a 175-gr. Bullet, the close-range problem largely disappears. Selecting the heavy-for-caliber bullet for hunting will increase penetration and deliver far more energy to the target. Velocity is a major factor in this discussion; the 175-gr. bullet moves at 2,800 fps or slower, dropping it into the moderate-velocity range.

For example, an experienced Canadian moose guide told Bob Fulton of Hawk Bullet fame, "A .30-caliber rifle, no matter '06 or any magnum, will take three shots on average to knock a bull moose down. Calibers .338 and up do not require follow-up shots nearly as often." That is another argument for choosing relatively heavy bullets. How many hunters select 220-gr. bullets in their .30 caliber? Look on the shelf of your sporting goods store. Popular loadings for .30-caliber cartridges will have bullets from 150 to 180 grains. The heavier bullet will have a higher sectional density and, if well-constructed, will penetrate deeper.

Velocity has its place. High velocity is excellent in a varmint rifle where meat loss is not an issue, and fast, humane kills are the main issue. Velocity can overcome wind in some shooting situations. Most of all, high velocity is about fun and driving a bullet faster than anyone else.

Comments on School #2 (mass times velocity)—It's not unusual for these adherents to be older, more experienced shooters. They've made the mistakes and seen the real-world results of extreme velocity. Muzzle blast and recoil are things they do not relish. They know that the killing effect is a direct result of the size of the permanent wound cavity in both depth and diameter. Experience has taught them that heavier bullets for caliber are far more likely to take an animal off its feet, anchoring it with the first shot. That's the name of the game: not to come home with a collection of perfectly formed mushroomed bullets.

Logical progression often takes this school down the road of big bores, lead bullets or blackpowder cartridges. These choices fit right into our model of moderate velocities and heavy projectiles. However, there is a wide variety of cartridges that fall into this category, ranging from obsolete calibers to very modern cartridge designs.

These folks have to put up with comments like:

"You don't need a chronograph. A sundial will do!"

"Wow, that thing looks like it will kill on both ends!"

"You must have more testosterone than brains!"

"What's the difference between being hit by a bus or a train?"

"But you can't use that for 'Shoot and Release.'"

All kidding aside, after many years of building custom guns for these "old-timers," they almost universally have the same attributes they look for in a cartridge.

A velocity range from the muzzle of 2,400 to 2,700 fps.

A point-blank range of 200 to 300 yards.

Recoil is roughly equal to a .30-06 with a 180-gr. bullet at 2,700 fps (this one is always negotiable).

They choose heavy-for-caliber bullets, but not necessarily the heaviest.

Efficient design, no wasted powder capacity. More powder equals more recoil.

John "Pondoro" Taylor was a member of this school of thought; when commenting on it, he stated that Elmer Keith put it so succinctly in his book *Big Game Rifles and Cartridges* that he felt it advisable to quote him. "Many hunters today," wrote Keith, "are apparently small-bore crazy, seemingly wanting to kill as large game as lives with a light and small a bore of rifle as possible, throwing the lightest bullet obtainable; even to hunting big game with the .22 Hornet. Such men need their heads examined. Certainly it is not sportsmanship they display."[6]

Taylor commented, "High velocity flattens trajectory and so to a great extent eliminates the bug-bear of judging distance. That was the primary object of boosting velocities. There are other advantages connected with penetration and expansion of bullets; but practically all these are in connection with long-range shooting. In fact, unless your bullet weight is carefully chosen, *too high a velocity at close range can be a decided disadvantage* by causing your bullet to disintegrate on impact if it happens to strike even a comparatively light bone.

"I (Taylor) have long been inclined to think that there has been too much of a rush to velocity whilst ignoring bullet weight."[7]

Taylor stated emphatically that the ideal striking velocity for dangerous game is 2,400 fps or higher, so he advocated a muzzle velocity of 2,500 fps.

Many calibers historically fit into this realm of moderate velocities. The 6.5mm Manlicher Schoenaur, 7x57 Mauser, .30-40 Krag and .303 British are a few relatively small-bore cartridges that had a reputation for being very useful and deadly way out of proportion to the ballistics they produce. A quick look at the loadings that helped build their reputation shows that heavy bullets for caliber were the reason for their success. High sectional density drove the bullets to deep penetration in game animals—160-gr. bullets in the 6.5mm, 175 gr. in the 7x57, and 180 gr. in the .303 British were reliable killers on medium-sized game. The introduction of higher-velocity cartridges of the same caliber caused the construction of bullets to be modified to work with the change in velocity ranges. So, the old stand-by calibers could no longer reliably expand the projectiles to create a large wound canal. This and the trend of using lighter bullets rendered these calibers less effective.

It's interesting to note that in the middle of the last century, the .32 Winchester Special had a reputation for being a better killer than its venerable twin, the .30-30 WCF (at one time the .32 Special was listed in the top five most effective calibers in a Canadian study). The reason for this is simple: bullets being made for .30 calibers at the time were constructed to perform at the higher velocities of the .30-06 or .300 H&H, so they tended to be too heavily constructed for the .30-30, which could not drive them fast enough for proper expansion. The .32 WCF, on the other hand, was the only caliber that used that caliber of bullet in

6 Taylor, John, *African Rifles and Cartridges*, 1948

7 *Ibid.*

the Winchester line. So, the bullets were made to work at the velocities that the .32 Special could develop, and they were far more likely to expand and perform well terminally.

The difference between the two schools is sort of like the tortoise and the hare. These tortoises have learned that velocity is not the only measure of a cartridge. Instead, the endgame of terminal ballistics is far more critical. Put another way, It's not how fast you get there. It's how hard you hit when you arrive that matters.

CHAPTER 10

Pressure

Significant changes have come to the reloading community in recent years, or as I have been waiting all my life to say, "Since the turn of the century." Affordable tools allow the average reloader to test their loads and rifles in ways that were not financially feasible just a few years earlier. Two affordable tools indirectly test for pressure using a transducer glued to the barrel, and a third is being readied for release. Several software packages predict starting loads based on case capacity, providing a safe starting point for a new cartridge (see Chapter 8).

What does this mean for the wildcatter? The pressure signs that most reloaders like to use are of limited value at best. Even with high pressure, an improved case design will have easy bolt lift and extraction. Experience tells the reloader that the condition of the fired primer is not necessarily a reliable source of information. The best indication of safe loads is case life and head expansion. If you can reload your brass five or six times without primer pockets getting loose, that is the final word on that particular load until you invest in a pressure testing system.

A Little History

Into the early 1960s, it was common practice to interchange the terms CUP and PSI—CUP means copper units of pressure, and PSI is pounds per square inch. Using PSI in this way was incorrect, but since there was no practical way to measure it in a firearm chamber at that time, no one bothered to correct the misuse of the term. When the piezoelectric and strain gauge systems came on the scene in the '60s, PSI suddenly became a real value, and it became essential to differentiate between the two. "For years, 52,000 PSI (CUP method with erroneous designation) had been published as maximum for the .270 Winchester. Suddenly, new publications were showing 65,000 PSI ... as maximum."[1]

How often have you read that CUP and PSI are not correlated and cannot be? It has often been pointed out that a .45-70 at 28,000 CUP will also read as 28,000 PSI, but it just so happens that the two systems cross at that point. But as you move up the pressure curve, the two systems supposedly diverge erratically or indefinably. However, that does not make logical sense: if both systems measure pressure in the chamber, they must be correlated simply because they measure the same thing.

PSI and CUP Correlated

According to Denton Bramwell in *Correlating PSI and CUP*, "If two variables are correlated, you can estimate one from the other. The opposite of this is 'statistically independent,' which means that you can't estimate one from another. It is very hard to come up with completely statistically independent or uncorrelated numbers. Usually, the question is not whether things are correlated, but how well they are correlated.

"It's a fact that two variables that are both well correlated with a third variable must be well correlated to each other. So, if the copper crusher system is well correlated with peak chamber pressure, and the piezoelectric PSI system is well correlated with peak chamber pressure, then CUP must be well correlated with piezoelectric PSI."[2]

The nature of measuring systems is that they all contain some error, identified as standard deviation (SD). The SD for the CUP measuring system is 2,000 PSI (correct usage) and the piezoelectric system is a little more accurate with an SD of 1,300 PSI. For example, the 7x57's published pressure is 46,000 CUP and 51,000 PSI, while the .300 Savage operates at 46,000 CUP and 47,000 PSI, according to published data. Standard deviation is the explanation for these apparent inconsistencies between the two cartridges. Variables in both systems make precise readings next to impossible, which is why SD is described for each system.

Denton Bramwell produced two formulas[3] for converting CUP and PSI values back and forth as needed. The first formula is for ANSI PSI and CUP values as used by SAMMI:

---

1 *Lyman Reloading Handbook, 47th Edition*

2 Bramwell, Denton, *Correlating PSI and CUP*, 2002

3 *Ibid.*

$$ANSI\ PSI = -17902.0 + 1.51586 \times ANSICUP$$

The CIP in Europe uses a different system, and it requires a second formula for accurate conversions:

$$CIP\ PSI = -2806.88 + 1.20911 \times CIPCUP$$

While Bramwell admits his formulas are not perfect, they are accurate to within 3,000 PSI, which makes them nearly as accurate as most measuring systems in terms of standard deviation. The bottom line is that the next time someone says you cannot compare or extrapolate PSI and CUP data, you have proof they are wrong.

No Free Lunch

Nearly every reloader asks the same question at some point, "How much faster can I push it?" or the ever-popular, "What pressure are you running in that wildcat cartridge?" It may or may not be surprising to learn that the answers are complicated and that many variables come into play while answering them, as they do every time you pull the trigger.

There is nothing wrong with the desire to push the projectile harder and faster. I designed a 4,000 fps cartridge just because fast is fun. If you understand the variables and learn to make them work in your favor where possible, pressure will not be a problem.

Cartridge Design

Many shooters think improved cartridges (increased capacity) or wildcats with significantly increased capacity can exceed the pressure limits of the parent cartridge. This assumption is a fallacy. If the parent cartridge was designed for 60,000 PSI, the wildcat or improved case will live by that same rule. Why? Simply put, the rifle will still have the same action designed to work at a specific maximum pressure. Changing the cartridge does not change this fact. Likewise, the brass has the same design limits as its parent design.

So, how do larger capacity cases get more velocity if they operate at the same pressure? Understandably, the higher case volume makes for a larger combustion chamber, creating a higher volume of gas at the same pressure. The bullet will be pushed out faster if more gas is in the bore. It's the same reason car enthusiasts like to overbore cylinders when they rebuild an engine: more horsepower. Think of a rifle as a single-piston engine with the bullet acting as the piston, albeit a one-time throw-away piston.

Empirical testing suggests that some cartridge designs have advantages over others. Some are more inherently accurate, and the .308 Winchester is an excellent example of this, which seems to shoot better than some other .308 calibers. This tendency has more to do with the capacity of the case being well balanced to the bore than with other design factors. P.O. Ackley found through years of testing that a 28-degree shoulder on his "improved" cartridges was generally more accurate than a 40-degree one. Over the years, however, customers were more interested in the sharp shoulder and perceived increased capacity, so the 40-degree cases became more popular. The only real advantage to the sharper shoulder is that it slows the flow of brass forward, reducing the need for frequent case trimming. The difference in accuracy is not huge; it would take a benchrest shooter to spot the discrepancy.

Testing has also shown that some designs are more efficient than others. You might ask, "Efficient? Why in Sam Hill would I want an efficient cartridge? I want power, accuracy and knockdown power, but efficiency?"

In this context, "efficiency" refers to the conversion of powder to ballistics. An efficient design will deliver more power from less fuel and less recoil for the same result from a similar cartridge. A good example of this effect would be the .300 Savage. It has a reputation for less recoil and delivers ballistics similar to the .308 Winchester. Where the .300 Savage falls short of the .308 is when you look at bullets that are 180 grains or heavier because the lack of fuel reaches the point of diminishing returns when using heavier projectiles. A desirable effect of these lower-capacity cartridges is that they tend to be accurate with a wider variety of bullets and powders—unlike overbore cartridges, which are often very particular about which load they will shoot. Therefore, efficiency can be desirable when it delivers sufficient power with low recoil, accuracy, loading flexibility and longer accurate barrel life.

Bullet Design

Bullet design will influence your ballistics. Today's bullets are available in more styles, materials and calibers than ever. Solid-base bullets, as a rule, will increase pressure. There are two reasons for this effect. First, the bullets, being homogenous, are relatively incompressible; they do not deform in the bore like a lead core bullet. Second, solids usually have a longer surface area because of the lower-density material used in their construction (lead is heavier than bronze or copper). To control the amount of surface contact a solid has with the barrel, some bullets ahead of the cannelure are bore diameter; the back half of the bullet engages the rifling. Most manuals show solids shooting

slower than lead-core bullets of the same weight because of the increased bearing surface area of the bullet. This difference in velocity between solids and lead-core bullets proves that the bearing surface is a significant factor for internal ballistics.

Bullets with a solid web of jacket material, such as the Nosler Partition, Swift A-Frame, Combined Technologies, H-Mantle and others, will also show this higher pressure to varying degrees. The thicker the web and the harder the jacket, the more noticeable it will be. Generally, this will not cause any real pressure problems; instead, it tends to make the bullets less accurate. Before you get all hot and write a nastygram, witness the number of benchrest matches won with these various projectiles (not many). That does not mean they are bad choices; on the contrary, they work well and deliver excellent accuracy in most hunting rifles.

Over the years, manufacturers have attempted to deal with these issues. Two notables are Nosler and P.O. Ackley, both of which experimented with putting groves on the parallel section of the bullet. Some only had a cannelure over the solid web area, while others had multiple grooves to control pressure to some degree. You might think the grooves will allow you to drive the bullet faster. The truth is, not really. Remember, solid-base bullets were going slower than similar lead-core ones, so at best, the grooves bring the projectiles close to their lead-core counterparts in velocity for the same pressure.

North Fork Technologies has done extensive testing on solid-based bullets with grooves. Mike Brady of North Fork shared some of his results to address why there is no free lunch (extra velocity) when you shoot grooved bullets.

Brady also explains why his company decided to go with grooved bullets. He is a meticulous tester, so when he expresses an opinion, it's based on experience and empirical data, not theory or guesswork.

"The purpose of the grooves is twofold," Brady said. "First, whenever a bullet passes down the barrel, the lands of the rifling must engrave the bullet. The material that is displaced by those lands must have a place to go. In a conventional bullet, with a thin jacket and a full-length lead core, the jacket and core can easily yield to the lands. In a monolithic bullet or one with a monolithic rear section, the only route of escape for the displaced material is to make the bullet longer. Considering the material in this area will not yield, as easily as if there was lead underneath it, the stresses, between the bullet and the barrel, will exceed the sheer strength of the jacket material. This increased stress sets up a galling action, which is one of the major causes of jacket fouling. What the grooves do is to allow the material that is displaced by the rifling lands, an easy escape route. This allows the stresses between the bullet and the barrel to stay below the point at which galling (fouling) occurs.

"The second advantage of the grooves on the rear section is that they allow the bullet to be more forgiving to variations in bore dimensions. The dimensions of different barrels commonly vary by plus or minus .0003 inch, and it is not unheard of that they can vary by more than .0010 inch. If you put a solid sectioned bullet down a barrel that is over standard size, you probably won't have too much of a problem; accuracy may suffer but, generally, it won't be dangerous. Unfortunately, the reverse is not so benign. A solid sectioned bullet, with no grooves, fired down an undersized barrel can cause dangerously high-pressure spikes as well as increasing the probability of severe fouling, it could even damage the barrel. The grooves lessen this problem, as they are designed to receive more than the standard amount of displaced material. The only true fix for an undersized bore would be bullets that match the bore.

"Chronograph. Chronograph. Chronograph. The chronograph is the most useful tool available to the average loader, at a reasonable price. In every box of bullets sold by North Fork, there is a slip of paper that recommends firing factory ammunition with the same weight bullet through your rifle to check the velocity. Using a reputable manual, choose an appropriately slow powder for the cartridge, using the same weight bullet, and reduce the max load by at least 8%. If that load does not give the same velocity, then increase the powder charge, 0.50 grain at a time, until it does match the velocity of the factory load. Obviously, watching all the time for any of the classic pressure signs. When you achieve the same velocity as the factory load, you will have an equal pressure. In addition, on the paper in the box, North Fork states that, *on average*, North Fork bullets require 3% to 4% less powder to achieve factory (or manual) velocities and pressures. In some guns, it's only 1% less, in others; it is the full 8% less.

"In testing we have not run across a case where we were not able to achieve the same velocity as a factory load at factory equivalent pressures or the stated velocity, from a reputable manual, with a particular bullet weight, in a particular cartridge, *at the same pressures*. It usually just happens at a slightly lower powder charge.

"To confirm that pressures are the same as factory loads, North Fork uses the Oehler 43 system of pressure measurement. Even with over 30 years of reloading behind me, it has been a revelation. Just remember, if you are generating more velocity than a factory load, or loads from a reloading manual (considering the weight of bullet, powder type and quantity, and the length of your particular barrel), then you are generating more pressure than that factory or published manual load. North Fork has found in testing that when dealing with cartridges from .277 through .338, at velocities of 2,700 to 3,100 fps (which covers 95% of all cartridges), that if a load is reduced to produce a 100 fps reduction from factory muzzle velocity, the pressure is reduced around 4,000 to 5,000 PSI. Adjusting the load to produce a 100 fps increase, over factory velocity, takes an increase of around 7,000 to 8,000 PSI. In many cartridges, that would put you well over 70,000 PSI. If you are comfortable with that, then so be it. Just don't kid yourself that you've come up with some magical loading, or that you own some magical rifle, that is producing that velocity gain; the gain is coming from increased pressure, period. The gun may handle it, the brass may handle it, but the pressure is there."

Brady must be right because just a couple of years after introducing the highly popular North Fork design, Barnes started marketing the "Triple Shock"—a three- and later four-groove version of the 'X' Bullet with a solid base.

Throat Design

You can influence pressure to some degree by modifying the chamber throat. A longer throat will produce less pressure and more velocity because the bullet is allowed to get moving before it engages the lands of the rifling. Many factory chambers today have long throats to give the manufacturer extra protection from various lengths of loaded factory ammo.

On the other hand, you can substantially increase the initial pressure spike by seating it close to or touching the lands. Benchrest shooters can load close the lands because they're operating—in most instances—at *lower pressure to begin with*. Generally, rifles shoot best with the bullet seated between .040 and .080 inch off the lands for hunting purposes. Seating closer only introduces variables that can cause dangerous pressure; besides, why not maintain a margin of safety for yourself?

Bottom line, no matter what improvement is made in bullet design, pressure is still the factor that governs velocity. In other words, when you hit 60,000 PSI on a .30-06 (let's say the velocity is 2,800 fps) if you were to test a variety of bullets of that same weight, you would discover that 2,800 fps very closely corresponds to 60,000 PSI regardless of the bullet design. One bullet design might require more or less powder to come up to pressure than another, but no design will allow you to achieve magic results. To put it another way, pressure is required to achieve velocity. If you design a projectile that has less friction in the bore, pressure can fall off more quickly as the bullet moves down the bore. To reach the same velocity, you must bring the pressure back up (by adding fuel). This is why advocates of moly-coated bullets find that, on average, they must burn more powder to reach the same velocity they did with a plain, uncoated bullet.

The Laws of Physics, or The Speed Limit

Bore diameter places an upper limit on velocity, at least for any reasonable powder capacity. The only way to exceed these limits is to use a smooth bore or play some other tricks with throat length and bore diameter, as mentioned above—all of which are impractical for real-world shooting, even though they are fun for experimental purposes.

Math will explain many things in life. Not surprisingly, it explains why there is a speed limit for any given caliber. As a reminder, the equation for pressure is $P=F÷A$ where P is pressure, F is force, and A is area. If we increase A, P will fall off instantly, provided F is constant. These factors are unchangeable. No amount of clever design, fancy coatings or special finishes will affect it materially.

Each cartridge, in turn, has a speed limit based on its case capacity and designed pressure limits. You can go through any number of machinations (i.e., custom throating, forward ignition) to try and get around this fact of life. Still, it's much easier to live within limits and choose the cartridge that offers the desired ballistics (see the comparison below).

CARTRIDGE	BULLET WEIGHT	MAXIMUM SAFE VELOCITY (FPS)	% OF POWDER ADDED
.30-06	180	2,800	Baseline
.300 WSM	180	2,900	11.75
.300 Ultra	180	3,200	14.21
.338-06	185	2,860	Baseline
.338 Win.	185	3,050	8.4
.338 Ultra	185	3,150	8.6

An interesting and valuable fact is that when you go up in bore diameter (increase A), the same weight projectile will move faster at the same pressure. Notice in the table above that the .338 180-gr. projectiles travel down the bore faster than the .308 bullets of the same weight. Why? Two reasons. First, the bullet's base area is larger in diameter, so there is more area for the gases to push on. Second, and less importantly, since the same weight bullet in the larger diameter usually has less contact area with the bore, there is less friction. Consequently, when you want a faster cartridge, one answer is to go for a larger bore diameter.

Sectional density (SD) comes into play here, too. Mass over area (SD) varies as to the square of the caliber (see Chapter 17 for more details). What matters to us is that applying identical force (pressure) for the same length of time to two bullets of the same SD, regardless of caliber, will result in the same acceleration. Therefore, the identical velocity will be achieved.

But... But... But...

What about Rocky Gibbs? Well, to put it simply, while Gibbs managed to wring a lot of velocity out of the old .30-06 case, many shooters of his cartridges consider it standard practice to load a case once or twice after fireforming and then throw it away because the primer pocket loosens. *That's too much pressure; it puts the rifle and the shooter at risk every time you pull the trigger.* Based on my research, it's unlikely that Gibbs favored loading such dangerous loads. He constantly preached that case life was the measure of safe loads.

What about P.O. Ackley? Ackley took the time and expense to test his ideas carefully. In his books *Handbook for Shooters and Reloaders, Vol. I & II,* he thoroughly describes the methodical experiments he used to test his "improved cartridge" concept. He contended that by straightening the body taper, he could run higher pressures in actions traditionally thought to be limited in strength. Therefore, in a small way, he found a way around the issue of pressure in some actions. However, trouble can come when a reloader decides this is a license to run the pressure up.

Ackley talked about this speed limit issue differently; he wrote about "bore capacity." The article on bore capacity from Ackley's Vol. 1 covers the subject thoroughly. In it, he describes several tests used to prove his point. The most interesting involved the use of a .270-caliber barrel chambered successively for larger cartridges, starting with a .270/308 Winchester, then rechambering to a .270 Ackley Improved, and finally rechambered to an unnamed .270 wildcat based on the '06 case, likely the .270 Gibbs. By using the same barrel for all three, Ackley removed many variables from the experiment. He wanted to show that there is a point of diminishing returns as you increase case capacity. In other words, once you surpass the ideal bore capacity for a given caliber, little is gained by the increased powder consumption. You give up accurate barrel life, and the resulting cartridge becomes more critical to load.

Ackley ran a comparison using 150-grain bullets and loads that were just one grain less than loads that blew primers for each cartridge.[4]

CARTRIDGE	BULLET (GR.)	POWDER CHARGE (GR.)	VELOCITY (FPS)
.270/.308	150	47	2,886
.270 Ackley Imp.	150	55	2,968
.270 Wildcat	150	60	2,972

Note that the increased powder charge resulted in a minimal increase in velocity—just a 4 fps increase in velocity by burning another 5 grains of powder. There is a speed limit for every caliber.

Interestingly, the factory .270 Winchester will push a 150 gr. bullet at 2,900 fps according to published data, and from this test, it appears that it is slightly overbore, a point Ackley made many years ago. Of course, various powders will produce different results, so the point of diminishing returns is not the same with all powders.

Ken Howell tells a story about his attendance at a ballistics seminar by Ken Oehler, the genius behind Oehler chronographs and other ballistic tools like the Oehler Model 43 pressure system. Oehler asked the attendees to estimate the pressure in the average reloader's pet load. Everyone guessed at a variety of numbers. Howell suggested that most were probably over 70,000 PSI, with which Oehler agreed. Think about that for a minute. That means that we, as

4 Ackley, P.O., *Handbook for Shooters and Reloaders, Vol. I*, pg. 177

Right to left: rounded, flat and reseated primers.

reloaders, underestimate the pressure we create in a given load all too often.

Pressure Signs

Recognizing pressure signs and knowing when "enough is enough" will make your guns last longer and keep you safe. Pressure and velocity generated in your specific rifle are affected by many factors, such as chamber dimensions, bore diameter and condition, throat length, the amount of bearing surface and hardness of the bullet, type and lot of primer, flash hole size, brass hardness, neck tension on the bullet, individual case capacity, ambient temperature at the time of firing and the powder lot selected for the load. Even this extensive list falls short of naming all the variables that can affect the resulting pressure when you fire a load.

If the handloader can recognize pressure symptoms, it does not matter what pressure a given load operates, at 57,000 or 59,500 PSI. What matters is whether the load is safe for continued use with that lot of brass in that particular rifle.

There are several common pressure signs that reloaders say you can watch for when testing a new cartridge case, or any reload for that matter.

- Flat primers
- Cratered primers
- Pierced primers
- Stiff or difficult extraction of fired cases
- Stiff bolt lift
- Extractor or ejector marks on the case head
- Smoked primers
- Primer pocket expansion
- Case life
- Case head expansion

Unfortunately, by the time the above pressure signs become evident, you have probably already far surpassed safe pressures. However, each is discussed below for clarity.

Primers are commonly called a "weak link," where pressure will be noticed first. However, the problem with using primers to spot pressure is that there are many manufacturers of primers, and all are made to different specifications. Primers are probably the worst method of detecting excessive pressures.

Flat primers are often a result of low-pressure loads and brass that have been resized too far, causing a mild condition of excessive headspace. When you fire such loads, and pressure builds, the brass begins to expand and stick to the chamber walls; at the same time, the primer is forced to the rear by the pressure in the case until the bolt face stops the primer. Still under pressure, the primer balloons up a small amount, and finally, chamber pressure builds enough to force the brass to stretch as the case head moves back to contact the bolt face. In the process, the primer is reseated when the case head moves back. As the expanded primer is reseated, it has to conform to the primer pocket and ends up with a flanged head.

Cartridges with case lube or oil on them will slip back into the chamber, which can produce flattened primers as described above. A lubed case will not grip the chamber walls, creating additional bolt thrust and an unsafe condition.

Cratered primers can be caused by oversized firing pin holes, firing pins that are too sharply pointed, damaged firing pins or a weak firing pin spring. Excessive pressure can cause a cratered primer, too.

Pierced primers are caused by excessive pressure most of the time. Poor firing pin shape can cause it. Firing pins cut by escaping gases can be sharp or irregular, causing pierced primers. The shape of the firing pin tip is critical. It must be rounded and smooth. The firing pin hole must be a close match for the firing pin to prevent the primer from flowing back into the hole under pressure. By the time you get a pierced primer, no matter what the actual cause, you will likely have exceeded safe pressure limits, as pressure would be needed to cause the primer to fail.

Stiff or difficult case extraction is more often related to pressure than other problems. Other reasons for difficult extraction include a rough chamber (you would notice this one with the first shot) or mechanical problems with the bolt, action or extractor. Again, if you have stiff or difficult extraction and this condition does not exist with lighter loads, then it's time to back off about 5% on your loads.

A stiff or sticky bolt lift is caused by excessive pressure expanding the case so far that it cannot shrink back. Because the expanded case is longer and larger in diameter than the chamber, it puts tension on the bolt, making it hard to open. As mentioned above, if you have this condition with a given load but not with others, then you know it's too hot for your rifle.

If inspection of the fired cases reveals that machine marks, extractor slots, or ejectors are imprinted on the brass, then pressures are high indeed. Sometimes, this condition is noted as shiny spots on the case head. There is no other cause for this condition. If you had soft brass, this condition would appear with much lighter loads than with quality brass. Soft brass is pretty obvious; when sizing, it will feel spongy in the reloading press and exhibit excessive pressure signs with relatively light loads. It will flow abnormally, lengthening the case with every shot and allowing thickening of the neck.

Smoked primers or soot on the case head are usually caused by cases that already have their primer pocket expanded too large. Because the primer cannot fully seal the primer pocket, a small amount of gas escapes around the primer—a clear indication that your brass has already experienced excessive pressure.

Shooters sometimes think case head separations are caused by excessive pressure; this is a fallacy. Poor quality or thin brass can exhibit signs of separation, but this is rare. Assuming your brass is quality, *there is only one cause of case head separations: excessive headspace.* Excessive headspace can be in the ammo just as easily as in the gun. When resizing brass, it's critical not to move the shoulder of the case back unnecessarily too far. Several companies offer case gauges of various styles, allowing a visual check of headspace on your sized brass.

Case head expansion is common to all high-intensity rifle cartridges. What matters is how much expansion occurs and if it continues after the initial firing. Before firing, measure the solid head area of five factory rounds around the circumference and note the high and low measurements. Fire these rounds and measure the heads again. It's not uncommon for factory loads to expand the case head .0002 to .0003 inch (2 or 3/10,000th of an inch). With typical pressures, the case head will stabilize after the first firing and not change much in subsequent loadings. With this knowledge, you can establish a baseline for your wildcat cartridge to track pressure as you work up loads.

As pressure increases, the case head will expand, too, but this is *not* a precise method of measuring pressure. Tests have shown that case head expansion can seem normal, and pressures can be as much as 8,000 PSI higher than the brass indicates. Brass can work harden so this method works best with new, unfired cases for the most reliable results. The bottom line is that measuring case head expansion is better than having no information, but it is not much better. A maximum load is the maximum pressure load that can be shot continuously, not the maximum load the rifle and case can handle.

One writer is using these new tools to test the validity of some of our old stand-by pressure signs, particularly case head expansion (CHE) and pressure ring expansion (PRE). Denton Bramwell wrote several articles for *Precision Shooting* magazine, and in one, used the Pressure Trace system to check pressures on given loads and matched that data to those gathered by looking at CHE and PRE on the same cases.

In the past, there was no economically feasible way to test the hypothesis of CHE and PRE. Ken Waters originated these two processes in his "Developing Pet Loads" column in *Handloader* magazine in September 1982. The basic concept is that you could categorize each load by measuring the amount that a case head or pressure ring expanded in firing. In other words, if you fired a factory load and it expanded the case head .0002 inch, that would be your maximum safe expansion for handloading with the same lot of brass, thus giving you a comparative pressure measurement. To Waters' credit, he made no great claims for this measuring system and offered it as a low-tech way to stay safe, avoiding loads that unnecessarily expand the case head through excessive pressures.

PRE is similar, except you measure the case where the head thins out into the body, where the brass fully expands to match the chamber wall. Here, the brass has limited elasticity and will only spring back so much that if you expand

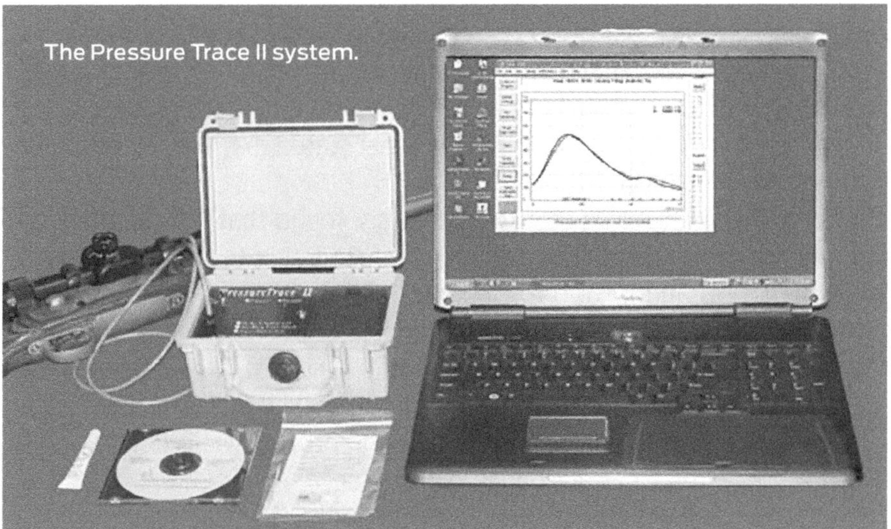

The Pressure Trace II system.

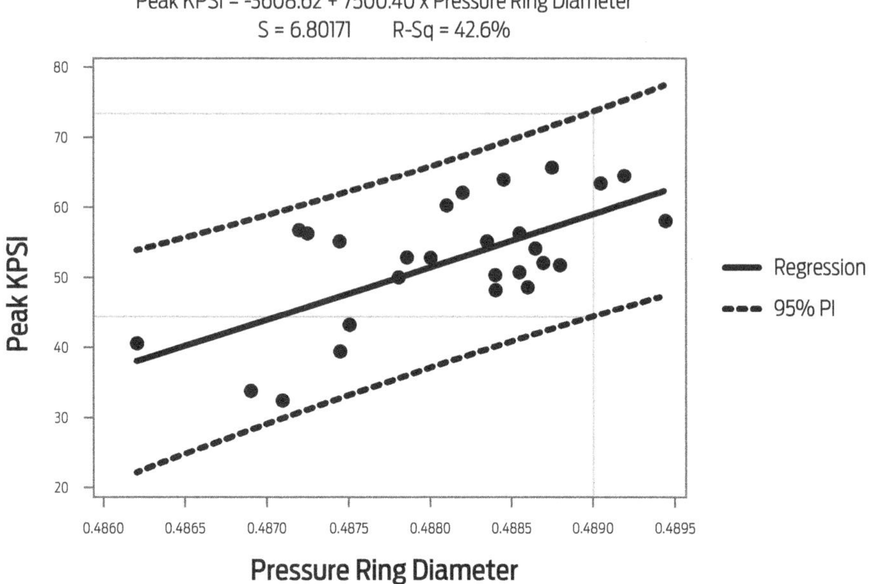

it further, it will end up larger in diameter at the pressure ring after firing.

Industry notables such as Hodgdon Powder support CHE. Hodgdon's *No. 27 Manual* states that a maximum load will produce an expansion of .0005 inch and that any expansion greater than that would indicate excessive pressure.

In *Practical Reloading Manual, 1st Edition*, Nick Harvey's method is to increase loads slowly until he sees .0005 inch expansion, then drop back one grain and test 10 rounds. He calls that his maximum load if none of the 10 rounds exhibit an expansion of .0005 inch. In 1958, when writing for P.O. Ackley's *Handbook for Shooters and Reloaders, Vol. 1,* Vernon Speer stated that "...any measurable expansion was too much."

In short, Bramwell, using statistical analysis, found that CHE and PRE are poor predictors of pressure, particularly if you're trying to tell the difference between 50,000 and 65,000 PSI, as most shooters would like to do. Using the Interclass Correlation Coefficient to compare results, in which a score of 1 is perfect or ideal, he found that PRE scored .359 in his test rifle, which was only slightly better than CHE. This score would indicate that both systems are about halfway to marginal in value. In the following graph, Bramwell compares peak KPSI pressure with case head change in diameter.

The above graph proves Bramwell's point that CHE is unreliable in predicting precise chamber pressure. However, he has unwittingly proven some limited value for the CHE measuring system. You will note that 22 of his test shots fell under 60,000 PSI—that's 78.58%; the remaining six shots in the test fell under 65,000 PSI, the test's upper limit, meaning that more than three-quarters of the time CHE correctly predicted pressures under 60,000 PSI. Then, statistically, 100% of the shots were under 65,000 PSI, and none showed case head expansion of more than .0004 inch, meaning that, barring further testing, you can still say that case head expansion of .0004 inch or less will keep you under 65,000 PSI, at least in the test gun used for Bramwell's test.

This author would suggest that a much larger sampling is required to determine the validity of the above tests. Simply testing one caliber in one rifle does not definitively prove the value of CHE or PRE. As stated earlier, CHE and PRE are better than no information, but not much better. It's only statistics.

As Benjamin Disraeli said, "There are three kinds of lies: lies, damned lies and statistics."

Tools for Measuring Pressure

The PressureTrace II device consists of a control module connected between a strain gauge (which is glued to your barrel) and a PC or laptop. The PC runs software that emulates an oscilloscope and adds analytical information to compare data.

A strain gauge is a small polymer material with a fine conductive grid on its surface. As steel around the barrel expands, the gage is stretched, altering current flow through the grid. The PressureTrace module samples these current fluctuations 300 times per shot, stores them in a memory buffer and automatically downloads the raw data to the PC, where it's analyzed and plotted. Up to 10 shots can be overlaid and compared on screen simultaneously.

The PressureTrace module contains a microprocessor, which reduces or removes noise and senses changes to current flow caused by barrel heating or other factors that would adversely affect the accuracy of measurements. The system has extremely high reliability and is easy to use. Once you've entered each firearm's dimensions and the "gauge factor" (provided with each strain gauge) into the software, plug the module into a firearm, select the gun from a pop-up menu, click "shoot," and it's ready to capture pressure curves. After each shot, a trace will overlay on the PC screen to a total of 10.

PressureTrace generates PSI estimates without calibrating the system to a factory load. Using factory ammo with a known pressure to verify results is always recommended, but RSI recognized that each chamber would produce different pressures, and wildcatters may have nothing for comparison. It uses thick and thin wall open vessel algorithms to provide reasonably accurate pressure estimates from barrel, chamber and brass dimensions. If a barrel is not cylindrical at the chamber (where the gauge is glued), you must calibrate the system against a load of known pressure. This is particularly true of double-barrel shotguns with a strong flare near the locking mechanism, octagonal barrels, etc.

The system can measure two pressure ranges. A standard pressure range setting for centerfire rifles will read from 0 to 80,000 PSI. A high-resolution setting for low-pressure blackpowder calibers and shotguns will read to 20,000 PSI.

No permanent modifications to your guns are required. Strain gauge kits include special glue, cleaning swabs, Teflon strips, instructions and gauge(s) soldered to a connection receptacle and pre-attached to plastic tape. PressureTrace does not require a ground connection to the firearm, so there is no need to ruin the barrel's finish. You can remove gauges with Acetone, leaving no indication the system was ever installed. Recreational Software, Inc., 1343 Navajo Dr., Cottonwood, AZ 86326. *shootingsoftware.com*

Now discontinued, the Oehler Model 43 was the first system available to the average shooter that measured chamber pressure using a small strain gauge glued over the chamber area. The Model 43 kit contained all the items and tools needed to use the system.

There' no need to drill any holes in the barrel, but the bluing will likely be marred where the grounding wire is attached. Measuring the inside and outside diameters at the gauge location provides a realistic pressure scale for the readings. You can reliably compare the pressure generated by your handloads with factory ammunition pressures. You can reliably compare the pressures from different handloads in the same gun. Also, you can measure the pressures generated by wildcats where no standards or factory ammo are available for comparison. The Model 43 is not intended to measure SAAMI pressures. Oehler offers another product, the Model 83, made for SAAMI applications.

The Model 43 can measure several velocity readings on each shot. With a few add-on items, you can measure both muzzle and downrange velocities, and you have two proof channels to go along with the primary readings.

You can use the optional acoustic target if your bullets are supersonic at the target. Special microphones record the bullet's passage, and the system displays the exact hit location, time-of-flight, ballistic coefficient and velocity at the target. The large window of the acoustic target makes it easy to measure actual ballistic coefficients over long ranges. Oehler Research, Inc. *oehler-research.com*

Close Focus Research offers third-party testing. Below is the address to an Excel spreadsheet that will help you mathematically calculate your pressure. This is a free offering from CFR. *closefocusresearch.com/calculating-barrel-pressure-and-projectile-velocity-gun-systems*

With the cost of these pressure-measuring systems less than the average rifle, the excuses for not owning one are getting pretty skinny. But, since relatively few reloaders will invest in pressure test equipment, we all need a reliable system for establishing safe pressure. No system is foolproof, but the most reliable method is simple and cheap. Once you have chosen a load, take five cases and load them with your recipe. Load and fire the five cases six times. If the primer pocket is still as tight as when you started after the sixth load, you have a safe load in your gun. How do we know it's safe? If the primer pocket opens up at any point during the process, that indicates brass flow and excessive pressure. If the pocket remains unchanged, the pressure is low enough that you're not 'proof testing' your gun with each shot.

So, choose the cartridge that best suits your desired velocity level. Don't try to make a .30-06 into a .300 Ultra. Work up an accurate load; velocity should always be secondary to accuracy. Now you know why "There is no free lunch."

CHAPTER 11

Smashing The Headspace Myth! The .400 Whelen

By Michael Petrov

Editor's note: *These articles, republished with permission, originally appeared in* Precision Shooting *magazine's February 2001 and December 2003 issues. They have been edited for stylistic consistency only. Thanks to Michael Petrov for all his research and willingness to share them with the shooting fraternity.*

Major Townsend Whelen was instrumental in the development of a line of cartridges that were based on the .30 Government Model 1906 cartridge case. In this article, I will try to trace the history and development of the Whelen-named cartridges until 1923. Much has been written about the Whelen-named cartridges as well as the many different adaptations of them in the last 80 years. I wish to return to the original source material as much as possible for the history of these cartridges. Much of the contemporary published material, especially on the .400, differs from what my research has turned up.

In the early 1920s, Whelen tested some of the big-bore British bolt guns, and although he was impressed with the power of these rifles, he was unhappy with their accuracy. He believed a rifle could be built in America with a more

WAR PLANS DIVISION

WAR DEPARTMENT
OFFICE OF THE CHIEF OF STAFF
WASHINGTON

August 23, 1919

Fred Adolph, Esq.
Genoa, New York.

Dear Mr. Adolph:

Your letter of the 18th instant relative to the barrels received. When you hear from Zischang please let me know. It is a pretty expensive job getting a new nickel steel barrel from the Winchester Company at the price they now ask ($20.), and then having it rebored for $18. However I now have on hand a .25 caliber Winchester single shot rifle, the barrel of which is getting pitted due to the smokeless primers in the small .25-20 shells. I may want, in the course of a month or so, to have this barrel rebored to .38 caliber with an 18 inch twist, groove diameter about .375, bore diameter about .365-inch. If I decide to do this, and Zischang can do the job, I will send it to him. I do not want this barrel chambered as Neidner will chamber it for me.

In addition to this I am anxious to get a heavy nickel or Krupp steel barrel, about 28 inches long, .38 caliber, bored exactly as above, for fitting to a Springfield action. Neidner and I have been trying to develop a .38 caliber high power Springfield for some time, to use the regular Springfield shell, obtaining the shells before they are necked down, and then necking them down to .38 caliber. This barrel will be chambered with the regular Mann-Neidner chamber, and will use the .38-275 Winchester soft point jacketed bullet slightly altered in form in a swedge. This will make a most excellent big game rifle. Now I imagine that we will have to go to Germany for such barrels, so as soon as you find out anything about getting barrels from Germany please let me know and I will take the matter up with you and let you know exactly what is wanted.

There is a market at present for reloading tools, particularly for tools for the .30-1906 cartridge, and for a press and resizing die which will resize .30-1906 shells once fired to standard size. This is just a suggestion.

Very sincerely,

Townsend Whelen.

How the prices have gone up! Winchester are now charging $60 for a .22 Single Shot rifle that they used to sell for $15.!

powerful cartridge than what was on the market following the First World War. At the same time, he wanted to use the 1903 Springfield and the standard-length Mauser action without going to the expense of using the larger and more expensive Magnum-length actions. His first experimental work on these was before either of the two big gun companies had introduced a bolt-action in .30-06 caliber (Remington M-30 1921 & Winchester M-54 1923). From 1923 to 1925, Griffin & Howe only offered its proprietary Whelen cartridges as its largest caliber rifles and not any of the English cartridges such as the .375 H&H. A .375

H&H bolt-action rifle From Holland & Holland would have set a sportsman back $400 in 1922.

.38 Whelen (.375 Whelen)

The first reference I can find that discusses the idea of necking up the .30-06 case is in a letter from Townsend Whelen to the gunmaker Fred Adolph of New York dated August 23, 1919. Whelen is trying to get a barrel for the .38 Whelen cartridge that he and Adolph O. Niedner are working on. The .38 Whelen is the .30-06 necked up to use the Winchester 275-grain .38-72 WCF bullet re-formed with a spire point.

In the January 1923 *American Rifleman*, Whelen is sending people to Niedner at Dowagiac, Michigan, because Niedner is now making the .38 Whelen. By April 1 of 1923, Whelen announces that Winchester is stopping the production of the 275-grain .38-72 WCF bullets and suggests that no more .38 Whelens be made. I am not sure if any of these rifles survived the last 80 years, but it's not because I have not looked for them. This cartridge was reintroduced in the 1950s and named the .375 Whelen. I have often wondered what the outcome of the .35 & .400 Whelen would have been if there had been a supply of good .375-inch bullets back in 1923.

.400 Whelen

The first notice I find of the .400 Whelen is in *Arms And The Man* on June 15, 1922, where Whelen tells about his work on this cartridge. The .400 Whelen is the .30-06 cylindrical case necked down to take the .405 Winchester 300-gr. .411-inch diameter round-nose bullet. Four test rifles were being made up, two on the 1903 Springfield and two on the Mauser action. Whelen estimates the velocity of the 300-gr. bullets at 2,350–2,600 fps. These test rifles, as well as the loading tools, were made by James V. Howe then of Philadelphia, Pennsylvania. The barrels were made and installed by A.O. Niedner in Dowagiac, Michigan. By November 15, 1922, Whelen was offering a circular by mail with information on the .400.

I cannot think of another cartridge with as bad a reputation as the .400 Whelen. From *Cartridges of the World, 6th Edition,* "The .400 Whelen was not a very successful development because when the .30-06 case neck is expanded to this size, it leaves only a very slight shoulder, and this gives rise to serious headspace problems." I have also read several reports of the firing pin driving the case forward over the shoulder.

I am not going to list all the negative things I have read about the .400, or

Cartridge	Weight of Bullet grs.	Muzzle Velocity f.s.	Muzzle Energy ft. lbs.	Trajectory 200 yards Height at 100 yds.
25 Special H. P....	86	3300	2080	1.7"
25 Special H. P....	100	3000	1998	1.9
35 Whelen.......	200	2835	3570	2.5
35 Whelen.......	250	2635	3855	3.0
400 Whelen......	300	2425	3918	3.5

there would be room for little else. As I began to collect information, there were two distinct schools of thought on the .400; one was by people who used the .400 and thought it was a fine cartridge; the other was by those who did not, telling you how bad it was. The first praise I read for the .400 was by (and it should be no surprise to the readers) Elmer Keith. A quote from *Big Game Rifles* by Elmer Keith, Samworth 1935. "I have used this rifle over a period of 11 years and have a lot of respect for it."

"Much criticism has been passed on this rifle and cartridge, some claiming that the front shoulder of the case was insufficient to hold its headspace against the blow of the firing pin. Such is not the case, and that forward shoulder is ample in correctly chambered rifles and used with correctly necked cases."

The biggest challenge I faced in learning about the .400 was to find and record chamber dimensions of the older original rifles. Although it was not a popular cartridge, there have been several .400s made over the last 78 years.

Most of the problems with this cartridge I have been able to trace to one factor. The .30-06, .25 Whelen (.25-06), .35 Whelen and .38 Whelen all have a shoulder diameter of .441. "The ORIGINAL .400 Whelen shoulder is .458 inch." When and how this information got lost to modern riflemen and writers, I have no idea. Many .400s that were made in later years for which I have measurements have the .441-inch shoulder; this is also true of many resizing dies.

I have wanted a .400 Whelen rifle for some time, and my search for an early .400 Whelen has not been easy. The rifles I found either had been modified, or the price was well out of my reach. Which brings up a good point. *If these things are no good, why are they so expensive?*

By the time I had resigned myself to the fact that I might never find what I was looking for, a chain of events began that you only dream about as a collector. Not only was I able to acquire what I believe to be the second .400 Whelen Made by Griffin & Howe in its first year (1923), it showed up unfired with a box of G&H cartridges. These early G&Hs had blued bolts, and there was not so much as a brass rub mark on the bolt face. The icing on the cake was when friends Mark Benenson and Russell Gilmore of The Rifled Arms Historical Association sent me Townsend Whelen's case-forming and loading tools for his .400 to use and take measurements from. These early loading dies are sometimes mistakenly referred to as "Pound Dies." Nothing could be further from the truth. They are not meant to be hit with anything but instead are to be used in an arbor press. The way Whelen made the cases for the .400 was to neck down cylindrical

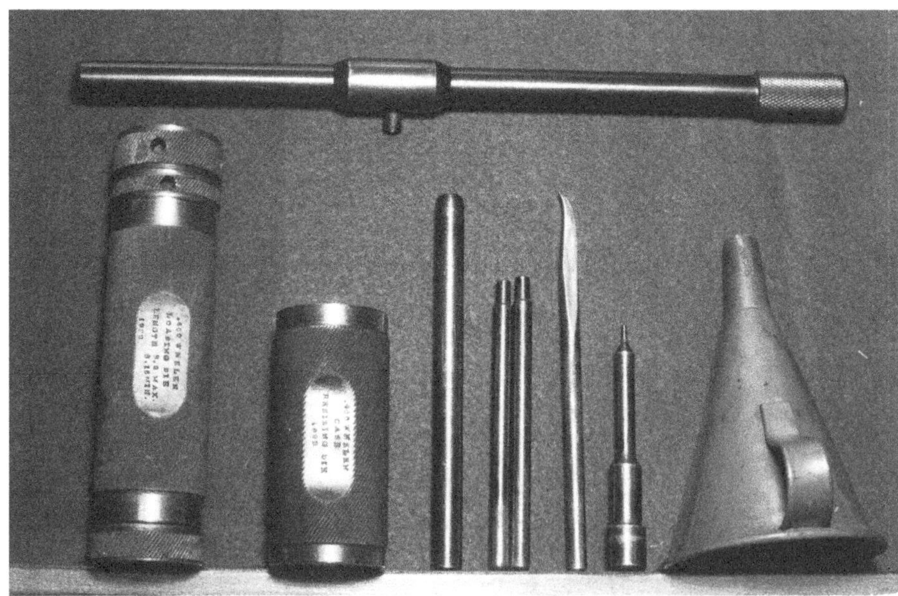

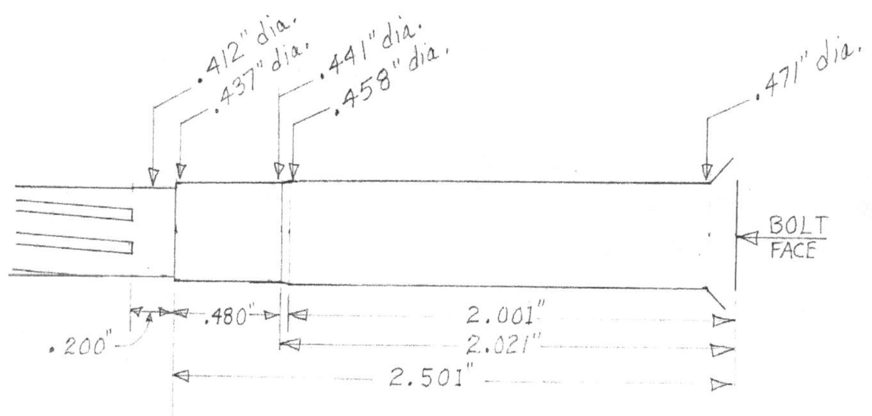

brass, and I was going to do it the same way. Today, there are several sources of cylindrical brass.

With gun and loading tools at hand but impatient while waiting for brass, I made a die for my lathe to hold annealed .35 Whelen brass. Using a tool that looked like a boring bar with a rounded side, I ironed some cases out straight. Using feeler gauges with Whelen's die, I found that when the case was .006 inch from bottoming out, I could not force the bolt home on an empty case. At .005 inch, I could get the bolt closed with resistance. *No way is a firing pin going to drive this case forward.*

I then trimmed the cases to a length of 2.470 inches. When you are using cylindrical brass, they are full size out of the die, and fireforming is not needed. I dumped in some IMR 3031 topped with a 300-gr. DKT round-nose bullet. I also loaded a few with the last of my supply of Barnes originals (the ones they no longer make) that shot so well in my .400 Niedner. As luck would have it, the Barnes originals worked much better than the DKTs, but in all fairness to DKT, I have yet to try its spitzer bullets. A local store did have some of the Barnes X-Bullets .411-inch diameter in 300 gr. so I gave them a try only to shoot a 5-inch group at 50 yards with them. If I had spent some time doing research on the X-bullets, I would have known that they work best when seated .050 inch off the lands. New loads and back to the range with the X's; results are

From left to right: Frankford Arsenal 1918, G&H .35 Whelen, .38-72 Winchester, .38 Whelen, .405 Winchester, G&H .400 Whelen, .30-06 cylindrical, .400 Whelen sized and .400 Whelen loaded.

close to MOA.

The loaner dies of Colonel Whelen's were perfect for the rifle, and everything worked great. Dreading the day that I would have to return the dies, I put out the word that I was looking for a set of .400 Whelen dies. A set was located, and when I received them, I resized a case only to find the dies had reduced the shoulder diameter back to .437 inch. After sending a Cerrosafe cast of the Whelen's dies and two fired cases to RCBS, I received a set of dies made perfectly for this rifle. If you have a .400 *anything*, I suggest that a chamber cast is in order and that .30-06 brass with the .441-inch shoulder never be used to fireform brass.

In one case, a person I was corresponding with was having all the problems that I have ever read about with his .400. It turned out he has the original .458-inch shoulder-chambered rifle, but his set of dies was for the '06 shoulder. (Update 10-2000; I just got off the phone with the owner of an early G&H .400 Whelen, who is having this exact problem. A quick check of a resized case showed the dies put it back to '06 size.)

How did all this get so mixed up over the passing of time? Did no one ever take the time to measure an early .400 Whelen? One bit of information I have looked for in the early articles written by Whelen was his telling about the larger .458-inch diameter shoulder. So far, I have not found it. Whelen did suggest that only G&H, Hoffman, and Niedner make the .400 Whelen, so maybe this was their trade secret. I have cataloged pre-1940 sporters in caliber .400 Whelen made by Griffin & Howe, Fred Adolph, Niedner, Hoffman Arms Co. and Krieghoff of Suhl, Germany. Because of all the bad press, many of these rifles have been rebarreled or modified in some way. An early engraved G&H I know of was rechambered to a belted magnum case so it would have the belt to headspace on.

With the proper chamber and loading dies to match, my rifle has performed flawlessly and is a tribute to Townsend Whelen, James V. Howe and the gunmakers of Griffin & Howe.

.400 Whelen Part 2

It was naive of me to think that I could write an article (*PS* February 2001) for a magazine called *Precision Shooting* about a rifle and cartridge and not publish loading information. I received enough inquiries about chamber dimensions and loading data that I had to do something. The fact was I wanted to play with this cartridge in a rifle that had a scope; what I did not want to do was modify my little-used Griffin & Howe rifle, so I built a new one.

For this project, I chose a pre-64 Model 70 Winchester (1951) action and my favorite classic scope, the Lyman Alaskan. This scope was introduced in 1937. It is a 2½-power scope made with Bausch & Lomb lens, has a 5-inch eye relief and is perfect for the .400 Whelen. Why this scope was ever discontinued is beyond me. In my opinion, this scope will work fine for 90% of all Alaskan hunting. Plus, I think having the windage adjustment in the scope is a handy addition. To explain that, I will say most of my classic custom rifles have the windage adjustment in the mount, and this is the most modern rifle and scope combination I own.

In building the new

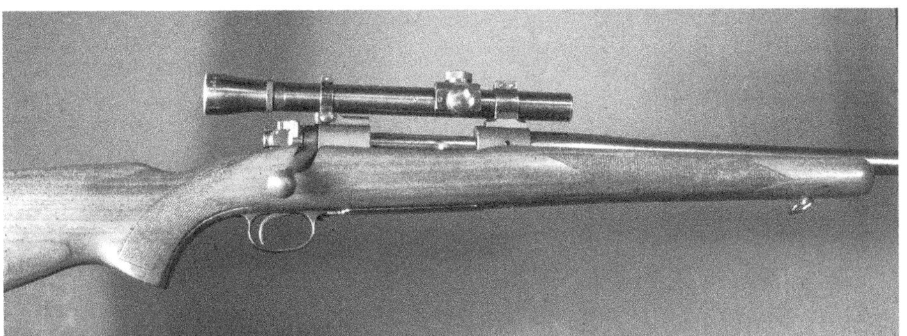

Top; Winchester 70 with Lyman 48 Peep. Middle: Model 70 with Lyman Alaskan scope. Bottom: Husqvarna custom belonging to Bob Zywna, stocked by David Christman Jr., all .400 Whelen.

rifle, my objective was to duplicate as nearly as possible the original Griffin & Howe rifle. The G&H has a 24-inch barrel, 1:14-inch twist and .411-inch groove diameter. There was no question but that I wanted my friend and gunsmith John Wills to do the work. John is one of the most careful workmen I know, and everything by him is done right. Word spread fast about the new project, and two friends, Dennis P. & Bob Z., wanted a .400 Whelen built as well.

I was delighted to learn that Winchester was reintroducing the .405 Winchester and that Hornady was to make the ammunition as well as the bullets for reloading. I saw my first Hornady bullets made for the .405 at the Shot Show in Las Vegas in 2002 and was relieved to learn that they were .411 inch in diameter and 300 grains like the originals. What I was not ready for was that they made them with a flat nose. The original bullets had a round nose. The Winchester Model 95 has a box magazine, so there is no need for a flat nose. No one at the Hornady Shot Show booth could tell me why they had a flat nose. In a reply to a follow-up letter to Hornady, I was told that the final decision was made by Mr. Hornady with no reason given for the flat nose.

I was surprised at the number of barrel makers who either did not know or had a different idea of what a barrel for the .405 Winchester should be. The original barrels were .411 groove diameter with a 1:14-inch twist. Luck was on our side because of a call to Shilen, Inc. Not only do they make a textbook barrel as far as dimensions, they had three on hand. My barrel also had to be chrome-moly, I could not justify a custom stock, but it would be rust-blued with real wood.

Before we ordered a chambering reamer, it was decided that we would have everything on hand, such as the barrel, bullets and brass we were going to use. Bob ordered basic brass from Quality Cartridge (PO Box 445, Hollywood, MD 20636) with the .400 Whelen headstamp. I believe this is the first batch in the 80-year history of the .400 Whelen to have the Whelen headstamp. When the brass arrived, I necked some down, and trimmed them to length and made several .400 Whelen rounds we could measure. From the loaded ammo and using the measurements from several original .400 Whelen rifles, the new reamer was drawn up. The chambering reamer was then ordered from Dave Kiff at Pacific Tool. The chamber was cut for a case with an overall length of 2.501 inches. I adjusted the neck-forming die until the bolt would just close on a case and trimmed it to an OAL of 2.495 inches.

I was determined to do everything by the book, and that included following the break-in instructions that came with the barrel. Most of my sporting rifles are 50 to 80 years old, and breaking in a barrel was new to me. The new and rebarreled guns I have worked with have all been lead bullet guns where breaking in is not needed. The sheet called for cleaning the barrel after every shot for the first five shots, then cleaning for the next 50 shots after every five shots. "Cleaning the barrel" means using a bronze brush saturated with solvent, making 20 passes through the bore, letting it soak for 10 minutes, then saturate the brush for 20 more passes, finishing up by pushing three patches through the barrel to clean it.

I got the original loading data for the .400 Whelen from a *Dupont IMR 3031 pamphlet*, a Griffin & Howe box of loaded ammo, and Philip B. Sharpe's *Complete Guide to Handloading,* all listed 61 grains of 3031, a 300-grain Winchester or WT&C bullet for 2,300 fps out of a 26-inch barrel.

The first go 'round, I loaded 58 grains of 3031 and a Hornady 300-grain bullet. Shooting at 50 yards, I was amazed to see the very first bullet print, then the next four print lower into a .320-inch group. I adjusted the scope and got ready for the next 50 rounds of barrel break-in. The brass was well formed, and I had no problems other than recoil. I was glad that my project was not a .505 Gibbs. During break-in, I tried a couple of different powders, but from what I could see at 50 yards, 3031 was doing a fine job. H4895 held a lot of promise, and I'm sure

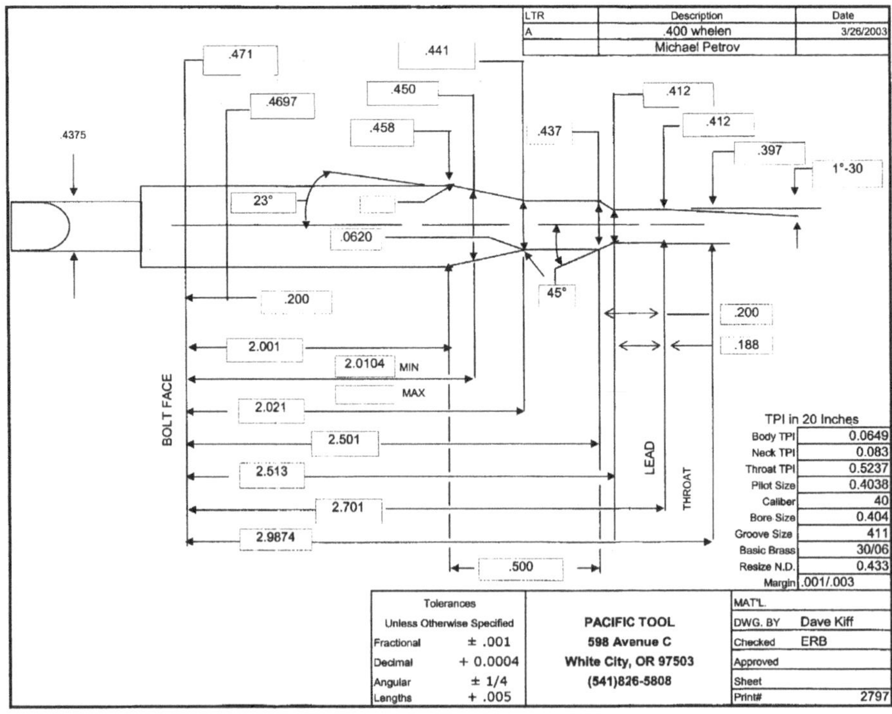

if I had worked with it more, I could have improved velocity.

My intent was to work with the reported velocities circa 1920s. I had no intention of ringing the last fps out of this cartridge. This is a fine cartridge with a 300-grain bullet at 2,260–2,360 fps. Besides, I am only shooting at paper bears. If I were to need more, I could grab my .400 Niedner, which shoots the same bullet at 2,700 fps. I had located a small supply of original Winchester bullets that I loaded to the same specs as G&H used; five shots at 100 yards into a 1.650-inch group. If I had a larger supply of these bullets and worked with OAL, I'm sure I could have improved on this. I used the RCBS full-length sizing die for sizing down the neck the first time on new brass. After that, I necked sized only.

It was apparent right from the start that this rifle likes a cold, clean barrel and Hornady bullets. With the barrel and me both broke in, it was time to move to 100 yards. The problem with the Lyman Alaskan 2½ power scope at 100 yards is that the cross wire was so big that it covered up the X-Ring of a standard 100-yard target. I had to use 200-yard targets to be able to see some white around the crosswire. Now was the time to try some different bullets. I decided right off that three-shot groups should be sufficient for a big-bore hunting rifle. I also was worried that I would develop a flinch, so I wanted to streamline the bench time as much as possible. My shooting friends did comment that they could not decide which was worse, the report of the .400 Whelen or my whining about the recoil.

Both Dennis and I used pre-64 Model 70 actions originally chambered for the .30-06. Once the actions were barreled and chambered, Dennis worked over my original model 70 stock. The barrel channel was relieved and floated approximately .030–.035 back to the "bell" on the barrel. A channel was milled in the wood directly behind the recoil lug on the receiver to receive a quarter-inch threaded rod. A slot was also milled in the stock directly in front of the trigger slot. A threaded rod was also placed therein. This was done for reinforcement; Micro-bed was used for bedding compound. The milled slots were filled with compound, and a small amount of it was placed in the recoil lug slot, under the bell of the barrel, behind the magazine well and the tang area of the stock.

The underside of the rails had to be opened up slightly for the spire-pointed bullets to feed properly, but the Hornadys would come off the left rail and hit the extractor cut in the barrel. This was not a problem for me because the Hornadys are fine for barrel breaking-in and paper punching, but with that blunt nose, I would always be worried about a failure to feed. Dennis, on the other hand, wanted to shoot them, so John worked on both the rails, feed ramp and

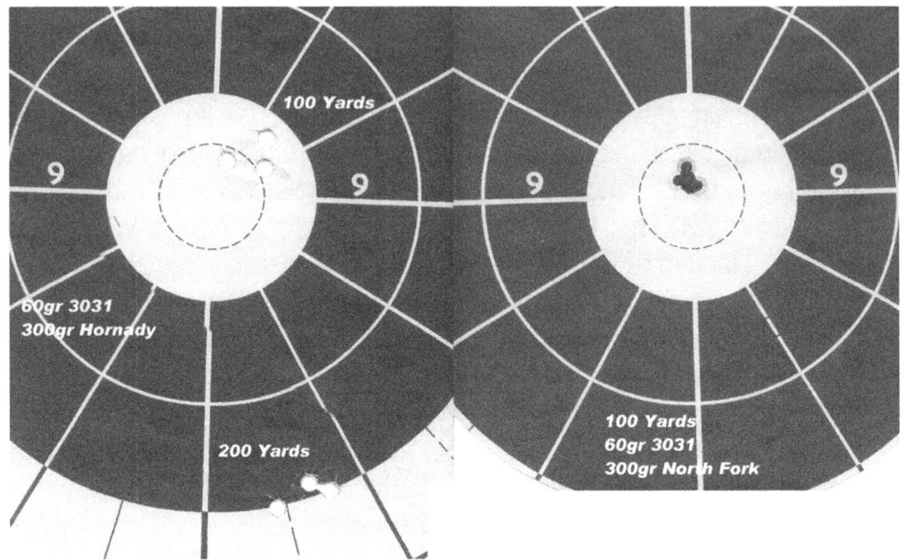

the extractor cut until they would feed reliably in his rifle. Bob's rifle was made on a Husqvarna action, and only a little work was needed for proper feeding.

I belong to an older school that believed a hunting rifle equipped with a telescope should have a precision adjustable rear sight as well. In Alaska, like other places, it can be a long way to the local gunsmith if your scope is broken or damaged. I removed the scope and mounted a Lyman 48, which I then zeroed for this rifle. I can remove the scope, replace the receiver sight slide and be right on target.

After I removed the rear sight and remounted the scope, I headed back to the range to re-zero the scope. For this, I used some of the Hornady bullets and also loaded three cases with the North Fork bullets. I knew the rifle liked a clean, cold bore. I wanted to try a three-shot group using North Fork bullets with the rifle fouled and the barrel warm. Keeping in mind that the largest group to date (see chart) at 100 yards with NF bullets was .848 inch. After firing several Hornadys, the barrel was fouled and warm. I fully expected to see something around an inch or more. Much to my surprise, after firing three shots with North Fork bullets, all I could see with the 2½ power scope was one black hole that turned out to be a .325-inch group.

WARNING! *This load data is for Petrov's Winchester Model 70 only! There are so many incorrectly chambered .400 Whelen rifles or dies that reduce the shoulder diameter you need to make sure what you have before you proceed.*

.400 Whelen 24-inch Barrel

BULLET	BULLET WEIGHT (GRS.)	POWDER	POWDER WEIGHT (GR.)	AVERAGE VELOCITY (FPS)	YARDS	THREE-SHOT GROUP (IN.)	FIVE-SHOT GROUP (IN.)	NOTES
Hornady	300	IMR 3031	60	2,260	100		1.100	
Hornady	300	IMR 3031	60	2,260	200	1.080		
Hornady	300	IMR 3031	60	2,260	100	0.880		
Hornady	300	IMR 3031	60	2,260	100	0.855		
Hornady	300	IMR 3031	60	2,260	100	0.415		
Hornady	300	IMR 3031	61	2,312				
Hornady	300	IMR 3031	62	2,337				
Winchester	300	IMR 3031	61	2,260	100		1.650	
Hawk	300	IMR 3031	60	2,210	100	0.960	1.700	
Barnes X	300	IMR 3031	56	2,040				
North Fork	300	IMR 3031	60	2,385	100	0.400		Cold, clean barrel
North Fork	300	IMR 3031	60	2,385	100	0.482		22° F
North Fork	300	IMR 3031	60	2,385	100	0.618		22° F
North Fork	300	IMR 3031	60	2,385	100	0.848		15° F
Hornady	300	H4895	60	2,543	100	1.145		22° F
Hornady	300	IMR 3031	60	2,282	100	0.971		15° F
Hornady	300	H4895	61		50	0.410		
North Fork	300	H4895	61		50	0.341		Best accuracy
North Fork	300	IMR 3031	60	2,362	100	0.325		50° F dirty barrel

Townsend Whelen wrote in *Wilderness Hunting & Wildcraft* (1927), "Confidence. A big-game hunter should have that confidence with his rifle, which comes only through perfect familiarity with it." I can say that I have owned few hunting rifles that I have felt as confident with as I am with this one. It has turned out to be one of the most accurate big-bore rifles I have worked with. It's rewarding to see the first bullet out of a cold and clean barrel go exactly where I place the crosswire. I have a lot of respect for the work of Townsend Whelen. I believe he helped the advancement of the American sporting rifle more than any other single person. The .400 Whelen has, for many years, been a dark cloud over his name. I hope these two articles have let in a little light.

CHAPTER 12

Reamers

If your buddy asked you if he could store his RV in your one-car garage, the response would be, "No way, it'll never fit!" The same applies when using 'finish' chamber reamers to make reloading dies. Think of the chamber reamer as a bus and the die as a one-car garage; you will understand how well they go together.

Where did this concept come from? It is probably from bullet seating dies and writers who have never made a reloading die. You can use a chamber reamer to make the bullet seating die because the case is already sized and can slip into the seating die. The close dimensions align the bullet to the case's mouth and neck. You can also make bushing-type neck-sizing dies utilizing the chamber reamer, but this is a newer concept and is not the reason for the confusion.

You cannot use a finish chamber reamer to make resizing dies. The idea that chamber reamers will work for reaming resize dies has taken hold and will not die. By their very nature, chamber reamers are larger in diameter than the ammunition. This is done for two sound mechanical reasons: First, so the ammo will feed into the chamber smoothly; second, when the brass expands under pressure, it will have enough room to shrink back. Even though brass is soft and thin, it still has some spring and will spring back from the full chamber dimension just enough so extraction is possible.

If you have a roughing reamer for your chamber, it might be suitable for cutting a resize die. More often, however, the wildcatter will order a separate reamer called a resize reamer. The resize reamer is ground to a smaller diameter along its entire length. This reduced dimension is what does the resizing.

Resize reamers are best ordered from the same reamer maker who provided your finish chamber reamer. Most reamer makers will produce one upon

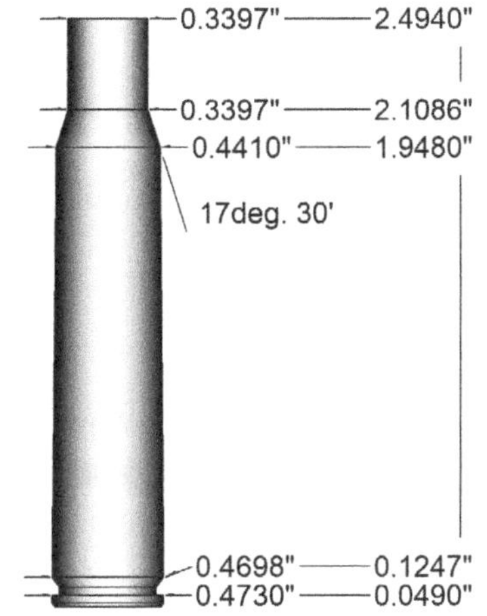

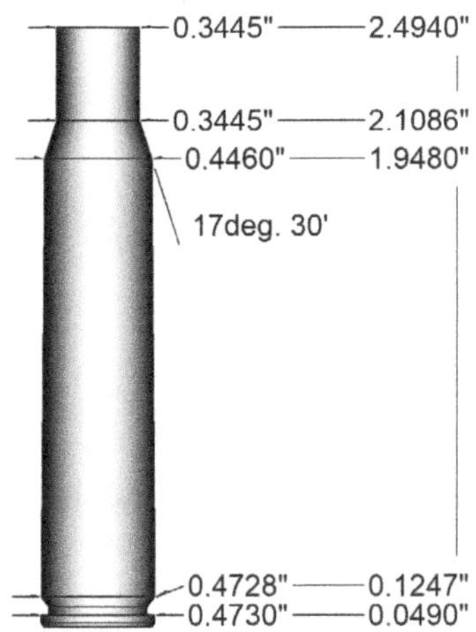

Ammo (left) vs. chamber (right) dimensions.

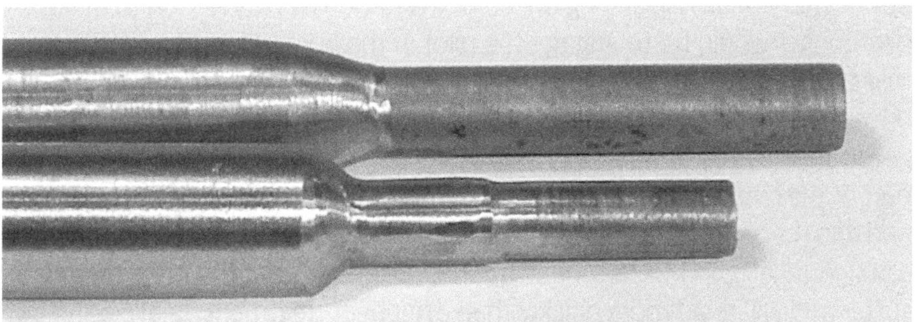

Cannon reamer pilots.

request for any available chamber drawing. Experience taught this author to ask questions about the resize dimensions the maker will use. Often, the neck is left too large, resulting in too little resizing of the brass, and the bullet will not have sufficient tension to remain stationary in the case. On average, the neck must be ground .007 inch smaller than the chamber dimension, providing enough resizing so the bullet will have reliable, even tension when seated (vital to good accuracy).

You can also make a "cannon" reamer for special one-time chambers or dies to try out your ideas. If they work, investing in a good finish reamer is justified.

You make cannon reamers by turning a blank out of tool steel on a lathe to the exact dimensions you need for the chamber or dies (an oil-hardening drill rod works well and costs very little). Once the blank is finished, set it up on a mill and cut away exactly half of it, leaving the pilot and the drive stem full diameter.

The relief grind below the cutting edge.

Cutting away half the blank creates a single cutting edge. If you cut away more than half the diameter of the blank, the reamer will be too aggressive and bite into the metal, cutting an oversized chamber. If you cut away less than half, it will not cut well, if at all. The tolerance is pretty broad; you can be plus or minus .010 inch either side of half, and it will cut just fine.

A pilot and drive shank are necessary for a working reamer. The pilot should not be more than ½ inch long ahead of the neck. The only reason to make the pilot longer would be to engage the pilot in the bore before the cutting edge makes contact with the barrel or die blank when the chamber is pre-drilled. The drive shank could be any length, but more than 1 inch may promote warping.

You should relief grind all but the cutting edge for the remaining blank. If any part of the reamer other than the cutting edge touches the chamber, it will gall and ruin the chamber or die. The most straightforward procedure is to perform a rough relief grind before heat treating the metal because the material is softer and will grind more quickly than after heat treatment. Leave 1/16th inch below the cutting edge untouched.

Follow the heat treat instructions for your reamer blank material. Choose the material that best suits the tools you have on hand. Again, oil-hardening a drill rod produces a good reamer; it's suggested for shops without a heat-treat oven. Keeping an even heat in the blank is critical to avoid warping it. Wire up the part so that you can use a rosebud tip to apply heat; the container of heat treat oil should be deep enough so the blank doesn't touch the bottom when fully submerged. Plunge the reamer end into the oil; do not swing the reamer back and forth in the oil, as this promotes warping. Submerge the blank quickly so that it's covered. Don't continually lift and plunge the reamer to cool it; keep it in the oil.

If you have a heat treat oven available, it is much easier to avoid warping. An oven also allows for choosing other materials, such as air-hardening tool steel. As previously mentioned, make every effort to avoid warping your reamer blank.

Relief grind on cutting face of cannon reamer.

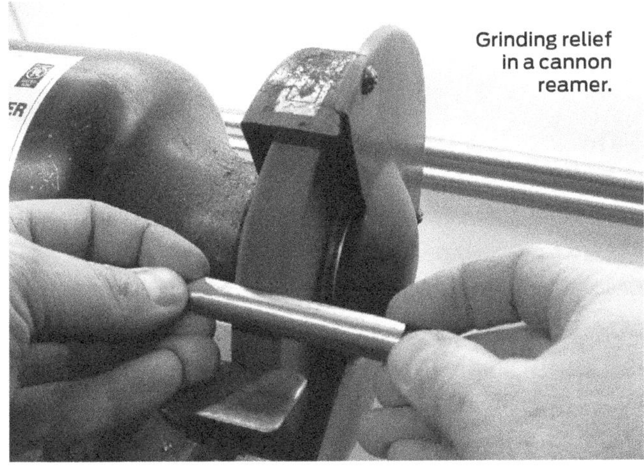
Grinding relief in a cannon reamer.

Once heat-treated, you're ready to finish grind your reamer. Start by going over your relief grind, being careful not to damage the cutting edge. Remember, you only have one. There are two ways to "point up" the cutting edge. The first is to hollow grind the entire flat of the reamer on a bench grinder. This works well, but it can take a fair amount of time to work the entire flat. The second method uses a die grinder to work along the cutting edge.

Now that the entire reamer is relief ground and the cutting edge is pointed up, you can sharpen the reamer. Hand stoning is the best sharpening method. I use diamond laps in my shop. They're available in three different grits—course, medium and fine. Medium and fine are all that you will need for this project. Start with the medium lap and, working from the relief grind toward the cutting edge, relieve the material up to the cutting edge, leaving just a few thousandths of an inch at the edge to finish with the fine lap. The idea is to taper that 1/16th inch edge away from the cutting edge on the relief side that was left untouched.

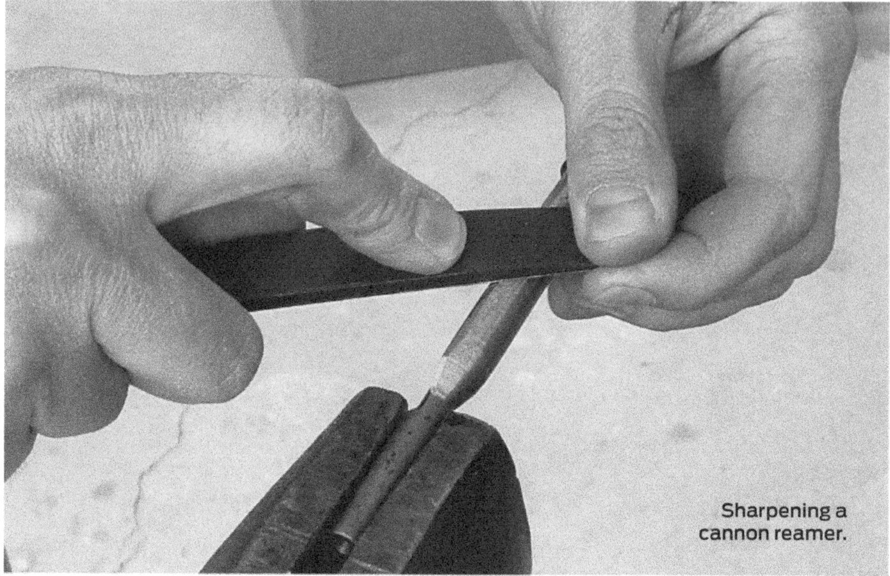

Sharpening a cannon reamer.

The first time you make a cannon reamer, you should create a dummy chamber or die to test your reamer in. Use the same material for the dummy that you'll use in your barrel or die so you know how the reamer cuts. The going will be slow; you only have one cutting edge as opposed to the six or so flutes on a typical reamer. Pre-drill the chamber or die in the body area so that the cannon reamer cleans up the chamber area. Leave about .050 inch for the reamer to clean up at the shoulder.

Chamber Reamer Dimensional Considerations

For the pilot diameter, think ahead and measure the barrel's bore. You want the pilot to ride on the barrel's lands (the smaller of the two diameters if you slug your bore and measure the lands and grooves).

If the corner is left sharp, it can cut the brass. For instance, if the neck and shoulder junction is left sharp, you can cut the neck off the case when you fire it.

Resize Reamers

For dies, the simplest method is to make the pilot the exact diameter you want your neck. Then, use a decimal reamer to create a pilot hole of the correct diameter. This has two advantages: It simplifies the cannon reamer's design and makes the pilot as large as possible, preventing warpage during heat treatment.

As mentioned, the neck diameter should be .007 inch smaller than the matching chamber. This will allow you to size the brass minimally but ensure sufficient tension to hold the projectile. (More than .007 inch will unnecessarily work the brass. Less will likely result in insufficient tension on the bullet.) Variances in brass thickness typically fall within the margin set by sizing the brass down .007 inch at the neck.

The diameter at the shoulder should be .003 inch smaller than the chamber. For the best accuracy, the base diameter should be only .002 inch smaller than the chamber. By keeping the base diameter close to the chamber diameter, the case is held closer to the center with less slop, which enhances accuracy. But you have to resize a little, or eventually, the bolt will become hard to close, interfering with smooth feeding and function.

The corners must have a slight radius where the shoulder angle meets the case body and the neck. The radius eases the forming of brass and prevents the corners from becoming weak points in the case. If a corner is left sharp, it will scrape the brass; the neck will try to curl around the corner like a ribbon pulled over a sharp edge. On top of that, the neck will be scraped, leaving it looking poor and building up brass in the die. The radius needs to be only slight, but it is essential.

Shoulder angles greater than 20 degrees are more difficult to form, and above 30 degrees are even more challenging. Trial and error will be a good teacher, but if you have a case requiring several form dies, use a shoulder angle in the form dies of 20 degrees or less. When this is done, the shoulder/body junction point should be maintained so that the finished headspace will be correct. Then, finish off the neck with the full-length size die.

Headspace in a reloading die is different from that of a rifle in one way. The headspace gauge should protrude from the base of the die .130 inch. The shell holder is .125 inch. The additional .005 inch is necessary to allow proper adjustment of the die to set the correct headspace for your chamber. Between the spring in the loading press and the spring of the brass, shoulder movement demands that extra .005 inch.

Below are comments from Dave Manson on the subject of "Dimensioning Chambers for Wildcat Cartridges." You will note that some of Manson's dimensions are different than those above; this shows that more than one method will work, and some dimensions are less critical than others.

When designing a wildcat, most shooters think in terms of cartridge dimensions. This makes sense—our reloading manuals and most magazine articles about wildcats or standard calibers show representative or maximum cartridge dimensions. Sooner or later, though, that wildcat cartridge you've designed will have to fit in a compatible chamber.

Knowing cartridge dimensions, how do we arrive at dimensions for the chamber in which that cartridge will be fired?

Before we can answer this question, more information is needed. First and foremost is the intended use of the wildcat: is the shooter a benchrest competitor, interested in shooting bug holes at 100 yards, or will they be engaging dangerous game at pucker-factor distances? Chamber dimension requirements in these two examples are quite different.

In the first instance, the chamber should fit the ammunition closely, often with the bullet hard into the rifling, to squeeze the last bit of accuracy from the rifle. The shooter wouldn't be too concerned with the possibility of dirt entering the chamber because they'd shoot the rifle in a controlled environment and clean it often.

A chamber designed for the second example wouldn't be fitted nearly so close to the dimensions of the ammunition. Optimizing reliability—so the rifle goes bang every time something is charging the shooter—is much more important than realizing the ultimate accuracy potential of the gun. When designing a chamber for this application, the wildcatter would also have to be concerned with large variations in temperature and the likelihood of dirt and other foreign matter entering the action and chamber because of the gun's use in less-than-clean conditions.

These examples represent two extremes in which wildcat cartridges might be used; you may want to build a rifle for one of these uses or some purpose that falls in between.

Wildcatting is not limited to creating new or "improved" cartridges. Often, a shooter will not be satisfied with the way factory ammunition fits a factory chamber. This is not unusual because SAAMI tolerances allow a possible clearance between the cartridge and chamber of as much as .011 inch. This doesn't occur all the time, but often enough that many veteran shooters have grown tired of seeing a bulge in their fired cases just ahead of the extractor groove and want to "tighten up" their chamber to reduce or eliminate it. Others may find that their necks expand excessively or want to turn cartridge necks for better accuracy and would like a chamber with a smaller-than-standard neck. Still, other shooters may use VLD (very low drag) bullets for long-distance shooting and need the throat brought back closer to the loaded round. A modified, standard-dimensioned chamber would likely meet the shooter's requirements in such cases.

This is where we come in. Based on your requirements and the dimensions of your cartridge, we'll draw on our experience to design a chamber reamer that will cut the chamber you need to meet those requirements. It's not rocket science, but it does require that we listen carefully to what you want to accomplish.

On a wildcat project, we'll usually ask you to send us a dummy round exactly as you wish to shoot it, from which we can take measurements. The dummy should be prepared so that all external dimensions are exactly as they will be when the gun is shot. Necks should be turned to the desired thickness, cases trimmed to the proper length, and the bullet seated to the desired depth. Place the bullet wherever you'd like it to be—you don't have to worry about it having too much freebore because the reamer we'll make for you will cut the throat to give the desired bullet-to-rifling relationship. If you want the bullet hard against the rifling, we can do that; if you want a .050-inch jump, we can do that as well.

Reaming primer pockets or deburring the flash hole in the dummy isn't necessary since these operations don't affect the cartridge's external dimensions. On "improved" wildcats or those requiring fireforming, the shoulder and body won't be fully formed, so you'll have to tell us what you want their final dimensions to be. We'll allow for this and will also allow for the length shrinkage that occurs during fireforming.

On any wildcat project involving a new chamber, unfired brass should be used. Don't try to save money by using old brass that has taken a set in a chamber cut to different dimensions. Buy enough brass from a single lot to last as long as you intend to shoot the gun. Take sample measurements from at least 10% of the brass, and then make the dummy you send us from the case with the largest base diameter.

Getting down to specifics, for a benchrest chamber, unless requested to do otherwise, we would make the chamber reamer larger than the dummy by the following amounts:

- *Base diameter: +.002 in.*
- *Shoulder diameter: +.003 in.*
- *Neck diameter: +.002 in.*
- *Base-to-shoulder length: +.001 in.*
- *Overall case length: +.010 in.*
- *Throat configuration: .0003 in. larger than the bullet, the leade angle to match the ogive and the location of leade angle to result in the bullet seated against rifling when chambered.*

I have seen benchrest comments on neck diameter that referred to the dimensions as near zero dimensions, meaning the tolerances are held so close that the cases hardly need any sizing. That would be tighter tolerances than those mentioned above.

A dangerous game chamber would be considerably more open:

- *Base diameter: +.005 in.*
- *Shoulder diameter: +.008 in.*
- *Neck diameter: +.005 in.*
- *Base-to-shoulder length: +.005 in.*
- *Overall case length: +.020 in.*
- *Throat configuration: +.001 in. larger than the bullet, the lead angle to match the ogive, and the location of the leade to result in the bullet .050-.100 in. off the rifling when chambered.*

On larger dangerous game cartridges, these allowances would be opened even more in the interests of reliability and keeping pressures from spiking due to high ambient temperatures. Finally, it should be said that all the dimensions we suggest are just that—suggestions. You, the customer, have the final say on the specifications to which we make your reamer.

Besides chamber dimensions, reloading die dimensions must also be considered when designing a wildcat cartridge. If your project is completely special and not an alteration of industry-standard dimensions, die design is a simple matter of sending the die maker of your choice a copy of your chamber reamer print and having them make dies to suit. Your chamber reamer can usually be used to make a seating die, but a special resizing reamer may have to be made if the die maker can't create the required dimensions with the tooling they have on hand.

If you want to "tighten up" your chamber to optimize the cartridge-to-chamber fit and still use off-the-shelf dies, additional factors must be considered. Standard dies are designed to bring the fired case back to within industry tolerances for the specific cartridge. To minimize working the brass, this usually means the dies will size the case to slightly smaller than the maximum case dimension. If your cases are, say, .006 inch. smaller than maximum, and you want a chamber that will allow them only .003 inch expansion, the fired case will end up smaller than the standard resize die. After several firings and reloadings during which the resize die has not touched the case, you'll find your cartridges won't fit your chamber.

Standard sizing dies also bring neck diameters down to just below maximum cartridge specs. If you order a reamer with a neck diameter reduced more than, say, .005 inch smaller than standard, you'll be better off buying dies that use interchangeable neck-sizing bushings. This feature allows you to custom-fit neck tension and realize the benefits of a tight-necked chamber.

In summary, optimizing (wildcat) cartridge-to-chamber fit requires careful dimensional coordination of the cartridge, chamber and reloading dies. If all are considered as part of a system and designed accordingly, your wildcat should be no more of a problem to live with than a standard chambering.

Reamer Makers

Numerous good reamer makers are working today, and it pays especially for the hobbyist to call around and ask about prices. Custom reamers from some makers cost more than others. If you fax or mail a drawing and request a quote, you may get a more accurate response.

Clymer Manufacturing Company
1645 West Hamlind Road
Rochester Hills, Michigan 48309-3312
248-853-5555
clymertool.com

JGS Precision Tool Mfg. LLC
60819 Selander Rd.
Coos Bay, OR 97420
541-267-4331
jgstools.com

Dave Manson Precision Reamers
8200 Embury Road
Grand Blanc, MI 48439
810-953-0732
mansonreamers.com

Pacific Tool & Gauge
P.O. Box 2549
White City, OR 97503
541-826-5808
pacifictoolandgauge.com

CHAPTER 13

The Accurate Chamber

Barrel quality is the first major factor in chamber accuracy. In 1945, J.B. Gebby told Charles Landis, "If the barrel borers hold specifications to within .0005 inch, then it's up to the gunsmith to chamber it correctly."[1] Today, tooling has improved, and we can expect even better quality in our barrels. For instance, Douglas air-gauge match barrels are uniform within .0001 inch; that's fully 80% better than in 1945. Gebby was right, however: the quality of the work performed by the gunsmith in fitting the barrel and chambering will make or break a rifle's accuracy.

You need a premium-quality chamber reamer. Solid pilot reamers work fine. However, using a floating pilot reamer for the best-quality chambers is common. Floating pilots have the advantage of turning with the barrel, while a solid pilot rides in the bore as chambering is performed and will slightly burnish the tops of the lands ahead of the throat. If the solid pilot causes any inconsistency, it will be insignificant, but we are discussing the best methods, so use a floating pilot for the best results. Another advantage of floating pilots is that you can precisely match the pilot's bushing to the barrel's bore for the best possible results. The sources for these tools are in Chapter 12, along with a complete description.

The primary difference between various reamer manufacturers' tools is in the degree of finish the reamer provides. It's not unusual to have to polish a chamber slightly when headspacing is complete to remove the minute lines left by the tool. If not removed, these will leave tiny circumferential lines on the brass when fired. These lines are unsightly and indicate to the reloader that the chamber is "rough." If a reamer is sharpened correctly, it will not leave them.

1 Charles, Landis, *Twenty-Two Caliber Varmint Rifles*, 1946

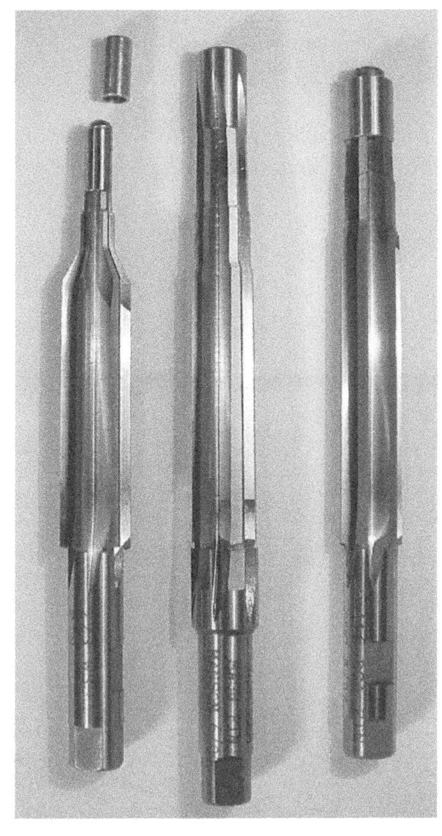

I had a friend who hung out in Paul Marquart's shop, and he told a story about the famous reamer maker Red Elliot walking into the shop just as he was polishing out a chamber with some emery cloth. Elliot asked what he was doing, and Marquart explained he was "Polishing out the chamber to remove tooling marks." Elliot confiscated the chamber reamer on the spot and chastised, "If the reamer leaves marks, it needs to be sharpened."

Setup accuracy for the threading and chambering of the barrel will deliver 90% of what is required for a precise rifle. You should carefully align the barrel to the bore's axis in the lathe so the threads will match the axis (an experienced machinist or gunsmith will know how to do this). Proper alignment in the lathe will also cause the shoulder and face at the breech to be perpendicular to the bore axis for the best results. The ideal thread will allow the receiver to be threaded onto the barrel by hand, but there should be very little (if any) axial thread movement while you screw the receiver on.

Thread fit is an area where novices often get into trouble. Engineers like to follow published specifications when assembling things. The problem with that approach in building a rifle is that gun manufacturers work within specified tolerances, which frankly are broad and forgiving. In the engineer's approach, we would use gauge wires and measure the treads for exact diameters according to the specifications for that particular thread. Unfortunately, the receiver (by Murphy's Law) will inevitably be at one of the extremes of the allowed tolerance. So, with a perfect barrel thread, the barrel may not even thread into the action if the receiver is at the minimum. On the other hand, if the receiver is at the maximum, the barrel will flop around as you thread it in, affecting accuracy. Neither result will deliver the best accuracy. You should fit the barrel thread to the specific action to achieve the most accurate groups.

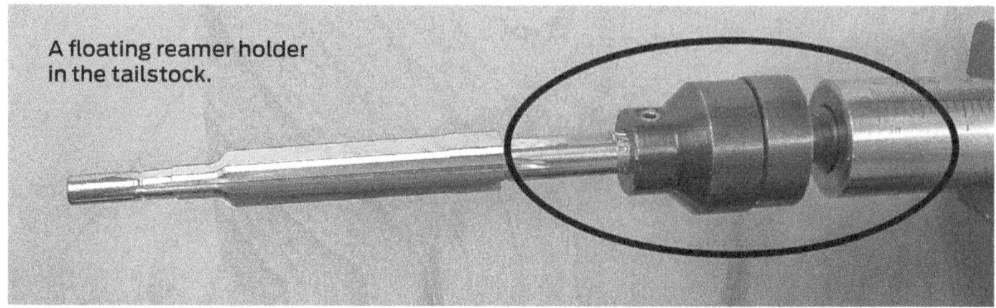
A floating reamer holder in the tailstock.

The spider on the headstock, outboard side.

Note the line left from the original chamber after rechambering.

Every shop has its proprietary method of chambering that it thinks is the best process. Often, these choices are dictated by the machines and tooling at hand. The simplest method, requiring the least setup time and tooling, will deliver the best results: First, thread the barrel for your action between centers to get the desired alignment. When you're done threading, take a light cleanup cut on the breech area of the barrel ahead of the threads so that the cylindrical area matches the axis of the bore. Then, set up the barrel in a three, or better yet, six-jaw chuck. (Alternatively, dial everything in with a four-jaw chuck.)

Dial in the muzzle so it sticks out the headstock, and lock it down with a spider. Next, use a floating reamer holder in the tailstock to take care of any minute misalignments. Achieving sub-half minute of angle precision is no problem with this method, and better results are typical.

Another method of holding the reamer in the tailstock involves machining a fixed holder to fit in the tailstock, which is machined in your lathe for a perfect match. This method is for the engineer types who like to try to control all the variables. It's as accurate as your machine, and your skills will allow.

Blueprinting the Action

Other accuracy tricks include "blueprinting" the action. Blueprinting involves several things: the locking surfaces must have even contact, and the locking surfaces must be at least 80% in contact with the locking recess; the more, the better. The receiver face must be 90 degrees to the bore axis (we use a tolerance of +/-.0005 inch across the bolt face). Check this by measuring from the face of the action down to the bolt face in the locked position. It should go without saying that if you can get a perfect 90-degree match, the measurement will be a dead .0000 inch.

On hunting rifles, threads are less critical because the barrel will be shouldered solidly against the receiver's face, which will take care of any minor misalignment. Benchrest rifle builders set the receiver up to "true" the treads by re-cutting them to ensure they are perfectly aligned with the bore. Finally and ideally, the firing pin should strike in the center of the primer for optimal accuracy.

It may seem strange that we're discussing all this peripheral work in a chapter about chambering a barrel. The reason is simple: All this preparation and careful setup work will provide the foundation for an accurate rifle.

Chamber Tolerances

In the two drawings below, note the differences between the brass/cartridge and chamber dimensions. The chamber must be larger than the cartridge

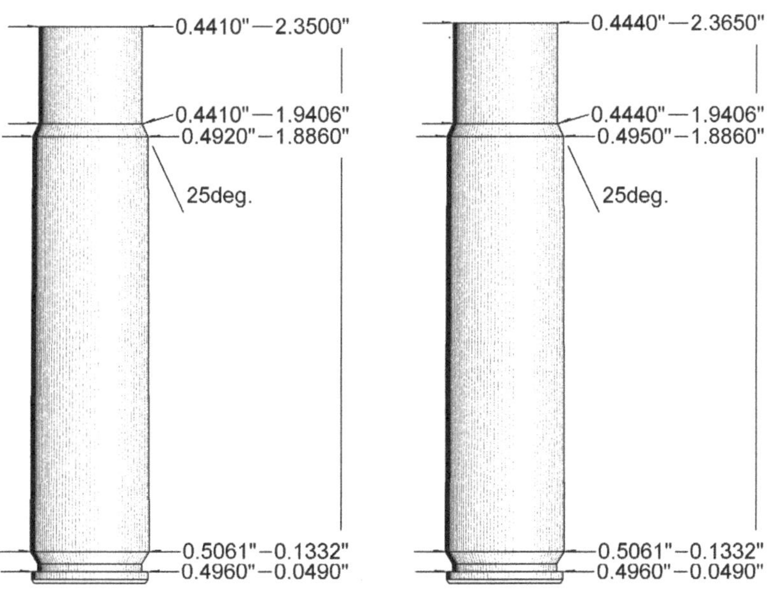

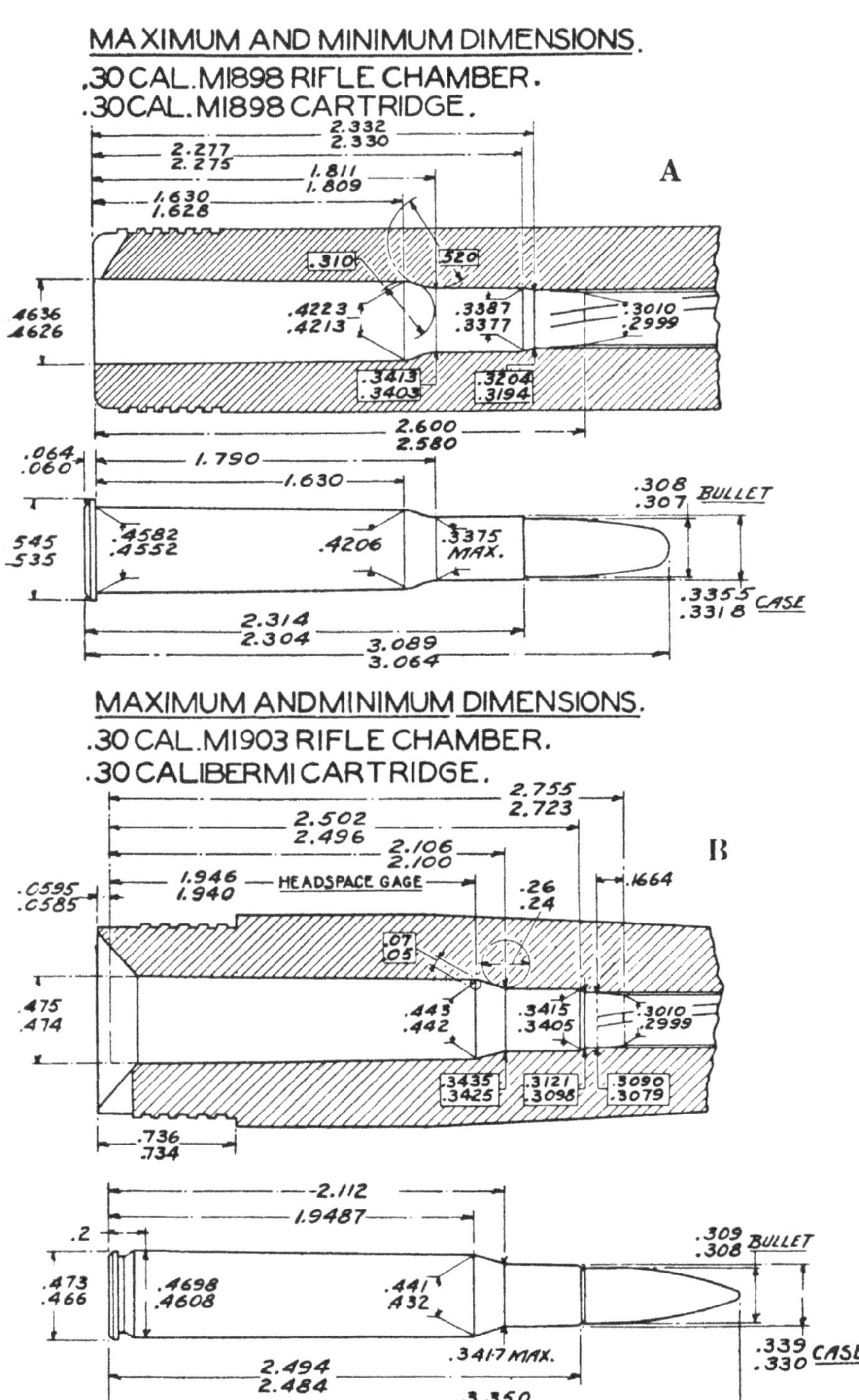
MAXIMUM AND MINIMUM DIMENSIONS.
.30 CAL. M1898 RIFLE CHAMBER.
.30 CAL. M1898 CARTRIDGE.
A
MAXIMUM AND MINIMUM DIMENSIONS.
.30 CAL. M1903 RIFLE CHAMBER.
.30 CALIBER M1 CARTRIDGE.
B
HEADSPACE GAGE
BULLET
CASE
.3417 MAX.

Note turning marks on the neck and how minimal material is removed.

for the firearm to function correctly. Smooth feeding is a function of these tolerances. If a cartridge is the same dimension as a chamber, it will not chamber properly, for if you have a hole and a plug the same size, forcing the two together will require some effort to overcome the friction between the surfaces.

We need to pay attention to a few dimensions in our example. For simplicity, these are the only dimensions included in the drawings on page 199, as they have proven to be reliable and accurate over time. The chamber breech must be .002 inch larger than the sized case at the same point. A .002- .003-inch difference works well where the case body meets the shoulder. The chamber's neck should be .004 inch larger than the case neck. The neck dimension is critical because brass varies in thickness, and this tolerance of .004 inch will allow for most anomalies in brass thickness. Note that the headspace dimension is the same for the brass and chamber.

If chamber dimensions are larger than those listed above, the result will be diminished accuracy and shortened case life as the brass becomes overworked. We're talking about an additional .002 inch. If tolerances are opened farther for the chamber, all sorts of problems become evident. When the breech is too large, the brass can fall to the bottom of the chamber, causing the firing pin to strike off center. This condition can start the bullet into the lands at an angle to the bore, not a condition desirable for accuracy.

Tight Chambers

Tight chambers have their place in the scheme of things, just like most anomalies. A tight chamber for use in competition or target guns where no one's life depends upon its reliability is fine. Townsend Whelen wrote three chapters in *Clyde Baker's Modern Gunsmithing* about chambering for rifle cartridges. Much of that information is as valid today as the day he wrote it.

Whelen had strong opinions on chambering based on his years of experience shooting, hunting, and working at Frankfort Arsenal.

On tight chambers, Whelen said, "A lot of foolishness has been written about minimum or tight chambers. Many shooters seem to think that tight chambers are very desirable and that they are more accurate. The truth is that tight chambers are very undesirable. They are accurate only when a bullet of the exact correct diameter is used, and it is often extremely hard to get such bullets. Chambers cut with the relative dimensions and tolerances shown in the drawings are the most accurate and satisfactory chambers known. Practically every American manufacturer is now designing his chambers for new cartridges with tolerances between maximum cartridge and minimum chamber very closely approximating those shown here, and we cannot too firmly impress upon the gunsmith that he should follow these as a guide.

"Very often a customer will write to a gunsmith or manufacturer, and state that he desires a barrel cut with an extremely tight chamber or a chamber of some peculiar shape. The gunsmith might very properly refuse to cut such a chamber from the standpoint of safety alone. But he can also plead the cost of making the necessary reamers."[2]

Whelen also discusses the cost of chamber reamers in the 1930s, which, while interesting, makes little difference to us today. However, the current cost for custom finish chamber reamers ranges from $145 to $250. Moreover, if you're going to have dies made, you'll need a resize reamer—which some gunsmiths use as a roughing reamer for the chamber—so that doubles the cost. Gauges are also necessary to set the chamber headspace properly. Custom gauges are $40 and up, depending on the size and manufacturer. The argument of cost versus a tight chamber is a real concern. The bottom line? Tight chambers have no place in hunting rifles.

Tight-necked chambers are no different than the tight chambers mentioned above; they have no place in a hunting rifle. A tight neck allows you to control neck tension on the bullet and uniform neck thickness. Typically, a tight neck chamber involves leaving all the body dimensions at standard dimensions and tightening the neck dimension. The most sensible tight necks are designed to allow for the absolute minimum removal of brass from the case's neck. Yet, even these "sensible" versions are unsafe with factory ammo because the brass around the neck will be pinched between the bullet and the chamber wall, increasing neck tension on the bullets and significantly increasing chamber pressure.

2 Whelen, Townsend, *Clyde Baker's Modern Gunsmithing*, 1933

For target and varmint rifles, tight necks can increase accuracy. However, nearly the same result can be had by turning the necks of your cases for uniformity. When turning for uniform thickness, you can set up your case-turning tool to remove material for about 90% of the neck circumference. By leaving that 10% area at its original thickness, you have a built-in gauge that shows that you have uniform neck thickness while leaving the maximum possible wall thickness. If you set up a tool to measure the wall thickness after such brass preparation, you'll find the measurable difference to be less than .0001 inch—closely approaching zero difference. This will deliver the benefits of a tight neck chamber without the expense of special reamers and allow you to shoot factory ammo when necessary.

Case Life and Chambers

Standard chamber dimensions (as described earlier in this chapter) will deliver the longest case life. Oversized chambers can cause the brass to expand in firing, so when it's resized, it receives too much work in the dies. Overworked brass requires more frequent annealing and will have a shortened useful life. As mentioned, oversized chambers will cause accuracy issues. One is that if a case lies in the bottom of a large chamber and is fired, the case head will conform to the angle between it and the bolt face. This will make the head slightly out of square with the body—and there is little chance the case will make it back into the chamber with the same orientation the next time you fire it.

When ideal chamber dimensions are used, the brass will work less in the die, yielding longer life. These dimensions and safe loading pressures will ensure long case life. If you're working out a new wildcat and are unsure which dimensions will work best, ask your reamer maker. They know more about these tolerance questions than your average gunsmith and can save you a lot of trial and error.

Chambers and Pressure

There are two primary ways the chamber can affect pressure.

1. Neck dimensions
2. Throat

I explained earlier how the neck of the chamber should be .004 inch larger than the brass cartridge case. This amount allows the brass to expand under pressure, releasing the projectile to move into the throat and down the bore.

A neck that is only .002 inch over the neck will work well in most instances but leaves little room for variation in brass. Such a neck will not increase pressure as long as the brass is uniform, .002 inch smaller than the chamber neck. Turned brass is essential for a tight-necked chamber. Tighter necks increase pressure unless you turn the brass to match because of added resistance as the bullet is released. Increased pressure can appear abruptly; it takes very little to push pressures up significantly.

In the early 1970s, some knowledgeable and experienced ballisticians collaborated with an entrepreneur to create the Apollo cartridges. These were Bob Forker, Bob Hutton and Bob Heiderich, respectively. They marketed a line of rifles and ammunition for their new-fangled cartridges: The .257, 7mm, .300 and .358 Apollo cartridges were all based on the .300 Winchester Magnum case. Other than necking them up or down for the various calibers, they made no other significant changes to the case. Now, are you scratching your head and wondering how this was any big deal? The truth is, the shooting public must have asked the same question, or we would all be shooting Apollo rifles today.

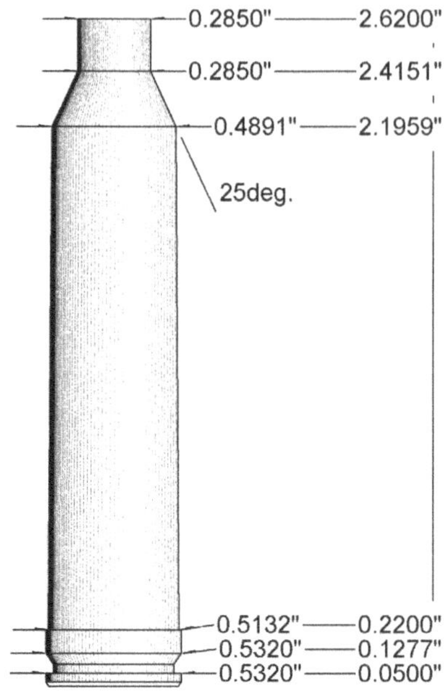

The .257 Apollo (.25/300 Winchester).

Apollo used a long magnum action instead of the standard-length magnum action typically utilized with the .300 Winchester Mag. Apollo's primary change was using freebore. The factory literature went to great lengths to explain the benefits of a long throat if properly applied.

Freebore is nothing new. Read this excerpt below from the Apollo catalog.

LET'S TALK ABOUT FREEBORE...

This term is generally misunderstood, if understood at all, by most rifleman [sic]. Consider a basic axiom of ballistics- "The more powder burned, the greater velocity." (up to the point of diminishing returns), Apollo cases hold lots of powder. To increase case capacity and velocity even more, a precisely determined amount of "freebore" is utilized in all but the 6mm Apollos.

Empty space or "freebore" is reamed from the chamber between bearing surface of the bullet and the rifling. This "pocket" fills with expanding gas as the bullet hesitates for a fractional mili-second as it engages rifling, thus acting as additional case capacity. If "pocket" is equal, say, to 5% of case volume, then the case may be loaded with 5% more powder. This results in a velocity increase without raising pressure.

When this additional freebore-gained capacity isn't fully utilized, chamber pressure drops. Freebore serves a secondary purpose- that of relieving peak pressure when bullet slows at the twist "barrier."

The question as to whether freebore impairs accuracy has long been debated. Suffice it to say that many benchrest groups with freebored Apollo rifles measure not more than 5/8 inch at 110 yards-as good or better than with comparable non-freebored weapons. However, because of this controversy and the fact precision varmint-accuracy is required of our 6mm Apollo, freebore is not used in this caliber.

To illustrate the advantages of freebore when used properly, we ran extensive chronograph tests on a .30 cal. Apollo rifle, 26-inch barrel, but chambered for the standard .300 Winchester Magnum cartridge. Rifle was first fired with 180 gr. W-W factory ammunition. Velocity was about 85 fps less than the factory-claimed figure.

This same rifle was then throated and freebored to exact Apollo specifications and fired again with both 180 gr. W-W factory fodder and medium intensity (77/4350) Apollo handloads. Velocity loss of the factory cartridge in now freebored chamber was minimal—55 fps—yet the Apollo handload, at about the same pressure level, clocked-off a grin-engendering 285 fps superiority over the factory load in standard chamber![3]

RIFLE WITH STANDARD CHAMBER (NO FREEBORE) 26-INCH BARREL[4]

CARTRIDGE	BULLET WEIGHT (GRS.)	MUZZLE VELOCITY (FPS)
.300 Winchester Factory	180	2,985
SAME RIFLE AFTER FREEBORE TO APOLLO SPECIFICATIONS		
.300 Winchester Factory	180	2,930
.300 Apollo Handload	180	3,270

Apollo tried to market the concept that it invented a new cartridge by changing something as simple as the chamber's throat length. Did these cartridges deliver improved performance? No doubt, but was it worthy of the hype that Apollo received? Who's to say? Did the designers deliver a new cartridge? Definitely not, at least in the case of the .300 Apollo, which was just a long-throated .300 Winchester for use in a long magnum action, which allowed the bullet to be seated to the base of the neck, preserving case capacity.

When you design your cartridge, you could incorporate this principle of a long throat to recover case volume lost to deep-seated bullets. However,

3 *Apollo Mach IV Series*, brochure, 1973

4 Ibid.

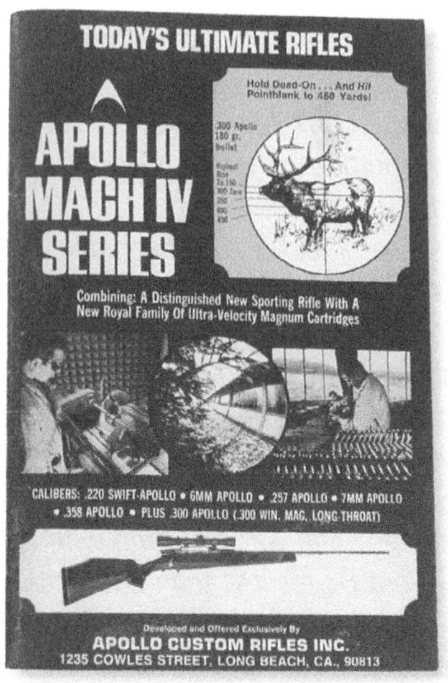

the problem with this tactic is that it limits you to heavy-for-caliber bullets. Light bullets will be substantially shorter in most cases, and then you will have a massive jump from the case to the lands. It's generally accepted that too much jump does not enhance accuracy, although many long-throated rifles shoot pretty well. Accuracy in freebored rifles is highly dependent upon the bullet fit to the throat as well as the amount of freebore. See Chapter 9 for a complete discussion of throat design.

Consider these factors in designing your cartridge: Is your design unique or just a minor adjustment to an existing cartridge? Even Apollo realized the difficulties and dangers of the .300 Apollo, so it never offered ammunition for that caliber. If someone had fired a .300 Apollo load in a standard .300 Winchester Mag. chamber, the results would have been devastating to the rifle and likely the shooter as well.

To distill it all down, accurate chambers result from careful setup of the barrel, action and chamber. If everything is plumb, square, and aligned along the axis of the bore, it's tough to make a mistake.

CHAPTER 14

Cartridge Design and Accuracy

To paraphrase the great Townsend Whelen, "Only accurate cartridges are interesting!" There is little point in designing and building a wildcat that is not at least as accurate as the many and varied factory cartridges you can buy off the shelf.

Accuracy is derived more from the precision and quality of the gunsmithing techniques used in assembling a firearm than from cartridge design, but for one caveat: When the cartridge design follows tried-and-true principles, accuracy can be taken for granted. If, on the other hand, a poor design is used, accuracy will be much harder to achieve.

For example, take the .219 Donaldson Wasp. Harvey Donaldson was an early pioneer, designing his case during the heyday of experimentation; he did not have the large volume of history to draw upon that we have today. Other experimenters and gunsmiths designed similar cases at approximately the same time. Charles Landis, a contemporary of Donaldson's, stated in his book *Twenty-Two Caliber Varmint Rifles* that he believed Donaldson arrived at his design independently and without direct knowledge of the competing wildcats.

In 1935, Donaldson began experiments that took 10 years to complete and culminated in the .219 Donaldson Wasp. The Wasp became a popular caliber among benchrest shooters because of its reputation for accuracy and flexibility in loading. It remained popular until the 1970s when the PPC and BR designs finally supplanted it from the top ranks of the benchrest world.

Donaldson had a different approach when he started his tests: he was purposely designing a case with specific characteristics. He wanted a small, convenient, high-intensity cartridge with accuracy, economy and flat trajectory. He also wanted to avoid other characteristics—long, heavy cases with problems like excessive throat erosion and pressure issues. In short, he was trying to design an "efficient" cartridge.

Donaldson's early attempt was based on the .25 Remington Rimless case, which had a case capacity roughly 22% greater than the final Wasp design. Very quickly, it became evident to him that this early design was grossly inefficient. With its large powder charge, the pressure was all out of proportion to the velocities achieved, and the increased case capacity did not deliver the expected velocity increase. Having learned this lesson, he set aside the barrel and began a new design.

Based on the results of this test, Donaldson determined that a case with a small diameter body about the neck diameter would not deliver the desired results. Next, he turned to a case of smaller capacity, with a short and fat body relative to the neck of the case. He used the .25 Remington case to form the shorter one for the next test but shortened it to 1.625 inches. It sported a short, fat design with little taper in the case body. Early tests with this case confirmed Donaldson's contention that the long case was correct.

Finally, the .219 Zipper case came along, and Donaldson saw it as an opportunity to prove his findings from the two earlier designs. First, he designed an improved .219 Zipper case left full-length that dimensionally matched the first design on the .25 Remington case. Results proved that this full-length case was not using the powder available, again proving the results from the first test.

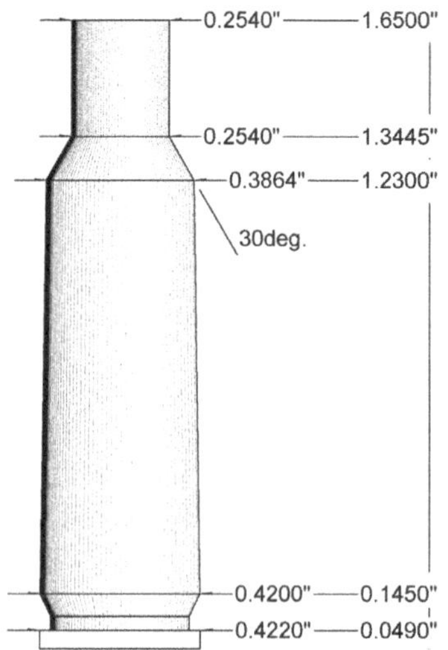

The .219 Donaldson Wasp original from the .25 Rem.

Next, Donaldson took all the data he had collected in building four test rifles and used it to design his .219 Donaldson Wasp. Unlike most wildcatters, he had used careful experiments and several years of work to create an efficient wildcat that produced exceptional accuracy. The only change he made from this point on was to add 1/32 inch to accommodate a graphite wad without sacrificing load capacity. If the wads had worked, we would still be using them today, but the final version of the Wasp includes this dimensional change.[1]

Donaldson believed that the shorter case with a relatively fat shoulder relative to the neck diameter and an abrupt shoulder angle of 30 degrees was key in efficiently burning the powder. The .219 Donaldson Wasp and the .219 Zipper have nearly identical case capacity, but the more efficient design of the Wasp is claimed to produce better accuracy and longer barrel life.

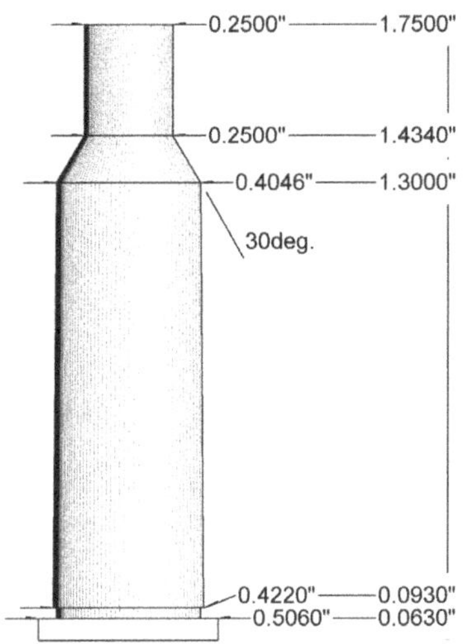

The .219 Donaldson Wasp (Landis).

Some pretty extravagant claims for velocity were made. When comparing modern data for the Wasp and contemporary cartridges like the .22-250, we see that the Wasp is an equal with a 45-grain bullet. It uses so much less powder that you could load 40 more rounds for the Wasp from a single pound of powder. However, with heavier bullets, the .22-250 produces more velocity: load 25% more powder with a 60-grain bullet, and you will pick up 300 feet per second over the Wasp with the same bullet (though the tradeoff would be barrel life).

Donaldson's meticulous testing and design work demonstrates how valuable research can be before you design a case. We have hundreds of sources for researching cartridges and case capacity these days, and carefully selecting a case for its capacity and shape can help you create a successful design without wasting tooling and barrels several times to get it right. Donaldson spent many years pursuing a .22 high-intensity cartridge with impeccable accuracy, barrel life and flexible loading characteristics. Knowing his lessons will help you accomplish similar results with less time or money invested.

Accurate Case Design Considerations

If you're looking for hard and fast rules for accurate case design, you may be disappointed; however, some guidelines are available. You can find accuracy in any bore diameter if the gun is well-built and the cartridge well-balanced to the bore volume.

Case capacity. Looking at load data for the .219 Donaldson Wasp, it becomes apparent that with a 45-grain bullet, virtually all .22 centerfire cartridges max

1 Landis, Charles, *Twenty-two Caliber Varmint Rifles*

Shoulder angles from left to right: 17 degrees, 30 minutes; 25 degrees; 21 degrees; 35 degrees; and 40 degrees.

out at 3,600 fps. However, the .220 Swift and .22-250 add 300 fps with heavier bullets (requiring up to 25% more powder than the Donaldson Wasp). The lesson is to consider how much more powder it will take to meet your desired result. As a general approximation, *a 10% increase in powder charge will deliver a 5% increase in velocity for the same bullet.* If you have to burn more than 10% to gain a 5% increase in velocity, your case is overbore. Selecting the smallest case that will deliver the ballistics you're after without pressure issues will always be the goal, and such cases are more flexible in loading, allowing the use of many powder and bullet combinations while producing excellent accuracy.

Bore capacity. Homer Powley ties bore capacity and expansion ratio together in case design. The expansion ratio is the ratio between the bore's total volume and the case's volume. The expansion ratio is the number of times the gas will expand by the time the bullet reaches the muzzle. High ratios mean good barrel life, while low ratios indicate shorter barrel life. Low ratios may result in the highest velocity, though in many instances, this slightly higher velocity is more than offset by significantly reduced barrel life, critical loading and general inflexibility.[2]

Powder selection is an essential factor in accuracy. Many reloaders try to use powders outside the correct range for their cartridge, either too fast or too slow. There are a couple of easy shortcuts if you're unsure how to select a powder. First, look up similar capacity and caliber cases to see which powders are typically used. Second, use a computer program to estimate loads, which will recommend powders at the appropriate burning rate. Ideally, you want the powder that will produce the most velocity with the least pressure, which can be easier said than done. This ideal powder will generally be more flexible in loading and often work with a wide weight range of bullets.

2 Ackley, P.O., *Handbook for Shooters & Reloaders*

Shoulder angles from 17 to 30 degrees will deliver good accuracy in nearly all designs. Such angles provide enough contact area and a mechanically positive shoulder to headspace against, and feeding is generally smooth and easy to adjust. A shallower angle of less than 17 degrees is less positive for headspace purposes and can be forced too far into the chamber, although it will feed nicely.

Steeper shoulders, above 30 degrees, are more critical on headspace fit, provide a less accurate cartridge case, and feeding will be rougher than with the shallower angles. It's agreed that 40-degree shoulders, as used in Ackley and other "improved" cases, impede the stretching of brass and do not require nearly as frequent trips through the case trimmer.

Extremely sharp shoulders above 40 degrees are particularly critical on headspace, and chamber reamers with such steep angles do not last nearly as long as more conventional angled designs. To prove these points, check the benchrest crowd to see what it uses, and you will not find any cases in the winner's circle with shoulder angles at either end of the spectrum.

P.O. Ackley believed from his testing that a 28-degree shoulder produced the best average accuracy. Brass is much easier to form in a die at these angles, and up to 25 degrees, most brass will form easily.

Short and fat is where it's at! Since World War II, the trend among accuracy buffs has been steadily toward shorter and fatter cases, mainly due to benchrest shooters finding that this shape produces more uniform ballistics and, consequently, more uniform groups. When we say fat we're talking about the difference between the shoulder and the neck of the case. While the Donaldson Wasp and its brethren from the 1930s and '40s led the way to shorter, fatter cases, interestingly, newer designs are not substantially different. For instance, the .22 PPC has nearly the same case capacity as the Donaldson Wasp; it's just on a rimless case. So, when you select a case for your design, a relatively fat case may improve your results. However, like everything else in life, too much of a good thing will not be beneficial.

Neck tension is one facet of accuracy that is often overlooked. Holding neck thickness to a reasonable level will aid in controlling neck tension. The energy required to overcome inertia and get the bullet moving out of the case is called "pull." A neck that is too thin will not provide uniform pull from shot to shot. Necks that are too thick will not resize well in the die because they tend to spring back more after forming. Neck wall thicknesses between .012 and .014 inch are typical on factory cartridges and provide uniform pull. You can ensure uniform pull by doing some simple things: anneal the necks about every

Neck turning.

fourth shot since the pull becomes less uniform as they work harden. Then turn all your necks for concentricity. Be aware that if you turn your necks too thin relative to the chamber and neck size die, you will not be able to get any neck tension at all, so take measurements before you get carried away. These two procedures will enhance the accuracy of any rifle.

Brass selection is a little-discussed but important factor in cartridge design. Recent tests with a wildcat prompted the weighing of various brands and lots of .30-06 brass. Weights varied from 174 to 204 grains for various makes of brass. The problem is that safe loads in the lighter brass will likely be excessive in the heavier cases because of the latter's reduced capacity. Military brass is often much thicker, thus reducing case capacity. One shooter pointed out that +P brass for his .45 ACP showed substantially increased pressure from reduced capacity in the thicker-walled case—probably double based on the velocities he reported.

Brass quality can vary widely. Brand names from the big manufacturers, Winchester, Remington, Federal, Hornady, and Starline, to name a few, are very consistent in quality. Norma, Lapua, Nosler and Alpha are currently associated with premium-quality brass.

Strange problems can arise from sub-par brass: Soft cases can cause pressure signs where no real problem exists. Hard or brittle brass will not form well or can crack, split, or buckle during forming or firing. Some hard brass will crack after one or two loadings. As for detecting the difference between normal, hard, and soft brass, experience is the best guide. After you've formed brass, it will not take long to spot stuff that does not work how it should.

Use brass from a single lot for consistency. Shot-to-shot pressure will be uniform, and velocities will show less deviation. A low standard deviation is not a guarantee of accuracy, but it is at least a sign that there are fewer variables to deal with in developing your loads. If a load gave a small SD when chronographed but did not group well, mechanical or bedding problems are likely the source, or the barrel's harmonics would also be a possibility.

With all that said, it's still important to say "but." Like most things in life, all these rules or concepts make for good guidelines, but at the same time, you may ask, "Just how much difference will I see on the target if I break these rules?" The truth is that most hunters will not be able to detect much difference if a cartridge does not sport perfect design accuracy-wise. While we read all the time about rifles that shoot 1 MOA or better, the percentage of guns that are capable of this with off-the-shelf ammo is small, and shooters who hold that well are an equally small percentage of the shooting public. So, most hunters will be hard-pressed to see the difference in accuracy from one design to another, yet we all want to remove any questions about our equipment to be assured of the best possible groups.

Let's say the kill zone on a deer-size animal is 6 inches (minute of deer), and the average deer-class rifle will produce a 2 MOA group. That means it would be reasonable to use the rifle for shots up to 300 yards. Likewise, a 3 MOA rifle is good for 200 yards in the same circumstances. A rifle that shoots under ½ MOA is not one bit more deadly than a 2 MOA one at reasonable hunting distances—it just adds to the hunter's confidence. Never has a deer, elk or any other game animal been impressed by accuracy figures or ballistics tables. Neither will they surrender or shout warnings to their buddies when they see you arrive with your new .595 Eargoschplittenloudenboomer. All this is to say that breaking the rules can be fun, too.

Once you've progressed to the point of wildcatting, you're probably looking for sub-MOA accuracy or better, though. If you live for the best possible accuracy, following the design principles in this chapter will aid in developing an inherently accurate cartridge. Benchrest shooters can tell the difference between high-performance target cartridges and hunting rounds. Accuracy buffs will go to great lengths to attain the best possible precision and find a 2 MOA rifle anathema. If you're a member of this accuracy-oriented fraternity, skip the comments about "minute of deer" accuracy above and design only accurate cartridges using the design principles in this chapter.

CHAPTER 15

Case-Forming Tools and Methods

Folks new to reloading and wildcatting are often intimidated by the prospect of forming brass for a new gun. Most of the information in this chapter relates to bottlenecked cartridges, mainly because 98% of all wildcats are in rifle calibers. Pistol cartridges are also wildcatted, though, and these same methods and concepts will apply where they use bottlenecked cases.

My first experience with forming brass was for a .25-06—the .30-06 case necked down to .257 inch. All we had available then was .30-06 brass, so forming was a necessary evil. Many helpful folks warned me about wrinkled necks or shoulders and dented cases. (Those with experience are either shaking their head or laughing by now.)

Forming .25-06 from .30-06 requires no special skills or tools. It's as simple as running a standard lubed case into a .25-06 full-length sizing die. The effort required is no more than that needed to size .30-06 in a standard full-length sizer. In short, sizing and forming brass is simple, even when the case is more complex to form than the .25-06. This experience taught me not to take the advice of shooting "sages" at the range to heart without testing the information (one of the first stages of Diplock's Syndrome). Much of the advice received from shooting buddies is not derived from personal experience, so much as it is gun gossip.

Gun gossip is just what it sounds like. Two or more shooters get together, and one tells the others why forming brass for an "Eargoschplitenloudenboomer" is so tough. Without any qualifying statement as to the source of the material or the degree to which the facts are recalled, our "sage" expresses "the facts" with all the authority of, "I've been shootin' for *thutty* (30) years" behind him. Never mind that our sage, if pressed, could not recall the magazine, the author, or even that the source of his input is just an old opinion. He will proudly tell you that what he says is the gospel, according to John Moses Browning. Of course, little of what he said proves accurate when you check his facts. That is a fair definition of gun gossip and another good explanation of why gunsmiths develop "Diplock's Syndrome." For a complete description of Diplock's Syndrome and its origin, see Chapter 5.

Forming Methods

Coldforming is the process of forming brass into a new shape without fireforming. It has some limitations. Coldforming works best when you make small changes to the parent brass to form the new cartridge case. The .25-06 mentioned above is an extremely simple case to form because all that changes is the neck. All other body dimensions stay the same.

When coldformimg more complex cases, start with parent brass larger than the new case so you have sufficient brass to form the new case. Coldforming requires dies of various configurations to form the new brass. Let's assume you're starting with cylinder brass to form your new cases. You'll need forming dies to create the shoulder and neck. As a rule, the most you can move a neck down without causing damage to the case is about .040 inch. Therefore, form dies must be made in increments to reach the desired size.

The photo below depicts the process of forming the .17 Shrew, which Max Dunlevy designed from .221 Fireball cases. The first step is to anneal the cases down to the location of the new shoulder and form the new shoulder. Next,

Designed by Max Dunlevy, the .17 Shrew-forming process.

trim it to length while still at .22 caliber. Then, form it to .17 caliber in the forming die and turn the necks to the shoulder. Finally, full-length resize, fireform and trim to final length.

In some cartridge cases, an additional step of neck reaming is required to make the brass serviceable. For this, you use a special die made for the purpose. Insert the formed and trimmed brass into the neck-reaming die and use a "chucking reamer" to remove the extra wall thickness in the neck area. (The thickness comes from the body of the case, which the manufacturer left thicker below the shoulder because there was no need to thin it out. That extra material gives you the desirable characteristics for extraction and overall case strength/life.) Neck reaming is unnecessary for many wildcat cases, so don't get too excited about it.

An excellent alternative to neck reaming is outside neck turning. This process requires a turning tool, which most reloading tool companies offer. A hand tool like the Forster Neck Turning Tool is fine for truing necks requiring minimal turning. However, if you remove large amounts of metal (as with the .358 Yukon), use a bench-mounted tool like those from Wilson, Forster or RCBS. The case neck is supported on a mandrel during the turning process, so the result is more accurate and uniform than with a neck reamer. If ultimate accuracy is the name of the game, neck turning is the way to go.

Once a case is fully coldformed, you can load and fire it in the wildcat chamber without needing a fireforming load because it is fully formed out of the die. This method has the added advantage of not wasting reloading components, barrel life or time at the range on a forming load that you will likely never use in the field.

Neck reaming in a die allows you to remove wall thickness during the forming process when the brass is too thick.

Fireforming Techniques

Have you ever heard of the "K.I.S.S." method? "Keep It Simple Stupid" is one of those little axioms that seem to hold no matter the situation. So, let's start with the simplest of fireforming methods.

Fireforming factory ammo in a factory chamber? I hear you saying, "You're kidding, right?!"

Here is an excellent opportunity to see how the chamber differs from the

SAAMI New Cartridge & Chamber – 338 WEATHERBY REBATED PRECISION MAGNUM

Maximum Average Pressure (MAP)* = 65,000 psi
Crusher pressure limits not established.
* Refer to SAAMI Z299.4 for pressure guideline interpretation description.

Instrumental Velocity: 225-gr @ 2,800 fps

CARTRIDGE & CHAMBER

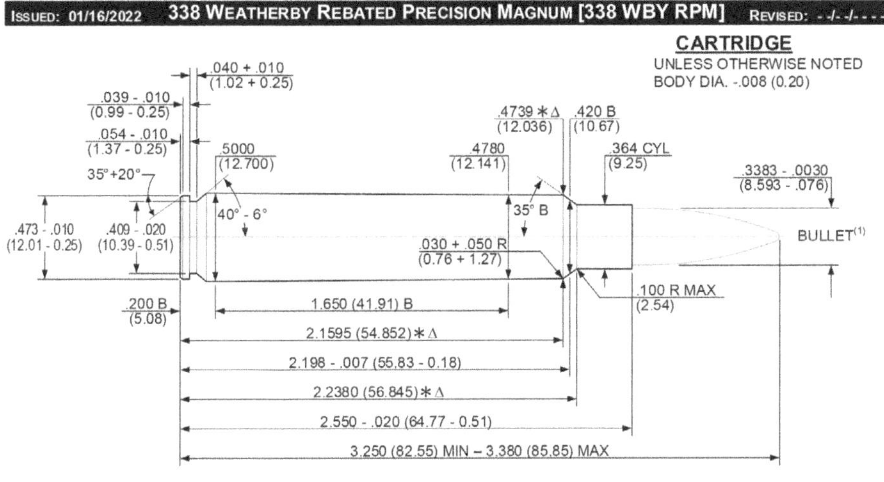

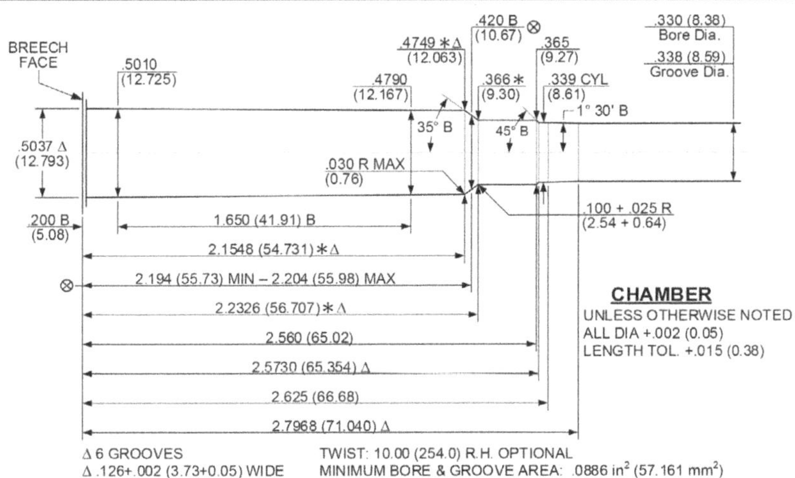

Δ 6 GROOVES
Δ .126+.002 (3.73+0.05) WIDE

TWIST: 10.00 (254.0) R.H. OPTIONAL
MINIMUM BORE & GROOVE AREA: .0886 in² (57.161 mm²)

NOTE:
B = BASIC
Δ = REFERENCE DIMENSION
(XX.XXX) = MILLIMETERS
* = DIMENSIONS ARE TO INTERSECTION OF LINES
⊗ = HEADSPACE DIMENSION
ALL CALCULATIONS APPLY AT MAXIMUM MATERIAL CONDITION (MMC)
(1) – BULLET PROFILE IS SHOWN FOR ILLUSTRATIVE PURPOSES ONLY

DO NOT SCALE FROM DRAWING

In the SAAMI prints (above), the top print is for the ammo dimensions. The bottom is for the chamber. Notice that there are tolerance callouts on both the ammo and the chamber. These tolerances allow the ammunition makers to build ammo that would always work in the factory chamber. Equally, the chamber is designed to accept ammo within the allotted tolerances. These are important and necessary mechanical principles used in manufacturing. Wildcatters and reloaders must understand how tolerances apply to their guns for safe function.

Credit to Clymer Manufacturing

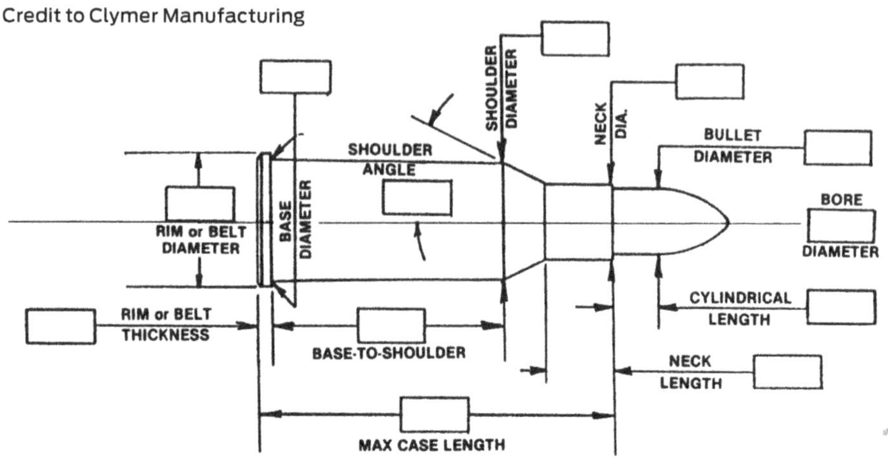

ammo. Take some unfired factory ammo and fired brass from one of your rifles. You don't need the gun for this, just some measuring tools, either a dial calipers or a micrometer. Sit down with some paper and a pencil, draw a diagram like the one below and fill in the blanks. Then read on.

An improved chamber with standard ammo before fireforming.

Now that you have those dimensions, you can see that your brass fireformed to your rifle's chamber. The dimensions on the brass drawing will be larger than those on the ammo drawing. The reasons for this are covered in depth in Chapter 9. Simply put, if you're nervous about fireforming, don't be. You have already done it each time you shot a rifle.

Improved Cartridges (Ackley)

Improved cartridges are the next level in fireforming. The headspace in an improved cartridge is .004 inch shorter than in the factory cartridge because the cartridge is tightly trapped between the bolt face and the chamber shoulder. However, no great amount of force is needed to close the bolt on such a round because the contact area between the brass and the chamber is so small.

When you fire a factory cartridge in an improved chamber, the body and shoulder of the case will stretch and expand to fill the chamber. A small amount of energy is lost in forming the brass, so any given load will lose 2% to 3% of its velocity, plus or minus a few fps. The real advantage of improved chambers is reloading the newly formed case to take advantage of the increased space. See Chapter 2 for more details. Fireforming in an improved chamber aligns with our "K.I.S.S." method. No special preparations are made for the brass before you fire it in the improved chamber.

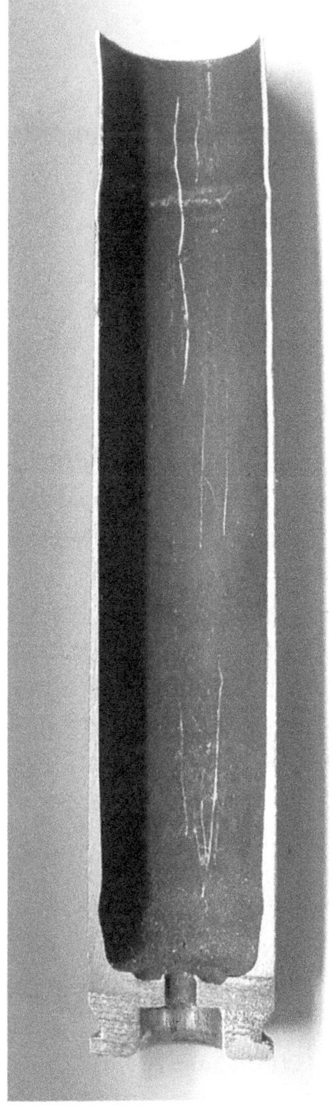

Thinning in the sidewall from the brass stretching due to excessive headspace.

Headspace and Forming Brass

Headspace is as crucial to your ammo as it is to your rifle. Shooters often assume that a headspace problem is limited to their gun; however, it can just as easily be found in the ammunition. When a shoulder is pushed too far back, excessive headspace results. If a shoulder is not pushed far enough down when forming the brass, it can cause a condition where the bolt is hard or impossible to close with the headspace below minimum.

Shoulder angle is an important issue when considering headspace. Rimless cases need a shoulder angle between 17 and 40 degrees for reliable headspacing. Sharp shoulders with angles greater than 40 degrees make it more difficult to control precise headspace. As a side note, such sharp shoulder angles are also hard

False shoulder.

on tool life. Accuracy will be more elusive in cases with super sharp shoulders because the angle requires the base-to-shoulder length to be tightly controlled, far beyond more conventional angles of 40 degrees or less.

We have a few options depending on the configuration of the parent brass. Rimmed cartridges are the easiest and most forgiving because the case is headspaced on the rim—so you can use nearly any reasonable design ahead of the rim.

Belted cases are similar in that they are supposed to headspace on the case belt rather than the shoulder. In practice, most reloaders headspace belted cases on the shoulder because it produces better accuracy. If you plan to use a belt to headspace your wildcat, carefully check to see how your belt matches up with the headspace gauge you're using. Modern belted brass is not precise, which could throw a monkey wrench into your plans.

Standard rimless cases present the biggest challenge for headspacing. The headspace between the formed brass and the chamber must be tight enough to hold the case steady during the firing process. Proper headspace allows the brass to fireform correctly. If the brass is two or three-thousandths of an inch (.002–.003) short on headspace, it will fire fine, but the headspace of the resulting fireformed brass will vary, causing inconsistency in accuracy. Carrying the condition even further, if it's too short, then either misfires or case head separations are possible.

Wildcat Forming

In Chapter 1, we defined a "true wildcat" as a cartridge that must be formed in a die before it can be fired in a chamber and that there is no factory ammunition that can be safely fired in the chamber. Now, let's look at what it takes to fireform a wildcat cartridge.

Assuming no cylinder or (basic) brass is available to form your cases, especially when forming belted or rimless cartridges, you should create a false shoulder on which the case can headspace. The idea is to partially form the new shoulder to provide a positive headspacing area.

Forming the false shoulder is pretty simple. The neck of the parent case must be a larger diameter than the desired neck of the new cartridge. This may require first necking the brass up: two calibers above the desired final dimension usually provide a substantial shoulder area.

Using the sizing die for the new cartridge, size the neck down to the new caliber.

Have the rifle handy. Remove the firing pin/striker assembly from the bolt so that the firing pin spring doesn't interfere with the closing of the bolt (assuming the rifle is a bolt-action).

Trial fit the formed case to the chamber and attempt to close the bolt. When the fit is correct, you will feel the bolt drag on the brass as the bolt closes. No excessive force should be needed to close the bolt.

Once you determine the proper die setting, load the brass for fireforming.

Then, with your fireforming loads and a trip to the range, you will have fully formed brass. Accuracy with this fireforming load is often reported as a minute of angle or better. It's usually challenging to get a full load in the case because it has not been blown out yet. As with improved cases, some energy is used in forming.

Shrinking Case Length

The fireforming process will shorten the case life if the parent case has a large taper. Brass must come from somewhere to fill the new, enlarged body and the sharper shoulder. For example, this author developed a cartridge for a client several years ago, a .35 caliber on the 8x57 case. The idea was to get maximum case capacity from the old Mauser case, so we blew out the body, sharpened the shoulder, and, in the process, shortened the case by .070 inch, which left us with a neck far too short. The solution was to shorten the headspace gauge by .070 inch to regain the material needed for a proper neck length.

I Smell Something Burning

Instead of wasting bullets, You can use inert filler material to fireform cases. This method uses a small charge of a fast powder like Unique in an unformed case. You fill the remainder of the case with something inert—the best I've found is Cream of Wheat. When you fire it, the filler transfers energy to the brass, forming it into the new chamber dimensions. As discussed above, positive headspace is equally important when using this method. If headspace is not maintained during this forming, the brass will be incorrect for full-pressure loadings.

In *Designing and Forming Custom Cartridges*, Ken Howell recommends a charge equal to 10% of a standard load for the given case. This is typically a safe starting point; add one grain of powder at a time until your case is fully formed. The Cream of Wheat is necessary to develop the pressure to form the case. I advise plugging the case mouth with some bee's wax or a ¼ sheet of toilet tissue balled up. The plug holds the filler and powder charge in place during handling and transportation and will be blown down the bore when you fire the forming load. The shoulder corners may not be as sharp as a regular load, but the finished brass will be formed to the chamber it is fired in, so it will only require resizing before loading.

Hydraulic Case Forming

Rocky Gibbs popularized hydraulic case forming for his line of wildcats. The tooling required is pretty simple, although nobody is currently marketing them. First, a 7/8x14 nut fits with a permanent threaded plug that blocks about half the nut's thickness. Fill a piece of brass with 30-weight detergent-free motor oil. Insert the oil-filled case into a standard full-length sizing die. Then, thread the die into the other end of the nut, creating a captive cylinder. The top bushing and decapping assembly are replaced with a plunger assembly that will act as the piston to pressurize the cartridge case inside the die. The result will be formed cases with slightly rounded shoulders. The corners will sharpen upon the first firing.

The Whidden Gunworks hydraulic form die.

The main problem with hydraulic forming is the mess it creates. You'll need to prepare a work area to capture the oil with minimal fuss. Cleaning the formed cases requires a couple of extra steps.

Degreasing in soapy water will take care of the oil, then rinse the cases in hot tap water and drain. The heat from the water will dry the brass quickly, or you can place it in the oven at 200 degrees.

Water will work if the fit of your

ram is tight, but because of the lower viscosity, it will often squirt out. Add an O-ring on the ram, and you can probably control the water escaping. Cleaning up the oil never bothered me, as I do all my forming in one sitting.

One significant advantage of hydraulic forming is that you need not go the range to fireform cases. It also saves on components and wear and tear on your barrel. Brass life is probably longer with this method since you need far less pressure to form the cases generated in fireforming.

Once upon a time, RCBS offered a hydraulic forming tool that accomplished the abovementioned results. It used water instead of oil and was by all accounts as much trouble to use. At this writing, Whidden Gunworks offers a custom hydraulic form die.

Seating Depth

Many seating depth gauges are available that allow the precise measurement of your rifle chamber. The results give you a measurement for a bullet lightly

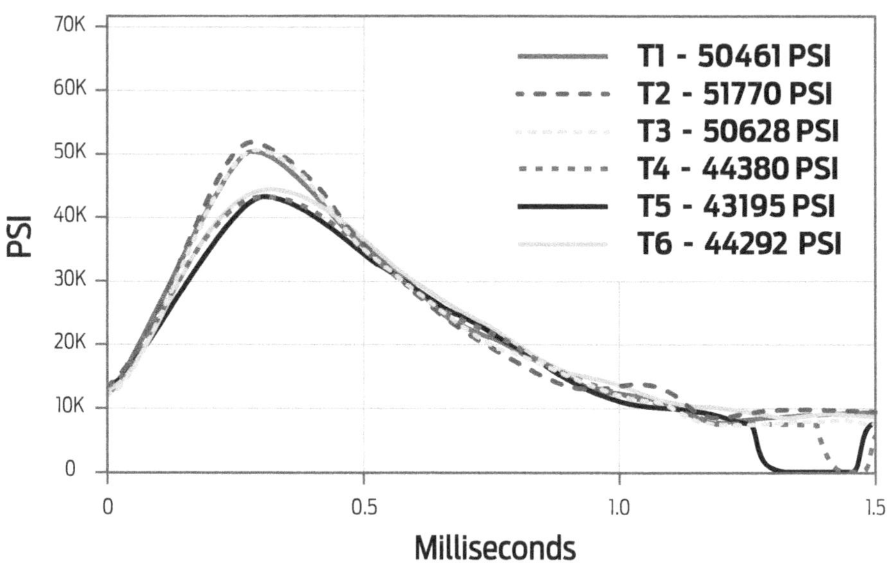

Pressure trace measurements taken from a 30-06. The three higher curves are for loads with the bullet touching the lands. The three lower ones are the same load with the bullet .020 inch off the lands. Note the average difference of 6,000 PSI.

touching the lands, allowing you to quickly establish the correct overall seating length for loaded rounds. The methodology varies depending on the specific tool you choose.

Using the measurements to set your bullet-seating die correctly and precisely is a simple matter. Bullet-free travel—often called "jump," "leade," or "free bore"—is typically .020 to .080 inch in hunting rifles for the best accuracy and reliability. If you shoot heavy-for-caliber bullets or monolithics, they are usually longer, requiring a longer throat than is standard.

As a rule, gauges are accurate to within .001 inch and will work with any bullet you choose. You can monitor throat erosion with them as well.

Another popular method of determining overall length with a given bullet is to seat a bullet partway into the neck, leaving it long, then closing the bolt on the case to seat the bullet to the maximum overall length of the chamber. This process works well, but on occasion, you may get a bullet stuck in the barrel's throat, so have a cleaning rod on hand. For more on how seating depth can affect accuracy, see Chapter 14.

Long Seating Bullets

Many writers have suggested another method of fireforming cases that will work, but it requires caution. Year after year, this method is mentioned in articles, and most of the time, you can tell by the details that the writer has never tried it! The idea is simple: leave the bullet sticking out of the case so far that it fully engages the lands and simultaneously forces the case head against the bolt. In effect, this method requires that you headspace on the ogive of the bullet rather than on the proper area of the case in question.

With the ogive of the bullet engaging the rifling, the case is unsupported and not headspaced by the brass. This method relies on the bullet forcing the case head against the bolt face.

Excessive pressure spikes are the concern when using this "bullet in the lands" method of fireforming. If you use a normal full-pressure load when fireforming this way, the results could be catastrophic, to put it mildly. When you fire a round, the highest pressure will occur during the first .750 inch of bullet travel. When the bullet starts while engaged in the lands, the initial pressure spike will rise higher and faster than if it has a running start as with a standard load.

Because the bullet is stuck hard against the lands, it cannot overcome inertia before friction is added to the equation. When a bullet engages the lands, it must be deformed to match the rifling. This deformation process is much easier for a bullet in motion, causing only a slight pressure spike when it engages. Bottom line, if you should find the method necessary, *be sure* to use light starting loads for your fireforming as pressure *will* be higher than you would typically experience if the bullet were seated off the lands.

Mixing Dies to Form New Cases

Wildcatters often use existing reloading dies to test a new idea. This is an acceptable method for testing and development. I initially tested the .411 Hawk using .41 magnum dies as a neck-sizer die. Was it a perfect solution? No, but it worked fine and allowed the testing to continue until the dies were ready for

The .411 Hawk test, neck forming in a .41 Mag. size die.

the cartridge.

Sometimes, you can use a succession of various unrelated dies to change the shape of the case or to neck it down. Many times, wildcatters will have existing dies shortened for these purposes. The only drawback is that you will probably need an extensive collection of dies to do much. Also, modifying reloading dies is tricky as they are heat-treated to be extremely hard, requiring carbide cutting tools for alterations. As a rule, modifying existing dies for a wildcat is not practical; instead, it is a stopgap until correctly made dies are ready.

If time is a bigger issue than money (a problem we should all have), several custom loaders can help make brass for your new wildcat. Remember that it takes these professionals nearly as long as it will for you to make formed brass, and they expect to be paid for their time. But, when your brass or ammo arrives, you can be on the range in no time, having fun instead of being stuck in the reloading room.

Here are a few reputable folks who supply brass and ammo for wildcats.

(Custom ammunition & brass)
Quality Cartridge
PO Box 445
Hollywood, MD 20636
qual-cart.com

(Obsolete and wildcat brass)
Buffalo Arms Co.
660 Vermeer Ct.
Ponderay, ID 83852
buffaloarms.com

E. Arthur Brown Co.
4088 County Road 40 NW
Garfield, MN 56332
800-950-9088
eabco.com

(Custom ammunition)
Superior Ammunition, Inc.
1320 Cedar St.
Sturgis, SD 57785
800-67-SUPER
superiorammo.com

Arizona Ammunition, Inc.
21421 North 14th Avenue, Suite E
Phoenix, Arizona 85027
623-516-9004
arizonaammunition.com

(Obsolete ammo and brass)
Old Western Scrounger
50 Industrial Parkway
Carson City, NV. 89706
775-246-2091
ows-ammo.com

Warner Tool Company
201 Old Homestead Hwy.
N. Swanzey, NH 03431
603-352-9521
warner-tool.com

Peterson Cartridge
17 Leonberg Road, Suite 100
Cranberry Township, PA 16066
724-940-7552
petersoncartridge.com

CHAPTER 16

Reloading Dies

Counting the cost, wildcatting can be expensive, and you should be aware of the costs before jumping into it. Moving your design from the drawing board to the range will require an investment in tooling, and you should also plan on ruining some brass while learning to form your new cartridge.

New folks always seem to hold the whole process in awe. Then, as the saying goes, "Familiarity breeds contempt." Or, to put it another way, "It doesn't take long for the shine to go off the apple." It sounds a little cynical, but it is good news for the beginner because that means they will be ready to move into forming brass for wildcats in no time.

A good example is my long-time shooting companion, Graydon Snapp. When we first met, Graydon was a client at the gun shop. He had been reloading factory calibers for a while and had experience in working up accurate loads. When we built his first .375 Hawk/Scovill, Graydon expressed some trepidation about the loading process. We discussed expanding .35 Whelen brass up to cylinder form and then resizing it to fit the chamber of his new rifle. The following week, he came into the shop with a big smile, saying, "I don't know why I was worried; forming .375 brass was really easy!" Another wildcatter arrives at the range.

Many books discuss using various dies but never explain how they work or how to use them. The purpose of this chapter is to take the mystery out of it and remove your fears so you can become a confident wildcatter. We'll start with the form die because it's the first one you typically use when forming a wildcat case. From there, we'll work through the various die types. However, it's assumed that you know how to lube cases and perform the basic reloading functions.

Form Dies

Various cartridge designs may require form dies to shape the brass for your new case. The form dies incrementally change the brass to the desired shape and correctly position the shoulder. How many form dies are necessary is a function of the case design; the maximum amount that brass can be sized down in a single pass is .040 inch plus or minus a few thousandths of an inch. The .358 Yukon, a cartridge I developed for Bill Kemmerer of Sarasota, FL, requires several steps to form and therefore makes a good example.

Parent brass for the .358 Yukon is the .300 Remington Ultra Mag., which requires three form dies to shape the shoulder. Form dies do not usually have a decapping rod; they only create a new shoulder and form a neck. Because the parent brass is often longer than the desired wildcat, the brass will often protrude out the top of the die when fully inserted, though this depends on the manufacturer's design. The typical setup for a form die is to thread it into the press to touch the shell holder when the press's ram is at its topmost position; then lower the ram and turn the die in about ¼ turn so the ram cams over the center. This process overcomes the spring in the press (all reloading presses will spring slightly when sizing or forming brass, some more than others).

Before forming brass, it is often beneficial to anneal it so that it will form more easily and avoid creating flaws or wrinkles in the case. Brass will work harden in the forming process, especially when many steps are required. If you note that the neck is curling back at the mouth or wrinkles appear, it's time to anneal it. If the brass collapses in the die after annealing, then you may have to work it without annealing until the final step in the full-length sizing die.

File and Trim Dies

A file or trim die is no different than a form die except that the brass will protrude out the top so that you can cut it off to the correct trim length for your

Notice how the wall thickness increases as you move closer to the head of the case. Thickness varies depending on the cartridge.

cartridge. In our example, the file/trim die is the final one in the process, saving the cost of an additional form die. To begin, install the die in the press as above and run the brass into the die; when the ram is at its topmost position, it will protrude from the top of the file/trim die. If it protrudes only slightly, use a smooth-cut file to make the brass flush with the top of the die, as the name suggests.

If the brass is long, as with our .358 Yukon, use a hacksaw to cut most of it off and file the brass flush to the top of the die. Once complete, you'll have brass trimmed to the minimum length for your cartridge. Deburr the case mouth, and you're ready to move to the next step.

Neck-Reaming Dies

The neck-reaming die ensures the neck thickness is correct and uniform for your finished brass. In most cases, an outside neck-turning tool will do the same job, though neck reaming is useful on very thick brass. When sizing brass down from larger or longer cases, the new material that makes up the neck will have come from farther down the original case's body. Brass tapers from thick at the head and web of the case to thinner toward the shoulder area. When you move the shoulder back, you'll often get into thicker material that won't provide proper neck tension on the bullet, causing the neck to be pinched in the chamber—a condition that can cause excessive pressure when you fire the gun. The neck also thickens when sizing brass down from a larger diameter, so check for thickness and uniformity when you neck down brass.

Neck-reaming dies have diameters that will hold the neck at its correct resized dimension (before the bullet is seated, in most cases). Install the die in the press so that it touches the shell holder. With the brass in the die (ram at its topmost position), insert the neck reamer at the top, which will guide the neck reamer. Using a long-handle tap wrench to drive the reamer lets you feel the cutting action. Run the reamer down, turning it clockwise until the entire neck is uniform. You will feel it when it stops cutting. Then, remove and clean the reamer for the next piece of brass. You can use a drill motor to drive the reamer, but be careful not to put side pressure on it as it can cut off-center.

The neck reamer is a chucking reamer of the correct diameter. The diameter that will work with the neck reamer dies described here is .002 inch smaller than your bullet diameter. This dimension sets up proper neck tension.

Full-Length Dies

Full-length sizing dies do just what the name says: they size the entire case length. A fully resized case is desirable for smooth and reliable feeding when used in lever-actions, pumps or autos. In bolt-actions or single-shots, you will need to full-length size your brass about every fourth time you load it because it gradually grows in length when you fire it. Full-length sizing returns the brass to the minimum dimensions relative to your chamber.

You can also use a full-length sizer to neck-size your brass by backing the die out about ½ turn from touching the shell holder. When neck sizing as described, the case body will be resized very little, if any, so if you do not want the body sized, you will need an actual neck sizing die as they don't touch the body or shoulder.

Neck-Sizing Dies

Neck-sizing dies, as mentioned above, do not change the body or shoulder of the case in any way. The advantage is that you can reload and fire the case several times before you must full-length size it. A neck-sized case will generally shoot more accurately than a full-length-sized one. That's because the case matches the chamber. Thus, the brass does not fall to the bottom of the chamber, misaligning the bullet and the bore.

Conventional Bullet Seater

Most commercial bullet seaters fall into this category: an adjustable seating stem on the top of the die to adjust seating depth. With these dies, you can roll crimp the bullet in the brass. The disadvantage? Typically, the bullet must be stood on top of the case, and then the two are raised into the die by the ram; as the bullet rides on the case mouth, it can get cocked at an angle and must be forced into position aligned with the axis of the brass. This forced straightening often causes the neck of the case to bend as the bullet is seated, a major cause of lost accuracy. Run-out gauges measure the misalignment of the bullet and the bore line.

Inline Bullet Seater

Several variations of the inline bullet seater work on the same principle of holding the bullet aligned to the case, preventing the neck from being bent in the seating process. The method of aligning the case and bullet varies from one die design to the next. Some die makers offer "Competition" dies that work as inline seaters, while others have an insert that matches the entire case body. Moreover, others work on the case mouth, shoulder and bullet.

Factory Crimp Die

Lee Precision offers a factory crimp die, which pinches the case mouth into the bullet laterally, much the same as seen on most factory ammo, thus the name.

The die's operation is simple enough; it is made to match the specific cartridge. You adjust the die according to the factory instructions: the insert in the die contacts the shell holder as you raise the ram. When the ram reaches the top of its stroke—where it has the maximum mechanical advantage—the insert hits a taper in the die body, forcing the insert (collet) to close on the case's mouth, forcing the brass into the bullet. Like most crimp dies, you will have plenty of mechanical advantage, and

Before—the neck without the crimp.

After—the neck with the crimp.

it's easy to ruin brass, so don't overdo it! Only crimp enough to ensure uniform neck tension.

Uniform neck tension on the bullet is desirable as the more uniform each loaded round is, the more likely it is to produce accuracy on the range. Crimping the bullet is one way to develop uniform tension on the bullet. Many cartridges are sensitive to the amount of neck tension. For example, in testing the .411 Hawk, Mike Brady of North Fork Bullets discovered that by crimping the bullet, he could reduce the standard deviation in tested loads by a substantial percentage.

The reason for neck tension's huge effect on pressure and standard deviation is straightforward. If tension is light, it will be more difficult to control the amount of energy required to overcome the inertia of the bullet and get it moving. Consequently, the energy used to start the bullet down the bore will vary from one shot to the next, resulting in a wider SD. When you crimp the bullet, the neck tension increases, and we know from empirical testing that the amount of energy needed to kick-start the bullet down the bore may be greater, but it will also be more uniform.

Die Dimensions

Chapter 12 contains complete information on the internal dimensions of your dies under the discussion of reamers.

Externally, the standard thread for reloading dies is 7/8x14. Other threads commonly used on dies are 1x14, 1¼x12, 1¼x18, 1-3/8x12 and 1 ½x12. The primary reason for larger-diameter dies is to accommodate larger-diameter cartridges. However, the 7/8x14 die will handle anything up to the .378 or .460 Weatherby case. Probably 95% or more of all dies will be in the 7/8-inch diameter.

Length Specifications for Reloading Dies

Resize Dies	Length of brass plus .750 in.
Form Dies	Overall length equal to brass, minus .130 in.
File Trim Dies	Minimum trim length minus .130 in.
Seating Dies	Length of cartridge plus 1 in.
Neck-Reaming Dies	Case length plus 1 in.

The sizing die must house the length of the cartridge case and the decapping assembly or seating stem above the case mouth. Form dies can be any length, as trimming is usually not necessary. For economy, cut the form dies close to the actual trim length. For a file trim die, its length will be determined by the minimum trim length for your finished case design; take the minimum trim length and subtract .130 inch for the shell holder and crush; this equals the length of the trim die. Different manufacturers may vary shell holder dimensions. For instance, Redding makes the "Competition Shell Holder Set," which varies in height so that you can adjust the headspace of your brass more readily.

Bullet seating dies must handle the length of a loaded cartridge, plus the ability to load a variety of bullet weights (lengths), so be sure to leave enough room to adjust the seating stem. If you use an inline bullet seater like the Bullseye MIS die mentioned earlier, length is less critical because this type of die is designed to be universal and can be adjusted to fit nearly any case length. The added length of the neck-reamer die guides the neck reamer, aligning it to the bore axis. The dimensions given here for die lengths are flexible; the decapping assembly or seating stem may require a change in length, so go with the flow.

A vent is essential to all sizing, form and trim dies. Just below the shoulder of the cartridge, you will find a small hole drilled through the die wall. This vent allows air to escape as the brass is forced into the die body and prevents the denting of shoulders for case bodies by releasing any compressed, trapped air.

A "Q" die and inserts for various neck diameters and shoulder angles. You can change out the body portion, making testing of new forms quick indeed.

When working with straightwall cases, place the vent above the case mouth in the die to prevent scraping brass.

The 'Q' Die

Here's a tip that can save you much time and money in testing a new wildcat. Impatience was the impetus for the design of the 'Q' die. The name stands for "Quick." When designing a new cartridge, it's often helpful to produce brass quickly, as waiting for tooling or making dies takes time. Originally, the die was made from a reject die body and a jam screw fabricated to hold the die together.

Inserts are made from tool steel, usually one for the body of the case and another for the shoulder/neck area. Because the inserts can be made in a few minutes on a lathe, you can produce a set of form dies to test a new case idea or shape with little expense. Accuracy is pretty good if you make the inserts with a shoulder that aligns them one to another. You can make any size die, but heavy forming is impossible with this die as it is pretty thin, but it will do a surprising amount of sizing. If you need more than a few pieces of test brass, it's simple to heat-treat the inserts in the shop with a torch.

CHAPTER 17

Testing Wildcats

Now that you have a design, it's time to prove it and see what it will deliver on the range and in the field. This chapter will provide you with some tools and information that will assist in the safe collection of data from your original designs. Accuracy will be the goal of our testing, and velocity will be treated as a natural outcome of good design, but it will not be the focus of our discussion.

Velocity and accuracy are not mutually exclusive, but neither are they synonymous.

Accuracy will most often show up with moderate loads, and cartridges are usually more flexible in loading at moderate levels; flexibility is defined as the ability to use a variety of bullets and powders to achieve acceptable results. When velocity is your goal to the exclusion of all else, tradeoffs will rear their head and demand attention, forcing you to pay for every foot per second you add. Inflexibility in loading is the first tradeoff to appear, soon followed by short barrel life or erratic results. Occasionally, one gets lucky and finds a rifle that likes hot loads, delivering the best accuracy with the highest velocities, though this is the exception, not the rule.

Defining Accuracy

In Chapter 14, we discussed the inherent accuracy of cartridge designs, while in this chapter, we cover testing to prove accuracy once you've built the rifle. Accuracy must be defined, as we do not all measure it the same way; in Chapter 14, "MOD" accuracy was mentioned, that's "Minute of Deer." Any rifle that will shoot into a 6-inch circle to 300 yards is an MOD rifle. That is not great accuracy if you're interested in sub-MOA rifles. For this chapter, we'll define accuracy as any rifle that shoots one MOA or better.

Remember, MOA stands for Minute of Angle. To define MOA more specifically, a full circle is divided into 360 degrees and each degree is divided into 60 minutes. Thus, there are 21,600 minutes in a full circle (360 x 60 = 21,600). A minute is a slight angle, but it's exactly what gun sights need. A rule of thumb is that changing a sight's elevation setting by 1 minute of angle changes the bullet's impact point by 1 inch at 100 yards. A more exact value and how it's arrived at is shown below:

A circle with a 100-yard radius (distance from the center to the edge) will have a circumference of 628.32 yards or 22,619 inches (100 x 2 x pi = 628.32 {pi is about 3.1416}). Dividing the circumference in inches by the number of minutes in a full circle gives a value of about 1.047 inches (22619 / 21600 = 1.047). Thus, changing a sight's elevation setting by 1 minute of angle changes the bullet's impact point by 1.047 inches at 100 yards. The bullet's impact point would change by 2.094 inches at 200 yards (1.047 x 2) and by 3.141 inches at 300 yards (1.047 x 3).

If you look back on articles written in the first half of the 20th century, you will notice that groups for accuracy included 10 shots. Then, it was desirable to shoot several of these 10-shot groups to prove the accuracy of a given rifle/load combination. Sometime after World War II, shooting a five-shot group to prove accuracy became the practice, and nobody asked if you could repeat the feat. By the end of the century, three-shot groups were the rule among hunters and gun writers bragging on accuracy. That's at least a 70% reduction in test data.

There are probably many reasons that today's shooters have accepted less information and still declare a rifle "accurate." Time and component costs are enormous factors. Statistically, a three-shot group will average about 50% smaller than a five-shot group, so we can fool ourselves into thinking our gun shoots better than it actually does. Most hunters figure that they will typically only shoot one or two shots at a time anyway, so if their rifle consistently produces acceptable accuracy in three-shot groups, they are satisfied. If you get one three-shot group measuring .500 inch and are never able to get that gun to shoot under 1 inch again, you do not have a ½ MOA rifle (if a rifle/load combination will produce sub-MOA three-shot groups over and over, then it is accurate). To be honest with yourself about the accuracy, average all your groups and realize that the average is what your rifle can be relied on to produce in terms of accuracy.

VihtaVuori states in its 3rd Edition *Reloading Manual*, "It is generally considered that variation in the powder charge plays the main role in the accuracy of a firearm cartridge. Fortunately, this is not true. In shooting tests, it has been discovered that a less than ±1% variation in the powder charge has no significant influence on accuracy. This means, for instance, that the load in the .222 Remington may vary as much as 0.01 x 18.5 gr.= ± .185 gr., in .308 Winchester ± 0.01 x 45 gr.= ± .45 gr., and a .338 Lapua Magnum ± 0.01 x 100 gr. = ± 1.00 gr. without ruining accuracy!"

The point here is that other factors affect accuracy more than slight variations in powder charge. VihtaVuori says that a good-quality powder measure will throw charges that fall well within this ±1% window when applying a uniform handling technique. Many benchrest shooters load by volume and do not weigh each charge. Other factors are far more critical.

Developing Loads

When developing loads, we try to optimize them for a specific purpose. Generally, optimum loads would be defined as those with the desired velocity, flattest possible trajectory, the highest possible impact energy at all ranges, and, most importantly, the best possible accuracy. Not all loaders have the same goals, but when you start testing, having a goal in mind will help you choose components for your loads that best suit your needs.

Case Selection

As a review, manufacturers of metallic cartridge cases in the United States follow the specifications set out by SAMMI (Since being founded in 1926, SAAMI has been actively involved in the publication of industry standards, coordination of technical data and the promotion of safe and responsible firearms use. SAAMI currently publishes more than 700 voluntary standards related to firearm and ammunition quality and safety). In Europe, the governing body is the "International Proof Commission" or CIP (the CIP has been working since 1914 for the standardization of proof, which also involves standardization of pressure measurements, chamber and bore sizes and cartridge dimensions. Members include Austria, Belgium, Chile, France, Germany, Hungary, Italy, Russia, Spain, Finland and the United Kingdom).

In any case, these organizations set specifications for the manufacture of cartridges and firearms so that all manufacturers will produce uniform products. As a result, ammunition for a specified caliber will fit in any firearm chambered for that caliber. Like all manufactured items, some tolerance must be allowed in the manufacturing process. When you select brass, it's essential to understand this and choose the brass that best suits your needs.

Military brass is nearly always thicker, so it will have a lower case capacity than its commercial counterparts. Makers offer brass that will vary in thickness and hardness. It's not essential who offers what variation as much as you understand that it is a fact of life. This is why you should always buy a supply of brass from one lot for uniformity, removing one variable from your reloading process. It's a good idea to buy enough of one lot of brass so that you will not have to replace it for a few years, if ever.

Primer Selection

Boxer-type primers are the industry standard worldwide. Berdan priming is quickly passing from the scene, so it will not be discussed here. Boxer primers come in two basic sizes: Small (.175 inch) and Large (.210 inch). Other variations are for Standard Rifle, Magnum Rifle, Standard Pistol and Magnum Pistol, and some makers also offer "Match" primers. Each manufacturer has its proprietary designation for its various primers, but the basic breakdown is the same from brand to brand.

Magnum primers differ from standard ones mainly in the duration, intensity, length of the flame, and, to a lesser degree, the heat generated by the burning primer compound. Primer cup construction varies from one manufacturer to another, too. Magnum primers improve ignition in large-capacity cases with slow-burning powders. Sometimes, when you use light-for-caliber bullets, magnum primers will create a more uniform powder burn. Magnum primers are also useful when the ammunition is fired in sub-zero temperatures because they are more energetic. Primers affect the pressure any given load develops, so it's a good idea to back down a few grains whenever you switch primers and work up again.

Modern powders will ignite equally well with standard or magnum primers under most conditions. So, the best way to decide if you need magnum primers is to start working up loads with standard primers, and if your results are erratic,

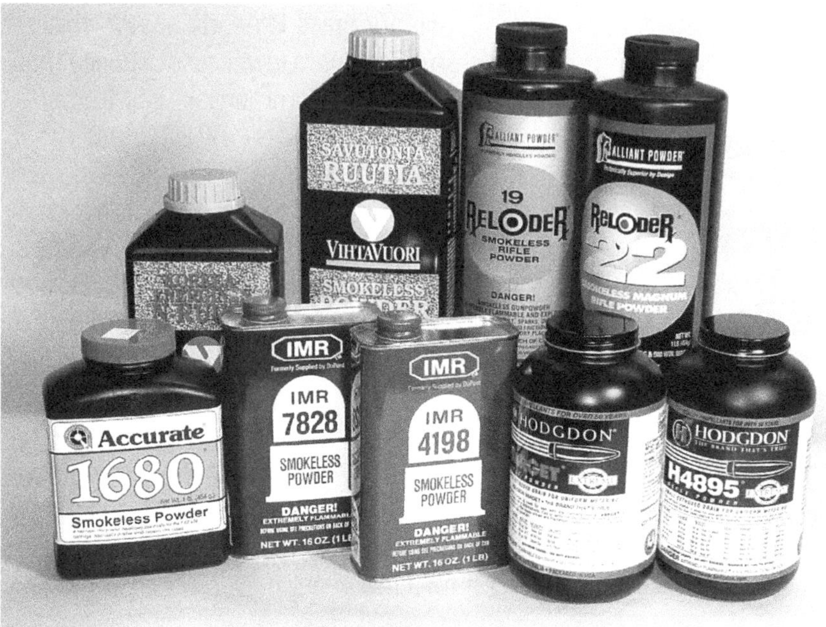

try switching to magnum primers to see if the load burns more uniformly. Since magnum primers tend to be slightly less accurate than standard, there is no advantage in using them unless your load calls for them.

The primer pocket can vary in diameter and depth. For this reason, nearly every reloading manufacturer offers tools to ream primer pockets to the correct depth and diameter. These tools have a built-in stop, so you cannot cut too deep, and the process is as simple as can be: follow the toolmaker's instructions. Accuracy fanatics will use primer seating tools that also allow for adjustable primer seating depth.

The flash hole is another area that can be modified to improve accuracy, and many toolmakers also offer flash hole uniforming tools. Similar to the primer pocket reamers, follow the toolmaker's instructions.

Like all other components in the reloading process, primers can significantly affect accuracy. You may want to try a variety of primers, especially if you're looking for the best possible accuracy. Of course, match primers should deliver the most uniform results.

Selecting Powders

Pressure is a paramount consideration when working up loads for any rifle. Think of it this way: a rifle, when fired, contains an explosion and directs it away from the shooter in a safe direction. In other words, if the rifle fails to contain the explosion of white-hot gases, they will be released next to the shooter's head—not a desirable effect. For details on how to recognize pressure problems, see Chapter 10.

The Powley computer, one of the software packages mentioned in Chapter 8, will help you develop a starting point for the loads in your new cartridge. Alternatively, you can check the water capacity of your formed cases and then use the data to compare your capacity to known cartridges. It's not unusual to find that your design closely matches the capacity of an existing cartridge. If it does, consider the bore diameter, and you have a starting point.

Here are some general rules that will guide your selection of powders when experimenting with handloads:

If the goal is accuracy...

Select an appropriate powder that nearly fills the case when the charge is less than the maximum. Typically, less than maximum loads that nearly fill the cartridge to a density of 75%–100% but not compressed (100% here is defined as filling the case to the base of the bullet when seated, leaving little or no air space). Such loads give more uniform velocities and pressures and, consequently, the best accuracy. Interestingly, the Powley computer is developed to deliver an 86% load density.

For all loads in small-capacity cases or light bullets with reduced loads in large rifle cases...

Use the fastest-burning powder that will deliver the desired ballistics within the pressure limits of the cartridge and gun it is to be used in.

Full-power loads in large rifle cases with bullets of high sectional density...

Choose the powder that will deliver the desired ballistics with the lowest possible pressure. In other words, slower powders usually work best with heavy-for-caliber bullets. The same is true for cases with large capacity vs. the bore diameter.

In cases with limited case capacity...

Choose the powder that will deliver your desired ballistics and stay within safe pressure limits but doesn't compress the powder. Switching to a spherical powder of a similar burning rate will often provide more loading flexibility and higher velocities with heavier bullets.

Guns are like snowflakes ... no two are alike.

Carefully test loads before jumping in and loading a bunch of ammo; a load safe in one gun may not be safe in the next.

Projectiles

An adage goes, "A chain is only as strong as its weakest link." Custom rifles cost thousands of dollars, and custom reloading dies can easily run several hundred dollars, with brass costing more than a dollar per piece, which is not uncommon. A guided hunt will also cost some substantial coin, so why do many shooters turn into a "Cheap John" when buying bullets?

It's easy enough to understand that if you're shooting prairie dogs or woodchucks, the quality of the bullet only relates to accuracy. Plenty of good varmint bullets shoot well and deliver the terminal ballistics required for humane kills. Even when hunting deer in the close cover of the eastern or southern U.S., most any bullet will suffice because you're shooting at under 100 yards most of the time. But what about when a record book trophy buck is on the line? Wouldn't you rather have a premium bullet you can rely on to open, causing a wide wound channel and dumping its energy in the animal?

We have been trained as a society to save money wherever possible. Here, another adage comes into play, "You get what you pay for!" The best-made premium hunting bullets you can buy cost, on average, a couple of dollars a shot. Accuracy and reliability are the main effects we want from hunting bullets. It's one thing to hit that royal bull elk at 250 yards, and it's quite another to *know* that the bullet will penetrate deeply while doing enough tissue damage to ensure a swift kill. Imagine you are on a guided elk hunt for which you paid $15,000. Your forty-five-cent bullet hit the most enormous elk you have ever seen but failed to penetrate, and the bull marches off into the black timber, leaving you to consider whether you saved any money on those bullets.

When selecting a bullet, it is of paramount importance to consider the purpose of the bullet in the planned load. For instance, no 1,000-yard match shooter would select a blunt-nosed hunting bullet, just as a hunter should never select a match bullet for hunting. The construction of these two types of bullets is different and, therefore, not interchangeable.

Bullet weight is a major factor in selecting the correct bullet for the job. Choose a bullet of the appropriate weight for the game you will be shooting. Recoil should not be a factor in the selection of a hunting bullet, except where the shooter cannot accurately shoot a heavy recoiling rifle. Choose the heaviest bullet the rifleman can shoot accurately if recoil is a factor. Often, the manufacturer will offer suggestions about using their product, as they know better than anyone how their bullet is constructed and what types of targets it will handle best. Make use of this free advice. Some bullet makers now indicate a recommended velocity range for their different designs. This useful information will help you select a bullet that will perform at the velocities you have in mind.

Inevitably, the sectional density and ballistic coefficient questions spring up when discussing the correct bullet selection for your specific situation. Remember that sectional density is a bullet's weight, in pounds, divided by the square of its diameter in inches.

$$SD = WA/d^2$$

Where; SD = sectional density
W = bullets weight in pounds
d = bullet diameter in inches

Sectional density is the expression used to describe the diameter of a projectile compared to its weight. You might say that SD is the weight that backs up the bullet's diameter. The shape of a bullet, along with SD, is the most crucial characteristic in maintaining velocity downrange. Consequently, bullets of the same caliber with higher SD will penetrate better than those with lower, assuming the bullets' construction holds together.

Higher sectional density will impart a flatter trajectory for a given velocity. Of course, like all rules, there are exceptions; the point is that you can use SD as a measure of how well a bullet will perform both in flight and on game. If two bullets leave the muzzle at the same velocity, the one with the higher SD will have a flatter trajectory. This is because mass (weight) overcomes air resistance. Also, the higher the SD, the less velocity reduction after the bullet exits the barrel because the higher SD bullet will have a lower ratio of air resistance to momentum. The wind has less effect in higher SD bullets as well.

The higher the SD, the lower the muzzle velocity you can reach at a given chamber pressure. It's pretty easy to understand: heavier bullets require more pressure to increase velocity. Also, heavier bullets for caliber (higher SD) will typically have a larger contact surface with the barrel, creating more friction while in the barrel.

Graydon Snapp, who was instrumental in developing Hawk Cartridges, says he uses SD to choose bullets when starting with a new caliber. He uses a .308 x

180-grain bullet as his baseline because it penetrates well, maintains velocity well downrange and is flexible in loading in most .30-caliber cartridges (the SD for such bullets is .271). Graydon then looks for similar SD when choosing bullets in unfamiliar cartridges. For instance, if you look at .375, a 270-grain bullet has an SD of .274, and the 270-grain bullet is a good choice for large-frame animals like moose, bears and elk. Graydon's rule of thumb works well with calibers from .264 up, providing a good starting point with hunting calibers. Sectional density is a useful measure of how well a projectile will perform.

Once SD is discussed, ballistic coefficients are sure to follow.

BC or BS?

What does that mean? BC is Ballistic Coefficient, and naturally, BS is Bull Shit.[1]

A ballistic coefficient is a number assigned to a hypothetically perfect bullet at a constant velocity under ideal and constant atmospheric conditions. Or a ratio that denotes a projectile's ability to overcome air resistance and maintain velocity compared to a standard (the hypothetically perfect bullet). Mathematically, it's the ratio between sectional density and the coefficient of form. Most manufacturers publish tables with the BC for each bullet they make.

The manufacturer's BC is often calculated from the form and nose shape of the bullet. Interestingly, when tested on the range, the BC is seldom the same as it was calculated. In other words, you can't assume the published BC from the manufacturer is correct. The BC derived from testing is the effective BC, but the problem is that every time a variable changes, so does the effective BC.

Laboratory conditions are required to record an accurate BC for any given projectile. Testing requires measuring velocity drop over a precisely known distance. The BC is the comparative ability of a projectile to push through the air and retain velocity. To make these numbers useful, it is a comparison to a standard multiplier. Another variable that can change BC is the starting velocity.

Ballistic coefficients are useless until the bullet passes about 300 yards. Why? Simply put, BC describes the projectiles' ability to retain velocity. So, until the bullet has time to shed some velocity, there is no critical difference between an efficient design and a fireplug of the same weight.

Why is the BC BS? Prescribed laboratory conditions for measuring BC are an altitude of sea level, temperature of 59 degrees Fahrenheit, relative humidity of 78% and a barometric pressure of 29.58-in. Hg. Temperature, relative humidity and barometric pressure are essential to calculating an accurate BC. These

1 http://stevespages.com/table3.html

atmospheric conditions influence air resistance and cumulative drag, creating an "*apparent change*" in BC. *This is apparent* because the projectile only behaves differently because of outside changes.[2]

"Apparent change"—to be intellectually honest, we should admit that an apparent change and an "effective BC" are the same. Let's see any shooter who can control outside factors when shooting or hunting. The BC of the bullet may be theoretically unchanged, but the effective BC certainly will change with these outside factors. The firearm and the barrel's bore dimensions and twist rate, can also affect BC.

Damage to the projectile can have a dramatic effect on the BC. Bullets with sharp tips are known to have higher BCs. If those tips are damaged in handling, the BC will be lowered measurably. To test this, load a magazine with sharp-pointed bullets and fire the first shot. The bullets lower in the magazine are bounced fore and aft under recoil, which can change the BC on all subsequent shots from the magazine. Want proof? Take a lot of loaded ammo and a chronograph to the range, fire five shots with sharp-pointed high-BC bullets, then randomly file the tips of five more bullets from the same lot and fire them. You will find that accuracy is not significantly changed but that the velocities will drop by as much as 10%. The BC in this test could be cut by as much as 50%. Of course, you must be willing to place your chronograph downrange, as this is a 300-yard+ test.

Today, most military munitions are guided in real-time or "smart bombs," there is little defense industry interest in further refinement of small arms' exterior ballistics. The ballistics research group (BRL) at Aberdeen has been closed. Yet, the final methods developed at Aberdeen could predict small arms trajectories to within a few inches at 1,000 or more yards ... for any projectile. You could argue that exterior ballistic science had developed to a point where unpredictable environmental factors such as wind eddies and temperature variations cause far greater error at long ranges than mathematics. Unfortunately, the shooting sports industry has failed to adopt the newer methods developed with our tax dollars—the same small arms method still used by the defense industry: the "Point Mass" and "Modified Point Mass" methods.

Shooting software that employs the "Point Mass" method developed at the BRL is available, with drag functions for most of the common bullet shapes. The results are superior to traditional "G1 fits everything" thinking, but shooters must learn that BCs differ for each "G" drag function. This is a scary proposition for bullet companies that understand many shooters pick bullets

2 Rinker, Robert A. *Understanding Firearms Ballistics*

that are based on high BCs. For example, a VLD bullet with a G1-based BC of .690 will have a properly calculated G7 BC of only .344, even though it is a more aerodynamic shape with less drag. I can sympathize with the bullet companies. Can you imagine explaining this to someone who thinks they can make a rifle shoot like a laser and thinks high BCs are the key? We call these shooters "the laser beam crowd."

Accurate modern ballistics (as defined by the BRL) use the coefficient of drag (CD) and speed of sound rather than traditional Ingalls/Mayevski/Sciacci s, t, a & i functions. The area of physics involved is sometimes called "aero ballistics." This method is closely aligned with aerodynamics, avoids velocity discontinuities, and is far more accurate to distances beyond 1,000 yards when combined with a proper drag function. A by-product of modern ballistics is that you can estimate the CD from projectile dimensions used to define custom drag functions for unusual bullet shapes.[3]

Calculating BC

The coefficient of drag for a bullet is an aerodynamic factor that relates air drag to air density, cross-sectional area, velocity and mass. One way to view CD is as the "generic indicator" of drag for any bullet of the same shape. You can then use sectional density (again, that's weight multiplied by its frontal area) to relate the drag coefficient to different bullet sizes.

Sectional Density = (Wt. in Grains/7,000) / (Dia.* Dia.)

You can see from the formula that a 1-inch diameter, 1-pound bullet (7,000 gr.) would produce a sectional density of 1. The standard projectile for all drag functions always weighs 1 pound with a 1-inch diameter.

Another term you'll occasionally find in load manuals is the bullet's "Form Factor." The form factor is simply the CD of a bullet divided by the CD of a predefined drag function's standard reference projectile.

Form Factor = (CD of any bullet) / (CD of the Defined 'G' Function Std. Bullet)

Ballistic coefficients are then the ratio of velocity retardation due to air drag (or CD) for a particular bullet to that of its larger 'G' Model standard reference projectile. To relate the size of the bullet to that of the standard projectile, divide the bullet's sectional density by its form factor.

ballistic coefficient = (bullet sectional density) / (bullet form factor)

These short formulae show that a bullet with the same shape as any standard bullet, weighing 1 lb. and 1 inch in diameter, will always have a BC of 1.000. If the bullet is the same shape but smaller, it will have an identical CD, with a

3 http://shootingsoftware.com/coefficients.htm

form factor of 1.000 and a BC equal to its SD. You often see articles declaring the BC is simply the SD divided by the form factor. They rarely explain that a form factor requires accurate CD measurements for the bullet and a standard reference projectile *of the same shape*. Indeed, if it were that easy to calculate BC, all software could do so for bullets, but few products can do it accurately.

Here are some drag models commonly used in small arms ballistics:

G1.1—Standard model, flat-cased with 2-caliber (blunt) nose ogive

G5.1—For moderate (low-base) boattails—7° 30' tail taper with 6.19-caliber tangent nose ogive.

G6.1—For flat-based "Spire Point" type bullets—6.09 caliber secant nose ogive

G7.1—For VLD-type boattails—long 7° 30' tail taper with 10-caliber tangent nose ogive

GS—For round ball—Based on measured 9/16-inch spherical projectiles

RA4—For .22 Long Rifle, identical to G1 below 1,400 fps

GL—Traditional model used for blunt-nosed exposed lead bullets, identical to G1 below 1,400 fps

GI—Converted from the original Ingalls tables

Remember, earlier, we mentioned that "prescribed laboratory conditions" are required to measure BC accurately. Here is how Stephen Ricciardelli, author of the web page stevespages.com, answers the question, "BC or BS?"

So what does this really mean? Let's say you live in Florida. You are enjoying your 90-degree temperatures, your 90% humidity, and your gentle gulf breeze. You decide to work up a new load for your favorite .30-06. As remarkable as it may sound, your first load prints groups of five shots at 200 yards of less than 1 inch! You're happier than a clam at high tide!

That fall you go to Colorado to hunt mule deer. You take your favorite .30-06, and those great new loads, with you. You are high in the mountains, you spot a great 18-pointer at around 400 yards, with a body weight of at least 500 pounds, squeeze off a shot, and miss the sucker by almost 5 feet ... but instead hit a scrawny little 95-pound doe with a severe case of hair-loss! You get so angry that you take a second shot, knowing that you are limited to only one kill, but what the heck, no one saw you ... and the second shot hits the game warden, who was standing around 3 feet from the poor old doe! (Unfortunately, you didn't kill the warden ... so off to court and jail you go ....)

How could that have happened? Here's an explanation, as best as I can do.

First of all, the 180-grain bullet you selected had a factory-rated BC of 0.431 (at the Standard conditions). Well, you tested the loads at 90 degrees instead of 59

degrees, the humidity was around 90% instead of 78%, barometric pressure that day was around 29.53-in. Hg. All these factors increased that factory rating of 0.431 to a little over 0.529. A difference of almost 25%!

So, you took your Florida loads, with their BC of 0.529 up to the mountains. The temperature is now 20 below zero, you are at 5,000 feet, and the humidity is only 35%. That Florida bullet with a BC of 0.529 now rates around a stinking 0.282. Impressed? You should be!

Do you wanna know why you missed? That magic number of 0.529 is now down to 0.282, and we haven't finished yet. Were you aware that combustibles behave differently at different temperatures? That bullet launched at, let's say, 2,600 fps in Florida is now only leaving the barrel at around 2,400 fps. And remember you fired your groups in a very gentle gulf breeze, you are now firing those bullets across 400 yards of crosswinds of up to 30 mph. (And you were probably shooting either uphill or downhill.)

How much of this miss is due to the BC? Very Little! Your .30-06, when sighted in while you were in Florida, dropped 50 inches at 400 yards, when launched at 2,600 fps. Now that you are in Colorado, the bullet is leaving the barrel at only 2,400 fps, it will drop 60 inches over the same 400 yards. The gulf breeze you enjoyed in Florida had no effect on accuracy, however, the 30 mph crosswinds up in the Colorado Mountains will cause that bullet to deflect almost 48 inches. So now your bullet is 4 feet to the side of your target, and at least 1 foot lower than you expected! That's exactly where the doe was standing! And the warden? Well, he was hiding next to a tree watching you, a few feet from the doe, and in your anger and haste, you pulled the crosshairs of your $39 scope just a tad to the right on your second shot. Well, the thick crosshairs of that cheap scope cover around 12 inches at 400 yards! You moved it two widths of the crosshair, and the warden caught that 180 grainer! So how come the doe died and the warden didn't? The doe weighed around 95 pounds, the warden 275. The doe had one layer of skin to protect her, the warden had his down jacket, wool liner, felt shirt, insulated underwear, and his beer gut to protect him.

When you get out of jail, the first thing you do is take your .30-06 to a range in Colorado. To your amazement, at 200 yards, five shots grouped around 2 inches ... that's how much the difference in BC actually made ... a stinking 1 inch at 200 yards! And that was for a B.C. difference of 50%.

Now you know the answer to the question, "BC or BS?"

One could argue that the BC of the bullet never changes; therefore, you should always choose a bullet with the highest possible BC to retain as much velocity as possible. In most cases, the same result would come from selecting a bullet with a high sectional density simply because we know that a heavier-for-caliber bullet will retain more velocity and penetrate better.

Here is a quick test to try if you still think BC is important at hunting ranges. Most hunters admit 300 yards is as far as the average hunter should shoot at game. Take your favorite hunting rifle and load 10 rounds with a high-BC bullet. Then, in the same lot of brass, load 10 rounds with a blunt round-nosed bullet of the same weight. Give them a fair test on the range at 300 yards. The two bullets on paper at 300 yards will shoot less than two minutes of angle apart, often closer (measuring center of group), but the difference in published BC can easily be .200 or more.

Just for fun, we conducted the above experiment. A good marksman, Steve Wright, ran this test. Our target pictured below consisted of a 3-inch black circle with a 1-inch white center; the vertical bar measured 1 inch, too. The gun was a .300 H&H magnum, and we selected 150-grain bullets because a wide variety of makes and styles were readily available. Once a load was developed for each bullet to attain similar velocities (average 3,125 fps at the muzzle), we sighted

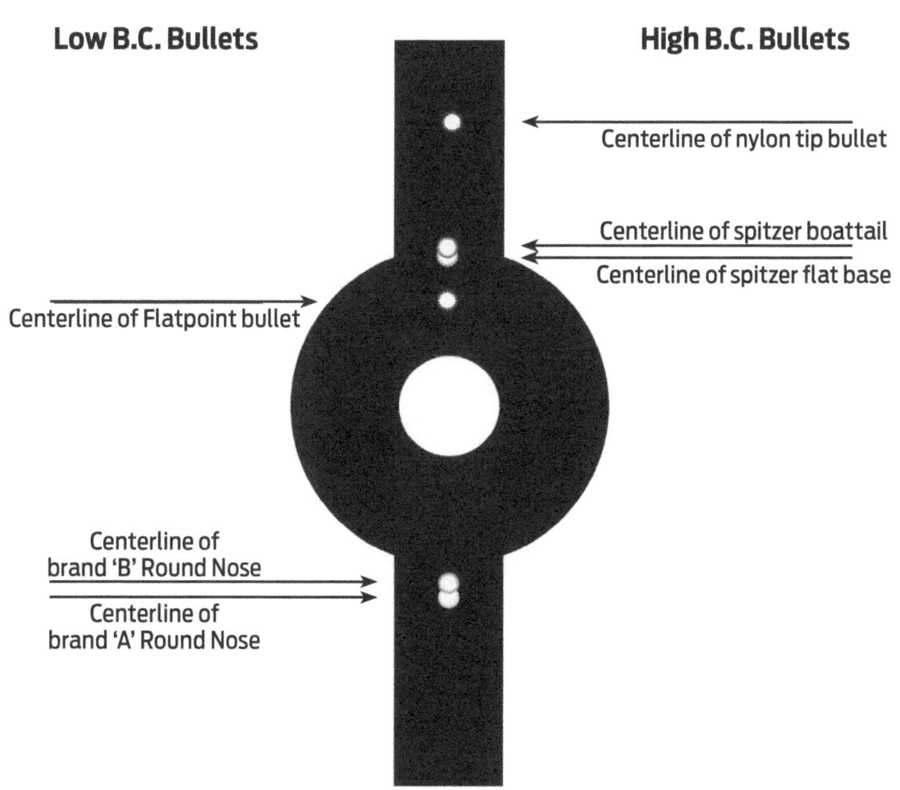

the gun at 300 yards and made no further sight adjustments.

All the groups landed within 1.7 MOA at 300 yards from a gun capable of 1 MOA accuracy with a good load, about 5.25 inches. As a side note, 50% of the groups we fired were under MOA in size for the given bullet. Bottom line? If you had a pocket full of our loads mixed up and randomly loaded your gun for a deer hunt, you could shoot to 300 yards and be assured of a hit, so long as you did your part; for that matter, you would still hit a prairie dog at 300 yards with that small a variation in elevation.

Do you still think BC is important at hunting ranges? Here are some comments from a couple of well-respected firearms experts. "The United States entered WWI in April 1917 using the .30-06 cartridge in rifles and machine guns using a 150-grain pointed, flat base bullet with a muzzle velocity of 2,700 feet per second and an extreme range of 3,400 yards. From machine guns, a sheaf of fire could be controlled only to 2,500 yards and was entirely outranged by the machine gun cartridges of our foes. It was discovered during the course of U.S. Army testing that the most effective bullet we could fire in our service cartridge while staying within chamber pressure limitations would weigh between 170-175 grains, be sharp-pointed, and have a taper or boattail at its rear end," said Robert Mermelstien in *Mermelstien's Guide to Metallic Cartridge Evolution.*

In *Small Arms Design, Vol. 1* (1945), Colonel Townsend Whelen stated, "Now for some of the facts about this bullet. Its angle of elevation for 1,000 yards at a muzzle velocity of 2,640 fps was 39 minutes (a minute is equal to 1.047 in. at 100 yards) compared with 48 minutes for the 150-grain bullet at 2,700 fps. A 172-grain flat-base bullet with the same point as the boattailed bullet, and fired at the same velocity required an angle of elevation of 44 minutes at 1,000 yards, but up to and including 400 yards the two angles of elevation were identical. Therefore the boattail did not show any advantage at all at short ranges where the velocities were very high, and it was not until 500 yards where their remaining velocity had dropped to about 1,800 fps that it began to show a slight advantage, and there only to about the extent of one minute. At 1,000 yards the boattail showed about five minutes less angle of elevation as compared with the flat-base bullet of the same weight. But beyond 1,200 yards, where the velocity had dropped below that of sound, the advantage of the boattail was very marked."

Back to the question of selecting the right bullet for the job ...

Cheap bullets are for plinking, varmints, practice and fun. Premium hunting bullets are for use in the field and are a small investment compared to all the other gear you will buy. Heavy-for-caliber bullets are more effective for hunting purposes. After all, there is no such thing as "overkill." Have you ever seen an animal that was too dead?

Working Up Loads

A descriptive term, working up loads means reloaders will spend countless hours developing a handload that will deliver the desired results by trying one load after another. Most often, these loads are a progression from a light starting load, well below the expected maximum charge weight, to the hottest load the gun will safely handle. Sometimes, the result is that the cartridge will not safely handle the combination of powder, primer, and bullet to deliver the desired result, so we start over with a different powder and bullet. Ideally, we want a load that will perform its appointed task with the lowest possible chamber pressure.

Many reloaders look upon reloading manuals as a starting point, assuming that the publisher has a team of lawyers that would not allow them to publish the "real maximum" loads. In reality, maximum loads in today's manuals indicate where the danger point lies; they are not intended as a suggested load to be shot day in and day out. If you choose a load about 5% below the published maximums for any caliber, you will get better life from your brass and barrel and probably better accuracy.

We have already discussed powder selection earlier in this chapter. If you have a pressure system like the PressureTrace or Oehler Model 43, you can take pressure readings from your gun that are pretty reliable, something that wildcatters could not afford to do 10 years ago. See Chapter 10 for more details. Such accurate pressure information will help you select the powder with the best burning characteristics for your particular load.

In the beginning, you need to test for the safe limits of the new cartridge and then look at the accuracy potential. Determine the likely maximum load for your cartridge case. If you're unsure how to do this, refer to Chapter 8, "Predicting Results." For simplicity, let's assume the maximum is 50 gr. Since we're working with wildcats, you should reduce that by 10% for a safe starting point. That way, if your calculations are off, you have an added margin of safety. With our reduction of 10%, your starting charge would be 45 grains. Load three rounds with this charge. Next, load three rounds with 46- and 47-gr.; at this point, increasing by only ½ grain on the subsequent loads would be prudent. In this way, you may have to pull a few bullets on the overloads, but you will not have nearly as many to pull as if you load large quantities only to find they are too hot.

Initially, seat the bullet at least .050 inch off the lands, yet make it uniform for all the test loads at this phase of the testing. You are looking for safe pressures now; you can vary seating depth later to improve accuracy. Keeping the bullet off the lands prevents pressure spikes while learning the pressure limits of the new cartridge. Freebore, throating and bullet jump are discussed in Chapter 9.

Another option requires a small investment and is extremely convenient when working up loads. That is, assemble a reloading setup you can carry to the range. One solution is to pick up the Lee Anniversary pack, which gives you everything but the dies and shell holder so you can load. Mount the press to a steel plate to clamp it to a shooting bench at the range. You can load just what you want to shoot at the range. Load the starting loads at home to save time. You can also size all your brass and prime them before you go to the range, so all you have to do is charge them and seat the bullets.

You may have to repeat this entire process with several powders. If you don't already know this, you will quickly learn that powders with similar burning

rates will deliver similar results. If you're looking for the lowest pressure with the best velocity, test powders just outside what you would typically choose for the cartridge, either a little slower or faster. Occasionally, the best results come from these powders on the fringes.

Once you've tested several powders and discovered the maximum load that can be safely shot regularly, you're ready to consider accuracy. Review your test data to see which powder/bullet combination gave the best accuracy in the first round of testing. Select the most accurate load within the test data for that combination of bullet and powder and begin loading with that charge while varying the bullet seating depth in or out in .005-inch increments. Soon, you'll find the "sweet spot" where accuracy is best. Varying the powder charge by a few 1/10 grains can enhance accuracy, though it's equally likely to decrease it. But don't vary the powder charge and seating depth simultaneously; if you do, there is no way to know which variable affects your results.

Load development methodology, as described, will require a fair amount of time if performed correctly. The process is as streamlined as possible because time is money, and the waste of the smallest components possible is considered. However, when you're done, you will know the limits of your cartridge and have accurate loads to brag about.

CHAPTER 18

Popular Wildcats Through 2004

We assembled the first edition of this book in 2004 and published it in 2005, thus the date qualifier on this chapter. Here, we added updates and corrections where needed. Chapter 19 covers the next almost two decades of wildcats.

Chapter 7 left off in the early 1990s with the wildcats of note up to that time, so this chapter is a snapshot of those that have appeared since then. Of course, this could be a massive list if every wildcat were listed, so we limited it to the popular ones. I left out one-of-a-kind experimental cartridges because they do not represent those of interest to the wildcat shooting public.

Left to Right: Calibers .10, .12, .14, .17 and .20.

Sub-Calibers

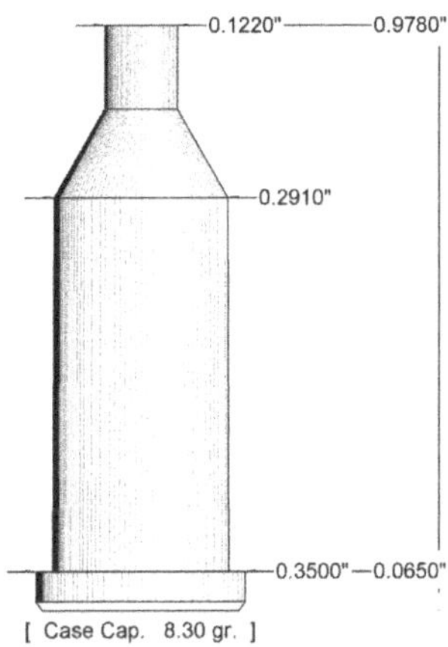

The .10 Eichelberger Squirrel.

Sub-calibers up to this time have been loosely defined, so it's high time we tied a specific definition to the term. "Sub-caliber cartridges are defined as any cartridge which uses projectiles of .224 inch or smaller diameter."

Sub-calibers are one of the fastest-growing areas of shooter interest. The introduction of the .204 Ruger in 2004 was a clear sign that the industry was beginning to see the market for small, light recoil calibers. Other cartridges that prove the market was growing are the .17 HMR, .17 Aguila, and .17 Mach II, all rimfire entries.

Many wildcats are in the sub-caliber category, and the following are the most popular.

.10 Eichelberger Squirrel

William A. Eichelberger is responsible for much of the proliferation and experimentation with sub-calibers that is going on today. He lists the .10 Eichelberger Squirrel among his three favorite designs and notes that its introduction caused "quite a stir." The .10 caliber is suitable for short-range work out to 50 yards. The actual bullet diameter is .103 inch, and a twist of 1:7 will stabilize the bullet. It can be superbly accurate and effective on small varmints like ground squirrels and pest birds.

.10 Eichelberger Squirrel ***21-in. barrel***

BULLET (GR.)	POWDER	CHARGE (GR.)	VELOCITY (FPS)
7.2	WW-748	6.5	3,924
7.2	H335	5.6	3,415
7.2	AA 2460	9.8	4,010
10	AA 2495	6.0	3,188
10	H380	6.4	3,290

.12 Eichelberger H&R Magnum

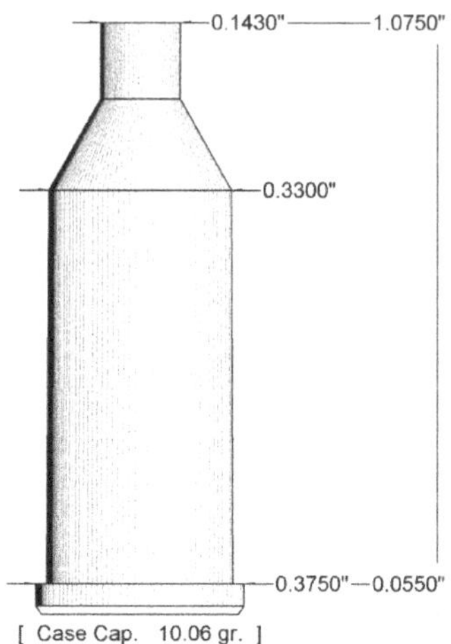

The .12 Eichelberger H&R Magnum.

The second of the three cartridges that Bill Eichelberger lists as his favorites is the .12 Eichelberger H&R Magnum. The bullet diameter for the .12 caliber is .123 inch, and the appropriate twist rate is 1:5.5 in. As you might imagine, locating bullets for the .10, .12, and .14 calibers is a challenge, so many shooters resort to making their own.

"It was in the early 1970s that I started getting serious about small calibers, particularly the .14s," Eichelberger said. "That interest was greatly influenced by chatting with many folks like Boots Obermeyer, John Walker, Bill Key, Bob Carpenter and Jim Cuthbert. During this time, I also managed to be in contact with some folks who were doing things with .14 calibers. I recall Tim Bolinger of Matco, Asa Davis, Bob Alexander of Viper Copper and Brass, and Chuck Richardson of DKT Industries. Nobody had much information, but we were all in the same boat toying with the project of making the .14 calibers work."[1]

.12 Eichelberger H&R Mag ***15-in. barrel***

BULLET (GR.)	POWDER	CHARGE (GR.)	VELOCITY (FPS)
10	AA 2230	9.6	4,125
10	H335	9.9	4,145
11.5	AA 2230	9.1	3,875
11.5	H335	9.5	3,890

1 http://www.saubier.com/eichelbergerinterview.html

.14 Eichelberger Dart

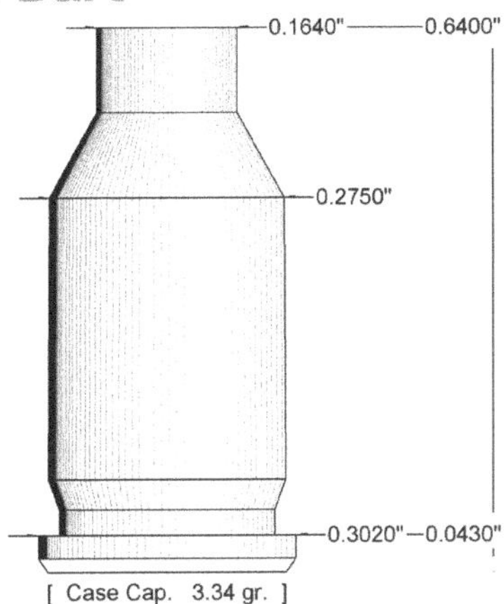

The .14 Eichelberger Dart.

In a letter, Eichelberger explained his involvement with the sub-calibers to me. "I became interested in smaller wildcat calibers, initially the .14s. Inspired by Alton Jones and Boots Obermeyer, we put together our first .14-caliber cartridge in 1979. The objectives were to design a small centerfire cartridge that was reloadable, thus our first attempt was the .14 Eichelberger Dart, based on the .25 ACP case. Based on need, available time, and available funds we proceeded to design other small cases, small-caliber wildcats in .14, .12 and .10 calibers. All of the cartridge designs were challenging but the ones using thicker walled brass were a bit more difficult. To date, we have designed a total of fourteen .14-caliber cartridge configurations, seven .12-caliber cartridge configurations and five .10-caliber cartridge configurations. The largest cartridge we have designed is the Eichelberger .14/222 Magnum and the smallest is the .10 Dart."

The Dart is included here because it started Bill Eichelberger down the design path. Eichelberger is widely recognized as *the* authority on sub-caliber cartridges and was a true gentleman. Update: Bill passed away on May 10, 2007. Hope to meet up at the range on the other side.

.14 Eichelberger Dart — ***15-in. barrel***

BULLET (GR.)	POWDER	CHARGE (GR.)	VELOCITY (FPS)
10	AA 9	3.5	2,967
12.7	H110	3.2	2,614
13	H110	3.3	2,692

.14/221 Eichelberger

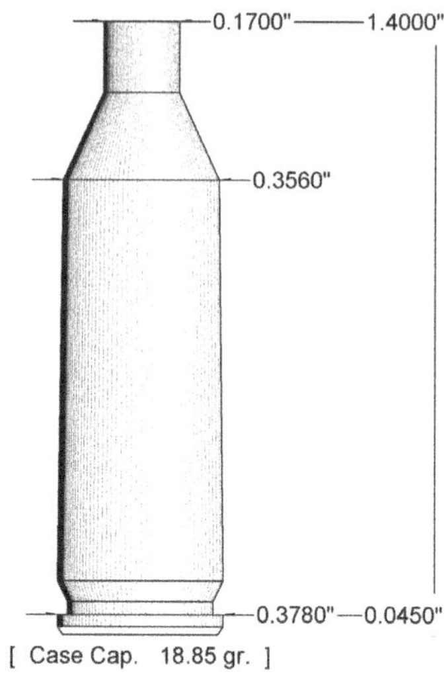

The .14/221 Eichelberger.

Bill Eichelberger also designed the .14/221 Eichelberger, which he listed among his three favorite designs. The bullet diameter is .144 inch, and a barrel twist rate of 1:8.75 in. is recommended.

When asked about his contributions to sub-caliber development, Eichelberger said, "I was intrigued with the possibility of shooting small-caliber ultra-lightweight bullets at high velocity. In the beginning, sometimes things didn't work as planned and as I said before, it was a bit frustrating because there was little reference material or information available. In fact, early on I gleaned a lot of valuable information through talking with Bob Carpenter who had worked on the Army's .14/.222 cartridge at their Aberdeen Proving Grounds in Maryland. In addition to my efforts, there were others doing some pioneering efforts in the .14-caliber arena as well. If I may indulge in a bit of trivia ... Asa Davis, Bob Alexander, Chuck Richardson, and I each had developed a .14-caliber cartridge based on the .32 ACP case and we each referred to them as 'Our .14 Flea.' A bit later I had managed to collect copies of the cartridge drawings from each of these three gentlemen of their .14 Fleas. Although there's not that much you can do different with the stuffy little .32 ACP cartridge case, each one of 'our .14 caliber Flea' designs was a bit different."[2]

Reloaders are advised that working with cases this small and bullets in the

2 http://www.saubier.com/eichelbergerinterview.html

range of 15 grains is challenging. Special equipment is required for loading and cleaning. Case capacities are small, and powder measurements starting around 5 grains allow little room for error. The bottom-line advice is "work up slow."

.14/.221 Eichelberger ***20-in. barrel***

BULLET (GR.)	POWDER	CHARGE (GR.)	VELOCITY (FPS)
13	AA 2495	17	4,183
15	AA 2495	17.8	4,042
18	AA 2700	16.7	3,703

.14/221 Walker (.14 Walker)

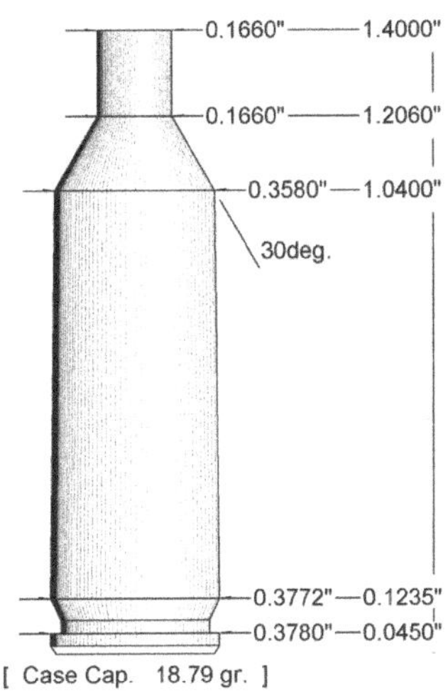

The .14/221 Walker.

The .14 Walker is a .221 case necked down to .14 caliber, which P.O. Ackley mentions in *Handbook for Shooters and Reloaders, Vol. II*. Jeff Lawrence of Lawrence Barrels is currently the best source for sub-caliber barrels, and he says that the .14 Walker is by far the most popular of the .14-caliber cartridges in use today, with the Eichelberger version coming in second place.

Walker wrote to Ackley in 1966[3], "The shooting was done with a sporting rifle of about seven pounds; the barrel length was 22 inches. The twist was 8.75 per inch. We have fired many groups at 100 yards measuring .312 inch and at 200 yards, groups measuring .700 inch. These are five-shot groups."

3 Ackley, P.O., *Handbook for Shooters and Reloaders, Vol. II*, 1966

.14/221 Walker			22-in. barrel
BULLET (GR.)	POWDER	CHARGE (GR.)	VELOCITY (FPS)
15	IMR 3031	17	4,215
17	IMR 4198	15	4,093
18	IMR 3031	16	3,830
20	IMR 3031	15	3,643

.17 Viper

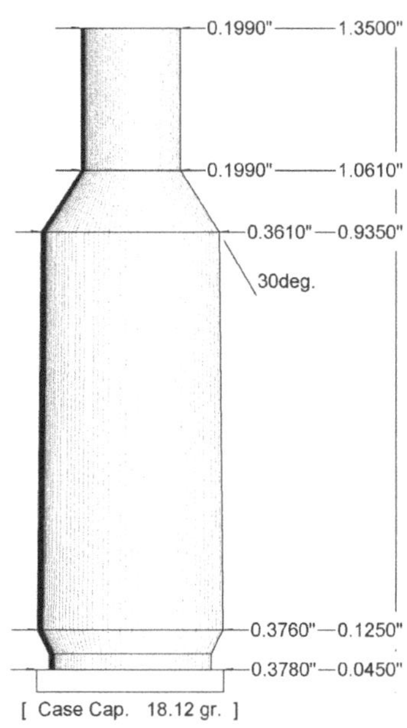

The .17 Viper.

Bob Davidson of Roswell, New Mexico, developed the .17 Viper concept from a desire to create a rimless case along the capacity of a .17 Ackley Hornet. He attempted to duplicate the performance of the .17 Ackley Hornet but with better brass. The case has more capacity than the .17 Ackley Hornet or the .17/30 Carbine. Forming .17/30 Carbine brass is difficult by comparison since every case had to be annealed to prevent losses. With the .17 Viper, annealing is optional. The .17 Viper fits sizewise right between the .17 Ackley Hornet and the .17 Mach 4. Davidson's sole purpose in designing the case was for fox hunting. The result is a cartridge that holds 15 grains of powder and will deliver 4,000+ fps from 20-gr. bullets, while at the same time, you can download it to 3,000 fps with 25-gr. bullets (to not damage the fox hides).

Davidson shortened a .17 Mach 4 case to a body length of .946 inch and lengthened the neck to .250 inch for an overall case length of 1.35 inches. He says, "A long neck on a cartridge is like long legs on a beautiful sports model, longer is better." Accuracy is excellent with groups well under ½ MOA for 20- and 25-grain bullets.

.17 Viper		*23-in. barrel*	
BULLET (GR.)	POWDER	CHARGE (GR.)	VELOCITY (FPS)
20 Vmax	N120	14.2	3,951
20 Vmax	N120	14.4	4,025
25 Hornady	RL-7	14.0	3,564
25 Hornady	RL-7	14.4	3,680
25 Hornady	RL-7	14.8	3,815
30 Berger	H4198	13.5	3,123
30 Berger	H4198	14.4	3,586
30 Berger	H335	17.8	3,629

.17-223

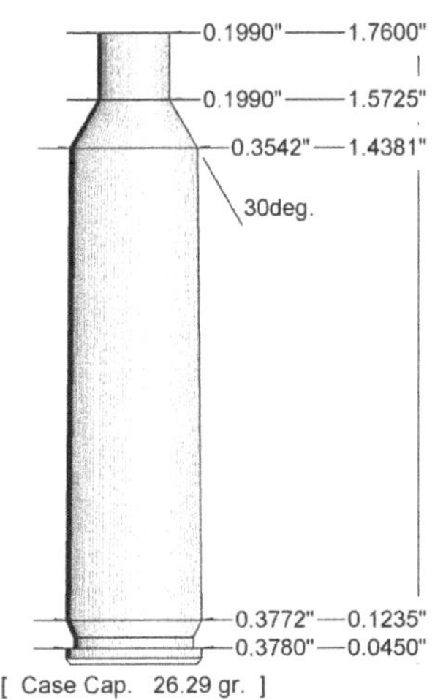

The .17-223.

The .17-223 enjoys the distinction of being the second cartridge in history to have a commercially chambered rifle marketed for it without a commercially available cartridge. This happened when Harrington & Richardson introduced the Model 317 Ultra Wildcat in this caliber; the gun used the Sako L461 action.

The .17-223 had several positives in the race for dominance in the wildcat market. First was the commercially manufactured rifle from H&R. Second was the massive quantity of 5.56mm NATO brass available worldwide. And third, the simplicity of forming the brass. Add in the fact that it's the ballistic equivalent of the .22-250 and is practically identical in performance to the .17 Remington, and you've got quite a combination. One disadvantage is that, like the .17 Remington, the .17-223 tends to foul the barrel in 10 to 20 shots due to the high case capacity vs. the caliber.

Let's sum up: a 6-pound rifle, 39 inches overall length, minimal report, no recoil, cheap available brass, velocities up to 4,000 fps, extreme accuracy, deadly on chucks and turkey. This cartridge has been around for a long time but is still very popular.

.17-223 ***20-in. barrel***

BULLET (GR.)	POWDER	CHARGE (GR.)	VELOCITY (FPS)
25	IMR 3031	20	3,660
25	IMR 4227	14.9	3,390
25	IMR 4198	20	3,700
25	IMR 4198	21	3,865

.19 Badger

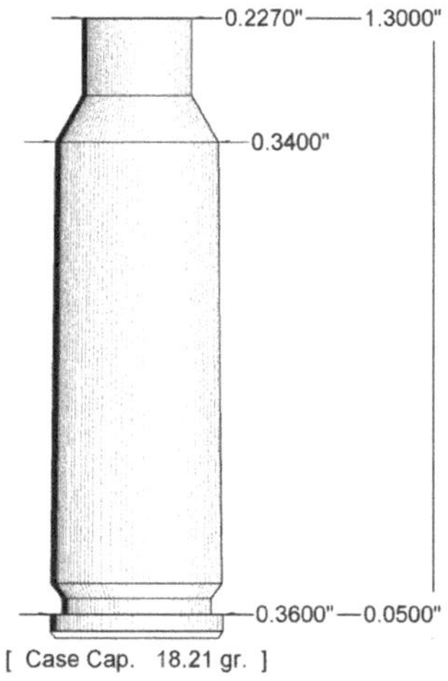

The .19 Badger.

A product from the folks at James Calhoon Bullets (4343 U.S. Hwy. 87, Havre, MT 59501), the .19 Badger is based on the .30 Carbine case. An associate of Calhoon Bullets, Jim Harrison, had a CZ 527 re-barreled to the newest entry into the .19-caliber family of cartridges from Calhoon. On the rifle's first outing in July 2001, seven badgers were taken; Andy Waritz witnessed this and nicknamed the cartridge the .19 Badger. The name stuck after that.

Cool operating, low fowling, .250-inch groups, with bullets near 3,550 fps, the .19 Badger is a slick-feeding rimless cartridge that reaches 300 yards with authority on varmint-class animals. Components and barrel kits are available from Calhoon.

.19 Badger		***24-in. barrel***	
BULLET (GR.)	**POWDER**	**CHARGE (GR.)**	**VELOCITY (FPS)**
27 Calhoon	AA 1680	16.6	3,725
27 Calhoon	N120	15.7	3,730
32 Calhoon	RL-7	15.7	3,530
32 Calhoon	N130	16.2	3,540

.19 Calhoon

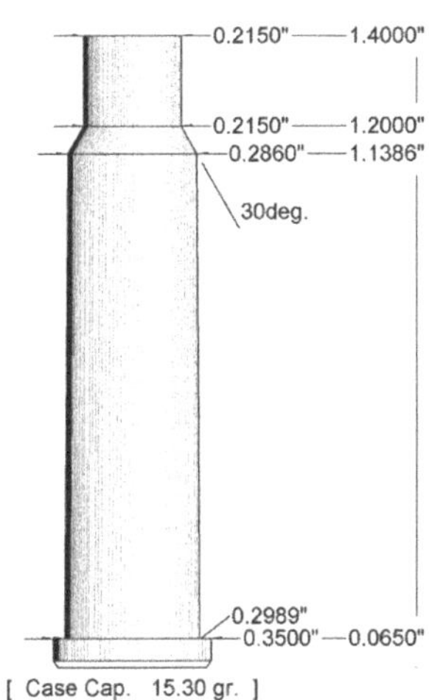

The .19 Calhoon.

Twice as popular as the .19-223 Calhoon (according to Calhoon Bullets), the .19 Calhoon—based on the Hornet—is an amazing performer, delivering velocities similar to the .17 Mach IV in an even more compact package. It utilizes "mini-sized" Hornet actions for a truly lightweight rifle platform. Cool operation, very low fouling and low cost make the .19 Calhoon the *ideal* gopher and squirrel cartridge.

Calhoon had tried various .17 calibers to locate a low-recoil round with sufficient energy to make clean kills on small targets. He ran into all the same problems most .17-caliber shooters complain about—fast heating and fouling. The .19 Calhoon's combination of a .198-in. bullet and the smaller case capacity produce far better ballistics than the parent .22 Hornet case, avoiding the fouling and heating problems of most .17-caliber cartridges.

This wildcat easily has twice the range and energy of the .17 HMR. It's easy to form: run a .22 Hornet case through the sizing die and fire. A compact design that is economical to shoot and has light recoil makes the .19 Calhoon an ideal choice when re-barreling any gun chambered in the .22 Hornet.

.19 Calhoon **24-in. barrel**

BULLET (GR.)	POWDER	CHARGE (GR.)	VELOCITY (FPS)
27 Dbl HP	AA 1680	14.7	3,610
	WIN 296	12.0	3,530
32 Dbl HP	AA 1680	13.5	3,340
	VIHT N120	13.3	3,270
36 Dbl HP	AA 2200	15.0	3,165
	AA 1680	12.5	3,000
40 Dbl HP	AA 2200	14.5	3,060
	AA 1680	12.0	2,860

.19-223 Calhoon

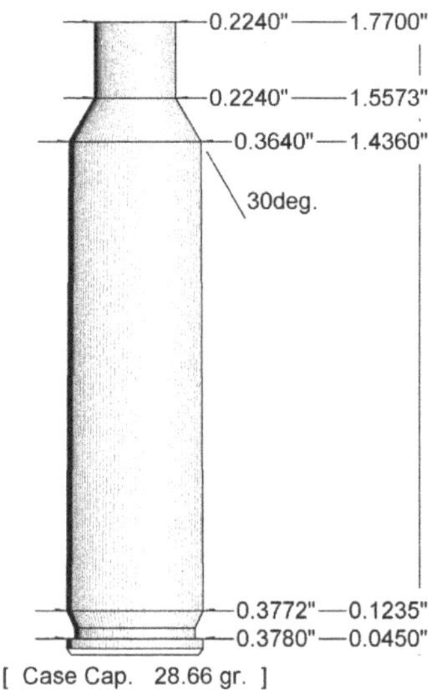

The .19-223 Calhoon.

In the early 1970s, when the NATO countries were holding field trials for a superior infantry round, of all the calibers that were tested to the 400-meter range (.14, .17, .19, .20, .22, .270, .30), the entry that won was the "4.85mm Experimental." That round was a .222 Mag. case using a .19-caliber bullet. It lost out to the .223 only because the military preferred a compact, jointed cleaning rod. Of course, we in the civilian crowd prefer a one-piece rod, making the .19 caliber the winner!

In Montana, where Jim Leahy of Calhoon Bullets lives, hunters spend a lot of time shooting ground squirrels and prairie dogs—targets that do not require an Eargoschplitenloudenboomer to do the job. In 1992, Leahy—an avid varmint hunter—read the NATO test results and saw an opportunity to design a new cartridge that filled the vital niche of low recoil and superior ballistics for the long-range varminters. By 1997, he finalized the dimensions, and testing was underway.

Compared with the .17 Remington, the .19-223 Calhoon will drive considerably heavier bullets (with much better ballistic coefficients) at similar high velocities. It is also more bullet-weight versatile, allowing as light as 32 grains for pelt hunting and as heavy as 44 grains for long-range performance. Compared to the classic .223, the .19-223 will shoot flatter and produce higher velocities with equal-weight bullets.

"With light bullets, awesome accuracy and scorching velocities, this former military round is a great varminter," said Holt Bodinson about the .19-223 Calhoon in his March 2000 *Guns* magazine article, "Calhoon's Amazing .19 Caliber."

.19-223 Calhoon

BULLET (GR.)	POWDER	CHARGE (GR.)	VELOCITY (FPS)
32 Dbl HP	AA 2520	27.0	4,025
	BLC-2	28.5	4,025
36 Dbl HP	AA 2015BR	24.5	3,840
	BLC-2	27.5	3,830
40 Dbl HP	VIHT N550	28.0	3,780
	AA 2520	25.5	3,680
44 Dbl HP	VIHT N550	27.5	3,670
	AA 2700	29.0	3,540

Tactical Twenty (Tact .20)

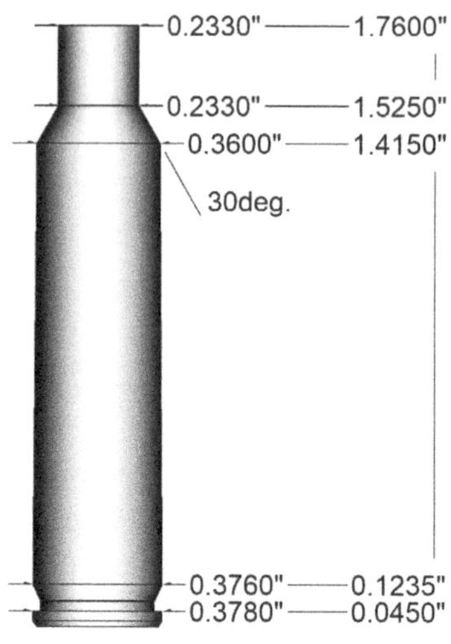

The .20 Tactical.

Todd A. Kindler, editor of *Small Caliber News* and owner of The Woodchuck Den, Inc., designed and developed the "Tact .20," based on a .223 Remington necked down to .20 caliber with a 30-degree shoulder. It moves the Hornady .20-caliber 32-gr. V-Max bullet at 4,200 to 4,300 fps. With the new Hornady 40-grain V-Max bullet (.275 BC) moving out of the Tactical .20 at 3,850–4,000 fps, the cartridge has much less wind drift and is flatter shooting at 500 yards than the big .22-caliber cartridges, including the .220 Swift and the .223 Winchester Short Magnum. The amazing Tactical .20 does all this with minimal powder, which means much less recoil and noise.

Dakota Arms licensed the Tactical .20 with premium brass and match-grade ammo and encouraged accuracy gunsmiths to chamber for it; however, with reamers made by Pacific Tool & Gage to their specifications. This way, the brass and loaded ammo matched the chamber and loading dies available from Redding and Wilson dealers.

It has proven extremely flat shooting and deadly on woodchucks and coyotes. The "Tact .20" has minimal recoil, so you can see your shots, and the Hornady 32-gr. V-Max bullet does not exit a large coyote or woodchuck. It has 500- to 600-yard potential from a rifle with a 24-inch barrel and predates the .204 Ruger by several years.

.20 Tactical		24-in. barrel	
BULLET (GR.)	POWDER	CHARGE (GR.)	VELOCITY (FPS)
31.5 HP Bishop	IMR 4198	24	4,221
32 VMAX	H4198	25	4,264
32 VMAX	X-Terminator	27	4,112
32 VMAX	N133	26	4,121
40 BT Lucas	Benchmark	26	3,762
40 BT Lucas	N140	27	3,775
45 BT Lucas	Varget	26	3,634

.20 VarTarg (VT)

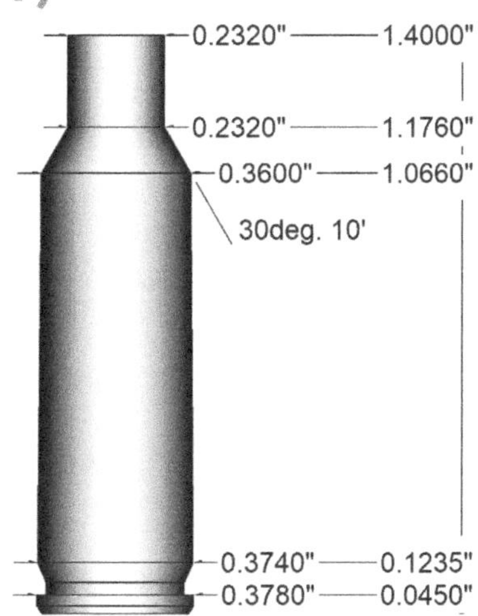

The .20 Vartarg.

In 1995, Todd A. Kindler, the editor of *Small Caliber News*, designed the .20 VarTarg (varmint/target), better known as the .20 VT for short, for varmint shooting in more settled areas and precision target shooting as well, hence the name VarTarg. Kindler necked down and improved a .221 case with the 32-grain Hornady V-Max bullet moving over 3,800 fps. The .20 VT is an outstanding, mild-mannered varmint cartridge out to 400 yards. A .20 VarTarg Turbo (VTT) is also based on an improved .222 Remington case.

The .20 VT may be one of the finest prairie dog and ground gopher cartridges ever designed. You can shoot it all day with little worry of overheating and with minimal cleaning, which adds up to more shooting time and fun! The wildcat has a mild report and little recoil, so anyone can enjoy shooting it.

When you crank up the new Hornady 40-grain V-Max bullets (.275 BC) in the

.20 VT to over 3,500 fps, you have a cartridge that almost equals the old .220 Swift (out to 400 yards, the .20 VT has slightly less wind drift than the Swift). That's amazing when you consider the .20 VT is doing it with about 20 grains less powder.

In 2004, Dakota Arms signed an exclusive licensing agreement with Todd Kindler. Dakota encouraged custom gunsmiths to build the .20 VT. However, it strongly recommended ordering chambering reamers from Dave Kiff at Pacific Tool & Gage to match Dakota's brass and ammo.

.20 Vartarg		***23-in. barrel***	
BULLET (GR.)	**POWDER**	**CHARGE (GR.)**	**VELOCITY (FPS)**
32	N120	18.6	3,880
40	H4198	18.8	3,518
40	N130	19.9	3,565
36	N130	16.9	3,042
36	N130	20.5	3,701
36	RL-7	19.3	3,674
36	H4198	20.0	3,728

.22 Reed Express

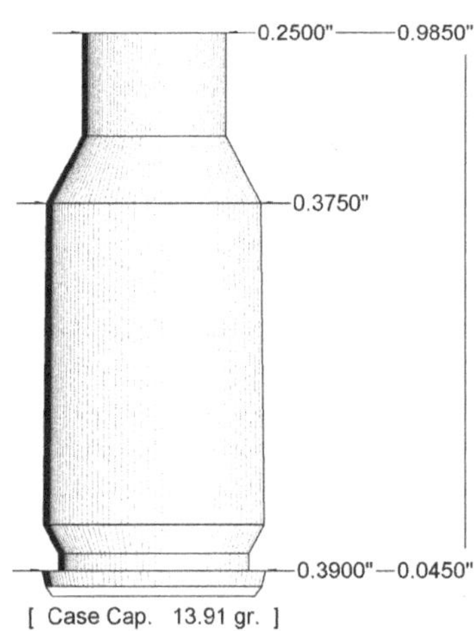

The .22 Reed Express.

Ron Reed of Ron's Ammunition and Research (RAR) instigated the .22 Reed Express cartridge, and my shop, Z-Hat Custom, did the legwork and testing. At the time of development, CZ 52 pistols were readily available as surplus, and the original caliber in these guns was 7.62x25. Starline offered 7.62x25, so quality brass for the .22 Reed Express was no problem. The idea was to create an optional caliber for the CZ 52 that would attract new shooters to these high-quality semi-autos.

As it turns out, the case capacity of the formed case is nearly identical to a standard .22 Hornet, though the Reed Express has a shorter, fatter powder column than the Hornet. (Custom barrels are obtainable from RAR at 1209 S.W. 129th St., Oklahoma City, OK 73170, reedsammo.com.) These barrels are made as a drop-in replacement for the original CZ 52, giving you a gun with two calibers for a minor investment. The .22 Reed Express feeds from the standard magazine, and no other modifications to the firearm are necessary.

.22 Reed Express ***10-in. barrel***

BULLET (GR.)	POWDER	CHARGE (GR.)	VELOCITY (FPS)
30 Berger	H110	12.7	2,782
33 TNT	H110	11.3	2,358
33 TNT	H110	12.5	2,677
35 Vmax	H110	11.3	2,339
35 Vmax	H110	12.6	2,721
40 Vmax	H110	11.6	2,550
50	AA 9	10	2,401

.223 Timbs

The .223 Timbs.

In a parallel development, the .223 Timbs results from collaboration between Quality Cartridge and Joseph Timbs just before the .22 Reed Express. Both were developed without knowing the others' work, proving again that "Great minds think alike, and fools seldom differ!" The Timbs loading is the American answer to the proprietary .224 BOZ, bringing the CZ-52 into the new millennium. The .223 Timbs is a special loading of the 7.62x25 round for use only in the CZ 52 pistol. It consists of a sabot like the Remington "Accelerator," pushing a 50-gr. bullet over 2,000 fps.

The concept was for a devastating multi-purpose round for small game, varmints and defense. Accuracy has proven to be on par with traditional rounds fired from the same pistol, and terminal ballistics are quite impressive, with initial tests showing devastating expansion from the varmint-type bullets. Once this specialized sabot loading proved the viability of such a cartridge, Timbs and Quality Cartridge planned to create their own wildcat for the CZ 52, called the 5.7mm Timbs.

.22 Squirrel

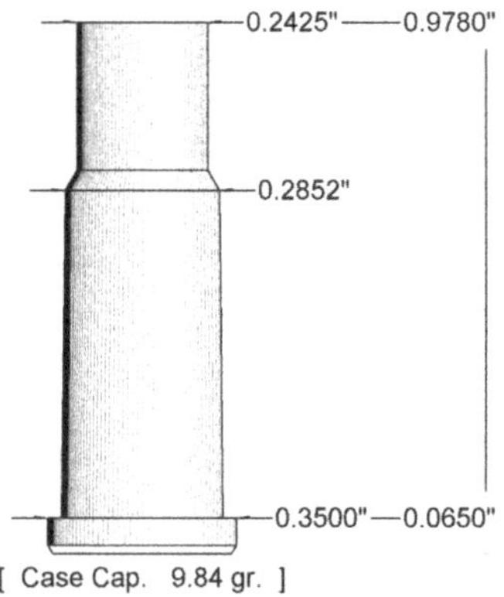

The .22 Squirrel.

The .22 Squirrel is a design from Todd Kindler of the Woodchuck Den, Inc., who noticed that one of the case-forming steps from the .22 Hornet to the .17 Squirrel produced a cartridge that looked close to .22 caliber. As surmised, the .22 Squirrel is based on the .22 Hornet with the case blown out and a 30-degree shoulder. Kindler's test results show that the .22 Squirrel can push a 40-grain bullet up to 2,400 fps and maintain an accuracy of 5/8-inch at 100 yards! With this accuracy and speed, the .22 Squirrel should be deadly on squirrels and could be just the ticket for turkey hunters who want to make that long-range headshot (where rifles are legal for turkey hunting).

.22 Squirrel		*22-in. barrel*	
BULLET (GR.)	POWDER	CHARGE (GR.)	VELOCITY (FPS)
30	N110	7.0	2,275
40	N110	7.0	2,230
40	WIN 296	8.1	2,345

.22 Dasher

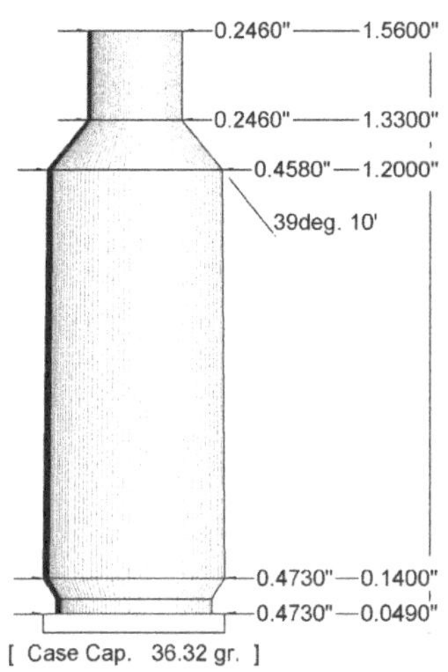

The .22 Dasher.

Sometimes, the first is not the best. The .22 Dasher was the product of a collaboration between avid shooter Al Ashton and precision rifle builder Dan Dowling, both of Colorado.

In the late 1980s to early '90s, cartridges like the PPC and the BR took over competitive shooting with their short, fat design and small primer pockets. One evening, Ashton wondered if a more modern, short, fat cartridge design with the .22-250's capacity would be a functional improvement. He looked at the idea of reworking the .22-250 and decided that was more work than a varmint shooter cared to deal with. At the time, the available BR brass quality was not good, so the idea sat on the shelf until Lapua began to offer BR brass.

Ashton took his idea to Dowling, who thought the project sounded interesting, so they designed a chamber to utilize the high-quality BR brass. Dowling ordered the reamer and headspace gauges from Dave Kiff at Pacific Tool and Gage, and soon, the first of many .22 Dashers was ready to test. It first appeared in an article by Al Ashton for *Precision Shooting* magazine in February 1999.

.22 Dasher		27-in. barrel	
BULLET (GR.)	POWDER	CHARGE (GR.)	VELOCITY (FPS)
50	Varget	35	3,850
50	Varget	36.5	3,975
50	IMR 4895	36.5	4,040
55	Varget	35	3,750
55	IMR 4895	35.3	3,870

.224 Texas Trophy Hunter (TTH)

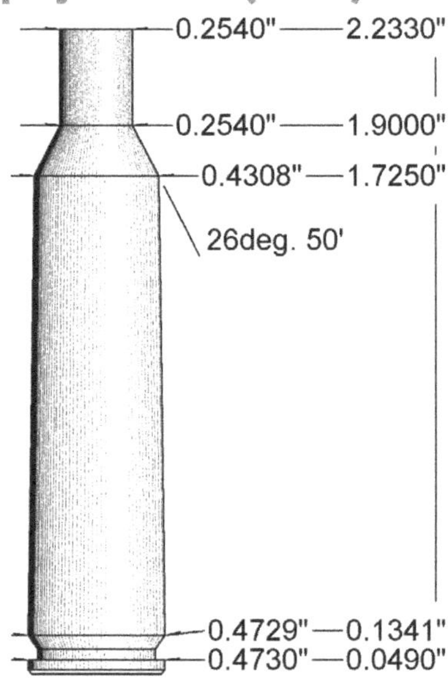

The .224 Texas Trophy Hunter (TTH).

In an apparent effort to reinvent the wheel, the Texas Trophy Hunting Association, for its 25th Anniversary, adopted the .22 Clark wildcat and renamed it to .224 TTH. Horace Gore and Ralph Lermayer devised the idea for an Anniversary cartridge for the association and selected this wildcat. In the tradition of Newton and Ackley, they suggest using heavy bullets to make the cartridge useful on deer-size animals.

Ken Clark of Madera, CA, introduced this wildcat in 1964; he necked down the 6mm Remington to .224 caliber. The plan was to use fast-twist barrels and heavy bullets. Back then, the choices of slow-burning powders and heavy bullets were extremely limited, so the popularity of the .22 Clark remained limited, although it has always had some following. Going back to the 1900s, the .22 Newton was an early cousin to it. The TTH also closely duplicates the

.22/243 Middlestead, a popular wildcat that originated in the early 1960s with gunsmith Paul Middlestead.

The stated purpose of the TTH is to drive a 75- or 80-grain bullet at 3,500 fps for use on whitetail deer and hogs in Texas. It's funny how a new name made an old idea popular. Of course, the availability of better bullets and slow powders did not hurt.

.224 Texas Trophy Hunter ***26-in. barrel***[4]

BULLET (GR.)	POWDER	CHARGE (GR.)	VELOCITY (FPS)
60 Nosler	IMR 4350	49	3,800
60 Nosler	RL-22	49	3,800
64 Win.	RL-22	49	3,750
75	RL-22	46.5	3,650
80	Ramshot	52	3,550
80	RL-25	50	3,550
80	RL-22	46	3,400

6mm Dasher

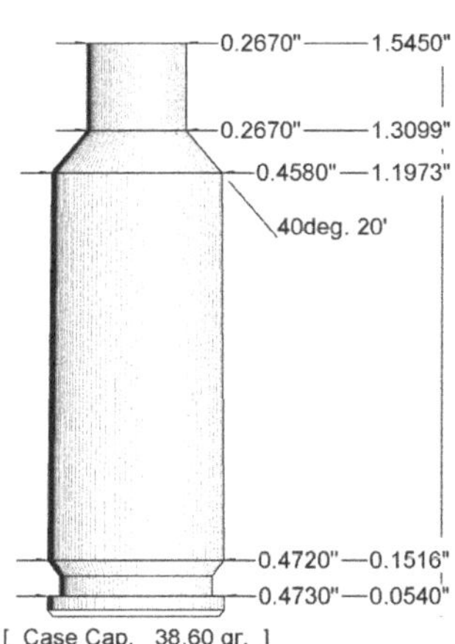

The 6mm Dasher.

The original Dasher was the .22 on the same case design. Al Ashton, a varmint hunter with a strong interest in precision long-range shooting, came up with the idea. The 6mm Dasher was an afterthought; Ashton said, "The .22 Dasher was still warm when it started looking for a bigger brother." Rifle builder Dan Dowling set about making the first 6mm Dasher immediately.

The Dasher name comes from combining the names of the two developers. Ashton's interest was mainly in varmint hunting with the new calibers. Dowling's

4 http://www.ttha.com/224tth.htm

interest ran more toward the possibilities for the cartridge in benchrest and with long-range shooting. The Dasher has an 11% increase in case capacity over the parent BR case. Dowling took some of the newly fireformed .22 cases to a match and sold several barrel jobs on the spot. One shooter said, "If it looks that good, it just has to shoot!" Early testing consistently produced groups in the low .300-inch range, so Dowling knew they had a winner.

June 2004, in Byers, Colorado, Richard Schatz steered his 11-pound 6mm Dasher to a new 6-target NBRSA 1,000-yard Light Gun World Record. His 6.125-inch aggregate eclipsed the previous World Record by ¾ inch (a considerable margin). Schatz broke the World Record with a compact Shehane Baby Tracker stock, unturned cases, Reloader 15 powder and a 26-inch Rem Varmint contour barrel with 1,500+ rounds through it. He set a new record without following conventional wisdom in the long-range benchrest game.

6mm Dasher			***26-in. barrel***
BULLET (GR.)	POWDER	CHARGE (GR.)	VELOCITY (FPS)
55	AA 2230	37	4,040
58	AA 2230	37	4,010
87	Varget	35.5	3,287
95	RL-15	33	3,000
95	Varget	34	3,050
10	RL-19	37	2,800
107	Varget	33	2,910
6mm Dasher			***27-in. barrel***
95	Varget	34	3,110
95	RL-15	34	3,100
105	Varget	33	2,980
105	RL-15	34	3,050

.240 Hawk

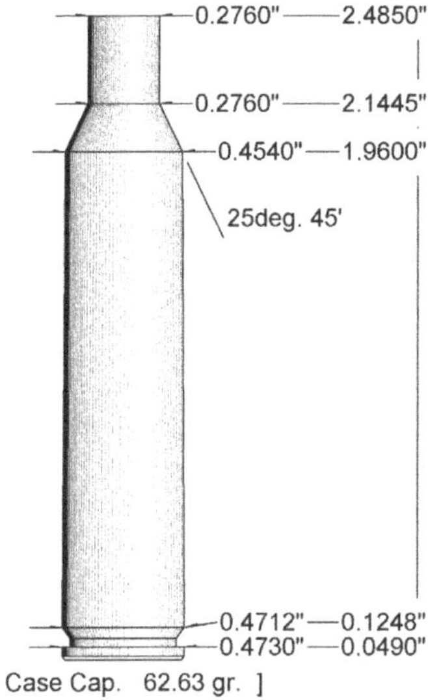

The .240 Hawk.

The .240 Hawk is for folks who love extreme velocity. I developed it as the extreme velocity entry for the Hawk line of cartridges. Contrary to the larger calibers in the Hawk line, this cartridge is totally overbore, which is not necessarily a bad thing. However, it means you can wring out unbelievable speed from it. The .240 Hawk's case capacity is about 4% greater than the .240 Weatherby, so use Weatherby data as a safe starting point.

Accuracy is exceptional; we shot many groups in the .300-inch range during initial testing. Prairie dogs and coyotes are in big trouble when this cartridge is around, or as a hunting buddy once said, "Now that's a flat shooter!"

Wayne van Zwoll wrote on the .240 Hawk, "Sure, this Hawk is inefficient. So is an F-16. Sometimes, performance matters the most. But I'll long remember that first 4,000-fps reading from an 80-grain bullet[5] ...."

.240 Hawk ***28-in. barrel***

BULLET (GR.)	POWDER	CHARGE (GR.)	VELOCITY (FPS)
60 Sierra	N150	53	3,968
60 Sierra	N150	52	3,922
70 Sierra	H4895	51	3,900
80 Remington	RL-15	53	4,055
80 Remington	H4895	52	4,037
87 Hornady	WIN 748	51	3,954

5 Van Zwoll, Wayne, *Deer and Big Game Rifles*, 2003

.257 Hawk

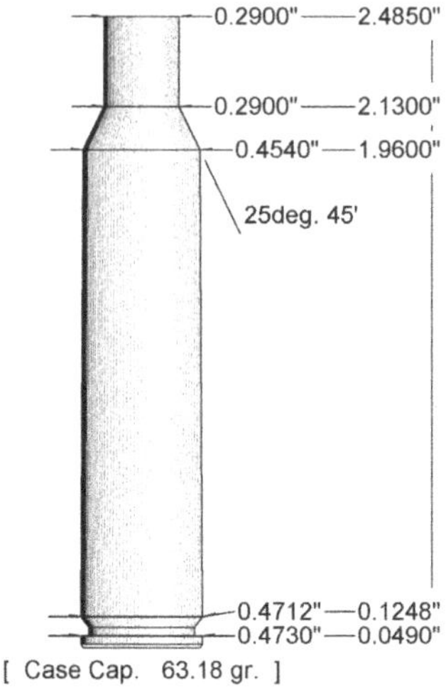

The .257 Hawk.

Is the .257 Hawk overbore? Yeah, a little. The wildcat is a flat-shooting cartridge for folks who love the .25-06 but want a little more without going to a magnum case. The case is based on the .280 Remington for its added length. Forming is simple: size .280 brass in a .257 Hawk die and load (the first shot will be a fireforming load). Accuracy with fireforming loads is usually very good, although top ballistics will come from fully formed brass.

Western hunters looking for a flat-shooting rifle for antelope and mule deer will be served well by the .257 Hawk. If you launch a 115-gr. Nosler Partition at 3,238 fps, it will remain plus or minus 3 inches of the line of sight to 311 yards. Now that's point and shoot! Varmints are no match for it, either. An 85-grain Nosler Ballistic Tip leaving the muzzle at 3,550 fps will be plus or minus 3 inches of the line of sight out to 330 yards, and at 400 yards, it's only 10.74 inches below the point of aim.

.257 Hawk — ***26-in. barrel***

BULLET (GR.)	POWDER	CHARGE (GR.)	VELOCITY (FPS)
75	H4064	48.1	3,444
87	WIN 748	50.0	3,748
90	H4831sc	57.0	3,800
120	N160	56.0	3,350

6.5 WSM

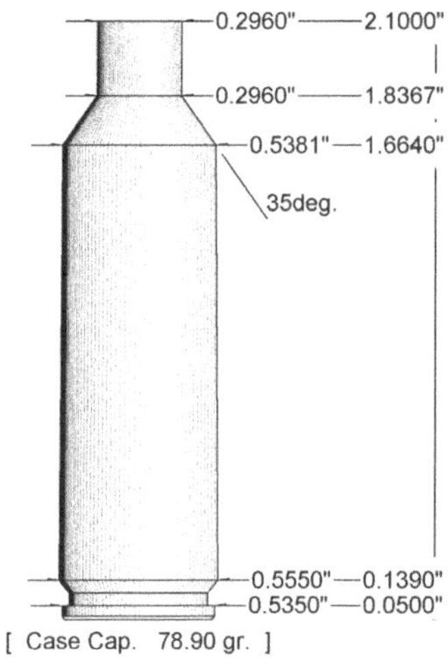

The 6.5 WSM.

Trends are interesting. The 6.5/284 Winchester is, at the time of this writing, undoubtedly the most popular wildcat cartridge in the U.S. However, the 6.5 WSM is gaining ground fast and will probably soon take over the number one slot. The 6.5 WSM uses a magnum case with more than 17% increased case capacity over the 6.5/284, so it has more recoil and report, which may hamper its growth in popularity. The deciding factor will be the 6.5 WSM's ability to deliver long-range accuracy better than the .284 case, though time will tell.

6.5 WSM ***24-in. barrel***

BULLET (GR.)	POWDER	CHARGE (GR.)	VELOCITY (FPS)
100	AA 4350	67.5	3,649
140	AA 4350	58	3,107

.264 Hawk

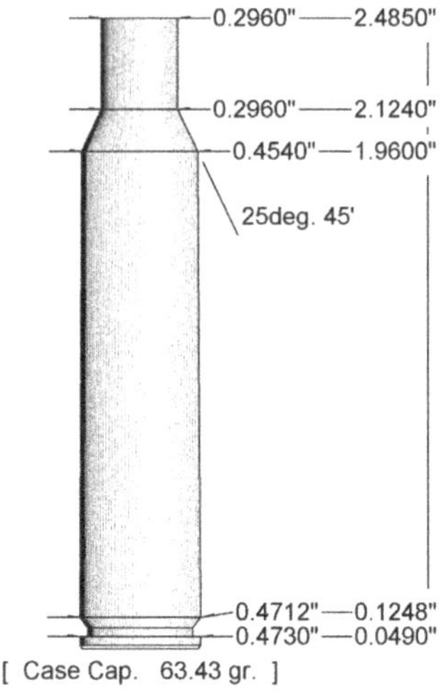

The .264 Hawk.

In 1997, your humble author designed the .264 Hawk as part of the entire Hawk family of cartridges. Correctly headstamped brass is available. The wildcat has drawn about as much attention from shooters as any Hawk cartridges. It sports a good relationship between case capacity, bullet weight and sectional density, making it an excellent choice for hunting in open country.

If you're a fan of the 6.5-06, you will like the .264 Hawk: recoil and report are identical for all intents and purposes, but the Hawk outclasses the standard 6.5-06 chambering. Brass is easy to form, affordable and plentiful. What more could you ask for?

.264 Hawk — ***26-in. barrel***

BULLET (GR.)	POWDER	CHARGE (GR.)	VELOCITY (FPS)
85	H4895	50	3,540
95	H4831SC	62	3,500
95	N160	57	3,435
100	N160	56	3,350
120	N160	57	3,440
120	IMR 4831	60	3,330
129	H4831	56	2,970
140	IMR 7828	55	2,934
140	IMR 4831	54.5	2,969
140	IMR 4350	53	3,090

6.5/284 Winchester

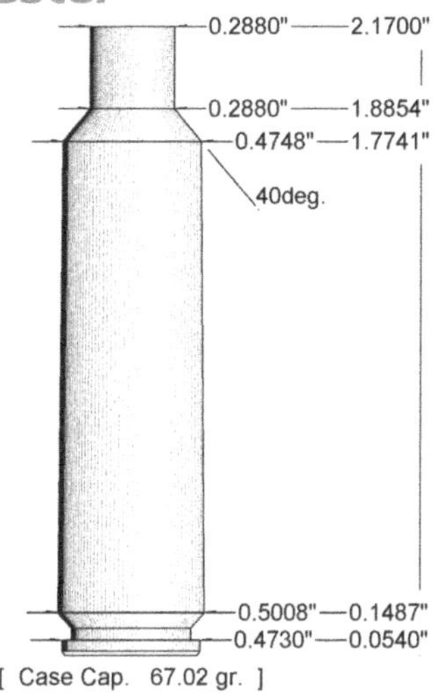

The 6.5/284 Winchester.

Nobody can say who first necked the .284 Winchester down to 6.5mm. Many popular wildcats are based on the .284 Winchester case (several are mentioned in Chapter 7). During the research for this book, it became apparent that the reining champion of popular wildcats today is the 6.5/284 Winchester. Much of the reason for its popularity is long-range benchrest shooting. However, the interest level in the cartridge is way out of proportion to the number of competitive shooters who might be using this cartridge.

The .284 case has slightly more capacity than an '06 case, and it fits the current thinking that short, fat cases are more efficient. 6.5mm projectiles of 140 grains or more have a reputation for deep penetration. This is an excellent cartridge for deer-class animals, and the 6.5/284 has a huge following and deservedly so.

6.5/284 Winchester

BULLET (GR.)	POWDER	CHARGE (GR.)	VELOCITY (FPS)
87	IMR 4350	57.9	3,503
100	IMR 4350	55.8	3,355
129	H4831	57.9	3,231
140	MRP	56	2,928
160	H870	63.3	2,750

.270 Hawk

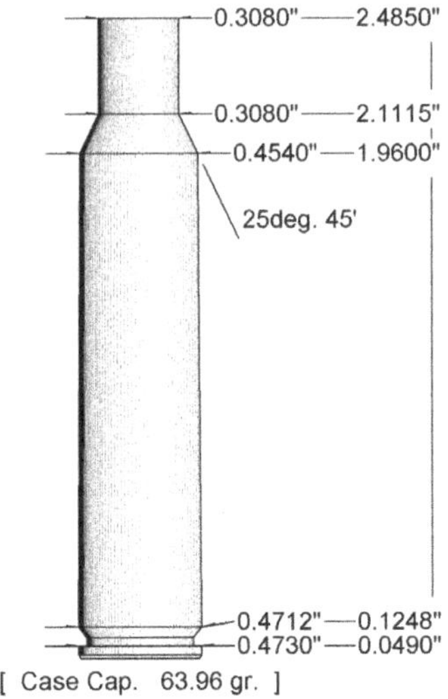

The .270 Hawk.

In his books, P.O. Ackley discussed the .270 Winchester and various .270 wildcats. Through testing different chambers behind a .270 bore, he determined that the Winchester was just about optimum for the bore size, if not slightly overbore.

When Doug Gregory expressed an interest in testing a Hawk cartridge—primarily for his own entertainment—I suggested he try the .270 Hawk simply because no data was developed for it then. Gregory is a detail-oriented reloader who keeps good notes and records comments with his results, a habit all reloaders should develop.

Developing loads for a new cartridge can be time-consuming, and Gregory spent lots of time on the .270 Hawk. Along the way, he contacted me to discuss developments and brainstorm alternatives. Initially, the results were precisely as Ackley predicted. The barrel throat was inspected for length and condition to see if it was too short or needed alterations to control pressure. It measured precisely as it should, allowing the bullets to jump .030 to .050 inch or more before engaging the lands, so no changes were made.

Eventually, he got around to testing H4350, which allowed greater velocity than any other without any signs of pressure. The results in the chart below tell the story. As for accuracy, his notes show MOA with every bullet he tried, often under. "The results with H4350 really surprised me," Gregory said. "It far outstripped the other powders I have tested so far in this cartridge, I really expected H4831 to be the best powder since it performs so well for many folks in the standard .270 Winchester. The .270 Hawk is easy to form and load, it had no strange idiosyncrasies to work out, just a pleasure to shoot. Recoil is virtually the same as a .270 Winchester."

.270 Hawk / 24-in. barrel

BULLET (GR.)	POWDER	CHARGE (GR.)	VELOCITY (FPS)
130	H4350	61	3,295
130	H4831	63	3,129
130	RL-22	62	3,131
140	H4350	58	3,161
140	H4831	60	2,967
150	H4831	59	2,855
150	H4350	57	3,051

.284 Hawk (7mm Hawk)

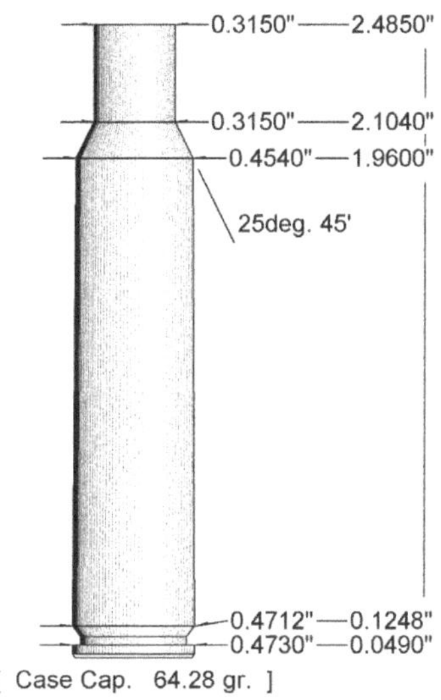

The .284/7mm Hawk.

The .284 Hawk is very similar to the .280 Ackley Improved. The primary difference is that the Hawk has a 25-degree shoulder. There is so little difference you could use starting loads for the .280 AI and be perfectly safe.

When we designed and tested the .284 Hawk, Nosler had not yet taken the .280 AI to SAAMI for standardization (it did that in 2008). I would be the first to admit that with the cost of dies and tooling, I would go with the .280 Ackley Improved over the Hawk.

.284 Hawk		***24-in. barrel***	
BULLET (GR.)	**POWDER**	**CHARGE (GR.)**	**VELOCITY (FPS)**
140	H4831	58	3,050
154	RL-22	59	2,827
160	RL-22	60	2,919

.300 Hawk

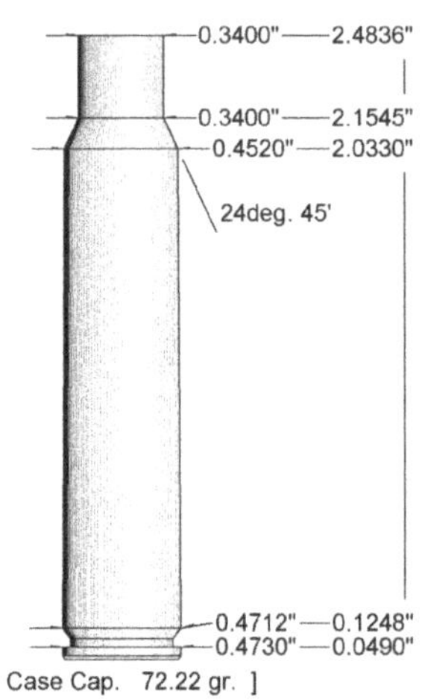

The .300 Hawk.

The first person outside the Z-Hat Custom shop to test the .300 Hawk was Steve Wright of Casper, WY, who said it best: "It seems to shoot whatever I put through it!" This cartridge is well-balanced and likes a wide variety of bullet/powder combinations, with slightly more than an 8% increase in case capacity over the venerable .30-06. Test results have shown it to be an accurate cartridge with near-magnum performance and recoil similar to the .30-06. Consistent groups well under ½ MOA show this caliber to be highly desirable.

If you could only have one rifle, this might well be it. A considerable variety of bullet designs and weights is available for .30 calibers from every bullet maker. Loads from 100 to 250 grains will allow you to take any game that comes your way. If versatility is essential in your caliber selection, the .300 Hawk fits the bill.

.300 Hawk		***22-in. barrel***	
BULLET (GR.)	**POWDER**	**CHARGE (GR.)**	**VELOCITY (FPS)**
150	Varget	57	3,095
168	IMR 4895	57	3,061
180	IMR 4350	61	2,938
200	IMR 4350	58	2,801

.300 BGA

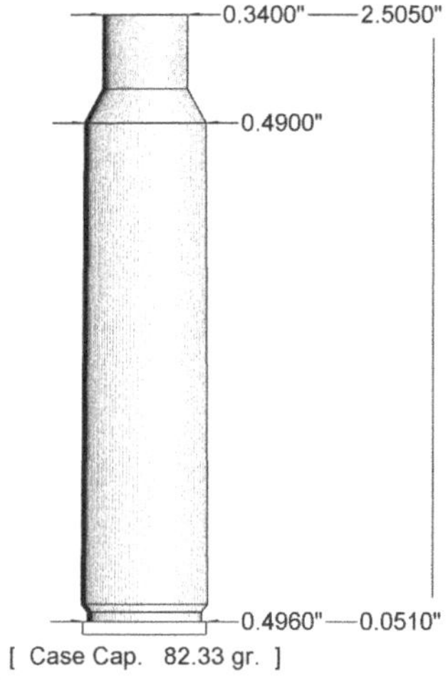

The 300 BGA.

In 1999, Raymond Oelrich, publisher of *Big Game Adventures* magazine, brought the idea for a new line of cartridges to me. Oelrich wanted cartridges with magnum power and total reliability, so he asked me to apply my experience with cartridge development to the project. The .300 BGA will easily keep up with the other .300 magnums in the .300 Weatherby, .308 Norma Mag, and .300 Winchester family, but with the advantage of using a standard-length (.30-06) magazine, which is common to all BGA calibers. The .300 BGA pushes a 180-grain bullet at 3,150 fps.

BGA cartridges include calibers from .257 to .416. Careful design allows owners of .25-06, .270, .280, .30-06 and .35 Whelen calibers to rechamber their existing rifles of the appropriate bore diameter to a BGA chamber and should see 150–250 fps increase in velocity and corresponding downrange energy, depending on the particular cartridge. The advantages of the BGA calibers include standard-length actions, magnum ballistics, moderate recoil and no belt.

Originally, Raymond Oelrich planned to market rifles and ammunition in these calibers. But life happens, and he moved on from publishing to other adventures. The cartridges remain, and I did make a few rifles chambered for these wildcats.

.300 BGA — ***23-in. barrel***

BULLET (GR.)	POWDER	CHARGE (GR.)	VELOCITY (FPS)
180	RL-22	75	3,121
220	IMR 7828	71	2,757
250	RL-22	64	2,524
250	H4831sc	63	2,411

3200 Hawk

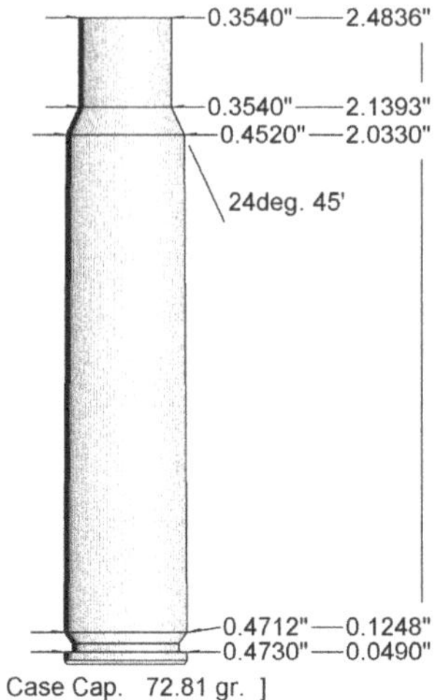

The 3200 Hawk (a 3,200 fps 8mm).

What? 3200? Well, it's an 8mm that will push a 150-gr. bullet over 3,200 fps. 8mm fans love the 3200 Hawk. You're not stuck with a belted case or an antiquated military cartridge. Here is a design that will deliver respectable ballistics without painful recoil.

Experience is a good teacher. The larger the bullet diameter, the harder it hits the target. That larger frontal area transmits energy to the animal more efficiently. When a hunter tries a larger caliber for the first time, the response is nearly universal, "I could not believe it; it took that buck right off its feet." Hyper-velocity is unnecessary to make clean, humane kills; bullet weight and diameter will do the same job and destroy less meat. Otherwise, those old boys with their muzzleloaders would have starved to death.

One 3200 Hawk owner wrote, "Not only is it going almost as fast as 8mm Remington Mag. factory ballistics, but I shot two 300-yard groups from a bench with this load. The first group measured exactly 2 inches I was pretty happy, but my second group measured 1 and 3/4 inches for three shots each. Brass life with these loads has been super, as a matter of fact, I am still using the same brass I started with a year ago and some have been reloaded 5+ times." That says it all!

3200 Hawk (8MM) ***22-in. barrel***

BULLET (GR.)	POWDER	CHARGE (GR.)	VELOCITY (FPS)
150	H4895	60	3,233
200	H4350	64	2,840
220	RL-15	56	2,707

.338 Hawk/.338 Scovill

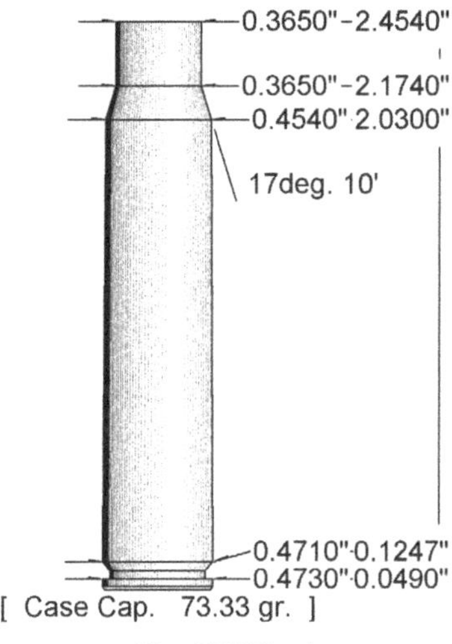

The .338 Hawk.

With nearly 10% more capacity than a .338-06, the ballistics of the .338 Hawk are what most .338-06 shooters wish they could get—a 230-grain bullet with the trajectory of a 180-gr. bullet from a .30-06. If high velocity is your game, the .338 Hawk can do that, too. It's a highly versatile cartridge with a 180-grain bullet at over 2,900 fps.

These two cartridges were featured in articles in *Handloader* magazine. (They appeared in subsequent issues, proving once again the adage, "Great minds think alike, and fools seldom differ.") Working separately and unaware of the other's work, Dave Scovill, editor of *Rifle* and *Handloader* magazines, was working on a .338 version of the .375 Hawk/Scovill simultaneously with yours truly. The two cartridges are not interchangeable dimensionally, but the load data is interchangeable. The shoulder angle is the main difference between the two cases.

I designed the Hawk version at the same time as the .358 Hawk, as I was a big fan of the classic wildcat .338-06 and wanted to see what a Hawk chamber would do in comparison to it. Scovill took a different approach to the project than me; he concentrated on the high-velocity loads possible with light bullets, emphasizing loads for the 180-grain Nosler Ballistic Tip and the Barnes 160- or 175-gr. X bullets. I was interested in a 225- or 250-grain bullet at moderate velocities.

Correctly headstamped brass and custom-loaded ammo are available for all Hawk calibers, something few wildcats can boast.

.338 Hawk/Scovill **24-in. barrel**

BULLET (GR.)	POWDER	CHARGE (GR.)	VELOCITY (FPS)
180	RL-15	60	2,941
180	N550	63	2,924
200	RL-15	58.5	2,863
225	IMR 4320	54	2,560
230	H414	60	2,615
250	N550	56	2,502
250	RL-19	63	2,545

.338/300 WSM (.338 WSM)

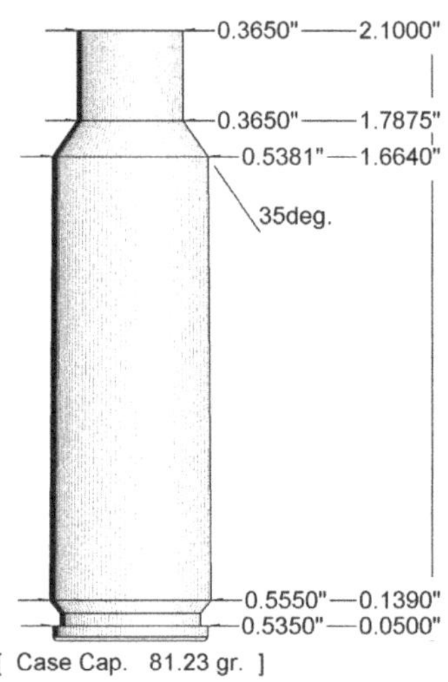

The .338/300 WSM.

Here is another cartridge that we cannot credit to any single gunsmith. Likely, the reamer makers had these reamers made up and on the shelf before brass was available to the shooting public. Perhaps this one should be called the .338 RM (Reamer Maker)?

The .338 WSM duplicates the .338 Winchester ballistically, so the factory is not likely to adopt it. Select starting loads for the .338 Winchester and work up from there. The .338 WSM has slightly less capacity than the .338 Winchester case. The short, fat configuration should allow the .338 WSM to equal or slightly outperform its older brother. As a hunting cartridge, the .338 WSM will handle anything in North America.

.338/300 WSM ***24-in. barrel***

BULLET (GR.)	POWDER	CHARGE (GR.)	VELOCITY (FPS)
180	–	–	2,850
200	–	–	2,725
225	IMR 4895	57	2,605

.338 Black Mesa Express

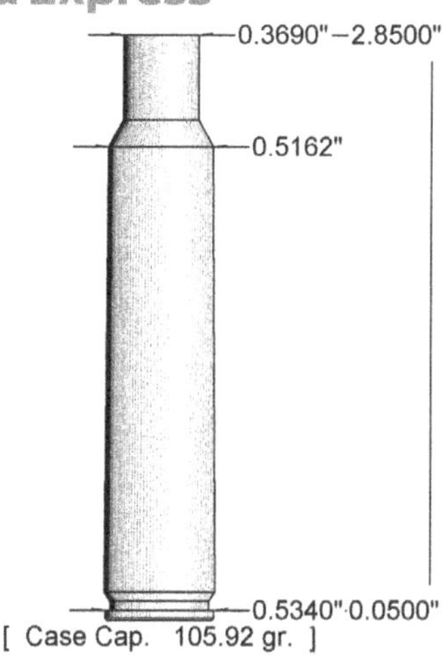

The .338 Black Mesa.

Brian McDaniels of the Black Mesa Rifle Company, Kenton, OK, developed the .338 Black Mesa Express by necking down his premier .375 Black Mesa Express. He intended to develop an accurate big game cartridge that would maintain its accuracy to 500 yards but have less recoil than the big .375 BME. He contends that his custom Black Mesa rifles chambered for this cartridge will easily hold ½- to ¾-minute groups at that range.

Pushing a 200-grain bullet at a velocity of 3,350 fps and a 250-grain bullet at 3,050 fps, the .338 Black Mesa Express provides all of the knockdown power needed for those long-range shots at mulies, elk and moose. Long-range accuracy with this wildcat is good enough that it won a 1,000-yard match at Williams Port, PA.

.338 Black Mesa Express ***26-in. barrel***

BULLET (GR.)	POWDER	CHARGE (GR.)	VELOCITY (FPS)
200 BTIP	RL-22	96	3,299
200 BTIP	H1000	94	3,072
200 BTIP	IMR 7828	90	3,259
250 SBT	H4831	90	2,973

.358 Hawk

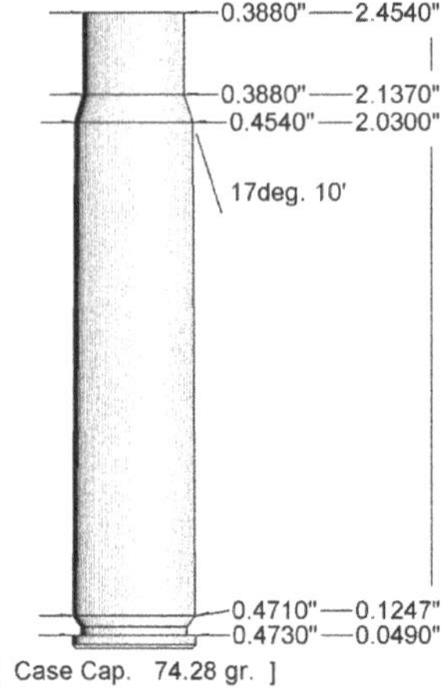

The .358 Hawk.

In 1995, Graydon Snapp walked into my gunsmith shop in Casper, Wyoming. Snapp had read the article in *Handloader* No. 166 about the .375 Hawk, and, being a fan of the .35 Whelen, was sure that a .358 Hawk would be the way to go. He had even written to Dave Scovill to ask about the idea. Since Bob Fulton lived just 25 miles away from him, Snapp had also looked him up and introduced Fulton and me.

I picked up a .375 Hawk/Scovill chamber reamer on sale from the reamer maker. Admittedly, I had a case of "Diplock's Syndrome" concerning the results reported in the article and was not sure I wanted to invest in expensive tooling for a wildcat. And finishing the range testing of the .375 Hawk was the first order of business. Pleasantly enough, the rifle reproduced the results in the *Handloader* article nearly perfectly.

Snapp was so pleased with the results of his new .375 Hawk/Scovill that he decided the .358 Hawk (his first choice) was now a must. At the same time, I was so impressed with the results of the .375 Hawk that I decided to build a .338 Hawk. So, I called Fulton and discussed the specifics of the design of both calibers. With Fulton's blessing, I ordered the reamers in September of 1996.

.358 Hawk — ***26-in. barrel***

BULLET (GR.)	POWDER	CHARGE (GR.)	VELOCITY (FPS)
200	AA 2700	65	2,857
225 North Fork	RL-15	61	2,796
225 North Fork	VVN133	55	2,660

225 Hawk	VVN530	55	2,687
225 Nosler	VVN133	53	2,606
250 Hawk	H4895	57.2	2,601
250 Hawk	VVN140	58	2,529
250 Speer	VVN530	52.5	2,490
270 North Fork	N550	64	2,566
280 Swift	N550	61.5	2,468

.358/300 WSM (.358 WSM)

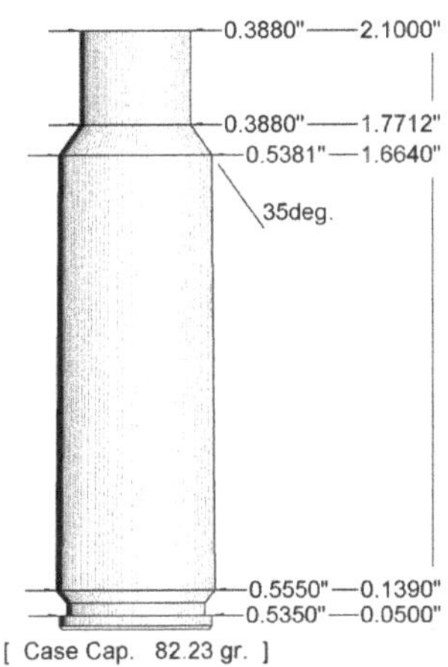

The .358 WSM.

Also known as the .358 Sambar in Australia, *Cartridges of the World, 11th Edition* lists the .358/300 WSM (.358 WSM) in its Wildcat Cartridge section. Breil Jackson developed it around 2002 with the help of a few gunsmiths.

Another cartridge that should probably be designated RM (Reamer Maker) instead of WSM, many different gunsmiths and wildcatters were working on this cartridge as soon as the .300 WSM was announced. The case capacity is nearly identical to the .358 Norma Magnum, so starting loads for the Norma can be used as a starting point. (The Norma case has about 2 grains more capacity by water weight.) The only advantage to this wildcat is the short case and lack of a belt.

.358/300 WSM — ***22-in. barrel***

BULLET (GR.)	POWDER	CHARGE (GR.)	VELOCITY (FPS)
225	–	–	2,825
250	–	–	2,740
286	–	–	2,450

.358 Yukon

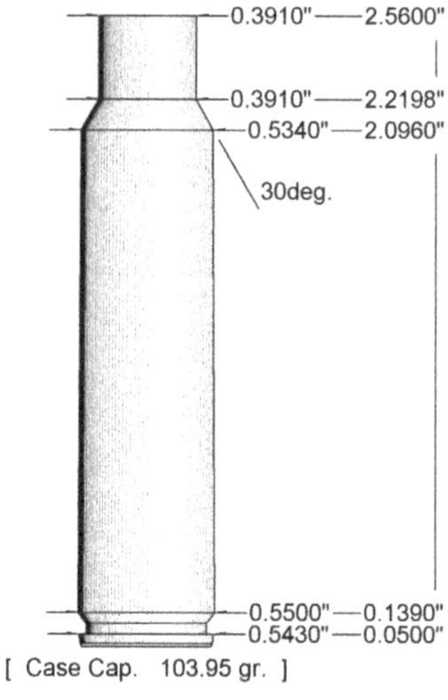

The .358 Yukon.

Bill Kemmerer of Sarasota, Florida, visited me at Z-Hat Custom, asking for a .35-caliber magnum case for his Browning BLR. His idea was to get 2,900 fps out of a 250-grain bullet from a cartridge that would fit in the BLR magazine. In effect, Kemmerer's new cartridge could equal the .375 H&H with the same bullet weight but with a shorter cartridge that he could feed through the Browning lever gun.

After some discussion, we selected a shortened Remington Ultra Case as the basis for the design because it's inexpensive, available and has the standard magnum rim diameter. We shortened the case to function in the chosen action and positioned the case shoulder so the rounds would feed well from the magazine. We used minimum case taper to increase case capacity so velocity goals would be more easily met without excessive pressure. Kemmerer selected the name Yukon, and the resulting cartridge deserves it.

Research before the project did not turn up any competitive cartridge that would fill the same purpose. Later, we noticed that we could easily make .358 Yukon cases from .330 Dakota or .375 Dakota brass, except that the Dakota uses the .404 Jeffery case for its offerings, so the rim diameter is too large—and the brass is more expensive. Dakota does not offer a .335 caliber, so the Yukon is safe in its niche. Headstamped and fully formed brass is available from Quality Cartridge.

The closest cartridge would be the .358 STA with about 5 grains more capacity by water weight—close enough that starting loads for the STA are probably mid-range loads for the .358 Yukon. The advantage of this cartridge over the STA is that it has no belt, and if you loaded it in a long magnum action, you could seat long heavy bullets out of the powder column and gain some performance.

.358 BOS (Boss)

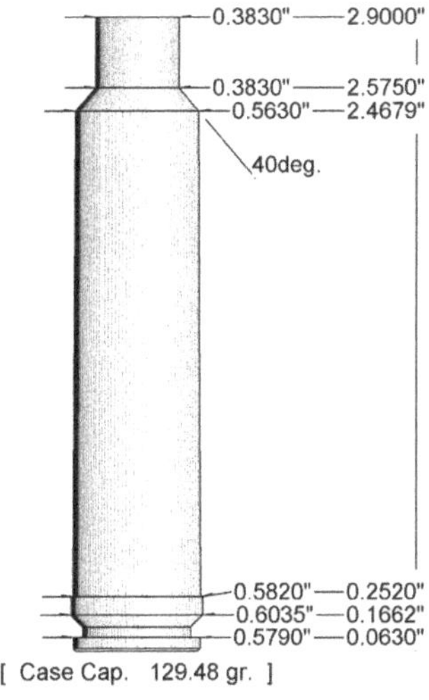

The .358 BOS.

Art Bosley, the designer of the .358 BOS (pronounced "boss"), started his design process the way many shooters do by progressing from one cartridge to another. First, he had an interest in the .30/378 Weatherby. The idea of 180-grain bullets at 3,400 fps seemed like something he would like for open country. In one summer, he shot out two .30/378 Weatherby barrels with about 500 rounds through each gun. When fall arrived that year, Bosley had two rifles that would not hold a 12-inch group at 100 yards. He was disappointed.

About this time, an article on the .358 STA caught his attention. It spoke of 225-grain bullets at 3,200 fps, which he thought would give him the best of both worlds: large-diameter bullets traveling over 3,000 fps. He had a tired .300 Mag. rebuilt with a new 28-inch Kreiger barrel in .358 STA. The short- and long-range results were impressive, so he was hooked on the big .35-caliber bore.

Those two shot-out .30/378s inspired him to design his own medium bore. Bosley wanted a minimum case taper, a 40-degree shoulder and a minimum neck length as he did not believe in the theories surrounding long necks. Upon receiving a chamber reamer made to his specifications, he worked up loads and found the new cartridge versatile. Most loads were under 1 MOA during the initial testing. Chronographing the loads showed consistent velocity increases for each half-grain of powder added, finally arriving at 127 grains of

RL-25 under a 225-grain bullet. This load produced 3,500 fps with only a 5 fps deviation between rounds from his 29-inch Douglas barrel. Bosley says he used a transducer to test the pressure of this load and found it was averaging 62,500 psi, which is equal to the parent cartridge.

Barrel life in these medium-bore rifles has proved much better than the .30-378 and is measured in thousands of rounds instead of hundreds.

.358 BOS (Boss) ***29-in. barrel***

BULLET (GR.)	POWDER	CHARGE (GR.)	VELOCITY (FPS)	PRESSURE (PSI)
225 NF	RL-25	126	3,600	60,000
237 Hawk	RL-25	120	3,319	58,000
250	H4831	118	3,210	–

.375 Hawk/Scovill

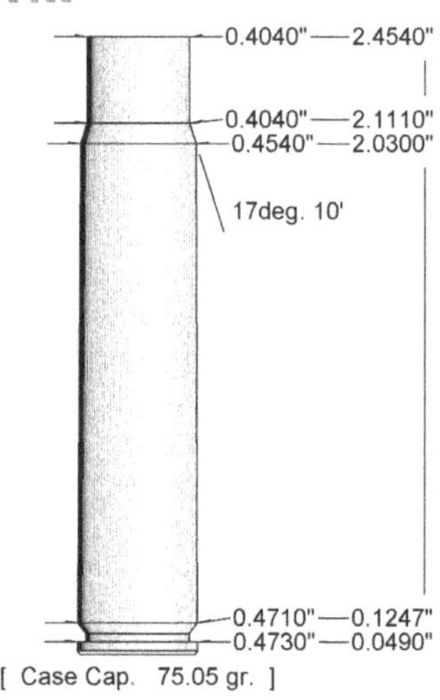

The .375 Hawk/Scovill.

The .375 Hawk delivers the same ballistics that made the .375 H&H famous in the early 1900s. In *The Rifle in America*, Phil Sharpe quotes ballistics for the factory-loaded 375 H&H as follows, "The 235 grain is loaded at a muzzle velocity of 2,775 fps, the 270 at 2,750 fps, and the 300 at 2,475 fps." You will note that the .375 Hawk/Scovill easily approaches these numbers. The critical difference is that the Hawk does it with less powder, no belt, less recoil and in a .30-06-length action!

In 1988, Bob Fulton, designer of renowned Hawk Bullets, had the idea to build a rifle suitable for dangerous game and anything in North America. Recoil was another major factor, and Fulton wanted an 8-pound rifle that would not beat him up. A friend gave him a rifle chambered in .375 Whelen Improved, but he was not impressed with the mediocre ballistics. So, he started looking for a better cartridge design based on the .30-06 case.

Fulton also wanted a case that was easy to form, so he decided to use the basic design of the 9.3x62 (often called the .30-06 of Africa). By moving the shoulder forward and reducing the body taper, he increased the powder capacity of the .30-06 by 9% over the original design. He used the original 17-degree shoulder angle to facilitate reliable feeding. When Fulton went to the range with his new gun and a chronograph, he was pleasantly surprised. His goal was to increase velocity to 2,600 fps with a 250-gr. bullet. He surpassed that goal by a wide margin, achieving 2,700 fps with a 250-gr. bullet.

In 1993, Dave Scovill published an article in *Handloader* No. 166 entitled ".375 Hawk/Scovill." Scovill converted the Hawk dimensions from those used on the 9.3x62 to the more common .30-06 base dimensions. Fulton had always used '06 brass for his .375 Hawk with no difficulty. The difference in dimensions serves an essential purpose, though. "The 9.3x62 follows the standard British practice of slightly looser chambering for use in Africa and other hot climates," Fulton said. "That improves the reliability of extraction; the extra room in the chamber is there to take advantage of the way that brass stretches and contracts."

Scovill noted that this left a slight case bulge on the web and cited concerns about stretching and possible head separations as the reason for using the smaller '06 case dimensions for his version. Ballistically, the two are identical, although ammunition cannot be interchanged. The .375 Hawk/Scovill superseded the original Hawk, and now we base all current Hawk chamberings from Z-Hat Custom on the tighter dimensions of the .30-06 case.

.375 Hawk/Scovill — ***24-in. barrel***

BULLET (GR.)	POWDER	CHARGE (GR.)	VELOCITY (FPS)
225	Benchmark	58.8	2,771
225	H4895	61.7	2,737
250 North Fork	H4895	61.5	2,695
250 Swift	H4895	57.7	2,606
250 Swift	IMR 4320	61	2,623
250 Hawk	H4895	59	2,669
270 North Fork	H4895	57	2,471
270 North Fork	IMR 4320	60.5	2,575
300 North Fork	BL-C2	57	2,358
300 North Fork	IMR 4320	57.5	2,383

.375 Black Mesa Express (BME)

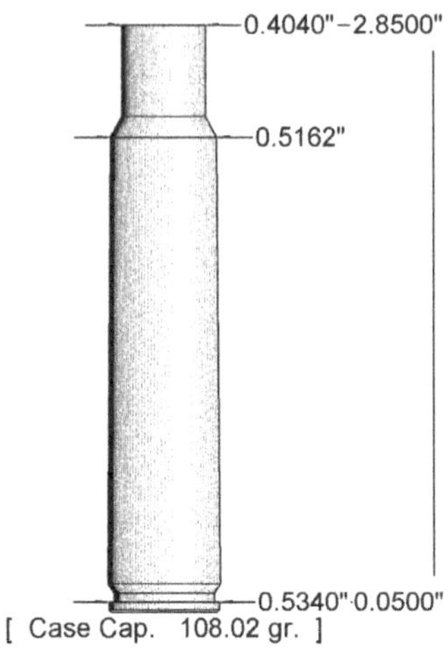

The .375 Black Mesa Express.

Brian McDaniels was the brainchild of the .375 Black Mesa Express, who cut his teeth working in the Aberdeen Proving Grounds. Years later, in 1994, he started the Black Mesa Rifle Company, producing the Black Mesa Express Rifle. The .338 and .375 Black Mesa Express are based on a rimless .404 Jeffery, having the rim altered to a rebated design with the exact dimensions as the .375 H&H to facilitate standard long magnum actions. Custom gunsmiths like McDaniels often develop good cartridge designs that are later emulated by factory offerings. Black Mesa, Dakota and others undoubtedly influenced the appearance of the .300 Ultra Mag.

Black Mesa Rifles is now owned by gunsmith Craig Smith of Boise City, Oklahoma, who is planning new cartridges in the same vein as the original BME designs.

.375 Black Mesa Express — 26-in. barrel

BULLET (GR.)	POWDER	CHARGE (GR.)	VELOCITY (FPS)
300 Sierra	RL-22	95	2,822
300 Sierra	IMR 7828	95	2,787
300 Sierra	H4831	93	2,792
300 Sierra	H4350	88	2,828
300 Sierra	RL-19	95	2,872

.411 Hawk

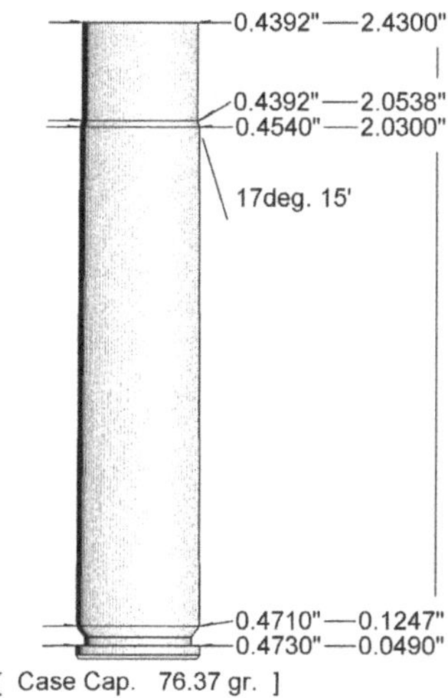

The .411 Hawk.

The .411 Hawk was the fourth cartridge of 11 in the Hawk line I designed and tested. When the .338 and .358 Hawk were finished, Bob Fulton called me. He had necked up one of his .375 Hawk cases to accept a .411 bullet and was sure it would work. Graydon Snapp and I played with .411 and .416 bullets in the Hawk cases, and it quickly became apparent that the .411 Hawk was the way to go.

The .400 Whelen could be considered a close relative of the .411 Hawk. Elmer Keith had strong opinions on the subject, "The .400 Whelen rifle and cartridge designed by Col. Whelen I consider the most powerful of all our American loaded big game cartridges ... Much criticism has been passed on this rifle and cartridge, some claiming that the front shoulder of the case was insufficient to hold its headspace against the blow of the firing pin. Such is not the case, and that forward shoulder is ample in correctly chambered rifles and used with correctly necked cases."[6] See Chapter 11 for more on the .400 Whelen.

Years of success in the field is the best testimony for the .411 Hawk. Of all the Hawk cartridges, we've chambered more guns for the .411 than any other. Like the other cartridges in the Hawk family, the .411 Hawk can be chambered in any '06-class action.

While popular in bolt guns, the .411 is also chambered in the 1895 lever-action. At our Z-Hat shop, we've converted many of the Winchester 1895 actions originally in .270 to it. Efficiency is typical with the .338 through .411 Hawk, and they usually vary in velocity only about 25 fps per inch of barrel length.

6 Keith, Elmer, *Big Game Rifles and Cartridges*, 1936

.411 Hawk		25-in. barrel	
BULLET (GR.)	POWDER	CHARGE (GR.)	VELOCITY (FPS)
300	H4895	64	2,553
325	H4895	64	2,479
350	IMR 4064	61	2,366
360	AA 2230	57	2,281
400	RL-15	57	2,159

.416 Aagaard

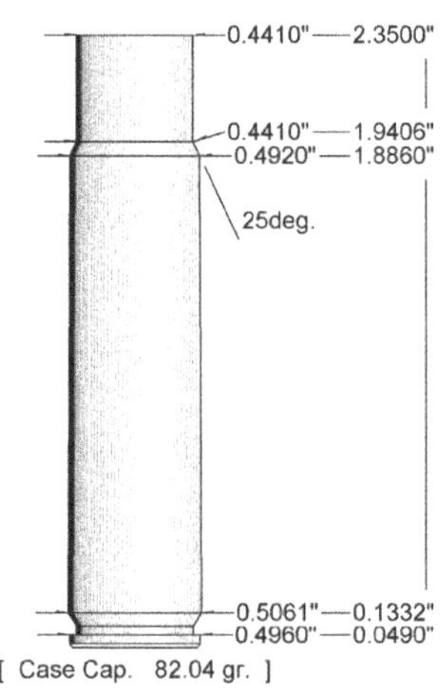

The .416 Aagaard.

I developed the .416 Aagaard for Z-Hat Custom client Frank Selman of Indiana. Selman was friends with Finn Aagaard, the well-known field editor of *American Rifleman* and Kenyan professional hunter (PH) from 1970 to 1977. Aagaard died in 2000. Selman had hunted with Aagaard on occasion and wanted to design a cartridge that he thought Finn would like, so we discussed a couple of parent cases before settling on the .376 Steyr.

A standard-length case and the ability to chamber it for a standard Mauser action were important considerations. Aagaard judged cartridge effectiveness not by kinetic energy, "knock-out value," or other theoretical numbers but by quickly delivered clean kills. The .416 Aagaard will deliver what its namesake would have called for on any North American game!

.416 Aagaard		21-in. barrel	
BULLET (GR.)	POWDER	CHARGE (GR.)	VELOCITY (FPS)
350	N133	62.0	2,239
350	H4895	65.0	2,316
400	RL-15	64.0	2,160

.416 BGA

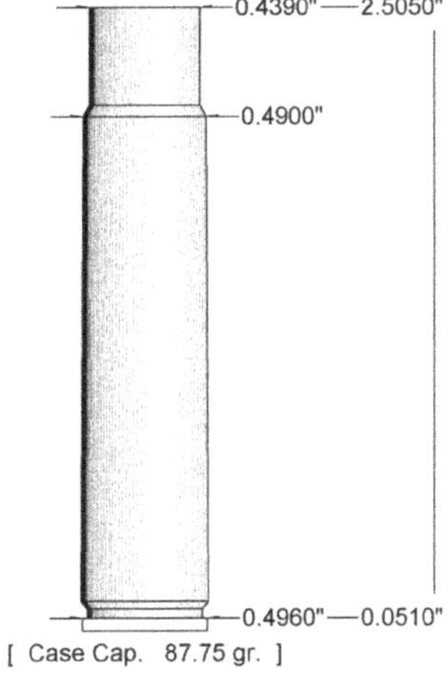

The .416 BGA.

The BGA cartridges are named for *Big Game Adventures* magazine and feature a range of calibers from .257 to .416. All are based on the same case, which will fit a standard-length action. Both Corbon and Superior Ammo load these calibers—the BGA cartridges are not limited to handloaders—although not all are readily available to the shooting public yet. The designer, Raymond Oelrich, searched for the proper parent cartridge for two years and teamed up with me to design and produce the first two prototypes. Ruger provided the first two test rifles, which have taken game from Stone's sheep to elk and functioned flawlessly.

The first two calibers produced were the .300 BGA and the .416 BGA, and both have had extensive testing in the field under actual hunting conditions. So far, they've exceeded expectations. The .416 BGA features a 400-grain bullet in the neighborhood of 2,350 fps. You can obtain faster speeds, but since it's likely the .416 will see usage in Africa, where high temperatures can cause dangerous pressures in cartridges loaded hot, there is no need for more speed.

The test rifle, a Ruger Model 77 with a standard 22-inch barrel, keeps the 350-grain bullet in one ragged hole at 100 yards. With a 3-inch high sight-in at 100 yards, it is dead on at 200 and only 8 inches low at 300 yards, yet it maintains over 2,400 ft-lbs of energy at that distance. It should do well on elk, moose, bears, and other large game where you need reach and retained energy.

.416 BGA **24-in. barrel**

BULLET (GR.)	POWDER	CHARGE (GR.)	VELOCITY (FPS)
300	IMR 4320	73	2,651
300	IMR 3031	70	2,604
400	H4895	71	2,348
400	RL-15	73	2,353

.416 UltraCat

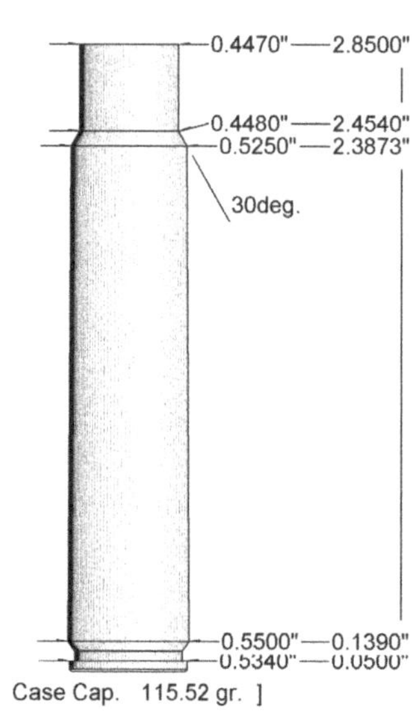

The .416 UltraCat.

Also known as the .416 UMT, the UltraCat is nothing more than the .300 RUM case necked up to .416 and originated in 1999 when the .300 Remington Ultra Mag (RUM) was introduced. Z-Hat Custom drew up a whole line of cartridges on the RUM case as soon as the .300 was introduced. Naturally, now that the .375 RUM is a factory offering, that would make a better source for brass.

Compare the ballistics for the .416 Remington Magnum to this cartridge. A 400-grain bullet in the .416 Rem Mag leaves the muzzle at about 2,450 fps. That means that the UltraCat can accomplish that velocity at much lower pressures. If you are planning on hunting in hot climates, that can be a significant benefit.

.416 UltraCat **26-in. barrel**

BULLET (GR.)	POWDER	CHARGE (GR.)	VELOCITY (FPS)
350	RL-15	91.0	2,800
400	IMR 4064	83.0	2,512
400	RL-15	86.0	2,580

.458 WSM

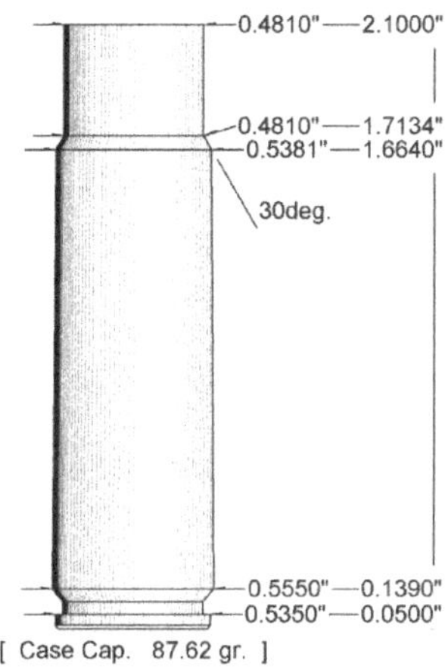

The .458 WSM.

Here is another candidate for renaming to the .458 RM (Reamer Maker), as no specific gunsmith can claim to be the first to produce this wildcat, and the reamers were available on the same day that the dimensions were released by the factory for the .300 WSM. The case capacity is virtually identical to the .458 Winchester Magnum, so like the .338 WSM, it's unlikely that the factory will offer this cartridge.

Ballistics are nearly identical as well; the fatter powder column may allow for the slightly more efficient burn, but load data is interchangeable with the .458 Winchester magnum (be safe and use published starting loads for the .458 Winchester as your starting point). The short case suits medium-length actions with lighter bullets, but if you're a fan of 500-grainers, you may lose powder capacity by the bullet intruding into the case too deeply.

This cartridge should make the .458 2" American obsolete.

.458 WSM — ***24-in. barrel***

BULLET (GR.)	POWDER	CHARGE (GR.)	VELOCITY (FPS)
300	IMR 4198	40.0	1,828
405	IMR 4198	51.0	2,112

.458 SOCOM

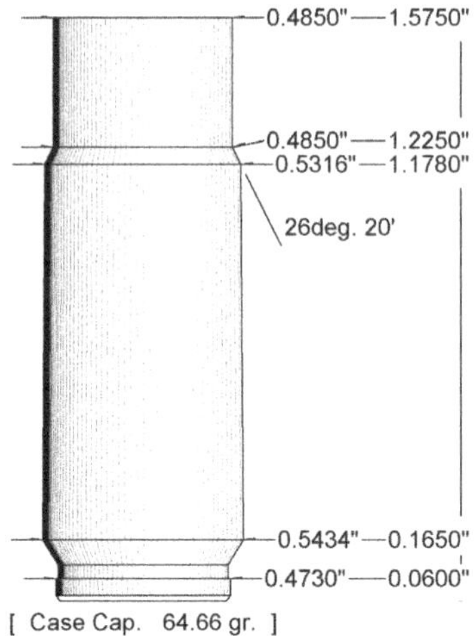

The .458 SOCOM.

Maarten ("Marty") P. ter Weeme developed the .458 SOCOM cartridge as a result of an informal discussion with a senior member of the U.S. Special Operations community following the Task Force Ranger debacle in Mogadishu, Somalia, as described in the book *Blackhawk Down*. In the book, several members of TF Ranger comment on the apparent ineffectiveness of 5.56mm ammunition in their engagement of the assailants, stating that multiple shots were required to disable a target.

Using the AR-15 or M-16 as a platform for this new cartridge was a primary design consideration. The designer looked at numerous options for parent cases and calibers, including 7.62x39 M43, 9x39 Grom, 6mm PPC and the .45 Professional as designed by LeGendre for the AR-15. This last round uses the .451-caliber pistol bullets, limiting the bullet choice to projectiles of no more than 300 gr.

To offer the greatest flexibility to the user, the decision was made to design the new cartridge in .458 caliber. This offered the user a vast choice of commercially available bullets, ranging from 300-gr. HP and spitzers, 405-gr. FN, up to 500-gr. solids and Tungsten-core RN. This decision was strengthened after a literature search revealed two similar designs, the .458 Whisper and the .458 x 1.5". Both had been designed to fire the heavy (500–600 gr.) bullets at subsonic velocities; the Barnes .458 x 1.5" also briefly saw service in Vietnam in the Special Operations community.

AR-15 bolt design was a limiting factor, so using a drastically rebated rim seemed the solution, and the 0.473-inch diameter rim employed by the .308-

and .30-06-based cartridges was chosen, as this would allow easy retrofit of bolt-action rifles in the caliber. Starline Brass was then contacted for "the impossible": a pre-production run of .50AE brass left unformed, untrimmed and with the rim rebated to 0.473 inch. Starline agreed.

With a stated purpose of hurling big chunks of metal at substantial velocity from unaltered AR-15 lowers and magazines—in full auto if desired—the .458 SOCOM is a successful wildcat. It has been dubbed "the .45-70 for semi-autos," as performance is right in line with the modern high-pressure loads for the venerable .45-70.

Starline offers brass, and Corbon lists loaded ammo for the .458 SOCOM with a 300-gr. JHP at a velocity of 1,900 fps and muzzle energy of 2,405 ft-lbs.

.458 SOCOM ***16-in. barrel***

BULLET (GR.)	POWDER	CHARGE (GR.)	VELOCITY (FPS)
Remington 300 HP	H110	37.0	1,867
Remington 405 SP	IMR 3031	48.0	1,654
Hornady 500 RN	IMR 4198	32.0	1,357

.470 Mbogo

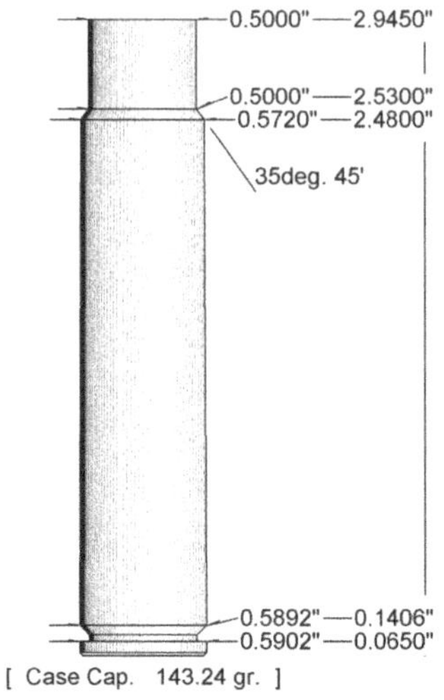

The .470 Mbogo.

What is a 470 Mbogo? This is a cartridge that Dave Estergaard designed to shoot a .475 bullet at an honest 2,500 fps from a 24-inch barrel at a moderate pressure level. Using the Load From a Disk program, the approximate pressures should be in the 53,000 psi area. A 500-grain bullet launched at 2,500 fps has 7,000 ft-lbs of energy at the muzzle.

It is an easy cartridge to form brass for and a snap to reload. You form the brass with one pass through the full-length sizing die using Mast Technologies' .416 Rigby cylindrical case. With the bullet seated to the overall length of 3.750 inches, the brass holds 9 grains more water than the .460 Weatherby.

The Mbogo has developed a following through a dedicated website and the availability of brass and ammunition from more than one source. A well-thought-out wildcat, it delivers all that the designer envisioned and more. Estergaard had so much faith in his new creation that he and a hunting buddy immediately arranged for a Cape buffalo hunt to test it. Now that's field testing the equipment!

.470 MBOGO ***24-in. barrel***

BULLET (GR.)	POWDER	CHARGE (GR.)	VELOCITY (FPS)
500	IMR 4895	110	2,490
500	RL-15	116	2,620
500	H4895	110	2,540

.50 BMD Short

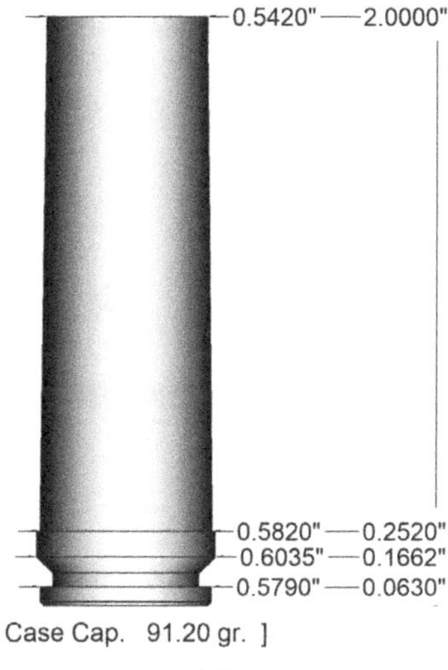

The 50 BMD (Short).

Belden Dampf developed the .50 BMD Short at the request of Charles Demos to provide a high-energy subsonic cartridge. Using information from the .50 BMD, Dampf shortened a large Weatherby magnum case to 2 inches and formed it with a straight taper to a .50-cal neck. Because of the Weatherby cases' fine quality and consistency and the BMD Short's unique design, no shoulder forming or neck reaming is required. The .50 BMD Short case is not likely to stick in the chamber under heavy loads like the .50-70 and has more propellant capacity.

The .50 BMD Short is designed as a maximum-energy subsonic cartridge using projectiles in the weight range of 700 to 800 grains. Firearms chambered for this round require a barrel with a twist rate of 1:16 or faster for the BMG-profile bullets. Rates of 1:9 have been used for slow velocities with the BMG projectiles. The cartridge headspaces on the belt and is compatible with cast bullets, which may require a crimp. Case forming is simple, and no neck reaming is required. Cases are cut to length, annealed, and sized, then checked again for proper length specifications.

Its initial purpose was to deliver 1,500+ ft-lbs of energy and sub-MOA accuracy in suppressed firearms at ranges under 200 yards. It's also an outstanding performer with conventional .50-caliber rifle bullets—considered a .50-90 on steroids. Chambering and die sets are available. Contact Belden Dampf, 3101 Beacon Road, Amarillo, TX 79118.

.50 BMD Short **24-in. barrel**

BULLET (GR.)	POWDER	CHARGE (GR.)	VELOCITY (FPS)
650 Ball	ACC-2200	55.50	1,346
650 Ball	ACC-2200	41.00	1,050
500 Ideal	ACC-2200	37.00	1,130
650 SAECO	ACC-2460	45.00	1,140
410 JSP BMD	IMR 4198	45.00	1,550
650 SAECO	IMR 4198	33.50	1,135
650 SAECO	IMR 4198	47.20	1,557
750 A-MAX	IMR 4198	38.00	1,250

Pre-2005 RCBS Die List

Below is the list of dies sold by RCBS in 2004; some surprising old timers are on the list, along with some new arrivals. They are in order, starting with the most popular at the top of the first column and continuing in descending order at the top of the second column.

.470 NE 3-1/4" FL DIE SET	.50-90 SS 2.5" 3-DIE SET
9.3X66 SAKO FL DIE SET	.308 ACK IMP 40-DEGREE
5.7X28 FL DIE SET	.338-300 WSM FL DIE SET
6.5MMX57R FL DIE SET	.50-110 WIN 3-DIE SET
.30R BLASER FL DIE SET	.500 NITRO 3" 3-DIE SET
.50-140 SS 3-1/4" 3-DIE SET	.50-70 WCF 3-DIE SET
.257 ROBERTS IMP FL DIE SET	9.3mmX57 FL DIE SET
.577-450 MARTINI-HENRY 3-DIE SET	9.3mmX64 BRENNEKE FL DIE SET
6.5mm-284 WIN FL DIE SET	6.5mm-300 WSM FL DIE SET
.17 ACKLEY HORNET FL DIE	.17 MACH IV FORM DIE SET
.404 JEFFERY FL DIE SET	6.5mmX55 SKANDINAVIAN
.450X3-1/4" NITRO EX 3-DIE SET	8MM-348 FL DIE SET

CHAPTER 19
Wildcats 2004 to 2023

12 Gauge From Hell (12 GFH)

In 2004, Rod Garnick, John McMorrow and Ed Hubel experimented with a full brass-cased 12 gauge and slugs. According to Hubel, Garnick originated the idea. They started by cutting a .50 BMG case down to 3.85 inches in length.

In later experiments, Hubel made his own case by using high-base cups from new unfired 12-gauge hulls. He tested loads at an extreme maximum of 3,400 fps with a 600-grain slug. The more realistic loads ran at 1,700 fps with the same slug.

You may ask how this lines up with ATF rules. As long as the gun fires standard 12-gauge loads, this wildcat is nothing more than specialized ammo. The chamber would have to be modified to handle these longer cartridges. I found comments on forums by Ed Hubel (now deceased, RIP). He also used modified .50 BMG cases at 3.5 inches, so they experimented with several variations.

12 GFH

BULLET WEIGHT (GR)	VELOCITY (FPS)
600	1,700

.17 Velociraptor (4.4x28mm) (17x28)

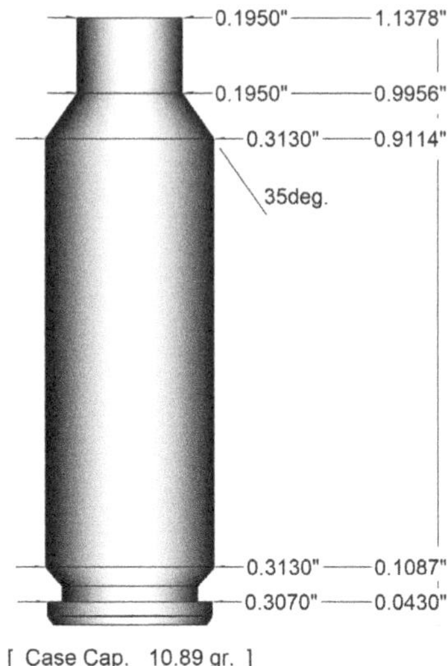

The .17 Velociraptor.

In 1991, the U.S. patent application for the 5.7x28mm was granted to Belgium's FN Herstal, with credit going to the inventors Jean-Paul Denis and Marc Neuforge. After NATO trials from 2002 to 2003, the 5.7 looked pretty good.

In 2005, Kevin Weaver designed the .17 Velociraptor, probably the most natural wildcat from this case. It produces velocity all out of proportion to the case size. With any small case capacity, be careful about load development. Just 2/10ths of a grain can push the pressures up fast.

.17 Velociraptor

BULLET WEIGHT (GR)	VELOCITY (FPS)
18	3,600
20	3,500
25	3,400

.17 TCM (30 Degree)/.17/22 TCM 30 Degree

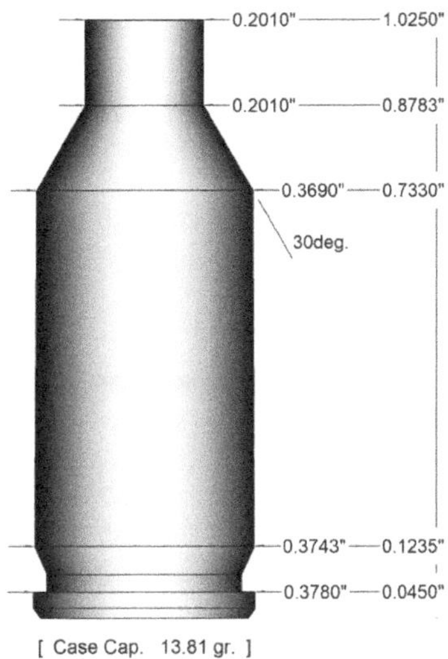

The .17 TCM 30 Degree.

I worked up the .17 TCM while working with the TCM rifle in .22 TCM. When I ordered the reamer and gauges to correct the .22 TCM chamber to fire the factory-loaded ammo, I also acquired a .17-caliber reamer of the same case design incorporating a 30-degree shoulder. Easy to form, I created a new neck-shoulder junction that allows the case to headspace; I then fireform the rest. This is a cute little .17.

.17 Mink

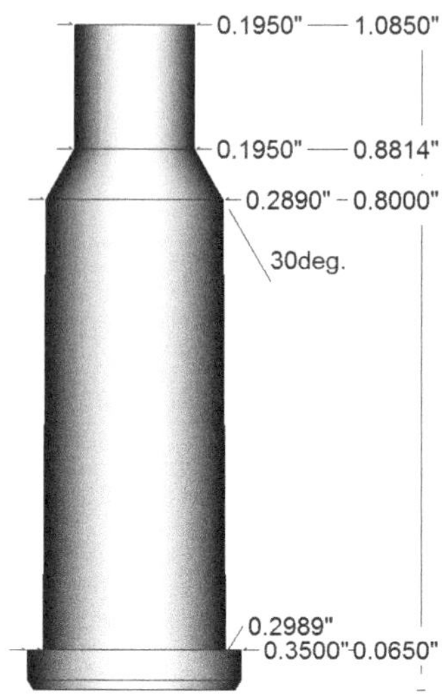

The .17 Mink.

The .17 Mink is a wildcat design created by Kevin Harrington in 2005. Kevin set the shoulder at .800 inch because Hornet brass easily supports that dimension and allows for a decent neck length. It also falls about halfway between the Squirrel and the K-Hornet in length.

Harrington wanted his designs to all have the same body length, making brass forming easy. This also means you only need one set of headspace gauges (Harrington uses the shoulder to headspace for better accuracy).

The .17 Mink was designed to increase the range of the Squirrel family of cartridges by 100–150 yards, meaning your outer range is more like 300 yards. First and foremost, Harrington sees the Mink cartridges as being used for hunting and plinking. He says the .17 is not as good terminally as the .20 or .22 Mink.

The .17 Mink propels a .172-inch diameter 20-grain bullet at 3,600 fps with 575 ft-lbs of energy. The energy at 200 yards is comparable to a .17 WSM at the muzzle. Harrington uses a 1:9 twist.

.17 Mink	***23-in. barrel***
BULLET WEIGHT (GR)	**VELOCITY (FPS)**
20	3,700

.17-32 Magnum

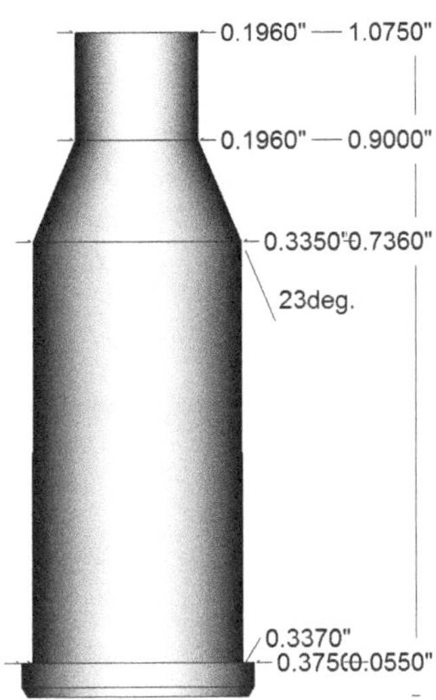

The .17-32 Mag.

I have known Carroll Pilant for many years. He was a technical advisor at Sierra, which is how we met. He created the .17-32 Magnum wildcat not to solve some need or problem but because he had about a thousand rounds of .32 H&R Magnum cases in his reloading room. He says he awoke late one night with the idea to neck them down to .17 caliber and chamber a Ruger No. 3 single-shot for the cartridge. Pilant gets about 3,300 fps from a 20-grain bullet.

.17-556 KAK

The .17-556 KAK.

Kurt Kosman designed the .17-556 KAK and admits it's not new. What is new and important is that his decisions for this cartridge are based on using it in the AR platform and making it readily available to anyone. Kosman wanted to put what is traditionally a wildcat cartridge into a package that any shooter who likes to reload could pick up without learning new skills. He started work on this project in January 2023 and tested it, and KAK—a U.S. company that produces OEM parts for the AR platform—had it on the market by August of the same year.

The .17-556 is similar to the longtime .17/223 (.17 Practical) but is not a direct crossover. The big difference is the chamber design. After looking at how the industry treated the old .17 Practical, Kosman found that the neck diameter on reamers and drop-in barrels almost all required neck turning. On top of that, throats were very short, which added to the probability of erratic pressure spikes with the old cartridge. His solution was to make several proprietary changes to the chamber, including a no-turn neck design with a leade that includes some freebore so the bullet doesn't jam into the lands. This mitigates erratic pressures, making the cartridge much easier to load.

Like the .17/223, you set headspace with standard .223 gauges. The overall case length is the same as the parent case as well. By my definition of a wildcat, brass forming is required before it can be fired in a wildcat chamber. KAK supplies barrels and uppers for the AR-15 platform, including dies and fully formed brass. That means the average reloader can shoot this cartridge the same day the parts and brass arrive. Seldom can a wildcatter do that, as usually, it takes some work to get the brass right and work out the first load for a safe starting point.

During experimentation, Kosman found that once-fired military brass works best for the .17/556 since commercial .223 brass is too soft from the factory annealing, causing shoulder collapses in the forming process. So, KAK used once-fired brass to form the new .17 cases and annealed them after forming. KAK's brass comes in 100- or 200-round containers, fully formed and ready to load. Load data is available on the KAK website (kakindustry.com). Of course, you can still do more case prep if you so desire, but for many shooters, time is money, and they would rather be shooting. Accuracy with the above-described system produces ½ MOA groups with a KAK upper right out of the box.

.17-556 KAK	***18-in. barrel***
BULLET WEIGHT (GR)	**VELOCITY (FPS)**
15.5 NTX	4,300
20 V-Max	4,100
25 V-Max	3,800

.20 Mink

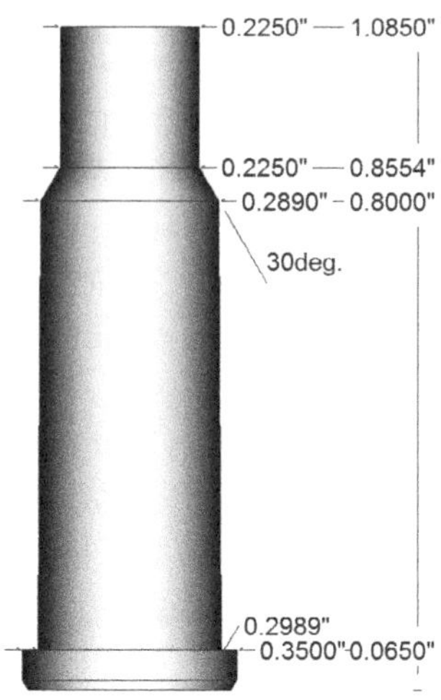

The .20 Mink.

Kevin Harrington, the .20 Mink's designer, says there is no need for neck turning unless you use European brass like RWS or Norma, which are next to impossible to get at the time of this writing. PPU brass is not great to work with, either, he says.

Harrington uses his custom-built Mink rifles with premium optics to get excellent results. He is interested in accuracy more than velocity. "If I only had one Mink, it would be the .20," he says. There is a broad selection of bullets, some with high BCs. Harrington likes shooting woodchucks at longer ranges and reports one kill with a .20 Mink at over 500 yards.

He does uniform the primer pockets and flash holes. But, no neck turning and no annealing. (He used to do these things but found they didn't affect his accuracy.) With the Mink line of cartridges, you can shoot all day without fatigue because the recoil is low, and you can watch the bullet hit the target.

Redding offers Mink dies, but RCBS no longer makes them (RCBS once made all three calibers, so you might find them used). Harrington's favorite powders for the Mink are WIN 296 or H110 (same burn rate). "There is a myth on the forums that making Squirrel brass is harder than the Mink. It is no more difficult to make Squirrel or Mink brass," Harrington said.

He recommends a 1:11 twist rate for the .20 Mink.

.20 Mink	***24-in. barrel***
BULLET WEIGHT (GR)	VELOCITY (FPS)
32	3,175
40	3,200

.20 Practical

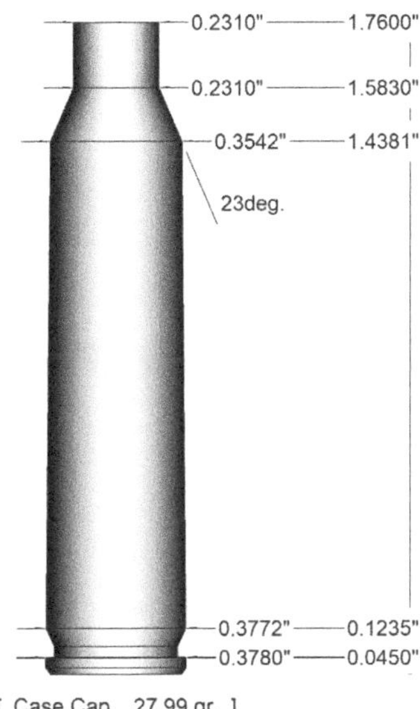

The .20 Practical.

The .20 Practical originated in 2004, so it missed the first edition of this book. Warren Brookman and Kevin Weaver, Brookman's gunsmith, cooperated on the design. The .204 Ruger was new to the market, and brass was challenging to locate. The two came up with a simple cartridge conversion with readily available brass.

They lit on the .223 Remington case and necked it to .20 caliber with no other changes. It's "Practical" because you don't need expensive dies. Use the proper bushing in your .223 dies to neck the brass down, load and shoot.

Ballistics are similar to the .204 Ruger and .20 Tactical, with 4,000 fps easily achieved using a 32-grain bullet. Like most cartridges in this velocity range, better accuracy often results below the magical 4,000 fps threshold. Of course, barrels last longer, too, when you stay below peak loads.

.20 Practical	***24-in. barrel***
BULLET WEIGHT (GR)	VELOCITY (FPS)
32	4,100
40	3,950

.20 NoZler (.20/22 Nosler)

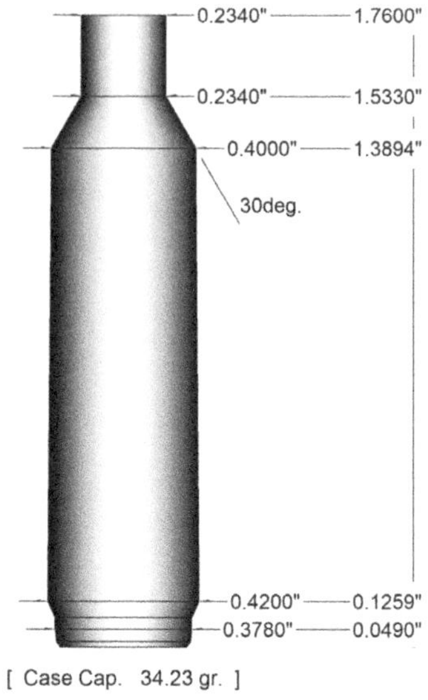

The .20 NoZler.

In researching this book, I discovered that the brass for the .20 Nosler, as it has been published, is a ghost cartridge (not really). Nosler took it to SAAMI in 2017 and will bring out the .20 Nosler someday, but the .20 caliber is a fairly small niche in the marketplace, so it might take some time (it's already been six years as I am writing).

Here is my solution: the .20 NoZler is nothing more than the .22 Nosler necked down to .20 caliber with no other changes. It allows you to use the .22 Nosler headspace gauges. Redding offers .22 Nosler bushing dies; you could easily resize brass with the appropriate neck bushing for .20 caliber. Better yet, Redding made me a set of dies for this caliber, although it spelled NoZler wrong. Go figure.

According to Nosler, the difference is that the .22 Nosler cases have 4.5 percent less capacity by water weight than the .20 Nosler. This may well be a good thing, as either cartridge is way overbore for the .20 caliber. That means velocity will not be in short supply, but barrel life may be.

Here is the trap that all wildcatters fall into: The .20 PDK is made from 6.8 SPC, with the rim unaltered at .417-inch diameter. The shoulder is .059 inch farther back than on the .20 NoZler. You must form the PDK in dies. Then, the .20 BR has the same case capacity as our new baby, the .20 NoZler, but the .20 BR is shorter and fatter. What makes our cartridge different?

Redding supplied the .20 NoZler dies for the author's tests. He accomplished sizing with a single pass through the sizing die.

The .20 NoZler has a .378-inch rebated rim, so it will work in guns with the 5.56 or .223 bolt face. I use .22 Nosler brass, which is very high quality and requires little prep work. It will work in any magazine that handles the 6.8 SPC, .224 Valkyrie or .22 Nosler, so it's AR-compatible. Forming is a simple single pass through a size die. It will feed better than the fat BR case. Because this case has plenty of capacity for a .20 caliber, I planned to use heavy-for-caliber bullets with a 1:8 twist barrel from X-Caliber Barrels.

The reamer arrived from Pacific Tool & Gauge with a .235-inch neck and .042-inch freebore, which requires neck turning. I used a neck and throat reamer and had to upsize the neck, resulting in a .237-inch neck diameter in the chamber. A sized case with a bullet seated had a .2355- to .236-inch neck with the lot of brass I have. So, neck turning is required with the .235-inch neck diameter on the PTG reamer.

When I test-fired the new chamber, it showed no problems with the neck diameter as is, so I skipped turning necks, but it might be better for accuracy to true them up.

The throat's freebore was extended to .106 inch. This length allowed us to start testing with the 40-gr. Hornady bullet .050 inch off the lands and seat it so the contact surface was about equal to the neck and shoulder junction. Test loads varied from .300 inch to just over 1 inch at 100 yards, so I can't wait to dig into this cartridge and try more bullets.

.20 NoZler ***24-in. X-Caliber barrel***

BULLET WEIGHT (GR)	CHARGE (GR/TYPE)	VELOCITY (FPS)	MAX CHARGE (GR)	VELOCITY (FPS)
32	32.5 VV N550	3,618	34.0	3,831
39	32.0 VV N550	3,448	34.0	3,795
40	32.0 VV N550	3,550	34.3	3,896

.20 Nosler

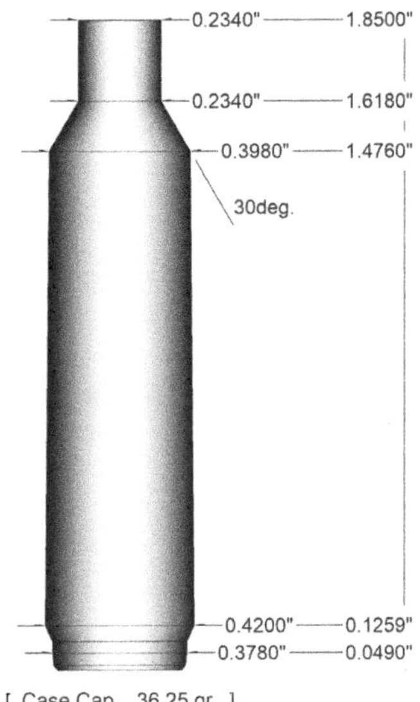

The .20 Nosler.

According to *Cartridges of the World, 17th Edition* (Gun Digest), Nosler took its .20 Nosler design to SAAMI in 2017. In 2023, as of this writing, it does not appear in Nosler's books or drawings on the SAAMI website. Nosler does publish cartridge dimensions and load data for it. The problem comes when you try to locate brass. The .20 Nosler is based on the 6.8 SPC, but the case length is 1.850 inches. That's .090 inch longer than the .22 Nosler brass and over .160 inch longer than the parent case.

I asked Hunter Pilant at Starline Brass about using a different cup to make their basic 6.8 SPC brass to get the extra length. He confirmed it could be done, but with current production demands, he suggested using .375 Winchester and turning down the rim to create the case. That suggestion makes sense, as the .375 Winchester brass is designed for higher pressure than .30-30 cases. To save labor and time, I chose not to go this route.

SAAMI requires the dimensional differences of the .20 Nosler vs. the .22 Nosler to prevent the interchange of ammunition. Nosler has staked out its territory for the .20 Nosler by publishing data, preventing confusion as much as possible. It should be evident that barrel life will be short with loads over 4,000 fps.

.20 Nosler	***20-in. barrel***
BULLET WEIGHT (GR)	**VELOCITY (FPS)**
32	4,225
34	4,100

.20 PDK (Predator Dog Killer)

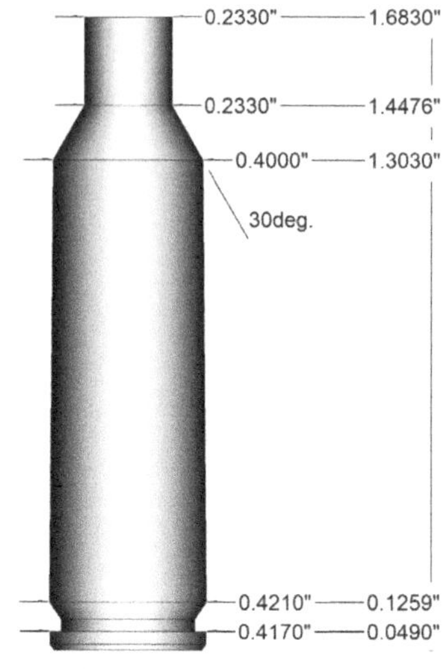

The .20 PDK (Predator Dog Killer)

Around 2004, Roy Winnett of Metamora, Illinois, created the .20 PDK (Predator Dog Killer) for AR-type rifles he built. The .20 PDK is made from 6.8 SPC with the rim unaltered at .417-inch diameter.

.20 PDK	***24-in. barrel***
BULLET WEIGHT (GR)	**VELOCITY (FPS)**
32	4,000
45	3,800
50	3,700

.22 Buckaroo

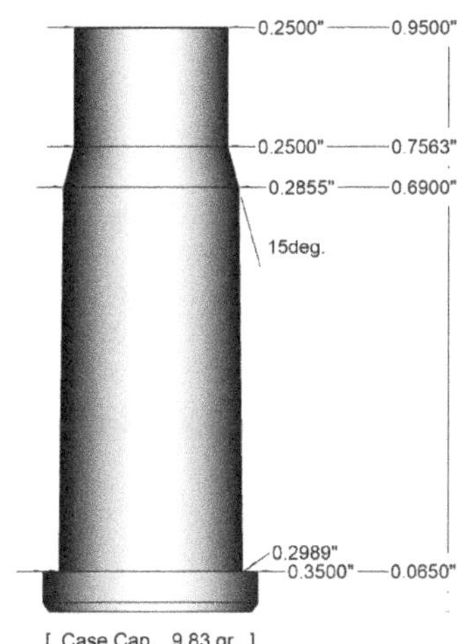

The .22 Buckaroo.

I always preach about knowing if it has been done before. When I researched the .22 Buckaroo cartridge in 2023, it was admittedly a follow-up after the fact. The Buckaroo is similar to the Kilbourn Junior Hornet and the .22 Mink. It's shorter than the .22 Squirrel by .028 inch, but the shoulder is farther forward so it has more capacity than the Squirrel.

The .22 Buckaroo is a necked-down .25 Dude, as seen later in this chapter. It has a considerable advantage over the .25 Dude because of bullet availability, not to mention barrels. Robart Schaefer and I were playing around with small .22 centerfire cartridges for the chapter in this book about alternative ammo for .22 rimfires. Switching to centerfire will be hard for most folks locked into rimfire .22s.

We were working on the .25 Dude when Schaefer suggested necking it down to .22. The .22 Buckaroo was the result. It will fit in any six-shot single-action cylinder that we checked—a completely different purpose than the designers of the Mink and Squirrel had in mind.

This cartridge makes more sense than the .22 LR centerfire case as an alternative to .22 ammo, mainly because of the cost and quality of brass. Custom cases for .22 LR centerfire have thin case heads and cost about $6 a piece at this time and will likely continue to rise.

On the other hand, .22 Hornet brass is much cheaper and usually easy to acquire. We used a shortened .218 Bee size die to neck down these cases, which worked like a champ, but Schaefer may decide on a sharper shoulder because he is considering using this wildcat in a single-action revolver.

.22 Mink

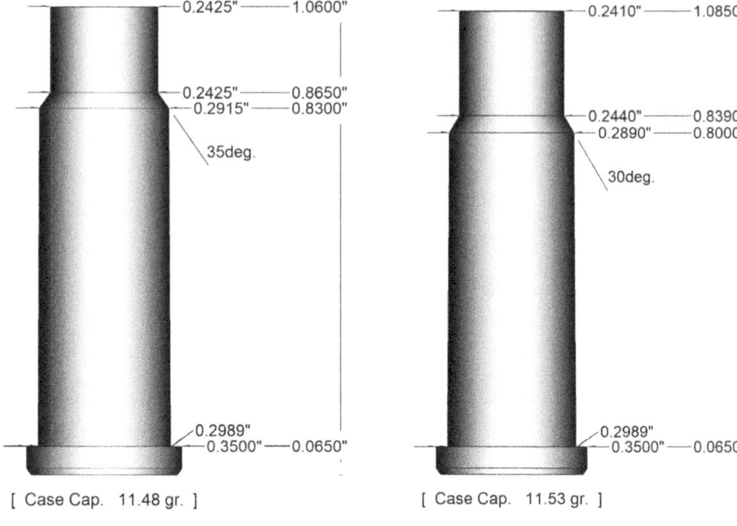

The .22 Kilbourn Junior Hornet.

The .22 Mink.

Like many wildcats today, the .22 Mink is a redesign of the old Kilbourn Junior Hornet. The KJH originated in the early 1940s. Fred C. Ness wrote it up for the May 1944 issue of the *American Rifleman*. The case length is identical. The location of the shoulder is .030 inch longer on the KJH, and the shoulder diameter is about .0015 inch larger. Still, the difference in case capacity between the designs is negligible. Kilbourn's purpose for his Junior cartridge was for use in low-pressure single-shots that were still pretty common and inexpensive in the 1940s.

Kevin Harrington of New York designed the .22 Mink. I doubt Harrington knew about the KJH. But he became a big fan of the .22 Squirrel and the .17 and .20 calibers. Todd Kindler said he thought Harrington had made more .22 Squirrel brass than anyone he knew. Harrington became well known as the guy to ask about reloading these cartridges. Many hunters wanted to extend the range of the Squirrel designs for shooting woodchucks and the like at longer ranges.

After shooting the Squirrel cartridges, Harrington thought a slightly longer case would do the job. He created the Mink series with a few things in mind: 1) Easy forming; except for the .17 Mink, you can use the FL die to form the case, minus the trimming. 2) No neck turning; the Mink case is headspaced on the shoulder datum. It has the same neck diameter as the Hornet. The case was designed to use Winchester brass with a neck clearance of .002-.003 inch in the chamber.

The 50-gr. Hornady V-Max in the .22 Mink will reach around 2,500-2,600 fps—and the 40-gr. V-Max really shines in the .22 Mink. Regarding the Mink family, the .22 is a better performer than the .20 and .17 simply because the bullets hit harder. Accuracy has proven phenomenal with reported group sizes between .250 inch at 100 yards and .500 to .750 inch at 200-250 yards, well under that magical MOA.

Kevin Harrington's Mink design was intended to deliver that extended range that hunters requested. He says one of the most significant advantages the Mink has over the .22 Hornet or K-Hornet is that it's designed for modern bullets. Modifying an old rifle from Hornet to K-Hornet, you still end up with a slow twist barrel of 1:16 or 1:14, depending on the rifle. A 1:10 Twist rate combined with shorter cases creates a more consistent cartridge. Not hampered by bullets of the old-school design, the Mink makes the best of what is available—high-BC spitzers. Some keyboard commandos claim that the fast twist will cause bullets to come apart. This assertion is a fallacy; the Mink's velocity range is much slower than a .223 Remington or .220 Swift.

Harrington says that if you want a nice, crisp, fully formed shoulder, use 50-grain bullets for fireforming. The .17- and .20-caliber Mink designs operate at low enough pressure that they seldom fully fireform the shoulder.

.22 Mink	***22-in. barrel***
BULLET WEIGHT (GR)	VELOCITY (FPS)
40	2,750
50	2,550

.223 Wylde

The .223 Wylde never really was a wildcat, but it deserves to be mentioned. In the 1990s, Bill Wylde, a gunsmith from Greenup, Illinois, who specialized in precision rifles, realized that because they shared identical case dimensions, specifications from the .223 Remington and 5.56x45mm NATO chamberings could be combined to achieve safe interchange of ammo. This lack of safe interchangeability is the subject of many articles, forums and YouTube posts.

The exterior dimensions of the .223 Remington and 5.56 NATO cartridges are identical. So why aren't they interchangeable? The 5.56 is loaded to 62,000 psi vs. .223 Remington, which is loaded to 55,000 PSI. Consequently, the answer comes down to chamber design. The dimensions of a .223 chamber are slightly smaller in general, but the real issue lies in the leade and freebore—the area between the front of the chamber (end of the case mouth) and the point where the bullet contacts with the lands of the rifling in the barrel. The .223 Rem. throat is shorter. The Wylde chamber makes it safe to fire either .223 Remington or 5.56 NATO in the same rifle and with better-expected accuracy.

Although SAAMI has not standardized this chambering, it has become very popular and is offered by nearly all makers of AR-15 barrels.

.22 PDK (Predator Dog Killer)

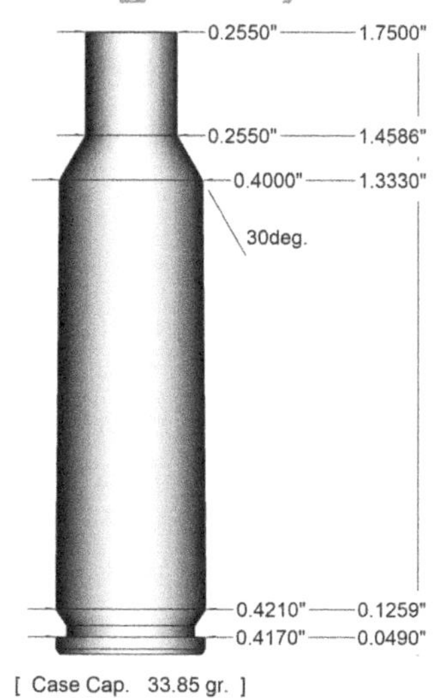

The .22 PDK.

Roy Winnett and John Hutchins joined forces to create the .22 PDK. When the 6.8 SPC came out, it spawned several wildcats. The .22 PDK will work in an AR-15 and an appropriate bolt-action. Richard Mann said Nosler copied the PDK with the .22 Nosler. It looks like Nosler maximized the design for all the case capacity it could get when it received SAAMI standardization in March 2022.

Nosler also used a rebated rim to work with a 5.56/.223 bolt face (.378 in.). This is a situation where the wildcat has been elevated to factory offering.

.22 PDK ***24-in. barrel***

BULLET WEIGHT (GR)	VELOCITY (FPS)
50	3,850
55	3,750
60	3,550
80	3,225

.22 Creedmoor (.22 CM)

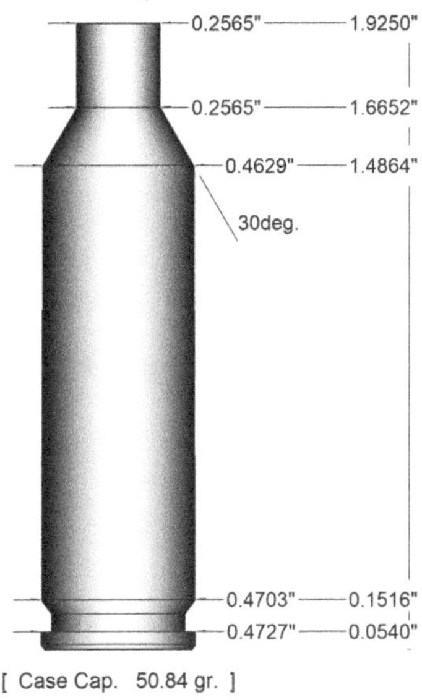

The .22 Creedmoor.

The .22 Creedmoor uses the standard 6.5 Creedmoor headspace gauges. In other words, it has the same body as the 6.5 and 6mm Creedmoor, but the neck and throat are different. Like any overbore wildcat (i.e., too much powder capacity), the .22 CM works best with fast-twist barrels and heavy-for-caliber bullets. How about an 80-grain Berger at 3,500 fps from a 26-in. barrel?

Hornady, Peterson and Alpha Munitions are already selling .22 Creedmoor brass. It's a safe bet that this cartridge will make it through SAAMI in the next few years.

.22 Creedmoor	***24-in. barrel***
BULLET WEIGHT (GR)	**VELOCITY (FPS)**
55 Hornady V-Max	3,814
75 Hornady ELD-M	3,457
80.5 Berger	3,296
95 Sierra HPBT 95	3,016

Peterson Brass published data for a 24-in. 1:7 twist barrel.

.240 Banshee

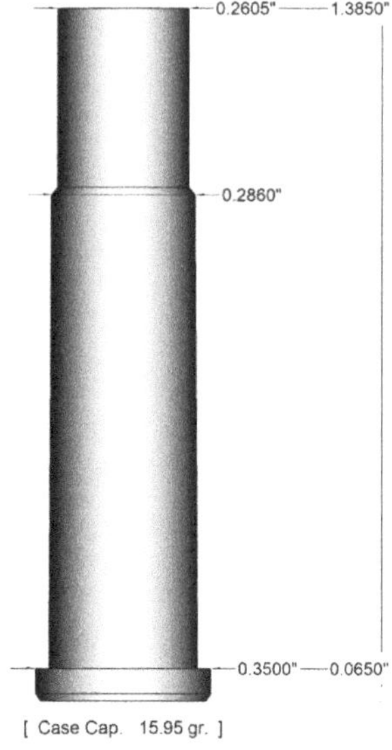

The .240 Banshee.

Gary Reeder envisioned the .240 Banshee as a pistol cartridge. It's similar to a .22 K-Hornet necked up to 6mm and performs best with light-for-caliber bullets because of its low case capacity compared to other 6mm cases. In 2008, Bill Oviatt of Lander, Wyoming, created what became known as the .24 Calhoon, which was the .19 Calhoon necked up to 6mm. Ballistically, these two cartridges are nearly identical. You know what they say, "Great minds think alike." There are dimensional differences, but ballistically, they are twins.

.240 Banshee	***12-in. barrel***
BULLET WEIGHT (GR)	**VELOCITY (FPS)**
55	2,400
60	2,200
75	2,100

.24 York

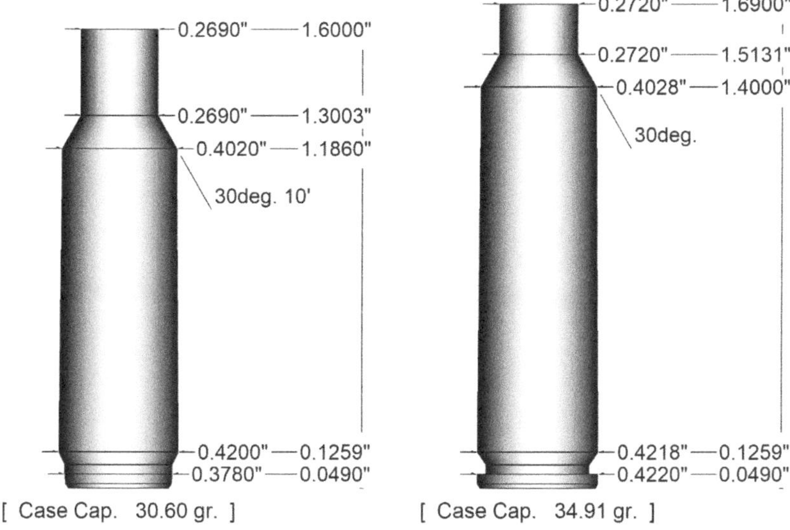

The .24 Nosler (left) vs .24 York (right).

In 2013, Wayne York of Oregunsmithing created the .24 York, necked down from his earlier 25 York. York said that he had noticed many customers ordering various 6mm cartridges and, since the .25 York was so much fun to shoot, it was natural to neck it down to .24.

Based on the 6.8 SPC case, this cartridge differs significantly from the .24 Nosler, which was last revised for SAAMI in 2017. The York has the standard SPC rim diameter and about 11.4 percent more case capacity by water weight.

Wayne York is an avid hunter and built two of these for his use. One is in a standard hunting rifle, and the other is set up with a heavy barrel for prairie dogs and coyotes. When his grandson needed a gun for hunting, he built a youth rifle in .24 York. "It's a versatile cartridge that works well for everything from varmints to deer-class animals, and the recoil is manageable for ladies and young shooters," York said.

.24 York	***24-in. barrel***
BULLET WEIGHT (GR)	**VELOCITY (FPS)**
57	3,250
100	2,800

6mm BRX

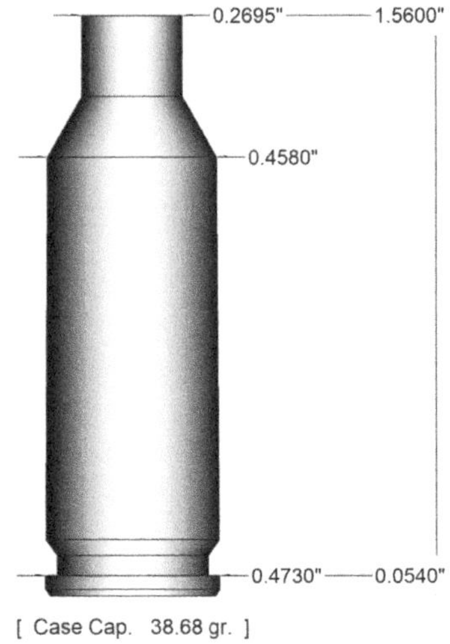

The 6mm BRX.

The 6mm BRX owes its existence to the competitive shooters who decided they needed more velocity to shorten the flight time. Since the 6mm BR has pretty low felt recoil, they could afford the increased powder charge without increasing fatigue. In short, a balancing act.

In 2005, Bob Crone came up with the 6mm BRX, which uses BR brass, but the shoulder is about 0.100 inch farther forward, thus shortening the neck to just under a caliber length. Bill Shehane made a version of this cartridge with the shoulder about .020 inch forward, but the true BRX is the Crone design. If you're trying to figure out where the cartridge fits, it has less capacity than the 6mm Dasher. Many shooters report velocities in the 3,000 fps range with 107-gr. Sierra bullets.

6mm BRX	***28-in. barrel***
BULLET WEIGHT (GR)	**VELOCITY (FPS)**
105	2,900
80	2,850

6mm XC

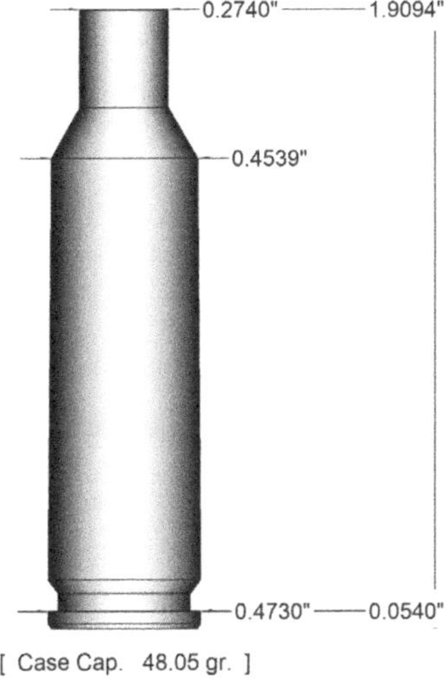

The 6mm XC.

Eleven-time NRA High Power National Champion David Tubb developed the 6mm XC specifically for NRA High Power match shooting. It is touted as one of the most accurate long-range 6mm rounds designed for repeating rifles. The 6XC is a CIP-standardized case.

In 2004, Tubb won three Camp Perry Across the Course championships and one Long Range Championship using it. Norm Houle won the 2004 Across the Course title, shooting 6XC in his TUBB 2000 rifle. Loaded with a 115-grain DTAC bullet in the XC, Tubb won the 2005 NRA High Power Long Range National Championship with the first-ever "perfect score" of 1450/1450 using this bullet/load combination.

The wildcat started gaining popularity outside competitive circles around the time, and factory brass became available from Norma and Peterson in 2007. Peterson Brass says on its website, "Tubb has won almost 30 different rifle championships and has proved to the world that the 6 XC is a highly effective, flat-shooting caliber."

Its 30-degree shoulder allows less case growth (less trimming required). Tubb found that velocities attainable with the 6mm XC are equivalent to the .243 Winchester. He reported that barrel life is much better than .243 Winchester because the XC has about 7 grains less powder capacity.

6mm XC	***28-in. barrel***
BULLET WEIGHT (GR)	**VELOCITY (FPS)**
115 DTAC	3,000

.257 Fox

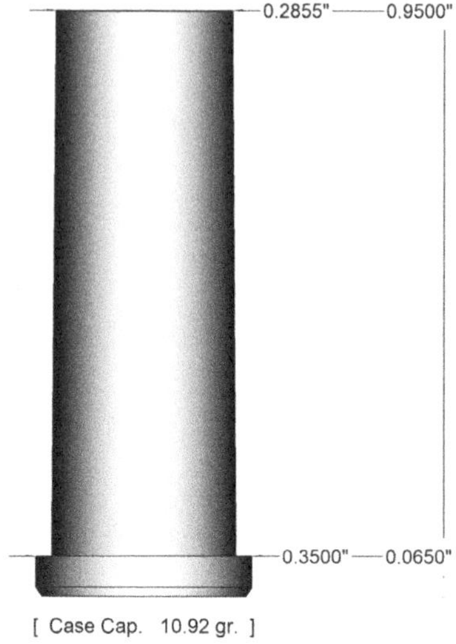

The .257 Fox.

Robart Schaefer and I get together occasionally and talk about our various projects, go shooting, do reloading and work on tools and guns for our entertainment. During one of these work sessions, we made tools for my version of the .22/25 ACP, which I call the .22 Mantis, prompting a discussion about other cartridges that might fit in a modified .22 LR single-action revolver.

I grabbed some .22 Hornet cases, and Robart measured the cylinder length of a Heritage single-action. We cut brass to .950 inch so loaded rounds would fit the cylinders. Running a .257-inch expander ball into the case mouth created a nearly straight case. That is how the .257 Fox came into being. I figured it would be good for clearing varmints out of the hen house since the lightest bullets in .257 inch are about 60 grains; it would never be a barn burner (pardon the pun).

.25 Dude

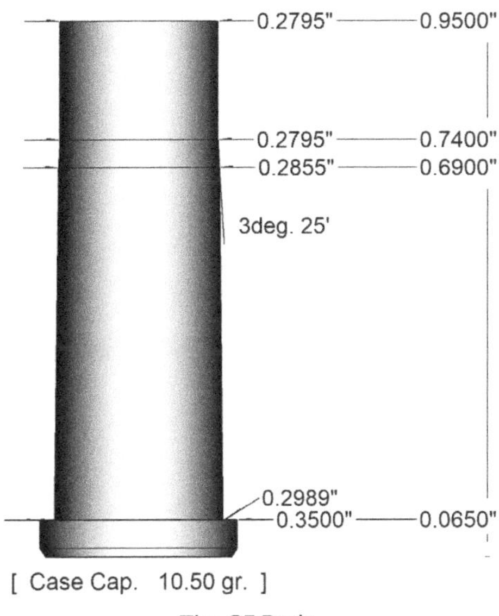

The .25 Dude

We created the .257 Fox first (see above), but bullets less than 60 grains were unavailable, making it a very limited cartridge. For that reason and because we had .25 ACP bullets on the loading bench, we immediately liked the idea of putting a little neck on the case and creating a cartridge with .251-inch bullets. It is almost 75 percent of the size of a .357 Magnum, so it looks very cool for a small cartridge.

Why a .25 "Dude?" Well, the likely guns include Heritage Rough Riders and Ruger Wranglers. A Dude in the cowboy world is sort of a pretender, a city dweller vacationing on a ranch in the West. The .25 Dude is certainly not a big, tough western round, thus Dude.

I ordered a few different .25-caliber slugs, which are swaged lead bullets for air rifles. Weights start at 36 grains. Bullets like the Hornady XTP for .25 ACP are currently unavailable but weigh 35 grains. Why a Heritage single-action that we converted to centerfire? Because it's cheap, and extra cylinders are readily available for experimentation.

In 2019, there was a version of this cartridge by Michael Tinker Pearce, a YouTuber, which he called the .251 TCR (Tinker Centerfire Rimmed). He arbitrarily cut Hornet brass to .980 inch, used a Uberti 1873 BP as the source gun for his first conversion, and then built other variations.

Barrel liners for air guns are readily available for conversions. I have an old Remington Model 6 single-shot that might convert well to this caliber.

.255 Banshee

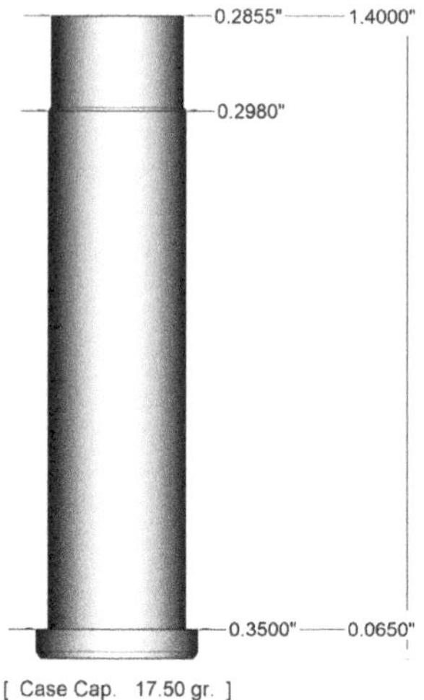

The .255 Banshee.

Based on the .22 Hornet, the .255 Banshee's case walls are straightened with no taper. Straight walls in bottle-necked cases aid in smoother extraction from revolvers. The straight case is necked down to .257 caliber with a 40-degree shoulder, giving it the look of a .22 K-Hornet. Gary Reeder designed the cartridge, wanting 2,000 fps from a 12-inch barrel and a 65–75 grain bullet. With the limited case capacity of the Hornet case, bullets over 87 grains will be moving slowly. This cartridge could be loaded subsonic with heavier bullets.

There have been numerous versions of the .25 Hornet over the years. P.O. Ackley said Herbert Longo had a version of the cartridge he promoted in the post-WWII years. There is very little new in the world of wildcats as old-time ideas become new because of specific guns coming on the market or the interests of the shooting public shifting. I found an article by Glen E. Fryxell, "Heading into the Hornet's Nest," about a custom Old Model Ruger Blackhawk in .25 Hornet. That version of the cartridge is a straight case with no shoulder.

.255 Banshee	***12-in. barrel***
BULLET WEIGHT (GR)	**VELOCITY (FPS)**
60	2,050
75	2,000
85	1,810

.25 York

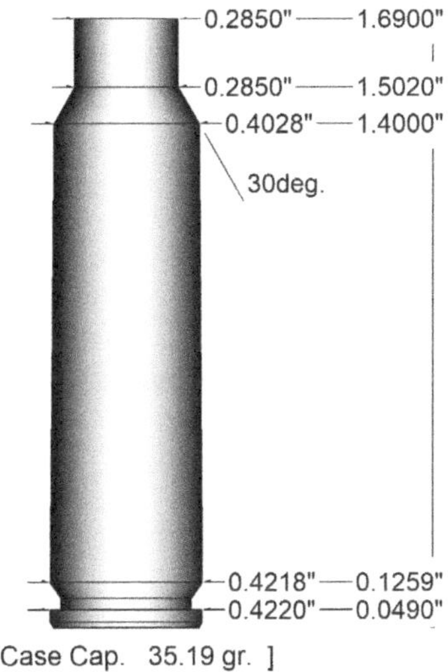

The .25 York.

In 2010, Wayne York of Oregunsmithing concocted the .25 York and a .22 based on the 6.8 SPC. That was 2010. Later, when Nosler released the .22 Nosler, he dropped the idea of the .22 as it was too close to the same cartridge. York was a fan of the 6.8 SPC and has used the factory cartridge for deer and antelope with great success at fairly close ranges. But he felt the cartridge suffered from limited bullet selection, so he necked it down to .25 caliber and blew the shoulder out to 30 degrees. There is a much broader selection of bullets in .257 than .277 inch. With the improved case, he went on to kill North American game up to elk. He felt comfortable extending his range on antelope and deer with the bullet choices available.

"The .25 York makes an excellent choice for an ultralight rifle. We have built a bunch of them on the Howa mini-action," York said. Oregunsmithing stocks headstamped brass with small rifle primer pockets, and York said that if you choose brass with a large primer, it will show signs of pressure sooner than a small primer. The place also stocks CH dies for the York cartridges.

.25 York	***24-in. barrel***
BULLET WEIGHT (GR)	**VELOCITY (FPS)**
75	2,980
100	2,800

.257 Raptor

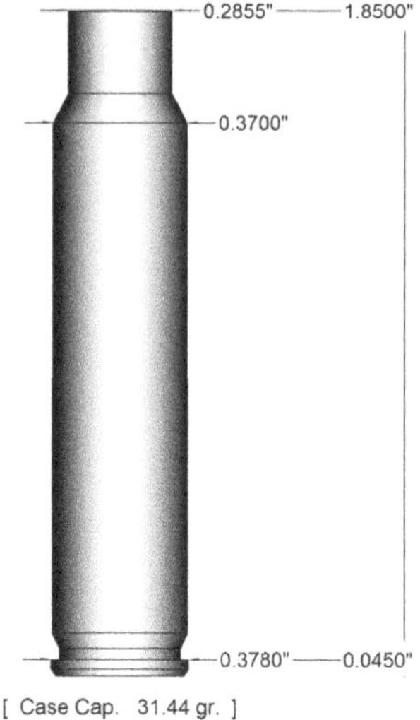

The .257 Raptor.

In 2009, Gary Reeder noticed shooters moving away from big cartridges and heavy bullets to those with less recoil. In short, cartridges that were fun to shoot and still did the job. Reeder consulted his notes and checked out the .204 Ruger for wildcat options.

Historically, the .204 Ruger comes from the .222 Remington Magnum case, with the shoulder moved forward and sharpened to 30 degrees. Reeder applied Ackley's design principles to the .204 case and necked it up to .257 simply because that is one of his favorites. Wildcats in the same family would be the .25/222 Copperhead and the 6mm x 47 (6mm/.222 Rem. Mag.). Reeder's cartridge has more capacity than the other two.

.257 Raptor	***13-in. barrel***
BULLET WEIGHT (GR)	**VELOCITY (FPS)**
75	2,700
85	2,500

.25 SAW

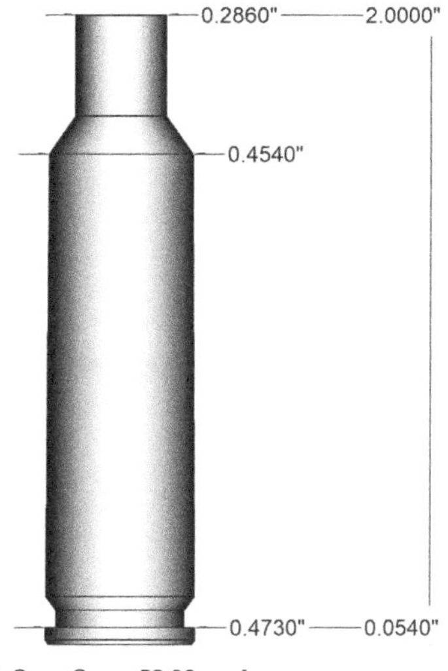

The .25 SAW.

In 2019, West Texas Ordnance (WTO) developed the .25 SAW three years after releasing its big brother, the 7mm SAW. The .25 SAW is a PRS cartridge designed to use heavy-for-caliber bullets. It thus works best with a faster twist barrel like a 1:7.5 or 1:8. This cartridge is a specialized variation of the .25 Creedmoor designed for use in MDT Extended OAL AICS-style magazines with the long ACE Bullet. It's hard to call this a wildcat since it's more like a proprietary setup for the PRS game.

Ballistically, the .25 Creedmoor is the same cartridge, although the cases are not interchangeable. The dimensions are proprietary, so the image here is for comparison only. A longer neck is the main difference from the Creedmoor.

.25 SAW	***26-in. barrel***
BULLET WEIGHT (GR)	**VELOCITY (FPS)**
131 ACE	2,950

.25 Creedmoor (2Fity-Hillbilly)

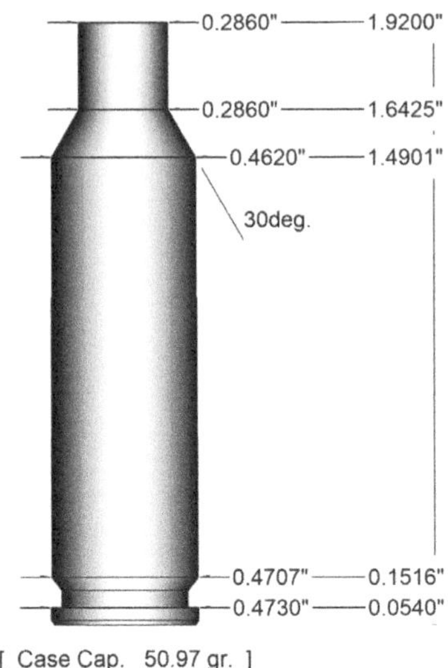

The .25 Creedmoor.

Gun writer Richard Mann lays claim to the .25 Creedmoor along with Mike Cyrus and Jerry Dove, who he named it for "two hillbillies."

It came along in 2017. Mann originally called it the .257 Wildcat "Because I couldn't think of a better name." To which I would say, "What about .25 Creedmoor?" Naturally, this name won out because it is nothing more than the 6.5 Creedmoor necked to .25 caliber. His cartridge's main advantage over the longtime wildcat .25 Souper (.25-308 Winchester) is the ability to seat long bullets out of the powder column.

.25 Creedmoor	***24-in. barrel***
BULLET WEIGHT (GR)	**VELOCITY (FPS)**
131 ACE	2,950
135 LRHT	2,860

.25-7 PRC

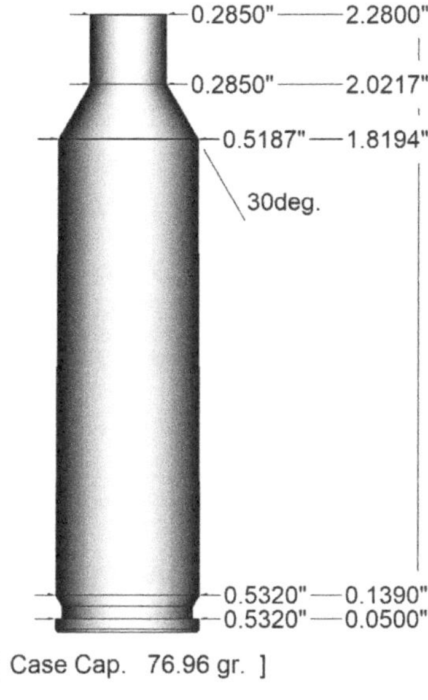

The .25-7 PRC.

The .25-7 PRC is a West Texas Ordnance (WTO) cartridge that hit the market in 2022–23. It compares to the performance of the classic .257 Weatherby Magnum and fits comfortably in a medium-length action. A 24-inch barrel can drive the 130-grain+ high-BC .25-caliber bullets at speeds of 3,200-3,300 fps. Like other WTO offerings, fast-twist barrels are needed to stabilize the heavy-for-caliber bullets.

Although seriously overbore for PRS-style matches, this cartridge could be very effective in lower round count hunter-style matches and even extended long-range competitions. With the 133-gr. Berger Elite Hunter at 3,240, the .25-7 PRC will hold 1,000 ft-lbs of energy and an impact velocity over 1,800 fps to 1,050 yards—more than enough for just about any shot on open country pronghorn or mule deer, and very capable on elk-sized game inside 600 yards. You can form the cases using off-the-shelf, commercially available dies, keeping operational costs low compared to other wildcats.

.25/7mm PRC	*24-in. barrel*
BULLET WEIGHT (GR)	VELOCITY (FPS)
133 Berger Elite Hunter	3,300
135 Berger LR Hybrid	3,270

.257 Allen Xpress vs. .257 Allen Magnum

In 2007, a new family of wildcats came out of the Allen Precision shop in Fort Shaw, MT. Kirby Allen stated the design goal of these wildcats was to offer a high level of performance as compared to the Allen Magnums (the older brothers of the Allen Xpress cartridges) but allow longer barrel life than their crazy overbore siblings, which used the .338 RUM as a parent case.

.257 Allen Express vs. .257 Allen Magnum

BULLET WEIGHT (GR)	VELOCITY 28-IN. BARREL (FPS)	VELOCITY 30-IN. BARREL (FPS)
100	3,850	4,050
110	3,750	3,900
115	3,700	3,800

Data provided by Allen Precision

Tire kickers interested in the Allen Magnum wildcats expressed major concerns about barrel life when they came out in 2005. Both cartridges are based on the .300 Dakota (.404 Jeffery). The Allen Xpress line of wildcats was designed to offer a similar performance option using much less powder, extending barrel life significantly. Even though the Allen Xpress wildcats are slightly less potent than their Allen Magnum big brothers, they produce extreme velocities in this .257 wildcat.

.6.5 Allen Xpress vs. 6.5 Allen Magnum

See the .257 Allen Xpress vs. .257 Allen Magnum for cartridge details. These are the same cartridge necked up to .264 inch. The parent case is the .404 Jeffery.

6.5 Allen Express vs. 6.5 Allen Magnum

BULLET WEIGHT (GR)	VELOCITY 28-IN. BARREL (FPS)	VELOCITY 30-IN. BARREL (FPS)
100	–	4,100
120	3,450	3,800
140	3,350	3,550

6.5 BC (Bitch Cat)

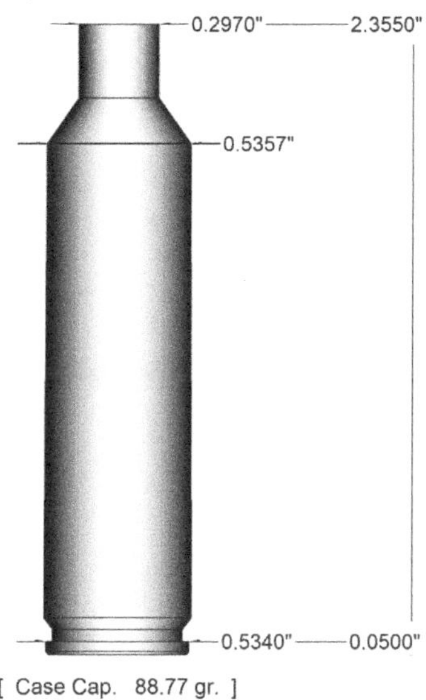

The 6.5 Bitch Cat.

In 2020, the Vortex Nation Podcast crew came up with this wildcat. The name Bitch Cat was defined as "one ferocious, fast-moving cat."

Based on the .300 RUM case shortened, the length makes it a perfect fit for standard-length magnum actions, and the rebated case fits the standard magnum bolt face. As they were getting ready to work up loads, powder and primers became hard to get. So, the load development was stalled until components became more available. They did get the first gun out in the field and took three antelope with it, pushing a 140-grain bullet at about 3,400 fps.

I asked Ryan from Vortex about the design process and why the podcast team got into wildcatting. He said, "Our main purpose was to show the shooting public that it's a fun and easy process to design your own wildcat. We wanted our audience to know that they can absolutely use their creativity to design and test a cartridge. We had no plan to fill a niche with our wildcat. It was really about learning and sharing the fun of the process."

From the outset, the design was for a hunting cartridge, designed and throated to work best with high-quality hunting bullets (instead of long, heavy competition bullets). Vortex selected bullets for their penetration capabilities. Exit wounds left a substantial blood trail.

6.5 PCC (Patriot Combat Cartridge)

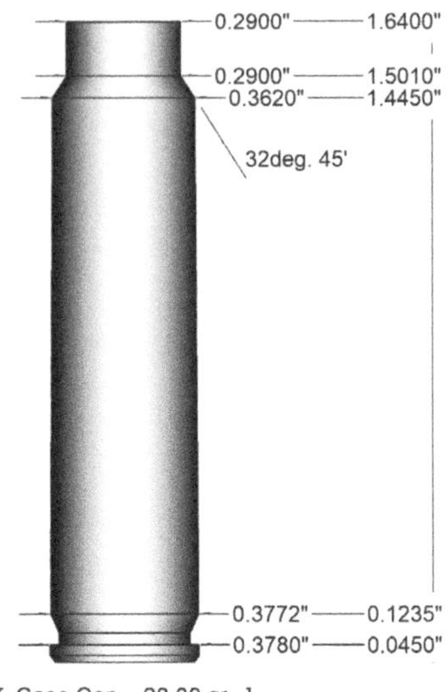

The 6.5 PCC (Patriot Combat Cartridge).

In 2012, Illirian Engineering and Design created the 6.5 PCC—a short-necked 6.5mm on the .223 Remington case that pushes a 100-grain bullet at 2,500 fps. These velocities seem pretty fast compared to other wildcats based on this parent case.

6.5 PCC	***20-in. barrel***
BULLET WEIGHT (GR)	**VELOCITY (FPS)**
100	2,550
120	2,200

6.5 Renner

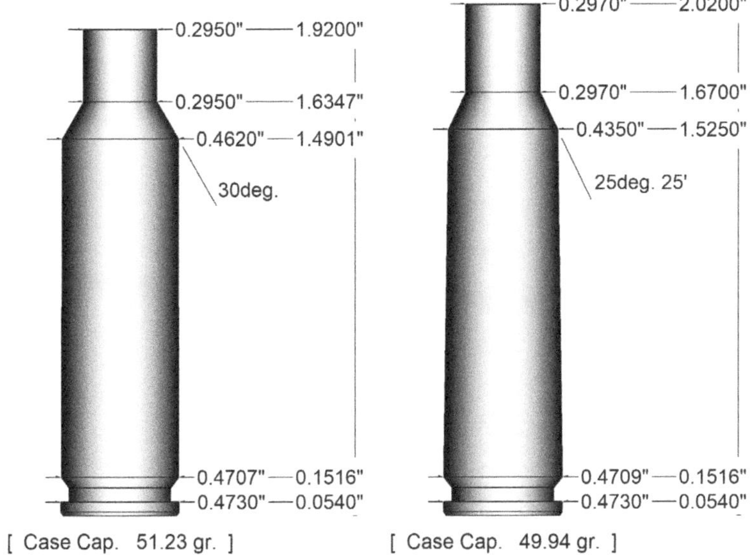

The 6.5 Creedmoor (left) vs. the 6.5 Renner (right).

R.J. Renner developed the 6.5 Renner for his hunting clients who wanted old-school designs for better feed and extraction and the ballistics benefits of the now-popular Creedmoor case.

Renner says modern "green" bullets are becoming the norm and present some issues with a short neck. Those grooves can be tricky in getting the crimp in the proper place with a short cartridge neck. The longer neck of the 6.5 Renner better holds those long cruise missiles. This rimless version is for bolt guns.

You can use load data for the 6.5 Creedmoor since the Renner has the same case capacity: Geometry, it's a thing.

6.5 Renner SS (Single Shot)

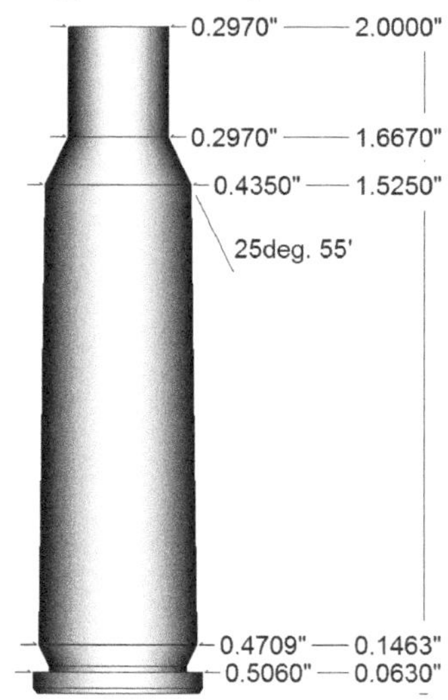

The 6.5 Renner Rimmed.

Based on the .307 Winchester, the 6.5 Renner SS is identical to the 6.5 Renner but has a rimmed case to make it a more traditional-style single-shot cartridge, allowing for positive extraction. You can use load data for the 6.5 Creedmoor, as this wildcat has the same case capacity.

6.5 Sherman

Here is a surprise entry in this chapter. In 2000, Rich Sherman designed the 6.5 Sherman based on the .270 Winchester case. So, how did it make it into this chapter? It gained popularity over time, so it did not come on the radar until several years later. Sherman has created an entire lineup of cartridges, which his customers call "Shermanized." I asked what that meant, and he said he uses minimal body taper, a 40-degree shoulder like Ackley, and moves the shoulder forward. So, these wildcats require you to form your brass in dies or buy Sherman's headstamped brass.

The 6.5 Sherman was Sherman's first wildcat due to his appreciation of the 6.5-06 Ackley Improved. He wanted a better case design with the same ballistics as the 6.5 Gibbs. The 6.5 Sherman accomplishes that with a .300-inch neck length (Gibbs' necks are typically .250 inch).

Sherman uses modern powders to chase maximum velocities in all his designs. The listed velocities were fired from 26-inch or longer barrels, but the cartridge is efficient enough to get impressive results from barrels as short as 22 inches. Sherman recommends fast twist rates; for the 6.5 Sherman, he specifies a 1:8 twist. Sherman cartridges are proprietary designs.

6.5 Sherman	***26-in. barrel***
BULLET WEIGHT (GR)	**VELOCITY (FPS)**
123 Matchking	3,260
140 Berger VLD	3,200
150 Matchking	3,000

.270 Allen Xpress vs. .270 Allen Magnum

The parent case for the .270 Allen Xpress and .270 Allen Magnum is listed as the .300 Dakota based on the old .404 Jeffery case. Like Allen Precision's .257 and 6.5mm designs, these .270 cartridges are overbore and will have limited barrel life. However, if you love velocity, this is your territory.

.257 Allen Express vs..257 Allen Magnum

BULLET WEIGHT (FPS)	VELOCITY 28-IN. BARREL (FPS)	VELOCITY 30-IN. BARREL (FPS)
130	3,500	3,750
140	3,400	3,650
169.5	3,200	3,450

.270 Sherman

The .270 Sherman is for those wanting that .270 Winchester nostalgia, but with the punch of a magnum on an '06 case size. This concept is even more appealing with new bullets like the 170-gr. Berger EOL. The parent case is the .270 Winchester.

The reported velocities put the .270 Sherman in the 7mm Remington Magnum class with much less powder, so it's suitable for medium to large game at extended ranges. Sherman cartridges are proprietary designs.

.270 Sherman	***27-in. barrel***
BULLET WEIGHT (GR)	**VELOCITY (FPS)**
150	3,200
165	3,000
170	3,000

.277 Wolverine

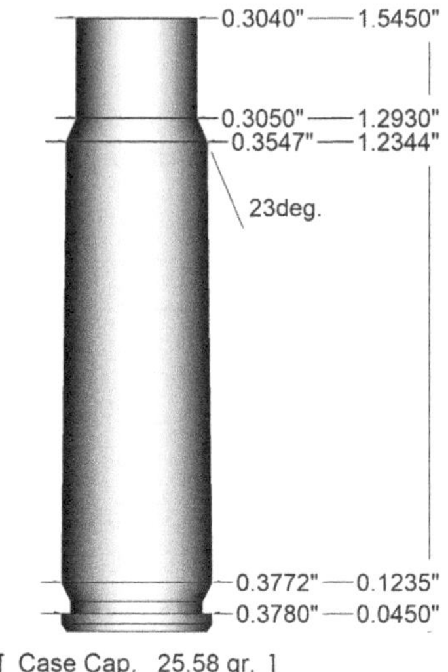

The .277 Wolverine.

Initially, the Wolverine was a proprietary cartridge by Mark Kexel and Mad Dog Weapon Systems, Inc. (MDWS). It's based on the 5.56 or .223 Remington case. MDWS released the dimensions in 2015, so anyone can copy and use the design. The Wolverine case is shortened to approximately 39mm from its 45mm parent brass, allowing loading heavier (longer) bullets to magazine length without the problems of seating the bullet's ogive into the case mouth. It can be loaded subsonic if that is your desire. You resize and form the case in a single-step operation to create a new 23-degree shoulder and oversized neck. This change makes it very different from cartridges like the TCU or the 6x45, and it will feed from standard AR magazines.

.277 Wolverine

BULLET WEIGHT (GR)	VELOCITY (FPS)
90	2,750
100	2,600
110	2,500

7mm Allen Magnum

The 7mm Allen Magnum is based on the .338 Lapua Magnum case with an improved shoulder. I have never been one to criticize others' design work, yet I cannot help but say, "Way too much powder capacity!" when I look at any cartridge like this. If velocity—at all costs—is your thing, then this one is for you. It will have considerable recoil, big noise and maximum velocity.

7mm Allen Magnum	***30-in. barrel***
BULLET WEIGHT (GR)	**VELOCITY (FPS)**
140	3,700
160	3,550
180	3,400

7mm Long Range Magnum (LRM)

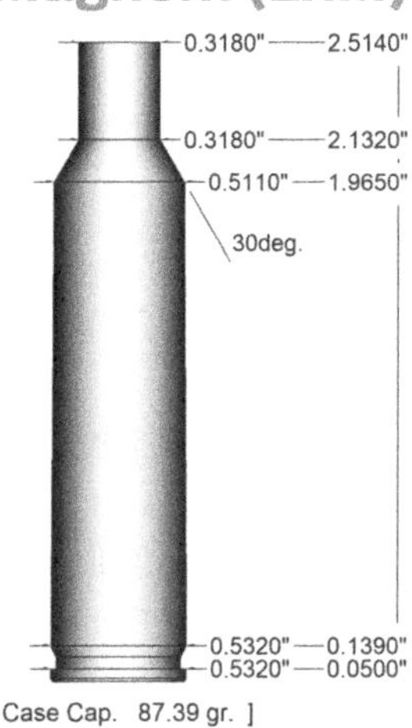

The 7mm Long Range Magnum (LRM).

In 2010, Gunwerks of Cody, Wyoming, brought out the 7mm LRM. Before that, in 2007, Ruger had introduced the .375 Ruger case with Hornady as a partner. Gunworks necks the case down to 7mm, creating what it calls the 7mm LRM. It fits in any standard-length magnum action but offers more case capacity because of the fatter case. The lack of a belt suits the trend away from that feature in cartridge cases.

When I contacted Gunwerks for this book, it stated, "We're on board and behind the finalized 7mm PRC cartridge. We will, of course, continue to support any customers who have LRM rifles." This statement suggests that Gunwerks considers the LRM to have been superseded by the PRC.

7mm LRM	***26-in. barrel***
BULLET WEIGHT (GR)	**VELOCITY (FPS)**
180	3,100

7mm Practical (7mm/300 Winchester)

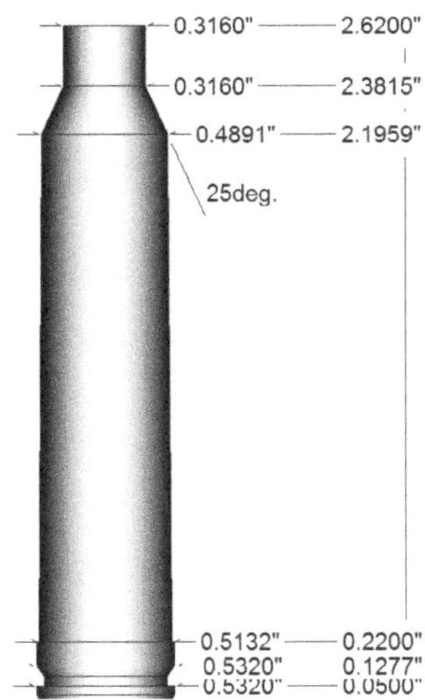

The 7mm Practical (7mm/300 Winchester).

Nathan Foster of Terminal Ballistics Research in New Zealand started developing the 7mm Practical in 2010 and, by 2017, was happy with his design. Why so long? Foster tested more than one throat configuration and finally decided on his chamber design. "Taking into account the many rifles in circulation and from a 26-in. barrel, extreme accuracy sweet spots for the 7mm Practical and 160-162-gr. bullets are generally between 3,200 and 3,225 fps," he said. That's about 200 fps faster than the 7 Rem. Mag. for the same accuracy sweet spot loads.

As of this writing, the 7mm PRC is the latest and greatest. It has the same case capacity as the 7mm Remington Magnum, depending on the lot of brass, within a grain or two. Statistically, they are the same. The difference is that the PRC is recommended with a faster 1:8 twist, and with the shorter, fatter case, you can load long, heavy bullets without eating up case capacity.

The 7mm Practical has about 10 percent more water weight capacity than the PRC. That is about what the best Ackley Improved case gains over the parent case. Foster recommends a 1:9 twist with the Practical, and it should perform well with heavy hunting bullets of reasonable length.

7mm/300 Win. Mag.	***26-in. barrel***
BULLET WEIGHT (GR)	**VELOCITY (FPS)**
160	3,200
180	3,000
195	2,900

7mm SAW

Born out of the Precision Rifle Series or PRS game, the 7mm SAW was to be a 7mm short-action cartridge that would reliably feed from AICS/AW box magazines and could drive a 162- or 168-gr. bullet to speeds at least equivalent to current 6.5mm competition cartridges such as the 6.5 Creedmoor, 6.5×47 Lapua and .260 Remington without the need to fireform brass.

There are two throat recommendations; the "7mm SAW I" chamber option is the short .045-inch throat for shooters who want to run standard AICS mags or Magpul. The "SAW II" chamber has a .150-inch freebore, which yields a maximum OAL of 3.090 inches with 183-gr. SMK bullets for F-Class shooters who single load. It was developed initially on Lapua's .308 Winchester Palma brass with a small rifle primer pocket. You can form brass in one pass through a 7mm SAW sizer die, and it's ready to load. You can also use standard large primer .308 brass.

According to West Texas Ordnance, the 7mm SAW can drive mid-weight .284 bullets like the 162-grain Hornady ELD-M and 168-grain Berger VLD to between 2,850 and 2,900 fps in a 26-inch barrel. You can push heavy bullets like the 180-grain Berger Hybrid and 183-grain Sierra MatchKing to around 2,725-2,750 fps. Those numbers give the cartridge a slight edge in drift and drop over the medium 6.5s while providing low recoil and excellent barrel life for PRS shooters. It's all about the tradeoffs.

7mm SAW	***26-in. barrel***
BULLET WEIGHT (GR)	**VELOCITY (FPS)**
162 ELD	2,850
166 A-Tip	2,850
180	2,725

7mm Valkyrie AR

In 2015, Bruce Finnegan—with help from a group of like-minded shooters called the Founders—designed the 7mm Valkyrie. The 7mm Valkyrie sits in the 7mm-08 power range but is for use in AR-15s. Cases are trimmed to 1.596 inches. Pressure testing was done with the pressure trace system along with accuracy testing. The recommended parent brass is 6.5x47 Lapua. You can also use .308 Winchester cases, but performance might suffer.

7mm Valkyrie AR	***24-in. barrel***
BULLET WEIGHT (GR)	**VELOCITY (FPS)**
110	3,025
140	2,800
168	2,600

7mm/6.5 Weatherby RPM

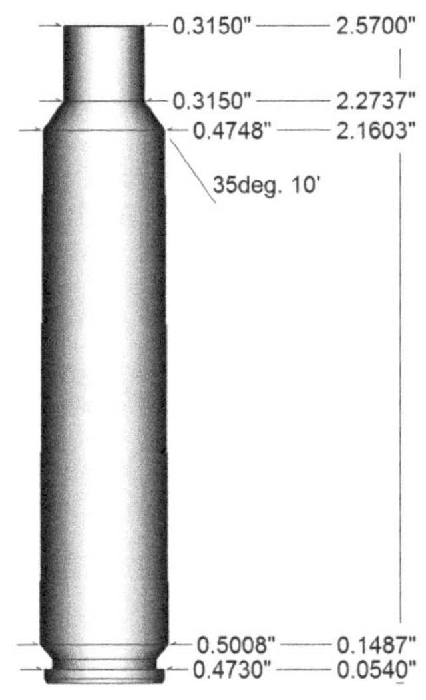

The 7/6.5 RPM.

The 6.5 RPM came out in 2020, but reamer makers designed the 7mm/6.5 RPM before brass was available. The case capacity is nearly identical to the 7mm Winchester Short Magnum (WSM). Using 7mm WSM starting loads for the same bullet would be a safe starting place. That puts this wildcat in the same class as the venerable 7mm Rem. Mag. In short, Weatherby will probably never bring this cartridge to the market as it has too many established competitors. Some would appreciate this wildcat for its combination of design features, chief among them the lack of a belt, which is considered passé by many shooters these days.

.300 Allen Xpress

.300 Allen Express	***30-in. barrel***
BULLET WEIGHT (GR)	VELOCITY (FPS)
200	3,500
210	3,450
240	3,250

The .300 Allen Xpress is based on the .338 Lapua case. Allen compares it to the .30/378 Weatherby. According to Kirby Allen, it uses 12 grains less powder to match the Weatherby's performance.

.30 ARX

In 2011, Robert Whitley of AR-X Enterprises created the .30 ARX based on the 6.5 Grendel parent case necked up to .30 caliber. Like the Grendel, the .30 ARX reportedly feeds flawlessly in AR-15s, offering excellent accuracy and better velocity than the original 7.62x39. (Oh yeah, that's the parent case for the Grendel). Whitley has created a slightly improved version of the 7.62 parent, or in this case, grandparent.

Compared to the .300 AAC Blackout (.300 BLK), the .30 ARX holds about 57 percent more powder, delivering more velocity. In a 20-inch-barreled AR-15, the .30 ARX can drive a 125-gr. bullet at 2,500 fps, and it can launch a heavier 150-gr. bullet at 2,400 fps, or about 200 fps faster than the 7.62x39. You can also load it to a subsonic level.

.30 ARX	***18-in. barrel***
BULLET WEIGHT (GR)	VELOCITY (FPS)
125	2,500
150	2,400

7.62x39 AI 28 Degree

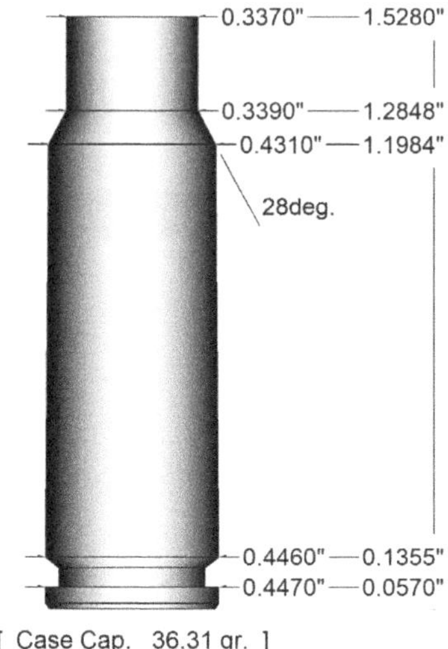

7.62x39 AI 28 Degree.

Dan Rawlings of Illinois informed me of his experiment with the 7.62x39 AI 28 Degree. He did not design it but took the time to wring it out and provide test data.

Rawlings said that no one listed a 7.62x39 40-degree reamer. Strangely enough, CH Tool & Die listed 7.62x39 improved dies with a 28-degree shoulder and had a set on the shelf. Rawlings bought them and began a quest into wildcatting. Utilizing a Howa mini in 7.62x39, he built a custom rifle. The Howa has the standard .311-inch groove diameter in the barrel. That rifle was enough to get him hooked on the cartridge, but he did not like hunting down .311-inch bullets for reloading. So, he traded that rifle off.

Rawlings ordered a New Ultra Light Arms Model 20 from Melvin Forbes. This new rifle has a .308 groove diameter barrel and is necked and throated to allow factory ammo with .311 bullets to chamber. P.O. Ackley's tests with bullets and throat diameters told me not to worry about the .003-inch difference in groove diameter. Dave Manson made a chamber reamer matching the above specs and die drawing from CH. Rawlings sent the reamer to Melvin Forbes at NULA to chamber his new Model 20.

The 7.62x39 AI 28 Degree is dimensionally different than the .30 ARX, .30 Grendel, .30 Major and several others, but the capacities are ballistic twins. The only difference Rawlings claims is that he can fire factory ammo in his improved chamber, so it's easy and cheap to feed. Using Lapua/Grendel brass, he says the water capacity of a formed case is 38 Grains.

7.62x39 AI (.311-in. groove)	*22-in. barrel*
BULLET WEIGHT (GR)	VELOCITY (FPS)
130	2,350
150	2,450

7.62x39 AI (.308-in. groove)	*21-in. barrel*
BULLET WEIGHT (GR)	VELOCITY (FPS)
110 Hornady	3,000
125 Nosler	2,950
150 Hornady	2,650
180 Hornady	2,200

.30 Raptor

The .30 Raptor is a Gary Reeder design on the .204 Ruger case. Like his other Raptor designs, it came about in 2009. Reeder had the Thompson/Center G-2 or Contender pistols in mind for this cartridge. You could consider it the .204 Ruger Ackley Improved necked up to .30 caliber. Reeder has a series of cartridges on this same case design—.240, .257, 6.5mm, 7mm and .30. This series is well-suited to whitetail hunting.

.30 Raptor	*22-in. barrel*
BULLET WEIGHT (GR)	VELOCITY (FPS)
100	2,300
125	2,200

.300 Raptor

Originating in 2010 and based on a .338 Excalibur case from A-Square in the 1990s, I have seen the .300 Raptor cartridge referred to as a "Monster Magnum." I cannot think of a better name, for pushing a 230-gr. projectile at 3,350 fps is a respectable accomplishment. There are darn few hunting bullets made to handle that kind of velocity. Kirby Allen designed it, and his company, APSrifles.com, offers custom actions for many of his monster-size cartridges, including the Raptor. At the time of this writing, brass is not available.

.300 Raptor	*28-in. barrel*
BULLET WEIGHT (GR)	VELOCITY (FPS)
180	3,650
200	3,560
240	3,275

.30 Remington AR

In 2008, the .30 Remington AR was a factory cartridge that came to the market just one year after the .450 Bushmaster, which may explain why it made it to the public. Remington purchased Bushmaster in 2006 to buy into the arena of AR-15 rifles and carbines. The .450 Bushmaster is based on the .284 Winchester case, and so is the .30 Remington AR or the .30 RAR, as it became known in the gun magazines.

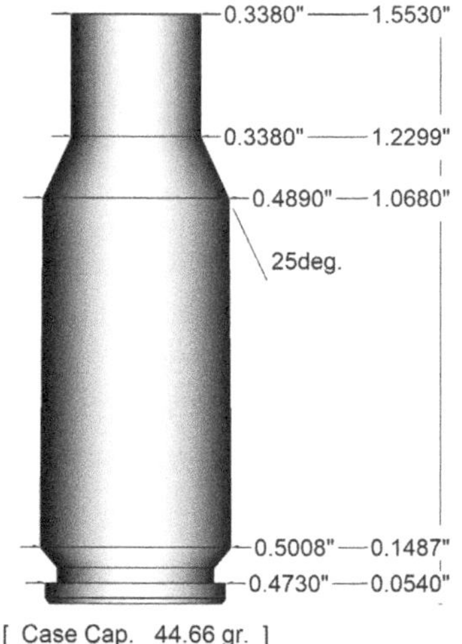

The .30 RAR (.30 Remington AR).

There are two options for forming .30 RAR brass: .450 Bushmaster or .284 Winchester. Remington's engineers disliked using SOCOM/Bushmaster bolt assemblies because the .30 RAR operates at 55,000 psi. In contrast, the two big-bores mentioned operate at only 38,000 psi. Remington created a special bolt head for its guns in the RAR caliber. Run it in a bolt gun, and there is no need for a special bolt head.

The .30 RAR has become obsolete or a wildcat through neglect and bankruptcy. It is an interesting cartridge because it follows the concept of Remington BR (Bench Rest) cases, with about 17 percent more case capacity due to the fatter case.

.30 Remington AR ***18-in. barrel***

BULLET WEIGHT (GR)	VELOCITY (FPS)
125	2,800
150	2,575

.300 Sherman

The .300 Sherman is a .30-06 wildcat with the exact case capacity as the .30 Gibbs. It is a simple rechamber conversion of your old '06. Like the other Sherman wildcats in the '06 family, it has a longer neck than the Gibbs, a body blown out to minimal taper and a 40-degree shoulder. The parent case is .270 Winchester. Sherman cartridges are proprietary designs.

.300 Sherman	*28-in. barrel*
BULLET WEIGHT (GR)	VELOCITY (FPS)
180	3,090
200	3,000

.30/6.5 Weatherby RPM

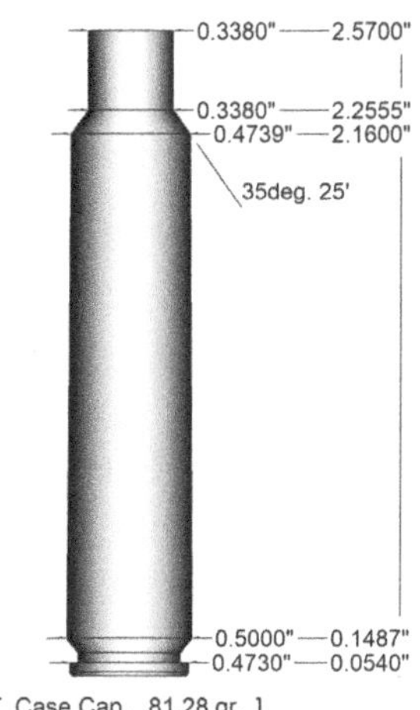

The .30/6.5 Weatherby RPM.

The case capacity of the .30/6.5 Weatherby RPM is identical to the .300 Winchester Short Magnum (WSM). Load data is easy to come by; use starting loads for the WSM, and you should be at a safe starting point. Velocity-wise that puts you about 100 fps faster than the .300 Winchester Magnum with the same bullet. This is one of those wildcats the reamer makers had ready to go before you could get brass.

.30/6.5 RPM	*24-in. barrel*
BULLET WEIGHT (GR)	VELOCITY (FPS)
150	3,150
165	3,000
180	2,925

.327 Martin Meteor

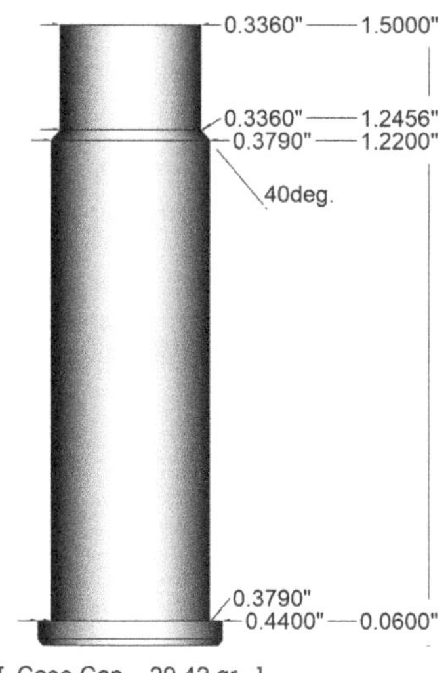

The .327 Martin Meteor.

Lee Martin of Arlington, Virginia, designed the Meteor in 2008. He used .357 Maximum cases sized in a full-length form die and trimmed the brass to 1.500 inches for use in a Ruger Blackhawk; however, it would also work well in a single-shot like the TC Contender. Wildcats for revolvers are not as common as for rifles or single-shots, so it's fun to entertain this concept.

This wildcat has considerably more case capacity than the .327 Federal, the whole point of the 15-minute conversation that spawned this design. At the time of this writing, there is a full write-up about the .327 Martin Meteor on SingleActions.com. I have to give props to Lee Martin: he knows cartridge history and did his research, the most important traits of a wildcatter!

.327 Martin Meteor ***8-in. barrel***

BULLET WEIGHT (GR)	VELOCITY (FPS)
85	2,200
100	2,100

.338 Allen Xpress

The .338 Allen Xpress is an improved version of the .338 Lapua Magnum. It could share load data with a .338 Lapua Ackley Improved, the shoulder angle and slightly different headspace being the only differences. Allen says this chamber can safely fire .338 Lapua ammo like other improved cartridges.

The .338 Allen Xpress matches the .338-378 Wby. and .338-416 Rigby chamberings but does so with about 10 grains less powder and a significantly shorter overall length.

.338 Allen Express	***30-in. barrel***
BULLET WEIGHT (GR)	**VELOCITY (FPS)**
225	3,400
250	3,300
265	3,200
300	3,000

8.6mm Blackout (BLK) (.338 Creedmoor/8.6 Creedmoor)

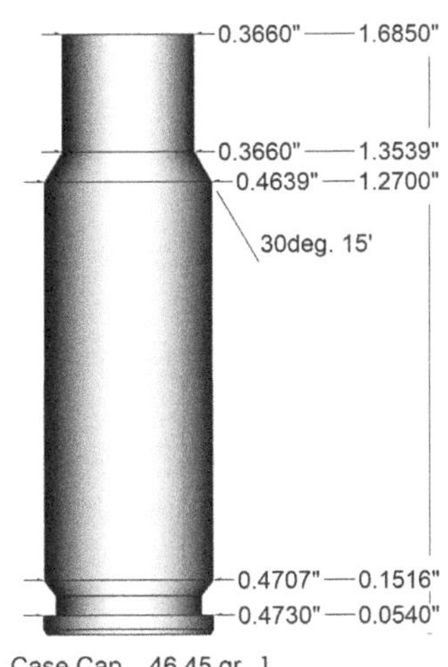

The 8.6mm Blackout (BLK).

To be very clear, the 8.6mm Blackout is not part of the Creedmoor family of cartridges. (It has its own specific headspace gauge.) The 8.6 BLK uses 6.5mm Creedmoor as a parent case and is trimmed to 1.685 inches and necked to .338 inch. As the name implies, it's designed for subsonic loads. Fast-twist barrels are required for the best results. The wildcat is an excellent example of why naming conventions matter, as the name has caused a great deal of confusion among the shooting public (the Creedmoor moniker should never have been used with this case).

8.6mm Blackout	***12-in. barrel***
BULLET WEIGHT (GR)	**VELOCITY (FPS)**
185	2,200
210	1,950
300	1,025

.338/6.5 Creedmoor

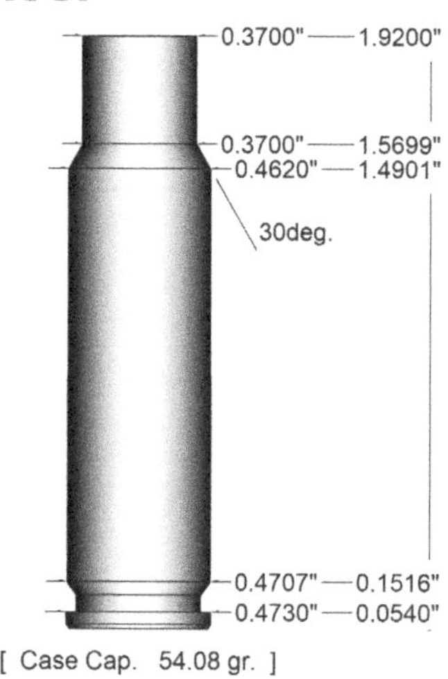

The .338/6.5 Creedmoor.

The .338/6.5 Creedmoor is a full-length 6.5 Creedmoor case necked up to .338 and uses the 6.5 Creedmoor headspace gauge. It's not designed to run subsonic. You seat bullets .080 inch farther out of the powder column, which is the main difference between it and the .338 Federal. Ballistically, the two are very similar.

Starting loads for the .338 Federal will undoubtedly work in the .338/6.5 Creedmoor.

.338 Enabelr

Applied Ballistics' .338 Enabelr is the same cartridge as the .375 Enabelr necked down to .338. Enabelr stands for Engineered by Applied Ballistics for Extreme Long Range. Nearly all cartridge designs, wildcat or proprietary, are based on some existing case that was necked down and some slight dimensional changes. However, the .338- and .375-caliber Enabelr cartridges are original designs with no parent case.

Like the .375 Enabelr, the goal was to utilize long, heavy match-grade bullets for sniper and competition applications. Applied recommends the Berger 300-grain OTM bullet. If you're interested in extreme long-range shooting, you probably already know about the Enabelr cartridges.

.338 Enabelr	***30-in. barrel***
BULLET WEIGHT (GR)	VELOCITY (FPS)
300	3,200

.338 Raptor

Kirby Allen designed the .338 Raptor based on a .338 Excalibur case, which originated from A-Square in the 1990s, and his company, APSrifles.com, offers custom actions for many of his monster-sized cartridges, including the Raptor. At the time of this writing, brass for this cartridge is unavailable.

.338 Sherman

Rich Sherman says, "There are countless old '06-sized bolt-action rifles around that will produce a very low cost 'poor man's magnum' that a rich man could also enjoy!"

The .338 Sherman is the largest bore in the '06 family of Sherman cartridges. With bullets ranging from 180 to 300 grains, the utility is endless. Barrel length choices are far less critical than most magnums because the Sherman is burning far less powder than competing .338 magnums. That wide range of bullet weights allows you to be unusually flexible in loading this caliber.

It can be a flat shooter for long shots or you can load heavy bullets to take your moose. Versatility is one of the best benefits of medium bores that is often overlooked. Sherman cartridges are proprietary designs.

.338 Sherman	***24-in. barrel***
BULLET WEIGHT (GR)	VELOCITY (FPS)
180	3,400
200	3,100
230	2,850
250	2,800

.338 Spectre

Marty Ter Weeme, founder of Teppo Jutsu, LLC, developed the .338 Spectre to deliver heavy, high-ballistic-coefficient bullets at extended distances. He based the Spectre—a proprietary design—on the 6.8 SPC case, necked up to .338 caliber. Specialty bullets from makers like Hawk and North Fork can expand at low velocity and will shine in this cartridge.

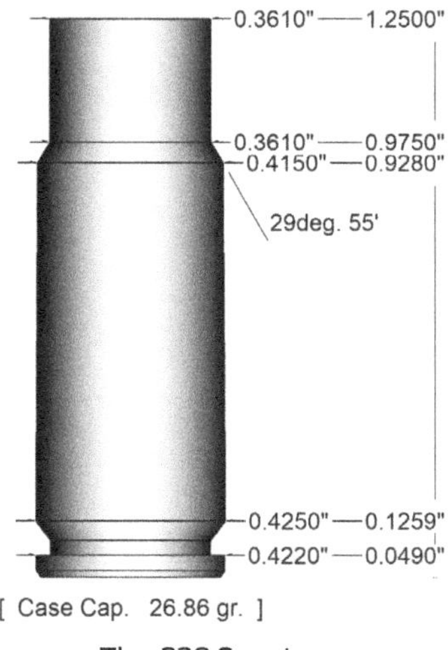

The .338 Spectre.

The .338 Spectre works with both subsonic and supersonic loads. If you're a .300 Blackout fan but want even more bullet, this is the next logical step (or you could jump to the .458 SOCOM). You can make cases from 10mm Magnum brass, but case life will be short. Brass made from the SPC case will last much longer as it's designed for higher pressures.

.338 Spectre	***16-in. barrel***
BULLET WEIGHT (GR)	VELOCITY (FPS)
225	1,680
300	1,050

.33 XC

David Tubb came out with the .33 XC (eXtra Capacity) in 2018. It has a 35-degree shoulder angle and .350 inch more body length with less body taper. The neck is .065 inch longer when compared to a .338 Lapua case. The case's total overall length is 3.087 inches (.415 inch longer than a .338 Lapua and slightly longer than a Cheytac case). By now, you have guessed this .338 is for the ELR (Extreme Long Range) competition, gaining popularity in the ELR Light Class. Tubb set a new ELR Cold Bore World Record at 2,200 yards on December 2, 2018, with the .33 XC, attested to by the Fifty-Caliber Shooting Associaton (FCSA).

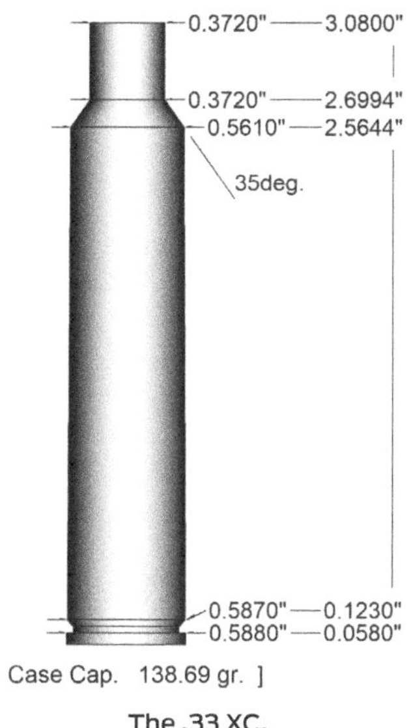

The .33 XC.

Tubbs' .33 XC has 139 grains of H2O capacity, approaching 130 grains of useable powder capacity, yet leaving the .393-inch neck unfilled (for bullet seating, as it should be)—depending on the powder density and drop tube length. Fired cases easily extract when using a properly polished chamber, even with a maximum powder charge. The .33 XC shares its headspace gauge with the .37 XC and the .41 XC: they all have the same body, just different bore diameters.

Reloading dies for the .33 XC are 7/8x14, which saves you money when buying dies, and a standard reloading press will work (.338 Lapua or Cheytac typically use larger diameter dies and require a larger press).

.33 XC	***33-in. barrel***
BULLET WEIGHT (GR)	**VELOCITY (FPS)**
250	3,400
299 DTAC	3,150

8.8x38mm

Dan Rawlings of Rantoul, Illinois, sent this example of his work to me shortly after the first edition of this book was published. I consider sharing info and like this to be an important part of wildcatting. Rawlings did not create the design; he received an old German single-shot from his wife as a gift. He describes it as a scaled-down version of the Mauser 71/74.

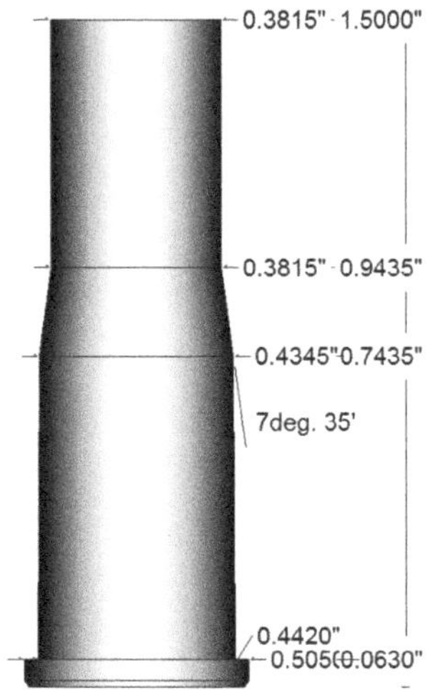

The 8.8x38mm.

He did some measuring and head-scratching, but most importantly, research. He found that the base and rim of the chamber matched the .303 Savage case. He cut the cases to length and sized them down so they would enter the chamber and headspace on the rim. Then, he fireformed them using the Crème o' Wheat method. He sent the fireformed cases off for a set of custom dies.

He also sent a chamber cast to a mold maker for an appropriate bullet. Rawlings is firing a 170-grain cast lead bullet over 18.5 grains of IMR 4198 at about 1,750 fps. He also has a blackpowder load that drives the same bullet to 1,250 fps.

With some know-how and ingenuity, Rawlings brought an otherwise obsolete rifle back to life, which is as entertaining as designing your own cartridge.

.358 BFG/358 IDC

The .358 BFG.

The Indiana Natural Resources Commission changed regulations in 2007 to allow hunting deer with a rifle as long as the cartridge was not longer than 1.625 inches and bullets were .358 inch or larger in diameter. Brian Farrington from Clinton, Indiana, lays claim to the BFG design based on the .25 WSSM.

Standing for Indiana Deer Cartridge, numerous gunsmiths came out with slight variations on the IDC theme. The rules have continued to change since 2007, so these wildcats have become less popular. Be sure to check the current rules if you're hunting in Indiana.

.358 IDC	***24-in. barrel***
BULLET WEIGHT (GR)	**VELOCITY (FPS)**
180	2,675
200	2,530

.358 Gremlin

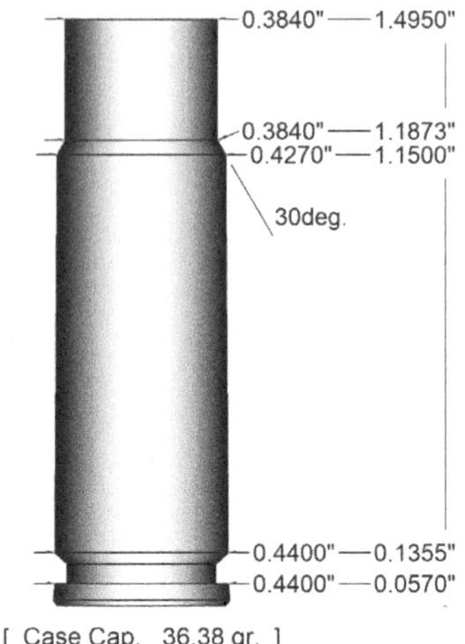

The .358 Gremlin.

In 2008, Brian Farrington, in response to the Indiana rule change in 2007 that allowed cartridges .358 inch and larger with a length under 1.625 inches for deer hunting, necked up the 6.5 Grendel. It was an easy way to meet the requirements of the regulations and have easy-to-form brass.

Farrington conceived this cartridge for the AR-15 platform, but it also became popular in bolt-actions. It's an excellent choice for deer at close range. It would be a good cartridge for lightweight rifles with low felt recoil and ballistics similar to the .35 Remington.

.358 Gremlin	***20-in. barrel***
BULLET WEIGHT (GR)	**VELOCITY (FPS)**
180	2,350
200	2,000

.35 Indiana

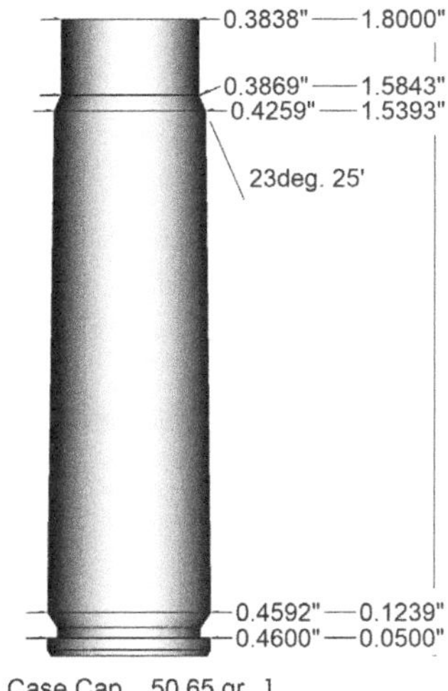

The .35 Indiana.

In 2011, the Indiana Natural Resources Commission changed the rules on deer cartridges once again. This time, the commission extended the length of the allowed cartridges to 1.80 inches, presumably to include the .460 Smith & Wesson. Scott Jones shortened the .35 Remington to 1.800 inches and loaded it to modern pressures since he was not limited by SAAMI specs.

.35 Indiana	*22-in. barrel*
BULLET WEIGHT (GR)	VELOCITY (FPS)
180	2,450
200	2,400

.358 Hoosier

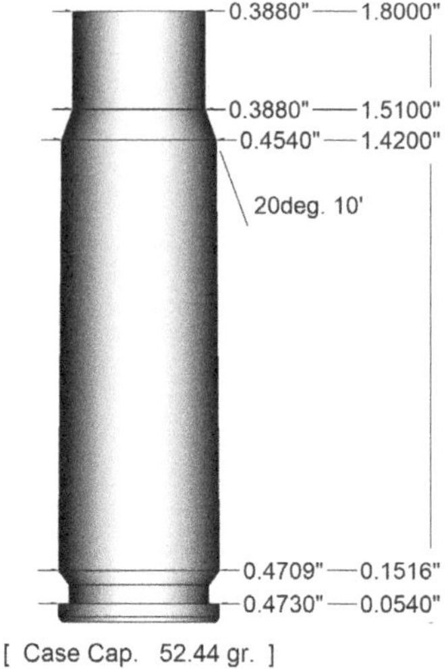

The .358 Hoosier.

Bill Herring shortened the .358 Winchester to 1.625 inches when Indiana first allowed rifles for deer hunting in 2007. Four years later, in 2011, the INRC changed the rule to allow cartridges of 1.800 inches in length. Herring responded by lengthening his wildcat to that length. So, the original Hoosier is 1.625 inches, and Version II is 1.800 inches. Only the gauges are different, and you can use the same reamer. However, the demand is for the latter version.

.358 Hoosier	***22-in. barrel***
BULLET WEIGHT (GR)	**VELOCITY (FPS)**
180	2,650
200	2,550

(Version II, 1.800 in.)

9.3mm BS (Barsness-Sisk)

John Barsness and Charlie Sisk headed out on a 2011 Texas hunting trip when the idea of turning the old .350 Remington Magnum into a 9.3 wildcat came up. They both liked the 9.3x62 cartridge, and the idea of creating a short-action version sounded fun. I'm unclear whether it started as a joke or became one along the way.

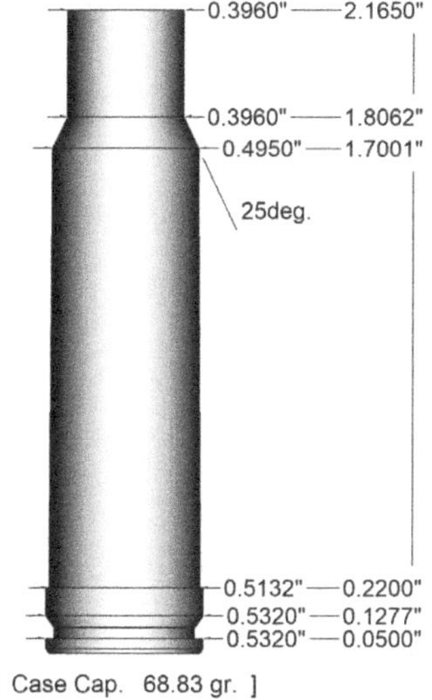

The 9.3 BS.

There are constant conversations among shooters about the need and value of wildcat cartridges. After all, there is not much new under the sun, so it's tough to find fresh territory. That's at least part of why they opted for the name 9.3 BS, to poke fun at their idea.

Sisk built a rifle for each of them in the wildcat. When they started testing, they were pleased that the results were exactly as they had hoped. They had reinvented the 9.3x62 ballistically in a short action, pushing a 286-grain bullet at 2,460 fps.

9.3 BS	***23-in. barrel***
BULLET WEIGHT (GR)	**VELOCITY (FPS)**
250	2,650
270	2,540
286	2,460

.375 Renner

The year 2012 saw the introduction of R.J. Renner's wildcat rimmed cartridge explicitly designed for single-shots—the Ruger No. 1, Renner's personal choice—and all North American big game. The .375 H&H is one of the most excellent cartridges ever conceived. While enamored of the .375 bore, Renner concluded that the .375 Winchester was not quite enough, and the .375 H&H was just a bit too much of a good thing. He sought something between them on the power scale.

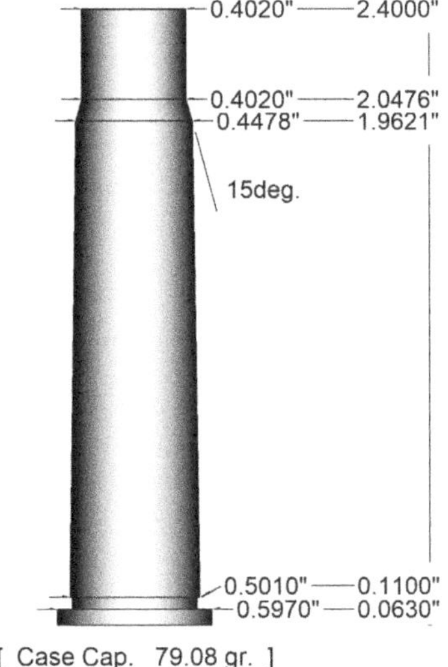

The .375 Renner.

Chambering is a simple matter of using a standard .375 H&H reamer to chamber, headspacing on the shoulder. Then, cut a rim recess in the back of the barrel. Renner does this on the lathe, but you can have a reamer made to specification.

The .375 Renner is based on the .45-90 case necked down with an appropriately shortened .375 H&H sizing die. It's that simple. The .375 Renner is easy to make and load; most any handloader will master it quickly.

The result is a flexible cartridge capable of taking anything from marmots to moose, and it does it all with less recoil than a full-size magnum. Renner's objective was to move 250-grain bullets at 2,400–2,500 fps at reasonable pressure levels that would not be hard on the brass, the rifle or the shooter. Renner admits that he is too busy building quality guns to wring out the .375 Renner thoroughly, so he published the chamber dimensions for anyone to play with.

He suggests starting loads for the .375 Whelen as a good place to begin.

.375 Renner

BULLET WEIGHT (GR)	VELOCITY (FPS)
235	2,575
250	2,545
270	2,420
300	2,381

.375 Raptor

Following the development of the .45 Raptor in 2014, the North American Sportsman, LLC, started work on the .375 Raptor, releasing it in 2016; it is either a .308 Winchester necked up and shortened or a .300 Savage necked up to .375, depending on how you look at it. Designed with the AR-10 in mind, the .375 Raptor is a big-bore cartridge with a 250-yard maximum point-blank range with lighter bullets.

.375 Raptor ***22-in. barrel***

BULLET WEIGHT (GR)	VELOCITY (FPS)
175	2,650
235	2,625
250	2,475
270	2,335

.375 Renner Belted Express

The .375 Renner Belted Express is a .375 wildcat spawned by customers shooting Ruger and Mark X magnums with the standard-length magazine box. Many customers want to know if we can make their 7mm Rem. Mag., .300 Win. Mag. or .338 Win. Mag. into a .375 H&H. Renner had to tell them no because the box was too short.

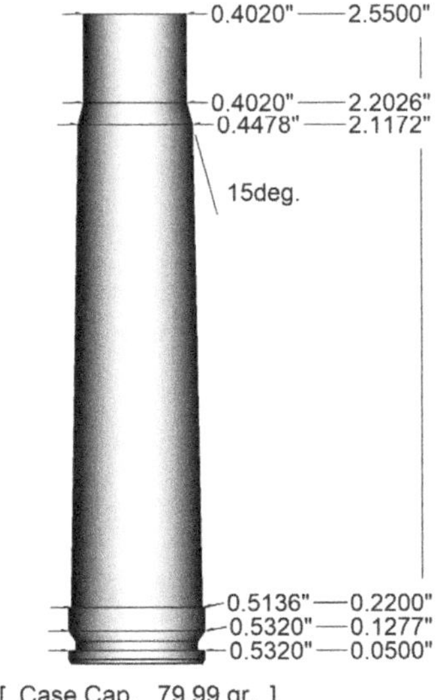

The .375 Renner BE.

Custom reamers and dies can add up to real money, plus waiting a year or more to get said reamer and dies usually kills the deal. I have suggested the .375 Taylor or other wildcats, but for the reasons above, clients were often unwilling to wait or pay for the special tools.

Renner came up with a simple solution. He shortened the .375 H&H to 2.55 inches. It looks just like the big .375 but a bit shorter. The beauty of this is that he uses a standard .375 H&H chamber reamer and cuts the chamber short. He then cuts the belt recess in the barrel as a secondary operation. Renner supplies readily available .375 loading dies and shortens them appropriately.

For brass, you can use either .375 H&H or .300 Win. Mag. Lube 'em, run 'em in the die, clean up the bit of trim ahead of the belt and shorten the neck. There you have it—.375 Renner Belted Express.

Easy-peasy, and you can have it all relatively cheap and quick. No waiting for custom tools or dies.

.375 Allen Xpress

The .375 Allen Xpress has the same body design as the .338 Allen Xpress necked up to .375. It was developed with two roles in mind. First, it's suitable for hunting any big game on the planet, and is a serious dangerous game load with a conventional .300-grain big game bullet. Second, you can also load it with the 350-gr. Sierra MatchKing and it performs exceptionally well as a long-range chambering in a medium- to heavy-rifle platform.

.375 Allen Express	***28-in. barrel***
BULLET WEIGHT (GR)	**VELOCITY (FPS)**
260	3,350
300	3,050
350	2,900

.375 Enabelr

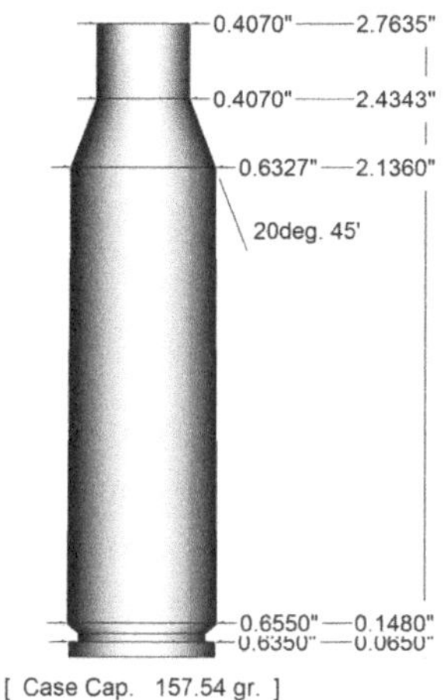

The .375 Enabelr.

Applied Ballistics designed the .375 Enabelr with the ballistics of the .375 CheyTac in mind. The design goal was to shorten the CheyTac case enough to feed the desired projectiles from the magazine without extending the length of the action. Applied Ballistics wanted to use the Berger 379- and 407-grain ELR Match solids or the Cutting Edge 402- and 427-grain Match/Tactical bullets for competition.

.375 Enabelr	***30-in. barrel***
BULLET WEIGHT (GR)	**VELOCITY (FPS)**
379	2,900
407	2,800

.37 XC

In the quest to find an ideal 2-mile cartridge, David Tubb devised the .37 XC, .33 XC and .41 XC—all on the same cartridge body, using the same headspace gauge.

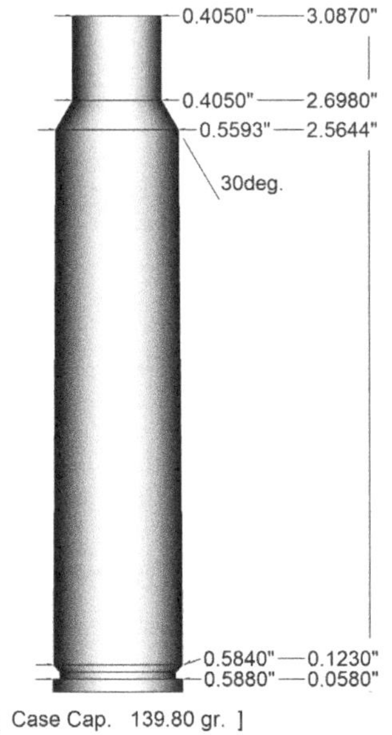

The .37 XC.

The target size for 2-mile competition is a 48x60-inch (120cmx150cm) rectangle fired at 3,200 meters—now synonymous with the King of 2 Miles competition. The .37 XC uses existing long-range .33-cal. platforms so you can keep your receiver and rebarrel it to this heavy hitter (utilizing the same bolt face as the .338 Lapua).

Many quality bullets for ELR are on the market now, so .375 is an excellent choice. The .37 XC bridges the gap between the .338 Lapua Ackley and the .416 Barrett. At the time of this writing, the .37 is a new offering that is stirring much interest in the 2-mile game.

.37 XC	***36-in. barrel***
BULLET WEIGHT (GR)	**VELOCITY (FPS)**
352 MTAC	3,150
375	3,000
400	2,900
500	2,825

.375 Bishop Short Magnum

The .375 Bishop Short Magnum.

Released at the 2022 SHOT Show, the .375 Bishop Short Magnum has a rebated rim of .473 inch and launches a 235-grain .375-caliber slug at a muzzle velocity of 2,950 fps and 4,542 ft-lbs of muzzle energy. Bishop Ammunition and Firearms compares it to the .375 Holland & Holland Magnum, except in an AR-10. Obviously, in an AR-10, the seating depth is a limiting factor.

Move this cartridge into a standard-length bolt, and ballistics will only improve because you can seat the bullets out of the powder column. RCC made the brass for Bishop.

.375 Bishop	*24-in. barrel*
BULLET WEIGHT (GR)	VELOCITY (FPS)
235	2,950

.400 Legend

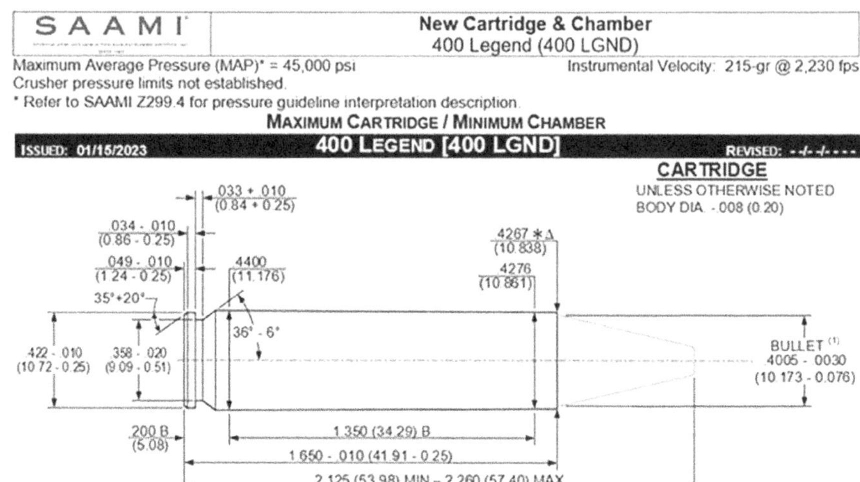

No, the .400 Legend is not a wildcat. But this new case will spawn some new wildcats. You might think of the case as a .220 Russian Basic or 6mm ARC Basic in more modern terms. The Legend brass has a rebated rim with the same diameter as the 6.8 SPC. It measures 1.650 inches long, so it's longer than the ARC, leaving plenty of room for wildcatters.

The .400 legend uses 40-cal. or 10mm pistol-diameter bullets. At the time of this writing, it has been on the market for a whopping three months. I asked Pacific Tool & Gauge, but no wildcats have been submitted for this new brass. The Legend is designed to operate at 45,000 psi maximum average pressure, so check the wall thickness and watch for pressure signs if you neck this one down.

.400 Marlin

Utilizing .40-caliber pistol bullets, the .400 Marlin is a necked-down .450 Marlin case. Scott Mayer designed this wildcat to use actual .400-caliber bullets, like those used in 10mm and .40-caliber handguns. In doing so, he ensured the availability of cheap projectiles instead of using the .416-inch bullets of most .40-caliber rifle cartridges. Mayer came up with this project before 2005, but it deserves to be reported here. It duplicates the .405 Winchester in a shorter package and is perfect in a lever gun. Mayer recognizes that nothing is new and points out that O.A. Winters wildcatted a similar cartridge on the .458 Winchester case decades before.

.400 Marlin	***24-in. barrel***
BULLET WEIGHT (GR)	**VELOCITY (FPS)**
210	2,150

.411 Strieby

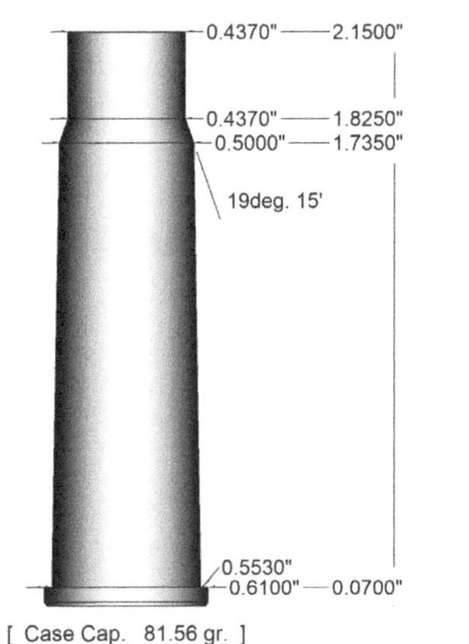

The .411 Strieby.

Ron Strieby of Syracuse, Indiana, created this variation on the .450 Alaskan (.348 WCF) case. In 2008, Strieby sent me sample cases to make a set of reloading dies for him. He used the .450 Alaskan to save the work of expanding the .348 cases. An active hunter, he took bears, elk, deer and antelope with this cartridge using a 350-grain North Fork bullet. Quality Cartridge offers headstamped brass for the cartridge in basic form.

.41 XC

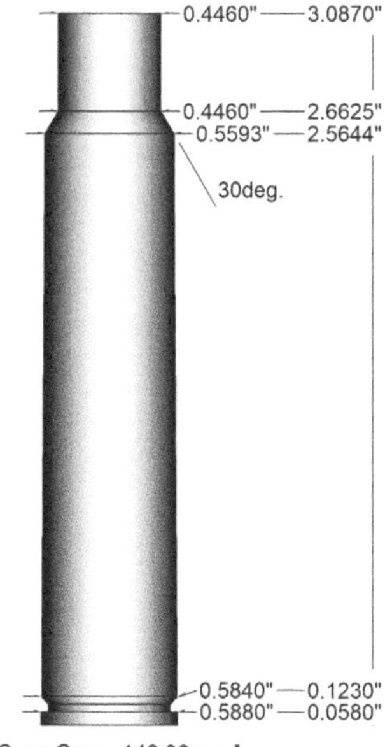

The .41 XC.

This is David Tubbs' .416 entry in the Extreme Long Range (ELR) game; the wildcat hit the market in May 2023. The .416 Barrett is the next logical step up, which uses 50 percent more powder to gain 290 fps over the XC. That is a lot of powder for a 10 percent gain in velocity.

Plus, the XC can utilize a .338 Lapua platform instead of a much larger and more expensive action for the .416 Barrett. The .41 XC pushes a 500-grain bullet at 2,900 fps. Tubb's company offers headstamped brass, dies and much more.

.41 XC	***33-in. barrel***
BULLET WEIGHT (GR)	**VELOCITY (FPS)**
500	2,850

.457 GNR

Gary Reeder is a prolific designer, and part of his ability to produce cartridges with tested load data comes from having people working for him. The .457 GNR is one of his more recent designs. Reeder had 25,000 rounds of .475 GNR brass custom-made several years ago, and he still has some in stock. This spawned the birth of a cartridge designed to deliver .45-70 ballistics using pistol powders.

Many folks have played with chambering .45-70 in various pistol platforms. Reeder says powders appropriate for the .45-70 do not fully burn in a pistol-length barrel. However, he *could* achieve .45-70-like ballistics with fast-burning powders by going to a bottlenecked case. Now you have a pistol delivering the ballistics you usually expect from a Marlin 1895 in .45-70—just about a holy grail for dangerous game hunters.

.457 GNR	*12-in. barrel*
BULLET WEIGHT (GR)	VELOCITY (FPS)
300	1,790
350	1,600
400	1,500
425 cast	1,450

.460 Alliance

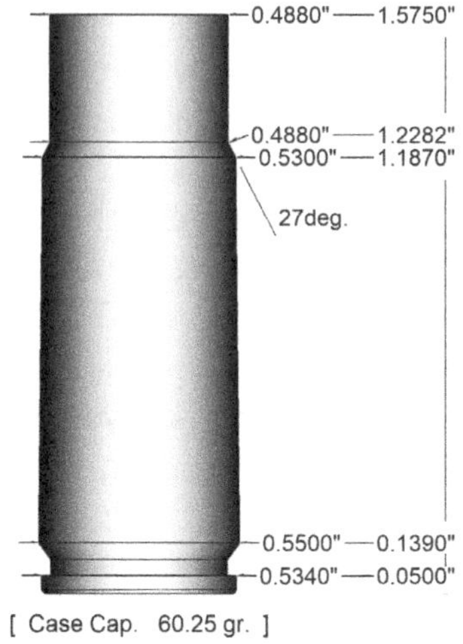

The .460 Alliance.

Developed by Michael A. Wayne of Alliance Armament, LLC in 2010 for use in the AK platform, the .460 Alliance is based on the RSAUM case. He intended to create a short-range hunting and tactical cartridge. Think of your AK as a repeating Trapdoor Springfield in .45-70 Government. That's pretty much what the ballistics look like, but now you can send multiple rounds from your AK. There's plenty of knockdown power from this little dandy.

.460 Alliance	***24-in. barrel***
BULLET WEIGHT (GR)	VELOCITY (FPS)
300	2,000
327	1,915
405	1,650

.45 Raptor

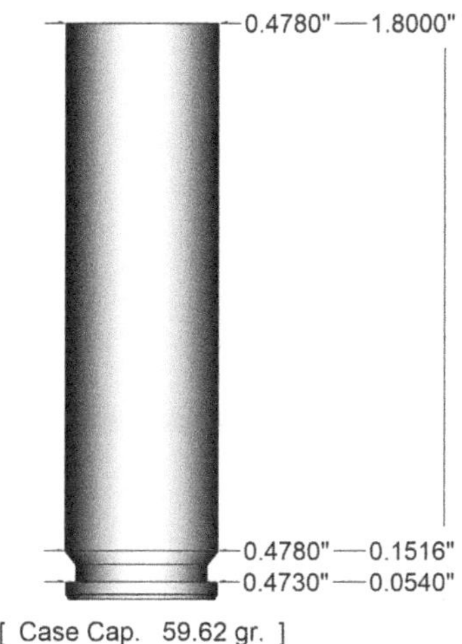

The .45 Raptor.

Introduced in 2014 by Arne Brennan of North American Sportsman, LLC, for the AR-10, the .45 Raptor uses pistol bullets and duplicates .460 Smith & Wesson and .454 Casull ballistics. Because it's a rimless case, it's well-suited to semi-auto operation.

The designer utilized cut-down .308 Winchester cases which headspace on the case mouth. The throating is designed with a shallower leade angle and more freebore than the typical .460 S&W SAAMI chamber. The rimless case feeds from standard .308 Win. magazines. With a wide range of bullets, it's a versatile cartridge with many applications.

You can use information from the .460 Smith & Wesson for load data. The Raptor has about 30 percent more 100-yard energy than other cartridges in this genre, such as the .450 Bushmaster, .458 SOCOM or .50 Beowulf. By holding case length below 1.80 inches, the Raptor automatically has a market in Indiana and Michigan where case length is mandated for hunting.

The .45 Raptor has a big enough following that Starline offers headstamped cases. The magazine capacity is identical to the .308 Winchester, i.e., if you have a 20-round .308 mag., it will hold 20 rounds of Raptor.

.45 Raptor	***18-in. barrel***
BULLET WEIGHT (GR)	**VELOCITY (FPS)**
200	2,350
250	2,125
300	2,000
395	1,750

.458 HAM'R

The .458 HAM'R.

By 2018, Bill Wilson had published data for his .458 HAM'R. Designed to compete against the .458 SOCOM and .450 Bushmaster, Wilson envisioned it in the AR-15 platform, which required special bolt and barrel extensions to deal with the shape and pressure of the cartridge properly. The shoulder of the HAM'R is .040 inch farther forward than the SOCOM, which prevents higher-pressure HAM'R rounds from chambering in a SOCOM chamber. If properly adjusted, you can use .458 SOCOM reloading dies for the .458 HAM'R.

The HAM'R should be DOA as a wildcat as it is barely distinguishable from the SOCOM and requires specially modified guns. The HAM'R only gets 100 fps more velocity, which is hardly worth the effort and expense. The .450 Bushmaster and SOCOM were long established with essentially the same ballistics in the identical platform. Alternatively, you could go to the .45 Raptor in an AR-10 without special mods.

However, the HAM'R belongs to a company that can afford to promote it, plus HAM'R is a cool name. So, it will likely stick around and maybe even go to SAAMI for standardization. Starline already offers formed headstamped brass.

.458 HAM'R	*18-in. barrel*
BULLET WEIGHT (GR)	VELOCITY (FPS)
250	2,125
300	2,100

.458 B&M Super Short

B&M added the smallest .45-caliber cartridge to its lineup in 2011. The .458 B&M Super Short is the Winchester WSM trimmed to 1.650 inches and formed in a sizing die. Hunting rifles are the core of the B&M cartridge concept, so B&M's action of choice was the controlled-feed WSSM-length Winchester M70.

B&M's rifle has a 16.25-inch barrel, 1:14 twist, and 36-inch overall length, weighing only 6.25 pounds. This setup would make an excellent rifle for hiking or fishing in bear country. The B&M "Super Short" line includes a .475 and .50 caliber on the same case; all B&M designs are proprietary.

.458 B&M SS	***20-in. barrel***
BULLET WEIGHT (GR)	VELOCITY (FPS)
250	2,600
300	2,180

.458 B&M

In 2005, Michael McCourry had a run-in with a hippo; the hippo tried to bite him. McCourry survived the attack with the aid of a .458 Lott, but it left him wishing for a lighter rifle that he could get on target faster. That experience led to the development of the .458 B&M and some other big-bore cartridges. By 2008, the .458 B&M was in the fields being tested.

The cartridge uses the .300 Remington Ultra Mag. case cut down to 2.240 inches and reformed and uses WSM magazine length. Several of McCourry's chosen loads produce over 5,000 ft-lbs of energy at the muzzle.

.458 B&M	***20-in. barrel***
BULLET WEIGHT (GR)	VELOCITY (FPS)
450	2,250
500	2,150

.45-70 Auto

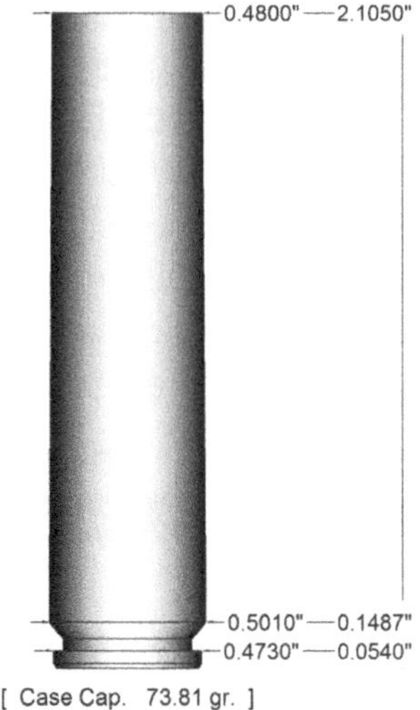

The .45-70 Auto.

In 2017, Phoenix Weaponry rebated the rim of the proven .45-70 case for use in the AR-10 platform. The modified case's rim is .473 inch, and the case length is unchanged from the standard .45-70. Standard .45-70 reloading dies paired with a shell holder for .30-06-class cartridges are all you need for loading tools. Phoenix sells pre-modified brass and even offers a cutting tool to make your own rebated cases.

Phoenix uses load data published for the Ruger No. 1 because this design will only be used in modern guns. You'll have to modify magazines to handle .45-70 Auto (a modified 10-round .308 AR-10 mag. will hold six rounds).

Another option for brass would be the .284 Winchester or Weatherby RPM cases.

.45-70 Auto	***18-in. barrel***
BULLET WEIGHT (GR)	**VELOCITY (FPS)**
325	2,300

.458 B&M Express (EX)

William V. Bruton joined forces with Michael McCourry of B&M Rifles and Cartridges to create a longer version of the .458 B&M. This 2.50-inch shortened .300 or .375 Remington Ultra Mag. case delivers ballistics equal to the .458 Lott in a standard-length magnum package. The load in the chart here produces almost 6,000 ft-lbs of energy.

.458 B&M EX	***20-in. barrel***
BULLET WEIGHT (GR)	**VELOCITY (FPS)**
450	2,440

.470 Turnbull

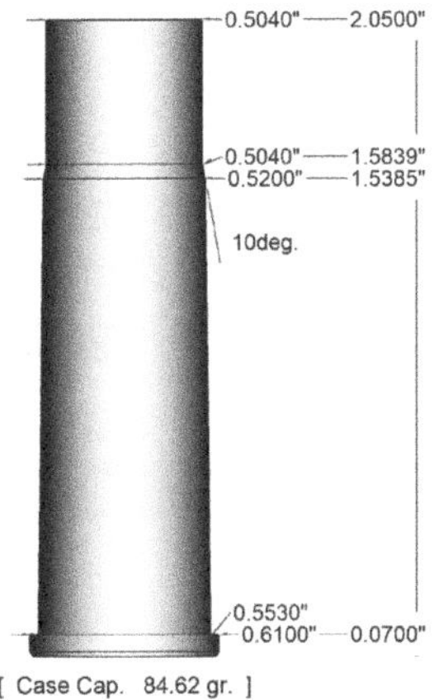

The .470 Turnbull.

The .470 Turnbull is slightly shorter than the .475 Turnbull for use in the Marlin 1895 lever-action. It will function in any vintage of Marlin 1895. The case is based on the .348 Winchester. The .470 Turnbull has an overall length of 2.55 inches with a 10-degree shoulder angle. Ballistics are similar to the .450 Marlin but with a larger diameter bullet and a rimmed case. The .475 Turnbull is its big brother, which Turnbull has SAAMI-standardized and designed to work in the 1886 or '71 Winchester or Browning lever guns. That cartridge case is 2.780 inches, has a shoulder angle of 17 degrees, 30 minutes, and achieves about 200 fps more than the .470.

.470 Turnbull	***20-in. barrel***
BULLET WEIGHT (GR)	**VELOCITY (FPS)**
350	2,000
400	1,850

.475 Lehigh

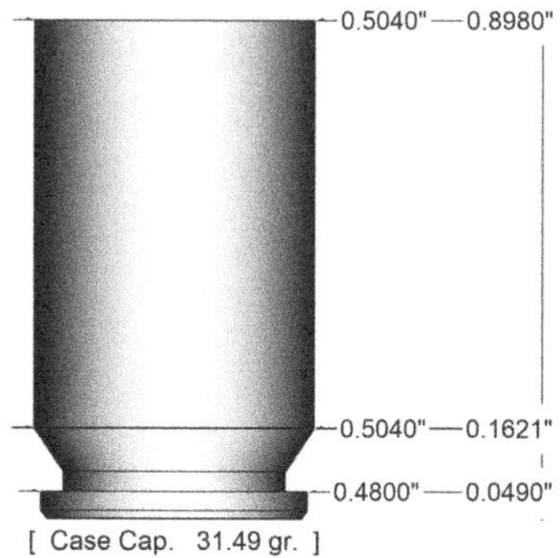

The .475 Lehigh.

The .475 Lehigh was designed for Lehigh Defense in 2011 by Michael Cyrus of Cross Outdoors, who later went to work for Lehigh. You make it by modifying the .480 Ruger case, turning the rim down to create a rebated case head, and trimming it to the same length as the .45 ACP. It offers larger diameter bullets in guns that currently run .45 ACP. It's intended to be a simple barrel swap in double-stack magazine guns to the larger diameter cartridge. Power levels are similar to the 10mm Auto but with a much larger bullet.

.475 Lehigh	***8-in. barrel***
BULLET WEIGHT (GR)	**VELOCITY (FPS)**
200	1,250
275	800

.475 B&M

Bruton and McCourry (B&M) put the .475 B&M into their lineup in 2011. They designed it for use in the Winchester Model 70 WSM controlled-feed actions. Like the .458 B&M, the case length is 2.240 inches—a shortened Remington Ultra Mag. case. They like to use short barrels on the guns built for these cartridges. After a close call with a hippo in 2005, McCourry advocated for fast-handling powerhouse rifles. This package produces what many consider to be the correct ballistics for dangerous game with well over 4,000 ft-lbs at the muzzle. B&M also has a .416 on this case; the significant advantage is more bullets to choose from, although the .416 maxes out at 400 grains.

.475 B&M	***18-in. barrel***
BULLET WEIGHT (GR)	**VELOCITY (FPS)**
425 North Fork	2,268
450 Solid	2,204

.475 Bishop Short Magnum

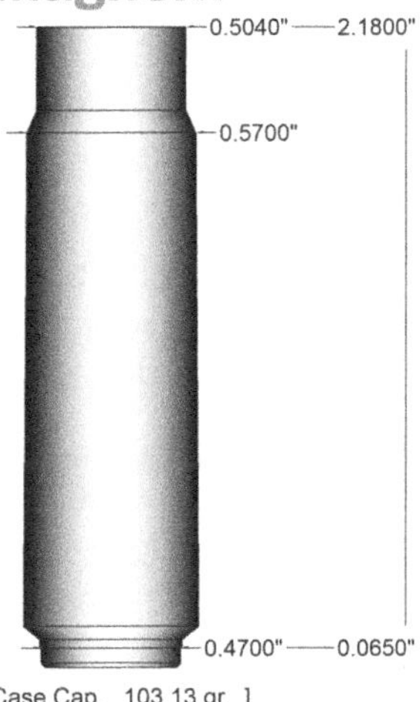

The .475 Bishop.

Released at the 2019 Shot Show, Bishop Ammunition and Firearms designed the .475 Bishop Short Magnum from the ground up specifically for its AR475GAR Semi-Automatic AR-10 platform rifle and .475 Safari bolt-action. A rebated rim of .473 inch allows for a standard .308 bolt face.

This cartridge was advertised as the most powerful in the AR-10 platform. It probably is to this day. RCC makes brass for Bishop. The .475 Bishop operates at 65,000 psi pressure, making it possible to launch the 390-grain .475-caliber projectile at a muzzle velocity of 2,500 fps. That's 5,500 ft-lbs of muzzle energy.

.475 Bishop | ***24-in. barrel***

BULLET WEIGHT (GR)	VELOCITY (FPS)
390	2,500

.500 Wyoming Express (500 WE)

Freedom Arms introduced this monster in 2005. The .500 Wyoming Express uses a 1.370-inch belted straight-wall case. Freedom Arms offers this chambering in its Model 83 single-action revolver. The best results will come from the recommended bullet weight range from 350 to 450 grains. The belt was necessary because of the intended platform; the rim diameter for a .500 would be too small for reliable headspace. Freedom believed it could provide better consistency with a belt formed on the case.

Depending on the loading, shooting the .500 WE in the Model 83 ranges from pleasurable to painful recoil, which should only be attempted by highly experienced big-bore shooters. Experienced shooters should start with low-velocity loads and work up in velocity to find their comfort level. In short, this cartridge can produce recoil that takes the fun out of shooting it, so why go there? Maximum loads operate at the 48,000 psi range.

.500 WE	***7.5-in. barrel***
BULLET WEIGHT (GR)	VELOCITY (FPS)
350	1,600
370	1,550
400	1,500
440	1,400

.500 Cyrus

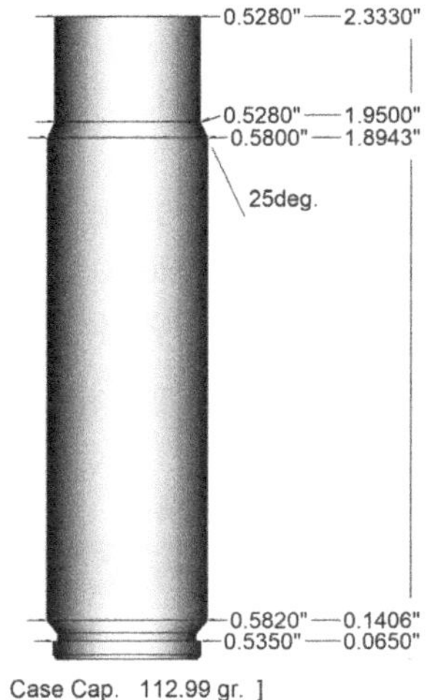

The .500 Cyrus.

Developed by West Virginian wildcatter Michael Cyrus, who worked for Lehigh Defense, the .500 Cyrus is a genuine .500-caliber cartridge. It will fit in an action sized for a .308 Winchester but duplicates .470 Nitro performance! Because it is a genuine .50-caliber, it is also compatible with pistol bullets for the .500 Smith & Wesson Magnum, and you can even load smaller-caliber sabot bullets like in a .50-caliber muzzleloader.

Cyrus took a .416 Rigby case, turned the rim from 0.586 to 0.531 inch, then shortened it and necked it up to .50-caliber. It will launch a 325-grain bullet at a sizzling 2,720 fps and, with a 500-grain bullet, generates nearly 6,000 ft-lbs of energy. It is a very odd but versatile cartridge that will cross your eyes and make them water every time you pull the trigger.

.500 Cyrus	***24-in. barrel***
BULLET WEIGHT (GR)	**VELOCITY (FPS)**
325	2,650
350	2,550
400	2,400
500	2,200

.50 TAC

In 2008, Michael Cyrus added the .50 TAC to his lineup. It's the same cartridge as the .500 Cyrus with one minor change: it uses .510-inch bullets instead of .500-inch. The .50 Tac is intended to be a subsonic wildcat with heavy .510-inch bullets.

The .50 TAC fits in a long magnum action. It provides a deep-penetrating round for tactical teams without the need for heavy rifles that come with the .50 BMG. This cartridge fits in a much more portable and convenient rifle and delivers about 70 percent of the power of the full-sized .50 BMG. It's capable of subsonic loading.

.50 TAC

BULLET WEIGHT (GR)	VELOCITY (FPS)
645 Lehigh	2,050
606 Lehigh	1,050

.50 B&M

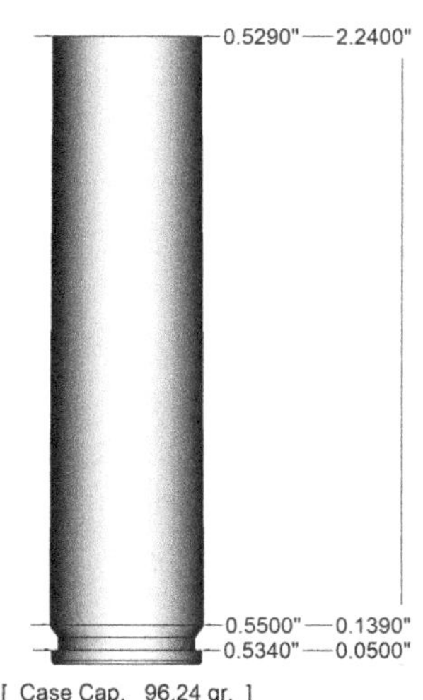

The .50 B&M.

The .50 B&M is a true .500-caliber cartridge designed for the Winchester M70 WSM controlled-feed action. The parent cartridge is the Remington Ultra case cut and trimmed to 2.25 inches. B&M offers rifles with 18-inch barrels weighing 6.5 lbs with the Winchester Ultimate Stock and 7.5 to 8 lbs. with Accurate Innovations wood stocks.

The .50 B&M can push 500-gr. bullets to 2,150 fps at maximum pressure. Regarding fast handling and heavy punch, it's in a class of its own.

While the .50 B&M can shoot all available commercial .500-caliber bullets, these projectiles do not all qualify as dangerous game bullets. Several custom bullets are suitable for dangerous game.

Cutting Edge Bullets and North Fork Technologies offer some that work well, according to B&M.

.50 B&M	*18-in. barrel*
BULLET WEIGHT (GR)	VELOCITY (FPS)
300	2,500
350	2,450
400	2,350
500	2,150

.510 Allen Magnum (.510 AM)

The .510 Allen Magnum is an improved chamber design for the .50 BMG. The goal was to increase the .50 BMG's ballistic performance by adding velocity. The .510 AM accomplishes this goal. Velocity gains in the 150 to 200 fps range are typical when using same-weight bullets. The Hornady 750-gr. A-Max or ELD are recommended because of their BC, ease of supply and accuracy.

.510 Allen Mag	*33-in. barrel*
BULLET WEIGHT (GR)	VELOCITY (FPS)
750	3,000

.585 Hubel Indiana (.585 HI)

We have mentioned many other Indiana deer cartridges in this chapter. Ed Hubel also created a cartridge to "comply" with Indiana's 1.800-inch cartridge length rule. Hubel used the .505 Gibbs case and shortened it to 1.785 inches. Hubel's recommended loads us cast lead Minnie balls as one would load in a muzzleloader. He liked the 440- to 540-gr. Minnie balls and used .58-caliber muzzleloading barrels with slow twists. You can expect a 440-gr. bullet to move at 2,200 fps.

.585 Hubel Express (.585 HE)

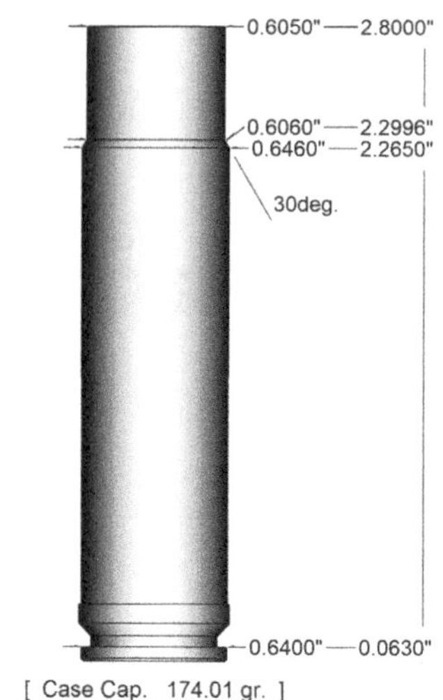

The .585 Hubel Express (.585 HE).

In 2004, Hubel swaged the belt on a .585 Nyati case to create a belted case that became the .585 HE. The .585 HE is a low-pressure cartridge; the first gun he chambered for it was a NEF Handi-Rifle. This finished gun was 15 pounds and had a 32-inch barrel and thick recoil pad. Recoil is in the neighborhood of 100 ft-lbs—more than three times as much as a .338 Lapua in a 10-pound rifle. However, it delivers more than 6,000 ft-lbs of energy at the muzzle.

.585 Short Hubel Express (.585 SHE)

In 2009, Hubel used a .505 Gibbs case to create a 2.70-inch case. Hubel says it's short enough to fit in a modified standard-length action. He claims 2,300 fps with a 650-grain bullet.

.585 Hubel Magnum (.585 RHM)

In 2010, using the 55 Boys anti-tank rifle case, Hubel created the .585 RHM. The cartridge's overall length is an impressive 4.60 inches long. The case alone is 4.00 inches long.

.700 Hubel Express (.700 HE)

The .700 Hubel Express is a natural outgrowth of Ed Hubel's work on the 12 Gauge From Hell. Using the .50 BMG as a parent case, Hubel expanded the neck out before swaging a belt on the case. Experiments that led to this cartridge started in the 1990s; however, the chambering of the first .700 HE took place in 2008.

He listed his 3.250-inch .700 HE as pushing an 825-grain projectile at 2,800 fps. His long version of the .700 HE was 3.870 inches, pushing a 1,000-grain slug to 3,200 fps. Hubel used a Vulcan Armament V50 action for the first .700 HE Long. The gun for the latter was 29 pounds in a thumbhole stock. Hubel typically did not use brakes on his guns; instead, he kept barrels long and heavy and added weight to manage recoil.

CHAPTER 20

Charles Newton, Ballistics Genius

Born January 8, 1870, in Delavan, New York, Charles Newton spent his first sixteen years on the family farm and attending school. He spent two years teaching school and six years in the New York National Guard. Eventually, Newton studied law and was admitted to the New York Bar when he was 26. He spent his spare time shooting and testing the "new smokeless" powders. Soon, he recognized the need for new cartridge designs to take full advantage of smokeless powder's different burning characteristics. By 1905, he had designed his first successful cartridge, which later became the .22 Savage Hi-Power.

Charles Newton.

It is incredible and somewhat sad that someone who contributed so much to modern cartridge design has become so anonymous. Ask your shooting buddies if they know who Charles Newton was; you will likely get a blank stare. To give you an idea of Newton's influence, look at the following list of cartridges he either developed or shared credit in designing.

.22 Savage Hi-Power	.30 Newton
.22 Newton	.33 Newton
.25 Newton	.35 Adolph Express
.250-3000 Savage	.35 Newton
.256 Newton	.40 Adolph Express
.280 Newton	.40 Newton
.30 Adolph Express	

At least a couple of those should jump out at you. To point out how much rifle cartridges have changed since Newton's day, in the 14th and 15th editions of the Newton catalog, an interesting fact was pointed out: "The American cartridges which develop over 2,200 fps velocity, aside from the Newton series, are but four: The Springfield Army (.30-06), the Ross .280, the Savage .22 High Power, and the .250-3000 Savage, the two latter of which, incidentally, were designed by Mr. Newton."[1] How many cartridges today exceed 2,200 fps? Nearly all popular centerfire rifles will perform far beyond this level. Oh, the difference a day makes.

Interestingly, Newton designed the .22 Savage Hi-Power in 1905/6. It was not until the fall of 1911 that Savage became interested in it. Savage chose a 70-grain .228-inch bullet at 2,800 fps, marketing it as the ".22 Savage Hi-Power" and "The Imp." So, here is an early wildcat that made it to factory acceptance.

Following the .22 Savage, Newton built another .22-caliber cartridge that could be classed as a big game round. He felt that "The Imp" could be improved upon. His goal was 3,000 to 3,100 fps with a long, heavy spitzer bullet. Thus was the birth of

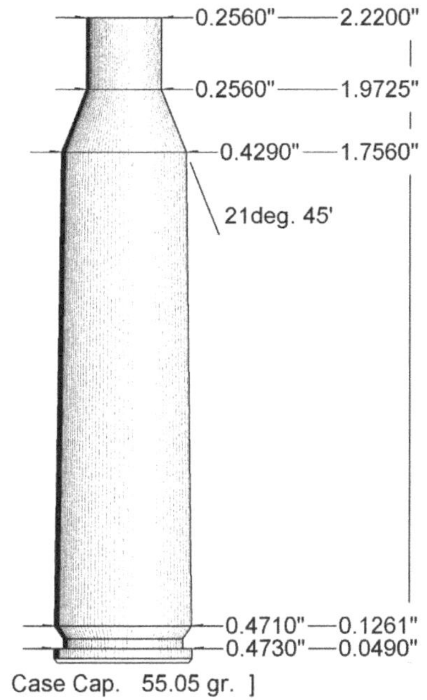

The .22 Newton.

1 Jennings, Bruce, Jr., *Charles Newton: Father of High Velocity*

the .22 Newton, using a 90-grain .228-inch bullet at 3,100 fps. The result was a 60 percent increase in muzzle energy over the .22 Savage Hi-Power. The spitzer bullet retained energy downrange.

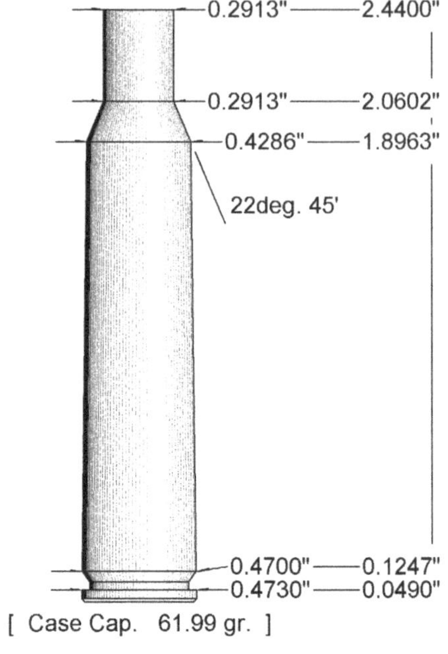

The .256 Newton.

Based on the 7x57 case, the .22 Newton was a full-capacity case necked to handle the .228-inch bullet. According to Ackley and gunsmith W.F. Vickery of Boise, Idaho, the .228-inch bore diameter is required for heavy bullets (70 to 90 grains).[2] This had to do with the construction of the bullets available then since velocities over 3,000 fps would often cause bullet failure. Designed long before modern powders were even thought of, the case worked better with the old slower powders, indicating they would be the best choice for building a .22 Newton today.

Long, heavy bullets like those used in the Newton come into their own at long range, as they maintain a higher percentage of their starting velocity. The disadvantage to a 90-gr. bullet in a .22 is the bullet's length, which requires a faster-twist barrel. It sacrifices initial velocity because of the energy eaten up in getting the higher rotational speed out of a fast-twist barrel. Even so, many shooters would say that the velocity at the target is more critical than the muzzle velocity.

Reports from the World War II era indicate that the .22 Newton produced no better ballistics than the .220 Swift, which is possible since the case would be well overbore. The Newton had 14.6 percent more case capacity than the .220 Swift. Falling in between the two was the .22/243 Middlested, with reported velocities of over 3,500 fps with a 70-gr. bullet. The Middlested beat the .220 Swift by nearly 200 fps, so the Newton did at least that well; based on capacity alone, it should produce another 100 fps with modern powders, likely delivering 3,600 fps with a 70-grain bullet.

It should be remembered that Newton envisioned his cartridge as suitable

2 Landis, Charles S., *Twenty-Two Caliber Varmint Rifles*, 1946

for hunting deer and black bears. Not many shooters today consider a .22 caliber a big game rifle. In many states, it would not be legal for big game. With the 90-gr. Bullet, the .22 Newton would be a lightning bolt on deer but try to locate such bullets today. Frankly, shooters would be better served with a larger bore, such as a .243 or .257, if bullets over 70 grains are desired. Newton never marketed this cartridge mainly because the .256 Newton was far superior for the stated purpose.

The .256 Newton—today probably the best known of the Newton cartridges—was loaded with a 123-grain bullet at 3,100 fps, making it a very flat shooter compared to the then-popular .30-06 with a 150-grain bullet at 2,700 fps. The .256 had the advantage of better ballistic coefficients, so it retained more energy than the stubby .30-caliber bullets. Newton claimed that the .256 Newton had 23 percent more energy at 300 yards than the '06 load mentioned above. At that time, the .30-06 was considered our most powerful American cartridge for big game. So, Newton enthusiastically touted his .256 as "Adequate for the largest of North American big game."

Introduced in 1912, the .250-3000 Savage was also a Charles Newton design. He had envisioned the .250 Savage with a 100-grain bullet at 2,700 fps but saw the advantage of marketing an 87-grain bullet at 3,000 fps—a pretty amazing velocity then. It's possible that Newton was the first to neck the .250-3000 down to .228 inch, but there is no record of it. Too bad, that would have given him credit for the .22-250, too.

There was a design for a .25 Newton. However, research for this book did not unearth any evidence that it was ever produced commercially. The .256 Newton would have done everything the .25 could do, so logically, Newton saw no reason to promote twin cartridges. It was around 1912 when these cartridges were being developed. A.O. Niedner did not begin marketing his version of the .25-06 until the

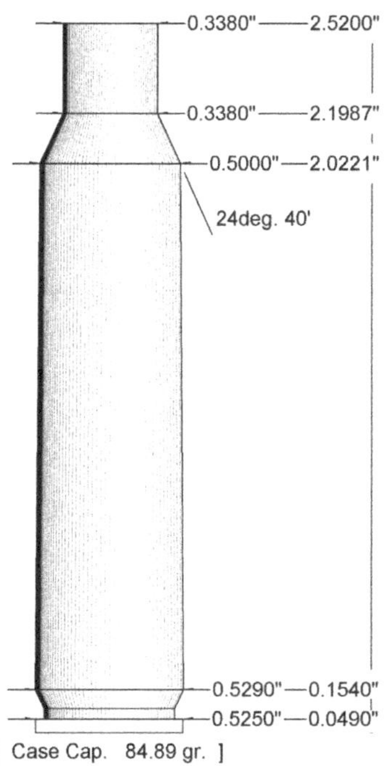

The .30 Newton.

early 1920s, although he may have worked on the development for some time before that.

Before World War II, the .30 Newton was the best-known cartridge of the Newton line. The lack of ammunition or brass forced it from the limelight, leaving the .256 Newton in the position of best-known at the beginning of the 21st century. Western Cartridge Co. produced ammunition for the .30 Newton in such sufficient quantity that it was still available in the 1930s. The .30 Newton was the most powerful hunting cartridge with any following in the United States from its inception in 1913 until 1925 when the Western Cartridge Company began offering .300 H&H and .375 H&H ammunition to the American shooting public.[3] Newton offered more powerful cartridges that never reached popularity, like the .30 Newton.

Fred Adolph was the first to chamber for the .30 Newton, which he marketed as the ".30 Adolph Express." There seems to be some controversy over the origins of the .30 Newton. Some claim it was Adolph's baby, while others say that Adolph asked Newton to design it. These two men regularly collaborated on cartridge designs, so this confusion is natural enough. If the source was Adolph, Newton finished the design process when he changed from Berdan to Boxer priming, eliminating the need to import the brass and primers. The case was larger in diameter and length than the .30-06 and delivered velocities we would associate with the .300 H&H or .308 Norma Magnum.

Townsend Whelen says, "The Adolph Express should prove a most excellent rifle for Western shooting where long shots often have to be taken. The velocity and energy, particularly of the 172-grain load, are so well retained at long ranges that it is doubtful if any other rifle now made can excel at ranges over 300 yards in game shooting. The recoil is so light that a good long-range target practice can be done with it even by a light man."[4]

Factory loads for the .30 Newton included a 170-grain spitzer bullet of Newton's design at 3,000 fps as advertised by Western Cartridge Co. Newton's velocities were nothing short of astounding in pre-World War I days when a .30-06 with the same bullet would have been loaded to something approaching 2,700 fps. With modern powders, the .30-06 is factory-loaded to 2,800 fps with a comparable bullet. Compared to modern cartridges, the .308 Norma Mag. has only about 2 grains less capacity by water weight than the .30 Newton. The Norma is factory-loaded to 3,160 fps with a 165-grain bullet; the Newton duplicates that in a non-belted case, which is not bad for a cartridge that is nearly 100 years old.

---

3 Van Zwoll, Wayne, *Modern Sporting Rifle Cartridge*, 1998

4 Whelen, Townsend, *The Outers Book*, 1913

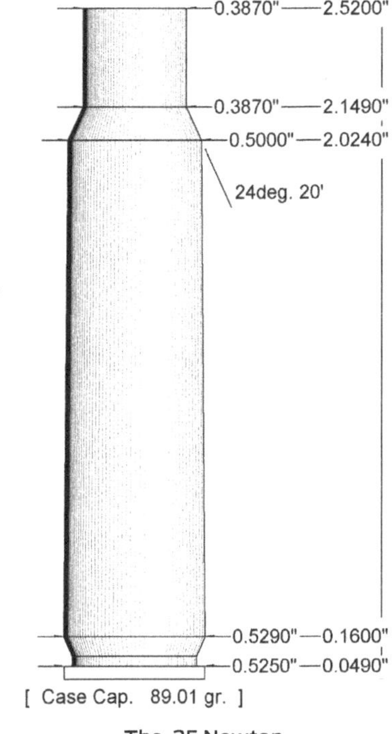

The .35 Newton.

Newton was at least 40 years ahead of his time in cartridge design. The .35 Newton, which he developed and marketed before World War I, advertised a 250-grain bullet at 2,975 fps and 4,925 ft-lbs of energy. An interesting comparison comes from factory ammo for the .375 H&H loaded by Western and Winchester during the same period, which advertised a 270-grain bullet at 2,720 fps and 4,438 ft-lbs of energy. Newton's .35 was 250 fps faster at the muzzle. It produced almost 500 ft-lbs more energy than the then-cutting edge .375 H&H. If you're looking for a modern equivalent to the .35 Newton, the .358 Norma Mag. is a virtual twin in case capacity, and based on today's published data, one would have to assume that the numbers for the .35 Newton were inflated a bit.

In *Outer's Book*, June 1915, Newton explained, "As to the .30, .33, and .35 Newton cartridges, these are frequently confused with the Adolph series. They differ only in the construction of the shell. The powder capacity and bullets used are the same. The Adolph series of cartridges was made by swaging down a foreign 11.2mm shell (11.2 x 72mm Schuler). This used Berdan primers, which had to be imported and the supply of which was somewhat problematical; also, the head was not only rimless but was turned down to fit the ordinary Mauser bolt head, this made it decidedly smaller than the body of the shell. This made the head weak around the primer cup and developed a tendency to stretch and loosen the primer when service pressures were used. The Newton shells have a head similar to that of the Ross shell, which is not only as large as the body of the shell, but slightly larger, giving a rudimentary flange which is quite a convenience at times and in no way interferes with the action of the shell in the magazine. This idea was borrowed from the Japanese, who use it in their military rifles. Thus, the Newton shell has a far stronger head than the Adolph, and uses ordinary American primers, reloading as easily as does the

CHAS. NEWTON
RIFLE CORPORATION

CHAS. NEWTON, President

IMPROVED HIGH-POWER
Rifles and Ammunition

STOP-GAP CATALOGUE

THIS leaflet is furnished to give some idea of the goods we offer during the time our regular catalogue is being gotten out. It will be superseded by a real catalogue as soon as the latter is ready.

CHAS. NEWTON RIFLE CORPORATION

Springfield. The ballistics of the two series of cartridges are in all respects the same."

Charles Newton underestimated the shooting public's will and ability to absorb recoil when he designed a 7.5-lb. rifle to house the .35 Newton. He was of the attitude that when you're hunting, you will only shoot once or twice, so a light rifle was a pleasure to carry, not a pleasure to shoot at the bench. However, Newton's major downfall was his inability to transfer his designs from paper to reality. The cartridges worked fine; it was his rifle that had trouble. Newton made two attempts at initiating manufacturing companies to build his rifles. Both failed, mainly because he could not control quality. His designs were sound, but he could not maintain the quality standards in mass manufacturing that would attract long-term loyal customers. Newton's rifle design was innovative; many think that multiple locking lugs like those used on the Weatherby Mark V are a relatively new idea, but Newton's rifles used multiple locking lugs before the First World War.

Charles Newton passed away in 1932 at 62, "the one-time designer, died discouraged. He had great ideas for his rifle and saw his business blossom and then rapidly fade. He made no money from it! But you can't blame a man for trying."[5]

Newton: In His Own Words

On bolt-actions vs. levers, he said, "One of the peculiarities noted in the communications of the advocates of bolt-action sporting rifles is the method used in presenting their arguments.

"Instead of explaining and emphasizing the points of superiority actually possessed by the bolt-actions, they forthwith proceed to abuse the lever-actions, charging them with being weak as the action, heavy, clumsy, ill-

5 Sharpe, Philip B., *The Rifle in America*, 1938

balanced, roughly finished, inaccurately bored, and that they will neither feed cartridges to the chamber or withdraw the empty shells; in fact, they have not a single virtue and all the vices imaginable. And they then proceed to print this arraignment to be read by men, most of whom have used these rifles for many years, and many of whom have used them for a lifetime.

"The writer [Newton] is an admirer of bolt-action rifles and is able to see some of their good points, points in which they are far superior to the lever-action, as well as the point in which he thinks the lever-action is superior.

"At Camp Perry, summer of 1910 a large number of new Springfield rifles were used in the national matches, using both the regular government ammunition, which developed a chamber pressure of about 45,000 psi, and also some made by the leading cartridge companies and which ran in pressure from 45,000 to 52,000 psi, the latter figure being the highest pressure ammunition furnished and being only 4 percent higher than the ammunition which the Winchester model 1895 rifle has used for the past six or seven years successfully.

"During those matches a bolt in one of the new Springfield rifles broke when firing the cartridge, the fractures being two, one beginning at the rear end of each locking lug and running forward and toward the center of the bolt to the face of the bolt and by which both lugs were broken off. It would be unjust to condemn a design of rifle because of the failure of a single weapon and the writer would be the last to do so, but the plain, hard, honest, cold facts are that after this bolt broke another broke in exactly the same manner, and another and still another until seven bolts broke, each exactly like the others.

"A little reflection will show clearly to a man who is not a mechanical engineer that the system of using front locking lugs is inherently weak for the reason that the rear face of the locking lug, being that portion which resists the strain, is but ½-inch from the face of the bolt and the lugs are but about 3/8-inch wide, consequently when the strain of explosion comes it tends to break off the lug together with a small wedge-shaped piece of metal running forward and diagonally toward the center of the face of the bolt. Were the locking lugs to be placed an inch or more from the face of the bolt or even at the rear of the bolt this could not happen for the reason that before the lug could give way it must either be cleanly fractured through or sheared, and if the metal were of proper strength it would not fracture, and of proper harness it would not shear."[6]

Newton followed up on his convictions years later when he designed his bolt-action: the locking lugs extended much farther to the rear and included multiple locking lugs, a design copied by several rifle makers since. He was correct that metallurgy and heat treating were paramount to a design's success.

He was an early proponent of smokeless powder and the cartridges developed for it. "For several years I have been a believer in the modern high power smokeless rifle, not only for sporting purposes but for the target as well. These cartridges are fully as accurate as the best target rifles made, and owing to the fact that the smokeless powder is clean and the bullets are shot from the shell without the trouble of muzzle loading or seating in the chamber ahead of the shell, and the absence of lubrication, that they are much more desirable as target cartridges from the standpoint of the Schuetzen rifleman than the regular lead bullets."[7]

On untested smokeless load data, "I think that people should not write and editors should not publish statements regarding such use of smokeless powders unless they are confident that the charges are within the limits of safety and then only when they explain fully all the elements entering into the experiment and warn the reader of the dangers of departing from the methods described in any detail."[8]

On wildcat development, "While writing the following description of a rifle the writer anticipates the first question asked by the reader will be, 'Of what use in this country is such a powerful weapon?' And we will frankly answer at this time that it is practically of none; that there are now on the market plenty of rifles and cartridges sufficiently powerful for the largest game to be found on the American continent.

"Then why devote time and money to developing, and space in this magazine to describing, such a rifle? And the answer, for a lack of a better, is

6 *Outdoor Life*, April, 1911

7 *Outdoor Life*, November, 1906

8 *Outdoor Life*, March, 1908

the distinctly feminine one 'Because.'"[9]

On Newton's first taste of success, the .22 Savage Hi-Power, "The cartridge is made by necking the .25-35 down to .228 at the muzzle (mouth) and loading it with 25 grains of Lightning Powder and a 70-grain metal-cased bullet having a soft sharp point.

"The instrumental velocity is about 2,760 feet per second, giving an actual muzzle velocity of 2,850 feet per second and a muzzle energy of 1,260 foot-pounds. Shooting at 200 yards the trajectory height at midway will be about 2.6 inches.

"... The actual muzzle energy of this bullet, although great, is far from being the true measure of its efficiency, as it is the efficiency which is utilized which counts, not that which is wasted after the bullet passes through the animal. This rifle being put up in the featherweight model, which weights but about six pounds, it might be expected to develop considerable recoil, but the recoil is about equal to that of the .25-35, and as for accuracy it is good for about a 4-inch circle at 200 yards."[10]

Newton discussed the desire for more power but not more recoil: "Once we all stood agape at the possibilities of the terrific velocity of the Krag, .303 British, .30-30 W.C.F., and similar cartridges, which so completely eclipsed the best of the 'old reliable' blackpowder cartridges. The war of the calibers waged long and hot, but when the dust cleared away the new type was seen to have come to stay, due to their superior trajectory, as an aid to hitting, and their superior power, as an aid to killing. But, not the least of their advantages was their ability to deliver a terrific blow without developing a distressing recoil. A powerful blow from a bullet usually involves a powerful backward thrust on the shoulder, the one being usually somewhat in proportion to the other, but the new small bores avoided part of this.

"However, the call for more power is growing, but the call for more recoil is not, and the cartridges of the future must furnish the power, without the recoil being proportionately increased. Many admirers of the New Springfield rifle have a wholesome respect for its rearward movement, even while they love it. How shall it be met?"[11]

On the .300 Remington Ultra Mag. and the .300 Dakota, Newton said, "Fred Adolph stepped in and helped ... we obtained some shells for the .404 Jeffery Mauser and necked them down and cut them off, and those heads fitted the larger bolts. Therefore, all that is needed to adapt your .30-caliber Springfield,

---

9 *Outdoor Life*, April, 1910
10 *Outdoor Life*, December, 1911
11 *Outdoor Life*, August, 1912

Mauser, Winchester, etc., to this cartridge, which was promptly christened the 'Adolph Express' (he said it 'Sounded like a fast passenger train') is to rechamber the barrel, and he will do this quickly and well.

"This cartridge was not designed with the expectation of regularly killing antelope at 1,500 yards, but for those of the Brotherhood of Cranks who have a desire to try really long-range shooting it affords a weapon far more adequate to meet the requirements made upon it than any other on the market."[12]

On heavy-recoiling rifles, "The advantages possessed by this type of rifle in hunting large and dangerous game, and such is the only game upon which it should be used, are two: First, it is very effective on the game if hit. Second, if the game be but wounded and should charge upon the hunter, he would not be compelled to make his retreat from a standing start; the recoil would have already given him a very tangible hunch to help him on his way, thus enabling him to make much better time than from a standing start. This advantage should not be overlooked and must be felt to be appreciated."[13]

Charles Newton loved a debate; he carried one on in the pages of *Outdoor Life* for years with then-Lieutenant Townsend Whelen and Edward C. (E.C.) Crossman. These were good old-fashioned gentleman's debates, arguing the differences between cartridges, lever-actions vs. bolt-actions, internal and external ballistics, and on and on. Although the debates occasionally became a little too personal, they still served the purpose of exploring the various subjects thoroughly from both sides.

Newton predicted the future: "We think the rifle of the future will have no materially greater velocity than at present in use, but that the improved powders will be utilized in propelling heavier projectiles, with consequent greater efficiency. The increase in length of the projectile will give greater striking power, not only at the muzzle but still more at the longer ranges. This will, in turn, result in further reduction in calibers as compared with the power obtainable and will be attended with still greater reduction in recoil in proportion to the energy of the bullet developed. All of which will be found someday embodied in our modern hunting rifle."[14]

I suggest two books on Charles Newton: *Charles Newton, Father of High Velocity* By Bruce M. Jennings Jr. (1985) and *The Newton Rifle* By Lawrence Wales (2012), ISBN 978-0-615-586-07-6. ⭘

---

12 *Outdoor Life*, September, 1912

13 *Outdoor Life*, April, 1910

14 *Outdoor Life*, September, 1912

CHAPTER 21

Jerry Gebby, Father of the .22 Varminter

When reading about wildcats, you often see the name J.E. Gebby of Dayton, Ohio, mentioned. Yet, details of his contributions to wildcatting and modern cartridge development are seldom given. His name is often mentioned in connection with the .22-250. Gebby was superintendent of the barrel plant of the General Motors—Frigidaire unit, one of the largest manufacturers of .50-caliber Browning machine gun barrels for the U.S. during World War II. He was a .22 target shooter of some reputation, and using his machinist skills, he began building .22 varmint rifles. Jerry Gebby was fond of saying, "I could hit a house fly at 100 yards if it would stay there for three shots." He could produce targets to back up that claim.

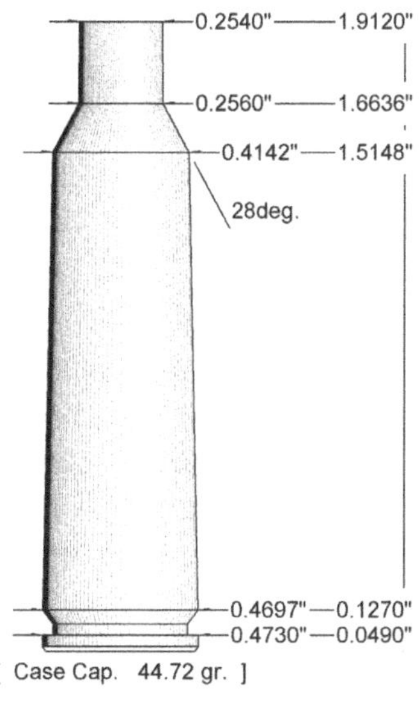

The .22-250 Remington.

Supposedly, Gebby copyrighted the name .22 Varminter and used it to market his cartridges. However, a copyright search turned up no such registered name, and a further search of trademarks also failed to produce anything under Gebby's name. This is probably just one of those myths that have been

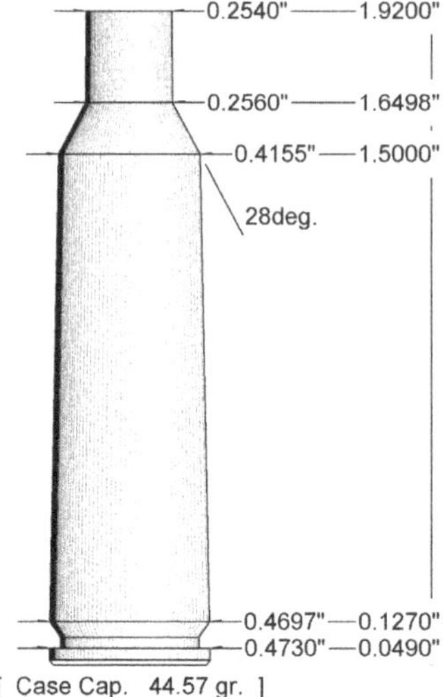

The .22 Varminter.

repeated so often that nobody bothers to check the facts.

According to Ackley, Capt. Grosvenor "Grove" L. Wotkyns originated the .22-250 as the .220 Wotkyns Original Swift (WOS).[1] Ackley then attributes the further development of the cartridge to Gebby and his associate, J.B. Smith. In *Twenty-Two Caliber Varmint Rifles*, Charles Landis says in about 1934, he was "deluged with a mass of targets, groups, and a number of manuscripts and suggestions on a .22-250 cartridge.[2] These communications came from Capt. Wotkyns who enthusiastically credited the .22-250 to Gunsmith J.B. Sweany; Landis says Hervey Lovell confirmed this as well. Captain Wotkyns' experiences with the .22-250 were chronicled in the May 1935 issue of *American Rifleman*.

Landis says that between 1925 and 1928, he personally visited Captain Wotkyns, who was then stationed at Frankford Arsenal. At the time, Wotkyns was seeking commercial attention for the .220 WOS. However, the manufacturers were trimming down their lines and were not interested in adding a new .22 centerfire. Years later, Wotkyns collaborated with Sweany to create what Landis dubbed the .22-250 Sweany-Wotkyns. They used a .223-inch groove diameter rather than Gebby's .224-inch groove and bullet. This change in bore diameter is an important credit for Gebby, as all modern .22 centerfire cartridges use the standardized dimension today.

Like so many of these early wildcats, many good gunsmiths and wildcatters were developing the same idea simultaneously, so the waters were pretty muddy. The .22 (standard) Varminter (as Gebby called it) came along in 1938.[3] On the other hand, Landis says that either J.B. Smith or J.E. Gebby or both were working on the .22 Varminter long before we have records of it, though he makes no guess at that date. In the May 1938 issue of *American Rifleman*, Gebby and J.B. Smith were advertising .22-250 rifles and custom-loaded ammo. By the following month, the name .22 Varminter had been attached to the cartridge.

1 Ackley, P.O., *Handbook for Shooters and Reloaders*, 1962

2 Landis, Charles S., *Twenty-Two Caliber Varmint Rifles*, 1946

3 Barnes, Frank C., *Cartridges of the World, 9th Edition*, 1997

Harvey Donaldson claimed to be the first to develop the .22-250, but in his writings, he admits that his design used a .228-inch bullet like the .22 Savage Hi-Power.[4] This meant he was also using 70-grain bullets. The .22 Varminter and the .22-250 of today were designed for lighter bullets. Donaldson submitted a version of the .22-250 to Savage Arms in 1935, which may well be the primary source for his claim to be first.[5]

Here is the kicker: In 1919, a young Jerry Gebby visited the Buffalo, New York, plant belonging to Charles Newton.[6] Newton gave Gebby a sample cartridge for an experimental case he had abandoned due to pressure problems. It was a .250-3000 case necked to .226 inch. Newton preferred heavy bullets, so his pressure problems probably came from heavy bullets and soft primers. When Gebby got around to working with the case years later, he selected lighter bullets in the .224-inch diameter, and by then, better cases, powder, and primers were available, combining to solve the pressure concerns.

The point here is not to belittle anyone or take credit away from any person connected with the development of the .22-250. The fact is that many people contributed to the design and eventual success of the cartridge. Some worked in collaboration, others worked alone, but none worked in a vacuum. Many of these experimenters knew of each other, and many crossed trails at some point.

Gebby did not limit himself to one cartridge but offered three different ones for the .22 Varmint rifle fan. The most popular was the .22 (standard) Varminter, which resembles the modern .22-250 adopted by Remington in 1965. Next in the line was the .22 Senior Varminter based on the .257 Roberts case. Lastly was the .22 Junior Varminter, which used the .32-40 Ballard-Marlin case. Drawings appear here based on dimensions taken from ammunition handloaded for Gebby rifles. The .22-250 Remington is added for comparative purposes.

The .22 Junior Varminter was based on the .32-40 Ballard, which Marlin and Winchester chambered. You could easily make brass from .30-30 Winchester. Dr. Mann produced a similar cartridge around 1910, if not earlier. Around the same time, A.O. Niedner offered a version of the cartridge. Hervey Lovell tried it in 1912; Niedner marketed a version again in 1922. The bottom line is that someone is always there before you in the wildcat world. So, Gebby made his variation of earlier wildcats when he introduced his .22 Junior Varminter, although, to be fair, he may well have developed his cartridges without prior knowledge of the earlier ones.

---

4 *Wildcat Cartridges Vol. 1*, Wolfe Publishing, 1992

5 Simmons, Dick, *Wildcat Cartridges*, 1947

6 *Wildcat Cartridges Vol. 1*, Wolfe Publishing, 1992

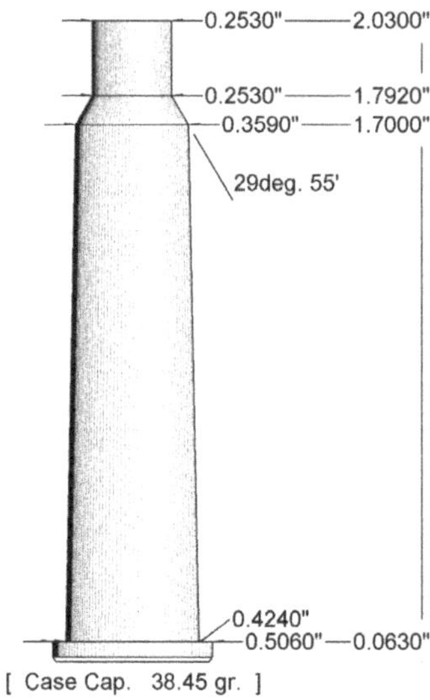

The .22 Junior Varminter.

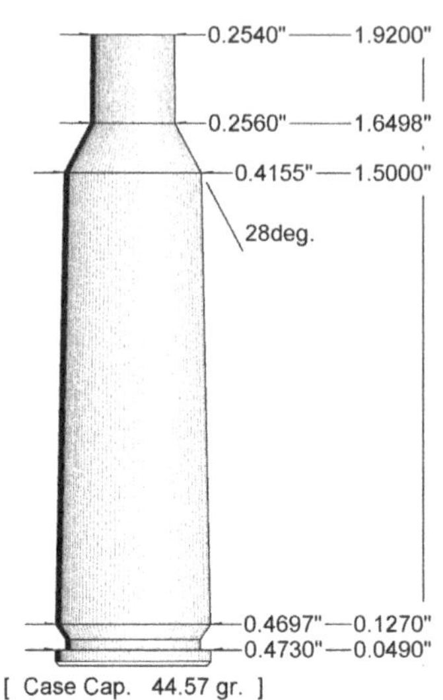

The .22 Varminter (Gebby).

Of course, Charles Newton covered this territory early on. Charles Landis corresponded with Newton in 1905 about just such a cartridge. For comparison, the water weight case capacity of the .22 Savage Hi-Power (Newton's cartridge) and the .22 Junior Varminter are 34.3 grains and 38.3 grains, respectively. So, Gebby's cartridge has slightly more capacity than the .22 Savage Hi-Power. The standard loading for Gebby's was a 60-grain bullet with an estimated velocity of 3,300 fps. Using the "Load From a Disk" software and our water weight capacity, reaching and exceeding that velocity today in this cartridge is possible. However, the pressures would indicate using a strong action like a Ruger No. 1. Gebby used the Winchester Hi-Wall, the Stevens 44 ½, Farquharson, and Sharps-Borchardt actions for the .22 Junior Varminter.

The .22 (standard) Varminter is very close to the modern .22-250; there is only about a .012-inch difference in the headspace. Otherwise, they're the same cartridge. This is why J.E. Gebby is credited for being the father of the .22-250.

The .22 Senior Varminter was based on the .257 Roberts case. Gebby conducted chronograph tests at Kings Mills on the Senior, showing a 40-grain bullet going 4,320 fps. That was in 1938—pretty impressive for the day. Well, it's pretty impressive on any day.

Jerry Gebby also worked regularly with the .22 Hornet, the R-2 Lovell and the .22 Swift. Barrel work and bluing were the mainstays of the Gebby shop. He was adamant that barrel accuracy lies mainly in the fitting, chambering, and throat of the barrel, to which he paid special attention. Regarding the tolerances and accuracy he expected from his barrels: "If the barrel borers hold specifications to within 0.0005 inch, then chambering and the bullet seat (throat) are the most important specifications and considerations."[7] Today's match barrels will measure within 0.0001 inch in variation from end to end—a 400 percent increase in precision by barrel makers since 1945. Gebby limited his work to metalsmithing, and by all accounts, he was very good at it.

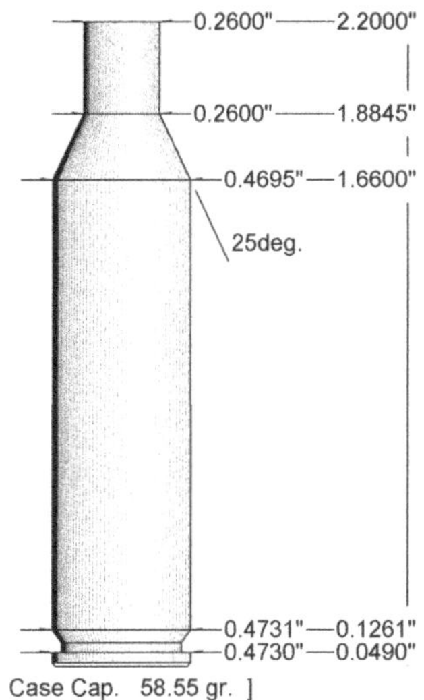

The .22 Senior Varminter.

After Gebby's work on the .22-250, he made another contribution to the wildcatting world. He was the first person of note to try to make a wildcat cartridge proprietary. By all accounts, that did not work any better for him than for later gunsmiths. The shooting public seems to be offended by gunsmiths' attempts to protect their works. This is strange because if a particular shop has taken the time to develop a concept fully, they are, by default, the experts in that specific cartridge. Why not avail yourself of that expertise? So, Gebby can be credited with the invention of proprietary wildcat cartridges.

At least Jerry E. Gebby understood that a good cartridge will go nowhere unless it is marketed. To accomplish that, a good name is necessary for success. For instance, a .22 Gebby would not have sold well, but J.E. Gebby had good luck selling the .22 Varminter. Never underestimate the power of a good name to sell a product or to interest shooters in your wildcat.

7 Landis, Charles, *Twenty-Two Caliber Varmint Rifles*, 1945

CHAPTER 22

Rocky Gibbs ... Living on the Edge

Rocky Gibbs with a Mauser barreled action. Photo: Roger Stowers collection

Apparently, Rocky Gibbs loved a mystery. At least, you would think so since he did everything he could to ensure a mystery surrounding his work. When folks would ask him about the shoulder angle of his cartridges, Gibbs would rattle off whatever number came to mind, ranging from 30 to 45 degrees. Then, when he died, he left instructions to burn all his records and research materials, a request his family honored. Even so, many sporadic records survived. Gibbs never published his case dimensions for fear that someone would capitalize on his work (more on this later). Rocky E. Gibbs died from Leukemia in September 1973 at the age of 58.

Born November 12, 1915, Mainlis Aamoen Gibbs contracted typhoid fever as a youngster, which resulted in the loss of sight in his right eye. So, when Gibbs became a shooter, he had to learn to shoot left-handed. Gibbs always preferred his self-imposed nickname, "Rocky." Not long after his High School graduation in Gainesville, Texas, Rocky boarded a train with the destination of Richmond, California, in mind. Gibbs wanted to be famous someday, and he figured that his given name would be a hindrance, so he determined to change it. While on the train to California, he asked the conductor what the mountain range in the distance was called. The conductor replied, "Those are the Rockies." Without hesitation, Manolis Aamoen Gibbs became Rocky Edward Gibbs on the spot.

Rocky Gibbs with the first elk he took shooting his .270 Gibbs.

In March 1955, he moved Gibbs Rifle Products from Richmond, California, to Viola, Idaho, about eight miles north of Moscow, Idaho, where he had purchased a 35-acre parcel with a blacksmith shop and enough room for a 500-yard rifle range. Soon, articles were published from such notables as Bob Hutton and Jack O'Connor, which helped to get the new business off the ground.

In addition to chambering for his line of wildcats, Gibbs also marketed several accessories for shooters and reloaders, including a booklet entitled *Front Ignition Loading Technique,* which covers the subject of duplex loading as developed by Charles O'Neil, Elmer Keith and Don Hopkins. Gibbs also advertised rifle muzzle stabilizers and hydraulic case-forming tools (Chapter 15).

On St. Patrick's Day in 1958, just three years after the move to Idaho, the family home burned to the ground, destroying all the records and remaining copies of the booklet. Gibbs never reprinted the booklets as sales had dropped off.

Initially, the Gibbs line of cartridges included seven calibers: the .240, .25, 6.5mm, .270, 7mm, .30, and 8mm Gibbs, which he developed between 1953 and 1955. Years later, he added the .338 Gibbs to the line. All Gibbs cartridges were based on the .30-06 case trimmed to 2.494 inches and of the same design

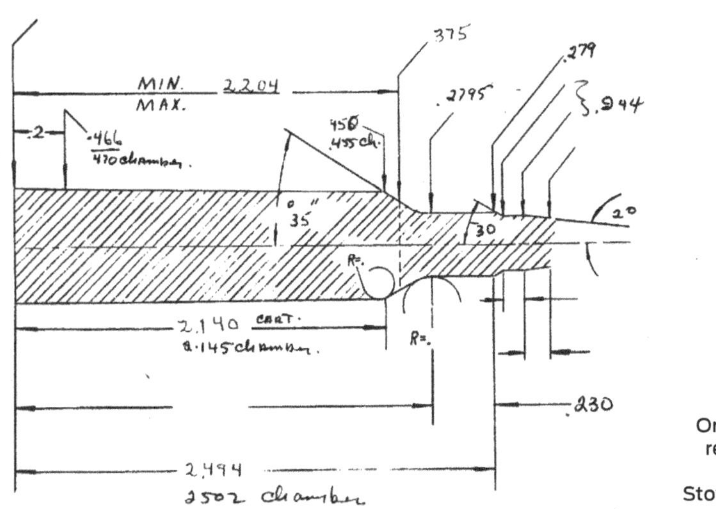

Original chamber reamer drawing. Photo: Roger Stowers collection

except for the neck diameter. Gibbs ordered all his chamber reamers with standard neck dimensions so reloaders would not have to turn or ream necks.

Nearly every wildcat comes about due to some experience or desire of the designer, and Gibbs' cartridges are no different. Gibbs belonged to a gun range in Richmond, California, and long about 1952, was a strong competitor in a local shooting contest but could not quite nail down the prize. Competition spurred the search for a cartridge to win the match the next time. The competition was based on multiple groups; first, shooters fired groups at 100, 200, 300 and 400 yards. Then, with the rifle zeroed for 100 yards, the group with the least bullet drop at 400 yards combined with the tightest group was the winner. Gibbs nearly won the competition with his .270 Winchester—he had the best group at 100 yards—but he lacked the velocity to win the second half.

Rocky's favorite gunsmith suggested that he try the .270 Ackley Improved in hopes of picking up the necessary velocity to win the second phase of the contest. In his Remington 721, the .270 Ackley gave him extraction problems with top loads. Disheartened, he sold the Model 721 so he could buy a Winchester 70 in .270 Winchester. Armed with this new rifle, Gibbs won the competition but still wanted a cartridge that would help him better his record.

For some unknown reason, Gibbs was sure that the 40-degree shoulder was to blame for his extraction problems, so he designed his own cartridge. In 1953, he ordered a .270 Gibbs reamer from Keith Francis' shop in Talent, Oregon (now JGS) with a 35-degree shoulder and a neck length of about .250 inch.

Gibbs believed the 35-degree shoulder would help prevent undue throat erosion. That .270 wildcat began a line of cartridges that proved commercially successful for Gibbs Rifle Products. It wasn't long before he had taught himself to perform barrel jobs and was chambering rifles for his shooting buddies. Near the end of his career, Gibbs estimated that he and his sons had chambered about 12,000 barrels for his wildcats.

The next time the competition came around at the Richmond Rod and Gun Club, Rocky Gibbs won it by a wide margin, setting a record that stood until the closing of the range. Based on research, it's a safe bet that his load for that competition was comparable to the ballistics of the .270 Weatherby Magnum, and pressures were likely much higher than he would have ever guessed.

By 1954, the other six cartridges in the original line were designed and available. It took little time for Gibbs to realize that, in the 1950s, .30-06 was more affordable and available than .270 brass, so his advertising took advantage of that fact. Gibbs cartridges are true wildcats in that you must form them first in a die before you can fire them in the chamber. Unlike an "improved" case design, there are no factory cartridges you can fire in a Gibbs chamber to fireform brass.

So, how do we know the correct dimensions for Gibbs' calibers if all the records were burned? The answer is pretty simple. Gibbs spoke highly of RCBS for supplying quality loading tools for his calibers in his booklet. So, RCBS's dimensions for the Gibbs line met Rocky's standards. Also, in various advertising materials, he made comments that serve as clues. For instance, he said that his chambers did not include freebore (long throating). In researching this chapter, some new documents came to light, including a drawing for Gibbs chamber reamers made by Keith Francis, the well-known reamer maker.

Gibbs' plagiarism fear was realized in some ways. Many of his contemporary gunsmiths and later ones never bothered to track down the correct dimensions for Gibbs' cartridges. They simply ran a 40-degree "improved" reamer in the barrel to move the shoulder forward. There are three major problems with this method: The shoulder angle is wrong, the neck will be too long, and the mouth of the chamber will be larger in diameter than it should be. This last one causes inaccuracy as well as a measurable bulge at the web of the case. Gibbs commented on such chambers, "a morphidite (*sic*) is produced." The result was a cross between an Ackley-improved chamber and a Gibbs chamber, receiving few benefits of either design and creating a batch of unique problems. So, if you're looking at a used rifle with a Gibbs chamber, carefully checking the fired brass or making a chamber cast is advisable.

Gibbs was adamant about the proper adjusting of loading dies. He stressed that the dies must be set to eliminate any headspace when the cartridge is chambered. Excessive headspace created by the loading die adjustment can allow the case head to slam against the bolt face and register an erroneous pressure indication by flattening the primer. Poor die adjustment with any cartridge will lay the groundwork for case head separations. The only cause of a case head separating is excessive headspace, either in the gun or in the ammunition. Be sure that the case shoulder engages the chamber shoulder and fully touches the bolt face when the gun is in battery. For details on properly forming brass for fireforming, see Chapter 15.

.240 Gibbs

The smallest caliber in the Gibbs line is the .240 Gibbs, marketed as the fastest 6mm in the world. In Gibbs' day, they formed .240 brass from .30-06, which was an easy process that took but a few steps. It's essential to have the rifle handy to check for correct headspace during the sizing process. Today, .270 Winchester brass costs no more than .30-06, so it makes sense to use .270 brass to save a sizing step. First, use a form die or a .25-06 die to neck the brass down to .24 caliber; remember to set the neck at about .250 inch in length. Then, size in a .240 Gibbs die. At this point, check the brass in your rifle's chamber: you should be able to feel the brass, yet close the bolt with undo effort. When checking the brass fit, remove the firing pin assembly from your bolt, as the spring tension will make it hard to feel the brass in the chamber when you close the bolt. Adjust the die down until you get

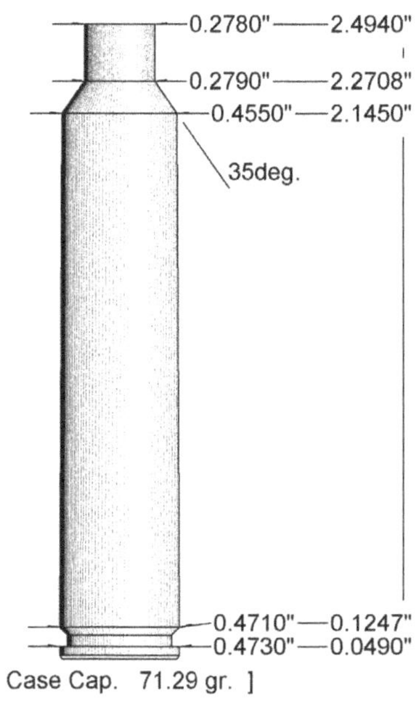

The .240 Gibbs.

proper headspace. Finally, load a fireforming load and head off to the range. The forming process is essentially the same for all Gibbs calibers.

It's interesting that of all the Gibbs cartridges, the .240 Gibbs is among the most enduring, yet it was the least advertised of the line. Gibbs made relatively few .240 Gibbs rifles compared to his other calibers. Overbore cartridges like the .240 Gibbs require special attention to detail, and minor problems can perplex the new reloader—they're finicky and tiny details can change performance and results. However, if you're looking for maximum velocity, such wildcats can deliver. But it comes at a price: you will burn more powder, choices of powders and bullets are often limited by results, and accurate barrel life will be relatively short. As always, these loads are for reference only. Always reduce them by 5 percent before testing in your rifle.

***.240 Gibbs*[1]**

BULLET (GR.)	POWDER	CHARGE (GR.)	VELOCITY (FPS)
75	H450	66	3,602
75	RL-22	63	3,665
85	IMR 4831	59	3,460
85	H870	69	3,500
105	RL-22	59	3,214
105	H870	67	3,255

Many articles about Gibbs cartridges mention the problem of the Secondary Explosion Effect (SEE). The concern is over light loads in sharp-shouldered cases with small neck diameters. Supposedly, powder, in such cases, can theoretically form a plug in the neck area and cause a dangerous pressure spike. However, no report of this effect being proven in a laboratory setting has come to light. There have been unexplained cases of rifles being destroyed and folks injured, but no way to conclusively prove the cause is related to SEE. I mention this here to point out that a light load is a bad idea in such cases. Select loads that will provide nearly 100 percent load density, and you will not have to concern yourself about it.

.25 Gibbs

Rocky Gibbs believed his .25 Gibbs was one of the best cartridges in the line-up. He said that the only wildcat that shot flatter was his .240 and described the .25 as an outstanding choice for deer and antelope. Since the .25-06 was still a wildcat (Remington standardized the .25-06 in 1969), it was a major source

1 Stowers, Roger, ".240 Gibbs," *Wildcat Cartridges, Volume I*, Wolfe Publishing, 1992

of competition for the .25 Gibbs. So, Gibbs' advertising claimed better velocity and less bolt thrust than the .257 Weatherby.

If clients were unsure which caliber they wanted, Rocky would recommend the .25. As a result, it ranked third in overall sales behind the .270 and .30 Gibbs. After 1958, Gibbs company envelopes were printed with a picture of the .25 Gibbs alongside a .257 Roberts cartridge. Charges listed below were maximum in the rifle tested; reduce 5 percent for starting loads.

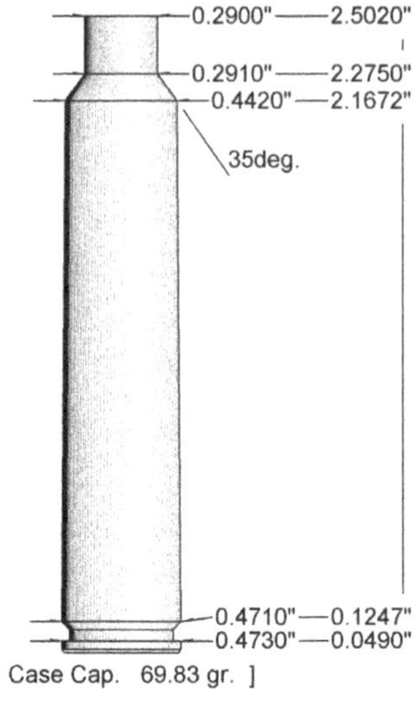

The .25 Gibbs.

.25 Gibbs[2]

BULLET (GR.)	POWDER	CHARGE (GR.)	VELOCITY (FPS)
75	IMR 7828	67	3,902
75	H4350	63	3,897
75	IMR 4831	64	3,910
87	IMR 7828	65	3,784
87	IMR 4831	60	3,768
100	IMR 7828	61	3,545
100	IMR 4831	57	3,502
117	IMR 7828	59	3,285
117	H4350	56	3,271
117	H4831	59	3,332

6.5 Gibbs

Although Gibbs marketed the 6.5 Gibbs as much as any of his wildcats, it never really took off. One of his long-time friends and hunting partners was Raymond Tarbox, an Idaho hunting guide. Tarbox described the process Gibbs used when testing a new rifle built for him in 6.5 Gibbs. "We used Speer 140-grain bullets and surplus 4831 powder. We added powder until the primer pockets loosened in Lake City cases. Those loads were then assembled in Denver 43

2 "The .25 Gibbs," *Wildcat Cartridges, Volume II*, Wolfe Publishing, 1992

cases and gave good case life,"[3] he said. Rocky Gibbs' approach to load development is the primary reason for the title of this chapter ... *Living on the Edge.*

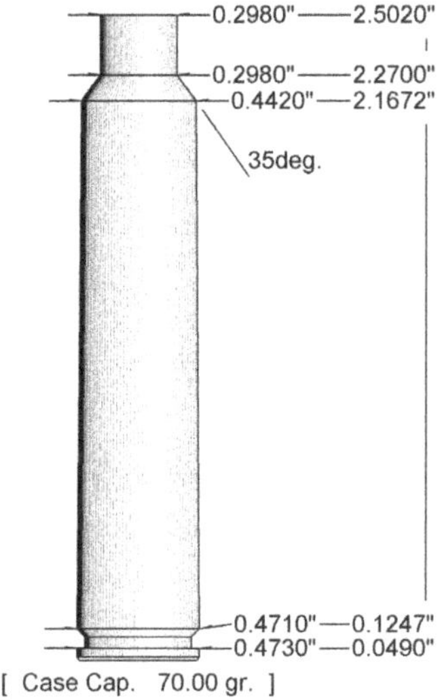

The 6.5 Gibbs.

In fairness to Gibbs, it is known that he tested a wide variety of brass to find the strongest available. He assembled loads in carefully selected cases and had many of them tested in Speer's laboratory. He then compiled load data for clients and sent it along with the rifles he built. However, his data was not pressure tested, and much of it was far too hot. The 6.5 Gibbs was advertised as "... a vicious big game rifle, fit for gophers to grizzlies."

Below is some load data from Charles A. Benke's tests of a 6.5 Gibbs. Benke was excited about the accuracy of his test gun. His testing produced groups under 2 inches at 200 yards with eight different powders.

6.5 Gibbs[4]

BULLET (GR.)	POWDER	CHARGE (GR.)	VELOCITY (FPS)
100	AAC 3100	61	3,433
100	RL-22	62	3,469
120	AAC 3100	58	3,264
120	RL-22	59	3,330
129	IMR 4831	58	3,099
129	RL-19	57	3,097
140	IMR 7828	58	3,039
140	H870	65	3,063

.270 Gibbs

In the May 1956 issue of *Outdoor Life*, Jack O'Connor described his experience with the .270 Gibbs. "As far as I can tell, Brother Gibbs doesn't do it with mirrors," said O'Connor. "I'm flabbergasted. So are Ray and Vernon Speer and all the right-thinking people who have seen what I've seen."

3 Benke, Charles A., "Sharp Shoulders, Case Life and the 6.5 Gibbs," *Wildcat Cartridges, Volume II*, Wolfe Publishing, 1992
4 Ibid.

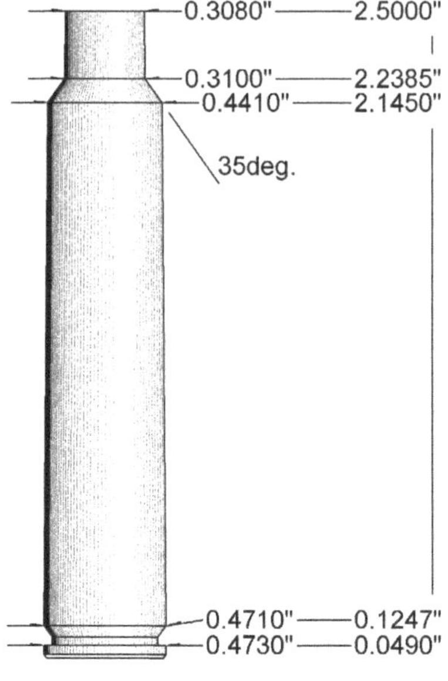

The .270 Gibbs.

The .270 proved to be one of the most popular of all the Gibbs cartridges during Rocky's lifetime. Gibbs himself called it "The best all-around cartridge for a handloader." In advertising, Gibbs said the .270 produced less recoil than the .30-06 and delivered more energy than a .300 H&H.

In 1954, Gibbs took a test rifle to Speer, which conducted testing but never published the results. Then, in 1963, Speer tested a .270 Gibbs on a Model 70 Winchester with a 24-inch barrel. Don O'Connor acquired that data for an article in *Handloader* magazine[5] many years later, which appears in the table below. Drop back at least 4 grains if you try these loads. They are maximum, and every rifle is different.

.270 Gibbs[6]

BULLET (GR.)	POWDER	CHARGE (GR.)	VELOCITY (FPS)
Speer 100	IMR 4350	65	3,673
Speer 130	H4831	66.5	3,400
Speer 150	H4831	62	3,165
Speer 150	H450	65	3,114
Speer 170	H4831	61.5	2,927

For comparison, here is some data from Roger Stowers' 26-inch-barreled .270 Gibbs.

BULLET (GR.)	POWDER	CHARGE (GR.)	VELOCITY (FPS)
110	IMR 4350	61	3,490
110	IMR 7828	67	3,467
110	IMR 4831	63	3,462
110	IMR 4320	54	3,391
130	H4831	63	3,287

5 "Don O'Connor's .270 Gibbs," *Wildcat Cartridges, Volume II*, Wolfe Publishing, 1992

6 Ibid.

130	H4350	60	3,265
130	IMR 7828	64	3,231
130	IMR 4320	53	3,178
150	H4831	60	3,054
150	H4350	57	3,015
150	IMR 7828	61	3,030
150	IMR 4831	56	2,994

7mm Gibbs

Like the 6.5 Gibbs, the 7mm Gibbs never sold as well as the rest of the line. Gibbs could not understand the lack of interest in these cartridges. He held a high opinion of 7mm calibers and their capabilities and praised Roy Weatherby for introducing the 7mm Weatherby Magnum. He said Joyce Hornady truly served the handloader when introducing Hornady's 175-grain bullet for the 7mm. Most of the 7mm Gibbs chamberings were conversions of Mauser 98s in 7x57. He expected the cartridge to take off when the .280 Remington was introduced, but to no avail. It made no difference who was advertising them; metric calibers were slow to catch on in the U.S.

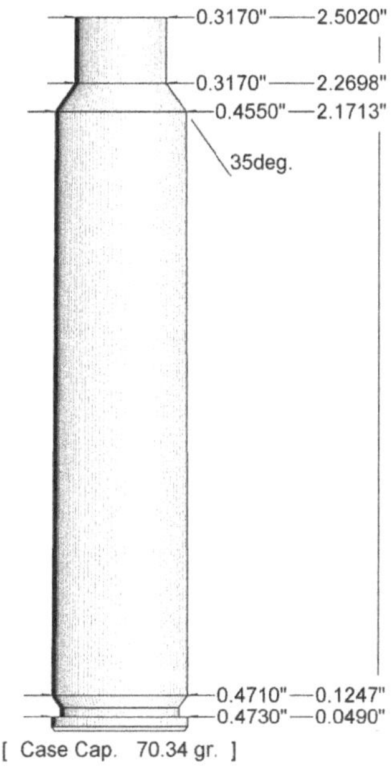

The 7mm Gibbs.

7mm Gibbs[7]

BULLET (GR.)	POWDER	CHARGE (GR.)	VELOCITY (FPS)
120	RL-19	65	3,488
120	H380	62	3,386
139	RL-19	63	3,296
139	H4831	66	3,321
154	H4350	60	3,096
154	H4831	64	3,141
175	H414	56	2,882
175	H4831	61	2,965

7 Stowers, Roger, "Gibb Metrics," *Gibbs Cartridges and Front Ignition Loading Techniques*, Wolfe Publishing, 1991

.30 Gibbs

The .30 Gibbs was the second cartridge that Rocky Gibbs designed and developed and is probably the best known today. In his *Front Ignition and Loading Technique* booklet, Gibbs said he initially selected the .30-06 case as a parent for his new cartridge "because of the ever-plentiful supply of .30-06 brass. Secondly, a case with standard head size delivers 40 percent less thrust to the locking lugs than a case with a large head, such as a Weatherby or a .300 H&H case."

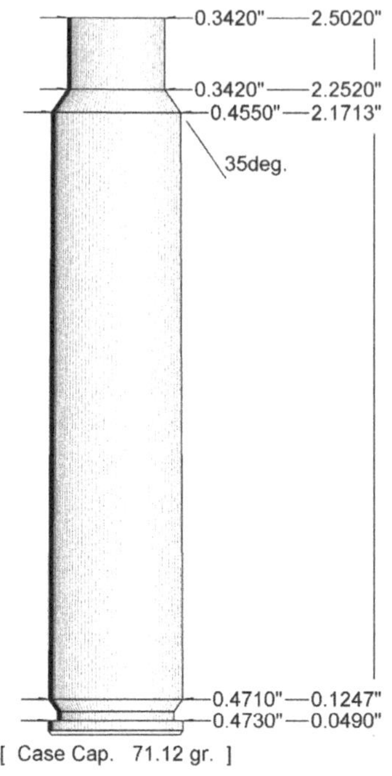

The .30 Gibbs.

Advertised as the "most economical .30-caliber rifle in the world, with recoil and barrel life comparable to the .30-06" and "The world's most powerful .30-06!" the advertising was primarily advocating conversion of existing .30-06 rifles. Gibbs did offer barreled actions, too, mostly 98 Mausers.

Bob Hagel wrote an article in *Handloader* No. 73 magazine entitled, "The .30 Gibbs, A Magnum-type Cartridge It Ain't," in which he says the .30 Gibbs loaded to the same pressures as a .30-06 would only deliver about 50 fps increase in velocity over the standard .30-06. In comparing his load charts for the .30 Gibbs to published data for the same powders in a .30-06, it appears Hagel did not make a fair comparison, or his method of determining pressure was flawed. The difference in velocity falls between 100 and 200 fps, depending on the source you check. The most interesting comparison is with a later article in *Handloader* by Roger Stowers, ".30 Gibbs." When comparing the load charts for these two articles, one notes that many loads are virtually the same, but the Stowers results are 100 fps faster than those in Hagel's chart. The main reason is that the Stowers' gun barrel was 2 inches longer.

Hagel says most .30 Gibbs conversions are on 24-inch-barreled rifles, so the claims of higher velocity are erroneous (strange because Rocky Gibbs always advocated long barrels). His comments completely ignore that the published data Hagel questions were for 26-inch barrels. For example, 180-gr. bullets

Rocky Gibbs testing a rifle with his son, Robert.

loaded with IMR 4831, 66 grains for Stowers' rifle and 67 grains for Hagel's, Hagel recorded 2,924 fps; Stowers with a grain less powder recorded 3,070 fps, an increase of 146 fps for 2 inches of increased barrel length. The *maximum* velocity for a 180-grain bullet with IMR 4831 listed in the *Nosler No. 3 Manual* is 2,760 fps for a .30-06 in a 23.5-inch barrel. Any way you look at it, the Gibbs produces a respectable increase over a standard '06.

.30 Gibbs[8]

BULLET (GR.)	POWDER	CHARGE (GR.)	VELOCITY (FPS)
150	IMR 4320	59	3,261
150	IMR 4064	59	3,225
165	H414	63	3,129
165	W760	63	3,106
180	IMR 4831	66	3,070
180	IMR 4350	64	3,054
200	H4831	64	2,871
220	IMR 7828	63	2,670

8 Ibid.

8mm Gibbs

The 8mm Gibbs was primarily developed to convert the large number of 8x57 Mausers that came home after World War II. It was a cheap way to convert bringbacks to readily available surplus '06 brass. With the Gibbs case design, you gain an additional 400 to 500 fps over the 8x57—nothing to sneeze at.

8mm Gibbs[9]

BULLET (GR.)	POWDER	CHARGE (GR.)	VELOCITY (FPS)
150	RL-15	64	3,346
150	IMR 4064	63	3,339
170	RL-15	63	3,202
170	IMR 4064	60	3,066
200	H414	68	2,913
200	IMR 4064	58	2,895
220	H414	65	2,797
220	RL-15	57	2,743

.338 Gibbs

The prolific wildcatter added the .338 Gibbs sometime after 1958. He understood all too well that any work he sold for this new offering would have to include a new barrel since no factory guns could be rechambered to his caliber.

The market for custom gun work was changing; surplus guns and ammo were less common, so conversion work was not as profitable as it had once been. Gibbs hoped that the fresh offering would bring new clients to his business. But the cartridge never really took off. At one point, Rocky considered changing the name of the .338 Gibbs to .338 MAG for his real initials, but he scrapped the idea. He believed the Gibbs name should be on all his work. In his view, "A tradesman should sign his work."

He believed that for the .338 Gibbs to shine against his 8mm Gibbs, it would have to use heavier bullets such as the 250-gr. pill. The problem was that he didn't think the case had enough capacity to take advantage of a heavy bullet—deep-seating projectiles

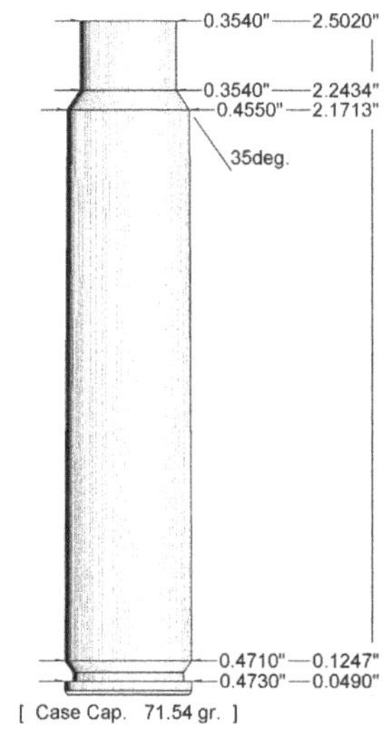

The 8mm Gibbs.

9 Ibid.

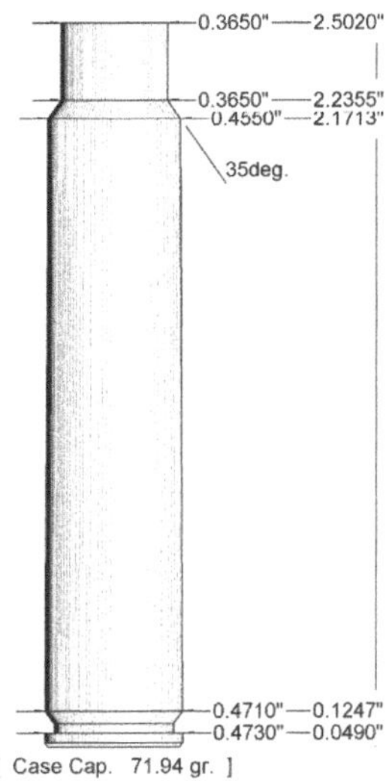

The .338 Gibbs.

robbed too much capacity. He felt that the .338 Winchester was just about the perfect capacity for the .338 bore. But because he did not have complete faith in his design, he had difficulty advocating that client's chamber for it. So, he allowed the cartridge to fall by the wayside. By 1961, Gibbs had dropped the .338 from his advertising due to lack of interest.

It's sometimes reported that he introduced the .338 Gibbs in 1968, but this is only half true. Gibbs reintroduced it when Norma released some slow-burning powders to the U.S. market, which Rocky believed would make his .338 Gibbs a viable contender. When marketing the .338 Gibbs, Rocky liked to talk about the reduced bolt thrust of an '06-diameter case head versus the magnums. He went so far as to make the comparison that a standard '06 case would have to be loaded to 83,000 psi to equal the bolt thrust of a magnum case.

***.338 Gibbs*[10]**

BULLET (GR.)	POWDER	CHARGE (GR.)	VELOCITY (FPS)
200	IMR 4320	61	3,059
200	RL-15	61	3,042
225	H414	65	2,843
225	W760	63	2,840
250	IMR 4350	65	2,727
250	W760	61	2,672
275	IMR 4350	62	2,567

Criticisms of Gibbs' Work

In later years, harsh criticism was heaped on the Gibbs line of cartridges. It was said that the designer overrated them and that the necks were far too short for good design. These same critics failed to note other cartridges with short necks, like the .300 Winchester and the .300 Savage, which have proven themselves through years of successful use in the field.

In his publication *Testing and Loading the Gibbs Rifles*, Gibbs wrote, "For

10 Stowers, Roger, ".338 Gibbs," *Gibbs Cartridges and Front Ignition Loading Techniques*, Wolfe Publishing, 1991

test loading the Gibbs rifles ... We have our own 'Copper-Crusher Gauge' for measuring peak chamber pressures but its all-round usefulness is impaired by the necessity of drilling a hole into the chamber through the wall of the pressure-gun barrel. Thus, ruining the barrel for any other use. In order to check peak pressures WITHOUT ruining the barrel, we developed a 'Pressure-Analyzer System,' then correlated it with the copper Crusher Gauge and under controlled conditions can now measure peak chamber pressures without any ill effects on the barrel being used."

This information means that R.E. Gibbs was one of the first—if not *the first*—gunsmiths to use strain gauge technology in his shop. However, it's far more likely that he devised a brass measuring method to correlate data. We know from more recent testing that this methodology would not be accurate or reliable. From his comments, Gibbs tested loads in his pressure barrel with the copper crusher unit installed while matching the pressure results with loads fired in a barrel not drilled for the cup gauge. He believed he could build up a comparative chart for his loads and the pressure they generated.

It appears that Gibbs did all his pressure test work in cup since he used a copper crusher to test his loads and the strength of various makes of brass. Then, he may have designed his own system using a transducer to record pressures without installing the crusher system on the barrel. He often referred to his results as psi (pounds per square inch), but it is doubtful he had the information or ability to convert his transducer results into psi. He likely used the terms interchangeably, a common practice at the time.

The problem is that psi and cup are different measuring systems, and the terms are not interchangeable. I contend that all the pressure data Gibbs mentions in his writings were actually in cup since that was the technology he had to work with at the time. Comparing his published information with today's data on a pressure system can easily check this. Factory loads for a .270 Winchester will typically read about 63,000 psi on an Oehler Model 43 pressure test system.

Gibbs tended to report only the highest velocities from his tests, a disease prevalent in the entire gun industry at that time and continues to this day. To measure velocity for his wildcats, Gibbs would work up loads that measured 53,000 cup on his test equipment, which would be a maximum load. Then, he would test those loads on Speer's Potter chronograph. One day, while chronographing loads at Speer, Gibbs was confronted by Ray Speer who asked him, "Why no one else could obtain the velocities that he (Gibbs) advertised?" In response, Gibbs asked if he was condemning him for cutting a good chamber or excusing the man who cuts a bad one.

Gibbs' velocities are questioned to this day as unattainable. He did several things to reach the numbers he reported. First, he corrected velocities from instrumental to muzzle velocity. He considered barrel length to be from the mouth of the case to the muzzle, which added about 2 inches to the length of his test barrels (a 26-inch barrel was a 28-inch one by all other standards). Finally, instead of taking the average of 10 shots, he took the highest velocity measured within a group and reported it as gospel.

Combining these items gave Rocky Gibbs well over 100 fps above what we would get using accepted standard techniques. Knowing all this and looking back on the .270 Gibbs data earlier in this chapter, the data in the first table was collected using Rocky's methods. The second table was generated using more conventional methods; the difference in velocities is unmistakable.

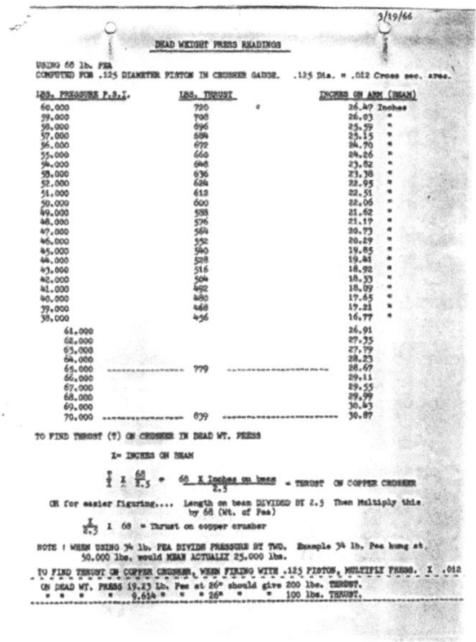

3/19/66

DEAD WEIGHT PRESS READINGS

USING 68 lb. PEA
COMPUTED FOR .125 DIAMETER PISTON IN CRUSHER GAUGE. .125 Dia. = .012 Cross sec. area.

LBS. PRESSURE P.S.I.	LBS. THRUST	INCHES ON ARM (BEAM)
60.000	720	26.47 Inches
59.000	708	26.03 "
58.000	696	25.59 "
57.000	684	25.15 "
56.000	672	24.70 "
55.000	660	24.26 "
54.000	648	23.82 "
53.000	636	23.38 "
52.000	624	22.95 "
51.000	612	22.51 "
50.000	600	22.06 "
49.000	588	21.62 "
48.000	576	21.17 "
47.000	564	20.73 "
46.000	552	20.29 "
45.000	540	19.85 "
44.000	528	19.41 "
43.000	516	18.92 "
42.000	504	18.53 "
41.000	492	18.09 "
40.000	480	17.65 "
39.000	468	17.21 "
38.000	456	16.77 "
61.000		26.91
62.000		27.35
63.000		27.79
64.000		28.23
65.000	779	28.67
66.000		29.11
67.000		29.55
68.000		29.99
69.000		30.43
70.000	839	30.87

TO FIND THRUST (T) ON CRUSHER IN DEAD WT. PRESS

X= INCHES ON BEAM

$\frac{T}{X} \times \frac{68}{2.5} = \frac{68 \times \text{Inches on beam}}{2.5}$ = THRUST ON COPPER CRUSHER

OR for easier figuring.... Length on beam DIVIDED BY 2.5 Then Multiply this by 68 (Wt. of Pea)

$\frac{X}{2.5} \times 68$ = Thrust on copper crusher

NOTE : WHEN USING 34 lb. PEA DIVIDE PRESSURE BY TWO. Example 34 lb. Pea hung at 50.000 lbs. would MEAN ACTUALLY 25.000 lbs.

TO FIND THRUST ON COPPER CRUSHER, WHEN FIRING WITH .125 PISTON, MULTIPLY PRESS. X .012

ON DEAD WT. PRESS 19.23 Lb. Pea at 26" should give 200 lbs. THRUST.
" " " " 9.614 " " " 26" " " 100 lbs. THRUST.

This chart was among papers from Gibbs' records, which escaped destruction in a house fire. It suggests the secretive wildcatter worked with a copper crusher pressure test system. Photo: Roger Stowers collection

Gibbs' Experimental Cartridges

In correspondence, Roger Stowers told me he had evidence for a .22 Gibbs, which Gibbs tested but never marketed. Actually, Gibbs never manufactured any .22 Gibbs for the public, as far as the available records indicate (see illustration). From the Speer Labs tests, the .22 Gibbs did 3,913 fps with a 60-gr. Hornady bullet. Note that Ray Speer signed the test sheet in the illustration. Stowers says, "I think he had problems with SEE (Secondary Explosive Effect) in the .22 Gibbs as he did with the .240 Gibbs, though he never admitted that."

Unfortunately, there is no record of the case design for the .22 Gibbs; it was likely on the .30-06 case since maximizing the '06 case and taking advantage of cheap brass interested him. One clue that he may have based it on the standard Gibbs design is that Denver 43 brass is listed as the case used in the Speer tests. The velocities listed below are appropriate for a 60-grain bullet in a .22-06.

Gibbs also tested a .300 H&H case with a Gibbs shoulder, presumably either to see if there was value in making a Gibbs magnum or, equally as likely, to duplicate the SEE condition.

"On many occasions through the past several months we have had many handloaders bring up the subject of 'unexplained dangerous pressures' using reduced loads of the slower burning powders," Gibbs said.

No record exists to indicate which cartridge the .22 Gibbs was based on, though likely it was .30-06, just like the rest of Rocky's line. Note Ray Speer's signature on the test results. Photo: Roger Stowers collection

Gibbs tested his version of a .300 H&H Improved case. Photo: Roger Stowers collection

According to Stowers, "There are quite a few notes in which Rocky was trying to prove or disprove the theory we call SEE. He could not create the situation because he did not use the large kernel slow burning powders for the test. He used ball powders and concluded, 'less powder-less pressure; more powder more pressure'... in his notes he never admitted any problems. There may have been more testing, but I only have a portion of the notes."

P.O. Ackley pursued the same issue to no avail; see Chapter 3.

There are no records of the case shape or dimensions for the improved design referenced on the above load sheet.

Another test cartridge that Rocky Gibbs worked on was the .240 Gibbs Jr. No records indicate the design or even the parent case he used.

Note: You may encounter other cartridges, such as a .35 Gibbs or a .375 Gibbs.

These are not Rocky Gibbs' work; they result from customers asking gunsmiths for them. They follow Gibbs' case design, so they are named for him as a courtesy and to make identification simple for the reamer maker and the gunsmith. Since they use the Gibbs headspace gauge, it only makes sense.

Rocky Gets the Last Word

Rocky Gibbs had a favorite comment when discussing his .270 or .30 Gibbs wildcats. So, he gets the last word: "My rifles make a magnum with a short barrel, just another rifle."

Author's note: I spoke to long-time gun writer Roger Stowers in preparation for this chapter. Stowers probably knows more about Rocky Gibbs than anyone in the shooting fraternity and has written numerous articles about his work. Wolfe Publishing assembled a book from Stowers' writings, which contained the summation of his research, entitled Gibbs Cartridges and the Front Ignition Loading Technique *(1991). Most of the information that makes up this chapter is taken from Stowers' work with his kind permission. Thanks, Roger, for preserving these records and for your help with this important chapter in wildcatting history.*

Test results for the .240 Gibbs Jr. Photo: Roger Stowers collection

More test results for the .240 Gibbs Jr. No cartridge drawings have been located. Note the pressure information recorded on this test sheet, proving Rocky did care about pressure. Photo: Roger Stowers collection

CHAPTER 23
Simple Math for Handloaders and Wildcatters

The purpose of this book is not to teach you ballistics but rather to design useful cartridges. I included the mathematical information in this chapter to save you time when researching possible designs. If you need more in-depth explanations of the formulas here, read *Understanding Firearm Ballistics* by Robert A. Rinker, who makes a complex subject understandable.

Equivalents and Conversions

Pounds to grains: pounds x 7,000 = grains
Example: 1 pound x 7000 = 7,000 grains

Grains to pounds: grains ¸ 7,000 = pounds
Example: 14,000 grains ¸ 7,000 = 2 pounds

Grams to grains: grams x 15.43 = grains
Example: 3.7 grams x 15.43 = 57.091 grains

Degrees to minutes (angles): Number of degrees x 60 = Number of minutes of angle
Example: ½ degree (.50) x 60 = 30 minutes

Inches to Millimeters: inches x 25.4 = millimeters

Example: .244 in. x 25.4 = 6.19 millimeters

Feet to Meters: feet x 0.3281 = meters
Example: 300 feet x 0.3281 = 98.43 meters

Feet to Yards: feet x 0.3333 = yards
Example: 300 x 0.3334 = 99.99 (you'll have to round it off)

Feet per second (fps) to miles per hour (mph): fps x 0.6818 = mph
Example: 3,000 fps x 0.6818 = 2,045.4 mph

Feet per second to meters per second: fps x 0.3048 = mps
Example: 3,000 fps x 0.3048 = 914.4 mps

Miles per hour to feet per second: mph x 1.467 = fps
Example: 2,000 mph x 1.467 = 2,934 fps

Meters to feet: meters x 3.281 = feet
Example: 100 meters x 3.281 = 328.1 feet

Meters to yards: meters x 1.094 = yards
Example: 100 meters x 1.094 = 109.4 yards

Yards to meters: yards x 0.9144 = meters
Example: 300 yards x 0.9144 = 274.32 meters

A *dram* is a unit of measure used to measure blackpowder. Smokeless powder cannot be measured in drams, and there is no known safe method of conversion to measure it for dram equivalence. It would be necessary to know the burning characteristics of a given powder to determine how many grains of that powder would deliver the pressure equal to one dram of blackpowder. Frankly, wildcatters will not have much trouble with this issue.

Formulas for Ballistics

Ballistic Coefficient: $C = W / id$

Definition: C = ballistic coefficient
W = bullet weight in pounds
i = form factor

d = bullet diameter in inches

Sectional Density: $SD = W / d^2$

Definition: SD = sectional density

W = bullet weight in pounds

d = bullet diameter in inches

Kinetic Energy: $MV^2 \div GC = KE$

Definition: M = mass

V = velocity

GC = gravitational constant (64.32)

KE = kinetic energy

Energy in Foot Pounds: $E. = WV^2 \div 450400$

Definition: E = energy (foot-pounds)

W = weight of the bullet in grains

V = velocity in feet per second

450,400 = accepted expression of gravitational constant and weight

Energy in Pounds Feet: $E = VW / 7000$

Definition: E = energy (pounds-feet)

V = bullet velocity (feet per second)

W = bullet weight (grains)

Cross-Sectional Area[1]: $XSA = \pi * R^2$

Definition: XSA = cross-sectional area

π = geometric constant (3.14159 is an accepted number for pi)

R = the radius of the bullet in inches

Spin Rate: RPS = V (12/barrel twist rate)

Definition: RPS = spin rate as the bullet exits muzzle in revolutions per second

V = bullet velocity

Greenhill Formula: $Twist = \frac{150 * D^2}{L}$

Definition: 150 = constant for bullets under 2,800 fps

D = bullet diameter in inches

L = bullet length in inches

(If your bullet velocity is greater than 2,800 fps, substitute 180 for the constant for a more accurate result)

Taylor Knock-Out Value: $\frac{(W * V)D}{7000}$

1 A-Square, *Any Shot You Want*, 1996

Definition: W = Bullet weight in grains
V = Muzzle velocity
D = Diameter of bullet
7,000 = Number of grains in a pound

On his "Knock-Out Value" system, noted African big game hunter John Taylor says: "Fifty of my Knock-Out values are necessary to bring an elephant down with certainty, but they won't keep him down other than momentarily; more than 60 values are needed to stun him. With values ranging between 60 and 80, you will probably keep him down for five or six minutes provided the bullet hits pretty close to the brain."[2]

Taylor was describing the power needed to stop an elephant, and many argue that his formula makes good sense when comparing apples to apples: the .444 Marlin to the .45-70 to the .50 Alaskan. They also maintain that it is less valuable when comparing a .22-250, .300 WSM and .458 Lott. If 60 to 80 TKO values are needed to stun an elephant, then who in their right mind would take a .22-250 with a value of 4.1 after anything other than varmint-sized game? Taylor devised a way to account for bullet weight and diameter when determining if a load was appropriate for a given use. He was concerned with elephants, but that does not mean the information is less valuable when considering other game.

Expansion Ratio: The ratio of the bore volume plus the powder chamber to the powder chamber volume alone. The volume is commonly expressed in cubic inches. You calculate the powder chamber volume by dividing the water capacity (in grains) by 252.4, with the density of water at 70° F.

Our example is a .358 caliber with a water capacity of 50 grains. This formula would look like this:

$U = W \div 252.4$, where U is the powder chamber volume (in cubic inches), and W is the powder chamber's water capacity (in grains).

$U = 50 \div 252.4$

$U = 0.198098256$

You will find the effective bore volume somewhere between the groove diameter and the land diameter, which depends on the height, width, and number of lands.

Or you can estimate it using this formula:

$Q = 0.773 * T * D^2$ where Q is the effective bore volume (in cubic inches), T is the bullet travel (in inches), D is the bullet diameter, and .773 is a barrel groove diameter constant (in inches).

---

2 Taylor, John, *African Rifles and Cartridges*, 1948

$Q = 0.773 * 22.399 * 0.358^2$
$Q = 0.773 * 22.399 * 0.138904$
$Q = 0.773 * 3.111310696$
$Q = 2.405043168008$ cubic inches of effective bore volume.

We now have enough to calculate the expansion ratio from the formula:

$R = (Q + U) \div U$ where R is the expansion ratio, Q is the effective bore volume, and U is the powder chamber volume.
$R = (2.405043168008 + 0.198098256) \div 0.198098256$
$R = 2.6031413728008 \div 0.198098256$
$R = 13.140657...$ expansion ratio.

Real World Ballistics by the Inch

If you wonder how much velocity you gain or lose with barrel length, I recommend the website *ballisticsbytheinch.com* (BBTI). As this book ages, if that site is taken down, you can find it through web.archive.org.

BBTI began in 2008. It includes valuable data that wildcatters and gunsmiths should know about. In September 2020, the site's authors announced they would no longer be testing but would maintain the site as an archive. There are four main sections of the site:

Calibers/cartridges—provides a list of 22 different datasets. You can browse the charts, click on a given ammunition type listed in the header of each chart for a graph of how that particular ammunition performed or download the raw data for your use.

Cylinder gap—the study's results, which used a Uberti Single Action Army clone in .38/.357 mag. to examine velocity differences between three different cylinder gaps (0.006, 0.001, and 'flush').

Polygonal rifling—documenting performance comparisons between polygonal and traditionally rifled barrels in 9mm.

Real-world guns—A comprehensive list of all the firearms used as 'benchmark' comparisons for results obtained from our T/C Encore test platform.

CHAPTER 24

Alternative Ammo for .22 Long Rifle Chambers

Ramset to the Rescue

I first started testing the idea of alternative .22 LR ammo in 2012. But the ammo shortages that overtook the country a few years later caused me to seek alternatives to burning up expensive ammo that was hard to replace. As a gunsmith, I search for a solution whenever a problem like this pops up, and with my background in wildcatting, I am probably a little more open to testing different types or styles of ammunition than some folks might be. Even so, the techniques I explain in this chapter should be handy for all rimfire shooters, reloaders and wildcatters.

When the ammo shortages began, I figured they would clear up quickly, like in the past. However, it was not to be, not this time. It would be more than two years before the shortage subsided noticeably in my neck of the woods. We occasionally saw shipments come in, but even with the stores rationing sales, it didn't last long, partly from regular demand and partly from hoarders sniping ammo as soon as it appeared on the shelf.

So, I decided to explore an idea I have had for a long time of using Ramset powder loads as a source for rimfire ammunition. A little research has shown that, at least in my area, you can find three of the five loads on the companies' charts. These are No. 2 (brown), No. 3 (green) and No. 4 (yellow).

The first and simplest test was to fire these loads (blanks) in a .22 LR chamber. (The rim and the lower portion of the body are the same as .22 LR cases.) They test-fired just fine: no signs of slitting, pressure or anomalies. No surprises there.

I started thinking outside the box because these loads differ in configuration from any rimfire case with which you usually fire a projectile. Many shooters are unaware that .22 rimfire barrels are a smaller diameter than .22 centerfire barrels. Rimfire barrels have a .222-inch groove diameter, while centerfires are .224-inch—just enough to quickly raise pressures and rupture case rims using centerfire bullets in a rimfire barrel.

Typically, when you overpressure a rimfire, the case rim blows out or ruptures. Case failure is dangerous for several reasons. First, hearing damage can occur. Second, bits of brass can be spewed out of any gaps in the action and can burn, cut or imbed in your skin or eyes. Third, releasing gas into the action can damage the bolt, barrel, extractor or ejector, depending on the gun's design.

There was no data on Ramset loads being fired in standard firearms, so I decided first to test for any damage to a typical .22 LR barrel. As you might expect, with no projectile, there was no damage to the barrel. I used a colored sealant to seal and identify the power level of the various loads on the crimp of each blank. I experienced no problems like the paint adhering to the chamber and increasing pressure.

Most shooters will want a simple and easy-to-use form of ammunition that will allow them to kill small animals and feed themselves in hard times. So, this first round of testing focused on a readily available system that anybody could use. For this reason, we used single-loaded single-shots or bolt-actions.

Pellets seemed like a possible source of projectiles at a reasonable cost. However, there was too much power even with the Brown loads (the lowest power); the thin skirt on the .22 pellets tore off and obstructed the chamber, so a second round could not be loaded. Accuracy with standard .22 pellets was worthless. Much of this problem is because pellets are too small and too light.

While at a sporting goods store, I found some Crosman Red Flight Penetrator pellets. They have a plastic sabot-like base that drives the pellet, and each

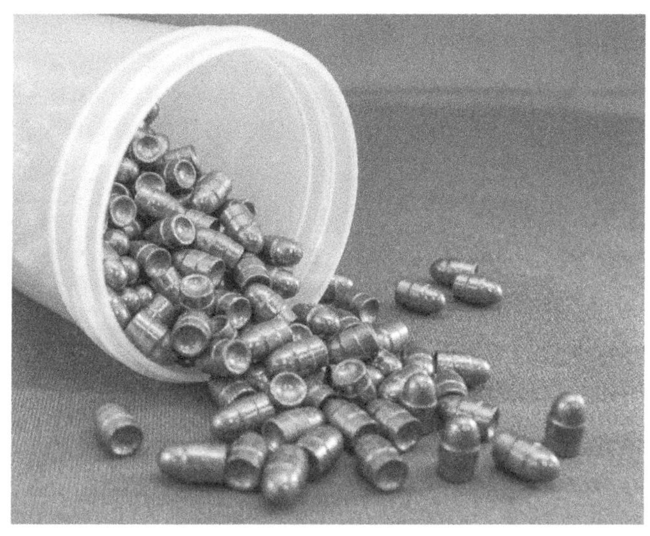

weighs 16.7 grains. I hoped the plastic base would protect the pellet and give us a viable projectile at minimal cost. It worked—if you're not looking for typical .22 LR accuracy.

I shot the test rifle with two brands of .22 LR ammo to determine the gun's baseline accuracy (see the groups below). Accuracy was good with 1/2 to 1-inch groups with various ammo at 50 feet. Naturally, the first shots with the powder loads and the pellets were fired with the gun behind a barrier to prevent any injury. Once the rifle fired safely, we progressed to accuracy and velocity testing.

The test rifle had a 20-inch barrel and iron sights. The Remington ammunition used for accuracy testing gave an average velocity of 1,185 fps. That's typical for sporting ammunition in a .22 LR with a 40-grain bullet.

The No. 2 (brown) loads produced a velocity of 1,624 fps; remember, that's with a 16.7-grain projectile.

The accuracy was not great, but it was the best of the three Ramset loads tested. The 10-shot group was 2.6 inches high by 2 inches wide, with eight shots going into a group of just over 1.5 inches. So, I would call that minute of rabbit at 50 feet. In other words, it would kill a rabbit with every shot.

Back to the rifle, next was the No. 3 green load. The group size was slightly larger than with the brown but hardly different enough to be considered poorer accuracy. Velocity was a surprise at a 2,047 fps average. So, even though these loads will not win any shooting contests, they will certainly hit hard.

Lastly, we tested the No. 4 yellow loads. These were the most potent, and performance indicated they were at the upper limit for a standard .22 LR firearm. There were no case failures, and the ejected cases looked normal. However, the bolt was noticeably stiffer to lift after firing, always a sign that the load was too hot. For this reason, I will not report the velocity as I consider the loads unsafe for general use. Accuracy was poor, and groups were erratic and much larger than the lighter loads.

When I decided to add this chapter to the second edition of this book, I looked to see what others had tried and had learned about using powder loads. There were several YouTube videos about the subject starting in about 2015. The results were similar: nearly all tests showed good accuracy with the Crossman Red Flight Penetrator and the No. 2 Powder Loads. It makes sense that the lower power loads would give the best accuracy, though the velocity with this combination is still very fast, around 1,450 fps, depending on the gun. Some YouTubers had better accuracy results than I did with this recipe in the area of 1-inch groups. Your particular gun will be the final judge of success with this ammo.

The next logical progression was to design a bullet that could be hand-seated into a standard .22 LR barrel with a Ramset load behind it. The expected weight for this projectile was about 30 grains. The reason for this bullet is simple: it allows the use of the powder loads without doing any work on the brass or using a specialized chamber in the gun. You might call it "field expedient." Since North American Arms made a bullet very close to what we needed for its cap and ball pistol, I ordered some.

I also revisited the problem of projectiles for improvised .22 ammo when I sat down to outline this chapter. Since I had some luck with pellets before, I decided to see what else is out there for air rifles that could be utilized with the Ramset loads. I found two options I wanted to test: A "hunting" pellet weighing 32.4 grains that looks like a traditional pellet but is longer, and the web is much thicker with a tiny hollow base. Second, "slugs" of various weights from the airgun world.

For this follow-up test, we used a 10-inch contender barrel with iron sights at 50 feet and Winchester Super X 40-gr. ammo as a baseline.

Schaefer theorized that the Ramset loads were inconsistent due to inferior priming. After all, they're used to drive nails into concrete. During the tests in the Contender barrel, I experienced two misfires. When I rotated the case and tried again, they fired. So, he may be correct about the priming. That 37-grain slug in the test below would be a decent hunting option.

LOAD	PROJECTILE (GR.)	VELOCITY (FPS)	ACCURACY @ 50 FEET (IN.)
Win. Super X	40	1,215	1
Ramset Brown	26 (Slug .217 in.)	1,376	2
Ramset Brown	37 (Slug .218 in.)	1,400	.700

Sharp Shooter Rimfire Reloader

Sharp Shooter makes a kit that is probably one of the smartest, if not the simplest, methods of producing .22 LR ammo at home (22lrreloader.com).

The kit includes a bullet mold to cast bullets in two weights, plus a crimper to ensure your projectiles are retained in the case. Additional tools include the primer cleaner and packer, primer funnel, measuring tool and eyedropper. Worth the price of admission is a detailed instruction pamphlet outlining the reloading process step by step, so there's no need to reinvent the wheel. Sharp Shooter's recommended powders included 700x, 7625, PB, Unique and Pyrodex P.

Priming fired .22 cases is the biggest obstacle I see in reloading .22 cases. Sharp Shooter has created a mixable compound to prime once-fired cases. You must clean the fired cases first and scrape out the rim recess before pushing the priming compound into the recess of the case rim. You wetten the compound with acetone or denatured alcohol so it adheres, and you can form it into the case rim.

Sharp Shooter also sells a resizing die and shell holder if you want your cases to work in various guns. Otherwise, the finished product will likely work only in the gun the cases were initially fired in. It's well worth the money to have the resizing die. You can try all kinds of experiments with it and the priming compound.

Many writers have reviewed these tools. All report good results and some sing its praises. I think the system is well thought out and works exceptionally well. Priming requires patience and attention to detail. Remember that this system is ideal when ammo is unavailable or difficult to acquire. It is not a production ammo system. Even so, the ability to cast your own heeled bullets for rimfire cases is valuable.

The best thing about the Sharp Shooter Kit is that you have actual .22 LR ammo.

209 Shotgun Primer Tests

Robart Schaefer wanted to see what could be done with 209 primers. He had some ideas, which we tested. First, he had the idea to put brass tubing on a 209 primer to create a case. Naturally, that would have to be a low-pressure setup, likely with no powder added. The idea was to see if we could use a 209 shotgun primer as a source of ammo for a .22. However, right up front, these loads would not work in a .22 LR chamber. The 209 with brass tubing seated on it is too large in diameter for the standard chamber. It's too large for the .22 Magnum chamber as well.

Tubing on a 209 primer to create a case.

That makes it less practical since you would need to modify the chamber or build a gun to work with the chambering. There are a few types of tubing available in the local hardware store. We started with brass in .010- and .014-inch wall thickness.

Initial attempts to seat the tubing onto the primer proved that we needed special tooling. Pushing the tubing onto the primer was easy, but it always stretched unevenly, causing major concentricity problems. We would need forming tools to produce reasonable accuracy.

As we worked on the tubing idea, I thought a better alternative must exist. Schaefer picked up a .25 ACP case and started taking measurements. Scoffing, I told him there couldn't be enough room for a 209 primer in that case. However, after deciding on a "B" letter drill, he went to the lathe, and soon, we had a test case with a seated 209 primer. The result is a rimmed case in .25 caliber.

Robart Schaefer testing accuracy. The 32.4-grain Seneca Hunting Pellet was the best projectile he and the author tested with the 209 Primer. Shown here is a 50-foot group. The gun has a standard .22 Magnum chamber with a rim cut added for the 209. You can still fire .22 Magnum with no issues.

To drill the .25 ACP cases properly, we needed to make a custom lathe collet to hold the cases securely. The outcome is a .25 ACP-shaped tube with no head. The extractor groove is present, so when you seat the 209 primers in the base end of the tube, the primer rim becomes the new case's rim.

Naturally, this is not a reloadable .22, but it's a fun experiment if you have a pile of .25 ACP cases in a coffee can. Even when primers and ammo have been hard to find, I have had no trouble locating 209 primers. These can be loaded with .25 ACP bullets, .25-caliber airgun slugs or, in my case, I plan to neck them down to .22 in my Mantis dies. We never tested this one as we had more ideas to follow up on.

The next idea was much simpler ...

The 209 primers will fit into the base of a .22 Magnum chamber. It will not headspace because the rim of the primer is about .021-inch thick versus the rim of a .22 Magnum, which is nominally .050-inch thick. The good news is that the 209 rim is wider than the rimfire case. A quick modification of a Contender barrel in .22 Magnum allowed the 209 primers to chamber and "headspace" on the primer rim, providing a well-sealed breech when the barrel was closed. Because you can use a Contender for rimfire or centerfire, it makes the testing easy. By the way, this modification did nothing to hinder the use of .22 Magnum ammo in the same chamber.

We did not add powder because there would be no case with the 209 primers seated this way. The first tests were with .22 pellets and then slugs. Airgun companies offer lead slugs in .22 caliber, so I ordered various weights for our tests, all in .217- and .218-inch diameters with hollow bases.

Dropping a projectile into the chamber is not likely to produce the best accuracy. Uniformity is the key to accuracy with all ammo and guns.

That's true with alternative ammo, as well. We created a bullet seater for each gun to give the best opportunity for accuracy and avoid mishaps due to inconsistent seating.

The first test of this barrel was a massive surprise to me regarding the accuracy of the Crossman Red Flight Penetrator and the heeled 30-grain lead bullets from North American Arms.

Using a seating rod to ensure we placed the projectiles in the exact location shot to shot, we started at just 10 feet. We started that close because we had not put sights on the barrel yet and to ensure the hits were on the paper. By aiming the top of the barrel at the target, we had groups with most of the shots in an inch and a half with the pellets. We switched to the lead bullets. The group shifted slightly to the right but was the same size with several flyers.

With sights installed on the barrel, I fired 10 shots for velocity. The group size at 15 feet was the same, about 1.5 inches. The barrel was dirty enough at the end of the 10-shot group that the primers no longer dropped out and required some effort to remove from the chamber, although the extractor easily pulled them out. The barrel length for the chart below is 9.5 inches with iron sights.

LOAD	PROJECTILE (GR.)	VELOCITY (FPS)	ACCURACY @ 50 FEET (IN.)
Fiocchi 209	(Red Flight Penetrators)	630	1.50
Fiocchi 209	32.4 (Hunting Pellet)	451	.900
Fiocchi 209	26 (.217-in. Slug)	403	.600
Fiocchi 209	37 (.218-in. Slug)	327	1.00
Winchester 209	(Red Flight Penetrators)	800	2.00
Winchester 209	32.4 (Hunting Pellet)	479	1.00
Winchester 209	26 (.217-in. Slug)	489	2.00
Winchester 209	37 (.218-in. Slug)	415	.750

.22 Mantis (.22 MMCW or .22-25 ACP)

My .22 Mantis wildcat is not a new idea. Many before me have made .22/25 ACP ammo. Bill Eichelberger had his .22 Dart. I had a customer, Dave Epperson, who created the .22 Epperson Cricket. Other names include the .22 Pokey and the .224 Montgomery. They all produce very similar results, with little room to play with. The Mantis has the shortest neck of all these variations. Robart Schaefer calls it the .22 MMCW, which stands for Montgomery, Mantis, Cricket, Whatever.

It's a very easy wildcat for which to form brass. Schaefer made a reloading die in my shop and heat-treated it. Using a TC Contender barrel, I carefully ensured the headspace was zero.

I have heard people complain of accuracy issues with the various versions of the .22/25 ACP. One creator used drill bits to make his chamber, which was not the best for accuracy. I used a chamber reamer and gauges, and my accuracy results have been under 1 inch with all the early test loads.

This wildcat may be one of the most useful .22 ammo alternatives, although it requires a centerfire gun. It works great in a Contender pistol.

LOAD (GR.)	PROJECTILE (GR.)	VELOCITY (FPS)
1.8 Bullseye	39 Armscorp	1,492
2.2 Bullseye	39 Armscorp	1,621

Tim Montgomery wrote to me about his .224 Montgomery. Having shot the

The .22 Cricket.

The author's .22 Mantis wildcat.

The .224 Montgomery.

cartridge extensively since 1990, He reports half-inch groups at 100 yards. His favorite load is VV 3N37 with a 40-grain bullet at about 1,650 fps, which gave good brass life and accuracy. He uses a .125-inch neck length and a case length of .615 inch. His gun is a 12-inch Contender pistol.

Bulk Rimfire Ammo Accuracy

This section discusses how to make the best of factory-loaded rimfire ammo. The short answer is yes; you can do a few things to get better accuracy results. It's an axiom that uniformity of ammunition improves accuracy.

Sorting by Rim Thickness

Neil Jones Custom Products offers a rim thickness sorting tool for rimfire ammo. The tool is simple, tough and maybe the fastest way to sort your rimfire ammo for rim thickness.

Neil Jones offers a standard rimfire tool, and you can purchase an additional insert for Magnum rims. This tool and *all* others used to sort rim thickness allow you to have the ammo in sorted lots for equal headspace (uniformity).

When firing groups, use ammo that all has the same rim thickness. Statistically speaking, this will produce better accuracy on the target than leaving the mixed-thickness ammo unsorted. The improvement in accuracy can vary widely but typically improves group sizes.

21st Century Innovation offers a rimfire gauge with a dial indicator to read rim thickness to check standard LR ammo or magnum rimfire with the same tool.

Bald Eagle Precision rim thickness gauges use a dial indicator and are about as simple as any tool in this market.

Raven Eye Custom's rim thickness gauge can be used with a dial indicator or a dial caliper, which you supply. The instruction sheet is well thought out and offers a lot of

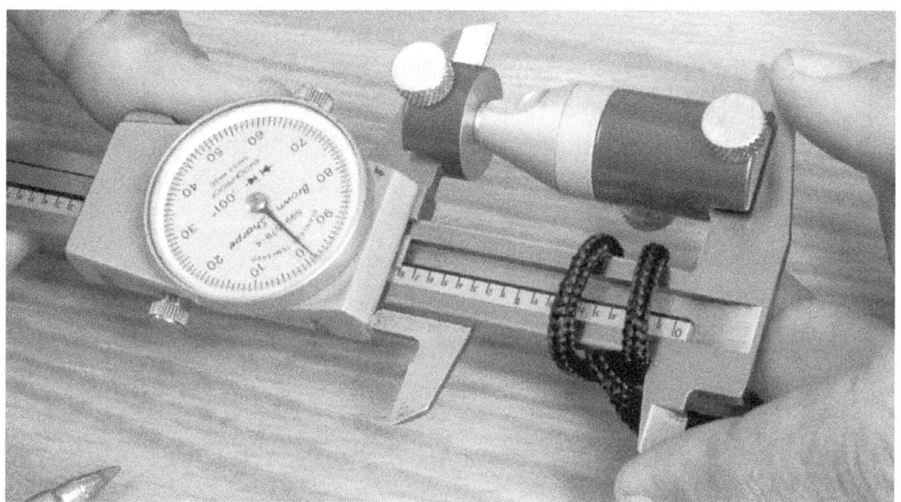

useful information, which indicates that the tool is well-designed.

Gehmann .22 LR rim thickness gauge. Gehmann is a German maker of Competitive shooting supplies. This gauge works the same way as the Neil Jones one, with a sliding bar, allowing you to sort your ammo visually.

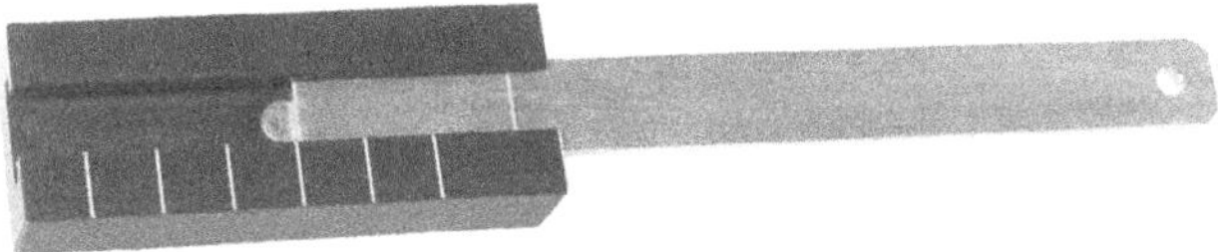

Hornady's Lock-N-Load 17-22 Rim Thickness Gauge is another tool to sort ammo by rim thickness. It attaches to your dial caliper and includes bushings for use with most .17- and .22-caliber rimfire ammo, except .17 WSM. The tool requires you to understand how to read a dial caliper, or you could opt for a model with a digital readout.

Sorting by Weight

Sorting cheap and medium-grade rimfire ammunition by weight will sometimes improve accuracy. The process is simple. Weigh each round of ammunition and sort it into batches by weight. An electronic scale will speed the process along. If you try this method, sorting by rim thickness first works even better.

However, if you're a competitive shooter, find the premium ammo that works best in your gun. By sorting it, the premium match ammo will be improved little, if any. Most shooters decide there is no reason to sort match-grade ammo—it's much better quality.

Another option is to measure the overall length from the case head to the bullet's ogive.

Check the Concentricity

Nielson Brothers Arms' Concentricity Gauge is the only gauge that measures bullet runout in rimfire ammo. On his website, Lester L. Nielson has a report of the tests he performed that proved the value of sorting for concentricity. Not many folks have the proof for their theory to go with the products they create, but Nielson does.

He says he sorts for rim thickness and bullet concentricity to the axis of the case. Measuring concentricity has proven to shrink groups, and competitive shooters looking for every edge should be measuring their ammo and sorting. Most concentricity gauges are set up for larger centerfire ammo and will not accommodate small rimfire cases. However, this tool by Nielson is designed just for small rimfire cases.

The bottom line is that all these methods involve sorting ammunition for uniformity. Uniform ammo is more accurate.

Options Beyond Sorting

Cutting Edge Bullets offers reloading dies and shell holders for .22 LR ammo and a handy loading tray for .22 LR. Most importantly, it offers several different rimfire bullet weights: 22-, 32-, 42- and 50-grain copper bullets. These bullets are lathe-turned, producing the best in uniformity, and all are the heeled type, which is necessary for rimfire cases.

Cutting Edge put its sense of humor out front with this product, marketing it as the cure for "Projectile Dysfunction." It ships with 200 pills in each prescription. I would bet the 50-grain match bullets are accurate in a 100-yard rimfire match.

Dies for Accuracy Improvement

The ammo shortage in recent years highlighted a couple of things concerning .22 ammo. One was it sucks when you can't get ammo. The other is that you want to make every shot count. When I was a kid, my Dad would buy a few boxes or a brick of .22 ammo, and we would shoot it all up on the weekend. I know he bought ammo for .69 cents a box, and I am sure it was $5 a brick on sale. When it was that cheap, we never worried about super accuracy because we would shoot until that pop can was *dead*.

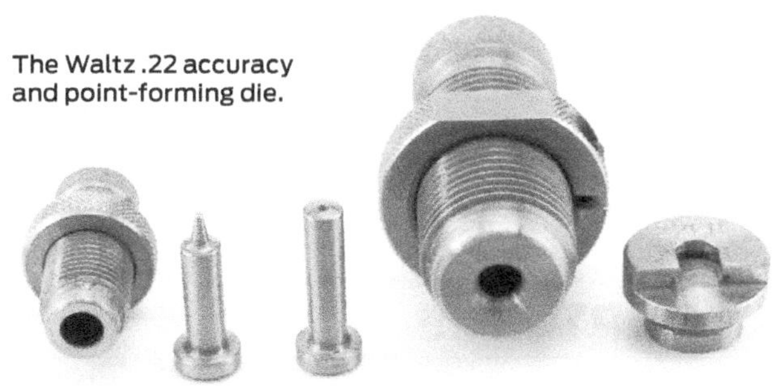

The Waltz .22 accuracy and point-forming die.

Today, the cost of ammo is a real factor in how much you can plink, so getting the most out of it is more of a concern. We need the can to die on the first shot. This is at least part of why the clever shooters develop tools to improve the cheap bulk ammo—so it shoots more accurately.

Neal Waltz is a retired machinist from Ohio who makes a swaging die that improves accuracy. The die swages a .22 bullet to a uniform size. (To be clear, we're working with loaded ammo here.) Waltz's die is ingenious because it can modify ammo with a target-style nose, like Eley's target ammo. Or you can create a hollowpoint of various depths, depending on your desire. The die comes with a shell holder for .22 LR and is self-storing for the two included nose punches. Set it up in any standard loading press and go to work.

The inside of the die is concentric and lapped to .225 inch so that you are also swaging the bullet up in diameter while repointing the projectile. It's less the increase in diameter and more the uniformity of all your ammo that improves accuracy. If you're shooting weekend matches with your buddies, this little trick could improve your score dramatically. Having seen this concept used in various guns, it nearly always reduces group size by about 50 percent with cheap ammo. The results will not be dramatic if you're already paying for match ammo.

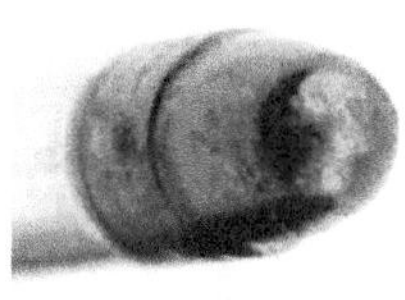

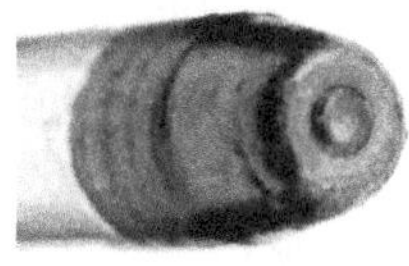

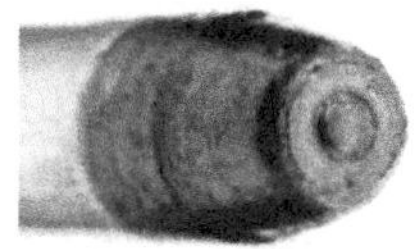

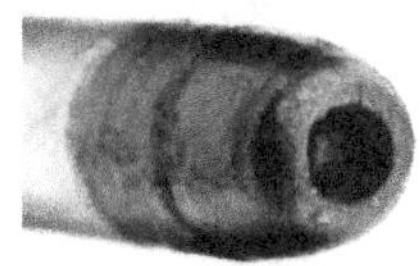

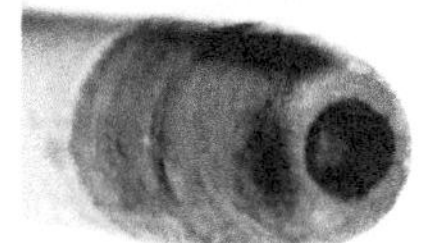

The two rounds at the top are unmodified bulk ammo. The center two are repointed with the target point, a semi-wadcutter form. The bottom two have been converted to hollowpoint.

CHAPTER 25

Armscor M22 TCM BA: Wanderings with a Micromagnum

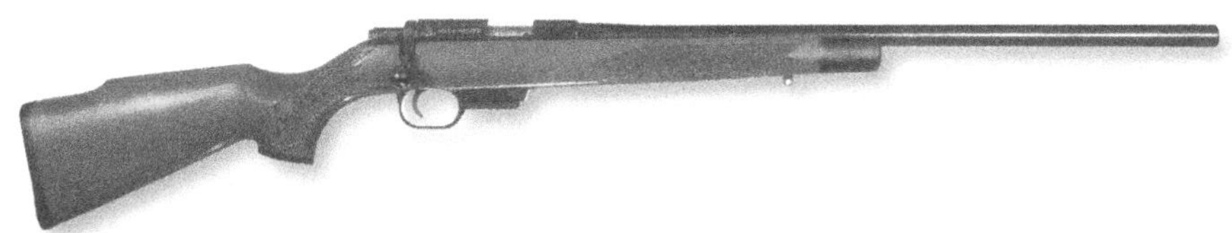

Confession time. I eagerly waited for the gun—announced in 2014 at the SHOT Show—to become available. Armscor designated it the M22 TCM BA. The caliber is .22 TCM, the barrel length is 22 inches, and it has a five-shot double-stack magazine. TCM stands for .22 TCM, for Tuason-Craig-Micromagnum.

Like any new gun, we cleaned and oiled the parts. I picked mine up the first chance I had, about two years after the announcement. The idea of a bolt-action rifle that handles pistol-length cartridges has long interested me. After all, if you're a wildcatter, it's a platform that could be a lot of fun.

If you're unfamiliar with the .22 TCM, it's about the same length as the .38 Super. Armscor uses 1911 double-stack magazines for this cartridge in its pistols.

Naysayers will complain that there is no real reason for such a gun because it lacks power and range. As a gunsmith, I will evaluate it with a professional eye toward making a good rifle out of it.

Frankly, most factory guns are lacking in some way from a custom gunsmith's perspective. The question is, is it cost-effective? In other words, is it worth the effort to work with the gun? I dove in, hopeful the Armscor TCM rifle would be

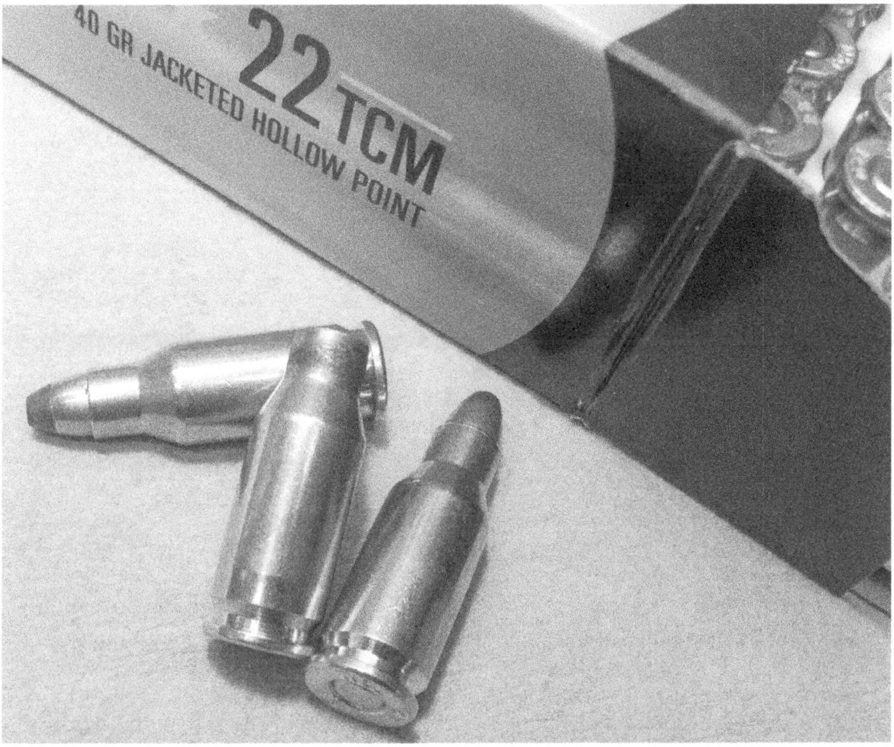

Factory ammo. The expansion of the fired cases is more than usual, but it is not a safety issue.

a good product. You may have guessed from my wildcat comment that this rifle will go through several calibers before I finish.

In this book, I have mentioned a young gunsmith, Robart Schaefer. Schaefer, a Trinidad graduate, also bought a TCM rifle and quickly began customizing the action and stock. We agree that the stock doesn't look bad, but it feels like a 2x4 in your hands. The grip is thick and oversized in every way. The stock is thick and bulky. Since it's a Philippine hardwood, I would bet it's a strong stock. The wood is soft

The neck area of the chamber. The large vertical shadow in the center of the picture is the case mouth area. On the left is the rifled bore. The chamber has a radius where it meets the bore. This is unusual as we usually see a 45-degree angle from the case mouth to the bore. Of more importance is the total lack of a throat in the chamber. Admittedly, the factory ammo uses light bullets with steeply tapered ogive bullets. However, that does not mitigate the need for a uniform throat to accept the bullet, giving the bullet the best possible launch into the rifling for accuracy.

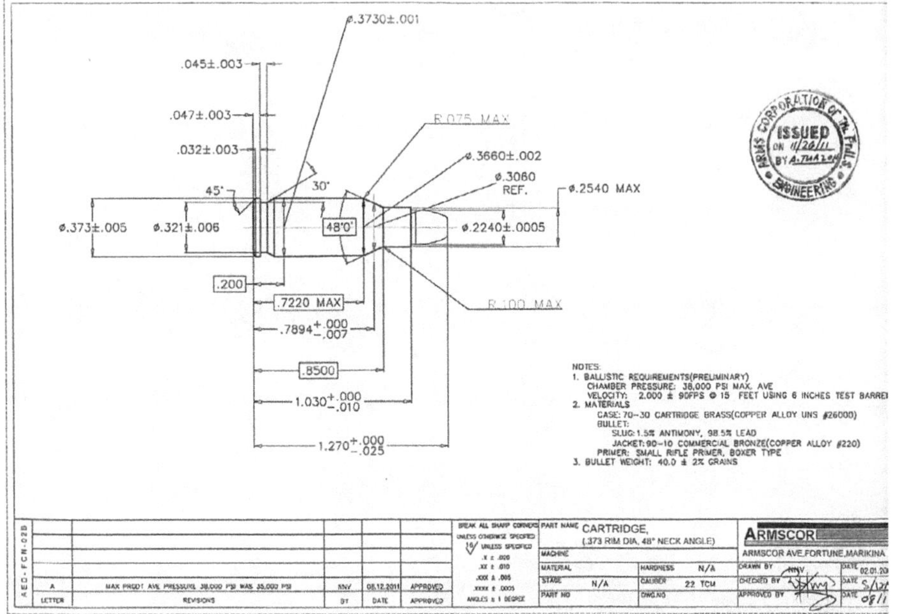

Factory ammo dimensions. It is essential to remind the reader that there are tolerances in manufacturing.

compared to walnut or other common gunstock woods, but considering it's designed for the .22 TCM's low recoil, it is functional and would make a good truck gun for the ranch or farm.

The gun has no typical recoil lug—the trigger/magazine housing acts as one. With a low-recoil rifle, it's easy to see why Armscor went this route. We added recoil lugs to our custom versions to improve accuracy and because we planned to test heavier recoiling cartridges.

The trigger pull from the factory on my rifle was about 4.5 pounds and reasonably crisp, a pleasant surprise as most factory triggers have a heavier pull weight and far too much sear engagement (creep). The striker fall was not authoritative, and it sounded like a rimfire action, which immediately made me wonder about reliability and accuracy. But, I firmly believe in range testing, not making assumptions without real-world experience. The safety is mounted on the right side of the tang behind the bolt knob. It operates quietly, if a little stiff, with no function issues.

Some shooters have reportedly been unhappy with the quality of the M22 TCM's barrel. (The 22.75-inch barrels have six-groove rifling with 1:16-in. twist.) One of the first things that Robart and I did was to borescope the barrels on our two guns. The results were *not* awe-inspiring.

I ordered five boxes of factory ammo, and the cost was very reasonable, with 50 rounds per box. I was glad to see that there was more than one lot of ammo: that slight variation allowed us to test reliability. (This was with standard brass before the 9R nickel-plated brass Armscor now offers.)

If you have a 1911 in the .22 TCM, the information here does not apply because the systems are different. The 1911 has a heavy firing pin that delivers a positive strike to the primer. The handgun is also a delayed blowback semi-auto with a large extractor, not to mention that the firing pin can travel as far as necessary to set off the primer. So, the ammo's headspace variances do not present any problems in the 1911.

The ammunition we received was all within normal factory tolerances. The neck diameter was .251 inch on loaded rounds, which, in my chamber, meant the brass expanded .007 inch in diameter when fired (.004 is considered standard among custom gunsmiths). I also noted that my fired brass measured .004 inch in diameter *over* the maximum chamber dimensions along the body. That's not a crisis, but it means accuracy will suffer slightly. Also, if dies were made to minimum dimensions, resizing would overwork the brass, reducing brass life.

Chambers have tolerances, and some shooters do not realize this. Typically, we allow about .002 inch of expansion on the case body and up to .004 inch on the neck for a quality standard chamber. A match chamber halves these numbers. However, tightening the dimensions is unnecessary if the dies match the chamber. Using a bushing-type neck-sizing die can reduce the amount of brass you must size to increase accuracy.

Range Time

On our first trip to the range, we wanted to shoot the rifle as it came from the factory with no modifications. We started shooting at 100 yards at an indoor range (no wind to contend with). We chronographed the factory ammo since people reported low velocities compared to advertised speeds. We fired 17 shots of factory ammunition to begin, 12 rounds from the

The primer on the left represents the average fired case. The one on the right was a misfire caused by insufficient energy to fire the cartridge reliably.

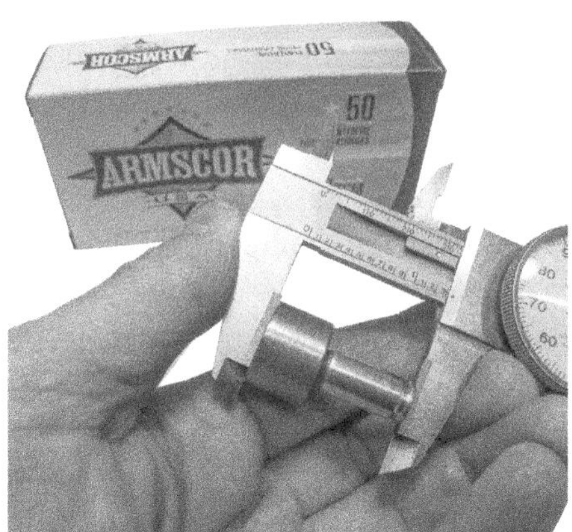

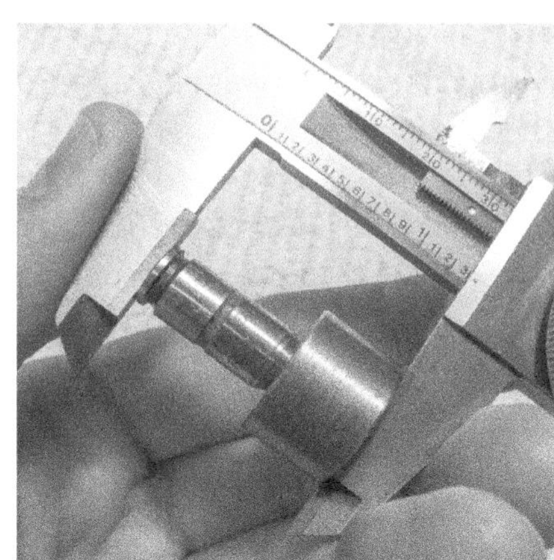

Checking the brass against the Go gauge.

first lot of ammunition in two strings. The average velocity for that first string was 2,802 fps—precisely as the factory reported. The extreme spread was 57 fps.

But the groups were nothing to write home about. (Although a better scope might have helped since we mounted a cheap 3-9x variable for the test. We used stronger glass to remove that variable during the next range test.) Groups for this test averaged 2.5 inches at 100 yards, or Minute of Coyote.

The second string, from the same ammunition lot, gave an average velocity of 2,816 fps, with virtually identical extreme spread. The standard deviation for both groups was in the 20s; nothing exciting to talk about there. The big news is that the factory gun with factory ammo produced the advertised velocity. Of course, every barrel is like a snowflake, so results would necessarily vary.

We switched ammo lots to see if there was any significant change in results. Five shots from this lot produced an average velocity of 2,821 fps, and accuracy was identical to the other lot. By this point, we had learned enough about the rifle and ammo to stop the test.

During test firing, we had a couple of problems that we needed to address before the tests could progress with any expectation of improvement. The bolt lift was stiff with all loads. There were no other signs of pressure, so it was likely a mechanical issue that we needed to track down.

We had three misfires. The first time, we re-cocked the rifle and fired a second time, and the round went off. The following two times, we retained the rounds for photos.

If I were trying to enhance accuracy at this point, I would have recrowned the barrel. However, I was still trying to improve the rifle's function and get the factory loads to fire, extract and eject as they should.

Back at the gunsmithing bench, we measured brass and looked for anomalies to help us diagnose mechanical and accuracy problems. In addition to the chamber cut somewhat oversized, we made a ring gauge and measured the fired cases for headspace. As you know by now, from reading about tolerances in headspace, they are specified to allow the safe operation of any given firearm with ammunition from any given maker or lot of the same caliber/cartridge.

There is only one maker of ammo and guns for the .22 TCM currently, but these rules still apply. The tolerances are as follows: Go gauges for a specified caliber could be considered a '0' measurement. This is the minimum and ideal for the chamber. The No-Go gauge is usually .004 inch longer—the bolt should not close on this gauge. When true, the gun has the best headspacing for accuracy and longevity. There is also a Field gauge, which is .004 inch longer than the No-Go. If the bolt will close on a Field gauge, it is considered unsafe and should be corrected or retired.

SAAMI's standard for ammunition and chambers defines how they should be measured even when the cartridge is not SAAMI-recognized, as with the .22 TCM. Generally, ammunition headspace is established about .003 inch shorter than the standard minimum chamber for a given caliber. This rule of thumb is a generalization but is a mechanically sound assumption. The Pacific Tool & Gauge (PTG) print for the .22 TCM follows this principle, and the ammo we bought from Armscor falls in this tolerance range.

The factory gun had an interesting result. It measured well with headspace gauges: we could feel the Go gauge when the bolt closed, and the bolt would not close on the No-Go gauge—precisely as it should be. However, fired

Photo shows the bolt handle after lapping, which increased the contact area by about 90 percent.

The opposing lug shown here is fully in contact. It has approximately the same area as the lapped area, and you can see where the bluing was removed during the lapping process.

brass headspace measured .009-inch long on average. This measurement is accomplished with a ring gauge. The gauge is .300-inch diameter inside and is .500-inch long. It measures on the datum of the case; subtract the gauge length, and you have the overall headspace dimension. If the gun headspaces correctly, how could this happen?

Remember how the bolt lift was stiff? That is a hint to this headspace problem. We looked at the bolt lugs and noted that they only touched on about 10 percent of one lug. That will allow a lot of spring in the action when fired. The bolt thrust forces the bolt lugs back against the locking recesses in the action. Since only one side was in contact, the lugs were twisted slightly—naturally, the case formed to fill the extra space created by the spring of the bolt. So, as we lifted the bolt handle, we must, in effect, resize the case slightly to get the bolt open. The solution? Lap the lugs. The M22 TCM rifle's design provides for large locking surfaces once they are lapped into contact.

We borescoped the barrel and found that there was essentially no throat in the chamber. This condition can promote pressure and is hard on accuracy. For best accuracy, the bullet needs a concentric uniform space to launch into the rifling. I decided to use my new PTG .22 TCM reamer and clean up the chamber, cutting a throat in the chamber and cleaning up the case mouth area to make it more conventional. I set the headspace with gauges to '0' again.

The keyboard commandos on forums suggest putting a second spring in the bolt to boost the firing pin strike. However, if the springs are not counter-directionally wound, they will eventually become tangled and reduce reliability. A new spring with a larger wire diameter is the ideal solution. We could not find one in time for this second test, so we used a field expedient repair, stretching the spring about .500-inch longer than the factory. This mod is a temporary fix, as it doesn't increase power but only ensures full travel of the firing pin

When the author faced the receiver, it was far out of square, which is common on production firearms. Note on the right of the photo the white metal where the cutter touched first while facing, indicating the face is not square to the axis of the action.

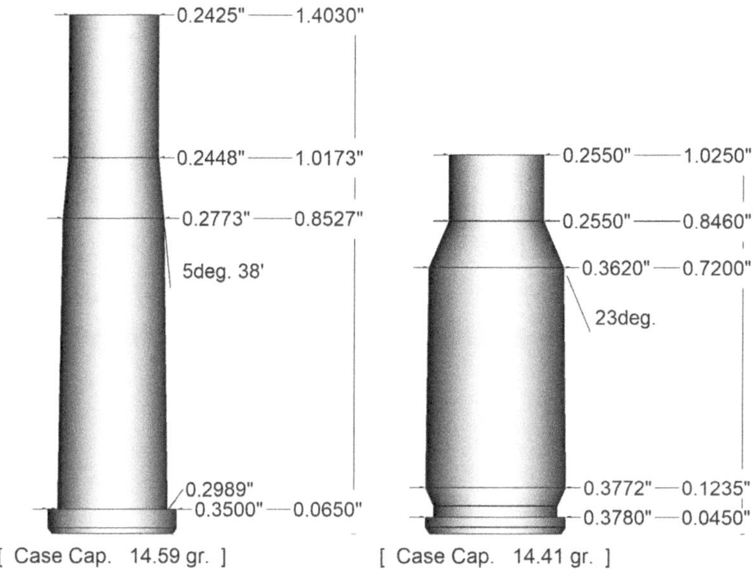

(and perhaps faster lock time).

The tunnel in which the firing pin spring rides was rough, and it rubbed. So, we polished the tunnel with 400-grit sandpaper on a mandrel until the spring moved in and out without interference. Then, we cleaned and oiled the bolt.

Second Trip to the Range

After changing the throat and firing pin spring, the average velocity was 2,764 fps. We experienced four misfires in about 25 shots—all fired when we re-cocked the action and shot a second time. So, this issue needed more attention. The bolt lift after firing was still stiff, although much better than during the first test. Even with the better scope installed, the accuracy was steady at 2.5 inches at 100 yards.

Inspecting fired cases indicated a slight Coke bottle effect on the brass, indicating that the chamber was not machined correctly, and the area near the shoulder was slightly larger than the area behind it on the case body. That made cases harder to extract, potentially adding to the bolt lift problems. We're only talking about .0002 inch, so it's not something you would see with your bare eyes. We took careful measurements to determine the actual numbers.

The fired cases' headspace was consistently .008-inch longer than the chamber, indicating some stretching of the action. The more serious concern was when we measured the factory ammo versus the fired cases, which grew an average of .016 inch. They were stretching dramatically.

I considered the factory barrel and chamber un-serviceable. So it was time to install a new barrel, a Green Mountain air-gauged blank, 1:14 twist. We also faced the receiver to ensure it was square to the action threads, which often improves accuracy.

Another accuracy issue was that the bolt handle was contacting the stock. We relieved the stock around the bolt handle so it no longer touched.

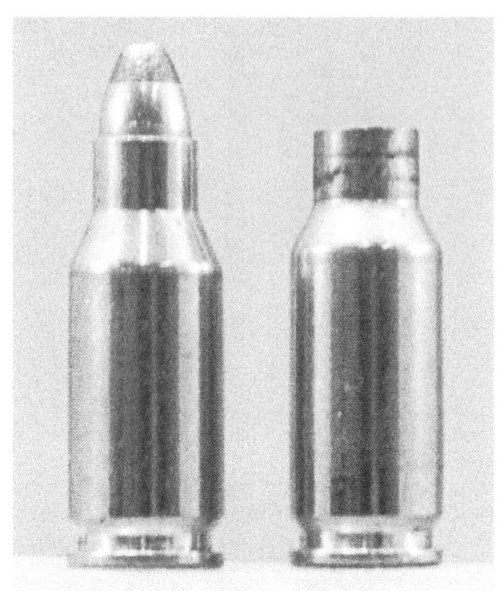

A factory round of ammunition next to a fireformed case in the new configuration.

Using the correct gauges, we carefully set the headspace on the new barrel to the minimum. Factory ammo cycled through it just fine. However, it appeared that the two lots of ammo we had both measured about .009 inch excess headspace, meaning that the factory set the shoulder down .009 inch from the specified chamber length. That is within the range of a field gauge, so it is technically safe to fire.

We test-fired two rounds. Both caused the bolt to stick and were very hard to extract. Even so, the M22 TCM's extractor is darn tough; it managed to extract these stuck cases without any ill effects.

The firing pin strikes were crisp and the correct depth into the primers. Still, the factory ammo showed signs of pressure. We considered lengthening the throat to alleviate it, but that would be getting ahead of the curve with reloading results. The fired factory cases measured 0.019-inch longer than unfired ammo, making them 0.010-inch or 10/1,000th longer than they should be (.009-inch headspace in the factory ammo allows for a slamming effect when the cases stretch, which may account for at least some of the additional length. Further tests will prove this out).

At that point, we began loading our ammo to get around the factory ammunition problems. We used Lee Pacesetter dies in .22 TCM to resize the fired cases in a Hollywood Turret press. We bumped the shoulders back to set the headspace to zero so the bolt would close effortlessly on each case. The case shoulders wanted to spring back a bit. So, I faced off the bottom of the sizing die to correct the headspace.

I wanted to try a few bullets just for function, so I only loaded two of each starting load. Research revealed that the TCM has a capacity nearly identical to the .22 K-Hornet, making it easy to find a moderate starting point for loads.

H110 STARTING LOADS	COL = 1.270 IN. (GR.)	COMMENTS
28 Kirksite cast	10.0	Easy bolt lift
40	10.0	Easy bolt lift
45	10.0	Stiff bolt, still too hot

A quick trip to the range yielded the above results. These were function tests to see if we were in a safe pressure range. The results indicated unusually high pressures with the 45-grain bullet, which should have been moderate. I used a Pacific Tool & Gauge precision throater to extend the throat by .025 inch (compared to the factory load). Now, with a 40-grain jacketed bullet, I have .110 inch of freebore. Of course, the freebore measurement can vary depending on the shape of the bullet's ogive, so the .110 inch is with the factory ammo only.

A longer throat will reduce pressure because the bullet can gain momentum before it engages the rifling. Secondly, the bullet easily moving into the freebore effectively increases the case capacity. Between the two, pressures with the same load can drop substantially. Some velocity may be sacrificed, but for the increased flexibility in loading, I'm more than willing to accept that. I looked at it this way: If a 45-grain bullet with 10 grains of H110, which should have come in as a medium-velocity load, showed pressure, the throat was too short.

Another change we made to the action was the installation of Talley scope mounts. I had a set on hand that matched the contour of the receiver; it eliminated the dovetail mounts clamped on the receiver, which is OK for rimfires but not too good for a centerfire with more recoil.

While we were installing the mounts, I also installed some set screws under the scope mount screws to remove some of the slop from the bolt fit to the receiver. I adjusted the set screws so the bolt was forced down onto the action's raceway but still moved freely for bolt cycling. From the factory, the bolt has significant movement in the receiver, which may hurt accuracy—it also seemed to promote our misfire problems.

The new scope mounts are very rigid, and we saw no accuracy issues that could be attributed to them or the scope in the latest test. We had no misfires on the next trip to the range; loads are listed in the following chart. Accuracy improved, so the removal of play between the bolt and the action with the set screws proved a success. This mod will lead to sleeving the bolt at a later date.

Below is the round of testing ammo with the longer throat. The velocities are the average of five shots of each load.

POWDER = H110	COL (IN.)	CHARGE (GR.)	VELOCITY (FPS)	COMMENTS
28 Kirksite cast	1.225	10.0	–	5.0 at 50 yards, wrong twist
40 Sierra #1100	1.290	10.0	–	1.10 at 50 yards
45 Hornady #2229	1.265	9.5	–	0.75 at 50 yards
40 TCM HP	1.270	10.0	2,662	3.00 at 100 yards
39 TCM JHP	1.270	10.0	2,654	1.25 at 100 yards
POWDER = UNIQUE	**COL (IN.)**	**CHARGE (GR.)**	**VELOCITY (FPS)**	**COMMENTS**
30 heeled lead	1.235	3.5	–	Shotgun accuracy at best
POWDER = WIN 296	**COL (IN.)**	**CHARGE (GR.)**	**VELOCITY (FPS)**	**COMMENTS**
40 TCM HP	1.270	10.0	2,654	0.50 at 100 yards, accuracy load
39 TCM JHP	1.270	10.0	2,672	1.375 at 50 yards
POWDER = IMR 4198	**COL (IN.)**	**CHARGE (GR.)**	**VELOCITY (FPS)**	**COMMENTS**
40 TCM HP	1.270	10.0	2,237	1.10 at 50 yards
39 TCM JHP	1.200	10.0	2,170	0.40 at 50 yards

Flat primers from factory loads.

Brass and bullets are available at excellent prices from ammosupplywarehouse.com and advancedtactical.com. They offer the TCM 40-grain hollowpoint with an exposed lead tip and the TCM 39-grain hollowpoint with the jacket to the hollowpoint cavity. Loads in the preceding chart with the TCM bullets starting at 10 grains extracted fine with no signs of pressure. So, one real solution to the problem is to drop the loads back to 2,650 fps or less for best results. However, that put the .22 Hornet ahead of the .22 TCM in velocity, so the testing continued.

I again tested some factory ammo on this last trip to the range, wondering if the changes to the gun might have solved the problems with the ammo—no such luck. Factory loads were overpressure, creating sticky bolt lift and expanded cases. There were no misfires, though.

You might be wondering about Armscor's 9R .22 TCM. I could not lay my hands on it at this writing. The only advertised difference is the seating depth of the bullet in the 9R ammo, which is deeper, so it will fit in a 9mm magazine. This feature might attract some conversion to TCM in other guns like Glock.

POWDER = H110	COL (IN.)	CHARGE (GR.)	VELOCITY (FPS)	COMMENTS
*40 Sierra #1100	1.290	10.5	2,792	Easy extraction
45 Hornady #2229	1.265	9.5	–	Easy extraction
40 TCM HP	1.270	11.0	–	
40 TCM HP	1.270	11.5	2,923	Overpressure
*39 TCM JHP	1.270	11.0	2,839	Functioned fine, maximum
39 TCM JHP	1.270	11.5	–	Overpressure
POWDER = WIN 296	**COL (IN.)**	**CHARGE (GR.)**	**VELOCITY (FPS)**	**COMMENTS**
40 TCM HP	1.270	11.0	–	Overpressure
39 TCM JHP	1.270	11.0	–	
POWDER = IMR 4198	**COL (IN.)**	**CHARGE (GR.)**	**VELOCITY (FPS)**	**COMMENTS**
40 TCM HP	1.270	11.5	2,569	Worked flawlessly
39 TCM JHP	1.200	11.5	2,496	Worked flawlessly

*These loads produced factory-advertised velocity with no stiff bolt lift.

My solution was to utilize the Ackley Improved concept. I had a reamer made with a 30-degree shoulder and headspace gauges to move the neck and shoulder junction back far enough to headspace properly with the factory ammo.

By then, I had decided to test the idea in a TC Contender barrel. It was a .22 LR originally, and I like the Contender for testing wildcats when appropriate. And this is certainly a time when it worked fine. After rechambering to the new TCM Improved specs, it was time to test-fire with the factory ammo first.

Factory ammo from the 14-inch Contender's test barrel shot well with a tight group at 50 feet using a 2x pistol scope. The average velocity was 2,784 fps. Extraction was stiffer than usual, and the brass showed some signs of pressure (flat primers). The primers were not as extreme as those pictured here. The rimfire bore is .222 inch in the grove rather than .224 inch, as with most centerfire .22s. This variance probably contributed to the velocity as it would increase pressure.

Factory ammunition did function in the contender barrel. The cases extracted, and I would consider that project a total success.

Next, I fired the same factory ammo in the TCM rifle with the new 30-degree shoulder. The pressure was very high, the bolt lift was stiff, and it required a mallet to open the bolt on the two rounds fired. Both bullets went into an oval-shaped hole. The average velocity of the two shots was 2,864 fps.

The whole point of this new chamber design was to get away from the pressure issues with factory loads. The test failed from that perspective. So, I cast the chamber to measure the actual freebore from the new reamer, which was .085 in. Usually, that would be enough, but when checking the ogive of the bullets used in the factory ammo, they were very close to the lands. The answer should be to extend the freebore to lower the pressure, then back to the range.

This bullet worked well to achieve velocity without pressure signs.

After reaming the chamber throat out to .125-inch freebore, we fired more factory ammo and found the velocity was down to about 2,790 average, but the bolt lift was still stiff. Extraction again required a mallet on the bolt handle. Not exactly the result we were looking for.

On the next page we toyed with the idea of a .17 TCM. Below is a picture of some dummies we made up; they are designed with the original shoulder angle of 23 degrees. The result is a short neck, but they would certainly work.

The final design included the 30-degree shoulder and improved case body like the .22 TCM Improved. That way, we could use the same headspace gauges for both cartridges.

Summing up, this is one time that the Ackley concept did not resolve the problem with factory ammo. Admittedly, I should have gone with the standard 40-degree shoulder, but I doubt it would have made any difference. I'm OK with that, but I would have liked to have factory ammo work in the gun. This is one of those times where there is no perfect solution. I did come up with reloads that produce the velocity as advertised without the sticky bolt lift of the factory ammo. So, partial success...

The reamer and gauges the author ordered from PTG for the .17 TCM Improved, 30 Degree. The neck on the reamer is noticeably longer than on the dummy rounds.

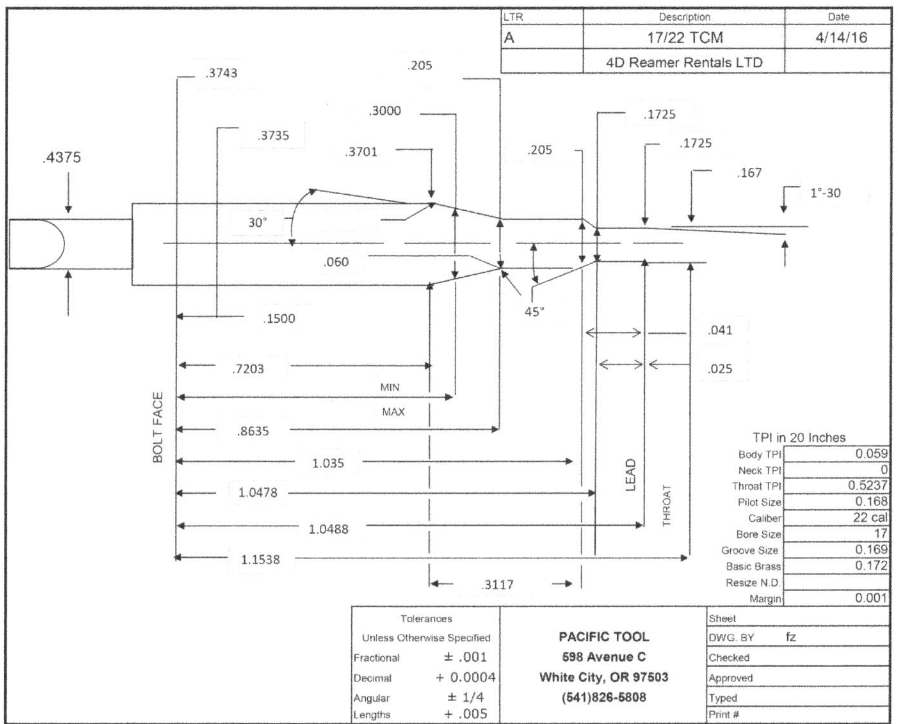

We have since decided to change our approach to the rifle with a sharp left turn. We may try a .24 TCM and have a 6mm barrel kicking around, and some light bullets would be fun in this cartridge—perhaps 60-grain Sierra BlitzKings or 75-grain Speer hollowpoints for varmints.

Some of the .17 TCM dummies the author made, which he designed with the original 23-degree shoulder angle. The result is a short neck, but they would certainly work.

Another Option

I considered trying the .17 TCM cartridge in the above print next in Armscor's M22. But for now, I'll chamber it in a contender barrel and have some fun. That's what makes wildcats intriguing ... always asking, "What if?"

AFTERWORD

The World's Most Accurate Wildcat

By Robart Schaefer

In the world of wildcatting, there are gods amongst men, those who are truly revolutionary and push the boundaries of what is possible. Greats like Kilborn and Newton were ahead of their time; Middlestead and Niedner had an eye for sophistication and refinement, while some like J.D. Jones squeezed every drop of case capacity out of cartridges—functionality be damned. Still, others created suitable little cartridges that have been around for years yet claim them as their own. Then, there is me, a great amongst greats—a genuine revolutionary, scholar, and genius—for I have created the world's most accurate cartridge.

Prepare to be amazed.

We must start with the most accurate caliber to make the most accurate cartridge. As we all know from years of advertisements and wankateering by firearms manufacturers and ammunition companies, 6.5mm is the most accurate bullet diameter (so long as it is in a new cartridge).

This revelation is a new development because 6.5mm has been around for years—even with a great selection of bullets, it wasn't until the 6.5 Creedmoor hit the market that it became a genuinely accurate caliber. The Swedes love 6.5mm; it has been their go-to caliber since the 1800s. As soon as the .308 Winchester came out, ten guys necked it down and stuffed a .264-inch bullet in it. Heck, Remington even made it a factory cartridge, but it made one colossal mistake: Remington gave it a lame name: The .260 Remington (ugh) ... no way could *that* be accurate.

However, the 6.5 Creedmoor has a pretty cool name. First, it's European-*ish* without being pretentious because they left out the metric-sounding part. And it has *Creedmoor* ... I don't know what that is, but I want one. It does everything that the .260 Remington does, except it's much harder to make the brass when you can't find it on the shelf. That also makes it better, I'm sure. To add to the 6.5mm's appeal, we also have the 6.5 PRC, which we know is accurate because Hornady says so right in the name: "Precision Rifle Cartridge." I know there are other PRC cartridges like the .300 and 7mm, and even though the 7mm is a little newer, the 6.5 hasn't lost all of its accuracy (yet). There are tons of high-BC bullets in 6.5mm, so even shooters who will never shoot past 100 yards at paper will feel like a real competitor or sniper. So, 6.5, it must be!

Regarding the case, I had to look into history to discover the true secrets of accuracy. You see, way back before jacketed bullets and smokeless powder, almost all cartridges used a rim to set headspace. I know what you're thinking: "Rimmed cases aren't accurate 'cause shotguns and revolvers have rims, and they aren't." But you see, this just isn't true. Back then, the rimmed cartridges were new and way better than paper cartridges, so hunters and competition shooters could get incredible accuracy and make outrageous shots. (Haven't you ever seen *Quigley Down Under?*) There are reports of hunters taking game at over 1,500 yds. These rimmed cartridges were capable of great accuracy and were the standard in precision shooting circles until most militaries moved to bottlenecked rimless cartridges.

Rimless cartridges use a prescribed diameter on the shoulder slope to set headspace, which was better at the time as it was all the rage. A few years later, Holland & Holland came out with a belted case, which it used for its headspace datum. The .300 H&H held records at Wimbledon for years and was so good that Winchester "Ackley improved" it, calling the cartridge the .300 Winchester Magnum (not an awesome name, but the magnum part is cool), and it became the standard for long-range shooting and is still used by military snipers.

These belts have another advantage: they give the illusion of extra strength. It looks more powerful; therefore, it is (in the minds of magazine writers and shooters alike). You would think that the cutting-edge technology at the time would have continued to be the best or would be supplanted by a new one. However, in recent years, there has been a fervent rejection of the belt, and almost all new rifle cartridges have regressed to the old rimless bottleneck style ... yet they have proven to be just as accurate.

Furthermore, the precision rifle crowd cannot agree on how to use headspace when resizing these bottleneck cartridges. Should you neck-size, bump the shoulder, or full-length size? Nobody knows; they say their way is better. It is only a matter of time before rimmed cartridges return—everybody knows how to headspace them. Therefore, I believe that headspace style, like accurate cartridge design, is fluid, changing with the turn of a magazine page or ad skip on YouTube.

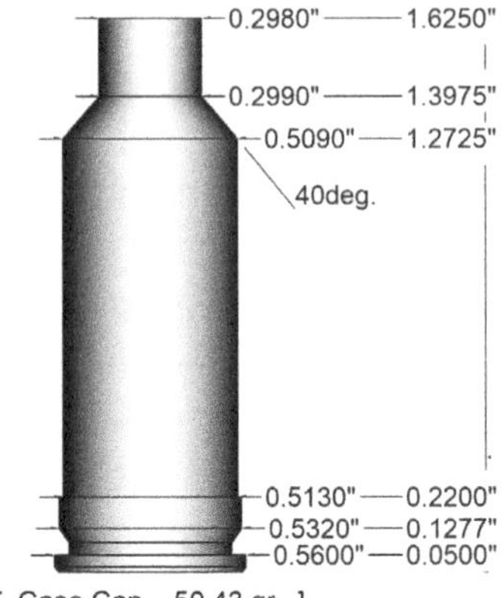

The 6.5 SSUPBRBRUM, pronounced *Soup-br-brum?*

So, to have the most accurate cartridge that can't fall out of favor, I had to use all three standard rifle headspacing techniques. Remington has "three rings of steel" for safety. My wildcat will have three rings of headspace for accuracy. Not only will it never fall out of favor with precision rifle shooters, but it will also always headspace correctly on at least one datum.

The 6.5 SSUPBRBRUM (6.5 Super Short Ultra Precision Belted Rimmed Benchrest Ultra Magnum) uses the .500 S&W as a parent case, which is high pressure and always has been, negating the need to find specific brands of brass, as one might need to do with an older rimmed cartridge like the .45-70. The rim thickness is trimmed to .050 inch to make it consistent. It has a belt swaged onto it, then it's necked to .26 caliber, with a 40-degree shoulder and minimal body taper. It has a maximum case length of 1.650 inches and a cartridge overall length of 2.5 inches. This profile (minus the rim and belt) is prolific in the precision rifle world today, with people claiming it is more efficient and provides a more consistent powder burn. I am of the mind that it looks cool; "*short and fat is where it's at.*"

As you can see, I have created the most accurate (probably the best) cartridge in the world and expect it to be picked up by a major manufacturer any day. With good looks, extreme accuracy, and headspace that never falls out of style, I expect it to be around long after I am gone.

Obviously, I'm being facetious (well, sort of). In all seriousness, wildcatting can be a never-ending source of entertainment. The hobby provides many hours at the reloading, shooting and gunsmithing bench. Do your research, learn from what came before and try to improve something.

What is your great idea going to look like?

–Robart Schaefer
Gunsmith & Comedian

APPENDIX I
Reloading Components and Dies

Alpha Munitions

Manufactures high-quality brass. The calibers offered will interest PRS and ELR shooters. Alpha has a process called "Optimized Case Design," which optimizes its designs' interior shape and case capacity. As part of this process, it touts "Optimized Case Head Technology."

In short, the case head technology refers to a proprietary alloy and heat treat of the brass. That process creates a grain structure and hardness in the case head that enhances case life, with primer pockets that do not deform as quickly as standard brass. Alpha says its field tests have shown case life that more than offsets the cost of this premium-quality brass. The 7mm SAW is the least well-known wildcat offering from Alpha.

Alpha also sells "Legacy" chamber reamers (carbide only), designed with its brass in mind. All critical reamer dimensions are guaranteed to be within 4 microns or 0.0001574803 inch, with most falling within 2 microns or 0.0000787402 inch. This means the reamer you purchase today will be virtually identical to the one you purchase in the future. That's a level of precision that is not common in the gun trade. *alphamunitions.com*

Bertram Brass USA

A master list of Bertram's cartridge cases can be found on its website. The more common calibers are usually on the shelf. Some of the more exotic offerings are on a special order basis and may take a few months to arrive. The list includes many obsolete and hard-to-find calibers.

Bertram USA rightly says that uniform internal case capacity is a better measure of potential accuracy than case weight. Of course, this assumes all the cases have the same characteristics within a brass lot. Mix lots, and all bets are off.

Bertram fills in voids in the market where other manufacturers fail to produce enough product to meet demand, making it a valuable source of brass. *bertrambrass.com*

Buffalo Arms

A reseller that stocks brass from many companies and carries tons of components for obsolete calibers, Buffalo Arms lists odd cases that some shooters have never heard of or have only seen in books. Best of all are the odd basic or cylindrical brass offerings, like .284 cases 2.40 inches long, .30-06 cylindrical 2.60 inches long, or .223 cylindrical 1.76 inches long, and even .30-30 Basic.

It catalogs brass shotgun shells in every gauge you could ever want for your low-pressure, large-diameter projects.

At the time of this writing, Buffalo carries reloading dies to match much of the brass it stocks. It's also a source of blackpowder and casting supplies. How about a .308-inch 98-grain TMJ projectile loaded in Nagant revolver rounds?

I have long used this company as a secret resource; I guess this wrecks the secret. In short, these guys are an excellent resource for reloaders and wildcatters! *buffaloarms.com*

Dixie Gun Works

Dixie Gun Works, or DGW, is a well-known reseller handling many blackpowder products. Where it serves wildcatters is with blackpowder basic cartridge cases. This lets you get your obsolete guns up and running and provides some rimmed cases in extra long basic form that you could wildcat on.

DGW is also an excellent source for bullet molds and cast bullets alike. *dixiegunworks.com*

Peterson Cartridge

Founded in Pittsburgh, Pennsylvania, by Derek Peterson and his two business partners, Peterson Cartridge began with a simple goal: producing extremely consistent, American-made brass rifle casings and precision ammunition designed for long-distance shooters.

You will not find any obsolete calibers here. Peterson is focused on the calibers that are currently popular with the mainstream of the shooting public. Think names like Creedmoor, Norma and Lapua. But it also has makes such as Weatherby, Nosler and others you would recognize.

While it primarily makes high-quality brass for the long-range and precision shooting crowd, Peterson has not forgotten the wildcatter and lists many cases that hold potential. Best, for readers of this book, Peterson has started offering what it calls "Wildcat Tubes." The rest of us call that basic brass. Do not overlook this brass resource on your next wildcat project. *petersoncartridge.com*

Quality Cartridge

I first met Pete Cardona of Quality Cartridge in the late 1990s while working on my own batch of wildcats—Hawk Cartridges—for which Cardona wanted to supply brass. At first, I had him make a bunter with "Hawk" on one side of the head and "Z-Hat" on the other. As demand made it worth the cost, we would add each caliber, so a bunter had to be made for each one.

Cardona produced brass for other wildcats then and was about the only place you could get headstamped cases for your wildcat without ordering 100,000 pieces. Over the years, we have stayed in touch, and every year at the SHOT show, we catch up on each other's work. It is downright amazing how much things have changed for both of us. But Pete has taken his business to the next level. He has continually added tooling, machines and automation to continue adding new products to his lineup.

You can find Quality Cartridge brass at Midway USA and Graf & Sons—two suppliers for wildcatters and reloaders to locate components and trust in delivery. Of course, you can order directly from Quality Cartridge, too. It's still in the wildcat game and has been helpful in the development of many popular wildcats over the years.

Quality Cartridge also catalogs a large number of obsolete cases with correct headstamps. If you're an avid reloader and collector, having properly marked brass is a real benefit, not just for obvious safety reasons but also for the simplicity of keeping things organized. It would be rough if you had 10 guns that all used .30-06 case heads but were in various bore diameters.

Expensive, you say? Not really, when you look at what factory ammo costs these days and then compare QC's custom brass. In most cases, it's a bargain, especially for obsolete cartridges. Reloaders often get caught up in quantity concerns, thinking they need several hundred rounds for each gun they own. While that can be true for the guns you shoot frequently, 100 rounds are enough for most folks. So, consider how much you will shoot that gun when deciding how much brass to buy. Often, the cost is much lower than you might guess.

Quality Cartridge offers an amazing variety. If time is short, the ready-to-load brass with the correct headstamp saves you much work at the loading bench. For those who want to do more of the work, Quality's basic brass (listed by the cartridge family) lets you control the forming and headspace to match your gun. And it offers most Ackley cartridges!

When I asked Cardona for a list of wildcat cartridges he has worked on since 2005, when the first edition of this book went to press, he sent the following:

- 5.7mm Demon
- 6mm Creedmoor
- 6mm Dirk
- 6.5 Grendel
- 6.5mm Creedmoor
- 6.5mm American
- .277 Wolverine
- .30 Hembrook Long
- .338 Baker
- .358 Baker
- .375 Bishop
- 8.6mm Blackout
- 9.3mm Baker
- .475 Bishop

Cardona included the Creedmoor and Grendel to highlight how fast a good idea can take off and become popular—not long after their introduction by many gun makers. *qual-cart.com*

Roberson Cartridge Company (RCC Brass)

While gathering information for this edition, Roberson Cartridge Company (RCC) announced it had ceased production. However, RCC produced many products, so the information below is useful as reference material since you may see it on the secondary market.

RCC manufactured brass cartridges for just about any cartridge you could imagine on CNC lathes and mills out of special C272 solid bar stock. Depending on the project, they were machined to SAAMI, CIP or customer specifications. Roberson had an extensive catalog of vintage drawings for customers seeking pre-SAAMI or CIP cartridges, often considered obsolete. It made wildcat brass from prints, fired cases and chamber casts, and you could have headstamped brass in hand before you even ordered your dies.

How RCC brass differed from traditional brass: The draw process has been used for cartridge manufacturing since the 19th century, and manufacturers have developed it to produce high volumes of brass cases. Draw cartridge manufacturers have tested many different types of materials over the years, and the best material for this process is a brass alloy with a mixture of 70 percent copper and 30 percent zinc.

When brass is cold-worked—by bending, drawing, compressing, and so forth—it hardens. Work hardening increases the tensile strength and decreases its elasticity. To accommodate today's high-pressure cartridges, brass must have a high tensile strength to withstand pressure spikes and elasticity to seal the chamber from gas blowby.

The draw process begins using a brass cup that is annealed and cleaned to remove any scale buildup that might have occurred. During the first draw, the cup is pushed through a die with a punch and extruded to lengthen it, which also work hardens it, so it must be annealed and washed for the second draw. Typically, a cartridge will go through four draws before it's ready for the next stage, where the case head will be turned, and primer pockets, flash holes, headstamps and necks are formed to complete the manufacturing process. After makers form the cartridge, they anneal it again and then polish it for shipping. During each annealing, they reduce the temperature to work harden the case for higher tensile strength and elasticity. The final annealing is to the case body at a lower temperature so it won't affect the hardness of the case head.

When brass is annealed at 250 degrees C, there is no visible change to the bonding of the grain structure, tensile strength or elasticity. At 300 degrees C, there is a microscopic change to the grain structure, and at 350 degrees, the work hardness becomes softer, and a fine grain structure can be seen. As temperatures increase, the brass becomes fully annealed and at 750 degrees C, you can see large crystals. Temperatures above this point will damage the brass.

The draw process facilitates mass production, but it's less consistent. That's why reloaders talk about using all one lot of brass; case weight, case volume, and concentricity are just a few of the variables that plague drawn brass. Test results have been positive for RCC-turned cases, with increased velocity and lower shot deviations versus C260 drawn brass.

RCC Brass had taken those variables out of the manufacturing process by having C272 cartridge brass hammer-forged into a tight molecular grain structure with high tensile strength, high yield strength and 15 percent malleability. By machining cases on CNC equipment, weight, volume and concentricity were among the best available in the industry. RCC didn't have to anneal case heads during manufacturing because the brass stock was hammer forged, providing the same hardness for each case.

C272 brass alloy has a much higher tensile strength, yield strength, and a tighter molecular grain structure than C260 brass yet retains needed malleability. But the real test was what you could do with RCC Brass reloading brass products. RCC brass met SAAMI and CIP pressure standards where applicable.

Once you placed your order, RCC processed it and forwarded it to the production queue, where an engineer reviewed it and emailed you a copy of the CAD/CAM cartridge drawing for confirmation. Customers were asked to review the drawing and submit changes if needed. Once the print was confirmed, the order went to the manufacturing process.

Services RCC Brass offered included:

- Manufactured to SAAMI, CIP or customer specifications
- Provided low-volume runs of 50 pieces
- Customized headstamps with a nominal setup fee and a 50-piece minimum order
- Manufactured wildcat cartridges; required a one-time setup fee and a 100-piece minimum
- Tested wildcat samples for a five-piece minimum (more expensive but cheaper than a new set of dies).
- Provided test samples for SAAMI, CIP, vintage or obsolete pricing available upon request

One important consideration. Do not use load data you developed with traditional drawn brass with RCC's machined cases. Start fresh and create new load data. My experience with turned cases involved low-pressure cartridges. RCC's use of hammer-forged material was how it handled higher pressures. As with all components, take things one step at a time and make no assumptions. Watch for stretch, expansion of the head and case life to know if you have safe loads.

RCC offered various wildcat cartridges in its listings, so you may find them at gun shows or online auctions.

.17 Cooper CCM	.22 Mink	.22/30-30 Win.
.17 Mink	.22 Newton	.22-303 British
.20 Mink	.22 Reed Express	.220 Jaybird
.20 Nosler	.22 Short–Centerfire	.220 Rook
.22 Cheetah MK I	.22 Spitfire	.220 Russian
.22 Chetah MK II	.22 Squirrel	.220 Wby. Rocket
.22 Cooper CCM	.22 WCF	.224 Harvey Kay-Chuk
.22 Dasher	.22 Win Mag - CF	.224 TTH
.22 Epperson Cricket	.22-15 Stevens	.225 Comet
.22 Hi-Power Ackley	.22-243 Middlestead	.226 JDJ
.22 LR-Centerfire	.22-243 Rayhill Rocket	

Starline

Starline Brass is a well-known company offering high-quality brass for reloaders. It has some obsolete calibers among its rifle brass but focuses more on mainstream cartridges. That makes sense when you think of Starlime as a production manufacturwer rather than a custom maker.

Starline lists a massive variety of rifle and pistol brass for nearly all current SAAMI cartridges. Some makers offer acceptable quality brass that will allow you to use your obsolete gun or create brass for your project. With Starline, you'll find the quality well worth the price—with consistency and accuracy you can count on from lot to lot.

Below are the more *unusual* offerings from Starline, which certainly catalogs many more than this. *starlinebrass.com*

.223 Basic	6.8 SPC Basic	Grendel Basic
.277 Wolverine	7.62x25 Tokarev	.300 HAM'R
.414 Super Mag.	.45 Raptor	12.7x42mm
.458 HAM'R	.500 Auto Max	.445 Super Mag.

Bullets

The bullet makers listed below produce bullets that are not in the mainstream of retail gun stores. Many make specialty bullets you will only find with small manufacturers as they fill a niche the bigger companies would not see as profitable.

Alco Bullets

Alco makes custom bullets for specialty uses. These projectiles are designed for off-the-shelf production guns, i.e., there is no need for special magazines or longer actions to accommodate them. Alco also produces custom pellets for large-caliber air rifles.

Alco's bullets and pellets are built on an Ultra-Low Drag (ULD) design and engineered with tight tolerances, which it says enhances accuracy. Alco precision long-range rifle bullets are available in .224, .284, .308, .338 and .457 calibers.

Alco Air Boss Ammo (pellet) was developed for Big-Bore PCP air rifles and is available in .308, .357, .457 and .510 calibers. *alcobullets.com*

Badlands Precision, LLC

Like many newer companies that have popped up in the last 20 years, Badlands specializes in lathe-turned copper bullets. Badlands claims to offer bullets with the highest ballistic coefficient of any solid copper bullet for any given caliber or weight combination. The bullets' profiles reportedly deliver performance on par with the highest BC lead core jacketed bullets.

The solid copper design reduces the contact surface area, allowing loading like any conventional bullet. No drive band restricts the COAL or requires single-shot restriction because they are too long to fit in the magazine box.

Check out Badlands' hunting bullets, called Bulldozers, and its long-range competition missiles, ICBMs. *badlandsprecision.com*

Berry's Manufacturing

Berry's offers more than 71 types of pistol bullets in 13 calibers ranging from .32 to .500.

Berry's pistol bullets are copper-plated and start with a swaged lead core formed under high pressure, which it says ensures uniform density and stabilizes bullets in flight. The core then undergoes a process known as electroplating, where it gets dipped in a copper sulfate solution, and an electric current is applied, depositing a layer of copper onto the lead core, effectively covering it and leaving no lead exposure. The copper plating provides a protective barrier for the lead, reduces barrel fouling and improves bullet performance.

After the electroplating process, the bullets are re-struck. This process involves passing the bullets through a die to ensure they meet precise specifications, such as overall length and diameter. The re-striking process reinforces the bond between the copper and the lead core and smoothens out any imperfections that may have been caused during electroplating. Finally, the bullets are thoroughly inspected for quality assurance.

Plated rifle bullets in .308 and .458 and a 123 gr. for 7.62x39 are all available. Berry's also stocks bulk-jacketed .223 bullets. *berrysmfg.com*

Cutting Edge Bullets

In 2001, Daniel Smitchko (Smitty) opened his CNC Swiss-style lathe shop, a machine known for machining tiny precision parts.

The shop was successful, but Smitchko realized that he wouldn't have proper control over its fate unless he developed a product line of his own. He combined his passion for precision machining with his obsession for long-range hunting.

After quickly coming up with a basic idea, research and testing began. A year and 47 revisions later, he had designed a bullet with a high ballistic coefficient and better-than-expected accuracy.

Cutting Edge's bullets are hollowpoint designs with a patented characteristic called a SealTite Band or Sealing Band, which seals the bullets into the barrel grooves. That prevents blowby in all but the most worn-out barrels. When fired, most other homogeneous copper bullets cannot upset, expand, or seal the bore. However, jacketed bullets can upset, so some solids do not shoot well in the occasional barrel.

As with all solids, start 10 percent below the published reloading data from a reputable source and work up to reach the desired pressure/speed. With careful development, you can often find a load that produces speeds equal to other bullets of identical weight. Sometimes, less powder will be needed because of the sealing band.

Cutting Edge offers a wide variety of bullet calibers and weights with many specialty designs for pistols and rifles. *cuttingedgebullets.com*

Warner Tool Company

Warner Tool Company, N. Swanzey, New Hampshire, offers high-BC Flatline bullets ranging from 6mm to .416 inch CNC lathe-turned into a monolithic solid copper design. These are long-range target bullets for competitions requiring high-BCs and surgical precision and accuracy. *warner-tool.com*

Hammer Bullets

Hammer Bullets are also custom-turned on a CNC lathe from solid copper. Each bullet is weighed and micrometer-measured as it's produced. The result is an incredibly consistent product with premium quality control for target shooting and hunting applications. The Hammer Bullets design has a U.S. patent.

Hammer can quickly produce virtually any custom caliber and weight your rifle can support. So, this is a zone for custom wildcat applications.

The hollowpoint design, intended for big game hunting, initiates expansion upon impact and sheds petals immediately, with the remainder of the bullet staying intact with a blunt front for an optimal wound channel.

As with all monolithic turned bullets, they tend to be long for their weight, so carefully note your barrel's twist rate. *hammerbullets.com*

Hawk Bullets

Hawk makes small runs of obsolete and custom bullets, including prototypes for many large bullet companies and the U.S. military from .245 to .700 inch. These excellent hunting bullets are available in diameters and weights that will satisfy some pretty wild requirements.

The perfect hunting bullet should expand soon after entering and retain a mushroom shape throughout the animal. In addition to the damage caused by the bullet's path, a properly mushroomed bullet will reverberate a hydro-shock extending outward to other tissue and organs. This is the basis of the Hawk bullet designs.

If you're looking for bullets in unusual diameters or weights, Hawk has them and offers a line of pistol bullets from .38 to .510 caliber. My personal experience hunting with them has been a delight. I have never had a Hawk bullet fail to do the job if I did mine. As a hunter, I test my loads to 300 yards, and Hawk bullets' accuracy has always impressed me. *hawkbullets.com*

James Calhoon Mfg.

Calhoon is the only source I know of for .19-caliber bullets. In 1997, it decided that .22-caliber rifles recoiled too much. Barrels overheated and fouled quickly, requiring additional time cleaning when you could be shooting.

Also, .17-caliber cartridges with capacities over 17 grains are finicky and more complicated to load than .22s. There were military tests of a cartridge halfway between the two—the 4.85mm with ballistics superior to the .223. Calhoon Mfg. adapted this ".19 caliber" to varminting. The maker devised the .19 Calhoon (Hornet), the .19-223 (19 Practical) and the .19 Badger.

Calhoon also supports its cartridges with barrels, cleaning equipment, loaded ammunition and reloading dies.

James Calhoon Manufacturing claims varminting to be its culture. The avid varminters on staff developed bullets for their own use and field-tested them. They started making bullets in 1987 and have developed a loyal following. Their "Double HP" produces dramatic hits and minimizes ricochets. The "Slick

Silver" plating on Calhoon bullets is advertised to cause less fouling and makes them unique in the marketplace. Bullets are offered in .19, .20 and .22 calibers in various weights. *jamescalhoon.com*

Lehigh Defense

Lehigh began manufacturing match solid bullets on Swiss CNC machines for competition. The manufacturer questioned how to push the limits of the technology and spent months in the shop working through many designs. Research and testing ultimately led to the development of a record-setting high-performance bullet. Being machined bullets, uniformity is excellent.

Lehigh Defense has continued to research and innovate and now offers a wide range of bullets for competition, hunting and self-defense. *lehighdefense.com*

Maker Ammo, LLC

Maker Bullets was launched in November 2014 by Paul Hendrixson and Constant Laubscher. In 2012, they began manufacturing a 220-grain solid copper bullet for .300 Blackout to address the limited availability of subsonic projectiles. Soon, they developed a fracturing bullet and an expanding design for hog hunting with subsonic calibers. As the designs progressed, they filed for patents on the fracturing projectiles.

In early 2015, Maker Bullets introduced a full line of match, expanding and fracturing projectiles available with or without polymer tips. They are CNC machined lead-free solid copper. Maker now lists more than 250 different weight and caliber configurations. *makerbullets.com*

North Fork Bullets

Originally made in Glenrock, Wyoming, by Mike Brady, North Fork Bullets has moved around a couple of times and is now owned and operated by Jorgen Bostrom in Sweden. The quality of the products is as good or better than in the past.

Bostrom has expanded the line to include a "Percussion Point," designed to rapidly expand for massive initial shock. It has a bonded core and a large solid copper base for deep penetration and is an excellent choice for hunting big cats or other large animals that are hard to stop.

North Fork still produces a full line of semi-spitzer bullets from .257 to .500 caliber in its bonded core hunting bullet series and solids and cup point solids for dangerous game hunters. At the time of writing, the U.S. distributor is "Reloading International." *northforkbullets.com*

Swift Bullet Company

Swift has been producing quality bullets since 1984. Among its popular hunting bullets are the Scirocco and A-Frame and now the most recently introduced Break Away solids. Swift's reloading manual has data specific to the Scirocco and A-Frame, so there is no need to guess the differences going from one design to the other.

In a time when so many companies are jumping on the ELR bandwagon and producing pencil-shaped high-BC bullets, Swift still makes premium hunting bullets you can rely on to penetrate deep and do their job in the field. *swiftbullets.com*

Custom Reloading Tools

CH Tool & Die, LLC

Founded in 1947 by Charles Heckman, CH Tool & Die has always been family-owned and operated—though not always by the same family (CH has changed ownership four times since its inception). In 1990, Dave and Dawna Davison purchased it. The Davison family then owned 4D Custom Die Company and merged the two companies to form CH4D. Over the next 30 years, CH4D developed a small-run, low-cost manufacturing process that allowed it to manufacture and stock a massive list of wildcat and obsolete caliber reloading dies economically.

In 2022, CH4D was passed down to the next generation. Rebranded and incorporated, CH4D became CH Tool & Die, LLC. The owners have decades of experience in the firearms industry and plan to continue production. On its website, the list of calibers at this writing contains 2,299 individual names, impressive by any standard.

Unique offerings include bullet-sizing dies so you can customize the diameter of projectiles for unusual or obsolete bore diameters. These allow you to reduce the bullet diameter. The bullets are pushed nose-first into the die and pop out of the top at the desired diameter. The maximum safe stepping size is .004 inch per die, and you can order them in any decimal diameter up to .570 inch in a 7/8x14 die. With larger diameter dies, you can size up to 1.170 inches.

You can size most down as much as .008 to .009 inch without damage to the jacket or dies, but do it in steps of no more than .004 inch per pass through the die. Of course, the jacket material and bullet construction will affect the results. *chtoolanddie.com*

Forster Products

Forster of Lanark, Illinois, offers numerous custom services for reloading dies and tools. At the 2023 SHOT Show, Forster introduced a .50-caliber version of the Co-Ax Reloading Press, which will easily accommodate large cartridges up to .50 BMG.

It also has various exclusive specialty reloading tools, including neck tension gauges and the Datum Dial, and is actively adding new tools to its lineup. *forsterproducts.com*

Hornady

Hornady makes custom reloading dies for any cartridge and will work from the chamber print for your chamber reamer or three fired cases. Providing a fired case is always preferable so the dies match your chamber.

Hornady offers two grades of dies: Custom or Match. Custom grade refers to conventional-style reloading dies. Match dies are bushing-style.

Hornady also makes hydraulic form dies. Say you have a wildcat that requires blowing the shoulder out a large amount. Hydraulic forming is ideal because of less loss of brass to split cases. It saves on components, barrel wear and, in the long run, a lot of time. Once hydraulically formed cases are ready to load and fire to their full potential, you waste no time fireforming. *hornady.com*

Lee Precision, Inc.

Well known for the Lee Loader and many other reloading tools, Lee also offers custom reloading dies for your conventional reloading press. These custom full-length dies require five fired cases and a few bullets you intend to load. You can get any cartridge with a base diameter of .555 inch or less in standard 7/8x14 dies. Cartridges over a .556-inch base diameter are offered in 1¼x12 die bodies. In either type, the maximum case length is 2.850 inches. Lee is probably the most economical of all the custom die makers, and its tools have always worked well for me.

If you need a neck-sizing die, Lee offers a custom collet-type one for your case.

Many reloaders like Lee's Custom Factory Crimp dies, which it can custom make for your wildcat. *leeprecision.com*

L.E. Wilson, Inc.

Longtime maker of arbor press-type reloading dies, Wilson also produces conventional threaded-type dies and various specialty loading tools like case gauges and trimmers. *lewilson.com*

Neil Jones Custom Products

Custom full-length sizing dies are bored out (machined) to resize your case to optimum chambering dimensions, eliminating excessive stretching and stress of the brass. Jones uses fired cases to determine dimensions for your dies. It also has a unique bushing that combines neck sizing and a shoulder bump to correct headspace while sizing.

Micro neck and seating dies allow you to adjust your die settings easily for precise results. *neiljonescustomproducts.com*

Newlon Precision

Bushing and non-bushing die blanks are available from Newlon Precision of Mariposa, California. This is different from what most makers offer, as these are blanks. The idea is for a gunsmith or hobbyist to make their own dies. The blanks are CNC-turned and of high quality.

You can use Newlon bushing and non-bushing die blanks to achieve a minimal amount of case sizing for accuracy and to extend case life. Die blanks allow the gunsmith to control the quality and delivery of dies to the customer. Newlon bushing dies use standard 3/8 x 1/2 Wilson, Redding and Hornady bushings. They are CNC machined from 416 stainless or 12L-14 steel (non-hardened).

You have complete control of how much sizing and where the sizing takes place: neck, length, base and body taper. Of course, this means you must acquire the appropriate resize reamers to make your dies. Your chamber reamer can be used only to make the bullet seating die. Newlon offers a micrometer head for its seating die as a valuable and useful upgrade. *newlonprecision.com*

Pacific Tool & Gauge (PTG)

Pacific Tool & Gauge (PTG) offers reloading die blanks for those who make their own dies. They're offered in standard 7/8x14 threads for common reloading presses and 1¼x12 and 1x12. Pacific also sells adapters for dies and small reloading tools. *pacifictoolandgauge.com*

Redding

Redding's custom dies come in the conventional type, bushing, or competition. Check the die reference charts in the Redding catalog; it has many dies for cartridges that will surprise you.

True wildcat cartridges with unique designs or unusual shoulder angles may require a tooling and engineering charge to partially cover expenses for making up special tooling. In the event such costs are required, they will be quoted separately. Send them your chamber reamer drawing, including all dimensions and the shoulder angle, for a firm price quote. Fired cases will work as well. *redding-reloading.com*

Short Action Customs, LLC

Short Action Customs, or SAC, sells a micrometer seating die with inline seating. It keeps the neck aligned with the projectile during seating for better accuracy and prevents neck bending. The neck bushing inside the die also allows the case shoulder to rest on the bushing. Thus, the seating depth is more uniform than with conventional bullet seaters.

The Infinity APS Bullet Seating Die is an arbor press die designed to give you the adjustability of the micrometer seating die above but in an even more accurate benchrest setup.

Also from SAC is a Modular Headspace Comparator, a tool to check the headspace on your loaded ammo. Before you scream, "Ammo doesn't have headspace!" go back to Chapter 15, Case-Forming Tools and Methods, and read the section about headspace and forming brass. This comparator has an advantage over others in that it measures cartridge OAL and headspace. *shortactioncustoms.com*

Vickerman Dies

The Vickerman is an outstanding inline bullet seating die. Originally designed and manufactured by Winn Vickerman, it's currently manufactured by Dayton Machine Shop. Inline bullet seaters prevent the side pressure on the case neck that occurs in conventional bullet seating dies, where the bullet must be forced into alignment as it seats.

These dies consistently seat bullets with little to no runout for improved accuracy. Parts are made with precision CNC machine tools to ensure their interchangeability. The Vickerman is fast and easy to use; whether you're reloading a .17 caliber or a .45-70, drop your bullet in the window and seat the bullet into the case. Vickerman also added a micrometer head for the die to easily adjust seating depth to your desired position. *vickermandie.com*

Warner Tool Company

In addition to the bullets it makes (see earlier in this appendix), Warner Tool Company also produces specialty reloading dies that are custom-made to match your specific chamber and are custom-ordered only. Since the dies are matched to your fireformed brass, wildcats are not a problem. Warner offers arbor press dies and threaded reloading dies for use in a press.

Features that WTC claims: Concentricity of .0005 inch or better from top to bottom. Precision headspace adjustment within the die via hardened and ground tool steel retainer rings (shims). Shoulder 'bump' 0.001 to 0.006 inch possible with the included shims. Two-part die insert construction—one for the body, one for the neck and shoulder, designed to 'cam over' on your reloading press.

WTC Dies are made from samples of your fired brass to full-length size only .001 to .0015 inch on the body diameter and just enough on the necks to get 30, 40, or even 50 reloads from your brass (neck annealing required). *warner-tool.com*

Whidden Gunworks

Whidden Gunworks of Nashville, Georgia, manufactures custom dies from your fired brass (provide three cases). Whidden understands fired brass may not be available early in a rifle build. Your reamer print will suffice in those circumstances, but please note the fired brass will usually yield the best results. That's because reamer prints have tolerances representative of the dimensions but do not show the finished dimensions. This is industry standard practice.

My favorite quote from Whidden is, "What others may consider 'Wildcat' is the norm for us." You can get custom sizers, seaters, hydraulic form dies and trim dies from .20 to .408 caliber.

Along with dies, Whidden catalogs specialty tools for the reloader. CNC toolheads for Dillon presses, click-adjustable universal die lock rings, bushings for the Whidden bushing-style dies, bullet pointing dies and several other accessories. *whiddengunworks.com*

Large Resellers of Reloading Supplies

- Black Hills Shooters Supply *bhshooters.com*
- Brownells *brownells.com*
- Bruno Shooters Supply *brunoshooters.com*
- Creedmoor Sports *creedmoorsports.com*
- Duck Creek Sporting Goods *duckcreeksportinggoods.com*
- Graf & Sons *grafs.com*
- Midway USA *midwayusa.com*
- Midsouth Shooters *midsouthshooterssupply.com*
- Missouri Bullet Company *missouribullet.com*
- Natchez Shooting & Outdoors *natchezss.com*

- Powder Valley *powdervalley.com*
- Reloading International *reloadinginternational.com*
- Shooters Pro Shop *shootersproshop.com*
- Top Brass *topbrass-inc.com*
- X-Treme Bullets *xtremebullets.com*

Organization of Interest

- International Ammunition Association *cartridgecollectors.org*
- Sporting Arms & Ammunition Manufacturers' Institute *saami.org*
- National Shooting Sports Foundation *nssf.org*

APPENDIX II

Comparing Parent Cases by Water Weight Capacity

When measuring a case's water capacity (volume), the standard method uses fired unsized cases. The results will be closer to the case volume when expanded at firing.

In preparation, I use distilled water to avoid any weight caused by impurities. Put one or two drops of dish soap in a half cup of water; this eliminates capillary action that can cause the water to cup (concave) at the case mouth—water should be level with the top of the case when full. An eye dropper works well for getting this correct.

Weigh the dry case with a spent primer in place. Cases vary widely in weight from one maker to the next. Frequently, modern cases are thicker in the case wall and heavier than older ones for the same cartridge. These heavier cases have less capacity, with every 8.5 grains of brass displacing about 1 grain of water. Small cases like the .22 Hornet may see up to 10 percent capacity differences. However, variations of 2 grains of water are more typical for medium-sized cases such as the .30-06 Springfield.

Once you know your case's dry weight and have that figure written down, fill it with the water/soap mixture, being careful not to introduce bubbles. Then, place the water and case into a scale pan. Subtract the dry weight of the case, and you now have its water capacity. Repeat the test with several cases from that lot of brass, and average your results for the best comparative information.

The chart below shows case capacity information taken from numerous reference sources. We tabulated these approximate case capacities in grains of water by collecting data from the listed sources and then averaging them. So, they are handy for comparing case capacity from one cartridge to the next. Remember, you will change the case's capacity as you neck up or down.

References used include ballistics programs QuickLOAD, LoadTech, RCBS. Load and Load-from-a-Disk. And the book *Handloading* by W.C. Davis (NRA, 1981). Cartridge collector Ed Reynolds, the author of LoadTech and AccuLoad software, shared his extensive list of case measurements. When creating LoadTech, Reynolds and his partners measured tons of cases to ensure their software accurately estimated load data.

Estimating Case Capacity

In his book *Designing and Forming Custom Cartridges,* Ken Howell provides a methodology for estimating case capacity. Howell's book is the best single reference on case dimensions. There are hundreds of cartridges, but he only included ones for which he had a reliable and accurate source for dimensions, such as reamer makers, SAAMI, CIP, RCBS, Triebel, original ammunition manufacturer's catalogs and other original drawings.

To estimate, take either the maximum dimensions of the outside of the case or the minimum dimensions of the chamber from a reliable source such as SAAMI or CIP. The maximum dimensions for the case body will approximate the chamber (fired cases are always slightly smaller than the actual chamber because the brass shrinks a tiny amount after firing). Better yet, get a chamber cast from your gun to match your chambering (fired cases are a better source of information).

Once you have the dimensional information, compute the water weight to fill this volume. Divide the weight of the brass by its specific gravity (between 8.44 and 8.56, depending on the source) to give the weight of the water it displaces; subtract that amount, leaving the internal case volume. This method allows you to estimate case volume if you don't have a fired case to weigh.

The listings below are arranged by caliber and then by volume (size matters). The water weight (in grains) is to the right of the cartridge name.

One last reminder: it is ideal to measure your brass when possible.

CARTRIDGE	WATER WEIGHT (GR.)	CARTRIDGE	WATER WEIGHT (GR.)	CARTRIDGE	WATER WEIGHT (GR.)
.14 Hornet	12	6.5x54 MS	50	.340 Weatherby	98
.17 Velociraptor	10.9	.260 Remington	53	.338/.378 Weatherby	132
.17 Hornet	14	6.5x55	57	.33 XC	138
.17 Remington	27	6.5-06	65	.357 Maximum	34
.17/222 Rem.	39	6.5 Rem. Mag.	68	.35 Remington	51
.20 Practical	28	.264 Win. Mag.	82	.358 Hoosier	52.4
.204 Ruger	33	6.5 Bitch Cat	88.7	.358 Winchester	57
.20 NoZler	34.2	.270 Ren	16	.358 IDC	58.8
.22 Buckaroo	9.8	.277 Wolverine	25.5	9mm Mauser	62
.22 Mink	11.5	.270 Winchester	68	.35 Whelen	71
.22 Hornet	14	.270 Gibbs	71.1	.350 Rem. Mag.	73
.218 Bee	18	.270 WSM	78.6	.358 Norma Mag.	88
.22 K-Hornet	21	.270 Weatherby	83	.358 Yukon	101
.221 Remington	21	7-30 Waters	45	.358 STA	105
.222 Remington	27	7mm-08	56	9.3x57 Mauser	64
.223 Remington	31	7x57 Mauser	59	9.3x72R	67
.222 Rem. Mag.	32	.284 Winchester	66	9.3mm BS	68.8
.22 PDK	33.8	.280 Remington	67	9.3x62	77
.219 Zipper	34	.280 Ackley Improved	73.4	9.3x74R	82
.22-250 Rem.	43	7mm WSM	81	.375 Winchester	49
.220 Swift	48	7mm Rem. Mag.	84	.375 Whelen (.375-06)	73
.22 Creedmoor	50.8	.30 Carbine	21	.375 Renner	79
.223 WSSM	53	.300 Blackout	24	.375 Renner Express	79.9
.22-06	65	7.62x39 Improved 28 Degree	36.3	.375 H&H Mag.	95
.240 Banshee	16	.30 Remington AR	44.6	.375 Bishop	96.3
.24 York	34.9	.30-30 Winchester	45	.375 Ruger	100
6mm BR	39	.30-30 Ackley Improved	46.6	.378 Weatherby Mag.	136
6mm XC	48	.300 Savage	52	.37 XC	139.8
.243 Winchester	54	.308 Winchester	56	.375 Enabelr	157.5
.243 WSSM	54	.30-40 Krag	58	.400 Whelen	73
.240 Flanged NE	58	.30-06 Springfield	69	.405 Winchester	78
.240 Weatherby	65	.30/6.5mm Weatherby RPM	81	.450/400 NE 3.25"	123
.257 Fox	10.9	.300 H&H Magnum	86	.41 XC	142.3
.25 Dude	10.5	.300 Win. Mag.	89	.45 Colt	42

CARTRIDGE	WATER WEIGHT (GR.)	CARTRIDGE	WATER WEIGHT (GR.)	CARTRIDGE	WATER WEIGHT (GR.)
.255 Banshee	17.5	.300 Weatherby	99	.454 Casull	47
.25-20 WCF	19	.30/378 Weatherby	130	.45 Raptor	59.6
.256 Winchester	22	.32-20 WCF	22	.460 Alliance	60.2
.25-35 WCF	37	.327 Meteor	29.4	.458 Ham'R	65.1
.257 Raptor	31.4	.303 British	57	.450 Marlin	74
.25 York	35.1	7.65 Mauser	58	.45-70 Government	77
.250 Savage	46	8x57 Mauser	62	.450 Alaskan	88
25 Creedmoor	50.9	7.62x54R Nagant	64	.45-90 2.4"	90
.257 Roberts	56	8mm-06	70	.458 Winchester Mag.	94
.25-06 Rem	66	8mm Rem. Mag.	98	.458 Lott	108
.25/7mm PRC	77	.338 Spectre	26.8	.460 Weatherby	140
.257 Weatherby	84	8.6 Blackout	46.4	.475 Lehigh	31.4
6.5 PCC	28.4	.338/6.5 Creedmoor	54	.470 Turnbull	84.6
6.5mm Jap	48	.338-06	70	.475 Bishop	103
6.5 Carcano	49	.338 Win. Mag.	86	.50 BMG	293

APPENDIX III

Specialty Reloading Tools for Wildcatters

Disclaimer: I am not being compensated in any way for the listings that follow. They are tools and products that I like and feel provide something useful, if not unique, for the reloader and wildcatter.

PMA Bullet Puller

As a reloader and wildcatter, you'll inevitably need to pull a few bullets occasionally. This task has always been a chore, requiring you to remove your loading die from your press and use a plier-type bullet puller or yank them in an even less savory method that often damages projectiles.

aPMA makes pullers based on Charlie Hood's original design. The idea came from a good friend and customer of PMA's, John Crawford, who made an excellent bullet puller that eliminated the need for pliers or a press—it was one piece and completely self-contained. With his permission, PMA adopted the design and offered it in popular sizes from .22 to .30 caliber.

To use it, drop the loaded or dummy cartridge into the false chamber, tighten the clamp on the bullet, and back out of the false chamber by unscrewing it from the main body. After a few rotations, the bullet is free from the case. Loosen the clamp, and the bullet drops free. Most importantly, the bullet comes out undamaged, maybe not competition-worthy, but certainly in varmint-shooting condition.

PMA Micro Die Adjuster

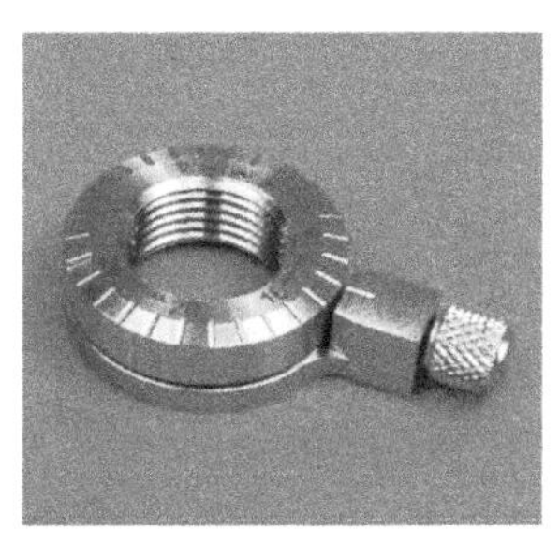

PMA's Micro Die Adjuster (MDA) replaces your existing lock ring, and you can use it with nearly any 7/8-14 full-length sizing die.

I used this tool with sizing dies from Redding, RCBS, Hornady, Lee, Harrells Precision, and any standard thread die. It allows you to adjust your "shoulder bump" as fine as .0005 inch. The engraved marks on the MDA are equal to approximately .001 of an inch of adjustment (actual adjustment .000992 inch) to the shoulder bump. Splitting the engraved marks is, therefore, approximately equal to .0005 inch.

The MDA does not work with the Forster Co-Ax press, and it's not intended for use with turret presses, progressive presses or the RCBS Summit Press. However, it works on most single-stage presses. Some custom dies for extremely short cartridges may require an extended shell holder, which you can order with or without the thumbscrew for locking your setting. It's also available in 1.25x12 and 1.5x12 sizes.

PMA 200 Line Tool

Chamber prints usually call out the point .200-inch up from the case head. The PMA 200 Line Tool makes measuring the .200-inch line a fast, repeatable exercise. It holds the case by the base and has a slot at the .200 line for calipers, so you get a repeatable measurement.

The .200 line on brass refers to the spot on the body of a cartridge commonly measured to evaluate sizing dies, monitor pressures, and eliminate "clickers," the annoying hiccup that occurs when brass isn't sized correctly. Usually, this symptom is fixed with a different FL die (possibly a tiny base or custom) or a ring die.

Available to fit nearly every case family, the sizes available include those listed below. Each is sized to be a couple of thousandths of an inch larger than the case diameter for ease of function.

A- .381-in. (.223 Rem. family)

B- .444-in. (.220 Russian, PPC, ARC and Grendel)

C- .476-in. (.308 Win., BR and .30-06 families)
D- .503-in. (.284 Win. family)
E- .535-in. (Standard Magnums, PRC family)
F- .558-in. (Rem. Ultra and Short Mags, WSM family)

PMA Ball-Bearing Drive Priming Tool

The ball-bearing drive in the PMA Priming Tool serves two functions. It fully supports the priming punch assembly and engages the linkage, keeping the punch assembly and link in perfect alignment and eliminating wear on the two parts. The ball bearing also smoothens the operation; if you appreciate fine tools, this is one.

PMA uses 17-4 PH stainless steel for all moving parts and grinds the contact surfaces of the priming punches flat and parallel. This keeps your primers entering straight and bottoming flat in the primer pocket for uniform results.

The priming tool has an adjustable head for minor adjustments to the primer seating depth. You adjust the head to where the handle will stop when the primer is seated correctly and bottomed out firmly in the primer pocket. The head is infinitely adjustable: no clicks, just a smooth thread, and secured by a friction o-ring. A secondary punch engages the case head, keeping it square with the primer and punch. It also fully supports the primer (keeping it straight) to enter the primer pocket.

Many hand-priming tools are larger than they need to be. The PMA tool fits well in hand and is 1 inch shorter and 4 oz. lighter than other stainless steel priming tools of similar design. An upward swoop to the handle adds comfort during priming and has plenty of leverage for the job.

PMA says that Redding shell holders have the most consistent through holes in the industry and are the most square. PMA inspects each shell holder sold with its tools to ensure they fit correctly. Your existing Redding shell holders should also work fine.

PTG also makes a primer pocket uniforming tool shown here with the basic die blanks.

Die Blanks and More

Dave Kiff at Pacific Tool & Gauge started making

die blanks for me in the late 1990s when I was producing reloading dies to match my customers' guns. Since then, he expanded his offering of die blanks to include ones with and without pilot holes. Pacific offers them with many different-size pilot holes, minimizing the hobbyist's tools.

Quick-change lathe fixture. No. 1 is the body, to be held in the lathe's chuck, No. 3 is a washer for tension, and No. 2 is the lock nut to hold the blank in position.

Available dies include 7/8x14 for standard reloading presses plus 1x12 and 1.25x12. This variety will allow you to make dies for nearly any caliber you can dream up without the time to machine the blanks from scratch.

PTG also offers a Quick-Change Lathe Fixture for machining 7/8x14 dies. To work on reloading dies, place the fixture in the lathe chuck and use a jam nut on the die threads to lock the die in place for machine operations. The tool prevents damage to the die blank during machining. It also allows for semi-production operations with the ability to quick-change dies to repeat duplicate operations on multiple blanks.

PTG has a few other simple reloading items and adds products frequently.

PTG Precision Throating Reamer

Pacific Tool & Gauge's Precision Throating Reamer is not a reloading tool, per se. Still, it can solve seating depth issues by extending the throat in your chamber to accommodate longer bullets.

This kit allows you to set the exact length you want because the sleeve over the reamer acts as a stop on the end of the chamber before the throat (case mouth).

F.W. Arm Auto-Centering Decapping Dies

F.W. Arm's Auto-Centering Decapping Dies simplify decapping done separately. The patented auto-centering shuttle captures the case neck, providing axial alignment of your brass before the decapping tip enters the brass.

You can use the auto-centering die on manual or automated reloading presses. There's no need to hand guide brass up to the decapping pin, no more nicked necks, and no need to slow down to protect the case mouth. It also

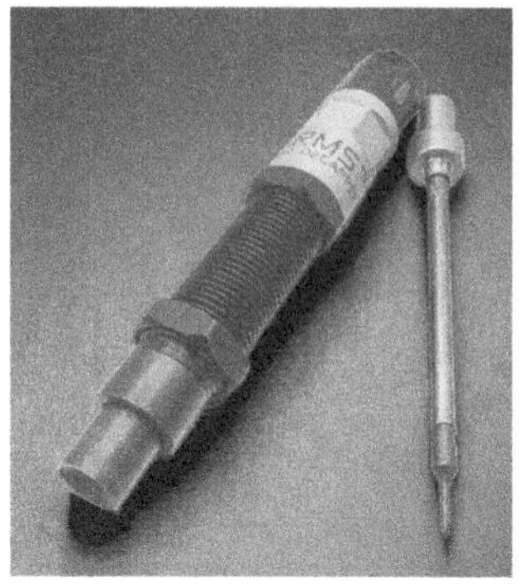

features an adjustable spring-loaded primer popper, which eliminates primer pullback (it always clears the primer pocket).

F.W. Arms offers two lengths of decapping dies; first, a standard length for most pistol calibers (calibers under .575 inch, which is the largest diameter), and rifle calibers up to .308 Win. in case length.

Decapping pin diameters are available for standard .080-inch flash holes and smaller-diameter pins for 1.6mm flash holes. Pro Tip: Get an extra guide rod if you run both standard and small flash holes, using it as a dedicated guide rod for each pin size. Guide rods and tips are easy to change, with all tools included inside the decapper package.

Badger Ordnance Chamber Gauge

The Badger Ordnance Chambering Gauge removes the guesswork and inconsistency of using a regular depth gauge tool while precision chambering your rifle barrels. It comes with a dial indicator and instructions.

It's designed to work on barrels for the Remington 700 (and its clones) and reduces the errors made with other measuring methods by taking the training and skill out of the measuring process.

Broken Case Extractors

Broken case extractors are simple tools that have been around for a very long time, yet I often find that shooters damage chambers because they are not aware of them.

They are caliber-specific, i.e., .30 caliber will work on most .30 caliber chambers if the tool is the correct length. The sharp shoulder near the tip catches the lip of the mouth in cases with a head separation in the chamber. Push the tool into the case until it clicks at the case's mouth. Then, use a cleaning rod to pop the stuck half of the case out of the chamber.

They come designed for many cartridges, but with a bit of understanding of the tool, you can interchange them for many others. I use the parts to make other calibers when working on customer guns. It's faster and cheaper than making the entire tool.

AMP Annealing Machine

While pursuing the best method for annealing brass, the developers of the AMP Annealing Machine learned something essential to reloaders and wildcatters alike: We have all been wrong about how often brass should be annealed for the best accuracy.

It turns out that brass work hardens with only one firing cycle. So, this tool is a must for you benchrest types who want to remove every alibi from the loading process.

You calibrate the machine to your lot of brass. Once that is accomplished, running all your brass through the machine at the prescribed setting is simple, ensuring your neck tension will be uniform, removing one more variable.

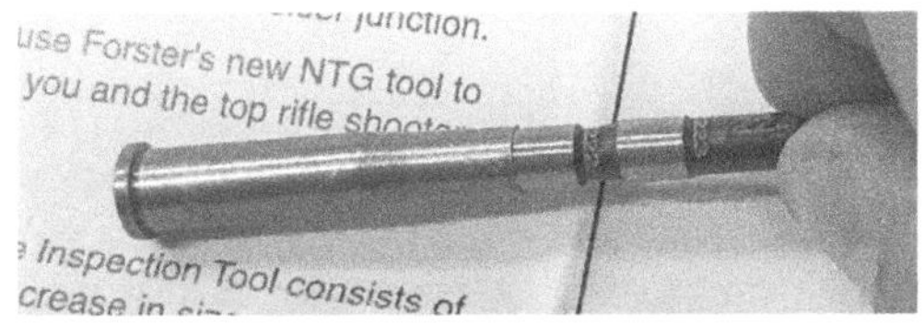

Forster Neck Tension Gauge

Use Forster's Neck Tension Gage (NTG) as an inspection tool to sort a batch of brass quickly and accurately. The NTG provides the information needed to create exacting neck tensions during the bullet seating operation.

Use it after case neck sizing and before bullet seating to determine the optimal inside neck diameter for consistently releasing a bullet from your reloaded rounds. It allows for inspection of the inside diameters of case necks to be sure a "donut" has not formed at the neck-shoulder junction. Donuts are caused by brass flowing up the shoulder into the neck as you cycle the brass through the firing and reloading process.

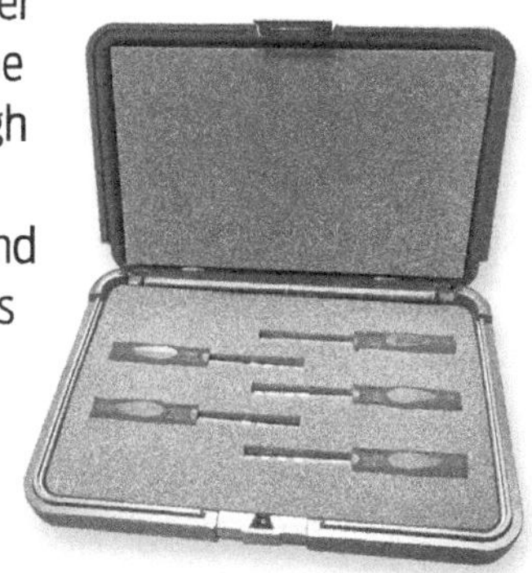

Available in five calibers—.224, .243, .264, .284, and .308—each NTG consists of four stepped diameters that increase in size until reaching the handle. Each diameter is etched on the metal tool. Insert the tool tip into your sized case neck, sliding it in until one of the diameters achieves a slip fit. Use the resulting value to fine-tune your case preparation.

Hollow Pointer Kits

Intended for use in the Forster Case Trimmer, the Hollow Pointer Kit comes in two diameters, 1/16 or 1/8 inch. Because you use it in a trimmer, the depth of cut is controlled to avoid inconsistency in the finished bullet weight. It provides the potential for better expansion with low-pressure lead bullet loads in about any caliber you can dream up.

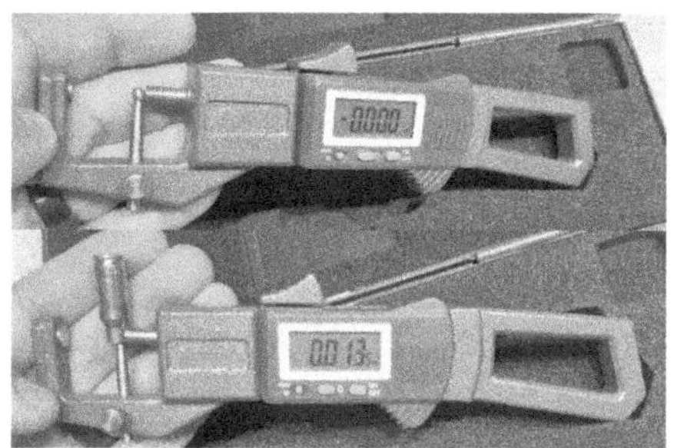

Pictured here is a Sinclair tool for measuring neck thickness.

Neck Thickness Gauge

Many companies make various neck thickness micrometers for checking the thickness of the brass of the neck. However, Sinclair's Neck Thickness Gauge uses a ball-shaped anvil. The ball is superior because the case mouth is often untrue, giving a false reading on a pin anvil.

Inline Fabrication Reloading Press Mounting System

Inline Fabrication says, "A challenge for the modern reloader is sometimes we have more presses, calibers, case prep tools or desktop gadgets than available bench space. Trying to work in a crowded, cramped space is not an enjoyable thing."

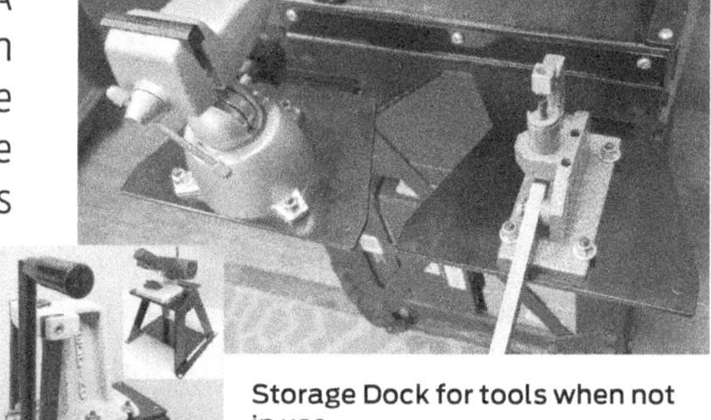

Storage Dock for tools when not in use.

This is where Inline's Quick-Change System comes in. Using the QC storage docks, you can have one press mounted using one or two quick-change Ultramounts and store the rest of your equipment up and out of the way on the wall.

This organization adds a layer of functionality that was not even a thought in the past. Maybe you bring your press into the house from the garage after reloading, take it to the cabin, a buddy's reloading room, etc. It takes 30 seconds to remove, stow and swap it out with another.

That gives you the rock-solid rigidity of a fixed mount with the convenience and efficiency of quick change. Bases come in three heights, and Inline has a vast database of mounting plates for various reloading presses, vises, and other bench-mounted tools that take up space. If you need a custom plate, Inline makes them for a minimal upcharge.

Inline also sells LED lighting kits for reloading presses and other accessories and gear that organize and improve the reloading process.

Flush mount inset into the work surface of the bench.

Another Source for Bench Optimizing

Total Vise offers a system for bench organizing that you can apply to reloading or gunsmithing. If you're working in a limited space, these systems are useful, allowing you to use the same bench for many jobs. Total Vise has added many tools since I first ran onto them, and I expect it will continue to innovate and add to its products.

Shaviv Ammo Burr

There are hundreds of tools on the market that do case prep. I put the Shaviv Ammo Burr tools on this list because they have much better ergonomics than most I've used. If you're prepping cases by hand, the last thing you want are blisters and sores. Note the handles are full-sized so that you can get a solid grip.

Available individually or in a kit, the tools have plastic/rubber handles for comfort. The kit contains a machinist-style deburring tool with a hook cutter that produces a radius on the deburred part instead of a sharp corner.

The ammo tools have extendable arbors for the deburring cutters. You can set them to the best length for your application with a positive detent lock. There is a gold-anodized handle with all metal parts to retain the interchangeable and extendable arbors. In addition, the handle has built-in ratcheting, so you're not back-dragging the cutter as you use it. The Inner chamfer tool works on anything from .17 caliber up to .470. The Outer chamfer tool can handle up to 1 inch in diameter so that you can use it on the 12 Gauge From Hell.

Expander Dies and Mandrels

Mandrel-type expander dies are available from many makers. Some offer mandrels in .0005-inch increments (5/10,000th of an inch), allowing you to dial in precisely for proper neck tension on the bullet. This means you could easily have a half dozen mandrels for each caliber. That can be expensive.

Some makers offer only standard-for-caliber mandrels, keeping costs down (L.E. Wilson is one). Be sure to take note of the selection of mandrels when you choose a die brand so you can get the tools you want.

Mandrels have several advantages over traditional expander ball assemblies offered by most reloading die companies. Because the nose of the mandrel is tapered, it's perfect for repairing dented case mouths or squashed necks (out of round).

Expander balls pull up on the case when you extract them during sizing. This process is more likely to bend the case or the neck inadvertently. Because the brass is stronger in form when force is applied downward into the neck, a mandrel is far less likely to bend the case—in short, giving you better accuracy. Additionally, their design compensates for any misalignment of the die or ram to the press. You achieve better results by self-centering in the case mouth than with a traditional expander ball.

K+M Precision Shooting Products is one of the "Cadillac" brands offering expander dies and mandrels. You can purchase them individually or in a kit with everything for a given caliber.

Falling somewhere between the two companies mentioned is 21st Century Innovation, with mandrel kits containing five sizes per caliber. The die bodies are sold separately and can be used with various calibers.

K+M die in a Forster Co-Ax press.

These are just a few of the examples. You will find many options when you start looking for expander mandrel dies. The choices have much to do with how precise you want to be with the mandrel size. If you're a competition shooter, you can dial things very close. On the other hand, if you are a varminter, you may not need to spend hundreds of dollars on mandrels when the standard size will suffice. It's all up to you.

Food Dehydrator for Drying Brass

If you wet-tumble your brass, the quickest way to dry it is probably a food dehydrator. This is not rocket science. But I have one tip: Check out your local thrift store for used dehydrators; you can probably pick one up cheaply. It's also something you can watch for at garage sales.

Sources:

21st Century Innovation, 420 Carol Ann Lane, Ossian, IN 46777, 260-273-9909, *21stcenturyinnovation.com*

AMP Annealer, 649-238-7798, *ampannealing.com*

Badger Ordnance, 816-421-4956, *badgerordnance.com*

Forster Products, 310 SE Lanark Ave., Lanark, IL 61046, 815-493-6360, *forsterproducts.com*

FW Arms, 510-306-8087, *fwarms.com*

Inline Fabrication, 3003 West 11th Ave. #252, Eugene, OR 97402, 541-246-4691, *inlinefabrication.com*

K+M Shooting, 616-399-7894, *kmshooting.com*

L.E. Wilson, 3745 5th ST NE, East Wenatchee, WA 98802, 509-782-1328, *lewilson.com*

Pacific Tool & Gauge, 675 Antelope Rd., White City, OR 97503, (541) 826-5808, *pacifictoolandgauge.com*

PMA Tool LLC, 1752 Summit St, New Haven, IN 46774, 260-246-5860, *pmatool.com*

Shaviv USA, P.O. Box 1698 Janesville, WI 53547, 800-828-8765, *shavivusa.com*

Total Vise, 406-830-5881, *totalvise.com*

About the Author

Fred Zeglin retired from building custom rifles after 30-plus years, during which he specialized in wildcat designs for his clients. He still dabbles in wildcats for fun. In 2005, his first book, *Wildcat Cartridges*, was published. Since that time, he has written six more books, including *P.O. Ackley, America's Gunsmith.*

Fred spent five years as the Firearms Technology Coordinator and Short-Term Gunsmithing Program Coordinator for Flathead Valley Community College in Kalispell, Montana. He wrote and implemented the curriculum for the firearms program at the college and still serves in an advisory role. He currently owns 4D Reamer Rentals, Ltd., so he deals with more reamers and headspace gauges than any other gunsmith you will ever meet.

He has taught NRA gunsmithing courses in Wildcat Cartridge Design at Murray State College in Oklahoma, Flathead Valley Community College in Montana, and Trinidad State Junior College in Colorado. Fred also worked with AGI to create the "Taming Wildcats" and "Reloading A to Z" instructional videos. He has written articles for *Precision Shooting, Guns & Ammo, Gun Digest, Cartridges of the World, Gun Digest Book of Exploded Gun Drawings*, and many others. His gunsmithing blog can be found at *gunsmithtalk.wordpress.com*.

Currently, Fred is writing and editing the *Gunsmithing Student Handbook Series*, which includes titles such as *Understanding Headspace, Chambering for Ackley Cartridges, Chambering Rifle Barrels for Accuracy*, and *Gunsmith Tools, Cutters & Gauges, A Primer.*

Fred has expanded from writing to publishing as well. Under the banner of Z-Hat Publishing, he is now acquiring copyrights for out-of-print books and bringing them back to the market. *The Bolt Action Rifle, Volume 1 & 2* by Stuart Otteson and *Stockwork for the Beginner* and *Checkering*, both by S.L. Mays, are among the titles he has revived. Visit *z-hat.com.*

NEW TITLES

ALLISTICS HANDBOOK
| $19.99

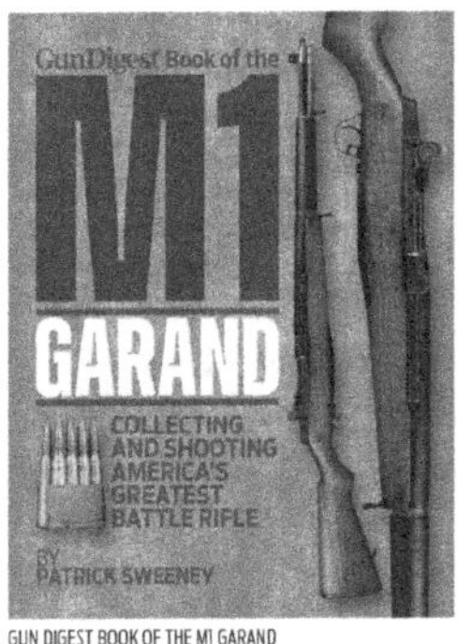

GUN DIGEST BOOK OF THE M1 GARAND
R8170 | $39.99

LEVER-ACTIONS: A TRIBUTE TO THE ALL-AMERICAN RIFLE
S8450 | $39.99

DIY SURVIVAL: BEST HACKS FOR WORST-CASE SCENARIOS
R8158 | $24.99

RID: THE BUG OUT BOOK
| $37.99

SUPPRESSORS: RECOIL MAGAZINE'S COMPLETE GUIDE TO BUYING, MAINTAINING, AND SHOOTING WITH A SILENCER • R8173 | $37.99

OVERLAND: PROJECT GUIDE TO OFFROAD, BUG OUT AND OVERLANDING VEHICLES • R8444 | $37.99

GUNSMITHING THE 1911: THE BENCH MANUAL
S8447 | $37.99

OTHER POPULAR TITLES

ARD CATALOG OF SMITH & WESSON, 4TH EDITION
| $54.99

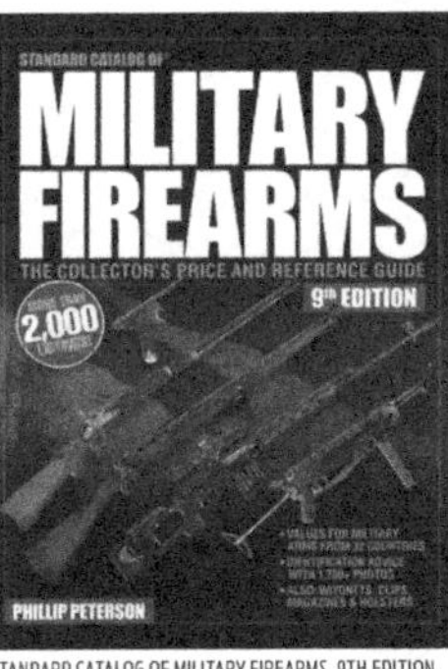

STANDARD CATALOG OF MILITARY FIREARMS, 9TH EDITION
R8070 | $36.99

THE OFFICIAL GUN DIGEST BOOK OF GUNS & PRICES, 14TH EDITION • R8077 | $34.99

DEADLY FORCE: UNDERSTANDING YOUR RIGHT TO SELF-DEFENSE, 2ND EDITION • R8161 | $25.99

GEST BOOK OF CONCEALED CARRY, 2ND EDITION
$29.99

DIY GUNS: RECOIL MAGAZINE'S GUIDE TO HOMEBUILT SUPPRESSORS, 80 PERCENT LOWERS, RIFLE MODS AND MORE • R8132 | $37.99

AR-15 SETUP, MAINTENANCE AND REPAIR
R8123 | $35.99

PRECISION RIFLE MARKSMANSHIP: THE FUNDAMENTALS – A MARINE SNIPER'S GUIDE TO LONG-RANGE SHOOTING • R8086 | $27.99